THE PARTITION OF INDIA

Policies and Perspectives

1935–1947

THE PARTITION OF INDIA

Policies and Perspectives 1935-1947

EDITED BY

C. H. PHILIPS

Director, School of Oriental and African Studies
University of London

AND

MARY DOREEN WAINWRIGHT

Research Officer, School of Oriental and African Studies

THE M.I.T. PRESS
Massachusetts Institute of Technology
Cambridge, Massachusetts

First Published 1970

ISBN 0 262 16043 9

Library of Congress catalog card number: 77-118351

Printed in Great Britain

PREFACE

It may well be said that an episode which cost so many families their lives or their homes, and which still arouses such powerful feelings of hatred and remorse, should be left to future generations to describe and assess. Certainly it is difficult, a mere twenty years after partition, for those Britons, Indians and Pakistanis who lived through those terrible months to look back on them with detachment. But it may reasonably be presumed that those who played some significant part in the episode or who saw what went on have at least some responsibility for setting down their evidence, so that future generations may achieve a closer understanding of the processes which have dramatically changed the history of their three peoples and countries.

The enquiry which led to the publication of this volume began as a simple attempt to collect evidence from those still alive who had taken an active hand in the partition and who had thus far not set down their share of the record. From this it grew into a regular series of meetings spread over three years between 'participants' and historians, young and old, of the three countries. An invaluable body of evidence and comment was thus brought together in London; and through the stimulation of a fresh surge of interest in Pakistan the papers of the All-India Muslim League covering the period from its origin in 1906 down to 1947 were rescued and stowed in safety in the University of Karachi, where they are now being preserved and sorted for use by scholars.

The partition seminar, as it came generally to be known, has also stimulated and encouraged a number of new studies relating to the subject, among which may be mentioned an analysis of British policy in the years between the two great wars, studies of the last three British viceroys, Linlithgow, Wavell and Mountbatten, the publication of British official documents on the transfer of power, fresh studies of Jinnah, the maker of Pakistan, and full-scale histories of the Indian National Congress and the All-India Muslim League.

This volume makes no claim to be a comprehensive study of the events and processes leading to the partition of India, but rather to present relevant evidence, along with an analysis of some of the more important aspects, with a view to indicating those major questions and areas of study on the subject which require and will repay early investigation. The introduction seeks to give a lead in this direction.

The papers included in this volume are presented in two categories, corresponding broadly with two main groups of contributors: on the one hand academic students of the partition and on the other hand actors in or interested observers of the events themselves. Thus the papers in the section *Policies and Parties*, relating firstly to British policy and then to the policies of the major Indian parties, are largely based on the study of records, while those in the section *Perspectives and Reflections* derive from personal experience and observation of Pakistani, Indian and British contributors.

We should like to express our great appreciation to the very large number of busy persons, in all three countries, who have gone to great trouble and given generously of their time, whether in coming to address the seminar, in private discussion, in answering detailed questionnaires, or in taking part in the conference which was held in London in the summer of 1967. The participants in the conference, many of whom travelled from India, Pakistan, and other parts of the world to attend, were Mr S. Osman Ali, Mr D. G. Austin, Dr K. K. Aziz, Professor K. A. Ballhatchet, Dr K. N. Chaudhuri, Dr D. G. Dalton, Mr Durga Das, Professor C. von Fürer-Haimendorf, Mr J. B. Harrison, Mr H. V. Hodson, Professor Mahmud Husain, Mr M. A. H. Ispahani, Dr N. S. Junankar, Professor Humayun Kabir, Khan Abdul Qaiyum Khan, Sir Muhammad Zafrulla Khan, Mr E. W. R. Lumby, Raja Sahib of Mahmudabad, Professor P. N. S. Mansergh, Professor A. C. Mayer, Dr S. R. Mehrotra, Sir Penderel Moon, Dr R. J. Moore, Professor M. Mujeeb, Dr B. R. Nanda, Mr H. M. Patel, Professor C. H. Philips, Dr I. H. Qureshi, Mr B. Shiva Rao, Professor K. B. Sayeed, Dr Percival Spear, Professor H. R. Tinker, Mr C. S. Venkatachar, Miss M. D. Wainwright, Sir Francis Wylie, Dr Z. H. Zaidi, Mr Maurice Zinkin, and Mrs Taya Zinkin.

We should particularly like to thank those who in one way or another shared in the work of the seminar but whose contributions are not directly, in the form of papers, represented in this volume: Mr Jamiluddin Ahmad, Mr Horace Alexander, Sir Claude Auchinleck, Professor N. K. Bose, Sir Ronald Brockman, Lord Butler, Mr Alan Campbell-Johnson, Sir Olaf Caroe, Major-General V. F. Erskine Crum, Sir Hugh Dow, Sir Ambrose Dundas, Mr Kanji Dwarkadas, Mr Stephen Garvin, Dr P. C. Ghosh, Lord Glendevon, Sir Percival Griffiths, Dr Zakir Husain, Sir Frederick James, Acharya J. B. Kripalani, the Earl of Listowel, Dr Syed Mahmud, Mr Humayun Mirza, Earl Mountbatten, Mr K. M. Munshi, Sir Archibald Nye, Viscount Radcliffe, Mr P. Kodanda Rao, Sir John Sargent, the Earl of Scarbrough, Lord Spens, Mr Ian Stephens, the late Sir Francis Tuker, Mr Geoffrey Tyson and Professor L. F. Rushbrook Williams.

We are also deeply indebted to the Leverhulme Trust which provided substantial funds both to get the seminar going and to bring participants to the conference in London.

The London School of Oriental and African Studies has throughout given general support to the venture.

School of Oriental and
African Studies
November 1968

C. H. PHILIPS
M. D. WAINWRIGHT

CONTENTS

INTRODUCTION

The outstanding political development in India in the ten years before the British decision to transfer power in 1947 was the emergence and political exploitation of Muslim nationalism. Independence for the peoples of the sub-continent was not at issue, for this had been the declared aim of British policy at least since 1917 and successive British governments had been honestly, though slowly, working towards self-government for twenty years. The Government of India Act of 1935, which had now come into operation, in spite of its numerous 'checks and balances' was in its provincial sections a considerable concession to self-government, while the federal part of the Act might well have been the first step in a complete transfer of power at the centre.[1] What was scarcely foreseeable in 1937 was that the final transfer of authority, within the short space of ten years, would be to two successor states, and those divided on religious lines.

The only all-India Muslim party of any significance and strength was the All-India Muslim League, which however had failed in the recent general election of 1937, attracting less than five per cent of the Muslim vote, and was, at this time, showing little sign of separatist policies. M. A. Jinnah, who had finally returned to India in 1935 after some years retirement in England to resume the leadership of the Muslim League and to organize the party for the election, was still calling for Hindu-Muslim unity, as he had done in the past. Though in the Legislature he had attacked the federal part of the 1935 Act as 'thoroughly rotten, fundamentally bad and totally unacceptable' as well as 'not workable', nevertheless he had re-affirmed that he was not opposed to all-India federation as such, but merely to the scheme put forward by the British government.[2] And even after the failure of his party in the elections, after the Indian National Congress had taken office in seven (later eight) provinces, and after his failure to negotiate any kind of Congress/League agreement in the United Provinces and Bombay, Jinnah, while attacking Congress policies and predicting that they would lead to 'class bitterness, communal war, and strengthening of the imperialistic hold', still went on calling publicly for a 'complete united front and honesty of purpose' to obtain 'full national democratic government for India'.[3] There was no suggestion of Muslim secession.[4]

Were India to be in danger of breaking up at all it seemed likely that disintegration would take the form of some kind of fragmentation or 'Balkanization' of the sort which haunted the mind of Jawaharlal Nehru. A pertinent question is therefore why, of all the political possibilities which were before India, this particular form of partition evolved; why it was the

[1] See R. J. Moore, 'The Making of India's Paper Federation', below, pp. 54–78 for a different interpretation.

[2] Speech in the Legislative Assembly, February 7, 1935 on the report of the joint parliamentary committee on Indian constitutional reforms.

[3] Presidential address, All-India Muslim League, Lucknow session, October 1937.

[4] But see S. R. Mehrotra, 'The Congress and the Partition of India', below pp. 201–4.

Muslims who came to found another nation state and not, for example, the Bengalis, the Madrasis, or any other of the linguistic, cultural, or racial groups of India. Was it that in India religion was the over-riding compulsion, rather than nationalism as understood in the west? Or was it that the conditions favouring the emergence of a distinct nationalism were to be found at this crucial period among Muslims rather than among other cultural groups? Or was it that only Muslims, among all possible break-away groups, found the necessary dynamic leadership?

In attempting an answer to these questions there is a danger as one looks back on the events of these years, of seeing them always coloured in the light of the final outcome; of judging every move in the knowledge that in August 1947 Britain would partition India and transfer power to two new dominions of India and Pakistan. Such hindsight tends to produce a restricted or fixed view, with an exaggeration of some effects and a dismissal of others. Moreover, in studying a near-contemporary episode which has aroused in millions the greatest fear and hatred, there is a temptation to take sides, to identify with one party or another, to marshal evidence to prove a certain case – albeit unconsciously – because of unquestioned assumptions deep in the minds of those who lived through those years, and who have been subjected to propaganda about them, either proceeding from the new nations themselves, particularly sensitive as these are about their historical past, or from the former imperial power concerned to justify its actions, or to see in withdrawal a 'victory' or 'fulfilment' not a 'defeat'.

The main course of events which led to the triumph of the Muslim League and the establishment of Pakistan – proceeding from the Act of 1935, through the elections of 1937 and the Muslim reactions to the Congress ministries of 1937–9, followed by the opportunities of the war years, the successes in the 1946 elections, the responses to the British initiatives of 1945–7, and the final triumph in August 1947 – is well known.

As the papers printed in this volume show, the interpretation of those events tends to vary with the preconceptions and present-day outlook of the contributors to the debate. A view widely held in India, for example, is that partition was a tragedy – a vivisection – and discussion in that country therefore tends to be concerned with discovering the reasons and apportioning the blame for this failure to maintain the unity of the sub-continent, as well as thinking up ways of mitigating the undesirable results of division. With admirable detachment the blame is often laid at the feet of the Congress leaders: had they done this, or refrained from doing that, partition could have been avoided. In Pakistan, on the other hand, where naturally it cannot be accepted that partition should have been avoided, there is a tendency to project the growth of Muslim nationalism into the depths of history, and with it the seeming inevitability of the establishment of a Muslim state. Among British writers there is of course some difference in outlook between generations, and within the generations between historians and those who actually served in India. Those brought up in the age of empire and concerned in the administration of that empire tend to differ from those of their contemporaries who were more influenced by the political climate of the thirties at home in England, while the generation to whom the *raj* is hardly even a memory, and who have seen without regret the rapid and seemingly inevitable break-up of empire, have yet another standpoint, not necessarily more objective. Past experience and present prejudice influence the very questions asked and before any new interpretation of partition can be put forward, before the myths which have already grown up on all sides can be understood and perhaps dispelled, many more detailed studies need to be undertaken.

In the introductory pages which follow it is proposed not to summarize the papers, and certainly not to give a full account of the partition, but to define some of the important questions to which detailed answers are needed if the making of partition is to be fully explained.

I. SOME PROBLEMS OF BRITISH POLICY

The making of the Government of India Act of 1935

Any enquiry into the course of events leading to the partition of India in 1947 into two sovereign states, India and Pakistan, must raise the questions why it had taken the prolonged period of thirty years from the Montagu declaration of 1917 to reach this point of independence, and why the main line of constitutional advance from that declaration, through the Government of India Act of 1919, the declaration on the proposed grant of dominion status within the Commonwealth, and the Government of India Act of 1935 had not led, as the British intended, to a federal solution, and the maintenance of the unity of India.

The broad and simple answer to the first question is that none of the principal parties in London or India had expressed and maintained, until a very late stage, an over-riding sense of urgency for the settlement of the political question. This was understandable because the future of a vast, heavily and diversely populated, tradition-riddled sub-continent was in question. The political problem seemed intractable, and the more the British administration of India studied and became more intimately informed on the complexity of Indian society, the more impressed it became by the difficulties of rousing the sleeping giant and the more convinced of the inevitability of political gradualness. Moreover, Indian leaders themselves seemed to accept an extended time scale of constitutional development. It was no doubt a coincidence, but not without significance, that in the late 1930s the British viceroy, Linlithgow, and the two principal Indian political spokesmen, Nehru and Jinnah on quite separate occasions should have expressed the view that another twenty to thirty years might well elapse before India would be free. Everyone seemed only too keenly aware that the grand old clock of empire was still beating with a slow, strong and measured tick.

The hopes aroused by the British declaration in August 1917 that there was to be a 'gradual development of self-governing institutions with a view to the progressive realization of responsible government in India', and by the Government of India Act of 1919 were soon dashed by the bitterness created by the Rowlatt Act, the disturbances in the Punjab and the Amritsar massacre. Losing faith in British intentions, Gandhi who had only recently assumed the leadership of the Congress, began his civil disobedience campaign, and as a result the British began to see the Indian National Congress as mainly a disruptive element. A rift opened which was never really closed until 1947.

These disturbances in India coincided with a period of political and economic upset in Britain, but by 1927 a period of stability seemed likely to emerge in both countries, and the prospects of political conciliation and rapprochement seemed, for a moment, bright. However, the chance of co-operation was soon lost in a controversy over the nomination of the wholly British membership of the Simon commission which was to advise on the future system of government. Congress responded by resuming its civil disobedience movement, and in an atmosphere of growing enmity the constitution-making process went slowly on its way through Round Table conferences, joint parliamentary committees and prolonged parliamentary debates on a new India Bill. Although the whole political talent of Britain appeared to be devoted to the task, not until August 1935 was the new India Act passed.

The ten years of real peace from 1925 to 1935 had given the British government ample time to take an important step forward on the road to responsible government, the last, as it turned out, before the final transfer of power. That this measure of constitutional reform took so long to complete is to be explained by the dissensions among Indian nationalists themselves, and not least, the delaying tactics of the dissident Conservatives in London led by Churchill, who was successfully though unhappily able to exploit the India question as part of his general attack on Baldwin's leadership.

Some writers feel that there was a body of moderate opinion in India which given an imaginative approach might have been mobilized to urge forward the constitutional approach,[1] and that such a development would have ensured the establishment of responsible government in India well before the outbreak of war in 1939. Had this happened it would have been unlikely to have involved partition for, although communal tensions had been rising, the Muslims were politically weak and divided.

In analysing the factors and influences determining the Act of 1935, some modern historians place the major responsibility for the delays in formulating that Act on Conservative politicians in London, also holding them responsible for the final shortcomings of the Act which, it is argued, made its failure a foregone conclusion.[2] This is to see these British politicians moved by imperial self-interest, yielding reluctantly to the pressure of Indian demands for self-government, and finally producing an Act heavy with safeguards, checks and balances: an Act not so much to free India as for the further government of India.

This was not the assessment made by distinguished historians at the time. Henry Dodwell saw the Act 'as a great experiment. No one can say whether it will succeed or not. But unless all Indian politicians are deceived in their belief that representative and responsible government is suited to the needs of India, it promises a political structure under which Indians will be free to develop those political institutions which they have never before possessed, and to forget that disastrous communal strife and division which from time

[1] See, e.g. P. Spear, 'A Third Force in India . . .', below, pp. 490–503.

[2] See, e.g. R. J. Moore, 'The Making of India's Paper Federation', below, pp. 54–78.

immemorial has always prevented the country from showing a united front to her enemies.' [1] Some five years later, Reginald Coupland, drawing attention to the care and attention devoted by parliament to India,[2] hailed the Act as 'a great achievement of constructive thought . . . which made it possible for India to attain Dominion Status without any more of those British discussions and decisions which had marked all the previous stages of her constitutional advance'.[3]

In their view the Act of 1935 stood a reasonable chance of succeeding.

The adequacy of the Act of 1935

Between 1937 and 1939 it was demonstrated that the provisions of the Act relating to the establishment of cabinet and responsible government in the eleven British Indian provinces could be made to work. But the unwillingness of the Indian states to federate with these provinces prevented the Act of 1935 from becoming fully effective.

On the face of it the federal prescription in the Act of 1935 appeared simple. The federation was to come into operation when an address to the Crown by parliament should ask for a proclamation to that effect, provided that a sufficient number of states should have acceded to take up fifty-two of the 104 seats allotted to the Indian states in the upper house of the federal legislature and to represent half of the total population of all states. A state was deemed to accede when its ruler executed an instrument of accession empowering the federal government and legislature to exercise authority over it in accordance with the Act.

By the outbreak of war in September 1939 these provisions had not been fulfilled, and in the light of their apparently straightforward nature it must be asked why Linlithgow, the viceroy, had failed to bring in the princes, or more precisely, even the relatively small group of big states, which in effect could have meant the difference between success and failure.

At the Round Table conference which opened in London in November 1930, there had been sixteen delegates from the states, including representatives of the important states of Hyderabad, Mysore, and Gwalior and including also the rulers of Alwar, Baroda, Bhopal, Bikaner, Kashmir and Patiala. Early in the proceedings the Maharaja of Bikaner agreed that India must be united on a federal basis and the other princes echoed his sentiments. But it was noteworthy that none of them suggested that federation was an early possibility or expressed any views about the question of responsible government at the centre.

The Act provided for a representation of 125 seats for the Indian states,

[1] H. Dodwell, *India*, vol. 2 (1936), pp. 265–6.

[2] Referring to the joint committee of both houses of parliament, which, under Lord Linlithgo was chairman, scrutinized the constitutional proposals for the future government of India, Coupland said, 'No more powerful parliamentary committee has ever been set up. It contained most of the leading men in British public life, including several who had held high office in India. It was in almost unbroken session for eighteen months, holding 159 meetings and examining 120 witnesses. . . . A remarkable part of its proceedings was the evidence given by Sir Samuel Hoare; he was examined for nineteen days and answered over 7,000 questions.' R. Coupland, *The Indian Problem*, 1833–1935, part 1 (1942), p. 132.

[3] *Ibid.* pp. 132–3.

one-half of the total for British India, which were to be distributed mainly in terms of population, with, for example, sixteen seats for Hyderabad, seven for Mysore, five for Travancore; but in fact comparatively few of the states were to be represented individually in this way, and in most cases groups of states were to be formed with one representative for each group. How this grouping was to be settled was not laid down.

In detail, therefore, before the federation could start, much remained to be worked out in India, no doubt on the initiative of the viceroy.

But in the five years between the first Round Table conference of 1930 and the passing of the Act, the princes had perceptibly changed their attitudes, dropping their initial warm approval of the federal idea and stressing rather their own autonomy. They raised objections to the infringement of their domestic sovereignty which the Act necessarily entailed, and questioned even the minimum powers which would be required within the Indian states by the proposed federal authorities. They went so far as to put the view that the princes' adherence to the federation would in effect constitute with the British government a bilateral agreement between allies and equals, and although the secretary of state firmly rejected this claim, it was clear that the princes, prompted by their army of legal advisers, had returned to the threadbare subject of their sovereign status and of the precise nature of British paramountcy over them.

In fact the British failure in the late nineteenth and early twentieth century to deal decisively with the claims of the princes, and to bring them and their states politically into line with the British provinces, had come home to roost. By the twentieth century the Indian states were a political anachronism even in India. At the start of the nineteenth century Richard Wellesley as governor-general had indicated that the right British policy was to bring the Indian states under complete political control, but this had not been done. Between 1936 and 1939 it would therefore have required dynamic pressure on the part of Linlithgow to transform this situation; and the touchiness on this subject of the right wing of the Conservative party in parliament, quite apart from Linlithgow's caution, effectively ruled this out, and still further encouraged the princes in their exaggerated notion of their own status and strength.

Linlithgow had expressed confidence before he left London for India in the spring of 1936 that the federation could be made fully operational within his five-year term of office, but on arrival he had become quickly aware that some of his governors and senior civil servants were deeply sceptical. It would have been surprising, too, if his skill as an administrator had not enabled him to see the obvious difficulty of working out an effective federal scheme involving over five hundred separate states, some vastly large, some minutely small, scattered throughout India. It was significant therefore that he chose the careful and leisurely method of sending a number of personal emissaries on a round of the princes not to cajole or hurry them but simply to explain the Act and discuss the proposed procedures and meaning of accession.

This was bound to be a slow and involved process, and it was not until early in 1939 that Linlithgow was able to formulate the terms on which the adherence of the princes to the Act was acceptable. Meanwhile the assumption of political power by the Indian National Congress in the British Indian provinces, following the general election of 1937, and its increasingly critical and aggressive attitude towards the princes made them regard the idea of federation with increasing apprehension and repugnance, so that the prospects of fulfilling the federal part of the Act of 1935 had receded even before the outbreak of war in September 1939 caused Linlithgow formally to bring the negotiations with the princes to an end.

In the circumstances of the period 1935 to 1939 a ruler as cautious as Linlithgow could never have provided an adequate answer to the political question of the Indian states, and there can be little doubt that the British government and the viceroy had gravely underestimated the complexity of this question. The issue was shirked until 1947–8 when Lord Mountbatten and Vallabhbhai Patel showed that the Gordian knot could be cut, but it required bold statesmanship and a combination of threats, promises and force.

The role of Linlithgow as viceroy

Criticism of Linlithgow's political policies in India by contemporaries and subsequently by historians has been generally adverse. It has been said, for example, that he failed to take the political initiative between 1936 and 1939 even when the context seemed right, that in particular the leisurely manner of his approach to the princes contributed to the postponement of the federation, and that he blundered egregiously in failing to consult the Indian political parties before taking India to war, thus throwing away the chance of Congress support in the war. Further, that he was always tepid towards any policy of associating the major parties with the war effort. He is charged with 'having found an obstacle for every solution'.

A full evaluation of Linlithgow's role must await the publication of his personal papers.[1] But already the evidence is available to show that in fact in the early period of his viceroyalty down to the war, Linlithgow was rather more enterprising in devising political initiatives than his opposite number, Zetland, in the India Office, and that it was not until after the outbreak of war that Linlithgow took up the stiff, apparently unsympathetic attitude to Indian political parties and politicians for which he is criticized.

Once war had been declared Linlithgow was and felt himself to be at bay. With Britain under attack, his personal responsibility at the head of the Indo-British empire was enormous. The test of his every action was the survival of Britain and the empire. He had not consulted Indian leaders before declaring war because he knew that they were intent on driving a political bargain, and he was uncertain what his course ought to be in the event of their refusal to participate. Firmly of opinion that in India time was on Britain's side, that the end of the *raj* was not even in sight, and that in the event of rebellion the Indian parties could be contained if need be by force (which he proceeded to demonstrate in 1942), he had no doubt that, come what may, the right British policy within India was strictly to maintain the political *status quo*. It can be argued not unreasonably that in such circumstances this was a defensible policy, certainly through the period when the future of

[1] Lord Glendevon, the son of Linlithgow, is at present engaged in writing a study based on his private papers.

Britain itself was in jeopardy. It must be noted, too, that in more favourable circumstances when the crisis of the war was past, his successor, Wavell, failed to get the Indian parties to agree at the Simla conference.

Nevertheless it was during Linlithgow's viceroyalty that the Indian National Congress rebelled, and the Muslim League declared for partition, which events must be accounted failures for a viceroy charged with the task of applying the Act of 1935 which was to fulfil the British political dream of a united, responsibly ruled India.

British initiatives during and after the war

The incidence of world war between 1939 and 1945 inevitably changed the context and the pace of constitutional development in India. Down to 1939 all parties in India appeared to have assumed that the leisurely progress towards self-government would continue, as it had done in the past, for perhaps another quarter of a century. And, after the outbreak of war – apart from the abortive Cripps mission in 1942 – constitutional questions took second place, in the policies of the British government, first to the effort to survive and later to the achievement of victory. But by late 1945 the British government was convinced that, for reasons more connected with British politics and Britain's changed place in the world than with conditions in India, Britain must withdraw from the sub-continent as soon as agreement could be reached with India's leaders on the details of the transfer of power. And all British moves thereafter were directed to what proved to be the impossible task of finding a plan acceptable to the major Indian parties, which would yet maintain the unity of the country.

British policy on India between 1945 and 1947 is already open to scrutiny in a wealth of published, official documents, and much secondary analysis from a variety of points of view has also appeared on the Simla conference, the cabinet mission and the Mountbatten viceroyalty. Further studies in depth will no doubt increase our understanding of the background to partition and of the role of those most concerned, but so much relevant evidence in published form is already available that it seems unlikely that access to the remaining archives which have not yet been opened to scholars will necessitate any fundamental reinterpretation of British policy in this period. British policy was now governed by a determination to hand over power to a strong and united Indian government as soon as practicable.[1] The factors militating against this aim rested in India not Britain, and it was conditions in India and the policies of the Indian leaders which in the end made partition seem the only acceptable solution.

Once partition had been agreed upon, events moved swiftly, and the transfer of power was completed in a dramatically short time. The actual speed of transfer has been held responsible – and no doubt correctly – for many of the disputes which later arose between the two new countries of

[1] Various contributors to this volume (e.g. B. R. Nanda and H. Kabir) argue that the British encouraged Jinnah and the League in the demand for Pakistan: but others (e.g. M. A. H. Ispahani and M. Hasan) accuse the British of wishing to frustrate Muslim aspirations. However, there seems little doubt that official policy was to maintain the unity of the sub-continent if at all possible.

India and Pakistan. Yet any scrutiny of the course and fate of the previous British attempts by Cripps and the cabinet mission must evoke the thought that had negotiations in this instance also continued in a more leisurely manner the Mountbatten plan would have gone the way of its predecessors, while the country sank deeper into communal chaos.

Mountbatten's two plans for partition, 1947

Alan Campbell-Johnson, press attaché to the viceroy, reported in his diary on May 11, 1947 'Mountbatten has had a shattering day. . . . It seems that last night Mountbatten gave Nehru the chance of reading the draft Plan as revised and approved by London, and that Nehru, having read it, has vehemently turned it down. He is convinced that it involves a major departure in principle from the original draft prepared by Mountbatten and his staff which Ismay and George Abell took back with them to London.' [1] On that same morning V. P. Menon, constitutional adviser to the governor-general, and an intimate of the leading Congressmen, reported, 'When I saw Nehru on the morning of the 11th I found that his usual charm and smile had deserted him and that he was obviously upset.' [2]

From the sharpness of these reactions some idea of the gravity of the situation may be gained; and out of this crisis Mountbatten hurriedly withdrew his first draft plan and devised a second, fresh plan which was presented to Jinnah and Nehru and their senior colleagues on June 2nd. It was this second plan which formed the basis of the partition of August 15, 1947.

Around this episode of the two plans there has arisen a good deal of confusion and misunderstanding. In a recent study a distinguished Pakistani, Chaudhri Muhammad Ali states that there was no difference between the first plan which was sent to London, and the second, revised plan, except an earlier transfer of power on the basis of dominion status,[3] and goes on to conclude that the revised plan represented a 'secret bargain' between Mountbatten and the Congress leaders to speed up the transfer of power – which 'was the price paid to Congress for agreeing to stay within the Commonwealth. . . . For this one gain to themselves, the British were prepared to pay any price – at the expense of Pakistan.' [4]

Some have found Nehru's reaction to the sight of the first plan extremely puzzling. One writer asks, 'What made Nehru react in this way to proposals which embodied a plan for determining the will of the people of India to a partition upon lines of religion, which only a few days before he had publicly recognized as the supreme question to be answered? At the time, it must have appeared baffling.' [5] And the conclusion drawn is that Nehru must have been suffering from a kind of 'political amnesia'. 'While going through the motions of consultation and discussion with Mountbatten on a plan for partition, he had remained entranced by the vision of a united India. Confronted by the

[1] A. Campbell-Johnson, *Mission with Mountbatten*, p. 89.
[2] V. P. Menon, *The Transfer of Power in India*, p. 361.
[3] C. M. Ali, *Emergence of Pakistan*, p. 136.
[4] *Ibid.* p. 138.
[5] H. R. Tinker, *Experiment with Freedom*, p. 112.

mechanism for partition in the inescapable context of the written page, his first reaction was to deny that such a development was possible.'[1]

But this is to be less than fair to Nehru, and to misunderstand the historical background. Congress and Nehru had long stood for the unity of India. They had fought the general election of 1937 on this platform; they had reaffirmed this in 1942 when rejecting Rajagopalachari's proposal to recognize Muslim separatism. It was not until May 1, 1947 that the Congress working committee formally accepted the principle of partition, on that day Nehru writing to Mountbatten, 'In regard to the proposals which, I presume, Lord Ismay is carrying with him to London, our Committee are prepared to accept the principle of partition, based on self-determination applied to definitely ascertained areas. This involves the partition of Bengal and the Punjab.'[2]

Nehru had not seen the text of the plan taken by Ismay to London, and when Mountbatten showed it to him on the evening of May 10th it was his first sight of the document.

In it he read that the provinces would have the right to determine their own future, and therefore Madras, Bombay, United Provinces, Central Provinces, Bihar, Orissa, Assam would formally have to reaffirm that they wished to remain within the Indian constituent assembly. Bengal and the Punjab were to determine their own future. Sylhet would be given the option to join a partitioned Bengal, and a referendum was to be held in the North West Frontier Province to ascertain the will of the people. There was provision for Baluchistan to express self-determination. Each of the successor states, it was proposed, should conclude independent treaties, presumably also with the British government.

Nehru's reaction to these proposals was immediate and vehement. 'Instead of producing any sense of certainty, security and stability, they would encourage disruptive tendencies everywhere and chaos and weakness.' He could not but be keenly aware that already H. S. Suhrawardy was actively campaigning for an independent Bengal, and that the larger Indian states were using the fact of British paramountcy to emphasize their separateness. Against the background of Congress policy and the cabinet mission plan, which had started with an acceptance of an Indian union, Mountbatten's plan appeared to reject the union as the successor to power and appeared rather to invite the statement of claims of a large number of successor states who would be permitted to unite if they so wished into two or more states.[3] Nehru in fact still saw the Indian union as the successor state, and Pakistan in the position of an area or areas that had seceded from the parent country.

Nehru's reaction to the plan was therefore intelligible, and completely in the context of his own and Congress's longstanding policy, and not in any way an aberration or taken in a fit of absence of mind or 'political amnesia'. He had always feared the fragmentation of India.

Mountbatten saw how closely he personally had come to disaster. As he said, he had shown Nehru the draft 'on an absolute hunch. . . . Without that

[1] H. R. Tinker, *Experiment with Freedom*, p. 112.

[2] Pyarelal, *Mahatma Gandhi. The Last Phase*, II, pp. 158–9.

[3] C. M. Ali, *The Emergence of Pakistan*, p. 136 says, 'There is no difference between the plan discussed at this conference and the partition plan taken by Ismay to London.'

hunch, Dickie Mountbatten would have been finished and would have packed his bag. We would have looked complete fools with the Government at home, having led them up the garden to believe that Nehru would accept the Plan.' [1]

This was tantamount to admitting that the plan had been loosely drawn. It may well be that the form was dictated by the day to day, discussion by discussion, piecemeal manner in which Mountbatten had proceeded.

When the final plan of June 3rd was drawn, it proceeded from the assumption that power was to be handed over to two successor states on the basis of dominion status. Nehru found no difficulty in accepting this formulation.

The second and final plan was therefore vitally different from the first, and assertions to the contrary with their accusation of secret bargains between Mountbatten and Nehru are wide of the truth.

The Radcliffe Boundary Commission

The continuous partition line which the commission was required to demarcate in both the Punjab and Bengal was bound in both provinces to cut across thickly populated and long-settled areas, each of which formed an integrated economy and system of communication. Injustice and great hardship could not be avoided, and the awards themselves were sure to be unpopular and to become the subject of controversy. What is surprising is that certain aspects of the process by which the award was made have attracted even greater attention and adverse criticism.

The Mountbatten time-table for independence constituted a crash programme and required that the boundary award should be carried through with the greatest speed; and in fact it was completed within six weeks. The boundary commission was originally provided for in the plan of June 3rd. Two groups, one for Bengal and one for the Punjab, were set up, each consisting of four members, two in each group representing India and Pakistan respectively. Nehru and Jinnah had both agreed that the members should be High Court judges. No progress was made on Mountbatten's suggestion that these members should select their own chairman, and Nehru and Jinnah asked him to request H.M.G. to use its good offices in making available a suitable person. Sir Cyril Radcliffe was selected with the full agreement of both parties, and both they and he agreed to the terms of reference.

Arriving in Delhi on July 8th Radcliffe at once sought interviews with Nehru, Patel, Jinnah and Liaqat Ali Khan separately, in order to ascertain that in their view the importance of having an award by August 15th, taking into account its inevitable imperfections, outweighed all other considerations. Each said that it did.

The Bengal and the Punjab parts of the commission met at Calcutta and Lahore respectively, and since it was plainly impossible for Radcliffe to attend all of their public hearings, he made his own headquarters in Delhi, where daily he received a full transcript of the shorthand notes of both sets of proceedings. This he reinforced by two visits of several days each to Calcutta, and similar, single visits to Lahore and Simla for discussions with his commission colleagues. One suggestion which he early made to them was

[1] A. Campbell-Johnson, *op. cit.* p. 89.

that any boundary line agreed by them between themselves would have far more weight than any arbital line drawn by himself, but unfortunately neither of the two groups was able to arrive at a common basis for their judgments, and Radcliffe therefore had to make the awards alone. Moreover, since the requirement was for a continuous line in each province, it was impossible to reserve areas of especial difficulty for more leisurely scrutiny, or to provide for subsequent change. Radcliffe has emphasized that the process of shaping the two continuous boundary lines was carried on throughout the six-week period and that the final definition remained open until the end.

Criticism from the side of Pakistan has steadily been directed against the objectivity and detachment of Radcliffe as chairman of the commission. Chaudhri Muhammad Ali says 'the award in the Panjab was of such a character as to arouse immediate suspicions of outside interference'.[1] Muhammad Zafrulla Khan has alleged that Mountbatten had known the likely nature of the award before publication and had got parts of it changed.[2] Such a process was easy, argues Chaudhri Muhammad Ali, 'since Radcliffe and his office were lodged in a wing of the Viceroy's house, it was possible to maintain discreet contact without any outsider coming to know about it'.[3]

We must note, however, that Mountbatten had foreseen the dangers in such an arrangement and had indicated that it was not suitable for Radcliffe when in Delhi to stay in the viceroy's house. In his press conference on June 4th he had stated that 'So far as it is humanly possible there will be no interference or dictation by the British Government', and throughout the award period Mountbatten's staff were keenly aware that he wished 'to have nothing to do with Radcliffe personally or with any representations that might be made in connection with the work of the Boundary Commission'. His press officer, Alan Campbell-Johnson, also reported to this effect; and both he and other senior members of Mountbatten's staff state that Ismay, too, took the same view.

It is true that on at least one occasion Mountbatten had suggested to Radcliffe that there might be advantage in presenting the award to the public if there was some overall 'balance' in the nature of the awards, perhaps between Bengal and the Punjab, but Radcliffe did not see how this idea of 'balance' could possibly be pursued or achieved consistently with his duties to each commission.

In pressing his charge of collusion Chaudhri Muhammad Ali has cited the instance of a sketch map known to have been made on August 8th by the viceroy's private secretary for Evan Jenkins, governor of the Punjab, which was apparently based on a telephone conversation between the viceroy's secretary and the secretary of the boundary commission. He argues that this provides clear evidence of collusion between Radcliffe and the British administration in fixing the boundary.

Chaudhri Muhammad Ali also reports that on August 9th or 10th he saw a pencil line already drawn on a map in Ismay's office. 'I said (to Ismay) that it was unnecessary for me to explain further since the line, already drawn on

[1] C. M. Ali, *op. cit.* p. 216.
[2] During conference discussions.
[3] C. M. Ali, *op. cit.* p. 217.

the map, indicated the boundary I had been talking about. Ismay turned pale and asked in confusion who had been fooling with his map.' [1]

It seems clear from the evidence that neither Mountbatten nor Radcliffe was personally involved. As for the existence of sketch maps and lines drawn on maps, the simplest explanation is that many such lines must have been drawn on maps at that period, not least in government offices for administrative purposes. It is not surprising, for example, that in this pre-partition period similar information was sought by and conveyed to the government of Bengal about the probable line of notional boundaries.

Chaudhri Muhammad Ali also sees something sinister in the fact that the commission award was withheld from publication until the day after independence. But a reasonable and simple explanation can also be offered for this. Radcliffe's report was actually ready and available on August 13th. But five days earlier, on August 8th, a strongly worded message from Liaqat Ali Khan, prime minister designate of Pakistan, had convinced Mountbatten of the possibility that the award would provoke a strongly antagonistic political and public response. However, he and his staff remained in no doubt of the important administrative advantages to be gained by immediate publication. On August 12th his staff (but not Mountbatten) saw an advance copy of the Bengal report and on a first appreciation they agreed that the award on the Chittagong Hill Tracts would upset the Congress. In discussion V. P. Menon emphasized the danger that as a result the Congress leaders might decline to attend the official independence day celebrations. Wishing to avoid this, Mountbatten therefore at once raised with Radcliffe the possibility that the actual submission of the report might be held back until after August 15th, but this Radcliffe declined to do, indicating that it would be submitted according to plan on August 13th.

Mountbatten had gradually become convinced of the superior advantages of holding back the report until August 16th, and of giving it to the rival parties simultaneously and together so that their anticipated counter responses might in fact cancel out, and be seen to do so.

On August 13th Mountbatten had to go to Karachi, before departing suggesting to Nehru and Jinnah that they should all meet in Delhi on August 16th to decide on the timing and method of publication and the enforcement of decisions.

Mountbatten examined the awards for the first time on his return from Karachi on August 14th and found that the main differences from the notional boundaries concerned the allotment in the Punjab of about three-quarters of the Gurdaspur District and a small part of the Lahore District to India; and in Bengal, besides the allotment of the Chittagong Hill Tracts to Pakistan various other districts or parts of districts to one or other state. Instructions were at once sent to the governors of Bengal and the Punjab that the governments of the two halves of the split provinces would have to take charge up to the notional boundaries on August 15th, pending publication of the awards, or failing this, of mutually agreed boundaries.

The meeting to consider the boundary commission's awards duly took place on August 16th, with both prime ministers and other ministers present.

[1] C. M. Ali, *op. cit.* p. 219.

Each side was given three hours to study the awards, and asked to meet at 5 p.m. The indignation of each side was intense. After two hours of bitter complaint, both sides could not but be aware of some of the general advantages of the proposals, and as Mountbatten had foreseen, were more easily able to agree that the awards should be announced and implemented forthwith.

II. CONGRESS AND LEAGUE, 1939–47: SOME QUESTIONS

The policy of the Indian National Congress

No one studying the swift movement of India towards partition in the years preceding 1947 can fail to be surprised at the tame manner in which the Indian National Congress in 1939 yielded the political initiative and position of power which it had so manfully and deservedly won for itself in the previous two decades. Almost equally surprising was its subsequent failure to restore its fortunes and reassert itself. It was this breakdown of Congress which opened the way for the Muslim League and Pakistan.

The Congress had taken the lead in the Indian freedom movement as an alliance of those Indians of all classes who were seeking a united and independent India. It prided itself on its claim to represent all significant Indian parties and interests; and the massive vote which it won throughout a large part of British India in the general election of 1937, followed by its ultimate assumption of political office in eight out of the eleven British Indian provinces, appeared to have justified its claims and its policies.

In the light of this success at the polls, there was justification in the refusal of its leaders to accept any policy of forming coalition ministries with other parties, and certainly not with the Muslim League which, in failing almost entirely to bring out even the Muslim vote, had been humiliated in the general election. On the contrary by offering places to many Congress Muslims in its new ministries Congress was able to point the moral, and in this context Nehru's declaration that Congress must actively pursue a policy of mass Muslim contact made excellent sense.

In the provinces in which it had taken office Congress, somewhat to the surprise of its critics, not least the British, proceeded to show a capacity for firm, progressive government, comfortably maintaining law and order, and initiating new economic measures. The style with which it assumed and used power and its bold assumption that the reins of all Congress ministries were to be firmly held at its all-India headquarters at Wardha, and that its viewpoint was continental not provincial, gave an impression of strength, unity, and single-mindedness of purpose. The political future of India seemed to be set safely within its grip.

Against this record of achievement and potential by 1939, the acceptance of partition less than ten years later, along with the recognition that the Muslim League under Jinnah had become the representative Muslim party, was a terrible defeat, mortifying and almost incomprehensible and unacceptable. Yet the fact was that within those ten years India was split and Pakistan was born. Even the most confirmed Congressman cannot fail to ask what went wrong.

It has to be said that despite earlier indications to the contrary, the leaders of the National Congress in the period between the outbreak of war in 1939 and the partition of 1947 showed in general a lack of realism, of foresight, of purpose and of will. In the face of setbacks from 1939 onwards, the unity and decisiveness of leadership, so conspicuous in the era when things were going their way, soon disappeared. It is true that in a party covering the spectrum of ideologies there were always bound to be internal strains and stresses, and divisions, but the extent to which the leadership fell apart during the war years is striking, and obviously deserving of detailed study which so far it has not been given. Most significant in this period was the gulf which opened up between Gandhi and many of his colleagues on the working committee. Earlier his traditional and independent role, exercised outside the committee and entirely in the context of domestic, peacetime and opposition politics, had served to provide and clarify issues and to focus the freedom struggle, and served as an incentive to action. But once Congress had gained some experience of the responsibilities of government, and had begun to appreciate how greatly the range of political issues had been extended by the commitment of India to war, Gandhi's role became an irritant, and a source of perplexity. By turns Nehru, Azad, Patel and others, took important initiatives but these were not sustained and no clear line of Congress policy was advocated or maintained. Once domestic politics had become communal, Gandhi's bewildering fertility of ideas and arguments had disrupting effects on Congressmen, confusing their sense of strategy and seemingly paralysing their will to reach decisions.

Two major decisions on policy, both of which showed a fundamental lack of appreciation of the realities of power, or at least of the extent to which those realities were bound to change in an India which had moved from peace into war, did more than anything to shake the foundations of Congress power. The first was the withdrawal of all Congress ministries from office in reaction to the decision of the British viceroy, Linlithgow, in 1939 to declare war on behalf of India. The second was the half-hearted attempt in 1942 to try by rebellion to force the embattled British to quit India.

In extenuation of the first decision it has been said that Congress had only assumed office in 1937 after great hesitation and by a narrow vote and in face of strong opposition from the left-wing, and that it could not honourably allow itself to be taken to war on behalf of an India which was not free. But these were considerations born of domestic and peace-time politics. The fact was that at a time when British power was being challenged throughout the world Congress had voluntarily sacrificed the gains of twenty years, had tamely surrendered the political initiative and position of authority for little apparent gain, and at the same time had opened to its opponents, especially Jinnah and the Muslim League, a route hitherto blocked to the centre of Indian government. The subsequent move of Congress into rebellion long before all other possible paths had been explored revealed its sense of frustration, and uncertainty of purpose, and proved to be a major miscalculation of the forces at play. By this act the leaders of Congress condemned themselves to a prolonged period of imprisonment with the result that the working committee, the power house of Congress, was put out of action for nearly three years and the Congress organization as a whole wound down.

It was a heaven-sent opportunity which Jinnah and the Muslim League could not and did not fail to exploit.

The climate of Congress opinion which conditioned all of the decisions taken by Congress relating to the Pakistan movement was largely created by Gandhi and Nehru. In response to the Lahore resolution of the Muslim League Gandhi wrote in April 1940, 'Unless the rest of India wishes to engage in internal fratricide, the others will have to submit to the Moslem dictation, if the Moslems will resort to it. I know of no non-violent method of compelling the obedience of eight crores of Moslems to the will of the rest of India, however powerful a majority the rest may represent. The Moslems must have the same right of self-determination that the rest of India has. We are at present a joint family. Any member may claim a division.'[1] This view he frequently repeated. In the same period Nehru's response to the Pakistan resolution was to say that 'if people wanted such things as suggested by the Muslim League at Lahore then one thing was clear. They and people like him could not live together in India. He would be prepared to face all the consequences of it, but he would not be prepared to live with such people.'[2]

The practical effect of both taking and announcing this attitude towards the Pakistan movement was drastically to reduce Congress's power of manoeuvre *vis-à-vis* the Muslim League, and to place total emphasis on persuasion and negotiation, without reference to Congress's power in the land. This being so it is startling to find Congress in April 1942 rejecting by a large majority Rajagopalachari's proposal that for the purpose of negotiation Congress should recognize Muslim separatism in some form, without closely defining what was implied. Not content with this rejection, Congress proceeded to declare that 'any proposal to disintegrate India by giving liberty to any component state or territorial unit to secede from the Indian Union or federation will be detrimental to the best interests of the people of the different states and provinces, and the country as a whole, and the Congress therefore cannot agree to any such proposal'.[3] This seemed to rule out some loose kind of confederation which was the most obvious, most practicable alternative to Pakistan and therefore the most promising line of negotiation.

If force or any threat of force was excluded and the main line of fruitful negotiation was closed, there remained either successful persuasion of the majority of Muslims to the Congress point of view or acceptance by Congress of Pakistan. Thus when the politics of mass communalism supervened, Congress found that the only course left open was not so much even to oppose partition as to try to limit so far as it could the area which was to be accepted as the state of Pakistan.

The emergence of Muslim Nationalism

How did it come about that the Muslims, politically weak and disorganized in the 1930s, were able within ten years to put forward a convincing claim for a separate state? Was Muslim nationalism a natural growth, a widespread movement of the grass roots which for long was not perceived in the centres

[1] D. G. Tendulkar, *Mahatma*, new ed. (1962), vol. v p. 269.
[2] *Leader*, April 15, 1940.
[3] Jagat Narain's counter-resolution.

of power, or was it the deliberate creation of the Muslim League? Did the League merely represent the feelings of the mass of the Muslims, or did its leaders create a nationalist movement by manipulating the many existing economic, social and political tensions until they were brought to focus on the one aim of seeking a separate homeland for Muslims?

The political ideal of nationalism, in contrast to the sense of community of Islam, was not widespread among Muslims until the last few years before the transfer of power. Moreover this Muslim nationalist movement did not show its head in those parts of north-west and north-east India where Muslims were in the majority, but arose first among middle and upper class conservative Muslims in the United Provinces, where they were in a minority. Perhaps this is no matter for surprise, for here Muslims were not a backward community as they tended to be elsewhere, but a substantial and fairly prosperous minority group, living in the centre of Muslim culture, and with strong memories of their days of power. Yet consciousness of past glories and culture, would not alone have been sufficient to provide the motive power to sustain an effective nationalist movement, even though such awareness of a proud past might have been the cause of an initial discontent. Present grievances were necessary to keep or bring alive and secure the expansion of such a movement.

The Muslims of the minority areas, among whom nationalist ideas first circulated, though not a depressed class, yet had their fears and grievances, and revolutionary ideas seem to stem more from frustrated expectations than from a state of total exploitation. A community aware of having lost power to the British only a century ago, was now, as the consequences of a British withdrawal became manifest, fearful of losing power permanently to the Hindu majority. The Hindus, throughout India and including the Muslim majority areas, were the successful community. They had early adopted western education and seized the opportunities open to them, while the Muslim community had hung back. But the Muslims, too – very late in the day – had been driven to adopt a form of western education, and were beginning to produce an intelligentsia to compete with the Hindus in government and the professions, lines in which, however, the Hindus had long acquired a hold.

The centre of this new Muslim education was Aligarh University in the United Provinces, and its young western-educated graduates formed an additional discontented element in the Muslim community of the minority areas. It would be natural for them to blame their minority status in the community for any lack of success in obtaining employment suited to their education, rather than to put the responsibility on the system itself, with its overproduction of graduates. The old might well be content to dwell on past glories and present culture, but the frustration of the young needed a political outlet. The Muslim League provided them with a cause.

And so, it was the minority provinces as Jinnah said in 1943 'who spread the light when there was darkness in the majority provinces. It is they who were the spear-heads. . . . It is they who . . . suffered for you in the majority provinces, for your sake, for your benefit and for your advantage. . . .' [1]

[1] Presidential address, All-India Muslim League, Delhi session, April 24, 1943.

The Muslim leaders in the majority provinces were slow to take advantage of these 'sufferings' and reluctant to adopt the hegemony of the League, dominated as it was by Muslims from the minority areas, and especially from the United Provinces, right up to independence. Muslims in these majority areas were mainly peasants and 'feudal nobility'. The peasants were not politically awakened and the politicians were for long inclined more to regional than to Islamic nationalism. It is true that after the shock defeat in the 1937 elections they joined the All-India Muslim League at its Lucknow session in October 1937, but their ideas on the role of the League differed from those of its president. Particularly in Bengal and Punjab they saw the League as having a role to play in all-India matters, but with no right to interfere in provincial affairs. The League had after all failed in the elections and had been unable to form ministries in any province, and Jinnah's claims of overlordship were resented by the provincial leaders. There was constant dissension between Jinnah, as president of the League, and the Punjab and Bengal ministries. In these two provinces Muslims with their slender majorities needed the support of non-Muslims to maintain stable governments and did not want to be heavily tarred with the communal brush.

The pact between Jinnah and Sikandar Hyat Khan by which Muslim members of the Unionist party in the Punjab joined the Muslim League while in return the League agreed not to interfere in provincial politics, did not settle relationships in the Punjab. For, once the Pakistan resolution of 1940 had been adopted it became essential for the League to gain control of Muslim politics in that province, which was, as Jinnah said, 'the corner-stone of Pakistan'. [1] Jinnah later denied that he had promised not to interfere in provincial matters and asked how there could be a 'pact' between a leader (himself) and a follower (Sikandar Hyat).[2] He called upon Muslim leaders in the Punjab to abandon their 'sectional interests, jealousies, tribal notions and selfishness' and to substitute devotion to Islam and 'your nation',[3] but as late as 1944 Jinnah's negotiations with Khizr Hyat Khan, the then chief minister, failed and as a result his prestige and that of the League suffered a setback in this vital province.[4]

In Bengal also there were constant clashes between Jinnah and the chief minister, Fazlul Haq, from 1937 until his defeat in 1943. In September 1941, long after the League, and by implication all Muslims, had officially adopted Pakistan as the goal, Fazlul Haq in a letter resigning from the working committee and council of the League, protested in the strongest terms against the manner in which the interests of the Muslims of Bengal and the Punjab were being imperilled by the Muslim leaders of the minority provinces, and complained of the way in which the principles of democracy and autonomy were being subordinated to the arbitrary wishes of a single individual.[5] When Fazlul Haq's ministry was defeated in 1943 Jinnah rejoiced at the fall of this 'curse to the politics of Bengal'.[6]

[1] Presidential address, All-India Muslim League, Delhi session, April 24, 1943.

[2] Speech at the Punjab Muslim League conference, Sialkot, April 30, 1944.

[3] Presidential address, All-India Muslim League, Delhi session, April 24, 1943.

[4] See Humayun Kabir, 'Muslim Politics 1942–1947', below, pp. 393–4, but this view has been challenged in discussion.

[5] See Ch. Khaliquzzuman, *Pathway to Pakistan*, pp. 255–6.

[6] Presidential address, All-India Muslim League, Delhi session, April 24, 1943.

At this date it might have seemed that the Muslim League had conquered the majority provinces, for there were now League, or League-dominated ministries in Assam, Bengal, Punjab, Sind, and the Frontier Province, but its position was still not as strong as this fact might suggest. In the Punjab the Muslim ministers were, in Jinnah's own words, members of the League in name only,[1] while in Sind, the Frontier, and Bengal the ministries were not stable, and in fact all were defeated early in 1945. At the same time the League leader in Assam formed a coalition with the Congress leader, so that by mid-1945 the political fortunes of the League in the provinces again seemed to be declining.

It was only by appealing to the people of the majority provinces over the heads of their old political leaders, and using mass methods similar to those introduced by Gandhi into the Congress organization, that Jinnah finally, in the 1945 elections, demonstrated that on the issue of Pakistan he had indeed the backing of the whole Muslim community. Yet to make sure of succeeding the League had to seek the assistance of the religious leaders in the election campaign,[2] and once Pakistan had been truly won the Muslim League began to fall apart, for it was not securely based in these old majority provinces.

Because Muslim nationalism conquered the majority areas only at a comparatively late stage in the campaign for Pakistan, the theory has been put forward[3] that had it not so happened that a number of powerful provincial Muslim leaders, notably Fazl-i-Husain, Sikandar Hyat Khan, and Allah Bakhsh, died when they did,[4] the Muslim League would not have triumphed in the Punjab and Sind, and that had not the League been seen to have been triumphant there, it would never have been able to capture the Frontier province from Abdul Ghaffar Khan and his Red Shirts. Critics of this theory point out that in point of fact these men were provincial rather than all-India figures, who would have been unable to withstand Jinnah's dynamism. But without Jinnah's leadership it seems likely that regionalism, such as the proposal for a united and independent Bengal, which was discussed by both Hindu and Muslim leaders there in 1947, would have competed seriously with Muslim nationalism as the political aim of these provinces. Fazlul Haq, for example, was never really reconciled to the partition of Bengal. As late as May 1954, when he was chief minister of East Bengal, he was reported as saying that he would not take notice of the fact that there was a political division of the province of Bengal into East and West Bengal,[5] and both he and H. S. Suhrawardy, while continuing to play important roles in Pakistan politics after partition, were from time to time suspected of intriguing for the reunion of Bengal and subjected to attacks as traitors to Pakistan.

Not until very late in the day did Jinnah's campaign to weld the Muslim community into a nation receive substantial help from the political leaders

[1] Speaking at the Punjab Muslim League Conference at Sialkot, April 30, 1943.
[2] See K. B. Sayeed, *Pakistan, the Formative Phase*, 2nd ed., pp. 202–6.
[3] See, for example, H. Kabir, 'Muslim Politics 1942–1947', below, p. 390.
[4] July 1936, December 1942, and May 1943 respectively.
[5] Quoted in K. B. Sayeed, *The Political System of Pakistan*, p. 188.

in the Muslim majority areas; nor was the movement at first launched under the banner of religion, though religious leaders were recruited later on to help in the 1945 election campaign. There had been no revival of faith among prominent Leaguers, nor had any serious thought been given to the structure of a specifically Islamic state.[1] Jinnah wanted a homeland for Muslims, not an Islamic state, and there was in fact on this issue a long difference of opinion between himself and the Raja of Mahmudabad, the youngest member of the League working committee.[2] Here we see perhaps a conflict between the generations, between the secular-minded constitutionally inclined Jinnah, and the more enthusiastic young who had responded whole-heartedly to the League's propaganda, including its religious aspect.

If, however, the original motivation for the emergence of Muslim nationalism was neither the backward condition of the masses in the majority areas nor an upsurge of religious feeling among Muslims in general, could it be, as has been asserted,[3] that 'national' sentiment as it first appeared in the minority areas was not merely the result of the dissatisfaction of educated Muslims with available opportunities, as suggested above, but the reaction of the landlord class to the realities of the democracy which would face them if and when the British withdrew? If this be so, it makes the achievement of the League the more remarkable.

Detailed studied of the politics of both minority and majority areas before the Pakistan bandwagon swept most Muslims into the League camp might help to show how a party of a conservative minority became a great mass movement. On the evidence at present available it seems most likely that it was the adoption of a simple and attractive slogan, the creation of an effective all-India organization, and above all the extremely capable and single-minded leadership of Jinnah, exploiting the separatist tendencies of the Muslims, and taking advantage of every opportunity offered both by the Congress and by the British to advance the League cause, which explains the success achieved by the League in the short space of ten years.

Many Pakistani scholars do not accept this view, believing that the demand for separation came up from the grass roots and would sooner or later have had to be taken account of, that it was not the creation of the Muslim League, but that the League leadership merely expressed the convictions of the masses. A study of the preoccupations of the Muslim community as a whole both in the years before and after the Lahore resolution would help to resolve the problem.

The organization of the Muslim League

The successful and swift dissemination of the idea and need for Pakistan, even the exploitation of religious feelings in an effective way, has conveyed the impression that the League was a well-organized party. Yet in the early thirties Muslims were hopelessly divided and the League was a negligible force, which in the 1937 elections gained a mere 4·8 per cent of the Muslim vote. Only in Bombay, where in any event the Muslims were a minority,

[1] See M. Mujeeb, 'The Partition of India in Retrospect', below, pp. 406–8.
[2] See Raja of Mahmudabad, 'Some Memories', below, pp. 388–9.
[3] By M. Mujeeb, below, p. 410.

did the League gain more than half the Muslim seats; and Bombay, too, was the home of Jinnah, the League president. In the United Provinces, the most important of the minority provinces, the League won less than half the Muslim seats; while only Bengal of the majority provinces returned any substantial number of League candidates. Even in Bengal only one-third of the Muslim seats went to the League, while in the Punjab the League won only two out of eighty-six Muslim seats, and in the Frontier Province and Sind none at all.[1] How therefore did the League come to be able to claim with credibility to be the sole representative organization of the Muslims in time for the elections of 1945 when it swept the board, capturing every Muslim seat in the central assembly, and 428 out of 492 Muslim seats in the provincial assemblies? Though even now the League was able to form ministries only in Bengal and Sind, and in Bengal the chief minister, H. S. Suhrawardy, needed the support of independent elements to form his ministry.[2]

A detailed examination of the Muslim League papers now deposited at Karachi University should show how the organization of the League was built up after 1937, how effective it was at various times, and in various areas, how strong it was in the majority provinces before 1945, and who were the effective organization men at different levels, how information flowed downwards from the working committee, what was the relative importance of student workers and others – for example, those who had formerly worked for the Khilafat movement in the twenties – and how methods differed as, for example, between minority and majority areas, between cities and rural districts, or in approaches to the educated and to the masses. What was the role of the secretary, Liaqat Ali Khan?

Khalid Bin Sayeed has described the structural organization of the League,[3] but detailed studies should show how the organization really worked in particular circumstances and in particular areas, especially in those most essential to the success of League policies. Jinnah felt it necessary time and again to call upon the League members to talk less and to work more, to adopt a more constructive programme, to create machinery to take some of the work off his own shoulders.[4] How did the League organization compare with that of other all-India or provincial parties? How effective was its propaganda in the early years – its literature, meetings, conferences, and press? It would seem not to have been overwhelmingly successful in the majority provinces before 1945, as it was found necessary to enlist the support of religious leaders to make sure of success in the elections of that year. Even

[1] See S. R. Mehrotra, 'The Congress and the Partition of India', below, pp. 189–192, and Z. H. Zaidi, 'Aspects of the Development of Muslim League Policy, 1937–47', below, pp. 251–4, for analyses of the 1937 elections.

[2] In the Punjab the League was unable to form a ministry as the Sikhs and Hindus refused to co-operate and a Unionist ministry was formed. In the N.W.F.P. the Congress won more Muslim seats than the League and formed a ministry.

[3] K. B. Sayeed, *Pakistan: the Formative Phase*, 2nd ed., pp. 176–219. See also Z. H. Zaidi, 'Aspects of the development of Muslim League policy, 1937–47', below, pp. 267–71, and Raja of Mahmudabad, 'Some Memories', below, pp. 386–9.

[4] E.g. Presidential address, All-India Muslim League, Karachi session, December 24, 1943 '. . . Now has come the stage when it is absolutely essential that we must undertake further steps and start our organizational machinery. . . .'

as late as June–July 1947 the support of the *ulama* was essential to the success of the Sylhet and Frontier referenda.[1] For Jinnah to use the cry of religion went against his whole previous career: did not the fact that this was required in order to obtain the support of the masses, indicate some failing in effectiveness of the League organization in the majority provinces?

Muhammad Ali Jinnah

Questions about the organization of the League lead naturally to what is the most interesting question of all relating to the events leading up to the partition of India in 1947, that is, what was the precise role of Jinnah? It is frequently said that without Jinnah there would have been no Pakistan, and he himself remarked that it was he with the help of his secretary and his typewriter who won Pakistan for the Muslims. No one doubts that he played the major part, and the positive part, in these crucial years from 1937–47. He dominated the League organization: to all intents and purposes he was the League organization. Yet he had many disadvantages as a popular leader, chiefly perhaps his inability to speak fluently in Urdu, combined with the austerity and fastidiousness of his personality. Once he had been established as the great leader – Qaid-e-Azam – the masses naturally flocked to see him, and to hear him, even though they could not understand his words. But how did he come to be so established? He was not a new star suddenly appearing to dazzle the mob, but on the contrary a prominent politician of very long standing. He had been the League's leading personality and president[2] during the period in the twenties when the party was at a low ebb, ineffective, with few members and those split into factions. It seems therefore that it was not Jinnah's personality alone which brought about the rejuvenation of the League after 1937. It was rather the combination of his drive and authority, his integrity and ability to inspire loyalty in his lieutenants, with the exhilaration of the call for Pakistan.

In the earlier part of Jinnah's political career, the success which he had enjoyed, culminating in the Lucknow pact between the League and the Congress in 1916, had been as leader of the liberal, left-wing section of the League, in the cause of Hindu-Muslim unity: he then attempted a *rapport* with the Congress (of which he was also a member) on the basis of a common nationalist policy. When he again led the League in a successful campaign after his long eclipse in the twenties and early thirties, the call was no longer for Hindu-Muslim unity, but for Hindu-Muslim separation. This complete reversal of Jinnah's role has prompted the question how a convinced advocate of Hindu-Muslim unity for most of his political career could become the foremost advocate of Hindu-Muslim separation. Exactly when did he change his views, and why?

Khalid Bin Sayeed puts the turning point in Jinnah's life in the period 1929–35 following both political rejection (at the All-Parties National Convention in December 1928) and failures in his personal life. He suggests that the needs of Jinnah at this time coincided with the needs of the Muslim

[1] See K. B. Sayeed, *Pakistan: the Formative Phase*, 2nd ed., pp. 204–5. But see also M. Husain, 'Dacca University and the Pakistan Movement', below, pp. 372–3.

[2] He was president of the League from 1919–30.

community: the Muslims needed a leader, Jinnah needed an instrument with which to achieve his aims, and to restore his self-confidence.[1] This view has been challenged[2] by those who point out that a great many people suffer personal failure at some point in their lives and that political failure is also almost bound to come at some time to those committed to politics over many years. Neither necessarily have far-reaching effects. Perhaps one should look not so much to changes in Jinnah, as to changes in circumstances, and the effects of these changes on Jinnah's political outlook, and political calculations.

Developments in British constitutional policies after 1919, along with the transformation of the Indian nationalist movement itself under Gandhi's leadership, had made Jinnah, his aims and his methods, as revealed in his political activities up to this time, irrelevant to the politics of the years between the wars. For Jinnah, though always a nationalist, was a believer in parliamentary democracy, certain that self-government could be achieved only by constitutional methods. And in the end independence was indeed won by constitutional not revolutionary methods. But for the greater part of the period between 1919 and 1945 (with the one major exception of the period of responsible government in the provinces from 1937–9) the nationalist movement under the leadership of Gandhi had abandoned the constitutional path for the way of direct action.

This abandonment of the constitutional path along with the transformation of the Congress party into a mass movement – in intention, if not entirely in fact – had alienated Jinnah from the beginning. In December 1920 he resigned from the party, as in the previous October he had resigned from the Home Rule League. He had then, in replying to Gandhi's invitation to him to participate in the new life opening up before the country, expressed in strong terms his opposition to the new methods. He rejected both Gandhi's programme and methods, convinced that they must lead to disaster, writing '... your methods have already caused split and division in almost every institution that you have approached ... your extreme programme has for the moment struck the imagination of the inexperienced youth and the ignorant and the illiterate. All this means complete disorganization and chaos. What the consequences of this may be, I shudder to contemplate.'[3] Jinnah never changed his opinion as to the disastrous nature of Gandhi's influence on the Congress, in later years frequently accusing him of being the cause of the failure of all attempts at Hindu–Muslim settlement.[4] His distaste for Congress methods was aggravated by the personality differences between

[1] See K. B. Sayeed, *Pakistan: the Formative Phase*, 2nd ed., pp. 289–94, and 'The Personality of Jinnah and His Political Strategy', below, pp. 276–93.

[2] By other Pakistan members of the conference.

[3] Quoted in H. Bolitho, *Jinnah*, pp. 183–4.

[4] For example, in his presidential address to the Muslim League session of December 1938 he said '... it is Mr. Gandhi who is destroying the ideal with which the Congress was started. He is the one man responsible for turning the Congress into an instrument for the revival of Hinduism....' And again in his presidential address of April 1943 '... from 1925 onwards ... many efforts were made for the adjustment of Hindu-Muslim differences. Every time we were the petitioners ... standing at the doors of Mr Gandhi and the Congress ... the reply was 'No'....'

himself and the new Congress leaders, not only Gandhi [1] but the other new men, especially perhaps Jawaharlal Nehru, between whom and Jinnah there was a complete lack of sympathy and understanding.

Moreover, the transformation of the Congress party into a mass movement meant that Jinnah's constant aim of attaining Hindu–Muslim unity no longer seemed an essential preliminary to any nationalist action, as it had while nationalist politics had been on a small scale and carried on in a constitutional manner. In this context to make political progress some sort of agreement between the two major communities had been essential, for Britain insisted on agreement before granting any measure of self-government. But now the dialogue with Britain was, for the moment, at an end. Furthermore, in a mass movement the Hindus were bound to be in a majority, and although it would be hoped that Muslims would join the movement, it was not essential that they should. Other matters than Hindu–Muslim unity preoccupied the Congress leaders in the inter-war period, and after the failure of the Khilafat movement Muslims generally took little part in nationalist politics.

In the provinces, however, it was a different story. The British decision to develop self-government first in the provinces, not at the centre, provided real opportunities for Muslims living in the provinces in which they were in a majority to play active political roles and to achieve power. Yet because the Muslim majorities in the two important provinces of the Punjab and Bengal were small, Muslim politicians had to co-operate with those of other communities and think on provincial not communal lines. Jinnah was an all-India politician from Bombay, a Muslim minority province: there was little place for him in provincial politics.

In these circumstances – alienated from nationalist politics, with no place in the development of the Muslim provinces, and, moreover, rejected by one wing of the Muslim League – it is a matter of no surprise that Jinnah should have played little effective part in the politics of the 1920s, even that he should have withdrawn completely for a time. Independence seemed very far off, the nationalist movement had developed upon lines of which he entirely disapproved, and the Muslims were so divided among themselves that they could no longer be taken seriously as a political force. In 1931 Jinnah settled in London.

Some two years later, however, in July 1933, he was approached by Liaqat Ali Khan [2] who begged him to return to India to lead the Muslims, and again it is surely no matter for surprise that an active man of only fifty-six, not long retired from politics, should have been tempted to make a last effort to build up the almost moribund Muslim League into an effective organization, especially after his rejection only a few years before. Yet Jinnah was slow in making up his mind to accept the challenge and visited India several times during 1934–5 in an effort to gauge the situation, before finally settling again

[1] At a reception given by the Gujarati community in Bombay in January 1915 for Gandhi on his return to India after his long years in South Africa, Jinnah made a speech of welcome in English. Gandhi replied in Gujarati and protested against the use of English at a Gujarati meeting. Jinnah could not have appreciated this rebuke at the outset of their acquaintance. See Tendulkar, *Mahatma*, vol. i, p. 158.

[2] See H. Bolitho, *Jinnah*, pp. 104–6.

in Bombay. He was elected permanent president of the League in March 1934, and at the end of the year he was elected to the Indian legislative assembly (in elections held under the old 1919 constitution). In 1935 he at last sold his London home and returned permanently to India. Yet his policy remained what it had always been. Speaking at a meeting of the Muslim League council in April 1934 he was still thinking in terms of co-operation between Hindus and Muslims,[1] and in the assembly he pursued a non-communal policy still in line with his policy of pursuing Hindu–Muslim unity.[2] There is no indication that in spite of the changes of the past fifteen years, and of his own personal failures, he had re-thought his position at all.

Was it therefore Jinnah's experience of practical politics during the 1937 election campaign and afterwards which changed him from an 'idealist' believing in the possibility of Hindu–Muslim unity, into a 'realist' who saw no future for the Muslims in India once the British had left? [3] There was no immediate evidence of this: in fact throughout 1938 he continued to talk as before of the necessity of a pact between Hindus and Muslims to settle the Hindu–Muslim question and to create a real united front.[4]

For Jinnah the moral of the 1937 election campaign and of the subsequent failure of the moves for coalition governments in the United Provinces and Bombay was first and foremost the imperative necessity of building up the Muslim League into a demonstrably strong party to justify his demand that it should be recognized as the sole representative organization of the Muslims. Given the League's failure to win the Muslim vote there was no reason for Nehru and the Congress to take Jinnah's claims seriously, nor could there have seemed to them any good reason for co-operation with the League except on their own terms, nor any obstacle to an attempt by the Congress to recruit the Muslim masses. Nehru refused to recognize the League as more than an important communal organization, and spelled out for Jinnah what he must do.[5] 'The more important the organization,' he wrote, 'the more attention paid to it, but this importance does not come from outside recognition but from inherent strength. . . .'

Thereafter Jinnah's constant aim was to build up this inherent strength, until he was able to demonstrate it conclusively in the 1945 elections. In this aim, the course of events and the policies and practices of both the Congress party and of the British government, worked to his advantage.

The period of Congress rule in its eight provinces created among Muslims a basis of resentment on which 'atrocity' charges could be built, thus giving Jinnah his first strong weapon in his attack on the Hindus. For however unfounded or exaggerated the accusations of Hindu atrocities might have seemed, there is no doubt that Muslim opinions and sentiments were disregarded by the Congress ministries, and that Muslims felt themselves

[1] Quoted in H. Bolitho, *Jinnah*, p. 109.

[2] See K. B. Sayeed, *Pakistan: the Formative Phase*, 2nd ed., pp. 79–80.

[3] See Z. H. Zaidi, 'Aspects of the Development of Muslim League Policy, 1937–47', below, p. 245.

[4] See, for example, Jinnah's letters to Nehru, March 17, 1938, and to S. C. Bose, August 2, and October 10, 1938. But see also, B. R. Nanda, 'Nehru, the Indian National Congress and the Partition of India', below, pp. 157–60, for a different view.

[5] During his abortive correspondence with Jinnah in 1938.

threatened. The realities of power, the advantages of office, were clear to all. Their fear of Hindu *raj* was reinforced and nothing was done to reassure them.

On the outbreak of war in September 1939 Jinnah received some evidence that he had achieved a certain measure of success in his policy of building up the Muslim League, for he was one of the leaders to be consulted by the viceroy on the day following the declaration of war. As he later said '. . . up to the time of the declaration of war the Viceroy never thought of me but of Gandhi and Gandhi alone. . . . I wondered within myself why I was so suddenly promoted . . .' and he concluded that the reason was that the Muslim League had now become a power to be reckoned with.[1] As Jinnah realized, this was a sharp blow to the Congress claim to speak on behalf of all India, and the British recognition that he was the leader of an important party increased Jinnah's stature, and that of the League, among Muslims. From now on the League's demands, particularly the demand for Pakistan after 1940, were taken into consideration by the British government whenever new proposals were put forward.

The Lahore resolution for Pakistan was adopted in March 1940. It has been suggested that Jinnah and the League needed a popular slogan to attract more support, and that the demand for Pakistan was at first merely such a slogan and a bargaining counter for use in negotiations with the Congress, and that the idea once launched aroused such enthusiasm, especially among the young, that it took control of the movement.

Was Jinnah working consistently and single-mindedly for partition from 1940 onwards? Was his strategy thought out and consistently followed, with the one aim of achieving Pakistan?[2] Or did he merely react to events, taking advantage of his opportunities as they occurred – the Congress resignations, the Cripps mission, the Quit India campaign, the British initiatives after the war? Why did he refuse to join the Congress in the Quit India campaign, against the arguments of the other members of the League working committee, who saw an opportunity for reaching agreement with the Congress leaders on the question of Pakistan?[3] Was it merely his distrust of the Congress leadership; did he forsee failure; or was he influenced by his life-long dislike of unconstitutional methods? Perhaps the Muslim League papers at Karachi and Jinnah's own letters will throw some light on his motives and policies in this period.

But had Jinnah been working single-mindedly for Pakistan from 1940 onwards why did he accept the cabinet mission plan in 1946: a plan which did not concede Pakistan? In March and April 1946 he continued to state publicly that Pakistan must be a fully sovereign state with complete control of its own defence and foreign affairs,[4] yet the League's own offer in May to the cabinet mission and to the Congress was for a federation in which the

[1] Presidential address, All-India Muslim League, Lahore session, March 1940.

[2] See K. B. Sayeed, 'The Personality of Jinnah and His Political Strategy,' below, pp. 282–93.

[3] According to Mr. Ispahani and the Raja of Mahmudabad, members of the League working committee. See M. A. H. Ispahani, 'Factors Leading to the Partition of British India', below, pp. 346–7.

[4] For example, in two interviews (March 3, and April 3, 1946) quoted in Jamiluddin Ahmad, vol. ii, pp. 379–80, and 382.

six Muslim provinces should be grouped together and deal with all subjects, *except* the vital ones of foreign affairs and defence, and communications necessary for defence.[1] It is true that after ten years the provinces were to be free to secede from the union, and that in the cabinet mission plan itself the possibility of Pakistan was similarly outlined. Yet Jinnah had more than once expressed his conviction that 'federation however described and in whatever terms it is put, must ultimately deprive the federating units of the authority in all vital matters. The units, despite themselves would be compelled to grant more and more powers to the central authority, until in the end a strong Central Government will have been established . . . once the units accept the basis of a Federal Central Government it follows that it will inevitably and out of sheer necessity resolve itself into an all-powerful Central Authority. . . .'[2] And, 'In a Federation, member states are compelled to grant more and more power to the central authority. Little by little they lose their independence. . . .'[3] Holding such views, could he really have believed that in ten years he would get his Pakistan?

M. A. H. Ispahani, a member of the League working committee, has told us how Jinnah welcomed the opportunity given to him by Congress deviousness over the cabinet mission plan to withdraw his own acceptance of that plan, and to reassert the demand for Pakistan; that he felt the acceptance to have been a mistake.[4] But given that the League itself had proposed a union of two federations, not two completely sovereign states, perhaps Jinnah's own explanation is sufficient. 'The League . . . sacrificed the full sovereign state of Pakistan . . . for securing the independence of the whole of India. They voluntarily delegated three subjects to the Union, and by doing so did not commit a mistake. It was the highest order of statesmanship that the League displayed by making concession . . . we were moved by a desire not to allow the situation to develop into bloodshed and civil war. . . . In our anxiety to try to come to a peaceful settlement with the other major party, we made this sacrifice . . . and accepted a limited Pakistan. . . .'[5] Is it not possible that, having at last demonstrated his strength in the recent elections, so that both the British and the Congress had been forced to accept the League as a third and equal party in the independence negotiations, Jinnah was now prepared to make some concessions on the issue of Pakistan? Could it not be that it was only after what seemed to Jinnah his betrayal over the cabinet mission plan that he finally lost faith in the possibility of any co-operation with the Congress leadership, as well as in the fairness of the British government? The Congress insistence on adhering to its own interpretation, while at the same time blandly asserting that it had in fact accepted the cabinet mission plan, together with the viceroy's invitation to the Congress to form an interim government, was perhaps the final disillusionment for Jinnah, the

[1] Gwyer and Appadorai, *Speeches and Documents on the Indian Constitution*, vol. ii, pp. 573–4.

[2] Presidential address, All-India Muslim League, Delhi session, April 1943.

[3] Jamiluddin Ahmad, *Some Recent Speeches and Writings of Mr. Jinnah*, vol. ii, p. 382 (April 3, 1946).

[4] See M. A. H. Ispahani, 'Factors Leading to the Partition of India', below, pp. 348–51, for his account of the League's response to the plan.

[5] At the meeting of the All-India Muslim League council, Bombay, July 29, 1946.

end of his faith in constitutional methods. He was, after all, now old and ill. Did he see himself finally losing, not in negotiation at the conference table, but by trickery? Was this the reason for the call for 'direct action'? 'We have learned a bitter lesson,' he said, 'Now there is no room left for compromise. . . .'[1]

But there is another explanation for Jinnah's action: perhaps the League welcomed the opportunity to withdraw its acceptance of the plan because it had come to realize that it no longer had complete control of the movement; the working committee might be willing to accept less than Pakistan, but possibly the rank and file were not.

What was meant by 'direct action'? According to the League, it was merely that the League would at last adopt the unconstitutional tactics of the Congress, albeit in a peaceful way. No one would suggest that Jinnah and the League working committee intended to let loose the orgy of violence which in fact resulted, one riot following another in a chain reaction throughout the country, sometimes initiated by one community, sometimes by the other. But, as has been said,[2] what can one think of the judgment of Jinnah, a man whose judgment was ordinarily so exceptionally good, if he did not anticipate violent outbreaks? 'Non-violence' was alien to Muslim thought, and the Muslim masses, called upon to take direct action to achieve Pakistan and to be ready for every sacrifice, must surely have understood something more than passive resistance. A study of the role of violence in Indian society would throw some light on the activities of both Congress and League in this turbulent period. The leaders did not advocate violence, but perhaps they did not look too closely at what was done in the name of the party among the lower ranks.

In the event the call for direct action was followed by the 'Calcutta killing', and from then on events moved swiftly towards the final solution of partition. Jinnah had made his point and had convinced both the British and the Congress leadership (with the exception of Gandhi) that partition must be accepted if the communal problem were to be solved. All that remained was to negotiate the terms. Jinnah had won the 'Muslim brief',[3] but not perhaps entirely in the manner which he would have wished, for, in the end, it rather looks as though he had been forced to adopt Gandhi's methods and to appeal to 'inexperienced youth and the ignorant and the illiterate'.

The decisive turning point, towards Pakistan

When was the crucial turning point in the events which led to the establishment of Pakistan? Certainly, after the call for direct action, with its sequel, 'the Calcutta killing', the communal situation got so out of hand that it seemed that only partition could assuage it. But the watershed in the movement has been put at various dates. Some see the Nehru Report (1928) as the parting of the ways, others point to the failure to form coalition ministries in the United Provinces and Bombay in 1937, while others again assert that the period of Congress rule from 1937–9 was more significant. But many

[1] At the meeting of the All-India Muslim League council, Bombay, July 29, 1946.
[2] By Percival Spear when introducing a session of the conference.
[3] K. B. Sayeed's phrase in a conference discussion.

put the crucial period at a much later date, as late as the Simla conference in 1945 and the decision of the British government to hold elections before negotiating a settlement, or even as late as the League's call for direct action itself. All these events played their part in bringing about the transfer of power to two dominions, rather than one, but whether the crucial period is put as late as 1946 depends upon whether one believes that Jinnah could at this time have controlled his followers and have persuaded them to accept something less than Pakistan: whether he was in complete control, or whether, in Humayun Kabir's phrase,[1] he was by this time riding a tiger from which it would have been impossible to dismount.

The essential element in ensuring the success of the League was for it to obtain control of the Muslims in the majority provinces, for as has been stressed,[2] had the Muslims been uniformly distributed throughout the sub-continent it is inconceivable that their political demands would have taken the form of a call for a separate homeland, however much they might have felt themselves to be a separate nation. It was because Muslims were in a majority in certain parts of the sub-continent that the idea of Pakistan could be put forward at all. But unless the Muslims in those areas were behind the movement there could be no possibility of its achievement: the Muslim majority areas were the key to Pakistan. It is therefore suggested that events mainly of importance to the minority provinces – the failure of coalition ministries, the outcry against Hindu 'atrocities', and the whole experience of Congress rule – although they have attracted much retrospective attention, were in power terms of much less importance to the movement for secession than those later years during the war when the League was establishing itself in Bengal and the Punjab, as well as in Sind and finally in the Frontier province, and winning the battle against the traditional provincial politician, with his regional loyalties. That the League now had the support of the Muslims in the majority provinces as well as those in the minority provinces was demonstrated in the 1945 elections. The campaign had been won. All that remained was for the League to stand firm on its demands: its strength had been made manifest. It is hard to believe that thereafter anything less than Pakistan would permanently have satisfied the Muslim community. And though there seemed, for a moment, when the League accepted the cabinet mission's plan, to be a chance for an agreement with the Congress, it is doubtful whether at that late stage any plan to maintain the unity of India could have succeeded.

[1] During the conference discussions.

[2] For example, by S. R. Mehrotra, 'The Congress and the Partition of India', below, p. 201.

POLICIES AND PARTIES

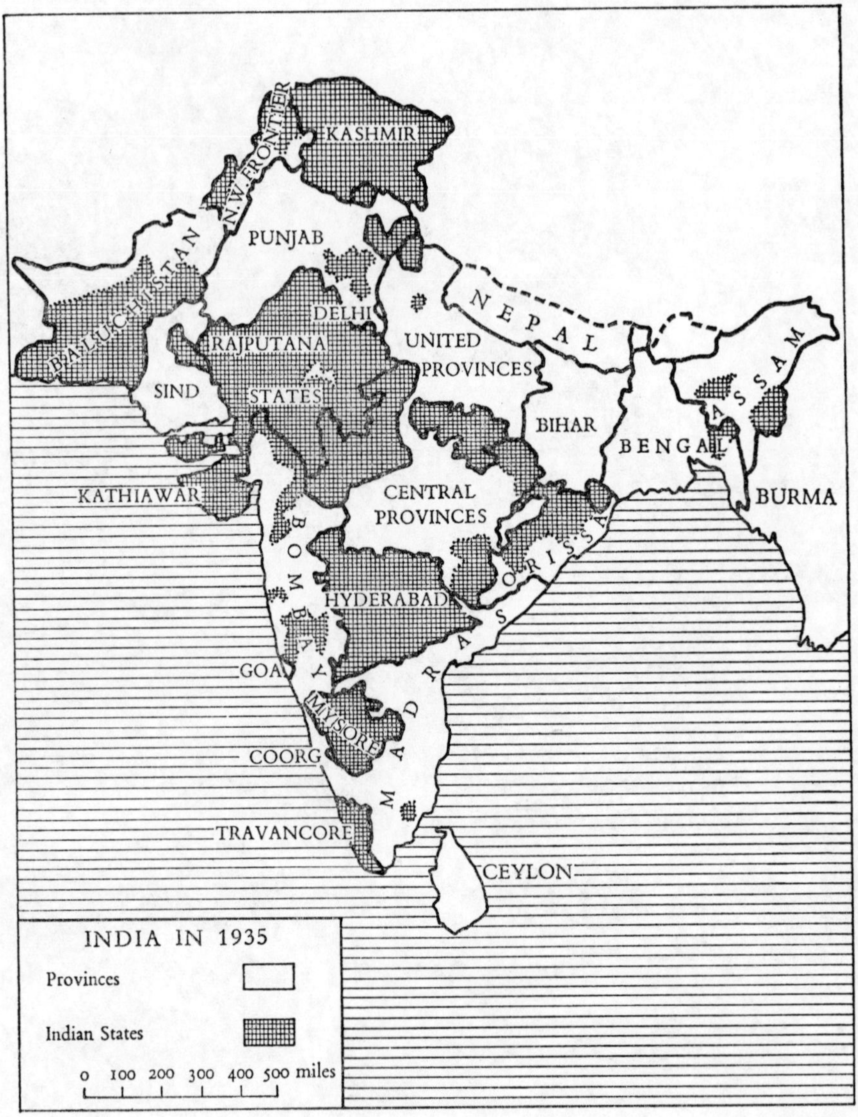
KASHMIR
N.W. FRONTIER
PUNJAB
BALUCHISTAN
DELHI
NEPAL
UNITED PROVINCES
RAJPUTANA STATES
SIND
BIHAR
ASSAM
BENGAL
BURMA
KATHIAWAR
CENTRAL PROVINCES
BOMBAY
ORISSA
HYDERABAD
MADRAS
GOA
MYSORE
COORG
TRAVANCORE
CEYLON
INDIA IN 1935
Provinces
Indian States
0 100 200 300 400 500 miles

SOME REFLECTIONS ON THE TRANSFER OF POWER IN PLURAL SOCIETIES[1]

by P. N. S. MANSERGH *

It would be of some interest to discover when the phrase 'transfer of power' was first used in its contemporary context. It was on occasion employed but at no time generally associated with the establishment of the Irish Free State in 1921–2 – possibly because of the Irish contention that power had always presided *de jure* in Ireland – nor earlier in South Africa, Australia, New Zealand or Canada. What happened in that first dominion instance was, as Professor Alexander Brady has noted, the transfer of the parliamentary polity from Britain to Canada. It was this that lay at the heart of the dominion precedent – which was itself an adaptation of earlier precedents in which certain constitutional forms had been transplanted from Britain to her colonies in the eighteenth and even the seventeenth centuries.

Does the common use of the phrase 'transfer of power' in respect of Indian independence then indicate a break with, or departure from, earlier dominion and colonial precedents? The answer would seem to be in the affirmative, provided, and it is an important proviso, the question is posed in its British setting. The word 'transfer' in common usage means the conveyance from one person to another of property or shares, or alternatively the removal of property or goods from one place to another. In conjunction with the word 'power', meaning in this context authority, or government over, the phrase signifies the handing-over of ultimate responsibility for government by one authority to another. This is precisely what did *not* happen in the case of the dominions. There was a progressive decentralization of responsibility but no abdication of formal sovereignty or final power. *Inter alia* this is indicated by the fact that all the dominion constitutions, including that of the Irish Free State, were embodied in British Acts of Parliament. Nor was the ultimate sovereignty of Westminster contested in the dominions other than the Irish Free State, the constitution of which exceptionally declared that all lawful authority came from God to the people. The British use of the phrase 'transfer of power', in 1947 and subsequently, may be thought to indicate British recognition of the nature of a departure from dominion precedents and of the political realities behind it. But important as it is to underline the difference, it is equally important to recognize how closely British thinking about this transfer of power was associated with earlier experience of transfer of the British parliamentary polity from Britain to formerly dependent territories within the British Empire.

[1] The theme of this paper is more fully developed in the author's *The Commonwealth Experience* (1969).

* Master of St John's College, Cambridge, and Smuts Professor of the History of the British Commonwealth, University of Cambridge; Editor-in-Chief, India Office Records project on the transfer of power.

A senior civil servant recently told me that in his first week as a new recruit at the Colonial Office just after the war an under-secretary of the department came to his room, threw a copy of *The Durham Report* on his desk and remarked 'This is still essential reading for all of us'. I doubt if this ever happened in the India Office. While not essential reading, the report, however, retains at least its relevance for an understanding of British attitudes to the transfer of power in India. John Stuart Mill, the exponent of the classical ideas of Victorian liberalism, wrote in his *Representative Government* that 'a new era in the colonial policy of nations began with Lord Durham's Report; the imperishable memorial of that nobleman's courage, patriotism and enlightened liberality'. That era has continued down to the present day and will no doubt continue to do so till the final end of British colonialism. The Indian experience was among its more important landmarks.

Lord Durham was sent out on a particular mission and his prime minister, Lord Melbourne, would appear to have been as pleased to see that moody nobleman with his dramatic good looks, aristocratic connections and uncomfortable radical opinions, depart for distant places, as was Winston Churchill a little more than a century later to see Sir Stafford Cripps leave for India on a not dissimilar but an even more taxing assignment. Yet the creative quality of *The Durham Report* was not geographically limited. Its two principal recommendations, responsible government and union of adjoining colonies, had equal validity at other times and in other places. In the perspective of 1947 the important things were first that these ideas were expounded in the report, and secondly, that in somewhat qualified form they had been successfully applied in a plural society in British North America. In the context of the transfer of power to India, what mattered was not that a Dominion of Canada had come into existence in 1867 but that it was successful. By that I do not mean so much that it has survived and that we are celebrating its centenary this year,*[1] but that its earlier achievements in the government and development of Canada and, not overlooked by imperial officials, in the consequent saving of imperial expenditure and effort made a deep impact upon the mind of British statesmen, and in a marked degree influenced their subsequent thinking about the future of dependent territories. When in more or less comparable situations they sought guidance from the past, they were apt to notice that there had been an experiment in Canada. It was deemed successful. There followed other experiments in Australia and New Zealand; they were deemed successful. There followed yet another experiment in an altogether more intractable and complex situation in South Africa; paradoxical as it was to seem to a later generation, it was deemed outstandingly successful especially by the Liberal government which was chiefly responsible for it, and their supporters. Each experiment was carried out with an awareness, on the British side, of earlier experiments. Gladstone, in drafting the first Home Rule Bill for Ireland, had a copy of the British North America Act before him; the architects of the Australian Commonwealth studied closely the same model before deciding to depart from it in important respects; Campbell-Bannerman, who thought of Canada as 'the greatest triumph of British imperial statesmanship' and 'of broad liberal views and nobly instructed imagination', wrote out in annotated form

*[1] 1967.

the lessons to be drawn from Canadian precedents for South African application. In its turn the South African example influenced British thinking about Ireland and in the autumn of 1921 Austen Chamberlain, occupying a position of critical importance in the Unionist party, inclined favourably towards an Irish dominion settlement, specifically because of the success of a dominion solution in South Africa. When finally power was transferred in India, this great departure from an hitherto exclusively European Commonwealth was commended to the house of commons by prime ministerial allusion to the success of earlier experiments, most of all in South Africa. Even if we may think now that Mr Attlee would have been wiser to stick to the safe, well-worn Canadian theme, the fact remains that in decolonization, as in other matters of politics, few things succeed like success. And to those responsible for the conduct of affairs in 1947, dominion status and the Commonwealth had been alike politically successful.

The essence of past dominion experience was thought to rest upon Durham's two principal conclusions – the first responsible, parliamentary government and second, where conditions made this applicable, the association of neighbouring dependent territories into a larger whole. What was their relevance to India? After 1917 responsible government was the professed goal of British rule. What did that mean in dominion terms? In the twenties some officials of the government of India considered the implications. Was the coming into being of a parliamentary system on the Westminster model they enquired, a necessary pre-condition of dominion status? Or could dominion status be considered as something apart from the nature of domestic government? By some it was suggested that there was no necessary connection between the two; that the association in effect was the product of particular Canadian circumstances. And as was well, or too well, recognized in some circles the fur coat of Canada was not suited to India's tropical clime. Yet if in all this there was much logic there was little history. How was dominion status to be divorced from responsible government? If there were not a parliament and a constituent assembly in existence or in immediate prospect with a government responsible through it to the majority of the people, to whom was power to be given? Where was the successor authority to be found? British administrators who felt most pessimistic about the prospects of parliamentary system in India looked elsewhere than Westminster for inspiration. In the minutes or published reports of the time, in consequence, there were apt to be references to other systems of government, to the American presidential system with its suggestion of strong, stable government, or most often to the Swiss non-party executive. These allusions were apt, however, to be more impressive on reading than on reflection. What did ordinary British administrators in India, or for that matter Indian leaders, know of the working of the American, let alone of the Swiss constitution? Were they really in a position to adapt something in its detail largely or altogether unfamiliar to them all? The answer was obviously in the negative and so as the years went by and the options narrowed, the British, with continuing reservations in many quarters, became reconciled to following the pathway of precedent, and the precedent which was most relevant was the dominion precedent with responsible government as an integral part of it. In a limited setting this was also true of politically conscious India. I remember the then secretary of the Indian National Congress telling me some ten or twelve years ago how carefully the works of Professor A. B. Keith on dominion status had been studied by the Congress secretariat and how discouraging they found all those surviving intricate and technical restrictions upon the dominion liberties which Professor Keith expounded with such unrivalled mastery. The secretary's reflection was that perhaps they would have been better advised to pay more attention to political trends and less to the professor's writings! But in any case the pertinacious and persistent appearance, or reappearance of dominion status was a feature of the Indian political scene despite all discouraging portents right down to 1947 when it provided the provisional means for the transfer with the Government of India Act, 1935 in part coming into its own at the last.

The Government of India Act, 1935 contemplated, as was consistent with the spirit of the second of Durham's conclusions, an Indian federation. In the Commonwealth tradition, since 1867 the British have had, indeed, a remarkable faith in federal constitutions. A chief reason for this may be that they have themselves had no experience of one. But here again the apparent success of the Canadian experiment, followed by that of the Australian, led British statesmen to repose what was at times well-nigh uncritical faith in federalism as a means of developing power in plural societies. The post-war Commonwealth is littered with the wreckage of British devised federal constitutions. It is a constant theme of British commentators that the greatest of the missed opportunities in the recent history of the Indian sub-continent was the failure to secure a federal solution for India. This is a view which also has its supporters in India and Pakistan. It rests on the assumption that a federal constitution once established is likely, so to speak, of its own momentum and by encouraging and developing a sense of belonging and working together to forge a sense of community that would not otherwise exist. This may well have represented over-simplification on a grand scale. How much closer has a century of federation brought French- and English-speaking Canada together? Furthermore if the foundation of Indian government was to rest on the popular will expressed through a popular franchise and if the electorate voted according to communal allegiance rather than economic or social interest, then certainly under a unitary system the will of the majority community would necessarily prevail. But in a federal system, however weak the centre, and however strongly entrenched the rights of the provinces, did not the alternatives in such circumstances remain government, with whatever qualifications, in accordance with the will of the majority or near political paralysis? Many of the plans for preserving the framework of Indian unity within a federal system displayed it is true at once the greatest ingenuity and the flexibility of federalism as an instrument of government. But at a deeper level, however, it is hard to escape from the conclusion that the arguments for federalism in India were essentially defensive, much indeed as Dicey conceived them to be. In political terms it was a second-best to the majority who preferred unity and also to the minority who preferred partition. In these circumstances little considered but deserving of more consideration than it would seem to have received, was the likely effectiveness and survival quality of a federal government, in the only form that seemed politically practicable, namely with a weak centre and strong constituent units. Nor is the possibility by any means to be discounted that preoccupation with federation in the thirties in effect excluded from consideration other and conceivably more realistic alternatives.

At a more particular level the coming into effect of the provincial sections of the Government of India Act, 1935, exposed some of the consequences that might follow from an approach to the transfer of power through adoption of the parliamentary system. In the first place it enabled Indian organizations or parties to register the extent of their popular support in electoral terms. In the second place, after dispute, it made possible the formation of governments. The way in which those governments were formed proved to be a major source of Muslim League grievance against the Congress. The nature of that grievance is not in dispute. It lay in the fact that the Congress, after its massive victory in the 1937 provincial elections, had formed one-party governments in provinces, in which the Muslim League had expected coalitions, in which they would be partners. This repudiation and rejection of the League derived fundamentally from the Congress conviction that it represented all-India. There was no need accordingly for political concessions to a minority grouping or, more particularly, for recognition of a ministerial role for the League which anyway had fared poorly in the elections. Muslims there would certainly be in the government – but they would be Congress Muslims or League Muslims who had renounced the League and joined the Congress as a condition of office. This general presumption was reinforced, so both Jawaharlal Nehru and Rajendra Prasad have told us in their recorded reflections, by a conviction that the conventions of British cabinet government should prevail. If there were League members of the provincial government in, for example, the United Provinces and Orissa, what then became of notions of collective responsibility? 'Congressmen', so Rajendra Prasad recalled, 'thought it contrary to the spirit of Parliamentary democracy to appoint any outsider in their Ministry.' If Muslims were to serve, then first claim, as party stalwarts were quick to emphasize, lay with those Muslims who were loyal members of the Congress and not with supporters of the League. Yet in retrospect, as written records suggest and personal conversations underline, most of the prominent Congress leaders remained preoccupied and even questioning as to the correctness of their 1937 conclusions. And at the time one of the Congress leaders, not surprisingly Maulana A. K. Azad challenged and fought in vain to prevent or reverse these exclusivist decisions dictated largely by party loyalists in the provinces. What was at issue was a question of political judgment, neither more nor less. On any reckoning the decision would seem in retrospect ill-advised. Whether it was more than that is a matter of opinion. Sir Penderel Moon deems it to have been 'the fons et origo malorum' and argues that the Congress leaders 'were responsible, though quite unwittingly' for the critical change in Muslim sentiment from readiness to contemplate co-operation in an all-India federation to insistence upon separation. The Congress 'passionately desired to preserve the unity of India. They consistently acted so as to make its partition certain'. But, it may reasonably be asked, did the partition of India then derive from so trifling a cause? Were there not fundamental forces at work? An error, or a series of errors in tactical judgment is one thing, the source of a political event so momentous as partition ordinarily another. Or to put the issue in another way – Was partition implicit in the Indian scene or not? If it were, tactics were of secondary importance but only if not, of first significance.

Without seeking to prejudge this question, it may be suggested that there is a greater element of determinism, or alternatively a more limited freedom of manoeuvre in situations where there is latent, or actual tension between communities, expressing their will through a parliamentary franchise and preoccupied with a prospective transfer of power than is apt to be allowed by contemporary observers or leaders. The pattern of events elsewhere in some parts of Africa, in Cyprus and earlier in Ireland by its very uniformity suggests this was so. The Irish precedents, now to be seen in historical depth, would appear especially relevant, and, if I may, I will quote from an analysis I made of them without thought of the Indian situation.[1]

'In theory the Irish Nationalist party in the eighteen eighties had a choice between the conciliation of the Ulster minority or its coercion constitutionally, or if need be, otherwise. A policy of conciliation carried with it one grave liability. It conceded, of necessity, the existence of two communities, . . . and by recognizing the separate identity of the minority community, almost inevitably encouraged a heightening of its claims. Could it be certain that conciliation, implying again of necessity, concession, would win Ulster minority acceptance of Home Rule even, for example, in a federal form safeguarding minority rights? In retrospect at least it seems unlikely. That being so, was not the wiser course to pursue a policy, not of conciliation, but of undermining the Ulster minority's will to resist and, as a corollary, their means of support?

'The question might have been – there is no evidence that it was – and may still be, debated in these terms. Historically if choice there was before the Nationalist leadership, there is no doubt what choice was made. From Parnell to Redmond, to Pearse and de Valera no Irish leader consistently pursued a policy of conciliation. For this there were many and by no means insubstantial reasons. Nationalists accepted as an article of faith that Ireland, like Mazzini's Italy, had "her own irrefutable boundary marks"; that the sea had made of her for ever one nation. They believed, given this premise, that in determining how self-government should be restored and exercised by that nation the will of the majority would, and should, prevail. The Ulster question was not a question between two countries, still less between two nations, but a domestic question for settlement by Irishmen and by Irishmen alone.

'Theoretic preconceptions were reinforced by tactical considerations. Ulster was not a solidly Unionist and Protestant province but a province so divided that in parliamentary terms a small majority of Unionist members was at best likely to be returned. Was not the right course once again, and especially for a highly organized, constitutional party, to seek, not to conciliate, but, in electoral terms, to capture the province? Here, the Protestant

[1] See N. Mansergh *The Irish Question, 1840–1921* (1965), pp. 189–90.

Parnell, that master of tactics, set the pattern by embarking on a policy of electoral "invasion", intended to consolidate support for Home Rule in the North and to convey the impression of its inevitability. The policy was crowned with significant success. Of the 89 contested Irish seats in the election of November 1885 the Nationalists won 85 and Ulster returned eighteen Nationalists as against seventeen Unionists. Here, if indeed required, was convincing and conclusive evidence that there was no question of a united northern province resolutely resisting Home Rule but of a minority concentrated in the north-eastern counties of that province whose co-religionists were strongly entrenched, but not numerically preponderant, in other parts of it. Yet electoral "invasion" exacted its price. By giving the appearance of an external threat, it contributed significantly to the closing of the anti-Home Rule ranks. More important, perhaps, it encouraged illusions in Nationalist thinking about the minority problem in Ulster.

'Electoral inroads in Ulster in fact reflected no weakening in Unionists resistance to Home Rule but were more simply the fruits of improved Nationalist party organization and of the response to Parnell's charismatic leadership among the party's natural supporters. In so far as they suggested otherwise, they were misleading. And the evidence suggests that, if not Parnell himself, then at least Parnell's successors were in fact misled. From his tactical approach to the Ulster question they never departed and superficially at least they had little reason to, for it continued to achieve notable successes on the road to ultimate failure. It involved almost of necessity, the discounting of minority misgivings, reasonable and unreasonable alike, the neglect of realistic preappraisal, in socio-economic as well as religious terms, of the true character of Ulster opposition and, in the period of the struggle over the third Home Rule Bill of the dismissal of threats of organized Orange resistance as "mere bombast". In all these things the impress of the personality of Parnell and the events of 1886 is clear. They determined, even pre-determined, the pattern of the future. And if the outcome was, as it certainly was, a failure to achieve unity, that is *not* to say other policies and other tactics would necessarily have succeeded.'

Irish experience invites certain questions, and reflections. How free are nationalist leaders, even an 'uncrowned king', to pursue 'other policies' given the sources of their political power? Nationalists, it might be argued, in situations such as the Irish and the Indian were bound to make 'mistakes', or a 'mistake' alleged to be conclusive. But were such 'mistakes' the necessary product of a historical situation, the contours of which were determined not merely by the interaction of majority and minority aspirations and fears, but also by the nature of the imperial factor. In this last respect there was, of course, one important difference between Ireland and India. Irish self-government was viewed in the context of domestic, Indian in the context of imperial or commonwealth policy. In that latter context concessions of responsible government to dependent territories had been made to indigenous political authorities, to whom power was generally conceded by stages. Had the British government, therefore, sought to conform to this precedent in India, their aim, once they had decided upon the transfer of power, would have been to constitute an authority, preferably a single authority, to whom it might be progressively transferred. In the predominant Congress view the British in India had followed, at least for some forty years before partition, another course, a policy of 'divide and rule'. 'It has been the traditional policy of Britain', complained Gandhi, after the Congress rejection of the August offer of 1940 'to prevent parties from uniting. "Divide and rule" has been Britain's proud motto. It is the British statesmen who are responsible for the divisions in India's ranks and the divisions will continue so long as the British sword holds India under bondage.' Even if it be conceded, and it may not be, that this was the language of politics and not of history, it is well to remember the importance of the time factor. On any reckoning circumstances changed and with circumstances interests. Once power was definitely to be transferred and there was no question of further imperial rule, then unity not division would seem in terms of precedent and British self-interest to have been the road to easy abdication in India, as it was not, by reason partly of party political considerations, in Ireland.

In the last phase before the transfer of power, chiefly because of the constricting, and in this case, triangular relationship implicit in all plural societies, the freedom of action of all parties declined. For the British in particular there was a progressively diminishing range of choice. Sometimes this is obscured, or partially obscured by the calibre and personality of those who dominated the final phase. The richness of personal records, the wealth of personal anecdote, the chronicling of colourful episodes and most of all long-range dialectical exchanges may drown in detail some of the purposes of historical enquiry. We are interested to know what happened certainly but even more why it happened. And in order to discover this it may be as well to pay rather less attention to what leaders said or wrote and to pay rather more to their actions and in particular to the progressive shrinkage of the options before them. This shrinkage is a commonplace in most triangular situations: for a variety of reasons it was accentuated in the Indian case as the time for the transfer of power approached.

The point may be illustrated once again by reference to the delaying effect of the communal problem upon a transfer. Gandhi argued that communal differences were insoluble as long as the third party, the British, remained. The British by contrast were apt to maintain that they could not leave India until it was resolved, which might, of course, mean that they would stay forever! Or to pose the dilemma in broader, less personal, terms, how was the British view that the resolution of the communal problem was a pre-condition of their departure to be reconciled with the Congress conviction that their departure was a necessary pre-condition of its resolution? The answer in fact proved to be, in so far as it was an answer, by partition, by a transfer of power to two successor authorities, a negation, that is to say, of the declared purposes of both. In essence it rested upon an analysis of a domestic situation entertained hitherto neither by the Congress nor seemingly by the British. It was suggested at the Round Table conference in 1931. For the 'divide and rule' of Congress, an Indian delegate substituted 'we divide and you rule'. Pushed to its logical conclusion, this meant presumably that the divisions at root were domestic. At the Round Table conference, logic was not pressed to such extremes. Princes and Muslims were at one in proclaiming that they had no wish to create 'Ulsters in India'. But was this really so? In respect of some of the princes (and their friends) it seems questionable; while as for the Muslims were they a community, the second largest within India, or were they a separate nation? If they were the former, then the pattern of a self-protective policy might have been expected to be, as indeed it was at least down to 1940, limited co-operation with the British and the Congress in the working out of a federal structure, in which the position of the Muslims, at least in Muslim majority provinces, was entrenched against a centre certain to be dominated, under any form of representative government, by representatives of the great Hindu majority in the country. But if the Muslims were not the second largest community in India, but a separate nation, then any such policy of limited co-operation was precautionary and preliminary to a demand for a separate national recognition. Was there a point in time at which they ceased to be the one and became the other – a point before which the options were in fact still real? Did the introduction of electorates on the British model, hasten their foreclosing and was this, one returns to the point, a likely consequence in all plural societies preparing to receive and if necessary to apportion power? In these matters words it may be underlined, are not conclusive. But they are important when invested with the force which Jinnah gave them at the Lahore meeting of the League in March 1940. It will be remembered that he castigated the British for their conception of government by parties functioning on a political plane as the best form of government for every country. He assailed *The Times* for having earlier concluded, after recognition of the differences, not only of religion, but also of law and culture, between Hindus and Muslims, that in the course of time 'India will be moulded into a single nation'. For Jinnah it was not a question of time, but of absolutes, of fundamental beliefs and social conceptions. 'Hindus and Muslims', he said, 'have two different religious philosophies, social customs, literatures. They neither inter-marry, nor even inter-dine. Indeed, they belong to different civilizations. . . . Their view of this life and the life hereafter are different. . . . The Muslims are not a minority as the word is commonly understood. . . . Muslims are a nation according to any definition of the term, and they must have their homelands, their territory and their state.' On this argument had the British, indeed, succeeded in imposing unity, then the consequence, again accepting the fundamentals of Jinnah's analysis, might well have been, as he threatened in 1947, the bloodiest civil war in the history of Asia. For at the heart of it was the contention that it was the unity of India that was artificial and imposed; the division natuıal. That, of course, presupposed a transfer of power to two successor authorities.

Transfer of power to two as distinct from one successor authority carried the implication of equality between the two successor states. Prior to the transfer, therefore, the League had to be equated with the Congress, or, as Jinnah would have phrased it, Pakistan with Hindustan. In numerical terms this meant the equation of minority with majority. It had happened in plural societies elsewhere. It had happened in Ireland when the six counties of Northern Ireland and the twenty-six counties of Southern Ireland were given equal representation in the Council of Ireland, that 'fleshless and bloodless skeleton', as Asquith termed it, proposed in the Government of Ireland Act, 1920. In arithmetical terms such parity could not be defended in either case. But, so Jinnah argued, the debate was not about nations. Nations were equal irrespective of their size. He secured his aim at the Simla conference, 1946. Jinnah was indeed the most formidable proponent of a two-nation theory yet to appear within the confines of the British Empire.

The two-nation theory with its emphasis on parity, however forcefully advanced, won political but not general psychological acceptance. Nor in constitutional-legal terms was parity indisputable. In view of Britain and Pakistan there were two successor states to the British *raj;* in the predominant Indian view there was rather a successor state and a seceding state. The distinction is more than one of semantics. If there were two successor states then each was equally entitled to division of resources and authority within the prescribed terms of reference. If, however, there was one successor state from which territories were carved to form a seceding state, then the presumption was that resources and authority descended to the successor state, except in so far as they were specifically allocated to the seceding state. In British statute law the issue may be readily disposed of. Under the provisions of the Indian Independence Act, 1947, described in its preamble as 'an Act to make provision for the setting up in India of two independent Dominions . . .' there were two successor states. Article 1(1) read: 'As from the 15th day of August, nineteen hundred and fortyseven, two independent Dominions shall be set up in India, to be known respectively as India and Pakistan.' But could the issue be settled by reference to British statute law alone? The Indian National Congress thought not. It claimed that the Dominion of India should continue as the international personality of pre-partition India, and the Indian reforms commissioner, V. P. Menon, advised the viceroy, after consulting the legislative department, that post-partition would remain identifiable with pre-partition India. 'It was our definite view', he wrote, 'that neither variation in the extent of a State's territory, nor change in its constitution, could affect the identity of the State'. In respect of international status this opinion was accepted (or in the case of Pakistan acquiesced in after protest and with reservation), with the result that India after independence remained a member of the United Nations and all international organizations whereas Pakistan, as a new state, sought such membership *ab initio.*

Less controversially it may be noted that power was transferred to two dominions. Given that partition had become inevitable it may well be that at this point the Commonwealth made its supreme contribution to history. It provided through dominion status the precedents through which power could not only be peacefully but also, and this was very important at the time, quickly transferred. The speed was conditional upon two things – first, the putting into motion of well-tried constitutional machinery, and secondly, the securing of substantial political agreement in Britain. There is no doubt that dominion status, even if only for a brief interlude, assisted British opinion in all parties in accepting the sudden and unfavourable transformation in their world position which independence for India necessarily implied. That was important negatively. Equally important was the fact that independence for India and Pakistan could open in an atmosphere of goodwill and indeed of hope which might well have been lacking had the transfer taken place outside the familiar Commonwealth framework.

There remains the question, academical in its ordinary presentation, but fundamental alike to the manner of the transfer of power to India and to partition there and elsewhere. What is a nation? How is it to be identified? Is there some criterion by which it may be judged whether or not in plural societies there are two nations within a single state to whom power should, or should not, be separately transferred? Or must one be reconciled to the fact that political science, despite the pretension implicit in its designation, does not deal in such absolutes and that only history by way of trial, error and much suffering can supply even a provisional answer?

THE MAKING OF INDIA'S PAPER FEDERATION, 1927–35[1]

by R. J. MOORE *

As a matter of historical record, when one looks back over the last few years it is surprising how late in the story it was that partition emerged as a practical and pressing political proposition, and the fact that it was never seriously put forward in the Round Table Conference debates, . . . or indeed in any of the discussions between 1930 and 1940, suggests that Federation, if only it could have been quickly implemented, might have saved the situation.

Lord Halifax, *Fulness of Days* (1957)

The 'ifs' of history tantalize retired statesmen no less than scholars. Conservative British statesmen who helped to make the Government of India Act of 1935 have aired an 'if' of central importance to students of recent Indian history: if the Act's federal provisions had become effective before the war then the partition could have been avoided. Attempting to explain the failure to set up a federation they have found fault with diehard colleagues and the executors of policy in India.

In their memoirs Lord Templewood [2] and Lord Halifax [3] have emphasized that Churchill's sustained attacks delayed by crucial years the preparation and passing of the India Bill. They also argued that more might have been done by the viceroys to secure the number of princely accessions required to bring the federation into being. In a private correspondence of 1953, when Templewood was preparing *Nine Troubled Years* (1954), they exchanged views frankly, freed from the restraints of loyalty to former colleagues. Templewood wrote:

'My general conclusion is that we were within reach of starting the All-India Federation, and that if it had not been first, for Winston, and secondly, for the slow-moving machine, we should have had it in operation by the time that the war started . . . My view in London was that most of the officials [of India], who were working quite loyally, did not believe in All-India Federation. If there was to be any federation they wished it to be a federation of British India . . . The Princes . . . were given very little help in making up their minds . . . When Willingdon [4] succeeded you and I became Secretary of

[1] This paper, relying heavily upon the Templewood Collection at the India Office Library, is offered as an interim account of the making of the 1935 Act until full access to the large range of relevant archival materials enables a history commensurate with the size and importance of the subject to be written.

* Lecturer in the Modern History of South Asia, School of Oriental and African Studies, London.

[2] Secretary of state, as Sir Samuel Hoare, August 26, 1931–June 7, 1935.

[3] Viceroy, as Lord Irwin, April 3, 1926–April 18, 1931.

[4] Lord Willingdon, viceroy, April 18, 1931–April 18, 1936.

State, I came to the conclusion that it was we in London who were pressing the reforms, and that the brake came not from Whitehall but from Delhi.'[1]

Halifax agreed that Churchill's opposition 'was undoubtedly one of the blocks in the road of Federation' and expressed the 'broad thought . . . that the brake was generally in India':

'I have often thought, though this was after my time and I may have been wrong about it, that a good part of the trouble and delay came from the fact that Freeman [Willingdon] liked the Princes and really disliked the British Indian leaders, and Hopie [Linlithgow][2] had not much use for the Princes and did not really get on human terms with anybody. The machine of course, moved slowly as all machines do, but I suspect the principal cause of obstruction lay in India rather than in Whitehall; i.e. Freeman and Hopie! If they has really been willing to push the Federation idea and had not been inhibited by one cause or another, either in approach to Princes or Congress, you would have been able to get the Cabinet and the Party to move more quickly.'[3]

That Churchill delayed the Act of 1935 and aroused hostility among Indian nationalists is clear. I have argued elsewhere that he also encouraged princely truculence after 1935 by insisting that the princes should not be bullied into acceding to the federation. There were sufficient diehard respecters of treaty rights among the Tories to make Neville Chamberlain[4] fearful for party unity. In consequence, Linlithgow was held tightly in leading-strings from home and cannot be adjudged primarily responsible for the failure to hustle the princes.[5] Again, it is difficult to see how Willingdon could have acted more expeditiously. During his viceroyalty the tempo of constitutional change was determined in Whitehall. However, the major weakness of the Templewood–Halifax interpretation of the failure to set up a federation lies not in its assertion of viceregal dilatoriness but in its assumption that the Act embodied a workable solution to the Indian problem. The valid criticism of the viceroys concerns not their speed but their insight into the political situation in British India. It is also the fundamental charge against the Conservative policy-makers of 1930–5: they failed to take sufficient account of the fact that the paper federation met the minimum demands of neither the Congress nor the Muslims. The story of the making of the federation, told against the background of those demands, suggests that the idea of an all-India federation was a chimera.

I

The process of constitution-making began inauspiciously with the appointment of the 'all white' statutory commission in November 1927. Lord Birkenhead's *Halifax* (1965) makes it clear that Irwin must be held chiefly

[1] Templewood to Halifax, July 7, 1953, Templewood Collection (hereafter referred to as T.C.). [2] Lord Linlithgow, viceroy, April 18, 1936–October 20, 1943.

[3] Halifax to Templewood, July 13, 1953, T.C.

[4] Prime minister, May 28, 1937–May 10, 1940.

[5] An account of Conservative policy towards implementing the federal provisions of the Act appears in my 'British Policy and the Indian Problem, 1936–40', below, pp. 79–94.

responsible for this blunder, which alienated the Congress, the Indian Liberals and a section of the Muslim League. While Sir John Simon and his colleagues tackled their task in the face of hostile public opinion an Indian all-parties conference met under Motilal Nehru's chairmanship to prepare constitutional demands. The Nehru report, published in 1928, and more moderate than a significant section of the Congress would have wished, called for dominion status for India under an essentially unitary system of government. The provincial governments would remain but a strong responsible centre would be created and residuary powers would devolve upon it. Separate communal electorates would be abandoned.

A minority of the Muslim League, under Jinnah's leadership, boycotted the Simon commission, attended for a time the all-parties conference and sought accommodation with the Congress on the heads of a constitution. However, the majority of prominent Muslims refused to join in the boycott and in December 1928 met under the Aga Khan's chairmanship as the all-parties Muslim conference, to formulate their answer to the Nehru report. In letters to *The Times* the Aga Khan had already fulminated against the Nehru report's unitary system. He favoured the recasting of provincial boundaries on racial, cultural and linguistic lines and an eventual federation of free states. These sovereign units, among which there would be Muslim and Hindu states, formerly in British India, and princely states, would even possess their own armies.[1] The Muslim League had, as early as 1924, resolved that in any future constitutional reforms India should be reorganized on a federal basis, with the provinces enjoying full autonomy and the authority exercised at the centre being confined to the minimum. It had resolved that separate electorates and the Muslim majorities in the Punjab, Bengal and the North-West Frontier Province must be retained. Again, no Bill affecting inter-communal matters should be discussed or passed in any legislature if three-quarters of the Muslim representatives opposed it. The conference of 1928 reaffirmed these demands and added others to them. Sind should be separated from Bombay, and the N.W.F.P. and Baluchistan should be given the status of governors' provinces. Muslims must have their share of the seats in central and provincial cabinets. In any central legislature one-third of the members should be Muslims. In essence, the Muslims demanded a belt of autonomous Muslim provinces extending across eastern and north-western India, together with statutory safeguards of Muslim interests in other provinces and a balance of authorities that implied the negation of majority rule and collective ministerial responsibility. Jinnah's fourteen points were more conciliatory than the conference demands only in as much as Jinnah was prepared to open separate electorates to negotiation.

In December 1928 the Congress resolved that if dominion status were not conceded within a year then they would demand complete independence and resort to civil disobedience. The Simon commission was proceeding deliberately and Britain intended that in due course its report should be considered by a joint committee of parliament and Indian assessors. In January 1929 Irwin was seriously worried by the unanimity of Hindu opposition. Sir Chimanlal Setalvad made him aware that the Hindu Liberals were

[1] *The Times*, October 12 and 13, 1928.

disturbed at the growing influence of extremism in the Congress and that they were anxious for him to make a conciliatory gesture. Irwin came to feel that whilst he could offer nothing by way of immediate reform he might win some Hindu friends by clarifying Britain's ultimate objective and by promising a liberal procedure for the review of whatever proposals Simon made. By June, when he returned to England on leave, he had drafted proposals for a declaration that Britain's intention was eventually to confer dominion status upon India and that after the completion of the Simon report a Round Table conference of Indian leaders and representative Britons should assemble in London to consider the reform of the constitution.

Irwin distinguished between 'purpose' and 'policy'. He held that the Simon commission's concern was 'policy', or the proposal of reforms, and that to declare Britain's ultimate 'purpose' would not trench on its work. He recognized that a declaration of purpose might precipitate Indian demands for its early accomplishment. He argued, however, that Congress demands were already so strong that to ignore them was to invite separatist agitation.[1] He believed that many Indians sought an assurance of the right to full partnership in the Empire rather than the immediate enjoyment of that right. Moderate Indians would rest content with the assurance of eventual parity, just as a minor looked forward happily to enjoying full rights within a family, or a junior member of a firm was satisfied with the knowledge that he would in time become a full partner.[2] He put his case before Simon, Wedgwood Benn, the Labour secretary of state,[3] and Ramsay MacDonald, the prime minister.[4] Simon was at first disposed to accept it but after discussing it with his colleagues and Lord Reading [5] he came to feel that such an avowal of purpose would prejudice the commission's enquiry. The minority Labour government recognized the advantage of obtaining Conservative and Liberal support for a declaration and Baldwin and Reading were sounded. Both agreed to endorse the declaration if the commission concurred. Knowing of the commission's opposition but impressed with Irwin's case MacDonald and Benn authorized Irwin to make his dominion status announcement on October 31, 1929.

The promise of a Round Table conference that Irwin's declaration contained had implications for the scope of the Simon enquiry. The commission's original terms of reference were confined to framing recommendations for the revision of the Act of 1919. They thereby excluded consideration of the Indian states. Immediately prior to his departure from India on leave Irwin met the standing committee of the chamber of princes at Poona. The princes had been shaken by two recent documents. First, the Nehru report had called for the transfer to an Indian dominion of the government of India's role in relation to the states. Then the Indian states commission report, whilst it assured the princes that paramountcy would not be transferred without their consent, proclaimed the paramount power's virtually unlimited right to

[1] A note by Lord Irwin on his proposed dominion status declaration, given to Hoare on September 25, 1929, T.C.

[2] A note by Lord Irwin on dominion status, November 1929, T.C.

[3] Secretary of state, June 8, 1929–August 26, 1931.

[4] Prime minister, June 5, 1929– August 25, 1931(Labour); August 25, 1931–June 7, 1935 (National).

[5] Viceroy, April 2, 1921–April 3, 1926.

interfere in the administration of the states. By June 1929 the chamber of princes was pondering the consequences for the states of constitutional reforms in British India. It behoved their highnesses to look ahead. They declared themselves 'in sympathy with the legitimate aspirations of British India . . . and willing to open avenues of negotiation with a view to the closer association of the two Indias in the future'.[1] The appearance of this 'new element in the Indian situation' required, as *The Times* of July 1, 1929 observed, a revision of the procedure for constitutional review. Clearly, the Simon commission must 'make recommendations as to the future relations between the States and British India' and the states should 'have their place in the subsequent discussions in London'. The editor of *The Times*, Geoffrey Dawson, was Irwin's Yorkshire neighbour and earlier in the year he had been a house guest at Viceregal Lodge in Delhi. Whether he was privy to the viceroy's plans at this time is uncertain. But there is no doubt that Irwin 'ghosted' the letter of October 16th in which Simon proposed the extension of his terms of reference to embrace British India's relations with the states and the summoning in due course of a Round Table conference. He also drafted MacDonald's acquiescent reply of October 25th.

Irwin's declaration of purpose and procedure was a qualified success in winning Hindu support. Whilst the Liberals agreed to co-operate the Congress refused to recognize Irwin's distinction between purpose and policy or to attend a Round Table conference, unless the function of the conference was stated to be the formation of a dominion status constitution. Despite Irwin's earnest statement of Britain's intentions, in December 1929 Congress chose to explore the wilderness of civil disobedience. For this Irwin blamed 'the clatter created in England by my Declaration, which . . . did so much to undermine the confidence of Indian leaders in our purpose, or at least in our capacity to give our purpose effective shape'.[2] For whilst Baldwin and Simon, though they disliked the disingenuous manner of Labour's authorization of the declaration, accepted the *fait accompli* with grace, such eminent Tory and Liberal authorities as Birkenhead,[3] Churchill, Reading and Sir Austen Chamberlain[4] condemned it as foolish and dangerous.

The Simon commission reported in June 1930. It recommended the early replacement of dyarchy by full responsible government in the provinces, though the governors should have large reserve and emergency powers. It also proposed far-reaching changes in the central government. The only constitution capable of combining 'elements of diverse internal constitution and of communities at very different stages of development and culture', the only constitution into which the states could be fitted, and therefore the only constitution that could provide for a central legislature 'capable of expansion into a body representative of All-India in the wider sense', was a federal constitution.[5] It is true that Montagu and Chelmsford had expressed

[1] *The Times*, June 26, 1929.
[2] Halifax to Templewood, September 1, 1953, T.C.
[3] Secretary of state, November 7, 1924–November 1, 1928.
[4] Secretary of state, May 29, 1915–July, 20, 1917.
[5] *Report of the Indian Statutory Commission* (Cmd. 3568–9, 1930), vol. ii (Recommendations), paras 24, 30.

a shadowy notion that the only form of government suitable to British India and the states was some sort of federation.[1] However, the 'Montford' central legislature, consisting of a council of state and a legislative assembly, included majorities elected directly by territorial, communal or special interest constituencies. The system was essentially unitary. The Simon commission denied the possibility of a unitary government of a democratic kind in India. A democracy of 250 million people was 'unprecedented'. 'If self-government is to be a reality, it must be applied to political units of a suitable size....'[2] The commission would change the name of the legislative assembly to 'Federal Assembly' and have it elected by the provincial assemblies through a proportional representation system. The council of state would be partly nominated and partly elected by the provincial legislatures. The central legislature was, in short, to be fundamentally reconstituted, on a federal basis.[3]

The commission shrank from proposing any measure of responsibility in the central executive. Responsible government must be tried first in the provinces, and for the trial to be fair a stable central executive was essential. It was argued, however, that the reconstruction of the legislature on federal lines would make the executive more 'responsive' to the legislature. Furthermore, it was proposed that the governor-general should himself appoint the cabinet, some of whom should be drawn from the legislature. This would leave open the possibility of an advance towards responsible government.

Whilst an all-India federation was the commission's ultimate objective, immediate federation was thought impossible. The most that seemed feasible was that British India and states' representatives should meet to discuss 'matters of common concern', in preparation for an 'eventual Federal Union'.[4]

It has become common to say that the Simon report fell stillborn from the press. Irwin condemned its failure to mention dominion status as exposing a lack of imaginative insight into the Indian situation. However, Irwin had played the dominion status card already, and Britain could scarcely accept that the purpose was capable of achievement at that time, as Congress had claimed. A constitutional historian of Sir William Holdsworth's weight commended this 'report of statesmen used to dealing with affairs' and its concentration on 'the actual operation of the Indian constitution in practice' rather than on 'constitutional theory'. Those who were obliged to consider its proposals should clear their minds of 'the tyranny of catchwords' such as 'Dominion Status'.[5] Irwin's declaration had indeed won the Liberals' co-operation. However, that it was the cause of some worry to Benn on the eve of the first Round Table conference is evidenced by a cabinet memorandum (dated November 14th) that he circulated on the alternative line to be taken if dominion status were demanded by Indian delegates.

Irwin, in fact, was prepared to offer little more than Simon was by way of immediate reforms. The government of India's despatch on the commission's

1 *Report on Indian Constitutional Reforms* (Cd. 9109, 1918), paras 120, 300.
2 *Loc. cit.* para. 23.
3 *Ibid.* para. 365.
4 *Ibid.* para. 235.
5 Sir W. S. Holdsworth, 'The Indian States and India', *Law Quarterly Review*, xlvi (1930), 407–46, esp. pp. 442–3.

report endorsed the ultimate object of all-India federation and agreed that it was a 'distant ideal'.[1] It questioned the wisdom of reconstructing the central legislature on federal lines by substituting indirect for direct election, chiefly because public opinion would be hostile to the change. It concurred in extending provincial autonomy, and denied the wisdom of central responsibility. Irwin's only significant advance on Simon was to propose the extension of the principle of 'responsiveness'. The government of India favoured the definition of the portfolios of continuing interest to parliament and their retention by official ministers. The remaining departments should be handed over to elected Indian members of the legislature, who were to be selected by the governor-general. Parliament's continuing interests would be defence, foreign relations, internal security, financial obligations and stability, the protection of minorities, the rights of the services and the prevention of discrimination against British trade. Irwin denied that he was proposing dyarchy at the centre. He expressly opposed any formal departure from a unitary central executive. Transferred departments should be capable of resumption.

Assuredly, the Round Table conference was not to be limited to the consideration of the Simon report. It was to be a free discussion of India's constitutional future. Nevertheless, as the British delegates prepared themselves it was clear that the non-governmental teams, the Liberals under Reading and the Tories under Hoare, the latter of whom were to be the chief makers of the new constitution, were basing their position on the leading principles of the Simon report: provincial autonomy, reconstruction of the central legislature on federal lines, no central responsibility and the eventual creation of an all-India federation.

II

Delegates invited from the Indian sub-continent to London to confer freely with representatives of the major British parties about their country's future polity naturally prepared themselves well. Princes and ministers of princes, Hindu Liberals and Muslims of all camps (save only the Congress) gathered together for preliminary discussions, on the ship that brought them, the *Viceroy of India*, at the Aga Khan's Ritz suite, with the Maharaja of Bikaner at the Carlton. Speeches and schemes were rehearsed and attempts were made to concert a common plan.

The Muslims had long favoured a loose federation and provincial autonomy. As early as May 1928 a conference of princes at Bombay had resolved to seek a union council of the states and the viceroy's executive. Within two days of Irwin's October 1929 declaration Bikaner stated that 'the ultimate solution of the Indian problem and the ultimate goal' was 'Federation, a word which had no terrors for the princes and governments of the States'.[2] When he and the ministers of the greatest Indian states, Akbar Hydari of Hyderabad and Mirza Ismail of Mysore, arrived in London

[1] *Government of India's Despatch on Proposals for Constitutional Reform*, September 20, 1930 (Cmd. 3700, 1930), para. 16.

[2] Bikaner's press interview of November 2, 1929, in K. M. Pannikar, *His Highness the Maharaja of Bikaner* (1937), pp. 321–2.

each had a different scheme, drafted in some detail, for an all-India federation. Long dormant potentates were now aware of the dangers to their sovereignty if the viceroy, enjoying undefined paramountcy, were to become responsive to a progressive British Indian executive. Negotiated entry to an all-India federation promised internal autonomy and a voice in affairs of common interest.

There was one group of delegates to whom an all-India federation had never appealed – the Hindu Liberals. Tej Bahadur Sapru, their leader, had joined with Motilal to draft the Nehru recommendations for a responsible, unitary central government. Now, however, to win Muslim and princely support for a measure of immediate responsibility at the centre he was prepared to back the idea of all-India federation. At that stage he could not assess the cost of central responsibility in terms of the powers to be retained by Muslim provinces and princely states, of Muslim and princely representation at the centre and of safeguards for communal interests. His colleague, Srinivasa Sastri, with characteristic pessimism and prescience, wrote on October 24, 1930: '... if there is agreement, it will be by surrendering to the Princes and the Muhammadans.'[1] Among Hindus of British India Sapru was outstanding for his readiness to avow the federal objective and leave the definition of terms for a later stage of horse-trading. He was prepared to give more to the Muslims for the sake of central responsibility than were his colleagues, and by the end of the year he had resigned from the National Liberal Federation over the issue. It was chiefly because of him that when the conference opened the Indian delegates were able to present a united appearance. At the first plenary discussion on November 17th, he called for an all-India federation and central responsibility. He was followed by princely and Muslim delegates who avowed the ideal with a show of enthusiasm.

Like the Indian delegates the British met to concert a common approach. MacDonald accepted Hoare's argument on the need to avoid 'a divided British front and a repetition of the Irish precedent'.[2] The Conservative and Liberal delegates were supplied with information by the India Office and with appropriate cabinet papers. The greatest Indian civil servant of the century, Sir Malcolm Hailey, had advised Hoare that the government of India's despatch, with its opposition to the reconstruction of the central legislature and its advocacy of 'responsiveness', was 'unreal and very transitory'.[3] He suggested that Hoare should seek an undertaking from the government that they would yield central responsibility for certain portfolios only if the legislature were reconstituted on the federal basis proposed by Simon. When Hoare and Reading met the government delegates at Downing Street on the eve of the first plenary session, Reading pressed in vain for MacDonald 'to define the limits beyond which they were not prepared to go'.[4] However, the prime minister did say that the government 'certainly could not go less far than the

[1] Sastri, to V. S. Ramaswami Sastri, October 24, 1930, in T. N. Jagadisan (ed.), *Letters of the Right Honourable Srinivasa Sastri*, 2nd ed. (1963), p. 199.

[2] Note by Hoare on 'a meeting with Govt. at Downing Street. Nov. 16th 1930', T.C.

[3] Note by Hoare on a conversation with Hailey, November 13, 1930, T.C.

[4] Hoare's note of November 16th, *loc. cit.*

Viceroy, but there must obviously be reserved subjects, e.g. defence, foreign affairs, Indian Princes, and, probably, finance'. A cabinet memorandum of two days previously suggests that the government was disposed to yield to the British Indian central executive the largest degree of self-government consistent with parliament's retention of responsibility over certain essential matters. The government seems to have done no detailed work on the reconstitution of the centre on federal lines and MacDonald seemed loth to press federalism if Indian delegates proved averse to it, though he did regard it as 'the most favourable line of advance'.

On November 19th, a cabinet memorandum recommended the encouragement of the all-India federation idea. Such a federation was 'right for India' and could be 'used to establish, with Indian support, a "safer" form of Government, thus making a transfer of power easier'. Under an all-India federation, the portfolios for all departments except defence and external affairs, and perhaps law and order and finance, would be transferred to responsible Indian ministers.[1] A week later Hoare spoke with Simon, who shrewdly pointed out the 'danger of our agreeing to an all-India framework with [the] Princes in it, and then a withdrawal of the Princes and a claim that our acceptance applies also to a Federal British India alone'.[2] From this conversation came an idea that was to be of cardinal importance in the making of India's paper federation. Simon advised Hoare: 'Try to get out of the Conference general resolutions in favour of federation of all-India and provided that all-India is federated, then a cautious acceptance of Government corresponding to responsible Government.' Here was the origin of the princes' 'veto' on British India's constitutional development, the central provision of the federal section of the Act of 1935.

On December 12th Hoare sought the Conservative party business committee's endorsement of the principle that Simon had enunciated: a measure of central responsibility on condition that an all-India federation was established. He stressed that the princes' declared willingness to enter a federation had merely shortened the time scale of the main principle of the Simon report. He reported that the federal structure sub-committee of the conference had agreed 'that there should be only one executive and one system of legislative Chambers for India and that the executive and the Chambers should be federal'.[3] This prospective elimination of the legislative assembly of British India was, he claimed, 'a very remarkable step to have taken. . . . And by taking it we have made it possible to rescue British India from the morass into which the doctrinaire Liberalism of Montagu had plunged it.' A fundamental shift in the polity of India, from a unitary to a federal structure, had been negotiated. Hoare urged that a federal government would be more stable than a unitary one, for it would operate under a written constitution and a supreme court, the system of representation would have a less popular foundation and the constituent governments would exercise a steadying influence on the centre. He regretted that the 'Montagu-

1 Cabinet paper circulated on the prime minister's instructions, November 19, 1930, T.C.
2 Note by Hoare on a conversation with Simon, November 26, 1930, T.C.
3 Memorandum by Hoare on 'Conservative Policy at the Round Table Conference', December 12, 1930, T.C.

Chelmsford reforms and the policies and promises of the last thirteen years' rendered impossible the creation of an irremovable executive separated from the legislature. It would be necessary to concede some responsibility. However, it was possible to transfer certain portfolios and yet retain the 'threads that really direct the system of government'. Britain could insist upon a broad definition of the viceroy's overriding powers. She could keep the army, 'the ultimate instrument of control, completely in our hands'. She could 'tie up' finance, with a statutory currency board to control the exchange and a reserve bank to manage the reserves. She could make the army, service salaries and pensions and the interest on loans permanent prior charges on the federal revenues. Thus could financial responsibility be circumscribed so that some eighty per cent of the federal revenues would be kept out of the hands of an Indian minister. Commerce could be safeguarded through a trade agreement. Again, the central legislature would be so constructed that the executive need be only technically removable: 'In actual practice an executive composed of such divergent elements as British India and the Indian States, the one dependent on election, the other upon nomination, could never be responsible or removable in the British sense of the word.' Hoare was advocating the mere semblance of central responsibility. Even that was to be 'entirely dependent upon an effective federation being in actual existence in India', a condition which would, he believed, take a period of years to fulfil.

Such was the spirit of the Tory agreement to the Indian demand for an all-India federation and central responsibility, and MacDonald's high-sounding declaration at the close of the conference must be seen against it. 'With a Legislature constituted on a federal basis', he announced on January 19, 1931, 'His Majesty's Government will be prepared to recognize the principle of the responsibility of the Executive to the Legislature.'[1] In an official statement of Conservative policy on February 5th Hoare could justly claim: 'During ten weeks of almost incessant discussion, basing ourselves upon the Simon Report, we steadily maintained our position.'[2]

Britain had indeed yielded little. She had diverted the Indian demand for dominion status by nodding assent to the nebulous formula; central responsibility with reservations and safeguards, upon the creation of an all-India federation. This was closer to Simon's recommendations than to the Nehru report. It was clearly very different from what Congress had demanded. For the Hindu Liberals it was a slim basis on which to attempt to persuade their Congress brethren that Britain was prepared to concede the substance of dominion status. In the month following the appearance of the Simon report Sastri had read to the East India Association in London a paper in which he insisted that the 'essential aspect' of dominion status, 'the very bond and cement of the Commonwealth', was 'the right of secession'.[3]

[1] *Indian Round Table Conference Proceedings, 12 November 1930–19 January 1931* (Cmd. 3778, 1931), p. 506.

[2] *Morning Post*, February 5, 1931.

[3] V. S. Srinivasa Sastri, 'The Report of the Simon Commission', *Journal of the East Indian Association*, xxi (1930), 252–80, see p. 253. Cf. Hoare's note of November 26, 1930 (T.C.), recording Simon's view: 'Dominion Status and Responsible Govt. with reserves and contradiction in terms.'

Sapru's claim now to have won dominion status subject to safeguards was unjustifiable, though it is explicable in terms of the mission that he had in prospect.

III

However nebulous the terms of the formula agreed at the Round Table it seemed at the time that a reservoir of goodwill had been built. The Indian parties had concerted a goal which the British had accepted. It had been agreed that there should be provincial autonomy and that the governor-general must retain, for some time, reserve powers over the army, law and order, external affairs and the rights of the minorities and the services, and hold safeguards over certain aspects of finance. A sub-committee had been set up to consider the knotty problem of defining the federal structure, including such difficulties as the size of chambers, the electorates, the powers of the centre over the provinces and finance. Another was to decide upon statutory safeguards for the minorities in the provinces and at the centre, which raised in particular the vexed question of separate electorates. The sub-committees' work had been inconclusive. Before the reassembly of the conference the Indian parties would need to determine their views on the matters that had not been resolved. 1930 had ended with euphoria at apparent accord. During 1931, as each of the Indian parties defined the Round Table formula in its own way, a gulf of discordance could be seen yawning between them.

The Hindu Liberals' reports to Gandhi of the atmosphere favourable to a constitutional settlement at the Round Table, their effectiveness as peace-makers between him and Irwin, and the latter's sympathetic disposition, brought the hopes of the Round Table to their apogee at Delhi in March 1931. Gandhi agreed to suspend civil disobedience and to consider 'the scheme for the constitutional Government of India discussed at the Round Table Conference'.[1] He acknowledged that federation was 'an essential part' of the scheme, as were 'Indian responsibility and reservations or safeguards in the interests of India, for such matters as, for instance, defence; external affairs; the position of Minorities; the financial credit of India, and the discharge of obligations'. Having reached this working agreement with the government, Gandhi had now to achieve accommodation with the Muslims.

The hopes of March faded in April, when Delhi saw a sign of the intractability of the communal problem. The all-India Muslim conference indicated the terms on which it would accept a constitution of the type proposed by the federal structure sub-committee. It demanded the 'autonomy of the constituent units and . . . complete residuary powers to be vested in them'.[2] '. . . all transfer of power should be made from Parliament to the Provinces, and . . . no subject should be made Federal without the previous mutual consent of the autonomous units of the Federation.' Further, 'there should be no difference between the powers of the various units', which meant that

[1] The Gandhi-Irwin agreement, March 5, 1931, in M. Gwyer and A. Appadorai (eds.), *Speeches and Documents on the Indian Constitution, 1921–47*, 2 vols. (1957), vol. i, p. 232.

[2] *The Times*, April 14, 1931.

internal sovereignty should be as strong in the provinces as in the princely states, that the Muslims would cede to the centre only such powers as the princes would relinquish. The Muslims must have one-third of the seats in the central legislature. This demand was not new, but before the Round Table proposal for an all-India federation it had concerned British India only. Now, with the predominantly Hindu princely states involved, the demand was for a third of the seats in an all-India centre. The old demand for a belt of Muslim majority provinces across eastern and north-western India was reiterated. There were to be separate Muslim electorates. Executive councils were to be so composed as to recognize Muslim interests. No legislature was to discuss any inter-communal matter if three-quarters of the Muslim members opposed the discussion.

In May Gandhi launched an initiative to open to negotiation the fundamental Muslim demand, separate electorates, Jinnah had long been prepared to negotiate the issue and in this he had not been alone among the Muslims at the Round Table. However, such delegates had been excoriated in private letters from the Muslim member of the viceroy's council, Fazl-i-Husain, and in the Muslim press. Gandhi was now dealing through the Nawab of Bhopal with Iqbal and other representatives of the Muslim conference, together with Congress Muslims. The proposals that emerged would have opened the way for the gradual withering of separate electorates; but again Fazl-i-Husain exerted himself to ensure their rejection. In consequence the problem of separate electorates remained. In September Muslim delegates returned to the Round Table wedded to the system.

Federal structure was less obviously a communal issue than electoral arrangements. The Muslim approach to the question of federation was investigated by a *Manchester Guardian* correspondent, who reported in June 1931:

'The Moslems see that the new Federal Government, if and when it comes into existence, will have a large Hindu majority. The entrance of the States has increased the majority, for the States are chiefly Hindu. There is a strong tendency to counteract the permanent majority by trying to form a large northern block of provinces which will be Moslem, and in which the Hindus will be, as it were, hostages for the good behaviour of their co-religionists in the centre and the South. . . . Many Moslems do not believe in the permanence of a Federal India, and they foresee a Moslem state in the North stretching from Karachi to North Bengal . . . This idea may help to explain their insistence on . . . the separation of Sind; . . . that the Moslem N.W.F.P. should become an ordinary province; . . . [and the securing of] a permanent majority in the Punjab, and if possible in Bengal.' [1]

A cabinet paper of September 1931 similarly probed the communal aspect of the central authority issue. It was, the paper concluded, a 'question whether the Muslim provinces, or the provinces in which the Muslims hope to consolidate their power, should be under any degree of control from a centre which will be predominantly Hindu'.[2] The paper considered the Muslims'

[1] *Manchester Guardian*, June 19, 1931.

[2] India Office departmental note on communal and minority problems, September 25, 1931, T.C.

'primary object' to be the creation of 'a Muslim India'; the secondary object was to secure Muslim interests elsewhere by the operation of the hostage theory.

At the second Round Table conference the Muslim delegates all sat pat on the resolutions passed at Delhi in April. Shafa'at Ahmad Khan insisted that the centre's power of interference in the provinces in case of emergency should rest with the governor-general alone, and that neither the federal cabinet nor the federal legislature should have such jurisdiction. The Aga Khan hinted that emergency powers should rest not with the governor-general but with the viceroy, as was intended for the paramount power's authority over the states. There was no inclination to allow potentially great powers to fall to the Hindu dominated centre. The Muslims opposed weightage for the states in the central legislature and adhered to their demand for one-third of the seats. The government was aware that the Muslim delegates were controlled tightly by Fazl-i-Husain and, behind him, orthodox Muslim opinion. Gandhi stood no chance of solving the communal problem. To make agreement even more difficult, the Muslims achieved a common front over safeguards with the delegates of the Depressed Classes, the Anglo-Indians, the Indian Christians and the European population.

At the second conference the stark realities of the Indian problem came into sharp focus. Whilst a deadlock occurred over the communal question the breach between Britain and the Congress over India's constitutional status was re-opened. The Congress had commissioned Gandhi to demand acceptance of their conception of the essence of dominion status: the right to secede from the Empire. This was firmly rejected and the responsibility with safeguards and reservations formula reiterated. Gandhi called in vain for complete Indian control of finance, without which he believed there could be no central responsibility 'worth the name'. In March he may have felt that if the goodwill of the Round Table prevailed then he might achieve a common front with the Muslims as a means of extracting from Britain the substance of dominion status. By December such hopes were seen to have been delusions.

As communal troubles mounted and the Delhi pact dissolved the princes showed themselves to be no enthusiasts for federation. Before the first session of the conference, when a British Indian constitutional advance had seemed imminent, they had been careful to avoid being cast as opponents of *swaraj*. They had appreciated that it would be difficult to do a favourable deal with a self-governing India. They had shrewdly supported the all-India federation scheme and gained a veto on British India's constitutional advance. It was a veto they would scarcely dare use against a united British India for fear of the unrest that would arise among their own subjects. Still, it was not long after the return of the states delegates from the first conference that some princes expressed anxieties about acceding to an all-India federation. The Maharaja of Patiala, chancellor of the chamber of princes, launched an alternative scheme, developed by Sir P. Pattani in 1930, for the union of a federated British India with a confederation of Indian states. The princes would then face British India as a body. The all-India authority would have minimal powers and it would consist of equal numbers of British Indian and 'Indian Indian' representatives. The scheme did not command widespread support, though Dholpur, Indore and Bahawalpur adhered to versions of it. However, it was indicative of the tendency of the princes to divide among themselves over federation. The scheme was calculated to appeal to small states, which could not expect to be represented separately in an all-India federation and which would take comfort from unity. On the other hand, states of a moderate size were probably attracted more by a scheme of Bikaner's for the separate representation of the states that enjoyed individual representation in the chamber of princes. The major Indian states, which did not belong to the chamber, wanted representation commensurate with their importance. The states also differed over the arrangements to be adopted for federal finance, and some began to show alarm at the financial implications of federation.

On the eve of the second conference, Sir Reginald Glancy, expert adviser to the Hyderabad delegation, wrote an illuminating account of the states' attitudes. He believed that sufficient states were committed to federation to make any general withdrawal impossible provided that British India agreed to reasonable terms. Yet just two months later, in a rueful supplementary paper, he observed that the cleavage in the British Indian delegation had caused a 'marked change' in the princes' attitudes:

'Now that the outlook is so gloomy and the chance of agreement between the British Indian parties so remote, the Princes have begun to hope that nothing will come of the Conference, and that they will be able to continue their sheltered existence while Hindus and Muhammadans wage communal war in British India.'

When the conference began there was not enough accommodation for the princes but by the end of October many of their chairs were empty. Some had gone home and others stayed in London only to see that they were not blamed for the failure of the conference. Glancy felt compelled to write that there was 'not one genuine friend of Federation left amongst the Princes'. The key to the situation was British Indian unity: 'If only agreement can be reached in that quarter, the States will very quickly fall into line.' The assessment was ominous.[1]

IV

Amid communal deadlock, the Congress challenged British policy and with the princes resiling the government had to determine a course of action. The political climate in Britain was not conducive to bold or enlightened statesmanship. Britain was licking her wounds. Prolonged economic depression had forced her off the gold standard in September. To many it seemed that an age in English history had ended. Ramsay MacDonald now headed a national (essentially Conservative) government, and from October operated with a 'doctor's mandate' accorded by a desperate electorate. To

[1] Memorandum by Sir R. I. R. Glancy on 'Attitude of the Indian States Delegates towards Federation', September 1, 1931, and supplementary memorandum of October 29, 1931, T.C.

the cabinet it seemed that imperial resources – of prestige no less than of finance – were incapable of supporting a liberal policy in India. In September the cabinet had complained to the viceroy that an increase of the Indian duties on piece goods was driving 'the final nail into the Lancashire coffin' in order to pour 'money into the pockets of Congress'.[1] On this issue the viceroy stood his ground; but when, to balance the budget, he supported the reduction of civil service salaries the cabinet overruled him. He vainly resisted to a point just short of resignation the cabinet's decision to keep the rupee tied to the pound, regardless of the price of gold. If in the circumstances of late 1931 the British government had little concern for the economic interests of India, she had no patience for the dissent of the Congress from the agreed formula for the reformed constitution. Imperial malaise must be added to communal antipathies as a reason for the evaporation of the Round Table's reservoir of goodwill.

It is known that in 1886, when Gladstone seemed to threaten the Empire by his announcement of a scheme for Irish home rule, Lord Randolph Churchill, remembering Ulster, observed that 'the Orange card would be the one to play'.[2] In 1931, when Gandhi's repudiation of the conference formula was added to the economic crisis ('the greatest Imperial emergency since the war', were Baldwin's words to Willingdon [3]), 'the Crescent card' became a trump in the hand of the Conservative and Unionist party.

Hoare, now secretary of state, considered future policy in a memorandum of November 9th. He reasoned that Britain could not afford to withhold all constitutional advance until the communities composed their differences, for fear of losing her friends, 'the 120 million Indians who have hitherto refused to take part in civil disobedience'.[4] The government should therefore determine the communal issue and proceed immediately with a Bill to confer provincial autonomy. The difficulties inherent in the federation question should be resolved subsequently. He thought that the Hindus could not 'afford to stay out' if Britain proceeded at once to 'the provincial autonomy stage'. He denied that he wanted to abandon the federal scheme, insisting merely upon the need to recognize that a Bill to implement it would take some time. Indeed, he would announce immediately the appointment of sub-committees to prepare for federation with investigations in India of the outstanding problems of finance and franchise. However, the following passage suggests his private thoughts:

'Few delegates would concede what history and logic suggest – that it is premature to consider federation till parties are in being in the shape of autonomous provinces, with experience and power to decide the form of the centre. To concede this would be to postpone federation for five, or, probably, ten years.'

If the circumstances proved favourable to it, Hoare would not, apparently, regret a return to the Simon report's leisurely approach to federation.

[1] Hoare to Willingdon, September 18, 1931 (secret telegram), T.C.

[2] A. T. Q. Stewart, *The Ulster Crisis* (1967), p. 21.

[3] Message from Baldwin in Hoare to Willingdon, September 24, 1931 (secret telegram), T.C.

[4] Hoare's memorandum for cabinet, November 9, 1931, T.C.

The viceroy could see no difficulty in a two-phase approach provided that provincial autonomy was clearly presented as only the first part of an integrated scheme; for there could be no going back on the undertaking to establish a federation as soon as possible. Neither Hoare nor Willingdon expected the determined opposition that the two-phase plan aroused, especially in Gandhi and the Hindu Liberals. Gandhi questioned the possibility of the provinces functioning effectively as autonomous units as long as an alien despotism persisted at the centre. Sastri was deeply suspicious of the Tories' motives. He feared that once central responsibility was relegated to a second phase Britain would find excuses for withholding it. The provinces would be required to prove their fitness for federation. Congress would boycott the first phase and Britain would call up the Muslims to govern the provinces. Provincial autonomy would raise leaders who would refuse to cede newly won powers to a central authority. Faced with such arguments the government abandoned for the moment the two-phase scheme, agreeing to embody provincial autonomy and federal provisions in a single Bill.

The two-phase plan was symptomatic of a British concern for Muslim support that grew as the possibility of reaching agreement with Gandhi receded. Early in November, Hoare had been responsive to the Muslim delegates' apprehension that in India Congress was trying to do a deal with the Muslims of Sind and the N.W.F.P. that would destroy Muslim solidarity. In his memorandum of November 9th he proposed the separation of Sind and the conferment upon the N.W.F.P. of the status of a governor's province. Ten days later he cabled to Willingdon that he was 'most nervous lest we should send them [the Muslim delegates] back discontented'.[1] Assurances were given to the Muslims that Sind and the N.W.F.P. would become full provinces.

On December 1, 1931 Ramsay MacDonald closed the second Round Table conference with a reaffirmation of His Majesty's Government's 'belief in an all-India Federation as offering the only hopeful solution of India's constitutional problem'.[2] To prepare the way for provincial autonomy the government would, if necessary, issue an award on the communal problem. Committees would be sent to India to report on the major practical problems involved in federation.

An old-fashioned Liberal like Willingdon found some difficulty in following the logic of this policy. Many of the obstacles to federation arose from the attempt to draw in the princes. Certainly the communal question was awkward but if an award would settle it in the provinces then surely its federal aspect could be decided similarly. In short, at the close of 1931 and early in 1932 he contended that a British Indian federation was the logical first step towards an all-India structure. He and his council were critical of MacDonald's pronouncement that an all-India federation was the 'only hopeful solution of India's constitutional problem': 'We think such a declaration unnecessary and dangerous, particularly as it leaves [the] fate of India

[1] Hoare to Willingdon, November 19, 1931, T.C.

[2] *Indian Round Table Conference Proceedings (Second Session). 7 September 1931–1 December 1931* (Cmd. 3997, 1932), p. 415.

at the discretion of the States.' [1] But of course the Tories had accepted central responsibility only on condition that the princes came into the centre as a stabilizing element. The all-India nature of federation was simply not negotiable. Even if Hoare's own inclinations had been liberal he was faced with a strong and growing diehard faction, drawing support from Lancashire, which disliked central responsibility on any terms, but more particularly in a British Indian form.

It was Willingdon, however, who determined British policy towards the political situation that arose in India after the second Round Table conference; and he was not altogether without influence on the development of the new constitution. When Gandhi returned to India he requested an interview with Willingdon to discuss the repressive measures that had been introduced to combat terrorism in Bengal and civil disobedience in the U.P. and the N.W.F.P. Willingdon required that Gandhi repudiate the local Congress manifestations of civil disobedience as the condition of an interview. When Gandhi rejected this demand Willingdon, unopposed from home, arrested him and declared war on civil disobedience. Now Willingdon too became solicitous of Muslim interests. In March 1932, fearing Muslim non-co-operation, he obtained permission to state categorically that the government would issue an award to settle the communal problem. And he was certainly effective in helping to ensure that the terms of the award were such as to retain Muslim goodwill.

Willingdon's strategy was to keep such Indian friends as Britain had whilst refusing adamantly to parley with the architect of civil disobedience. Doubtless his attitude towards Gandhi was inspired partly by personal animosity. But he did believe that Irwin's conciliatory policy had increased Gandhi's influence by conceding him apparent equality of status. Again, any weakening before civil disobedience would discourage the loyal elements in India, the services and the Muslims, and the agents of law and order, the army and the police. If Congress were given no quarter they would eventually come to heel. This policy the home government questioned occasionally but never with conviction. At the same time, Willingdon was always anxious to give evidence of Britain's good faith and liberal intentions in order to win the support of moderate men. In January 1932, soon after incarcerating Gandhi and bringing full-scale civil disobedience down upon his head, he cabled home: '. . . . it is essential at this juncture to show our *bona fides* by strengthening Indian representation on my Council.' [2] Hoare placed before the cabinet the viceroy's proposals on the matter. They were rejected, as he recommended, for they would have weakened the government of India without appeasing the Congress demand for central responsibility. Willingdon took the rebuff with doubtful good grace.

Willingdon's government enjoyed a notable success in constitutional controversy when, in April–May 1932, Hoare, with cabinet support, tried to revive the two phase plan. Hoare stressed that the India committee of the cabinet was concerned at the delay that would fall between the issue of the communal award to prepare for provincial autonomy and the completion

[1] Willingdon to Hoare, November 29, 1931 (telegram), T.C.
[2] Willingdon to Hoare, January 23, 1932 (secret telegram), T.C.

of the India Bill. However, Willingdon emphasized that reversion to a two phase approach was bound to arouse suspicion of Britain's motives. Only the Muslims would be satisfied; and the newly autonomous provinces would insist upon a further round of consultations before a federation was established. Sastri heard of the cabinet's proposal and protested pleadingly to MacDonald. He wrote to a friend: 'Imagine what will happen if provincial autonomy is granted and four provinces under Muslim rule oppose central responsibility (or stipulate impossible conditions) while seven Hindu provinces wish to go ahead.' [1] In the face of Willingdon's appreciation of the situation, and shaken perhaps by Sastri's representation, the cabinet backed down. Willingdon welcomed this development and pressed for an announcement on the programme for preparing the reforms. He was certainly anxious to hasten the India Bill. Indeed he caused consternation at home when, on one occasion, he publicly expressed a hope to leave India a constitutional viceroy.

V

Gandhi's departure in disappointment from the Round Table marked the failure to concert reforms by a consensus among the major British and Indian parties. So little had come of the second conference that Hoare was disposed to proceed unilaterally. Early in 1932 the promised committees visited India and reported on the franchise, federal finance and financial relations between the centre and the states, whilst a consultative committee containing nominated representatives of the conference was set up in India. On June 27th, partly no doubt in response to Willingdon's plea for a policy declaration, Hoare announced the government's programme to the house of commons. The first step would be the issue of a communal award. Next, whilst he did not close the door to further consultation with Indians, Hoare indicated that the government would itself proceed to frame proposals in the form of a white paper, which would be placed before a joint committee of parliament with Indian assessors. The Hindu Liberals accepted the need for a communal award but regarded the further programme as offensively authoritarian. Sastri saw it as evidence of Tory reaction and Sapru resigned from the consultative committee. Willingdon became anxious that abandoning the conference method would alienate the Liberals utterly. Sapru, Sastri, Jayakar, Setalvad, Joshi, Sethna, Chintamani and others condemned Hoare's procedure for doing 'away with ideas of equality during discussions between British and Indian delegates and agreement between them on [the] basis of proposals to be laid before Parliament'.[2] The Liberals demanded a further conference session in London as the condition of their co-operation. Willingdon cabled of the gravity of losing the vital support of the Liberals and intimated that if British India's Hindus denounced the new constitution then there was 'reason to fear that the Princes will not do business'.[3]

[1] Sastri to P. Kodanda Rao, July 2, 1932, *Sastri's Letters*, pp. 231–2.

[2] 'Manifesto' issued by the Liberals, reported in Willingdon to Hoare, August 18, 1932 (telegram), T.C.

[3] *Ibid.*

Quite apart from tactical factors, Willingdon considered it essential to bring British India and the states together to resolve the outstanding problems in federation. The reports of the federal finance and states finance committees had seemed to favour the states and had widened the cleavage between the two Indias. Agreed solutions to questions of finance and central representation and powers must be found:

'Without such a Conference it does not seem possible to make progress in determining a workable Federal scheme to be placed before Parliament, and without such a Conference the responsibility for failure to evolve a workable scheme . . . will fall solely on His Majesty's Government.' [1]

Hoare yielded. The Round Table was assembled for a third session in November 1932. It was a depleted gathering for none of their highnesses appeared. In their absence no firm decisions could be taken on federal finance or the states' representation, though the proportions of princely and Muslim seats at the centre were agreed. The states would have two-fifths of the seats in the council of state and one-third of those in the assembly. The Muslims would have a third of the British Indian seats at the centre and Britain would use her best endeavours to secure a fair representation of Muslims among the princes' nominees. Agreement was also reached on two other important matters. The assembly would be elected directly by all-India constituencies; and where doubt arose whether a subject was central or provincial the power of decision should lie with the viceroy. Hoare adjourned the conference after five weeks.

From the end of 1932 the Hindu Liberals, now the only firm friends of federation, became increasingly anxious about the reception of the proposed white paper.[2] Sapru and Jayakar pressed Hoare for the release of Gandhi and the civil disobedience prisoners in advance of the publication of the white paper. Failure to make this gesture would seriously impair the prospect of the white paper's acceptance. Hoare sounded Willingdon, who had his answer ready. In November, at his request, Sastri had in vain pleaded with Gandhi to suspend civil disobedience, which must, Willingdon insisted, remain the condition of releasing prisoners. At home the diehards would have quickly condemned any tendency to truckle to sedition.

At the close of the third conference the Liberals were also anxious 'lest through indecision and inaction of [the] Princes [the] launching of [the] Federal Constitution might be indefinitely delayed'.[3] Hoare saw that such fears arose because of the princes' failure to attend the conference, their disagreements among themselves over representation at the centre, and the lukewarm resolutions of the chamber of princes. From the beginning of 1933 Hoare began to prod Willingdon to obtain assurances from the princes of their intentions to accede.

Independently of Liberal anxieties, Hoare had good reason for concern about the princes. He was uneasy about the joint committee's reception of

[1] 'Manifesto' issued by the Liberals, reported in Willingdon to Hoare, August, 18, 1932 (telegram), T.C.

[2] Issued as *Proposals for Indian Constitutional Reform, March 1933* (Cmd. 4268, 1933).

[3] Hoare to Willingdon, January 6, 1933 (telegram), T.C.

the federation scheme should members feed that princely accession was unlikely. There was a strong group of Conservatives, including the esteemed and influential Marquess of Salisbury, that was hostile to central responsibility and would seize evidence of princely apathy in order to destroy the federal proposals. Hoare toyed with federal chambers of various sizes and with the minutiae of princely representation, seeking the formula most likely to ensure the accession of rulers who accounted for half of the seats and half of the population of princely India. Large chambers would give individual representation to more states and were therefore more attractive to smaller states but less so to the more substantial ones. On this problem Willingdon failed to give the firm, judicious lead that only the viceroy could. In 1932 he had put the merits of a scheme that would attract the large princes. The case might have been argued convincingly, for the eight largest princes represented almost half the population and area of the states. However, early in 1933, when Hoare proposed a small centre, Willingdon seemed to see safety in numbers. A small centre would deny individual representation to seventy-two per cent of the members of the chamber of princes. He dismissed almost lightheartedly the difficulty of obtaining firm assurances of princely intent:

'They have always said they would decide when the picture was filled in, and their ideas of a picture are pre-Raphaelite rather than futurist.' [1]

Carried away by his optimism, he asserted that if Hoare could pass a Bill 'without more definite assurances of adhesion but also without definite resolutions condemning [the] federation scheme as set out in the White Paper, I hope and believe that the passage of the Bill will make entry of most of the important States practically inevitable'.[2]

Hoare was not to be put off with generalities. He asked that political officers commend the federal scheme, with a large centre (as drafted in the white paper), to the princes and that they secure wherever possible 'provisional assurances of . . . intentions to federate'.[3] Willingdon did come to appreciate Hoare's apprehension of difficulty with the joint committee in view of the 'somewhat nebulous attitude of [the] Princes'.[4] After further investigation he sent home some reassuring calculations. Of the white paper's 104 princes' seats in the council of state, 65 would, he computed, be taken up, and by princes who accounted for 33 million of the 70 million states' peoples. He cabled: '. . . there seems definitely assured prospect that [the necessary] majority, measured in terms of population, will be attained.' [5] Ominously, however, he reported that some of the larger states – Hyderabad, Mysore, Travancore, Udaipur, Bhopal – were still standing out. Once Willingdon had obtained these intimations of the princes' intentions regarding the white paper scheme he felt committed to a large centre. He thought, too, that the temporary abstention of the big southern states would be less inconvenient administratively than that of the smaller but more numerous northern ones.

[1] Willingdon to Hoare, January 26, 1933 (telegram), T.C.
[2] Willingdon to Hoare, February 9, 1933 (telegram), T.C.
[3] Hoare to Willingdon, February 16, 1933 (telegram), T.C.
[4] Willingdon to Hoare, August 20, 1933 (telegram), T.C.
[5] Willingdon to Hoare, November 16, 1933 (telegram), T.C.

Willingdon was doubtless over sanguine that the princes would eventually toe the line. He did see the force of the argument that if British India repudiated the India Bill then the princes would recoil. But he seems to have thought that provided the Liberals and the Muslims stood by the government the Congress would eventually see the advantage of co-operation. Since January 1932 his policy had been to suppress civil disobedience and wait for moderate counsels to prevail. In 1934, when the Swaraj party decided to contest the central assembly elections under the 1919 constitution, he looked forward to the return of moderate Congressmen with whom he could open the constitutional dialogue. Despite occasional misgivings Hoare proposed no alternative to this policy of waiting hopefully.

It is unlikely that a more conciliatory viceroy could have influenced in essentials the form of the constitution, in a bid for Congress goodwill. Nor could he have pressed the princes harder. For in England a Tory backlash menaced even the modest white paper scheme for federation and central responsibility. During the years 1933–4 occasions were frequent when Hoare felt that the federal provisions would be lost. He, the prime minister and the cabinet were so nervous that they became obsessively concerned about minor Indian questions that might affect reactions to the federal scheme at home.

The attitude of the Lancashire interest seemed of critical importance. In 1933 Hoare delayed the presentation of Lancashire evidence before the joint committee pending the outcome of a Lancashire trade delegation's visit to India. Concern for Lancashire opinion affected the selection of an acting-viceroy during Willingdon's home leave. The secretary of state and the viceroy agreed that Hailey was the very best choice. However, the governor of Madras was then Sir George Stanley, brother of Lord Derby, whose support for the white paper was vitally important. Besides being influential in the party Derby was paterfamilias in Lancashire. Hoare discussed the matter with MacDonald and a secret telegram was sent to Willingdon confiding the decision to appoint Stanley. Again, towards the end of 1933 Japan pressed India for arrangements more favourable to her cotton textiles, under threat of cancelling orders for Indian cotton, of which she was the largest buyer. Hoare cabled Willingdon that acceptance of Japan's demand 'would evoke the relentless opposition of [the] Lancashire members on an issue in which they command wide support here, and there would be a risk, the gravity of which can not be exaggerated, that the Government's proposals for constitutional reform could not be carried'.[1] Willingdon was incredulous of the cabinet attaching such significance to a minor tariff adjustment. But so seriously did the cabinet take the matter that they demanded the rejection of Japan's terms and undertook to indemnify India against loss from any cancellation of the orders for raw cotton. In the event Japan backed down and settled for a face-saving concession. Hoare's problem was to steer a course that would enable the moderate majority of the Manchester chamber of commerce to remain ascendant. Extreme members of the chamber were prepared to go to almost any lengths to defeat central responsibility in India. In February 1934 Hoare acquainted Willingdon that a textile magnate had solicited Patiala's support against the federation scheme.

[1] Hoare to Willingdon, November 28, 1933 (telegram), T.C.

In April 1934 Hoare and his colleagues were apprehensive of the effect that an election campaign for the legislative assembly would have upon the reception of the India Bill. Extreme speeches would furnish the diehards with ammunition. 'We all felt', cabled Hoare, 'that this would almost certainly be fatal to the Bill.' [1] At this stage he was apt to jump at shadows. A few days earlier Churchill had accused him of a breach of parliamentary privilege. He stood charged with having exerted undue influence upon the Lancashire witnesses to the joint committee, causing them to alter the evidence that they had intended to submit. He defeated the motion but only after months of distracting toil and anxiety. It seemed to Willingdon that consternation in the face of difficulties at home led Hoare and the cabinet to an unrealistically gloomy appreciation of the Indian situation. He strove to overcome the cabinet's aversion to holding elections, arguing that to postpone them would prejudice Indian opinion against the Bill. In reply, the cabinet asked him whether he would not prefer to face hostile public opinion at that stage rather than hold elections and risk a campaign that would rouse British opinion and force the government to withdraw the federal provisions of the Bill. Willingdon claimed that the danger of a violent election campaign was being exaggerated, and he carried his point.

When the white paper came before the joint committee Hoare was forced to make significant amendments to its federal section. Salisbury proposed the abandonment of central responsibility whilst such non-diehards as Derby, Zetland and Austen Chamberlain sought a centre that would be more certainly stable, i.e. conservative. The white paper proposed a council of state with 260 members, up to ten nominated by the governor-general, 100 appointed by the princes, and the remainder elected by the provincial legislatures; and a federal assembly with 375 members, 125 appointed by the princes and the remainder elected directly by all-India constituencies, arranged territorially, communally and by special interests. Direct election was a sop to the democratic pretensions of British India. The large houses reflected an attempt to satisfy a substantial number of princes. There was a strong body of opinion on the joint committee which believed that small houses and a system of indirect election would be more stable. Hoare had to compromise in order to save the federal scheme. Whilst Willingdon set his face effectively against any modification that would give the princes an excuse to resile, he counselled that the sacrifice of direct election, while it would cause disappointment, was not crucial. In consequence, Hoare accepted that the assembly should be elected by the provincial lower houses and that the council of state should be elected by the upper houses or, where these did not exist, by *ad hoc* electoral colleges. These changes brought the centre closer to the Simon model; and, of course, they made the scheme less palatable to the Congress. Considering the balance of power in the Conservative party at this time, the passing of a Bill more liberal than that which was enacted in 1935 is inconceivable.[2]

[1] Hoare to Willingdon, April 18, 1934 (telegram), T.C.

[2] For an account of the divisions within the Conservative party over the Indian question see S. C. Ghosh, 'Decision Making and Power in the British Conservative Party: A Case Study of the Indian Problem, 1929–34', *Political Studies*, xiii (1965), 198–212.

VI

The Templewood–Halifax interpretation of the failure of the paper federation makes much of the weakness of British approaches to the princes. Before the passing of the Bill Hoare was already stressing the priority of the states problem. He pressed it on Willingdon frequently, for example in November 1934:

'The problem is in one sense more difficult and important than any connected with the views that may be expressed in British India, since if there were anything in the Act as passed to which most of the Princes were irreconcilably opposed we might find it impossible to bring the Federation into being.' [1]

Willingdon was misleadingly optimistic, even after the chamber of princes' resolution of February 1935, which attacked the draft instrument of accession's failure to limit paramountcy sufficiently and the statutory power of the viceroy to interfere in the states in the event of a threat to India's peace and tranquillity. In September 1935 he told Lord Zetland,[2] the new secretary of state, cheerily: 'My own opinion at present with regard to the Princes is that they will come in and not try and delay the proceedings.' [3] He might himself have cajoled the princes to accede. However, his similarly sanguine but misguided appraisal of Congress attitudes – he assured Zetland in June 1935 that he had 'every reason to think that when the Bill is through even Congress will work it, and work it properly' [4] – gives little ground for confidence in his judgment. He favoured approaching the princes through the political officers, on a regional basis, and in October 1935 wanted to appoint a political adviser to begin preparations. Zetland, however, insisted upon leaving the incoming viceroy, Linlithgow, free to determine his own approach. This was commendably liberal but of doubtful wisdom in view of Linlithgow's lack of experience in Indian administration and the acknowledged complexities of the case. Then Zetland certainly applied a brake from home for fear of a diehard revolt, and he viewed the inauguration of a federation as a process requiring some years to complete. Linlithgow was permitted neither the carrot nor the stick to bring the princes into a federation, and he was denied expert assistance.[5] Templewood and Halifax were right to stress that negotiations with the princes were not handled expeditiously, but the viceroys were less culpable than they suggest.

Furthermore, it is difficult to escape the conclusion that the task of landing the princes could not be isolated from the British India problem. The princes' attitudes to federation were conditioned by events in British India. In 1929 and 1930 the princes espoused the federal idea chiefly because they feared the exercise of paramountcy, large and undefined, by a viceroy subject to the influence of a strong, reformed British Indian centre. After the first Round Table conference, when their right of free accession was recognized and their accession was made a condition of central responsibility, they had

[1] Hoare to Willingdon, November 2, 1934 (telegram), T.C.
[2] Secretary of State, June 7, 1935–May 10, 1940.
[3] Willingdon to Zetland, September 1, 1935, Zetland Collection, India Office Library.
[4] Willingdon to Zetland, June 24, 1935, *ibid.*
[5] See my 'British Policy and the Indian Problem, 1936–40', below, pp. 79–94.

less to fear from British India, though they at once began to seek substantial safeguards of their sovereignty under a federal polity. In early negotiations they obtained weightage at the centre and a strict limitation of the central legislature's powers. To some extent they traded assurances of their accession for a restricted definition of paramountcy. But their fears for their sovereignty could never be assuaged. When the second Round Table conference revealed a deep communal cleavage in British India their enthusiasm for federation cooled rapidly. Glancy's analysis of their change in attitude was perceptive. The princes could only be brought into a federation if British India were first seen to be united and if public opinion were felt to be irresistibly favourable to federation. In the long term they paid dearly for their assumption that they could remain in splendid isolation as long as the communities were estranged in British India.

In retrospect, the agreement of the first Round Table conference to proceed by way of an all-India federation can be recognized as condemning India to a constitutional dead end. The scheme came from the princes, who did not really want federation. It was accepted by the Muslims, who were not, for the most part, enthusiasts for central responsibility but who would support it if their interests were fully protected. Nothing would have come of the scheme had Sapru not backed it. Without his support Britain could never have proceeded with the princes and the Muslims to devise a constitution so anathema to the spirit of the Nehru report as to have no real chance of being accepted by the largest party in British India. But given his enthusiasm and authority a well-meaning Labour government could draft an apparently historic formula. Clever Tory strategy made any central advance dependent on princely accession and made the central responsibility to be ceded the semblance not the substance of power. Hoare saw the formula for what it was: the diversion of the demand for dominion status; the retreat from Montagu's liberal goal of a democratic, unitary polity.

The steady recoil of the princes from an all-India federation suggests that Britain would have done better to address herself to the British India problem. The enlightened MacDonald–Benn–Irwin triumvirate did attempt to draw Congress into the constitution-making process. However, when Gandhi withdrew from the Round Table, the essentially Tory government proceeded with a scheme to retain Muslim support, conciliate the princes and ignore Hindu British India. Willingdon's counsel avoided the alienation of the Hindu Liberals. However, from late 1931 until the passing of the Act nothing was done to bring together the major parties of British India. Indeed the tendency of policy was to alienate rather than reconcile the communities.

Whilst the Congress went to gaol the Muslims fared well. They obtained full provincial status for the N.W.F.P., the separation of Sind, a virtual statutory majority of seats in the Punjab and an assured 48·6 per cent of the seats in Bengal; in short, they achieved power in four autonomous provinces. They also obtained separate electorates. However, there was little in the federation scheme to attract autonomous Muslim provinces, though Muslims would have one-third of the British Indian seats at the centre. Residuary powers were not left with the provinces. Through a system of lists powers were distributed as far as possible, but the central powers would be substantial and the federation would be strong rather than loose. Fears of a Hindu *raj* would still seem justified and communally inclined Muslims would reject the federation.

In 1936 the Congress condemned the federal scheme as giving too little responsibility to India. Indian democrats could scarcely accept a constitution that yoked the future of the Indian people to the princes. In the interests of the minorities and of stability the constitution imposed stern checks on majority rule and collective ministerial responsibility. If Congress were true to its principles it could only seek to destroy the scheme.

Between 1930 and 1935 Britain pursued a chimerical federation. In so doing she brought into being a powerful block of autonomous Muslim provinces in eastern and north-western India, a strong base for Muslim bargaining when the question of central government emerged in more real terms after the federal scheme collapsed. It made Pakistan plausible. Britain's truckling to the princes left them in their medieval dreamlands. This invited the Congress attacks that began in 1937 and sealed all hopes of princely accession. Powerful forces had been created and confirmed to thwart the growth of Indian unity.

The paper federation failed not because of the weaknesses in the viceroy's execution of the Act, nor because diehard opposition delayed its passing by a year or so, but because it was flawed in essential respects. It was not the viable alternative to partition that Templewood and Halifax suggest. Perhaps there was no alternative approach for Britain to have pursued with profit from the early thirties. There are indications that the cards were stacked against a communal settlement that would preserve Indian unity. The Muslims already wanted a block of autonomous eastern and north-western provinces, and a loose federation of sovereign states. However, it would be rash to knock down the 'if' of federation only to set up the myth of the inevitability of partition. If Britain wanted Indian unity her main problem in the early thirties was to achieve accord between the communities. This may not have been impossible. Amity might have been encouraged. Jinnah, who was prepared in 1934 to bargain separate electorates for a common nationalist front, was not treated with the same cordiality as, say, the Aga Khan. Tory policy recalls the playing of 'the Orange card' in Ireland. One can only speculate upon what might have happened if, after the failure of the second Round Table conference to solve the communal problem, Britain had declined to proceed unilaterally. The alternative was the Congress proposal to call together some kind of constituent assembly to draft a constitution that provided acceptable safeguards for the minorities and for British interests. One suspects that the proposal was thought to be tainted at its source. Such a procedure would never have been condoned by the Conservatives of the thirties. Even in the perilous summer of 1940 the cabinet modified a promise of India's right to frame her own constitution that a cautious Conservative viceroy proposed to give.

BRITISH POLICY AND THE INDIAN PROBLEM, 1936–40[1]

by R. J. MOORE

I only wish that between us we might have been able to make a greater contribution towards the solution of the problem with which we have been grappling, but the dice have been heavily loaded against us . . .

Zetland to Linlithgow, May 14, 1940

The lumbering machinery of parliamentary democracy strained and laboured to produce the Government of India Act of 1935. A commission of enquiry, sent to India pursuant to the statute of 1919, was succeeded by Round Table conferences with Indian leaders in London, and they in turn were followed by a joint committee of parliament. The dimensions of the Indian problem were at last circumscribed by the longest statute in British history. Probably the Act satisfied nobody completely, which reflects the complexity of the constitutional issues. Two future prime ministers attacked it for opposed reasons. For Churchill, leading the diehards, its federal clauses represented a precipitate rush towards self-government. For Attlee, it gave insufficient scope for the operation of 'the living forces of India'.[2] To the policy-makers it seemed that both objections ignored the realities of Indian politics – the need to conciliate the Congress, which demanded self-government, without alarming or alienating the minorities and the princes. They hoped, subject to providing safeguards for the interests of the Muslims, to give the Congress a fair field of action in autonomous provincial governments. They planned to create a central government in which the Congress would be counterbalanced by the representatives of the Muslims and the nominees of princes who ruled over a majority of the peoples of the states.

The Act followed the drift of British policy. Consistent with the declarations of Montagu and Irwin, Hoare introduced the Bill with a reaffirmation that Britain's aim in India was to create a self-governing dominion. The Act approached constitutional progress by devolving responsibility upon the provinces, a policy which, as Curzon observed in 1911 and Attlee in 1935, naturally fostered separatism. It aimed at the representation of interests, not of numbers, and as the most vocal interests in India were communal it encouraged communalism. The separate electorates of Minto, introduced at least in part out of a respect for minority interests that would have delighted John Stuart Mill, had been perpetuated, though criticized, by Montagu and Chelmsford. The communal award, embodied in the Act of 1935, wove together the strands of communalism and separatism by giving to the Muslims virtually perpetual majorities in the legislatures of the Punjab, Sind, the North

[1] Without the kind permission of the Marquess of Zetland to use his late father's private papers (now deposited at the India Office Library) this paper could scarcely have been written.

[2] Attlee's speech on the Government of India Bill, June 4, 1935, in C. H. Philips (ed.), *The Evolution of India and Pakistan, 1858–1947: Select Documents* (1962), p. 318.

West Frontier Province and Bengal. The Act also pandered to the princes, whose absolute authority resting upon treaties had remained uninfringed by the paramount power since the Curzon era. Now they had it in their power to veto Britain's plan for a federated India. If the federal sections of the Act were ever to be brought into operation, British diplomatists would need, between 1936 and 1940, to inspire political India with a new spirit of goodwill and compromise. Consummate care would be required if the infant federal constitution were not to die of neglect whilst the *enfants terribles* developed by policy in the past – communalism, separatism and princely petulance – received further nurture.

I

From Willingdon's departure in April 1936 until the fall of Chamberlain four years later British policy was essentially the policy of the Conservative viceroy, Lord Linlithgow, though he was frustrated by the home government's leisurely response to his attempts to open negotiations with the princes. Linlithgow's chairmanship of the royal commission on Indian agriculture and of the joint committee on constitutional reform had given him a certain standing in Indian affairs. Nonetheless, the extent of his authority during this crucial period is arresting. The secretary of state, Lord Zetland, had been governor of Bengal during the similarly critical years from 1917 to 1922 and had remained keenly interested in India. The cabinet contained Lord Halifax, whose stock had risen high during a distinguished viceroyalty, Sir Samuel Hoare, Zetland's predecessor at the India Office, and Sir John Simon, who had been chairman of the statutory commission. Linlithgow was competent, conservative, confident and industrious. Given an established constitution he would have ruled an empire creditably. Later when Japan overran Burma and Gandhi launched his 'Quit India' movement he did govern with great courage. However, from 1936 until 1940 it was his misfortune to be confronted with a constitutional conundrum, and his want of political insight and constructive imagination gave his somewhat Victorian virtues the appearance of complacency, pomposity and insensitiveness. He was loth to hasten democratic change and he was sobered by the complexity of the Indian situation. He esteemed the advantage to Britain of her Indian empire and he stressed Britain's responsibility to the minorities and the princes. To Zetland he was 'wise, cautious Hopie'.[1]

It was the viceroy who stood firm when after the elections of 1937 the Congress refused to take office in the provinces unless Britain agreed to waive the governors' reserve powers to safeguard the rights of the Muslims and the services and to impose law and order. He remained averse from truckling to the Congress although Halifax criticized his 'stonewalling' as showing a 'lack of imagination'.[2] Zetland became overawed by the situation as British relations with the Congress seemed to approach 'a turning point'.[3]

[1] Zetland to Willingdon, March 22, 1936, Zetland Collection (hereafter referred to as Z.C.).

[2] Zetland to Linlithgow, May 3, 1937, Z.C.

[3] Zetland to Linlithgow, June 28, 1937, Z.C.

He warned Linlithgow that if the Congress did not take office Halifax would probably persuade the cabinet to insist upon a peace offer being made to the Congress before it authorized the government of India to assume authority in the provinces under the emergency powers conferred by section ninety-three of the 1935 Act. The Congress decision to take office was a personal triumph for Linlithgow. This early success of a policy of immobility no doubt encouraged Linlithgow to attempt to call the bluff of Congress at an even more critical stage of his viceroyalty, when the Congress stated steep conditions for their co-operation in the war.

It was Linlithgow, too, who determined the tenor of British negotiations with the princes and drove forward the attempt to bring the federal scheme into operation. Hoare doubted the possibility of enticing the required number of princes to accede and shrank from hastening the day when the scheme would be pronounced a failure. Zetland was distracted from Indian affairs by the abdication crisis and by his natural interest in events in Palestine and Europe. But towards the princes his leisureliness of approach was studied. He failed to press parliamentary counsel ahead with the preparation of an instrument of accession. The princes were 'shy birds . . . and might easily take fright'.[1] Haste would surely 'frighten them off'.[2] He was also apprehensive that any hustling of the princes would give the Conservative diehards a 'handle to make use of' against the federal scheme.[3] Linlithgow insisted that the princes would not accede unless they were allowed to retain the excise duties collected in their states. Zetland was reluctant to bribe them by conceding revenues or powers that the Act had proposed to transfer to the federal authorities. The offer of a financial concession to one prince would lead others to raise the price of accession. Any concession would offend the provincial governments of British India. Zetland acquainted the prime minister of his dispute with the viceroy and found him averse from a course that, because it involved legislation, might revitalize the diehards. Eventually, in the summer of 1938, Linlithgow came home on leave and convinced Zetland of the need for concessions over excise, customs and salt duties and the corporation tax. An unwilling Zetland at last obtained cabinet approval for an Amending Bill that would make the concessions possible.[4]

It was January 1939 before an offer of accession was sent to the princes. They had six months in which to reply. In June a large and representative gathering of princes at Bombay declared the offer inadequate. By the end of July the necessary number of acceptances had not been received. Linlithgow, Zetland and the cabinet agreed to extend the offer to the beginning of September. To spur the princes Linlithgow suggested that Zetland contrive to have a question asked in parliament that would enable the government to announce their policy on the establishment of a federation as soon as

[1] Zetland to Linlithgow, September 25, 1936, Z.C.

[2] Zetland to Linlithgow, June 28, 1936, Z.C.

[3] Zetland to Linlithgow, January 25, 1937, Z.C.

[4] For Zetland's denial of dilatoriness towards implementing the federal sections of the Act see '*Essayez*' (1956), pp. 241 ff. Zetland as autobiographer was more fatalistic than as secretary of state. His account of this question is characteristic of a tendency to emphasize the intractability of the political situation and play down the weaknesses in British diplomacy. See also below, p. 92, n. 2.

possible. But Zetland shunned this device. He remained fearful of pressing the princes lest the certain reaction of the diehards encourage them in their lassitude. Linlithgow continued to search for a line of compromise that would draw the recalcitrant rulers into the federation. Zetland was mildly responsive to a suggestion of Halifax's that federal subjects might, for a time, be administered by states' officials. But Linlithgow doubted the appeal of any merely *pro tem* accommodation. Zetland was ever mindful of the danger of baiting the hook to draw in the princes. Breaching the spirit of the Act would alienate the provinces. However, neither Linlithgow nor Zetland really expected that enough of the princes would accede within the extended term of the offer, and Zetland did accept that some further concession might then be required. He believed that a change of mind might also be effected in the princes if they could be made to realize the drift of public opinion in modern India. He had in preparation a white paper on the offer and the princes' replies. The folly of the princes in rejecting such favourable terms would, he hoped, bring widespread condemnation upon them and so make them more tractable. This was how matters stood when, on September 11th, Linlithgow announced to the central legislature that the outbreak of war gave Britain 'no choice but to hold in suspense the work in connection with preparations for federation'.[1]

Certainly, then, negotiations over the accession of the princes were prolonged by disputation over the surrender of revenues and powers to a federal authority, until the war brought them to a close. However, the states' accession was not simply a matter at issue between the government of India and the princes. It came to acquire a communal dimension. The activities of the Congress and the Muslim League were largely responsible for the failure of the princes to accede. The federal clauses of the Act provided for a central government in which the influence of the princes and the Muslims would outweigh that of the Congress. So would the autocrats' fears of democracy and the minority community's apprehension of Hindu domination be assuaged. So too would the Tory diehards be appeased. But the Congress set out to democratize the constitution by a *tour de force*. No sooner had they agreed to take office in the provinces than they opened a campaign against the princes. Their object was to ensure that the states' representatives at the centre should be elected by the states' peoples and not simply nominated by the rulers.

Britain could not forbear from clarifying her policy towards reforms in the states. The Congress attached importance to a statement by Lord Winterton, a member of the cabinet, that 'the Paramount Power would certainly not obstruct proposals for constitutional advance initiated by the Ruler of a State'.[2] That was in February 1938. Ten months later, the cabinet decided that Britain was bound by the spirit of her treaties to support her princely allies if their position were clearly threatened by agitation for reforms. At the same time, it was thought necessary to impress upon them the wisdom of introducing administrative reforms. Zetland and Linlithgow tried to steer a middle course by encouraging administrative improvement and the creation

[1] Marquess of Linlithgow, *Speeches and Statements, 1936–43* (1945), pp. 200–3.
[2] *Commons Parliamentary Debates*, vol. 332, col. 4, February 21, 1938.

of advisory bodies whilst retarding constitutional changes. They sought 'a holding position'.[1] The states should neither gallop under the Congress spur nor remain absolutely stationary. Perhaps on paper this seemed a nice compromise, but in practice it was no answer to the question of how to reconcile the new India and the old. In the late thirties no solution was in fact possible. The contradictory policies of the past had produced an intractable problem. Britain was, in Zetland's phrase, 'on the horns of a painful dilemma'.[2] As a democratic nation she could scarcely oppose the Congress programme for reform in the states. Yet the activities of the Congress were bound to drive the princes to reject the federal offer.

The prospect of a Hindu dominated centre was also bound to alarm the Muslims. The Muslim League could, and did, play on the reluctance of princes such as the Nizam to help impose a Hindu *raj* upon their co-religionists. Early in 1940, the Aga Khan, who had supported the federal scheme in 1935, admitted to Linlithgow that 'the sugar had all come off the pill the moment the States' representatives were to be elected by the States' peoples rather than nominated by the Rulers, for under such an arrangement the Muslims would not get from the States in the Central Legislature the support they required to balance the Congress votes'.[3] The Muslim League was offended by the Congress refusal to form coalitions in the provinces that the Congress could govern alone, and it was alarmed by the mass contact movement. In the tenor of Congress provincial rule the League found, exaggerated or imagined incidents sufficient to confirm the Muslims' aversion from a Hindu *raj*. The growing probability of a Congress dominated central legislature generated a corresponding increase in Muslim opposition to the proposed federation.

From 1937 until the suspension of negotiations with the princes, the states question became an ever larger part of that wider Indian problem which ultimately proved to be soluble only by partition: how could the Congress demand for a self-governing democracy be reconciled with the Muslim League's insistence upon safeguards for Muslim interests? For the perceptive observer the transmutation of the states question brought this problem into ever sharper focus. Zetland was such an observer, and it was unfortunate that the more prescient member of the governing partnership during this period was able to exercise so little influence upon policy. Towards the end of 1937 he began to perceive that 'the strongest opposition' to the federal scheme would come from the Muslims.[4] In his memoirs he claimed that during 1938 'my mind travelled back to my experiences in Bengal twenty years earlier, of the almost irresistible centripetal force of Islam as such; from this time onwards I could not resist a steadily growing conviction that the dominant factor in determining the future form of the Government of India would prove to be the All-India Muslim League'.[5] The assertion is well-supported by his correspondence.

[1] Zetland to Linlithgow, March 21, 1939, Z.C.
[2] Zetland to C. Heath, December 19, 1939, Z.C.
[3] In Linlithgow to Zetland, February 27, 1940, Z.C.
[4] Zetland to Linlithgow, December 6, 1937, Z.C.
[5] '*Essayez*', p. 247.

In December 1938 Zetland wrote to Linlithgow:

'. . . if one thing is certain it is that the Muslims are uniting in their determination not to be dominated by the Hindus in any form of Central Government which may come into being.'[1]

He remarked then and during 1939 that eminent Muslims were sketching plans for grouping provinces into communal blocs, which might federate under a weak central authority. The separatist logic of the situation created by the Act of 1935 was developed in schemes such as that of Sikandar Hyat Khan. By April–May 1939 Zetland was 'almost certain' that the Muslims would refuse to work the federal scheme of 1935.[2] He was considering what should be done next and sounded Linlithgow about the wisdom of conferring with representatives of the Congress, the League and the princes. The viceroy, an incorrigible optimist, chose to 'let the situation develop'.[3] In July he had 'little doubt' that the Muslims would accept the federation if it were 'imposed upon them'. He did 'not expect serious trouble' from that quarter. A private letter of October 16th contains an admission that he had failed to discern the gradual sharpening of the outlines of the Indian problem during the preceding two years:

'I had not, possibly, fully realized till now how greatly the gap between Hindu and Muslim has widened since April 1937, or the extent to which experiences . . . since then have undermined altogether belief in the possibility of common and united action on which the Act of 1935 was so essentially based.'[4]

What made Linlithgow belatedly aware of the true nature of the Indian problem was the crystallization of the demands of the Congress and the League soon after the outbreak of the war, and his subsequent interviews with the party leaders. Even then he was lamentably slow to take effective action, despite the promptings of Zetland. It seems possible that during the early stages of the war an outstanding diplomatist might have developed a formula to solve the Indian problem. It is true that as early as September 5, 1939 Jinnah expressed to Linlithgow his concern over the prospect of Hindu domination and advanced partition as an alternative objective to democracy in a united India. However, even if Jinnah was already sincerely opposed to Indian unity, the Muslim League was not committed to Pakistan until March 1940. Britain should have been planning for a free united India and negotiating safeguards that would accommodate the Muslims within it. Certain initiatives were indeed taken during the first year of the war and it is worth recounting in some detail the story of their failure. As that most dedicated of British ministers for India, Edwin Montagu, remarked at a psychological moment during the first world war, 'opportunities lost in India cannot be recovered except at great cost'.[5] In the absence of effective diplomacy during the first year of war, the gap between British policy and Congress

[1] Zetland to Linlithgow, December 13, 1938, Z.C.
[2] Zetland to Linlithgow, May 22, 1939, Z.C.
[3] Linlithgow to Zetland, July 7, 1939, Z.C. [4] Letter to Zetland, Z.C.
[5] Montagu to Asquith, December 22, 1915, in S. D. Waley, *Edwin Montagu* (1964), pp. 82–5.

demands became a gulf, the communal rift became a chasm, and party resolutions hardened into ultimata.

II

Within a fortnight of the outbreak of war, the working committees of the Congress and the League had framed resolutions on the crisis, and Linlithgow had decided that it would be desirable to associate representative Indians with the conduct of the war. On September 14th the Congress determined not to support a war for the perpetuation of imperialism and called for a declaration of the implications for India of Britain's claim to be fighting for democracy and freedom. What, asked the Congress, are Britain's 'war aims in regard to democracy and imperialism and the new order that is envisaged', and how are 'these aims going to apply to India and so be given effect to in the present'? [1] The Congress wanted an undertaking that Britain would concede to Indians 'the right of self-determination by framing their own Constitution through a Constituent Assembly without external interference'. In the short term, they wanted to participate in the conduct of the war through representation in the viceroy's executive. On September 17th/18th the League condemned the federal scheme of the 1935 Act as giving the majority community power to trample on the rights of the minorities, requested the revision of the entire problem of India's constitution *de novo*, required that Britain make no declaration nor adopt any constitution without its approval, and claimed to be the only organization that could speak for Muslim India. Linlithgow recommended to Zetland that he should consult the leaders of the Congress and the League and offer them membership of a consultative war committee. Britain should then issue a statement reiterating her intention to establish dominion status in India, and declaring that after the war she would be 'very willing to enter into consultation with representatives of the several communities . . . with a view to securing their aid and co-operation in the framing of such modifications [to the Act of 1935] as may seem desirable'.[2] After some hesitation, chiefly owing to the fear of any consultative committee's trenching on the proper authority of the viceroy, the war cabinet approved of Linlithgow's proposed approach.

It seems probable that, even after meeting Gandhi and Rajendra Prasad, the president of the Congress, Linlithgow was sanguine of his approach enlisting the support of the Congress. He was overconfident, perhaps because of his victory over the Congress in 1937. He may also have overestimated the influence that Gandhi, who had initially and emotionally pledged his personal and unconditional support for the war effort, exercised in the Congress of 1939. He led Zetland to conclude that the Congress would be satisfied if their statement of September 14th were 'taken at a good deal less than its face value'. On the other hand, the British Labour party tried to impress upon Zetland that the Congress were in earnest. Cripps, who was in touch with Nehru, told Zetland that the situation was 'grave' and argued for the direct

[1] Congress Working Committee Resolution, 14 September 1939, Gwyer and Appadorai, *Documents*, ii, 484–7.

[2] Linlithgow's statement of October 18, 1939, *ibid.* ii, 490–3.

association of Indian representatives with the central government.[1] Attlee pressed the need for 'imaginative insight' into the situation and saw slipping past the last chance of bringing India freely into the British Commonwealth.[2] Linlithgow eventually made his proposed declaration on October 18th. It failed to satisfy the Congress. Linlithgow seemed unrepentant and explained to Zetland:

'. . . I do not think that either you or I, or for that matter the Cabinet, can feel that there is anything which we have left undone which we ought to have done . . . The fact is that the price has been put up a good deal by the other side.'[3]

Yet Linlithgow's conscience was not clear. When his declaration provoked the Congress to reaffirm their demands of September 14th and to call for the resignation of their ministries in the provinces, he soon had Zetland obtain the cabinet's permission for a fresh approach. He now intended to enlarge his executive to accommodate representative Indians, and early in November he asked Gandhi, Prasad and Jinnah to discuss with him, and among themselves, the means of doing so. He threw upon the Congress and the League the onus of reaching agreement about the reconstruction of the provincial governments as a preliminary to their framing proposals for representatives of their parties to join the central executive. This approach was unacceptable to the Congress, for their demand that Britain concede India's right to devise her own constitution at the end of the war had still not been met.

Britain's ostensible main reason for rejecting the Congress demand was that it ran counter to the League's insistence that no declaration be made or constitution imposed without its approval. Linlithgow had found Jinnah adamant that the League be recognized as the sole representative of the Muslims, and antagonistic to the Congress scheme for a constituent assembly. However, the Congress was deeply suspicious of Britain's motives. Gandhi and Prasad contended that all communities would be represented, on a basis to be agreed, in the proposed constituent assembly. The Congress, they argued, appreciated that to be satisfactory any constitution had to provide safeguards sufficient to commend themselves to the minorities. In consequence of Linlithgow's determination not to be 'bounced' by Congress into making arrangements that would be disliked by the Muslims or the princes, British policy approached an impasse.[4] But it was not long before the viceroy was jolted into activity.

About the middle of November, Zetland began to ponder ways and means of launching a new initiative. The Liberal, Raghavendra Rao, suggested to him that Britain send a parliamentary mission to India to investigate the nature of the proposed constituent assembly and of the safeguards that the Congress were prepared to concede. Halifax and Lord Snell, the Labour leader in the house of lords, also suggested sending out a non-government mission at this time. Zetland was attracted by the idea of accepting the

[1] Zetland to Linlithgow, October 2, 1939, Z.C.
[2] Zetland to Linlithgow, October 11, 1939, Z.C.
[3] Linlithgow to Zetland, October 22, 1939, Z.C.
[4] Linlithgow to Zetland, November 27, 1939, Z.C.

Congress proposal for a constituent assembly. Was it, he asked Linlithgow, a 'practicable proposition' to agree to ratify any constitution that such an assembly produced, provided that the minorities and the princes accepted it?[1] Whilst he procrastinated, Cripps acted. On November 28th Cripps acquainted Zetland of the purpose of a visit that he was about to make to India. He intended to explore the possibility of creating a constituent assembly. If the scheme seemed feasible then he believed that Britain should allow such a body to frame a constitution, and that she should deal with her outstanding obligations and interests in India by way of a treaty with a term of some fifteen years. Zetland was much taken with Cripps's proposals and sounded the prime minister on them in general terms at the beginning of December. He then elaborated upon them in a letter to Linlithgow and enclosed a draft of a restatement of policy. Britain, he argued, should call upon the major parties in India to agree the composition of an all-Indian body to determine a constitution for a self-governing India. She should announce her willingness to legislate along the lines suggested by the body at the end of the war. He thought that Chamberlain seemed 'quite ready to consider favourably what not so long ago would have been regarded as a revolutionary proposal', and he went on to speculate about attitudes in the cabinet.[2] Halifax, and probably Hoare, would be 'favourably disposed', but Simon might be 'rather sticky'. Churchill would 'clearly have to be approached with very great caution'.

Linlithgow's reaction to Zetland's proposal was decidedly hostile. Linlithgow was not convinced that the Indian situation warranted any 'radical' move.[3] He felt that the Congress were overbidding their hand. They had been unresponsive to his earlier overtures and unprepared to adjust their differences with the Muslims. Linlithgow believed that he held the trump card. For, as long as the Congress failed to secure the amity of the Muslims it remained impossible to meet their demand for self-government. The existing discords between the communities could strengthen Britain's control in India 'for many years'.[4] If, on the other hand, Britain conceded the Congress demand for a constituent assembly, then the Congress would be confirmed in their recalcitrance and would drive an impossibly hard bargain over the minorities question and over such matters as Britain's commercial interests in a self-governing India. Linlithgow counselled allowing the Congress time to sober, believing that they would then welcome a government move to settle the communal difficulty in the provinces.

Zetland's initiative did, however, elicit an alternative plan from the viceroy. He suggested that, in due course, he should extract from Jinnah minimum terms for the accommodation of the Muslims, and then appeal to Gandhi to agree to them. Thereupon, he would call together a dozen or so Indian leaders to ratify proposals for safeguarding the minorities in the provinces, and to accept a temporary expansion of the viceroy's executive. He would, finally, announce Britain's intention to introduce a scheme of federation as

[1] Zetland to Linlithgow, November 22, 1939, Z.C.
[2] Zetland to Linlithgow, December 6, 1939, Z.C.
[3] Linlithgow to Zetland, December 21, 1939, Z.C.
[4] Linlithgow to Zetland, December 18, 1939 (telegram), Z.C.

soon as possible, 'with a view to proceeding with the minimum delay . . . into the Dominion Status stage, and if possible before the conclusion of the war'.[1]

On January 10, 1940, Linlithgow delivered at the Orient Club, Bombay, a speech so conciliatory in tone that Gandhi at once seized upon it as presenting a better prospect of agreement between the Congress and the government than the offers of October 18th and early November. Gandhi sought an interview with the viceroy. At the beginning of February, the cabinet approved Linlithgow's proposal to meet Gandhi and to offer: a reassertion of Britain's intention to introduce dominion status as soon as possible; the expansion of the viceroy's executive to include Hindu and Muslim politicians; the inauguration of the federation as soon as the states agreed to it; the revision of the federal constitution in consultation with Indians. On January 13th Linlithgow had met Jinnah and obtained his conditions for an agreement with the Congress. Apart from demanding that *Bande Mataram* be abandoned as the national anthem, that the Congress flag should not be flown from public buildings and that the Congress should stop trying to 'wreck' the League, Jinnah required the formation of coalition ministries in the Congress provinces and a provision that no measure should be passed by the provincial legislatures if two-thirds of the Muslim members opposed it. Jinnah would not accept a democratic central government based on a popular vote, or the collective responsibility of ministers to a legislature. Surprisingly, Linlithgow felt that if Gandhi were 'prepared to be reasonable then there is . . . some chance of a settlement'.[2] Not surprisingly, his meeting with Gandhi lasted only two fruitless hours. Gandhi would not accept Jinnah's suggested provincial coalitions and he reiterated the Congress demand for a constituent assembly.

Linlithgow concluded that the Congress reckoned that 'if they can but hold out for a little longer . . . we shall be prepared to offer them a better bargain'.[3] 'As for the future', he advised Zetland, 'there is nothing for it now but to lie back for the present.' He continued to proffer this advice until the end of June. His letters during this period reiterate that Britain should 'refrain from action', 'wait upon events', 'avoid running after the Congress', 'lie back and not move'.[4] She had, he considered, offered all that she should. At the end of February, he observed that the 'opposition to the Congress' among the minorities and the princes was 'hardening rapidly'.[5] He anticipated 'a situation in which the Muslims are prepared to accept Dominion Status or Self-Government only on terms which cannot be accepted by Congress'. He wrote:

'. . . the more I watch the reaction of people here to developments since the breakdown of my conversations with Gandhi, the longer, I judge, is likely to be the process of advance towards self-government in India.'

The chances of agreement among Indians seemed 'negligible'. As agreement was a prerequisite of constitutional advance there seemed no possibility of

[1] Linlithgow to Zetland, December 21, 1939, Z.C.
[2] Linlithgow to Zetland, February 3, 1940, Z.C.
[3] Linlithgow to Zetland, February 6, 1940, Z.C.
[4] Linlithgow to Zetland, February 13, 21, 27, March 8, (telegram), 1940, Z.C.
[5] Linlithgow to Zetland, February 27, 1940, Z.C.

Britain's withdrawing from India in the 'foreseeable future'. Linlithgow saw clearly enough the steady deterioration of Congress League relations. But he refused to take a step that would alienate the Muslims, who had not resigned from the provincial governments, and he regarded a Congress retreat as the essential preliminary to a constitutional advance.

Zetland had never abandoned the line of approach that he had begun to pursue in November 1939. Just before Linlithgow's February meeting with Gandhi, he told the cabinet of his conviction that there was no chance of Linlithgow's proposed plan proving the basis of fruitful discussion. Gandhi, he explained, would simply see it as a further British rejection of the Congress demand. The federal scheme would prove impossible to revive because the Muslims would insist upon amendments that the Congress would find unacceptable. If the talks with Gandhi were not to break down almost as soon as they began, the viceroy must be prepared to offer a closer accommodation to the Congress point of view. Zetland argued that Britain should be prepared to accept a constitution framed by Indians themselves, provided that the states and the major parties in India agreed to the composition of the constitution-making body. He believed that until discussion amongst Indians of their communal problem and the possible solutions for it was undertaken in the clear knowledge that they and they alone were responsible for finding and maintaining a solution communal agreement would never be forthcoming. Zetland had wanted the cabinet to consider his views, and, if it accepted them, to advise Linlithgow of the fact before he met Gandhi. He hoped to induce Linlithgow to convene a small conference of Congress and League leaders, as a first step towards the framing of a constitution by the Indians themselves. However, the cabinet was divided on the matter and there was some criticism of Zetland's attempting to urge Linlithgow to go further than he considered wise. Linlithgow was left to his own devices. After his unsuccessful approach to Gandhi, Zetland returned to the charge, pressing him to bring the party leaders together.

Whilst Linlithgow 'lay back', Zetland laboured to bring the cabinet to a realization of the need for action to prevent the Indian situation from reaching a stage of utter intractability. On March 11th he told the cabinet of his anxiety to have some constructive plan of action. He presented a draft announcement which he hoped that the cabinet would allow him to send to the viceroy with the comment that His Majesty's Government was disposed to give favourable consideration to it. The draft envisaged the creation of an all-Indian body to prepare a constitution for India as a separate member of the Commonwealth. The body would include representatives of the states and the minorities who were acceptable to the states and the minorities. After the war it would appoint delegates to meet representatives of the United Kingdom for the purpose of agreeing the constitution, which it and parliament would then ratify. The draft announcement stated that the British representatives would be concerned only with ensuring that the constitution would be stable and enduring. Those matters in which Britain had an abiding interest – defence, the sterling debt, commerce, the services and the states that elected not to join the dominion of India – should be settled either in the constitution or by a treaty. On this occasion, the cabinet postponed taking a decision until it received Linlithgow's appreciation of the political situation after the meeting of the Congress at Ramgarh. When, on March 20th, the Congress demanded 'complete independence' (the catchcry that had swept India into the non-co-operation movement in 1930), and, four days later at Lahore, the League adopted the Pakistan resolution, Zetland was forced to admit that further time for reflection was required. Accordingly, he let his initiative lapse for the moment. Chamberlain's government fell before he could revive it, and L. S. Amery replaced him at the India Office.

On July 1st Amery wrote to Zetland that he had been 'working in substance along the lines which you suggested to the War Cabinet some months ago and which were not acceptable to that body at that time'.[1] He conveyed the news that Linlithgow had now 'come round very markedly to our point of view'. The gravity of the war situation in Europe had led Linlithgow to appeal for unity in India. At the end of June he sounded Jinnah and Gandhi on the probable reactions of the League and the Congress to a further statement clarifying Britain's intentions in India and to an offer to participate in the viceroy's executive. He found Jinnah anxious to join the government and 'indifferent' as to any statement, 'so long as it did not compromise him over Pakistan'.[2] Gandhi remained unprepared to modify the Congress demand for 'complete independence'.

Linlithgow suggested that Amery seek the cabinet's approval for a declaration to the following effect: (1) that Britain's aim in India was dominion status; (2) that the 1935 Act would be opened to discussion at the end of the war; (3) that the fullest consideration would be given to the views of all interests; (4) that Britain's continuing interests in India would be dealt with apart from the main constitutional scheme; (5) that, subject to Britain's continuing interests being suitably protected, 'His Majesty's Government would be perfectly content to abide by [the] conclusions of any representative body of Indians on which [the] various political parties could agree'; (6) that His Majesty's Government 'would spare no effort to bring about Dominion Status within a year after the conclusion of the war, and to set up whatever machinery those concerned agreed on as appropriate to work out [a] new constitution immediately on [the] conclusion of the war'. Linlithgow telegraphed that he recognized these ideas to be 'somewhat revolutionary' but that he felt it desirable to implement them with all possible speed.[3]

Amery placed Linlithgow's recommendations before the cabinet early in July and advocated their adoption. Britain had announced previously that her aim was to establish dominion status. However, as long as she indicated neither date nor method, she remained open to the charge that she was insincere and was merely playing for time; until she did so her exhortations to Indians to agree amongst themselves would meet with no response and only add to the suspicion that she was deliberately procrastinating. Amery speculated that Gandhi must at once have realized the danger to the Congress, both in the eyes of the public and from the viewpoint of Congress unity, of refusing an offer so reasonable as that which Linlithgow had adumbrated.

[1] Letter in Z.C.

[2] Linlithgow to Amery, June 28, 1940 (telegram), Z.C.

[3] Linlithgow to Amery, July 1, 1940 (telegram), Z.C.

He anticipated that the proposed declaration would take the sting out of the Congress opposition, and he even believed that a split might appear in the Congress ranks. Amery's draft statement followed the lines of Linlithgow's proposal: at the earliest practicable moment after the war India should become an equal partner in the Commonwealth; immediately after the war the Indian constitution should be examined anew by whatever constituent body Indians might agree upon; given agreement among Indians themselves, Britain would accept any constitution adopted by the constituent body; Britain's continuing obligations and interests would be arranged through a treaty; Indians would forthwith be invited to join the viceroy's executive and an advisory war council.

Unfortunately, Amery had 'a lot of trouble' with his draft, 'mainly owing to the Prime Minister's strong dislike of any move in connection with India'.[1] In Churchill's hands Amery's 'clear-cut draft' became 'a much more long-winded and imprecise document', and he told Zetland that 'for the style of it' he wished, 'in private at any rate, to disclaim any responsibility'.

Amery's draft finally appeared as Linlithgow's offer of August 8th. The statement surveyed, by way of self-justification, the various unsuccessful attempts of the viceroy, since the outbreak of war, to reach agreement with the major Indian parties. It offered places in the executive council and in a war advisory council to representative Indians. It stressed that in any revision of the 1935 Act full weight would be given to the minorities, and that 'the fullest practical expression' would be given to the wish of Indians to frame any new constitutional scheme.[2] 'With the least possible delay' after the war, Britain would agree to the setting up of a body of representative Indians to devise the framework of the new constitution, and would 'lend every aid . . . to hasten decisions on all relevant matters'. Clearly, the statement did not go as far as Zetland, Linlithgow and Amery had wished towards placing on a constituent assembly set up by Indians themselves the onus of making a constitution acceptable to Indians at large. Britain's responsibilities in India were emphasized and the time within which they were to be discharged was expressed evasively. The offer was presented not as a fresh approach to the Indian problem but as a continuation of past efforts to secure India's co-operation. As neither the date nor the method of introducing dominion status was specified, Britain remained exposed to the charges of insincerity and procrastination. The Congress observed that the British government had 'left no doubt that they had no intention to recognize India's independence, and would, if they could, continue to hold this country indefinitely in bondage for British exploitation'.[3] The August offer, in the words of Tej Bahadur Sapru

'far from easing the tension in India . . . has given rise to grave misgivings and has caused a great deal of resentment . . . Hedged in by so many conditions, [it] is so incomplete in the enunciation of the aim [of British rule] and so non-committal in regard to its being implemented within any reasonable

[1] Amery to Zetland, August 3, 1940, Z.C.

[2] *Linlithgow's speeches*, pp. 250–2.

[3] Resolution of All-India Congress Committee, September 15–16, 1940, Gwyer and Appadorai, *Documents*, ii, 505–6.

distance of time that it can afford no satisfaction whatever to the people of this country.'[1]

The offer was rejected by all parties. It was ironical that when Linlithgow, who had himself frustrated Zetland's liberal attempts to solve the Indian problem, at last took an enlightened initiative it should have been practically defeated from home.[2]

III

By July 1, 1940 Linlithgow was prepared to offer what for six months after the outbreak of war the Congress had asked as the price of co-operation. But in March the Congress had raised its price, and Linlithgow had forfeited his opportunity. It is difficult to justify his slowness to act. He argued that conceding the Congress demand for a constituent assembly to frame India's post-war constitution would alienate the Muslims and the princes. That objection was certainly no less real in July, yet he then set it aside. He had misjudged the attitude of the Congress in October, and when his offer of a consultative council was rejected he had hastened to suggest the expansion of his executive to include representative Indians. That overture and his approach to Gandhi in February were also rebuffed. His hopes of achieving a compromise were shown to have been based upon a miscalculation of the mood of the Congress. It is true that he sincerely doubted the practicability of the Congress scheme for a constituent assembly. If his doubts were well-founded there was surely advantage in confronting Congress with the shortcomings of their scheme. There was a strain of obstinate pride, a concern for viceregal prestige, in his long refusal to admit the case for a constituent assembly, which was destined to be the machinery to produce a constitution for an independent India. A more skilful diplomatist would have found a means of maintaining imperial prestige that did not inhibit his freedom of manoeuvre. Linlithgow defended his aversion from 'running after the Congress' by pleading that official implacability would make the Congress more tractable. The argument reads as a rationalization of an attitude, rather than as a dispassionate appraisal of political probabilities. It took the end of the 'phoney war' to humble him. Only then would he accept the constructive approach that the Congress, the Labour party and Zetland had so long advocated. It must be said, too, that he was certainly not eager to hasten the end of the *raj*.

Whilst he was slow to make an adequate response to the Congress demand, Linlithgow did little to allay Muslim apprehensions. He had not grasped until October 1939 the extent of the Muslims' discontent in the Congress-ruled provinces and their consequent fears of a Hindu *raj*. Even then, he failed to investigate the Muslims' alleged grievances, the logical first step towards a serious consideration of the safeguards for which provision would need to be made. The League contended that the governors had refrained from

[1] Statement of November 1–2, 1941, *ibid.* ii, 518–19.

[2] In '*Essayez*' Zetland is less critical of Linlithgow's policy during the early months of the war than one would have expected from the disagreements evidenced by their correspondence (pp. 262–85).

using their reserve powers for fear of offending the Congress. The charge should not have been left unanswered. From late in 1939, Linlithgow seems to have thought that his refusal to concede the demands of the Congress was sufficient to assuage Muslim fears. He looked to the Congress to compose their differences with the League, without having any clear understanding of how that could be done. It is difficult to avoid the conclusion that Linlithgow was more interested in pursuing a policy to retain the support of the League than in solving the problem of devising safeguards to accommodate the Muslims within a united India. In the absence of any British initiative on this problem, the Muslim imagination leapt forward to a future, evisaged by the Congress, when the *raj* would be no more. The communal dialectic that had become the dynamic force of Indian politics between 1937 and 1939 meant that each major Congress resolution provoked a Muslim reply.

The Ramgarh demand for 'complete independence', the result of Britain's failure to treat with the Congress, was quickly followed by the Lahore resolution. Linlithgow refused to take the claim for Pakistan seriously:

'I do not attach too much importance to Jinnah's demands for the carving out of India into an indefinite number of religious areas. . . . And I would judge myself that his attitude at the moment is that, as the Congress are putting forward a preposterous claim which they know is incapable of acceptance, he equally will put forward just as extreme a claim.' [1]

It was, he judged, 'merely put forward . . . for bargaining purposes'.[2] He may have been right. But the important point is that once the Congress and the League had taken up their extreme positions of March 1940 they could not recede without loss of face. Furthermore, the longer these positions were held the greater the number of their firm adherents.

The war acted as a catalyst in Indian politics. The Congress were encouraged by Britain's difficulties to set their claims high, and in the absence of an effective British response to take up an extreme position. The League raised its bids correspondingly. Perhaps in the early months of a war a great viceroy could have brought the parties into effective communication as the condition of a large constitutional advance. Perhaps, on the other hand, the Indian problem was an inextricable muddle and not a soluble riddle. The point is difficult to decide and must be left to students of the freedom movements. But certainly Linlithgow failed to test the situation with imaginative statecraft. He was unable to refute the logic of events that Britain's past policies had set in train, incapable of mastering the communal and separist forces that were shaping India's destiny. Though not an ineffective man in ordinary circumstances, he was too wedded to the ways of the imperial past to fashion a nation of the future. The situation ran away from him. In February 1940 he recognized that 'things [had] . . . advanced at a far more rapid pace than anyone had imagined' six months previously.[3] 'War', he reflected sadly, 'has imposed upon Indians and upon our plans . . . a stern and searching test, and . . . neither has emerged . . . as we would have wished that they might.'

[1] Linlithgow to Zetland, March 25, 1940, Z.C.
[2] Linlithgow to Amery, June 30, 1940 (telegram), Z.C.
[3] Linlithgow to Zetland, February 27, 1940, Z.C.

In June he realized that the Pakistan demand was sinking into the minds of 'rank and file Moslems'.[1] There is no doubt that he failed to arrest a serious deterioration in the situation.[2] Within two years Britain, by accepting in principle the right of provinces to secede, granted the need for a Muslim escape route from a united India. Perhaps the Ramgarh and Lahore resolutions marked the beginning of the end of Indian unity. Or perhaps the end should be dated from Churchill's frustration of Linlithgow's belated initiative. Though consonant with poetic justice, it would be fanciful to cast the arch-diehard as an unwitting architect of Pakistan. But by his intervention in July 1940 the bricklayer of Chartwell did help to build the foundations for the wall of partition.

[1] Linlithgow to Amery, June 30, 1940 (telegram), Z.C.

[2] K. Veerathappa, in an article based on the Zetland Collection ('Britain and the Indian Problem (September 1939–May 1940)', *International Studies*, vii (1966), 537–67), sees Linlithgow as more Machiavellian than inept. He is somewhat less than just to Linlithgow and makes too little of the difficulties in the situation.

BRITISH POLICY TOWARDS THE INDIAN STATES, 1940–7

by E. W. R. LUMBY*

The federal scheme in the Act of 1935 embodied a clear intention that in the future constitutional structure the princely states should form an element of conservatism, stability and loyalty to the British connection. Although they contained only about a quarter of the population of the sub-continent, they were allotted over a third of the seats in the federal legislature and these would most probably be filled by princely nominees rather than by popularly elected representatives. But the suspension of the negotiations with the princes on September 11, 1939 marks the beginning of a decline in the importance of the states in British thinking on the future of India. At first the federal scheme held the field simply because it had not been superseded; and the assumption could still be made that the British government might again attempt to rally the princes as a counterweight to Congress. Even in 1947 a public servant of the distinction of Sir Akbar Hydari might think it possible still to invoke Part II of the Act of 1935.[1] In reality it had been dead since 1942, when the Cripps offer not only foreshadowed the revision of the treaties but abandoned weightage for the states. In the proposed constitution-making body the states representatives were to bear the same proportion to their population as the British Indian representatives to theirs. In Britain people were growing accustomed to the idea that India would soon be fully independent, and that that it would be wrong or futile to attempt to perpetuate British power there; from being a buttress of that power the princes became a tiresome incident in its demission. They and their ministers might express their views on the constitutional future of the country; but the crucial negotiations soon came to be conducted by three parties only, the British, the Congress and the Muslim League. In the constitutional marathon even the Sikhs, numbering not much over 5½ million, stayed the course longer than the princes, who could claim, rightly or wrongly, to speak for their 93 million subjects. The object of British policy towards the states was now to prepare them to take their place in the new India by enabling them to negotiate with the successor authorities from as strong a position as possible. In this way the Crown would be able to renounce its association with the princes as gracefully as the circumstances permitted, and would save its face from the charge of abandoning its protegés who had so recently supported it in war.

The problem of disposing of the states was without precedent. 'It is generally agreed', the Butler committee had observed, 'that the States are *sui generis*, that there is no parallel to their position in history, that they are governed by a body of convention and usage not quite like anything in the world'.[2]

* Assistant Editor India Office Records project on the transfer of power; author of *The Transfer of Power in India 1945–1947* (1954).

[1] A. Campbell-Johnson, *Mission with Mountbatten* (1951), p. 54.

[2] *Report of the Indian States Committee*, 1928–29 (Cmd. 3302) para. 43.

There was some apparent resemblance between the position of the Indian princes and that of the princes of the Holy Roman Empire at the beginning of the nineteenth century. At the suggestion of the Indian political department, a memorandum was prepared in the India Office on the unification of the German states. But the mercenary intrigues of Talleryand and the *real politik* of Bismarck provided no useful guidance for dealing with the Indian princes in the conditions of the mid-twentieth century. Lord Mountbatten, we are told, made use of the example of Germany, with special reference to his own family, when persuading the princes to sign instruments of accession.[1] It is not clear how he was able to make this argument convincing.

Lord Linlithgow had been 'against doing anything that would alarm or dishearten' the princes, whom he considered 'the only solid and dependable elements so far as the British relationship with India was concerned'.[2] As Dr Moore has show, this attitude was very much in evidence during his long dialogue with Lord Zetland over the federal negotiations. It was also apparent in his disagreement with Amery's proposal for dealing with the smaller states, which will be described below. Before the end of his viceroyalty, however, events were to produce a change of tone. Addressing the chamber of princes on March 16, 1942, a few days before the arrival of Sir Stafford Cripps, he spoke for the first time of the 'survival' of the states 'as valued and respected elements in the new Indian polity which has yet to be evolved'.[3] From his departure to the final transfer of power there seems to have been little difference of view, so far as the states are concerned, between the viceroy and the secretary of state; nor did the coming of the Labour government bring any marked change of approach. In the last stage Lord Mountbatten's technique for inducing the princes to sign instruments of accession may have been too drastic for some people in London, and was certainly not to the taste of his political adviser; but he had been given maximum discretion in carrying out the relaxation of paramountcy, and so had his own way.

The relative absence of change and internal controversy in British policy during the period under review makes it possible to abandon chronological treatment and instead to deal with the three main aspects of that policy: (i) the encouragement of reform; (ii) how far a uniform policy should be adopted towards all states, large and small; and (iii) the lapse of paramountcy.

I

Because the Crown's relations were with the rulers of the states and not with their subjects, and because it did not normally intervene in their internal affairs, its promotion of reform was necessarily limited to advice and encouragement. For years the viceroy and the political department had been preaching the desirability of such administrative reforms as a fixed privy purse, security of tenure in the public services and an independent judiciary. However, many small states had insufficient resources to meet the costs of a

[1] Campbell-Johnson, *op. cit.* p. 264. See H. V. Hodson, 'The Role of Lord Mountbatten', below, p. 125.

[2] V. P. Menon, *The Story of the Integration of the Indian States* (1956), p. 54.

[3] Marquess of Linlithgow, *Speeches and Statements 1936–43* (1945), p. 320.

modern administration. It therefore became British policy to promote both the absorption of small states in larger neighbouring states and the combination of smaller states for administrative purposes. In his speeches to the chamber of princes Linlithgow urged the creation of joint services and the necessity of reform. Addressing the chamber for the last time in October 1943 he warned them that the Crown's obligations to protect carried with them equally binding responsibilities to ensure that what was protected continued to be worthy of protection.[1] Wavell made it clear that the internal autonomy of the smaller states could no longer be regarded as inviolable when, in his speech to the chamber on January 17, 1946 he advised that states which could not provide their subjects with modern administrations should either join larger units or combine with other small states to form political entities of sufficient size. Similar advice was given by the cabinet mission in the memorandum on states treaties and paramountcy which they presented to the chancellor of the chamber on the following May 12th.[2] In reply the standing committee of the chamber explicitly endorsed the suggestion that small states should form or join administrative units large enough to be fitted into the constitutional structure.[3] However, the inhibitions which prevented the Crown from compelling the princes to act, the princes' insistence on their sovereignty, their personal and dynastic rivalries, all combined to prevent effective amalgamation. Although in the last few months before independence there was a rush to form unions of states in various parts of India, it was now too late.

The only area where the Crown had gone further than moral suasion in promoting mergers and administrative reform was one in which the rulers did not in any case exercise full powers. In Kathiawar and Gujarat there were hundreds of small units which came within the category of Indian states although they were usually referred to as 'semi-jurisdictional' or 'non-jurisdictional' estates or talukas because of the powers which the political officers were able to exercise in them. In 1943 the Crown attempted to put into effect a scheme for transferring these powers to Baroda and other larger states, to whom the small units were to be 'attached' and who were expected to raise the standard of their administrative and social services. Even this project provided for 'the continued integrity of the "attached" units and of the existing powers and privileges of their talukdars and shareholders in so far as may be compatible with modern requirements'.[4] Nevertheless the estate holders stubbornly resisted attachment, which never became effective.

The question of promoting constitutional and democratic government in the states was more difficult. The Butler committee had more than hinted at the Crown's dilemma when it said that if 'attempts to eliminate' a prince were due 'to a widespread popular demand for change, the Paramount Power would be bound to maintain the rights, privileges and dignity of the Prince; but it would also be bound to suggest such measures as would satisfy this demand without eliminating the Prince'.[5] What the committee did not say, however, was that if these measures went so far as to deprive the prince of

[1] Marquess of Linlithgow, *Speeches and Statements 1936–43* (1945), p. 387.
[2] Cmd. 6385, pp. 11–12. [3] Cmd. 6862, p. 7.
[4] Political Department Communiqué of April 16, 1943 (reproduced as Appendix V to R. Coupland, *The Future of India* (1943)). [5] *Report of Indian States Committee*, para. 50.

some part of his sovereign powers, he might be unable to fulfil his obligations to the Crown and the whole basis of the treaty relationship would be undermined. Such considerations prompted Linlithgow to draw back in 1938 when, faced with the agitation for the extension of responsible government from the provinces to the states, he would have liked to urge the rulers to introduce constitutional government and representative institutions. In the event he was obliged to echo the assurances given by the secretary of state in parliament that while the paramount power would not obstruct proposals for constitutional advance initiated by the rulers, it had no intention of bringing any form of pressure to bear upon them to initiate constitutional changes. It was for the ruler himself to decide what form of constitution was best suited to the needs of his people and his state.[1] British authorities subsequently took a moderate step towards pressing for democratic reform. Wavell spoke to the chamber of 'effective association of the people with the administration'; and the cabinet mission's memorandum recommended that 'the various governments which have not already done so' should 'take active steps to place themselves in close and constant touch with public opinion in their State by means of representative institutions'. Such admonitions fell considerably short of advocating the responsible government which Congress was demanding so insistently.

On the other hand, British policy never went to the other extreme of countenancing or supporting the idea of a union of states entering into independence simultaneously with, but separately from, the British Indian provinces. Once the Cripps offer had opened the possibility that Britain might hand over power to more than one successor, it became conceivable that the princes might follow the example of the Muslims. In his letter to Cripps of April 10, 1942, the Jam Saheb of Nawanagar, chancellor of the chamber, asked for an assurance 'that in the event of a number of States not finding it feasible to adhere, the non-adhering States or group of States so desiring should have the right to form a union of their own, with full sovereign status in accordance with a suitable and agreed procedure devised for the purpose'.[2] Amery seems to have been more inclined to consider this idea than was Linlithgow.[3] When it was put to the cabinet mission by the nawab of Bhopal, the Jam Saheb's successor as chancellor, Lord Pethick-Lawrence surprisingly said it seemed to him an interesting and apparently feasible suggestion and he did not want to rule it out. Cripps however thought there might be geographical difficulties.[4] Perhaps Pethick-Lawrence was thinking of Coupland's discussion of the idea, in which he argued that a union consisting of several blocks of state territory might be a practical proposition, though it would be undesirable, especially if it relied upon the continued protection of the paramount power.[5] The announcement in the mission's memorandum that with the independence of British India paramountcy would lapse, and that British troops would not be retained in India to uphold it, deprived the project of a states union of much of its attraction for the princes. However, in the spring

[1] Linlithgow, *op. cit.* pp. 155 and 179.
[2] Cmd. 6350, p. 16.
[3] Menon, *op. cit.* p. 54.
[4] *Ibid.* p. 64.
[5] Coupland, *The Future of India,* chap. xii.

of 1947 Bhopal was still trying to muster a number of central India states into a union; and in May the secretariat of the chamber found it necessary to issue a statement denying press reports that a separate constituent assembly or sovereign Rajasthan was in contemplation.

II

The pledges and promises with which the Crown had been so lavish had been made to the states without distinction between great and small, full-powered, semi-jurisdictional and non-jurisdictional. 'Uniformity of terminology', the Montagu-Chelmsford report had remarked, 'tends to obscure distinctions of status; and practice appropriate in the case of the lesser Chiefs may be inadvertently applied to the greater ones also.'[1] It seems to have been this danger which led the greater princes to identify their interests with the smaller, so that any proposal which, like the attachment scheme, threatened the position of even the pettiest chieftain could be regarded as an affront to the whole princely order. British authority therefore tended to adopt a uniform policy towards all states, large and small, in so far as it was practicable to do so. When actual constitutional arrangements had to be made, it was clearly impracticable. The federal offer had not been sent to the smaller states, with an aggregate population of some three million, referred to in paragraph 12 of the first schedule of the 1935 Act. Similarly, the instruments of accession offered to the rulers in August 1947 were of three types: one for the 140 rulers of the full-powered states, one for the talukdars and estate holders of Kathiawar and Gujarat, numbering over 300, to whom the attachment scheme had applied, and one for an intermediate group of over seventy who exercised wide but not quite full powers.

Between these two occasions on which it became necessary to exercise a realistic discrimination, the problem of the small states was recognized, but not tackled with any notable resolution or success. Amery proposed to Linlithgow that where smaller states could not be merged in bigger states (a process to which there were obvious limitations), the separate jurisdiction of individual rulers should be replaced by the single administration of the viceroy. He suggested that the Orissa states should be selected for this experiment in the first instance. In his view it was unnecessary to consider what would be the ultimate political status of any such newly formed units; conceivably they might continue for some time to be administered by the viceroy, and not improbably their ultimate destiny would be merger with British India.

However Linlithgow felt disinclined, in war conditions and at a time when the larger constitutional questions were postponed by common consent until after the war, to embark upon far-reaching changes in the relations of the Crown with the rulers of the small states involving large-scale reactions throughout the entire princely order and in British India. He preferred to continue to carry out the policy of absorption or combination already described.[2] The most positive result of this policy was the ineffective attachment scheme.

[1] *Report on Indian Constitutional Reforms* 1918 (Cd. 9109), para. 302.

[2] The correspondence is summarized in Menon, *op. cit.* pp. 55–6.

Evidently, then, the British authorities were still apprehensive that any interference with the sovereignty of the most insignificant rulers would lead to protests by more considerable members of the princely orders. Henceforth, apart from the brief recommendation of administrative mergers in the cabinet mission's memorandum of May 12th, to which reference is made above, all declarations of British policy treated the states as a single whole.

III

British policy had long recognized that lapse of time and change of circumstances might affect the implementation by the Crown of its treaty obligations to the princes. The Montagu-Chelmsford report had found 'that the position hitherto taken up by Government has been that the conditions under which some of the treaties were executed have undergone material changes, and the literal fulfilment of particular obligations which they impose has become impracticable. Practice has been based on the theory that treaties must be read as a whole, and that they must be interpreted in the light of the relations established between the parties not only at the time when a particular treaty was made, but subsequently.' This remark was made in the context of the princes' fears of further encroachment by the paramount power in their internal affairs; but it could also be read in the contrary sense, that a time might come when the Crown would be unable to fulfil any of its obligations to the states and would have to repudiate them. Far from drawing this conclusion, the report proceeded to recommend in the next paragraph 'that the Princes should be assured in the fullest and freest manner that no constitutional changes which may take place will impair the rights, dignities and privileges secured to them by treaties, *sanads*, and engagements or by established practice.'[1]

The discussion of proposals for self-government in British India, however, forced a realization that it might become impracticable to maintain this uncompromising stand. Ten years later the Butler report hinted at the possibility of revolution by consent when it recorded a strong opinion that the princes 'should not be transferred without their own agreement to a relationship with a new government in British India responsible to an Indian legislature'.[2] The federal scheme was an attempt to implement this principle.

By 1945, with the federal scheme a thing of the past, the assurance which could be given to the princes had to be further modified. The standing committee of the chamber had resigned in a body as a protest against the 'gradual deterioration of the position of the States and the disregard of their legitimate interests'. Wavell was able to get the resignation withdrawn by giving an assurance, on June 25th, that there would be no future transference of the states' relationship with the Crown to any other authority without their consent, provided the rulers on their part gave the assurance that their consent to any changes which emerged as a result of negotiations would not be unreasonably withheld.[3] Wavell repeated this undertaking in his speech to the

[1] *Report on Indian Constitutional Reforms* 1918, paras. 304–5.

[2] *Report of Indian States Committee*, para. 58.

[3] Menon, *op. cit.* pp. 57–8.

chamber on January 17, 1946; and so did the cabinet mission in the opening words of their memorandum of May 12th. The final paragraph went further and described the situation which would follow the lapse of paramountcy; it is here quoted in full:

'When a new fully self-governing or independent Government or Governments come into being in British India, His Majesty's Government's influence with these Governments will not be such as to enable them to carry out the obligations of paramountcy. Moreover, they cannot contemplate that British troops would be retained in India for this purpose. Thus, as a logical sequence and in view of the desires expressed to them on behalf of the Indian States, His Majesty's Government will cease to exercise the powers of paramountcy. This means that the rights of the States which flow from their relationship to the Crown will no longer exist and that all the rights surrendered by the States to the paramount power will return to the States. Political arrangements between the States on the one side and the British Crown and British India on the other will thus be brought to an end. The void will have to be filled either by the States entering into a federal relationship with the successor Government or Governments in British India, or failing this, entering into particular political arrangements with it or them.'

In paragraph 12 of the statement of February 20, 1947 the British government once more undertook not to hand over paramountcy to any government of British India.[1] And paragraph 18 of the statement of the following June 3rd, affirmed that their policy towards Indian states contained in the memorandum of May 12, 1946 remained unchanged.[2]

In spite of the clear assertion in the memorandum that on the lapse of paramountcy political arrangements between the states and the Crown would be brought to an end, Lord Mountbatten found it necessary to deny, at his press conference on the June 3rd statement, that the British government intended to confer dominion status on any state which declared itself independent.[3] The suspicion – expressed by the Nehru committee in 1928 and frequently thereafter – that the British were planning to convert the states, or some of them, into an Indian Ulster, evidently died hard.

When paramountcy lapsed, what would be the situation then? Would the states become independent sovereign units even though they had never enjoyed this status before, and even though the majority had never exercised full powers in their internal administration? Did the 'particular political arrangements' referred to at the end of the memorandum imply relations between the successor authorities in British India and the states as autonomous units, as the political adviser claimed and as Jinnah was prepared to allow; or did it imply something short of independence for the states, as Nehru contended? Would the agreements on such matters as railways, customs, posts and telegraphs lapse with the lapse of paramountcy? On the last point Nehru and V. P. Menon argued that these agreements had been concluded with the government of India or the British government, did not involve paramountcy, and would therefore remain in force. Sir Conrad Corfield

1 Cmd. 7047.
2 Cmd. 7136.
3 Menon, *op. cit.* p. 84.

denied the possibility of differentiating between the two classes of agreements, since all functions connected with the states were exercised by the Crown representative[1]; and the secretary of state took his stand upon the pronouncement in the cabinet mission's memorandum that political arrangements between the states on one hand and the British Crown and British India on the other would be brought to an end. In his view 'political' should be interpreted as including financial and economic, therefore all agreements would have to be dealt with in the same way.[2]

The practical issue was that if nothing was done to prepare for the situation which would follow the lapse of paramountcy, the result would be political and administrative chaos. The solution which Lord Mountbatten so persuasively urged upon the rulers was in the nature of a compromise between those who claimed that on August 15, 1947 the states would become completely independent and those who contended that paramountcy must pass to the successor governments. The princes were insistently advised to sign instruments of accession surrendering to one or other of the new dominions three subjects – defence, external affairs and communications. They should also conclude standstill agreements in order to keep in force economic and financial arrangements, which in any case would be continued for the time being by the proviso to clause 7(1) of the Indian Independence Act.

In recommending his scheme to the princes in his speech of July 25th Lord Mountbatten said that it left them 'great internal autonomy' and 'all the practical independence that you can possibly use'. But he must have known that Congress would not leave the matter there. If you drop something useful, the probability is that someone else will pick it up. Admittedly Congress was speaking with two voices. On the one hand, it complained that the outcome of British policy would be the balkanization of India; and to prove its point it could quote the declarations made at the beginning of June by Bhopal, Travancore and Hyderabad that on the British departure they intended to set themselves up as independent sovereign states. On the other hand, there was a long series of pronouncements by Congress and other nationalist leaders to the effect that either *de jure* or *de facto*, or both, a government of independent India must inherit paramountcy whenever the Crown relinquished it. As long ago as 1928 the Nehru report had claimed 'there is no constitutional objection to the Dominion Government of India stepping into the shoes of the present Government of India'.[3] Ten years later, on the eve of his campaign against the princes, Gandhi had said that 'the Congress bids fair in the future, not very distant, to replace the Paramount Power'.[4] By June 1946 even an ex-premier of Kashmir, Sir Gopalaswami Iyengar, was arguing that it was a 'pure myth' that if the British Crown withdrew from India its powers over the states would automatically revert to them. He reasoned that the Crown representative could only fulfill his obligations to protect the states because he was also the governor-general, which enabled him to send military or police forces to their aid. Hence it was the governor-general in council who was the real paramount power, and on his departure paramountcy would inevitably devolve upon those who inherited his authority.

[1] Menon, *op. cit.* p. 86.
[2] *Ibid.* p. 103.
[3] *Ibid.* p. 25.
[4] Coupland, *op. cit.* p. 138.

Nehru's speeches on the eve of the transfer of power showed that he too appreciated the situation in terms of power politics. At a press conference in July 1946 he asserted that once the states ceased to be supported by British power, no local state army could carry on independently against the rest of India, because it was a physical impossibility. He told the all-India states people's conference on April 18, 1947 that any state which did not come into the constituent assembly would be treated by the country as a hostile state and would have to bear the consequences.[1] In his speech to the All-India Congress Committee on the following June 15th, he said: 'There is a certain inherent paramountcy in the Government of India which cannot lapse . . . which must remain because of the very reasons of geography, history, defence etc.' The states, he continued, could not remain in a void; if they did not join the union, there must be a suzerain relationship. The committee thereupon passed a resolution denying that the lapse of paramountcy would lead to the independence of the states and refusing to admit the right of any state to declare its independence and live in isolation from the rest of India.[2]

To set against such pronouncements – and there had been many others to the same effect – there was only Patel's conciliatory statement on taking charge of the new government of India's states department: 'The States have already accepted the basic principle that for Defence, Foreign Affairs and Communications they would come into the Indian Union. We ask no more of them than accession on these three subjects, in which the common interests of the country are involved. In other matters we would scrupulously respect their autonomous existence. . . . I should like to make it clear that it is not the desire of Congress to interfere in any manner whatever with the domestic affairs of the States.'[3]

Lord Mountbatten's policy achieved its objects of effecting a graceful demission of the obligations of paramountcy and avoiding accusations of betrayal by the princes. More important, it soon became clear that he had contributed to preventing the emergence of more than two successor states; Hyderabad was unable to hold out for long, Kashmir had to accept *de facto* partition in accordance with the geographical compulsions which he had emphasized. But whatever his policy and methods might have been, the states were an obvious anachronism, and their destiny was clearly to become subordinate to the successor government or governments of British India, provided only that these were sufficiently strong and determined. It could be assumed that the rulers' 'consent to any changes which emerged as a result of negotiations would not be unreasonably withheld' if circumstances gave them in practice no other choice. In every sense except the legalistic, paramountcy *was* transferred.

[1] Menon, *op. cit.* p. 78.

[2] *Ibid.* pp. 90–1. M. Brecher, *Nehru: A Political Biography* (1959), p. 354.

[3] The summary in Menon, *op. cit.* pp. 99–100, does not include the last two sentences.

THE CABINET MISSION AND ITS AFTERMATH

by A. G. NOORANI *

India's freedom was an inevitability. Despite what some might now say with the advantage of hindsight, India's partition was *not* an inevitability. True, in some form or other the partition of India had been urged by a few individuals, but until 1940 no political party of any significance had put forth that demand. At any rate, in 1946, the cabinet mission's plan did afford a chance of retrieving the lost situation, for, despite the fact that this plan decisively rejected the idea of partition, the Muslim League accepted it. This paper seeks to examine how it came to be that so fine an opportunity for an amicable settlement was missed, and why, in the aftermath of its failure, both sides were confronted with a situation which neither could willingly accept and which was altogether different from anything that they had imagined.

There were two forces at work, one, led by the Indian National Congress, aspiring for the transfer of power from British hands to a central government in India, and the other, represented by the Muslim League, seeking nothing less than the partition of India along religious lines. In fact, however, as will be pointed out, neither of the two had really considered the implications of its ideal in the light of the situation actually prevailing. M. A. Jinnah, the president of the Muslim League, had skilfully and successfully avoided spelling out the details of the demand for Pakistan on the plea that the details would arise for consideration only if and when the principle of partition was first accepted. However, as Dr B. R. Ambedkar pointed out,[1] from the Lahore resolution itself, which formulated the demand for Pakistan, a good many questions could legitimately have been asked. In the speeches that he made over the years 1940–6 Jinnah advanced many an argument to explain and justify the Lahore resolution. But the very explanations he offered make one doubt whether he had understood just what they implied.[2] Thus in his letter to Gandhi dated September 17, 1944, Jinnah said 'by all canons of International Law we are a nation'. It is not pedantic to point out that the concept of nationhood belongs to the discipline of political science, not to that of international law, because in developing the two-nation theory, on which he based the demand, Jinnah gave further evidence of the same lack of understanding. If Pakistan was to be a 'homeland' for all the Muslims of India, what was to be their status in the rest of India and what, indeed, was to be the status of the non-Muslim minorities in Pakistan? When it was argued that an avowedly Muslim state would exclude, or at least curtail, the participation of the other communities, Jinnah's reaction was an angry denial and

* Lawyer and journalist, Bombay.
[1] B. R. Ambedkar, *Pakistan or Partition of India* (1946), p. 411.
[2] See Ambedkar, p. 374 on Jinnah's theory of sub-nations.

a pledge of the fullest participation. To his legalistic mind the mere incorporation of statutory safeguards was enough. But perhaps the most striking contradiction lay in his reference to an 'India' to which both Pakistan and Hindustan (as he called the rest of India) were to belong. 'Let us, therefore, live as good neighbours; let the Hindus guard the South and West and let the Muslims guard the frontiers. We will then stand together and say to the world "Hands off India; India for the Indians".'[1] India's first High Commissioner to Pakistan Sri Prakasa pointed out[2] that Jinnah wanted the two states to be known as parts of India. Indeed, in his presidential address to the constituent assembly of Pakistan on August 11, 1947, Jinnah remarked 'no power can hold another nation, and specially a nation of 400 million souls, in subjection'. As is well-known, in this very speech he gave a go-by to the two-nation theory and spoke of the day when the Hindus and Muslims would cease to be such; not in the religious sense, but in the political sense as citizens of the state.

If in Jinnah's mind partition was a simple pragmatic solution with the two-nation theory as a mere temporary ideological justification, and with a marked sense of unity, despite the fact of partition, the Congress, as an advocate of unity, made little allowance for the diversities in India and, in effect, followed policies which impaired that unity. Little thought was bestowed on just how much autonomy should be allowed to the members of the Indian federation. The famous Jagat Narain Lal resolution of the All-Indian Congress committee passed in 1942 opposed the grant of the right of secession to any member of the federation. However, in September 1945, the Congress working committee, while recalling this very resolution, said in the same breath that it could not think 'in terms of compelling the people in any territorial unit to remain in an Indian Union against their declared and established will'. The one person from the Congress side who had given some thought to the problem was Maulana Azad. As he has written in his memoirs[3] he had come to the conclusion that the Indian federation should just deal with the three subjects of defence, foreign affairs and communications, thus granting the maximum autonomy possible to the provinces. According to the Maulana, Gandhi accepted his suggestion, while Sardar Patel disagreed with him.[4] Maulana Azad issued a statement on April 15, 1946, containing a masterly critique of the Pakistan demand and advocating instead a centre with very limited power. But there can be little question in the light of later events that this represented an expression of his personal opinion rather than the stand of the Congress.

When the cabinet mission arrived in India in March 1946, its task was to reconcile the two rival standpoints. In the opinion of one of the members, Sir Stafford Cripps, 'the gulf between these two points of view is by no means unbridgeable'.[5] The League wanted common subjects like defence, and foreign affairs, to be dealt with by treaty arrangements. The Congress wanted a federal centre for administering them. At the very outset, the cabinet

[1] Speech at the Muslim University Union, Aligarh on March 10, 1941, in *Speeches and Writings of Mr. Jinnah*, ed. Jamil-ud-din Ahmad, vol i, p. 242.

[2] *The Indian Express*, February 19, 1966.

[3] A. K. Azad, *India Wins Freedom* (1958), pp. 140–2.

[4] See Sudhir Ghosh, *Gandhi's Emissary* (1967), p. 196, for evidence to the contrary, however.

[5] Sudhir Ghosh, p. 96.

mission told Jinnah that he had to choose between an Indian union confined to defence and foreign affairs having under it two federations of Pakistan and Hindustan, and a sovereign Pakistan, but from which large blocks of territories inhabited predominantly by non-Muslims, would be excluded.[1] 'Sovereignty and a small area or on the basis of a Union and a larger area for Pakistan' was the choice. The cabinet mission put forward a plan for partition which both sides rejected.[2] Curiously enough, this is seldom recalled, but it was a significant move. Thereupon the two sides proceeded to put forward their proposals which are noteworthy in the light of what was to happen later. Thus, on May 6, 1946, the Congress president informed the cabinet mission that it was totally opposed to the idea of sub-federations within a federation.[3] Eventually the Congress proposals formally put forth on May 12th, provided that 'groups of Provinces may be formed'. But what was truly remarkable was that while on April 29, 1946, Jinnah forwarded to the mission a copy of the resolution passed by the subjects committee of the All-India Muslim League legislators convention adumbrating the Pakistan demand in its most extreme form, the formal proposals he forwarded to the mission on May 11, did *not* provide for the partition of India, but for a confederation of Pakistan and the rest of India. These were the approaches of the two parties, but Gandhi wrote to the mission a letter outlining the position to which he consistently adhered later. It was that the constituent assembly to be set up under the agreement would not be bound by the terms of the settlement but would be free to alter them.[4] Since the parties failed to agree, the cabinet mission put forward its own proposals in its statement of May 16, 1946. These proposals envisaged a union of India dealing with the subjects of foreign affairs, defence and communications, with the residuary subjects vesting in the provinces. The provinces were free to form groups with executives and legislatures and each group could determine the provincial subjects to be taken in common. The statement laid down in paragraph 19 the procedure for the election and the working of the constituent assembly to draw up the union, group, and the provincial constitutions. Very briefly, paragraph 19 contemplated that after the election a preliminary meeting should be held to decide the general order of business, elect officers and appoint committees. Thereafter the provincial representatives were to divide into three sections, one comprising Bengal and Assam, another Punjab, North-West Frontier Province and Sind and the third comprising the rest of British India. These three sections were to settle provincial constitutions and also to decide whether to have a group constitution and if so, with what provincial subjects the group should deal. After the constitutional arrangements had come into operation it was to be open to any province to elect to come out of the group in which it had been placed by these deliberations. The basic provisions of the proposals could be varied by the constituent assembly

[1] V. P. Menon, *The Transfer of Power in India* (1957), pp. 247–51.

[2] *Ibid.* p. 253.

[3] *Papers relating to the Cabinet Mission to India* (Delhi, 1946), p. 13.

[4] *Gandhiji's correspondence with the Government 1944–1947* (1959), p. 187. Letter of May 8, 1946. Sir Stafford Cripps in his reply of May 9th stated that if the Congress and the Muslim League did agree to a certain basis for the new constitution, they would be bound to do their utmost to see that that settlement was adopted by the constituent assembly.

only by a majority of the representatives of each of the two major communities.

The Congress president, Maulana Azad, complained to the secretary of state on May 20th[1] that while the provinces were given freedom to form groups, procedurally they were compelled to sit in a section. He was not unmindful of the liberty given to a province to opt out of a group later, but said that a dominating province in a section 'may even conceivably lay down rules, for elections and otherwise, thereby nullifying the provision for a province to opt out of a group'. He also contended that the constituent assembly would be a sovereign body and therefore free to vary 'in any way it likes' the recommendations and the procedure suggested by the mission. The day before Gandhi had taken up a similar point in a letter to Lord Pethick-Lawrence, the secretary of state. Jinnah issued a non-committal statement on May 22nd[2] analysing the mission's proposals against the background of the negotiations preceding it. In the main, it was a detailed criticism of those features of the mission's proposals which departed from the League's proposals of May 11th. Jinnah ended his statement by saying that the decision would have to be taken by the working committee and the council of the All India Muslim League.

The Congress working committee passed a resolution on May 24th, in which, among other things, it reiterated its interpretation of the grouping provisions put forth earlier in Maulana Azad's letter dated May 20, 1946, 'in order to retain the recommendatory character of the Statement, and in order to make the clauses consistent with each other, the Committee read paragraph 15 to mean that, *in the first instance*, the respective provinces will make their choice whether or not to belong to the section in which they are placed. Thus the Constituent Assembly must be considered as a sovereign body with final authority for the purpose of drawing up a constitution and giving effect to it'. [Italics mine throughout.]

The Cabinet mission issued a statement on May 25, 1946, dealing with the criticisms made by both sides. On the question of grouping which was to assume such critical significance later, the mission said 'The interpretation put by the Congress resolution on paragraph 15 of the statement, to the effect that the Provinces can in the first instance make the choice whether or not to belong to the Section in which they are placed, does not accord with the Delegation's intentions. The reasons for the grouping of the Provinces are well known and this is an essential feature of the scheme and can only be modified by agreement between the parties. The right to opt out of the groups after the constitution making has been completed will be exercised by the people themselves, since at the first election under the new provincial Constitution this question of opting out will obviously be a major issue and all those entitled to vote under the new franchise will be able to take their share in a truly democratic decision.'

The council of the All-India Muslim League accepted the mission's plan on June 6th to the surprise and relief of many. Soon negotiations began for the formation of an interim government and these proceeded simultaneously with clarifications of the long term plan by the cabinet mission to the Congress

[1] *Cabinet Mission Papers*, p. 33. [2] *Ibid.* p. 25.

leaders. Maulana Azad wrote to the viceroy on June 14th regretting that the Congress view-point on the grouping formula in the mission's plan had not been accepted by the cabinet delegation in their statement of May 25th. The viceroy wrote back the next day, 'The Delegation and I are aware of your objections to the principle of grouping. I would however point out that the statement of 16th May does not make grouping compulsory. It leaves the decision to the elected representatives of the Provinces concerned sitting together in sections. The only provision which is made is that the representatives of certain Provinces *should meet in sections* so that they can decide whether or not they wish to form groups. Even when this has been done the individual Provinces are still to have the liberty to opt out of the group if they so decide.' The viceroy was clearly drawing a distinction between the provinces sitting together in *sections* and forming *groups*. The first was mandatory under the mission's plan, but whether a province should remain a member of the group or not was purely optional since it had the right under the mission's plan to opt out by vote of its legislature *after* the first general election under the new constitution. There really was no contradiction in the mission's statement of May 16th.

On June 25th the Congress working committee passed a resolution agreeing to participate in the work of the constituent assembly. The resolution said, 'The limitation of the Central authority, as contained in the proposals as well as the system of grouping of Provinces, weakened the whole structure and was unfair to some Provinces, such as, the North-West Frontier Province, and Assam, and to some of the minorities, notably the Sikhs. The Committee disapproved of this. They felt, however, taking the proposals as a whole, that there was sufficient scope for enlarging and strengthening the Central authority and for fully ensuring the right of a Province to act according to its choice in regard to grouping, and to give protection to such minorities as might otherwise be placed at a disadvantage.' How the Congress working committee was persuaded to accept the cabinet mission's plan is narrated in detail in Pyarelal's memoirs[1] and in Sudhir Ghosh's memoirs.[2] Having regard to its interpretation of the grouping provisions of the proposals, the Congress leaders felt that the greatest obstacle to their acceptance of the mission plan was the declaration which each candidate for election to the constituent assembly had to sign to the effect that he was willing to serve as a representative of the province 'for the purposes of paragraph 19 of the Statement', which outlined the procedure making it obligatory for a province initially to sit in a section and only later to opt out of the group set up by the section.[3]

The cabinet mission having secured the League's acceptance was naturally anxious to secure the acceptance of the Congress as well. In the course of negotiations between the mission and Sardar Patel, Sir Stafford Cripps offered to amend the declaration by substituting the words 'for the purposes of the declaration of May 16' in place of 'for the purposes of paragraph 19

[1] Pyarelal, *Mahatma Gandhi*, vol. i, pp. 224–8.
[2] Sudhir Ghosh, *op. cit.* pp. 170–3.
[3] Pattabhi Sitaramaya, *The History of the Indian National Congress*, vol. ii, p. ccxvii (Appendix).

of the Declaration of May 16'.[1] From Pyarelal's account[2] it would seem that one of the members of the mission, Lord Pethick-Lawrence, thought that Sir Stafford was going too far and said, 'No, that presents difficulty'. However, Sir Stafford Cripps seems to have prevailed and the Congress working committee proceeded to pass a resolution of acceptance on June 25th. The cabinet mission's amendment of the declaration, designed so clearly to accommodate the Congress's ambiguous stand, was due to its enthusiasm to get the Congress to accept the plan; for, the mission had earlier consistently rejected the Congress interpretation and, indeed, later again did likewise.

The same day, June 25th, the Muslim League working committee passed a resolution commenting on the letter of the Congress president to the viceroy and the cabinet delegation, intimating the Congress decision with regard to the proposals. The League working committee contested the Congress's right to adhere to its interpretation of the mission's proposals, which was rejected by the cabinet delegation, and yet to profess to accept the cabinet's mission's plan. Indeed, the viceroy himself in his letter of June 27th, in reply to the Congress president, referred to the Congress's reiteration of its interpretation and pointed out 'the procedure for dividing up into sections can only be altered by a resolution of the Constituent Assembly passed by a majority of both communities under paragraph 19(7) of the Statement of May 16'. The Congress, while accepting the mission's long term plan, rejected the mission's proposals of June 16th for an interim government, which the Muslim League accepted. The mission, however, felt that since both sides had accepted the long term proposals, there was no point in going ahead with the formation of the interim government and decided to scrap its proposals of June 16 and make a fresh attempt at the formation of an interim government. Jinnah was very sore about this decision and accused the mission of breach of faith. In his statement of June 27 he took strong exception, once again, to the Congress adherence to its own interpretation of the grouping formula, while accepting the mission's proposals and said 'if they persisted in this and adopt measures to set at naught what is described by the Statement of May 25 to constitute the essential feature of the scheme, the whole plan will be wrecked at its very inception'.

It is clear in the light of the foregoing that the Congress acceptance of the cabinet mission's proposals was a conditional one and that Jinnah had publicly complained of it. It is necessary to stress this because later the legend spread that the League withdrew its acceptance of the cabinet mission's proposals because of an outburst by Nehru.

The Congress working committee's resolution was ratified by the All-India Congress committee on July 6, 1946. At this session Nehru took over the Congress presidentship from Maulana Azad. Speaking at a press conference thereafter, Nehru stressed that the constituent assembly was a sovereign body and that in all probability there would be no groups at all. The non-Pakistan provinces (Section A) would decide against grouping and so would the North West Frontier Province and Assam, leading to the collapse of the other groups as well. To be sure, Jinnah raised an uproar about this statement. Later in the month, Lord Pethick-Lawrence in the house of lords and Sir

[1] Sudhir Ghosh, *op. cit.* p. 170. [2] Pyarelal, *op. cit.* p. 225.

Stafford Cripps in the commons repeated the cabinet mission's interpretation of the grouping formula and rejected the Congress interpretation. However, Jinnah had the council of the All-India Muslim League convened in Bombay on July 27. The council withdrew its acceptance of the cabinet mission's proposals and passed another resolution authorizing its working committee to draw up a plan of 'direct action'. The Congress working committee met in Wardha in August 1946 and passed a resolution seeking to allay the Muslim League's misgivings. The effort was a futile one in view of what the working committee said, 'The Committee wish to make it clear that while they do not approve of all the proposals contained in this Statement (May 16), they accepted the scheme in its entirety. They interpreted it so as to resolve the inconsistencies contained in it and fill the omissions in accordance with the principles laid down in the Statement.'

It is not necessary for the purpose of this paper to go into the details of the negotiations leading to the formation of the interim government and the League's later participation in it. Our main purpose here is to trace the parties' differences regarding the principal question arising out of the mission's proposals, namely, the grouping of provinces.

Soon after making the announcement that an interim government would be formed by the Congress alone, the viceroy visited Calcutta to acquaint himself with the violence that erupted on the 'direct action' day, August 16th. While in Calcutta Lord Wavell met Sir Khwaja Nazimuddin, an eminent Muslim League leader, who suggested that if the Congress could yet unequivocally accept the grouping formula and the British government and their viceroy declare that no other interpretation would be countenanced save that authoritatively put forth by the mission, the Muslim League might retract its resolution withdrawing its earlier acceptance of the mission's plan. He also made a suggestion regarding the League's participation in the interim government which is not material for the purposes of this paper. The viceroy was much impressed by Nazimuddin's suggestion and on his return he handed over to Gandhi and to Nehru the draft of a declaration which he wished the Congress to accept. The declaration read: 'The Congress are prepared in the interests of communal harmony to accept the intention of the Statement of May 16, that Provinces cannot exercise any option affecting their membership of the sections or of the groups if formed, until the decision contemplated in paragraph 19(8) of the Statement of May 16 is taken by the new Legislature after the new Constitutional arrangements have come into operation and the first general elections have been held.' The viceroy was also of the opinion that it would be best not to convene the constituent assembly until this point was settled. The declaration,[1] however, was not accepted. Nehru's reply was that the Congress was prepared to abide by the verdict of the federal court on the dispute as to the interpretation of the clause relating to the grouping. The British government overruled the viceroy on the summoning of the constituent assembly and suggested that in the event of no agreement being reached on the grouping formula, Nehru and Jinnah, along with the viceroy, might be invited to London for fresh discussions. Thus, there was a deadlock between the Muslim League and the Congress with regard to the

[1] V. P. Menon, *op. cit.* p. 302.

grouping of provinces. Subsequently, the viceroy started negotiations with Jinnah for the League's participation in the interim government which were concluded successfully on the basis of the terms outlined in the viceroy's letter to Jinnah dated October 4, 1946. One of the terms was the Muslim League's acceptance of the mission's proposals of May 16th. Shortly after the Muslim League entered the interim government, the viceroy took up with Jinnah the question of summoning the League council for that purpose. Jinnah, in reply, contended that the Congress had not yet accepted the cabinet mission's proposals and that, therefore, there was no question of his convening the League council. He also asked the viceroy not to convene the constituent assembly.

On November 20th, the viceroy overruled Jinnah's objections and issued invitations for the meeting of the constituent assembly. He also sent for Liaqat Ali Khan, the senior-most Muslim League member of the interim government and told him that he could not agree to the representatives of the League remaining in the government unless the Muslim League accepted the mission's proposals. Predictably Liaqat Ali Khan took the stand that the proposals had not in fact been accepted by the Congress and, therefore, it was for the viceroy to secure the Congress's acceptance first. Meanwhile, the Congress took up the stand that the Muslim League should either accept the cabinet mission's plan or leave the interim government. To resolve this deadlock the British government invited representatives of both parties to London for consultations. The upshot was the British government's statement of December 6th in which the British government urged the Congress to accept the cabinet mission's interpretation. The last paragraph of the statement was very significant: 'There has never been any prospect of success for the Constituent Assembly except upon the basis of the agreed procedure. Should a Constitution come to be framed by the Constituent Assembly in which a large section of the Indian population had not been represented, His Majesty's Government could not, of course, contemplate forcing such a Constitution upon any unwilling parts of the country.' In retrospect, this was nothing but a recall of the alternative of the smaller Pakistan which, as we have noted, the mission had put to Jinnah in May 1946. What was now happening was that, thanks to the Congress insistence on its own interpretation of the grouping formula, the possibility of partition, which had hitherto been relegated to the background, was now being revived.

Nehru criticized this statement of December 6th as a variation of the mission's proposals. The Congress working committee in its resolution of December 22nd criticized this statement of December 6th, expressed its readiness to abide by the verdict of the federal court and decided to refer the matter to the A.I.C.C. This body met in Delhi and passed a resolution on January 6, 1947, advising action in accordance with the interpretation of the British government. But it added, 'it must be clearly understood, however, that this must not involve any compulsion of a Province and that the rights of the Sikhs in the Punjab should not be jeopardized. In the event of any attempt at such compulsion, a Province or a part of a Province has the right to take such action as may be deemed necessary in order to give effect to the wishes of the people concerned.' The Muslim League working committee, which met in Karachi at the end of the month, regarded this as yet another qualified acceptance and called upon the British government to dissolve the constituent assembly.

The constituent assembly, as a matter of fact, had met on December 9th, and had proceeded to frame certain rules to which the League's working committee's resolution took great exception. One of them was rule 63, whereby, the League argued, it was sought to assume control of the sections. The evidence that has since come to light suggests that this was, indeed, so designed. K. M. Munshi, one of the principal legal advisers of the Congress writes in his memoirs of his decision 'to exploit the rule-making power of the Constituent Assembly'.[1] He elaborates, 'If properly framed, the Rules would enable the Constituent Assembly as a whole to exercise control over the Sections and Provinces so as to safeguard the rights of the minorities in each of them. I discussed the matter with Gandhiji and Sardar, and also spoke about it to Jawaharlal Nehru. These talks, however, produced unforeseen results, not necessarily unfortunate. Later I learnt that, by some devious means, Lord Wavell had come to know of the advice that I had given to Sardar and Jawaharlal Nehru. *This confirmed his belief that the Congress had not in fact accepted the May 16 Plan and was exploring every avenue to circumvent the autonomy of the Sections – the only provision of the Plan which was attractive to the Muslim League*' (italics mine). The move was as unfortunate, though not from Munshi's point of view, as it was misconceived. Munshi himself writes, 'Under the Cabinet Mission Plan, the Constituent Assembly as a whole had no control over the constitution-making powers of the Sections and the Provinces. But it could frame its own rules, through which effective control could be exercised.'[2] How the procedural rules could modify the terms of the basic scheme Mr Munshi does not explain.

The League working committee's Karachi resolution adopted on January 31, 1947, strongly criticized the decisions of the constituent assembly, including the rules it had adopted, as *ultra vires* of that body. The deadlock remained and a final break-up between the Congress and the League appeared inevitable. Once again, the Congress members demanded resignation of the League members from the interim government. Once again, on the viceroy's demand that the League accept the plan, the League rejoined that the Congress itself had not accepted the plan and, therefore, was in no position to call upon the League to do so. As a way out of the deadlock the viceroy proposed to the secretary of state[3] that the British government should issue a statement calling upon the Congress 'to confirm that the relevant passage in its resolution dealing with sections and grouping which have given rise to the Muslim League's doubts were not intended to limit or qualify the Congress acceptance of the Cabinet Mission's plan'. The secretary of state did not agree with this suggestion. Very soon the Congress representatives declared that if the Muslim League's representatives were not asked to resign, the Congress representatives themselves would. This presented the British government with a veritable dilemma and it got out of it by issuing the famous statement of February 20, 1947, announcing its definite intention to take necessary

[1] K. M. Munshi, *Pilgrimage to Freedom* (1967), pp. 117–18.
[2] *Ibid.* p. 111. [3] V. P. Menon, *op. cit.* p. 337.

steps to effect the peaceful transfer of power into responsible Indian hands by a date not later than June 30, 1948. If it should appear that by then an agreed constitution had not been worked out the British government would consider to whom it should transfer the powers of the central government 'whether as a whole to some form of Central Government for British India or in some areas to the existing Provincial Governments or in such way as may seem most reasonable and in the best interests of the Indian people'. The Congress working committee welcomed this declaration in a resolution passed on March 8th. The working committee also passed on that date two other resolutions, one calling for the partition of Punjab and Bengal on communal lines, and the other inviting the Muslim League to direct negotiations.

That the British government did not regard the A.I.C.C.'s resolution of January 6th as an acceptance of its interpretation is evident from the fact that as late as March 1947 Sir Stafford Cripps asked Sudhir Ghosh to persuade the Congress 'to tell the world quite bluntly and in detail what they really mean when they say they accept the British interpretation of the Cabinet Mission's plan as set out in the Statement of December 6'.[1] As Sudhir Ghosh reported to Sardar Patel, the British government thought that Jinnah 'will soon realize that the Pakistan he is likely to get is not worth anything; if on top of this realization in Mr. Jinnah's mind the Congress is in a position to say in detail what is meant by its acceptance of the British interpretation of the Plan, then it will be possible for them to give Mountbatten such instructions and directions as would enable him to get the Muslim League into the Constituent Assembly'.

Lord Mountbatten succeeded Lord Wavell as viceroy of India. The directive he was given by the British government was to secure implementation of the cabinet mission's plan.[2] Maulana Azad was also anxious that the new viceroy do something to this end. He suggested that Mountbatten issue his personal interpretation on the grouping formula which would be acceptable.[3] Indeed, at a staff meeting of the viceroy on April 12, 1947, 'Mountbatten went to the root of the dilemma, and put the proposition that he should try to get Congress to accept the Cabinet Mission's plan in full, and then confront Mr Jinnah with giving in or accepting a truncated Pakistan'. The viceroy was trying various alternatives. On April 19th the viceroy felt that Pakistan was inevitable, but three days later he came round to the view 'that the Cabinet Mission Plan can somehow be resurrected in a new form and name. As originally presented it was psychologically wrong. If the principle of two sovereign States could be accepted union might be achieved through sovereignty.' However, as the viceroy put it 'my object is to create the effect of two sovereign States or separate blocks negotiating at the Centre rather than having a system of majority voting'. This was nothing but Jinnah's old proposal for confederation which he presented to the cabinet mission in May 1946.

But by now the rift between the Congress and the League seemed unbridgeable. On April 20th Nehru said that the Muslim League could have its

[1] Sudhir Ghosh, *op. cit.* p. 203.
[2] A. Campbell-Johnson, *Mission with Mountbatten* (1951).
[3] *Ibid.* Diary Entry, April 23, 1947.

Pakistan if it wanted, but it had no right to demand to be included within it areas which did not wish to join Pakistan. The cabinet mission's plan was dead. Partitioning India was only a matter of time.

It is clear from the resumé of events that the Congress's persistent refusal unequivocally to accept the grouping provisions of the cabinet mission's plant led to its collapse. Repeated British efforts, which continued till as late as March 1947, to get an unambiguous acceptance from the Congress failed miserably. Each time there was the same acceptance hedged in with a proviso or expressed subject to its interpretation, and with the right to interpret the document in its own way. Willingness to refer the issue to the federal court was of little avail since the grouping provisions were an essential part of the bargain with the League, indeed the only concession to it.

The reason for this reservation lay in the Congress's unrealistic and extreme concept of an All-India federation. Maulana Azad alone was prepared to accept a relatively weak centre, but he was unable to carry his colleagues with him. There was Gandhi's strong opposition. 'In face of Gandhiji's opposition, the Congress leaders did not dare to accept the May 16 plan, but neither did they want to reject it. So they put their own interpretation on grouping by taking recourse to two conflicting clauses of the May 16 plan.'[1] Of course, there really was no conflict in the provisions as was repeatedly pointed out. The main reason for Gandhi's opposition, and which the Congress leaders shared, was the fear that the plan would pave the way to Pakistan. Sardar Patel, writes his biographer,[2] 'was convinced that it would set India on the slippery slope of fragmentation'. The very fact that the League saw in the plan the 'basis and the foundation of Pakistan' and pointed them out to its adherents, in justification for its acceptance of a federal India despite years of agitation for Pakistan, was ground good enough for the Congress to disapprove of the plan. The pity of it is that the rejection of the plan, which in effect it was, was based on a total misappreciation of the document. Thus, we are told, Sardar Patel thought that the two groups comprising the Pakistan provinces 'would probably exercise their option of seceding from the Union'.[3] This option the groups were manifestly *not* granted by the mission's plan. In contrast to the clear right [para. 19 (viii)], of 'any Province to elect to come out of any group in which it has been placed' all it could do *vis-à-vis* the union was [para. 15 (6)] to 'call for a reconsideration of the terms of the Constitution after an initial period of 10 years and at 10 yearly intervals thereafter'. Significantly Jinnah publicly complained, on May 22nd, that 'our proposal that the Pakistan group should have the right to secede from the Union after the initial period of ten years, although the Congress had no serious objection to it, has been omitted and *now we are only limited* to reconsideration of the terms of Union Constitution after the initial period of ten years'. It is worth recalling in this context that while the Cripps proposals of March 1942 envisaged a federation, they provided expressly for 'non-acceding Provinces'. The cabinet mission's proposals, in contrast, did not. Indeed, Sardar Patel's own early reaction was one of enthusiasm. He wrote to K. M. Munshi on May 17, 1946, 'Since many years for the first time an

[1] A. K. Majumdar, *Advent of Independence*, p. 226.

[2] K. L. Punjabi, *The Indomitable Sardar*, p. 116.

[3] *Ibid.* p. 116.

authoritative pronouncement in clear terms has been made against the possibility of Pakistan in any shape or form.'[1]

It was this which emboldened Maulana Azad triumphantly to conclude that as a result of the cabinet mission's plan 'all schemes of partition of India have been rejected once and for all'.[2] As Mr Lele, himself a Congressman, asked, 'Could a triumph like this come without a price, without some sacrifice?' The price of a grouping of Muslim provinces the Congress was unwilling to pay. It was a singularly short-sighted and unimaginative decision. Once a federation had been set up, it would have inevitably gathered strength. We have seen, moreover, that earlier in the day Jinnah was offered the choice between a 'truncated' Pakistan and a federation with limited powers. That later he accepted the federation and publicly characterized it as the greatest success of the Muslim League's agitation shows his preference.

But if the Congress policies made partition an inevitability, it was the League's distrust and lack of statesmanship which ensured that partition came in an embittered atmosphere.

On March 8, 1947, the Congress working committee passed three important resolutions. One welcomed the British government's statement of February 20th, and another demanded partition of the Punjab and Bengal on religious lines. The third curiously enough, has gone largely unnoticed in the memoirs and chronicles of the period. It read thus: 'In view of new developments which are leading to a swift transfer of power in India, it has become incumbent on the people of India to prepare themselves *jointly and co-operatively* for this change, so that this may be effected peacefully and to the advantage of all. The Working Committee therefore invite the All-India Muslim League to nominate representatives to meet representatives of the Congress in order to consider the situation that has arisen and to devise means to meet it.'

Jinnah had always maintained that negotiations with Congress were possible if the principle of partition was first accepted. The logical corollary of the partition of the Punjab and Bengal was the partition of India on the same, that is, religious, basis.

It would have been natural to expect Jinnah to respond positively to the Congress resolutions. Hopes were raised when on March 27th, he called for a 'truce on the basis of Pakistan, the elimination of the British in India and India for Indians'.[3] But before long Nehru complained of the absence of any response from the League to the Congress invitation. A spokesman of that body, in reply, claimed that the League had enquired of the Congress the basis for the proposed negotiations. Refuting the claim, Shankerrao Deo, general secretary of the Congress, published the correspondence[4] exchanged between him and Liaqat Ali Khan, general secretary of the Muslim League. It appears that on March 9th Deo forwarded the Congress executive's resolutions

[1] K. M. Munshi, *Pilgrimage to Freedom*, p. 103. Munshi's comment, 'It was evident that Sardar was prepared to pay a price for averting the partition of the country, and was willing to share power with the Muslim League' credited the Sardar with greater statesmanship than he actually displayed. It is only fair to point out that the frustrations in the interim government followed and did not precede those about the complete acceptance of the mission plan.

[2] P. R. Lele, *Constituent Assembly* (1946), p. 62. This is an able but unnoticed work.

[3] *Dawn*, March 28, 1947. [4] *Ibid.* April 18, 1947.

drawing pointed attention to the invitation. Four days later Liaqat replied to say that the letter would be placed before the working committee of the League 'for their consideration'. On April 11, Deo sent a reminder requesting 'you expedite your decision'. On April 14, Liaqat replied 'no date for the next meeting of the Working Committee of All-India Muslim League has been fixed yet. In view of the discussions which are now in progress between the Viceroy and the Indian leaders, *it is not likely that a meeting of the Working Committee will be called* until a definite stage in the talks has been reached.' Since such a stage is reached only on the conclusion of the negotiations, the only and fair inference to draw from the letter is that the League was not a bit interested in direct negotiations with the Congress.

On June 6th, Gandhi suggested to the viceroy that he 'should speak in the following sense to Mr. Jinnah, when he found him in the right mood to listen: Now, therefore that the decision has been made and you have your Pakistan, why do you not go yourself and talk with the Congress leaders as friends, and try to get a settlement between yourselves on all the various points at issue? This would make for a much better atmosphere than adhering to the practice of only meeting together under my chairmanship.'[1] The viceroy at first promised to do so, but later asked Gandhi to communicate directly with Jinnah.[2] Nothing came of it however. 'Let it be a partition as between two brothers, if a division there must be', Gandhi had written to Jinnah on September 22, 1944. But that was not to be. Effected even in cordiality, partition would have created its own and difficult problems – the minorities and the Indian states. But the fact that it came in an embittered atmosphere rendered these problems intractable.

In perhaps the most perceptive essay on the times then written,[3] the veteran Liberal leader Sir Chimanlal Setalvad deplored that the agreement to partition India had not been reached as a result of 'mutual goodwill and understanding'. All the parties concerned were to blame for this. The cabinet mission's scheme 'had been killed by the wobbling and vacillating attitude of one party' (the Congress). He added, 'The cherished boon of a united India had fallen into their lap, but they by their own want of political wisdom threw it out and made it beyond their reach.' The British were to blame for not firmly standing by their own proposals.

As for the League, what had happened was a great personal triumph for Jinnah. 'But has he succeeded in doing good to the Muslims themselves and to his country?' He predicted 'this division of India has laid foundations of interminable quarrels and chaos which will bring untold suffering to generations yet unborn'.

Much has happened in the two decades since partition to confirm this, but accepting the realities as they are, it is yet possible to reverse the trend, not, indeed, by an undoing of the partition, but rather by applying, however belatedly, the lessons the events teach: that harmony is possible only by an acceptance of diversities and that the partition itself will work well but only in a recognition of the links between the two halves of the entire sub-continent which till the very last Jinnah regarded as one.

[1] *Gandhiji's Correspondence with the Government*, p. 255.
[2] *Ibid*. p. 260. [3] India Divided, *The Times of India*, June 15, 1947.

THE ROLE OF LORD MOUNTBATTEN

by H. V. HODSON *

One is often tempted, in looking back on the events of 1947 in India, to regard them as pre-ordained in their main shape, and the principal characters in the drama as mere actors of parts already written by fate and moving to an inevitable dénouement, although the players might sometimes vary the dialogue a little from the lines in the prompt-book. Such a view of Lord Mountbatten's role is the opposite extreme to that which was held of him by some people at the time, both detractors and admirers, who believed that he personally should be blamed or praised for the end of the British *raj*, the partition of India, the absorption of the Indian states, and the strife and bloodshed among Hindus and Muslims, Indians and Pakistanis, but not between them and the British, which accompanied those events.

His personal influence on the major historical happenings can, of course, be exaggerated. Before he was ever associated with the governance of India it was certain, first, that independence would come in some way within a couple of years or so of the end of the second world war. That statement is based, not only on the promises made on behalf of the national government by Sir Stafford Cripps in 1942 or on Labour's electoral victory in 1945, but on the foreseeable fact that the British electorate had lost its will to rule India, or at any rate its stomach for the means of doing so. The question was not whether, but how; and when, but only within fairly narrow margins.

Secondly, it was certain that India would be constitutionally partitioned. This certainty became fixed somewhat later, perhaps no earlier than the failure of the cabinet mission in 1946. The effort, which Lord Mountbatten himself pursued, to salvage some kind of minimal centre for all India was foredoomed to failure, in my view, before the end of 1946, when even the façade of an interim national government under the old régime was manifestly cracking up. The then president of the Indian National Congress, Acharya Kripalani, told me that many of the Congress high command had reconciled themselves to partition in some form by December, 1946, though they hoped to have some kind of central machinery for defence at least. The decisive moment was probably the Punjab provincial elections in February 1946, which reduced the Unionist party to a rump; for if the Punjab, through the voice of its assembly, had continued to want to remain whole it would have been next to impossible to divide India completely.

Thirdly, it was certain that decisive action to settle the constitutional problem, and to transfer political power to those who could take responsibility for exercising it far into the future, would have to be taken within a matter of months. Not only was central government politically on the verge of breakdown; administration in the civil service and police was getting

* Provost of the Ditchley Foundation since 1961; Reforms Commissioner, Government of India 1941–2; Editor, *Sunday Times*, 1950–61.

steadily weaker, the British element being exhausted by many years without home leave or reinforcement, and dispirited by the future prospect, the Indian element unsure who would next be their masters, and reluctant to expose themselves to political or communal reaction. The intense communalism of national politics was seeping into the police and even into the army. The pendulum of communal violence – Calcutta, Noakhali, Bihar, Rawalpindi – was swinging out of control. If not Mountbatten then Wavell or some other viceroy would have had to move far more quickly than was generally foreseen in Britain if there was not to be complete disaster. Lord Wavell's plan of British retreat, province by province, envisaged evacuation of India by March 1948.

Nevertheless, I do not accept a cataclysmic or determinist view of history. History is made by individual human beings, and as an individual Lord Mountbatten beyond doubt canalized and deflected the course of major events, although he could not stem their flood. I would like to analyse his personal contribution under three heads: his mandate, his character and experience, and his relations with the Indian states.

The first point to make about Mountbatten's viceroyalty is that he wrote his own ticket. The announcement of February 20, 1947 was not dictated by him, but it was agreed word by word with him and it arose out of the conversations that he had with Mr Attlee when the latter invited him at the end of 1946 to go out to India and in effect end the British *raj*. There is some dispute as to whether, in those conversations, the concept of a time-limit within which independence would be granted was first put forward by the one or the other, but it is certain that Mountbatten insisted against all arguments by ministers and officials that the terminal date should be precise. Sir Stafford Cripps proposed to say 'the summer of 1948'; Mountbatten demanded and received 'June 1948'. As it happened, the date became operatively null, but who would deny that its precision had a profound psychological effect in convincing Indians that the British government really meant business, and in forcing them into decisions from which they would have shrunk if they had not known that the sands were running out of the hour-glass?

Equally important, Mountbatten caused to be written into his mandate that fateful sentence declaring that if no constitution had been worked out by a fully representative constituent assembly by June 1948, H.M.G. would have to consider whether to hand over power 'as a whole to some form of central Government for British India, or in some areas to the existing provincial Governments, or in such other way as may seem most reasonable and in the best interests of the Indian people'. It may be said that this comprehensive list of possible alternatives was merely the logical corollary of fixing a terminal date. True, but by so spelling them out the statement was a public open licence for the creation of Pakistan. For Jinnah had only to continue to keep the Muslim League out of the constituent assembly, and to make central government impossible, to force partition on provincial or other lines as the only way in which H.M.G. could keep its promise. It might be the 'moth-eaten Pakistan' which he had spurned, but Pakistan it would be if he insisted on it and could hold his followers together. Hopes that he might not insist on it, or that, if he did at the price of partitioning the Punjab and Bengal, his followers would split, continued to be held by Mountbatten and many others almost until the last minute, but they proved wholly false.

There was, however, something in Mountbatten's mandate which was peculiarly his own. He did not want to go out to India. He feared it might ruin his naval career and be the death-knell of his life-long ambition to become First Sea Lord. So he made the steepest terms. He began by demanding a guarantee that afterwards he be taken back into the navy without loss of seniority and in an equivalent post to that which he would leave. The Admiralty, which objected, was over-ruled, and he had his way. He then made a more extravagant condition. He demanded plenipotentiary powers. Within the terms of his instructions (which he would agree) he must be allowed to act in his own way and without interference from London. 'You are asking', exclaimed astonished ministers, 'to be over the Secretary of State for India.' 'Exactly,' said Mountbatten. Attlee personally granted his demand. Of course Mountbatten sent back his proposed plan for the transfer of power, by Lord Ismay's hand, for cabinet approval. But when he virtually withdrew that plan, to the confusion of Ismay and the cabinet alike, he refused to accept a ministerial visitation, as the cabinet proposed, for that would have undermined his unique personal authority in India, and instead went himself to London, where he persuaded the cabinet in a couple of days to accept his revised plan. It is impossible to believe that the negotiations could have been carried out and the decisions taken as they were in India if the viceroy, like every one of his predecessors since Dalhousie, had been obliged to consult with and seek authority from the secretary of state in Whitehall at every turn. From his first days in Viceroy's House, Mountbatten's Indian visitors – princes and politicians – sensed at once that he was a different sort of viceroy, one who was able and prepared to take his own decisions and responsibilities and act with full powers. Of course it was theoretically unconstitutional, but it worked as probably nothing else would have worked.

I do not intend here to attempt a full analysis of Lord Mountbatten's personality and abilities. It is hard to do so when the subject is alive, and unnecessary when his career and character are so well known. But I want to refer to certain traits which were of special importance in determining his influence on events. They are his self-confidence (associated with an infectious display of energy), his political flair, his readiness to talk (associated with a readiness to change his mind) and his great speed of adjustment and decision in face of changes in events (associated in turn with a certain impetuousness which sometimes led him astray).

Manifestly it needed great self-confidence to go right out on that limb in the first place. Here was the most difficult and momentous task that had faced a British ruler of India since Warren Hastings, and he insisted on taking the whole responsibility himself. He liked the praise and resented the blame but he knew that he would get them both. He took over from a man who was aware of his failure and was seeking only an honourable route of escape. He came to work among British soldiers and administrators who were disillusioned and dispirited. The first among them, the commander-in-chief, Sir Claude Auchinleck, was one who always saw great difficulties and hated what had to be done, though he worked devotedly to overcome both difficulties and disinclinations. Mountbatten brought a sense of dominance over events, an effortless superiority to which no doubt his royal ancestry contributed but which must have been reinforced by the success of his own naval career. It had a tonic effect even among those who were prejudiced against him. On his relations with Nehru and Jinnah respectively it had opposite effects; with the latter, the magnetism that irrestibly drew Jawaharlal to Mountbatten was polarized into a force of repulsion between two would-be masters of destiny.

Mountbatten's confidence helped likewise to mould his relationships with the Indian princes and the heads of the political department which normally handled their affairs on the Crown representative's behalf. I shall come again to the states later, noting here only that Mountbatten never doubted that he could handle their highnesses and the immense problems raised by the lapse of paramountcy, and so the more readily pushed Sir Conrad Corfield and the political department into the background when he felt that they were working not on his lines but for an independent future for the princely states.[1]

I have avoided using words loaded with applause or opprobrium for this quality of Mountbatten's, words like leadership, conceit, courage, egoism, for it is not my purpose here to make moral or personal judgments. But it would be wrong not to mention the physical courage both of Lord and of Lady Mountbatten. His readiness to expose himself to the crowds and to the personal danger which that involved enriched his power both with the political leaders and with the public. The episode in Peshawar on April 28, 1947 was fateful in a more direct fashion. When the viceregal party arrived from the airfield they learnt that there was an immense Muslim League demonstration less than a mile away and about to march on Government House. The situation would be very dangerous, for the local police and troops were quite inadequate to deflect a menacing horde of 70,000 Pathans, and caution counselled retreat while there was time. Instead, Lord and Lady Mountbatten, with the governor, Sir Olaf Caroe, and a small entourage, went out to meet the crowd, and for nearly half an hour the viceroy of India stood on a railway embankment and waved greetings to this mass of frontiersmen until the cries of 'Pakistan Zindabad' changed to 'Mountbatten Zindabad'. It may well have been the turning-point in the Frontier Province away from the civil war which then threatened it.

Mountbatten's personal charm was an adjunct to his political flair but was by no means the same thing. Either quality can exist in public affairs without the other. He knew instinctively who was important and what was important, and did not waste much time on men of little weight or matters of no consequence, though he sometimes followed too far his interest in detail. He handled that strange triumvirate of power in the Congress, Gandhi, Nehru and Vallabhbhai Patel, with discriminating skill, dealing on a philosophical plane with the one, echoing the Mahatma's note of gentle chiding, and basing himself on the tacit assumption that they were seeking the same goal; persuading Jawaharlal with friendly intellectual argument, and recognizing

[1] [Editors' note: cf. Sir C. Corfield, 'Some Thoughts on British policy and the Indian states', below, pp. 530–3.

the Sardar's hard political realism and quest for power. The flair, but not entirely the charm, failed him with Jinnah. Jinnah seems to have admired and respected him, but they never got on terms of understanding. A hard task with Jinnah, one for a lawyer rather than a sailor; for Jinnah was a professional advocate of the first order, and not only used sharp points of constitutional law to back his case but also knew well how to win a case on a weak brief by tactical procedure. Perhaps Mountbatten realized too late the strength of Jinnah's position. I sometimes wonder whether things might have gone differently if the viceroy had accepted from the start Jinnah's purpose of Pakistan as no less valid and right than Nehru's purpose of independence, for both ends were equally implicit in his mandate; in other words had disarmed rather than confronted the champion of the Muslim League.

At any rate Mountbatten did not make the mistake – which many a political figure might have committed – of trying to move the masses below rather than the few at the top. The masses, even if he could have swayed them, could not deliver the goods he needed; only half-a-dozen leaders could do that, and he must keep them on his side, never allowing them to feel he was working beyond or behind them. When a national call to stop violence was needed, he did not make it himself; he demanded and received it of the leaders of the Congress and the Muslim League. He may be excused his failure to pacify the Sikhs because they had no effective political leadership; he dealt successfully with Baldev Singh, but Baldev Singh could not deliver the goods. The real leadership of the Sikhs was multiple, and (apart from state rulers) spontaneous and irresponsible; for a hundred years the Sikhs had accepted British paternal authority, but it was not the viceroy's role to become their father-figure.

It was, I think, an example of political flair, not of deception or evasion, as some in India and Pakistan believed, that Mountbatten so manoeuvred as to have the boundary awards announced on the day after independence. It could have been two or three days before, but why have the hangover before the celebration? For Indians and Pakistanis, no less than for the last viceroy, the day of independence had to be one of triumph, not of lamentation and strife. The awards were out of his hands, and he scrupulously kept them so (a forecast of the probable but not yet determined north-west boundary sent to the governor of the Punjab through the respective private secretaries was unknown to him in substance, though he was aware of its existence a few days before the awards reached him). He could not alter them; their consequences would be what they would be. To postpone their publication for more than a day or two after they were in his hands would have been to expose himself and the political leaders close to him to grave pressures. Political flair told him to contrive not to see them until he judged their publication to be most timely, and this he did.

Mountbatten loved talk and discussion. It was the essence of his method. Often he made up his mind by the process of putting up an idea or a problem to his intimate staff at one of their near-daily meetings, listening and contributing to their arguments, and observing their reactions. Detailed minutes were kept of these staff meetings, and they form a fascinating record of the development of his policies, though it is not always easy to distinguish the *ballon d'essai* from the formed opinion or intention. Let me quote a remarkable example outside the main stream of policy. When the idea of dominion status as the mechanism of independence (with or without partition) began to take hold, it was first thought of as an interim measure, not a total solution. It was therefore a natural assumption that for this interim period the same governor-general would continue in office, though as a constitutional instead of an autocratic vicar-monarch. When the actual plan was promulgated, and partition became certain, the bogey of a divided governor-generalship reared its ugly head. Mountbatten repeatedly said that he would not accept the governor-generalship of one dominion only, and when Nehru and the Indian quasi-cabinet invited him to stay, while no word came from Jinnah, very strong pressure was brought to bear on the latter to accept the same governor-general. Jinnah's decision to nominate himself (he said he could not resist the desire of his colleagues for that course, but no one could believe that in this matter among all others he was not dictator of the League) therefore caused the utmost dismay. Mountbatten's powerful inclination was to refuse the Indian request, for the reasons which he had long embraced, but he felt at the same time that he could not let the Indian leaders down and that his continued presence was really needed in the interest of the country, including that of settlement with the Indian states. In this dilemma, even on so personal and elevated a matter, he debated the problem with his staff. After considerable discussion they broke up and prepared among themselves a memorandum listing in turn the arguments for and the arguments against accepting the single governor-generalship. In the light of after-events the list of adverse reasons, though cogent so far as it goes, is seen to be light or silent on some of the objections that eventually emerged in practice, though the favourable reasons were certainly strong. The staff then voted, and all but one were in favour. Mountbatten was strongly impressed, and on the basis of these pros and cons put his problem to the king and Mr Attlee, both of whom urged him to accept the Indian request, as indeed did Mr Churchill, whose advice was sought through Lord Ismay. It was typical of the way Mountbatten dealt with problems and made up his mind, and sometimes changed it.

My belief is that his inclination to talk matters over rather than take written or formal advice had something to do with his famous 'hunch', as he called it, in showing to Pandit Nehru, in the strictest confidence, the first plan for the transfer of power, which he had recommended to H.M.G., as it had been amended during Lord Ismay's discussions in London. Nehru's hostile reaction caused him virtually to tear it up and frame a new plan, with the invaluable help of V. P. Menon, on the basis of early dominion status. Mountbatten regarded his action as inspired by a flash of premonition, but a man with different inclinations and habits would surely have reacted in a different way to a sudden doubt. Nehru was staying with the viceroy in Simla, and what was more natural for the host than to take his guest into his confidence and talk over what would otherwise emerge as an unalterable *firman?* From that decision sprang immense consequences.

The incident was also typical of Mountbatten's flexibility, agility and speed in face of new circumstances. This characteristic, however native to him, had undoubtedly been fostered by his training and experience as a naval officer and military strategist. The captain of a ship, or a commander in battle, must be ready to react at once to the unforeseen – the unexpected emergency, the miscalculated movement of the enemy, the sudden change in battle fortune. Rapidity not only of decision but also of action may be absolutely vital to the safety of his ship or men or to the gaining of victory or the avoidance of defeat. Apart from political and constitutional decisions (of which the change of plan in early May 1947 was outstanding) the most remarkable examples of this swiftness of action occur in Mountbatten's conduct as governor-general of India after the transfer of power, over the refugee problem and the threat to order in Delhi and over the tribal invasion of Kashmir.

By a strange paradox Lord Mountbatten as constitutional governor-general of independent India exercised more direct executive authority in certain spheres than he had enjoyed as autocratic viceroy. It may indeed be argued that his personal contribution to the determination of history was more decisive after than before the transfer of power.

Let us now, however, turn back to pre-transfer events and consider his role in regard to the Indian states. His Majesty the King had charged him personally with special responsibility in this respect, knowing as he did that the major princes cared deeply for their direct relations with the Crown as monarchy, which they felt lay behind their necessary dealings with H.M.G. and the government of India. Of course Mountbatten's liberty of action in regard to the future constitutional position of the states was strictly limited by the policy laid down by the cabinet mission and incorporated in his own instructions, that paramountcy could not and would not be transferred to successor governments, but would lapse on the demise of British power in India, leaving the states to make their own relationships with the new independent government or governments of former British India. This fact was sometimes forgotten by those who protested that he had let down the states, abandoning them to their fate and failing to establish for them a secure and independent part in the new constitutional structure. If circumstances in India had radically changed – if for instance the major parties and communal leaders in India had been ready to agree on a federal constitution including British India and states similar to that in the 1935 Act but with independent national sovereignty, as a solution to their conflicts and a satisfaction of their demands – then H.M.G.'s policy and the viceroy's instructions could no doubt have been changed accordingly; but one has only to frame that hypothesis to see how remote and indeed inconceivable it was.

Within the terms of reference of the lapse of paramountcy and restoration of constitutional independence to the states, only two broad possibilities were theoretically open. The first was that the major princely states, and groups of lesser states, might form sovereign nations of their own. The second was that they should remain subordinate entities, internationally speaking, retaining as much internal independence as they could but submitting to the successor national governments, by way of treaty or otherwise, in matters like external defence and foreign policy which had long been determined for them by the British power. The two solutions could possibly have been combined; indeed this would have been necessary if the first had been adopted for major states, since the smaller and more fragmented principalities could not in practice all have been incorporated into new princely dominions. But the broad choice was clear, and Mountbatten very soon decided upon the second solution as his policy. There were those in the political department who strongly favoured the first solution [1] and it was because Mountbatten felt that the department was working against rather than for his policy in this respect that he kept them at arm's length and dealt more and more on states matters with the embryo Indian states ministry in the persons of Vallabhbhai Patel and V. P. Menon, than with his political adviser and the department. If one were to restrict one's sources to the viceroy's papers one would get the impression that the standstill agreements and the draft instruments of accession were the work of the former team, rather than the latter, whereas in fact they were drawn up in the political department. But it is, I think, true that the basic policy of inviting prompt signatures of a simple instrument of accession for purposes only of defence, foreign policy and communications was the creature of Menon and Patel rather than the Crown representative's normal advisers.

The main point, in any case, is that the policy of dissuading the princes from any pursuit of independence or separate dominion status and of persuading them to make terms with the new régimes was essentially Mountbatten's. He used all his diplomacy to get Vallabhbhai Patel to agree to treating with the princes on the basis of limited accession, combined with continued possession of their thrones and revenues, when all the momentum of Congress policy was towards overthrow of these monarchies and the appropriation of their powers and wealth for democratic régimes. Patel said his terms for acceptance were 'a full basket of accessions', and this Mountbatten was almost able to give him. Only three apples – two of them very big and the third very awkward – were left out of the basket on August 15, 1947. As late as July 25, 1947, addressing the chamber of princes, Mountbatten said of the draft instrument of accession, 'I must make it clear that I have still to persuade the government of India to accept it. If *all* of you will co-operate with me and are ready to accede, I am confident that I can succeed in my efforts.'

That bargain between Mountbatten and Patel – it was perhaps more a bet than a bargain – demonstrates one of the two basic reasons why the former adopted the policy he did towards the states. It was the only one with hope of acceptance by the political leaders of British India. And an agreed, not an imposed, solution of the problem of ending British rule was the essence of his objective, though he did not shrink on occasion from threatening political leaders with an imposed solution worse from their point of view than the propositions to which he was asking them to agree. This runs right through his policy from March to August. As a realist, too, he knew that after the British had quit as rulers of India there was no hope or possibility of their remaining or returning or intervening to defend régimes which they had left in the states, whatever their past pledges had been. The states would in any case have to bed down sooner or later with the successor nation or nations

[1] [Editors' note: but see Corfield, below, p. 532.]

of former British India, and the sooner they did so the better terms they were likely to secure.

Secondly, Mountbatten repeatedly stressed the risk of Britain's being committed defensively to one part of India as a dominion of the Commonwealth and not to other parts, and the danger of a settlement which would leave the frontier of the Commonwealth running through the Indian subcontinent. For this reason he fenced, not only with princes who pleaded for dominion status or some form of continued treaty association with the British Crown, but also with Jinnah when the latter baited his demand for Pakistan with the offer to remain in the British Commonwealth; for the Indian constituent assembly had already resolved in favour of a sovereign independent republic, which in the thinking of those days automatically meant secession from the Commonwealth. And again in the thinking of those days the Commonwealth was still an association for mutual defence. Whether Mountbatten's approach to the states would have been different if he had foreseen that both the successor states would remain in the Commonwealth may be a matter for speculation. My guess is that it would not, for the argument from political realities would still have been decisive: certainly there was no change of front at all between early June and mid-August 1947, nor did the governor-general give any countenance thereafter to thoughts of Hyderabad or Kashmir becoming independent dominions of the Commonwealth – the two states for whom such a status might have appeared most plausible.

In another respect Mountbatten imparted a personal twist to policy in regard to the states. He often referred to the experience of his own family as a mediatized princely house of imperial Germany. He made no secret of his belief that this example could be applied in India. The principalities, as independent constitutional entities, had become out of date in the modern world of large nation states, but they could still form governmental units and their ruling families could still play a role. This approach may have made him more complaisant than he would otherwise have been towards the pressure tactics employed by the states ministry after the transfer of power to induce the smaller states to merge into unions, the precursor, as it proved, of total absorption into the national constitutional system. But it is doubtful whether a more critical attitude would have done more than slow down the process, once the realities of power asserted themselves in independent India.

That reflection brings me back to my starting point. It is possible to see Mountbatten as one who in a measure deflected, hastened or moderated the course of Indian history in 1947 but in no wise determined it; or he may be seen as a decisive master of major events. The truth lies somewhere in between. He made certain decisions, and pushed through certain policies, which might well have been quite different in the hands of another viceroy given the same facts and forces, and some of these decisions and policies were of great and lasting importance; yet even where his leadership was most crucial he was no Olympian dictator. His character and methods of work were, as I have tried to show, such that he always sought to carry with him those who shared in the formation of policy or would have to carry it out. There were occasions, for instance in his relations with Field Marshal Auchinleck over the Indian

National Army trials or the partition of the army, when this was not easy, even on the British side. The triumphant virtue he claimed for his constitutional plan was not its political perfection but its acceptance by the Indian party leaders. And he was always sensitive to changes in events and in opinion, ready to change his mind as quickly as he often had to make it up. At the same time, his adaptability was joined to an astonishing drive and energy, which carried along both colleagues and critics in India in a sort of slip-stream from which they could not escape even if they would, and which swept and churned minor personalities and events into a frenetic constructive turmoil. When the aircraft had passed into the distant sky and the air was still again, many of them fell back into their old immobile places. But history had been made.

KEEPING THE PEACE IN INDIA, 1946–7: THE ROLE OF LIEUT.-GENERAL SIR FRANCIS TUKER IN EASTERN COMMAND[1]

by MARY DOREEN WAINWRIGHT*

The post-war negotiations between the British government and the Indian nationalist leaders culminating in the final transfer of power in August 1947 took place against a background of general disorder, not at first entirely communal in nature, but after August 1946 degenerating more and more into a state of civil war between the two major communities. Whether or not the administration had lost control, whether or not the British members of the services had become demoralized or indifferent owing to the ending of their careers, has been much discussed, but not seriously investigated. Whether or not the army, given a free hand, could have enforced order, is at present a matter of opinion. But these questions are irrelevant: the administration might have been quite capable of functioning effectively, the army quite capable of imposing order, but the British people and government at home were no longer willing to settle the Indian problem by force. All that could be done by the British authorities therefore was to contain the situation as far as practicable, and to restore order as quickly as possible once disturbance had broken out.

Though the maintenance of law and order was considered by the British in India to be the most important task of government, the nationalist leaders seem to have been singularly unconcerned over such problems, until it became quite impossible to ignore them from August 1946 onwards. Perhaps the bitterness, non-co-operation with the imperial power, and frequent civil disorders of the inter-war years had accustomed the leaders to a state of civil disorder; perhaps it was merely, as has been argued, that violence was a common and accepted part of Indian life; or perhaps leaders such as Nehru and Jinnah were isolated and remote from everyday life and not really aware of what was going on; or perhaps they were just content still to leave such matters to the British. Only Gandhi, who himself had been responsible for much of the pre-war disturbance – for his non-violent demonstrations had frequently led to violence – only Gandhi took practical steps to control the communal violence of 1946–7. And Gandhi's methods were so eccentric and personal to himself, and moreover never tested in any actual context of

[1] This paper could not have been written without the co-operation of the late Sir Francis Tuker, who took a great interest in the work of the partition seminar. He allowed me to consult his personal papers, and discussed the whole episode with me at length. His personal account is contained in his book *While Memory Serves* (1950) which, in spite of its title, was based on documents from command archives and elsewhere. He began collecting his material before independence, and began writing the book before leaving India in November 1947, though most of it was written in England between December 1947 and February 1948.

* Research officer, School of Oriental and African Studies, London.

violence before independence, that it is impossible to judge the extent of his achievement in preventing violent outbreaks. The situation in Noakhali was already under control when Gandhi arrived there, and he did not move on to Bihar until the outbreak there had also been contained. And though he has been given credit, both at the time and since, for preventing an explosion in Calcutta in September 1947, other factors were at work, perhaps of equal or greater importance, and it is impossible to determine how far his methods helped to restore peace. Yet though it is impossible to estimate the effectiveness of Gandhi's efforts to stem the growing tide of communal violence, his concern was obvious to all.[1] Other leaders were absorbed in their constitutional negotiations. The task of maintaining law and order was left to the civil authorities, who in turn came to rely more and more upon the army.

For military purposes India was divided into commands, and this paper is concerned only with eastern command, within which the major communal outbreaks occurred before independence, and with its G.O.C. in C., Sir Francis Tuker. General Tuker was G.O.C. in C., eastern command, from January 1946 to November 1947, engaged in keeping the peace in a huge area of northern India – at its maximum size 1,500 miles wide and 800 deep – with inadequate troops and in difficult terrain. He was not, however, solely concerned with peace-keeping activities. As a military strategist, he was particularly interested in the defence of India in the post-war world, and with its place in the larger context of an Asia seemingly threatened by Russia on the one hand, and by an emergent China on the other. This paper is, therefore, divided into two parts: the first relating to Tuker's role in eastern command, and the second to his plans for the defence of India and for the maintenance of internal peace during and after the period of British withdrawal from the sub-continent.

EASTERN COMMAND, 1946–7[2]

Eastern command in January 1946 consisted of Assam, Bengal, Bihar and Orissa, but in October 1946 the United Provinces were added, and from August 1, 1947 Delhi and the eastern Punjab were also included in Tuker's parish. During 1946, when the whole political and military activity of the command centred round Calcutta, command headquarters were in the Rani's palace at Tollygunge (south Calcutta), but, early in 1947, when political troubles had travelled north and the situation in the United Provinces came to be considered more critical than that in Bengal, headquarters was moved to Ranchi in Bihar.

General Tuker arrived in Calcutta to take charge of the command on January 21, 1946, after a distinguished war-time career in the Middle East and Burma as commander of the 34th Indian Division, later of the 4th Indian Division and IVth Indian Corps. He had been an officer in the Gurkha Brigade from 1914, and like many British officers in the Indian army had a

[1] For Gandhi's role during this period see D. G. Dalton, 'Gandhi During Partition . . .', below pp. 222–44.

[2] This section is based on a number of documents collected by General Tuker and used by him while writing *While Memory Serves*, including confidential and secret reports, intelligence reports and notes, returns, correspondence, with other similar papers.

deep affection for the Indian soldier and peasant, rather less for the Indian politician and townsman. He believed, as many of them believed, that 'he knew the true India better than many of those Indians who spoke for her'. Nevertheless, he rightly conceived his task as a soldier to be to avoid all political entanglements and to confine himself to his military duties. These, in 1946–7, came to mean chiefly 'action taken in aid of the civil power' to help maintain, with a constantly decreasing force and in very difficult circumstances, law and order throughout eastern command.

The army, of course, could not take any action to maintain internal security until called in by the civil authorities. Tuker, however, who was extremely well-served by his intelligence staff, first under Colonel T. Binney and then under Lieut.-Colonel C. E. C. Gregory, and well-informed of conditions throughout his command, made his dispositions in advance of trouble, and himself informally approached the civil authorities when he considered it time for the army to be called in. He was a great believer in strong, even ruthless, action to put down outbreaks of violence before they could get out of control, and he had confidence in his own judgment, not only advising the civil authorities when he thought it necessary to call in the troops, but also refusing troops when he thought, on the basis of his own information, that they were not necessary. This occurred, for example, during the Muslim squatter trouble in Assam in March and April 1947. As the number of troops available for internal security was limited, and inadequate, it was essential to deploy them where they were most needed, and Tuker considered that he was the best judge of that.

Tuker's method of keeping control of the vast area under his command was to send in all available troops to an area where disturbances had broken out, restore law and order as quickly as possible, and then move the troops to those places where he judged that trouble might next be expected. This meant leaving some areas temporarily 'troopless', sometimes to the distress of the civil authorities, who feared outbreaks once the soldiers had moved away. But Tuker had confidence in his information, and backed his judgment, and though he sometimes 'took a chance' he was on the whole remarkably successful in keeping control of eastern command. This was done by anticipating events. All the intelligence received was pieced together, and from it, almost daily, reports were prepared describing the situation throughout the command. From these reports Tuker drew up forecasts of what might be expected to happen next. In addition, he was constantly on the move, making long journeys by air, rail, and by road, in all weathers, to discuss local situations with area commanders and their intelligence staffs.

When Tuker took over eastern command the Burma troops were passing through for demobilization, and at first there were some 300,000 British and Indian troops in the command, although the majority of these were not available for internal security duties. Demobilization continued throughout 1946 and 1947, so that by August of the latter year there were only some 5,000 British army troops in the command (and they could not be used to keep order after independence), in addition to between 120,000 and 140,000 Indians and Gurkhas in the Indian army – and this figure included soldiers stationed at a huge mechanized transport depot who were not available for internal security duties, and about 50,000 non-combatants (women's services, recruits, boys, civilians, etc.). Of the *total* number, about 30,000 were stationed about the time of independence in the two areas of Bengal and Assam, and Bihar and Orissa, while the rest were stationed in the United Provinces, Delhi and the eastern Punjab.

During the period of the disturbances there were not only difficulties caused by this demobilization but the experienced British war-time troops were being replaced by young inexperienced soldiers sent from England to make up the deficiencies in the British regiments in India. And a further difficulty, from July 1947 onwards, was that the Indian troops were in process of being classed into Hindu and Muslim units, making their use for internal security an administrative as well as a communal problem.

There was another factor causing concern to Tuker and his senior officers throughout 1946–7, and this was the fear that the latent communalism in the Indian army would break out, especially if, as was expected, serious trouble overwhelmed the Punjab and those other areas of northern India from which the army recruited most of its soldiers. Reliable and impartial though they might be away from home in Bengal and Bihar, there was a fear that once their own homes and families were threatened, the Punjab regiments would break. The reliability of the men from these regiments was already somewhat suspect, as most of those who had joined the Indian National Army were from Punjab and Sikh regiments. Because of this fear, that communalism would infect the army, Tuker pressed upon the commander-in-chief the necessity for classing the army into Hindu and Muslim units before communal feelings became too fierce. He believed that this could have been done quietly, without causing any alarm, in all the confusion caused by demobilization and the re-forming of regiments.

Tuker was quite convinced that the threat of communalism in the army was a serious one in 1946–7, and that those senior officers who believed otherwise were out of touch with the realities of the situation as it existed in the Indian army at this time. The men were subjected to nationalist propaganda, they read the vernacular press and attended political meetings, and political agitators were at work within the army itself – and politics were communal. To counter all this propaganda 'talking points' were published to all troops from eastern command headquarters, to keep them informed, to put over a temperate view on puzzling matters, and to help retain the confidence of the men in their unit commanders.

Peace-keeping duties in disturbed areas were made more difficult where the soldiers being used were mainly Hindus in a Muslim majority area, or Muslims in a Hindu majority area. They were constantly accused of partiality, and the sometimes fierce attacks upon them in the press had a bad effect on morale. This seemed to Tuker another good reason for classing the army, and siting Muslim units in Muslim areas, and Hindu units in Hindu areas, thus making the task of keeping the peace much easier from a military point of view. He had no doubts about the complete reliability of the soldiers in enforcing law and order, as long as communalism did not infect the army, but obviously the task would be less difficult if Muslim soldiers were putting down Muslim rioters, and Hindu soldiers Hindu rioters.

In the event, communalism did not break out in the army in eastern command, perhaps because Congress propaganda aimed at the forces' discipline declined from mid-1946, but the possibility had always to be borne in mind, adding to the problems of the commander – one more element to be taken into consideration when trying to anticipate and prepare for future incidents. From about May 1947, eastern command felt that it had to be particularly careful about how troops were handled in communal situations, and, when preparing for possible partition troubles, so far as it was possible, Muslim troops were sited in the Muslim areas.

Yet one more circumstance adding to the difficulties of eastern command in the first part of 1946, and causing concern about its effect on the loyalty of the Indian army, was the furore over the Indian National Army, especially the trials of its leaders, aggravated by the presence of the I.N.A. camps near Calcutta. Not only were the British regimental officers alienated from the higher command by the trials, and the returned loyal Indian prisoners-of-war angered and bewildered to find the 'traitors' not merely leniently treated by the army authorities, but held up as heroes by the nationalist politicians and press, but the camps themselves were a constant source of trouble. And once the I.N.A. men had been discharged and returned to their villages they continued to cause trouble in those very districts from which the greater part of the Indian army was recruited. Others were active in Calcutta, particularly among the Sikh community, which had hitherto not taken much part in political disturbances. From the middle of 1946 ex-I.N.A. men were busy in Bengal and the Punjab, and in 1947 they were helping to train the Congress volunteers, the R.S.S. Sangh, and the Muslim League national guard, while in August 1947 ex-I.N.A. Sikhs were active in organizing the attacks of their co-religionists on the Muslims in the Punjab.

But it was particularly in the first part of 1946 that the former members of the I.N.A. affected eastern command. Large numbers of them were held in camps in Bengal, waiting to be dealt with, and their presence had a disturbing effect on a part of the country already seething with political unrest. Their treatment was extraordinarily lenient. Apart from the thirty-six men who were brought to trial for acts of gross brutality committed upon their fellow countrymen, the men were put into camps and there divided into *Whites*, *Greys*, and *Blacks*. The *Whites* (3,880) were exonerated from any act of disloyalty other than that of joining the Indian National Army, received no penalties, and were treated in all respects as recovered prisoners-of-war. The *Greys* (13,211) were considered to have been only lukewarm adherents and to have taken no active part in the movement. They were discharged the service and forfeited all pay for the period when they were prisoners-of-war, and their war gratuities, but were allowed to keep family allowances already paid out and any pensions earned other than during their absence as prisoners-of-war. The *Blacks* (6,177), whose loyalty had been permanently affected and who were considered a danger to security, were dismissed the service, forfeited all pay and allowances (except family allowances) from the date of capture, all gratuities and all pension rights. Tuker thought that the *Greys* should have been re-enlisted in the army, after a period of rehabilitation in segregated communities, otherwise they would go to swell the numbers of disgruntled unemployed men in the villages in that part of the country (the Punjab) where communal tension could be expected to increase. The I.N.A. trials, continuing throughout the first part of 1946, increased the unrest in the camps and added to the troubles of eastern command.

In January 1946 every Indian unit in the command was in a touchy and highly strung condition, and when the first of the serious riots of that year broke out on February 11th Indian troops were not used in the restoration of law and order. Tuker had been attending a conference in Delhi, and only arrived back in Calcutta after the rioting had begun, on the evening of the 11th. The trouble had begun when the Muslims held a protest meeting against the sentence passed on Abdul Rashid of the I.N.A., but soon developed, with the active help of the Sikh community, the Communists, and the criminal elements in the city, into wholesale rioting, arson, and plunder. Military help was asked for on the evening of the 12th, and although rioting continued on the 13th, by the next day the situation had greatly improved, and by the 16th all was normal again.

Tuker learned several things from this riot: firstly, that the police could no longer be expected to control widespread disturbances and therefore the army must be ready to intervene much earlier in any future riots; secondly, that police intelligence had failed – although it was difficult to understand why, if they had had the necessary agents in the right places, the police could not have received earlier warnings of impending trouble – and therefore in future the army must find its own sources of information to obtain the warning of impending trouble which was needed, and not rely on the civil police intelligence system; and thirdly, that for the sake of their morale Indian troops must be used in any future riots. Because only British and Gurkha troops had been used,[1] there was a growing feeling among the Indian soldiers that they were not trusted. Therefore, although fears about the dependability of the armed forces were increasing following the naval mutiny in Bombay and the less serious outbreaks in the Indian air force and in the army itself, Tuker decided to replace the Gurkha battalion in Calcutta with an Indian battalion from Ranchi. There was one case of mutiny in eastern command when in Calcutta, in late February, two of the Indian pioneer units refused to obey orders. The incident was settled quickly and in secrecy: the mutineers were rounded up by British and Gurkha troops at night, to avoid causing trouble in Calcutta, and the leaders were soon afterwards tried by court-martial and sentenced, all without any news of the episode leaking to either politicians or press.

There was no more rioting in Calcutta on the February scale until August, but there were frequent incidents, and every week held its crisis days when the army authorities were prepared for trouble.[2] After the February riots army intelligence had investigated the Calcutta police, and in a confidential report to Tuker stated (with details of cases and sources of information) that although the officers were incorruptible, bribery and corruption amongst

[1] The Green Howards, Yorkshire & Lancashire Regiment, 4/3 Gurkha Rifles, and a composite battalion from personnel in transit, with 1 North Staffordshire Regiment and 25 Gurkha Rifles in reserve.

[2] For the situation in Calcutta during 1946–7, cf. Dalton, below, pp. 222–31.

the inspectors, sub-inspectors, sergeants, and constables was rife, and that the detective department was notorious for bribery and corruption. It was said that during the communal riots some members of the police force made enormous profits for their personal gain by demanding money for rescues. The Punjabi police imported by H. S. Suhrawardy were a particular cause of concern to the army. Knowing, therefore, that the police could not be expected to control serious rioting, the army made its own preparations to meet these 'crisis days' well beforehand.

Two of the 'crisis days' expected in August 1946 were the 9th, the anniversary of the 'Quit India' resolution of 1942, and the 16th, the Muslim direct action day. Tuker, having been called to a conference at Quetta and then to England for discussions, ordered reinforcements into Calcutta at the end of July. These reinforcements consisted of the 7th Worcesters from Ranchi, the 1/3 Gurkhas from Chittagong, and the 3/8 Gurkhas from north Bengal, and they brought the total number of battalions in the Calcutta garrison to nine (four British, and five Gurkha and Indian), plus one artillery regiment. There had been unrest throughout the whole command during July, with strikes in Calcutta, and lawlessness in Bihar, where the police, who had mutinied the previous March, were considered quite unreliable. And throughout Bihar and Bengal the Congress volunteer corps, the R.S.S. Sangh, the forward bloc volunteers, the C.S.P. volunteers, and the Muslim League national guard were all busy drilling and training. Even in the army there was restlessness in the Gurkha regiments, concerned over their future in an independent India. Yet because there had been many crises during the past months neither the civil nor the local military authorities expected any rioting on August 9th or 16th to get out of hand. The worst they expected was a riot comparable to that of the previous February.

Remembrance day, August 9th, passed off peacefully. It was expected that any trouble would be anti-British, affecting a comparatively small area, and widespread picketing by the army proved successful in preventing trouble from starting. Later, during the communal rioting, it was found that this method of control was ineffective, as large areas were left open where murder and arson could be committed unseen, and a combination of patrolling and picketing was then adopted and proved much more effective in controlling a wide area.

The communal riots (later called the 'Great Calcutta Killing') broke out on the morning of direct action day, August 16th. It was unfortunate that not only was Tuker away in England, but the officiating army commander, General F. R. R. Bucher was in Ranchi (from the 12th to the 19th). The officer in temporary command of Bengal and Assam area, Brigadier E. Sixsmith, had been in the Calcutta area for only one month, and very properly took the view that it was for the civil authorities to judge the moment when military aid should be asked for, and when asked for could not be refused. On this occasion the civil authorities delayed calling in the army until the second day of the riots, being apparently unaware of the extent of the butchery, looting and arson going on in the streets and alleys of the city's slums, information which should have been supplied by the police intelligence system. Yet the police cannot be held responsible for the delay in calling in the troops; they asked for military help as early as 2 p.m. on the first day. As a result of this request the governor, Sir Frederick Burrows, accompanied by Brigadier Sixsmith, made a tour of the city. There were crowds everywhere but 'no sign that there had been bloodshed' and the governor decided that the time had not yet come for military aid, although preparations must be made. The official request for military aid was written out and handed to Brigadier Sixsmith, to be used when the civil authorities decided that the police were no longer in control of the situation. The police themselves again urged that the military should be called in immediately. A second drive through the city was made during the evening of the first day of rioting, after which it was decided that the situation still did not warrant the use of troops, and it was not until the early morning of the next day (the 17th) that the troops began patrolling in support of the police. Later they were used effectively to gain control of the worst affected areas, and on the 18th more troops were ordered into Calcutta from Ranchi (the 4/7 Rajputs) and from Ramgarh (the Norfolks). Reinforcements arrived on the evening of the 19th. From August 19th the situation was under control, and all that was left for the army to do was to carry out the terrible task of clearing the streets of the bodies of the victims of the killing. This was done by the men of the Yorkshire and Lancashire regiment, the Green Howards, and the 7th Worcesters, with the help of Indian scavengers, who were paid Rs. 5 for each body found and disposed of. The dead numbered about four thousand.

For the next year troops were hardly off the streets of Calcutta, although the number of battalions in the garrison was reduced because of the call for reinforcements from eastern Bengal, Bihar, and the United Provinces. Between November 1946 and July 1947 the number of battalions in Calcutta varied from four to seven.

After the Calcutta killing it was confidently expected that the next outbreaks would be in East Bengal, and therefore in the third week of August the 1/3 Gurkhas were sent back from Calcutta to Chittagong. During the next six weeks reports received at eastern command headquarters indicated tension in the rural areas, especially in Noakhali and Chittagong, but civil intelligence was completely lacking. On October 2nd the governor of Bengal asked for troops to be sent to Comilla to provide some additional backing for the police there, and a company of the 4/2 Gurkhas was despatched from Calcutta. On October 7th a company of the 1/3 Gurkhas was sent to the Fenny area where there were symptoms of trouble breaking out. Nothing further was heard of any disturbances until the 14th when press reports indicated trouble in the Noakhali district, although the only indication of trouble received by the military authorities were reports of a general nature. On the 16th alarming reports appeared in the Hindu press, and troops were sent into the Noakhali district. Information continued to be scarce and the soldiers were handicapped by bad communications. However, it was found that the statements in the press had been very much exaggerated and the loss of life small, but because of widespread panic among the Hindu minority, who had fled from their homes, sometimes evacuating whole villages, there had been considerable destruction of property. The trouble had been fomented by a gang, including some ex-soldiers, of about one thousand hooligans led by Ghulam Sarwar. The gang had split up into smaller groups of from 150 to 200, which had terrorized the Hindus of the district, extracting money from them by threats of death. The gangs had been joined in the looting and burning of abandoned houses by some local Muslims. Noakhali district had rather a bad reputation for lawlessness and dacoity, and the gangs were exploiting the communal tension. Ghulam Sarwar was arrested and the army quickly gained control, though patrolling and movement were greatly hampered by the natural flooding of the roads and by a general lack of road communication. The greatest problem was caused by the thousands of refugees, for whom the army organized food, medical supplies and clothing, and then tried to persuade them to return home. Relief workers, moved by the press reports, flooded into the country and hindered the work of the military to such an extent that, on October 22nd, General Bucher sent a message to the Bengal government urging the absolute necessity of preventing any further relief workers from moving into East Bengal, and attempts were made to send unauthorized workers home. There were at this time more relief workers than refugees.

The trouble in Noakhali was over by October 20th, but the military remained to keep order for another ten months. For part of this time Gandhi was in Noakhali waging '*satyagraha* against large-scale communal rioting'.[1] His presence there from early November until the beginning of March was a cause of anxiety to the military who feared that he would come to some harm and be the unwitting cause of even greater riots than those which had already occurred: already the troubles in East Bengal had been responsible for a retaliatory outbreak in Bihar, followed immediately by more communal riots in the United Provinces. Naturally the estimates made of the value of Gandhi's activities in Noakhali by soldiers who already felt that they had the situation under control and who felt themselves responsible for his safety, differ from those of his disciples: reports from British officials keeping an eye on Gandhi's progress suggest that his influence was less than has been sometimes claimed. Yet there is no doubt that he brought comfort to the frightened Hindu minority, and that his example was an inspiration to millions in the rest of India.

While Gandhi was still in Calcutta waiting to begin his journey to Noakhali,[2] the grossly exaggerated accounts of atrocities coming out of East Bengal, and their exploitation for propaganda purposes, led to a retaliatory outbreak in Bihar. This time the Muslims were the victims, and the death roll reached seven or eight thousand. There had been disturbances in Bihar off and on throughout 1946, and it was known that the police were unreliable. As early as March General Tuker had been told by the inspector-general of police in Patna that the police would be useless in any trouble, and that the army would have to be used. Soon afterwards there had been a police mutiny. Therefore sufficient troops had been kept in the Bihar and Orissa area to meet any anticipated requirements until August 1946, when, however, reinforcements had had to be sent to Bengal to deal with the Calcutta and Noakhali riots. The depleted forces carried out flag marches in all areas of

[1] Cf. Dalton, below, p. 240.

[2] Gandhi was in Calcutta from October 29th to November 6th.

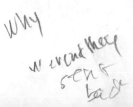

too bad

Why

w went they sent back

Bihar during September and October when outbreaks seemed probable following the Calcutta killing, and peace was kept until the news began coming in from Noakhali. Then Hindu attacks on Muslims began. The first incident was reported on October 27th, but the peak period of the disturbances was from November 1st to 6th. After the latter date the situation was under control, and by the 12th it was possible to discuss the withdrawal of troops.

The difficulties facing the military authorities in this operation were formidable. Not only was manpower limited, but the flooded condition of the country made troop movements difficult. Trains were not available to move troops within Bihar immediately the outbreak began, because they had been used to move troops into Bengal and had then been employed in troop movements within that province. Therefore the troops had to move from Ranchi to north Bihar by road, and because the Bararkar Bridge had been destroyed by floods, this route entailed a long diversion: it took two days to move troops the 280 miles from Ranchi to Patna. Moreover, many DUKWs and their drivers had been sent into East Bengal, and this meant that movement in flooded areas was hampered. In addition to these physical problems of terrain and limited resources, it was, from the army point of view, a misfortune that the governor of Bihar, Sir Hugh Dow, was absent from the province and that consultations had to be carried on directly with the prime minister, Sri Krishna Sinha, and the chief secretary, who were unfamiliar with the technique for employing troops in aid of the civil power. Much time was wasted in discussion. The prime minister objected to the use of British troops, and at the same time pressed for reinforcements, which were difficult to provide owing to the situation in Bengal. He also continued to press on the military commander his own plan, which involved splitting the troops into groups of four to six men, one group to be sent to each Muslim village. Apart from being tactically impossible especially in the flooded conditions obtaining in the countryside, this would have meant finding large numbers of magistrates, as one had to accompany each detachment and be present before the soldiers opened fire. Such troops as could be spared were sent into Bihar from other parts of eastern command, but not enough to satisfy the demands made upon the army by the prime minister and civil authorities. Many calls for aid were made, based on exaggerated and sometimes completely false information, or on rumours which had been unchecked and unconfirmed, resulting in troops being sent to deal with non-existent situations. Moreover the special magistrates hurriedly sworn in, were not very well informed as to their duties with reference to the use of military forces, and the V.C.O.s and N.C.O.s were not at first prepared to take firm and drastic action, although they later did so. They were afraid that after the withdrawal of British officers from India they might be subject to retaliatory measures if they acted too drastically.

Nevertheless, the army brought the disturbances under control in a short time in spite of their wide distribution and the limited military resources. They were helped by the police, who belied their reputation and proved unexpectedly reliable; by the lack of sensational press reports until after control had been effected; and by the influence exerted by Nehru, who with other leaders, visited the disturbed areas. Later the suggestion was made that the attacks on the Muslims of Bihar had been carefully planned by the marwaris of Calcutta, in revenge for the Calcutta killings, but no evidence ever emerged in support of this accusation, and it is more probable that agitators took advantage of the emotions roused by the news from Noakhali.

The last serious outbreak in the eastern command area in 1946 was at Garhmukteswar in the United Provinces, which had been added to the command in October. Large numbers of Muslims were killed by Hindu pilgrims, mainly Jats from about Rohtak and Hissar, followed by a retaliatory killing of Hindu villagers by Muslims. But the affair was minimized by the United Provinces government, and the army was not called in.

As 1946 passed into 1947 there was trouble threatening everywhere in eastern command. Although the prestige of the army was high, many senior officers, including General Tuker, wondered how long it could stand the strain. There was a fear that wide-spread rioting would lead to civil war. It was at this time, January 1947, that Tuker began to make preparations to implement a plan which he had drawn up for action in the event of the complete breakdown of law and order, one of a number of plans drawn up to deal with various possible eventualities. This involved putting down stores of arms and ammunition at pre-determined points along the northern frontier. The supplies were moved up secretly at night by 'reliable' men. In the meantime military tattoos and demonstrations were staged in all the important places of the command throughout January and February. Soldiers were still patrolling the streets of Calcutta, and technicians were standing by to take over essential services affected by the industrial unrest which had broken out in Bengal – seventy-two industrial concerns were either on strike or expected to strike. Infantry was sent to the mining areas. In Bihar the internal defence units were still out restoring the peoples' confidence after the disastrous winter disturbances, but the troops were being gradually withdrawn and by mid-March responsibility for law and order had been handed back to the civil administration.

In spite, however, of the apparently threatening situations in Bengal and Bihar, and the outbreaks of the previous year, Tuker was confident of the ability of the army to keep, or restore, order in this part of his command. This was partly because he had the soldier's contempt for the fighting qualities of the men of Bihar and Bengal, and partly because his intelligence reports convinced him that there would be no outbreaks which could not be brought under control. What he did fear was disaster in the Punjab overflowing into the northern and western United Provinces. He determined that whatever happened in the Punjab he would keep the United Provinces under control, even if it meant taking risks elsewhere by removing troops. The headquarters of the command was moved to Ranchi, and after the British government's announcement of February 20, 1947, Tuker moved troops up into the United Provinces to prepare for the storm which he expected to break out in the Punjab.

During March and April 1947 disturbances continued but there were no riots comparable to those of 1946. Various outbreaks in Calcutta were controlled by the police and troops, and though from April to August there was a chronic situation in the city, there were no serious disorders. In Bihar, after the troops had been finally withdrawn, there were police mutinies, beginning on March 24th, in Patna, Gaya, Monghyr, Jamalpur, Arrah, Chapra, Dharbanga and Jamshedpur. The troops were called in once again and put down the mutiny by April 3rd just in time to deal with communal riots which had broken out in Ranchi town itself. In Assam the government, fearing a Muslim invasion from the Mymensingh district of East Bengal, demanded troop reinforcements. The situation appeared on the surface critical and Tuker flew to Shillong to consult the area commander and his intelligence staff. He decided that there would be no serious trouble in Assam and refused the extra troops. His resources were by now too stretched to waste a single man: all the provincial governments in eastern command, except for Orissa, were relying on the army to keep law and order. There was criminal lawlessness in Noakhali and Tipperah, industrial unrest throughout Bengal, Bihar and the United Provinces, and on May 1st the troops had to take over part of Calcutta.

Political speculation centred round Bengal, and many thought that military attention should be given exclusively to that province, but Tuker was quite convinced that the safety of eastern India depended upon preventing the Punjab contagion from spreading to the United Provinces. There were again riots in the Punjab, and northern command was forecasting that within two months the Sikhs could be expected to start their war of revenge. The soldiers in eastern command were worried about their relatives in the riot areas, and to reassure them, enquiries were made in northern command about the whereabouts of all families from whom the men had not heard for some time. There were short communal riots in the United Provinces, in Agra and Cawnpore, but on the whole peace was kept in that province. General Curtis sent out the troops on flag marches to keep the people mindful of their presence and to give confidence to the police. He was helped by a large body of special armed constabulary: in the United Provinces the police were reliable, and in Lucknow, for example, they never once found it necessary to call in troops throughout the whole disturbed period 1945–7.

As the demands on the army were increasing, its resources were decreasing, because of disbandment and demobilization, and by this time no area in the command could easily spare a man to help its neighbour.[1] However, the situation improved slightly when eastern command was promised a reinforcement of up to one infanty brigade from southern command. Although this brigade was never called upon, Tuker felt that he could take more risks in the movement of his troops, with a brigade to call upon in case of emergency. For as all parties were coming to see that partition was inevitable it was expected that the calls on the army would increase even more.

In May 1947 while waiting for the British announcement, the two communities were busy preparing for what was commonly talked of as the coming civil war. The militant volunteers of the various parties were busy training, the R.S.S. Sangh being particularly active in Bihar and the United Provinces, and the Muslim League national guard in Calcutta, East Bengal and Assam. From various parts of the command came reports of the buying of arms and ammunition. A report on illicit arms in India, prepared in May, concluded that vast quantities of unlicensed arms and ammunition were in

[1] Between April and May 1947 alone total strength dropped by 19,149.

the possession of unauthorized persons, and that in Bengal and the Punjab the accumulation was on a scale beyond the power of the executive police forces and the provincial security authorities to check. In Bengal vast quantities of ammunition had been abandoned by the United States army, in spite of its responsibility to destroy surplus stocks before leaving India, and this had fallen into the hands of the public. In Calcutta there was an illicit traffic in arms from abroad. There had been a certain sale of weapons by military personnel, though eastern command had made strong efforts to check these transactions and from early 1946 had investigated all 'losses'. There was strong evidence that the Muslims of Bihar were obtaining arms from Bengal and that they already possessed a large number of American rifles as well as country-made weapons, and bombs were being manufactured. In the United Provinces there were great numbers of firearms, mostly locally made. In the Punjab arms were easily obtainable, and it was rumoured that the Sikhs had collected stocks of firearms in the gurdwaras of Amritsar, in addition to an armoury of rifles and revolvers which they had amassed in Patiala state. An unconfirmed report stated that an ex-I.N.A. officer was training a group of ex-I.N.A. Sikhs.

While awaiting the announcement expected on June 3rd, Tuker surveyed his command, trying to estimate where trouble would be most likely to break out. He considered the prospect of serious disturbances arising out of any boundary award between Assam and Bengal to be unlikely: neither the Congress nor the Muslim League would be likely to make trouble over the anticipated fate of Sylhet, and Assam might be expected to be glad to get rid of a troublesome Muslim population. In eastern Bengal, despite constant reports of serious trouble impending, Tuker did not expect any serious outbreaks. In Bihar there was unrest and industrial strife, but the police, helped by troops, were in control. The two danger spots were the United Provinces – where in May there were outbreaks in Bareilly, Benares, Cawnpore and Kosi – and Calcutta, which was the immediate problem. The chance of rioting following the June 3rd announcement seemed good, especially if the city were awarded to either community, therefore on May 23rd secret instructions went out for the reinforcement of Calcutta. Other troops were prepared to go to east, west and north Bengal, if necessary. As a further precaution Tuker asked Delhi that no definite announcement concerning the fate of Calcutta should be made on June 3rd, and this assurance was given. On June 2nd the streets of the worst affected areas of Calcutta were thick with soldiers, and there was virtually military government in the city, with thirteen major units stationed there.

With Calcutta under control General Tuker turned to the United Provinces. To block the intrusion into the province of violent bands from the Punjab, he threw out a border cordon, and behind it operated mobile columns to stamp out any outbreaks within the United Provinces itself. There were a few isolated incidents, and nearly 30,000 refugees from the Punjab, many of them Sikhs and a potential source of trouble, flooded into Dehra Dun, but there were no major outbreaks.

In July plans were made to deal with any disturbances likely to break out on or after independence day, which had been fixed for August 15th. To cope with the expected outbreaks on the Punjab boundary a Punjab boundary force was established, and at the end of the month Tuker was asked by the viceroy whether he wished for a Bengal boundary force. He declined it. He thought that it was much more likely that there would be trouble in Calcutta than on the new boundary, but even there he felt that there was a good chance that independence would be greeted peacefully. Communal clashes had become less frequent in Calcutta, the 7,000 Muslim Bihar refugees had already been sent back to Bihar, the senior Muslim police officers were to leave for East Bengal by August 7th, and the 'pestilential Punjabi police' would all have gone by the 6th. There were already large numbers of troops maintaining law and order in the city, and when the civil authorities began to clamour for more, Tuker felt justified in refusing. Independence day passed off peacefully in Calcutta, and afterwards the troops were gradually moved off the streets, until only four battalions remained.

In the last weeks before independence Bengal kept more than usually quiet. The referendum held in Sylhet on July 6th and 7th went off without incident, supervised by two battalions of the Assam regiment, and the troops were withdrawn on July 24th, although remaining on twelve hours notice to move out of their barracks in any direction until after the boundary commission award was published. General Tuker made a tour of East Bengal, and after conversations with officials, both civil and military, decided that there was little fear of any serious outbreaks, and that after August 15th a garrison of two battalions would be sufficient. Therefore on July 12th the Gurkha battalion was moved out of Chittagong, while at the same time a Pakistan battalion, the 2/8 Punjab regiment from north Bengal, replaced the 3/2 Punjab regiment at Comilla. Tuker did not consider it necessary to station a force on both sides of the new boundary. He nominated Major General D. Russell, commander of the 5th Indian Division, to keep an eye on the border, allotting to him for this purpose the 9th infantry brigade. They were to concentrate however at Barrackpore, near Calcutta, where, if, as was confidently expected, nothing happened on the frontier, they could move quickly into the city to reinforce the troops there. There were no riots in Bengal on independence day.

Meanwhile in the United Provinces in the weeks immediately before independence there were a number of outbreaks of violence, but the premier, Pandit Pant, acted decisively in imprisoning the leaders of the riots, and the soldiers kept the situation under control. However, on August 1st Delhi and eastern Punjab were added to eastern command, and the strain on the resources of the command became greater than ever. Troops were sent into the Delhi area and to help the commander of the new east Punjab area, into Rampur to be used against Muslim insurgents, and to deal with the Meo situation which had now come partly within the command's area. It was impossible for eastern command to control the new areas operationally, they were too remote from headquarters, and army headquarters in Delhi took over operational control. The Punjab boundary force was from the beginning under the control of supreme headquarters.

After independence there was a threat of serious trouble in the United Provinces, caused by the influx of refugees from the Punjab, at a time when the number of troops was inadequate to deal with a serious situation, because of the number of units which had been recently sent to the east Punjab. The particular danger was caused by the large number of Sikh refugees wearing kirpans. Early in September the area commander, General Curtis, approached the U.P. government to ask that the wearing of kirpans should be banned. He was supported by General Tuker, but while the situation rapidly deteriorated the government took no action, until finally in the last week of September, Curtis told the cabinet that unless the government took strong measures he personally would impose martial law. He was hardly in a position to do so but the bluff worked and the government itself then imposed measures tantamount to martial law. They banned all kirpans over nine inches, conferred wide powers on the commissioner, Meerut, ordered the segregation of the refugees into separate camps for Sikhs, Muslims and Hindus, and put all the police under military control. As Tuker reported to his successor (November 15, 1947) when he relinquished his command 'it was touch and go in September' until the U.P. government was persuaded to take strong action.

In September too, Tuker faced his last Calcutta riot, but in spite of his spare resources (because of the demands of the United Provinces and the Punjab), the rioting which broke out on September 1st was quickly brought under control, and on the 3rd all was quiet again. Gandhi had been in the city since before independence, having been persuaded to stay while on his way to Noakhali, where he expected violence to break out once more, though, as has been shown above, the military did not. After the first day's rioting he began a fast which was to continue until sanity returned to the city, and which in fact lasted seventy-three hours until the evening of the 4th. Though Gandhi was credited with bringing peace to Calcutta, and Tuker later wrote that 'the Mahatma had been worth two battalions to me', it is impossible to determine how far his fast had any effect on the actual rioting. The troops were already out in the streets restoring order, and the premier, P. C. Ghosh, also acted decisively, letting it be known that the police would shoot to kill if it seemed that one life could save many. Perhaps Gandhi's influence was greater in preventing violence in the future or at least in arousing feelings of shame for past misdeeds, than it was in the actual context of violence.[1]

General Tuker continued to carry out peace-keeping operations until November 1947, when he left India. For almost two years he had been engaged in that duty, of all duties the most disliked by soldiers, of maintaining internal security: and he had been successful. With a constantly decreasing force and in very difficult circumstances and terrain, he had succeeded in controlling the disturbances which had frequently broken out in his command during 1946–7, and, on partition had prevented a disaster in Bengal which might have matched that in the Punjab. At the same time, by suppressing the outbreaks among refugees from the Punjab, he had prevented the Punjab violence from spreading into the United Provinces. There had been no disaster in eastern command to match that in the Punjab.

[1] For Gandhi's Calcutta fast see Dalton, below, pp. 234–8.

GENERAL TUKER'S PLAN FOR THE DEFENCE OF INDIA'S NORTHERN FRONTIERS IN THE EVENT OF PARTITION[1]

Throughout 1946–7 Tuker tried, without much success, to persuade the military authorities, and others, to consider the coming independence of India from the strategical as well as from the political point of view. He had drawn up a plan for the defence of India's northern frontiers and for the maintenance of internal peace after the British withdrawal, in the event of partition, which he thought to be inevitable. This plan would have necessitated the immediate division of the Indian army into Muslim and Hindu units, and this no doubt was the main reason why it was never seriously considered before partition had been accepted politically. And once this had been done events moved too swiftly for the implementation of any long-term strategy. Yet Tuker always believed that had his plan been considered, and adopted in time, it might have forestalled any serious collision in the Punjab, and that, moreover, many of the later differences between India and Pakistan would then never have arisen.

Tuker believed that whatever solution to the independence problem might be found, India must be left with strong external defences, and internal tranquillity, so that she would be able to concentrate on her economic development, free from both external threat and internal discord, and at the same time take her rightful place in the wider context of Asia. A strong, united India would be the key to peace in Asia. This ideal seemed, however, impossible in the conditions obtaining in 1946–7 and Tuker's plan accepted the division of the country while at the same time aiming to ensure that the sub-continent would not be weakened strategically.

When General Tuker returned from Burma at the end of 1945, to an India well on the way to independence, he was so impressed by the growth of communalism during his absence at the war, that it seemed to him to be the one important factor in the situation, overshadowing the independence issue itself. He was particularly concerned at the time with the whole question of achieving stability in Asia and the Pacific, and especially in southern and south-east Asia, and therefore he had hoped that when the British withdrew from India they would leave a strong country, which would then be a major factor making for peace in the region. Now, however he became convinced that when the British left there was every possibility of India plunging into civil war. And therefore, even before taking over eastern command he drafted a plan, purely to clear his own mind, for the defence of India's northern frontiers, concentrating chiefly on the northern and north-eastern borders, rather than the north-west frontier which had always been Britain's major concern, because he believed that in future it would be China, rather than Russia, which would present the greatest threat to the security of India.

Partition of the country seemed to be the only way to prevent the catastrophe of civil war. But partition, unless carefully prepared for well beforehand, could lead to disaster. Instead of one united country there would

[1] This section is based on the two papers sent by Tuker to headquarters in Delhi in 1946, on personal notes written by Tuker, and upon a memoir giving the more personal side of events described in *While Memory Serves*, with various associated papers.

be two antagonistic states, obsessed with their fear of each other, turning their whole attention inwards upon each other, engaged in an impoverishing arms race, yet leaving the strategic northern frontiers unguarded, at a time when, because of the development of new military weapons and techniques, the mountain barrier of the Himalayas could be more easily breached than ever before. The problem as Tuker saw it, was that in an undivided India there would be civil war, leaving the country wide open to attack by external enemies: while in a partitioned India there could equally well be war between the two successor states and an undefended northern frontier inviting aggression, particularly from China. Internal tranquillity was therefore the key to external defence.

After careful consideration Tuker came to the conclusion that it would be easier to enforce and maintain peace within the sub-continent if it were partitioned, than if it were not, if only because neither a Hindu nor a Muslim state would permit lawlessness within its own boundaries to be stirred up by the minority groups which each would inevitably contain. Equally, if planned for well in advance, it should be possible to devise a scheme for keeping the peace between the two successor states, whereas to control a civil war would be much more difficult, needing many more troops: the sites of possible clashes between the two states would be limited and known, the sites of possible outbreaks in the civil war unlimited and unknown. He therefore decided that not only was partition the inevitable political solution, but also that it would be the lesser of two evils and strategically preferable. Two tranquil states would make the defence of the sub-continent easier than would a disturbed and uneasy unity.

Tuker's plan outlined in detail how to secure internal peace and external security in a partitioned India, emphasizing that plans would have to be made and accepted by both communities well in advance of any political decision. This seemed to be the most sensible and safest way of handing over India to independence.

The basic features of Tuker's plan were that the Indian army should be divided into Muslim and Hindu units as soon as possible, that these units should become the nuclei of the independent armies of Hindustan[1] and Pakistan, and that in addition there should be set up an external defence force, primarily to defend the northern frontiers, but available also for peace-keeping duties between the two new states if necessary. His view was that the frontier defence should be a common defence agreed between the two states, but because he did not believe that the two could live at peace with each other at first, nor that all would remain entirely peaceful within each country (because of their minority problems), he suggested that the defence of the frontiers should be undertaken in the first instance by an impartial external defence force, based primarily on the Gurkha battalions of the Indian army. The new states would be bound to be suspicious of each other at first; each would probably have territorial ambitions against the other; Pakistan might be tempted to attack Hindustan with the help of other Islamic states; and if faced with a war on her eastern boundary as a result of Chinese aggression, Hindustan would always fear a Pakistani attack over her open frontier.

[1] Tuker referred to the two states as Pakistan and Hindustan throughout the paper.

This impartial force was envisaged as an interim measure only, until the two new states had settled down peacefully together. Tuker's plan was that in addition to the large Gurkha contingent, there should be included a mixed force of about 10,000 Hindus and Muslims provided by the two states, and that this force should become the nucleus of a joint Hindustan–Pakistan defence force, responsible for the defence of the northern frontiers. This was the long-term objective. The immediate plan was for an impartial force under impartial control. Tuker suggested that this external defence force might be administered by the United Nations, but as it was not known in late 1945 how, or even if, the United Nations intended to organize world security, he expounded an alternative plan of Commonwealth control: the forces should be under an eastern Commonwealth joint staff, on which Great Britain, Australia, New Zealand, Burma and Ceylon would all be represented. This joint staff would arrange external defence with Hindustan and Pakistan, and the forces would be controlled by a British or Commonwealth commander-in-chief. Any British contingent would be limited to a small number of specialists, the force consisting essentially of the large Gurkha contingent, and the smaller Hindustan and Pakistan contingents. The impartial agency would also be used to prevent war between the two states, whose artificial boundaries would provide no sort of natural protection.

Tuker was convinced that both states would realize that it was in their own interest to contribute towards the maintenance of an impartial force, which would keep them safe from external aggression from a foreign state, while at the same time keeping them safe from each other. Their own forces would be used initially for internal security. Tuker wrote: 'My own impression is that so long as national dignity is satisfied and so long as the Commanders are regarded as the servants of the two States . . . political opinion will accept a degree of control . . . over their Defence Services.'

The external defence force should be stationed in 'non-communal' areas where the troops would not become involved in internal politics 'for although we hope that they will not be called upon, yet there is a great possibility that they may have to enter either state in order to restore peace. They must be stationed where they are able to enter without difficulty.' The areas suggested were Baluchistan and part of the north-west frontier, Dehra Dun, Kashmir, and the Assam Hills, with a general reserve and base area at Poona. From these sites the external forces could both enter disturbed areas quickly and look outwards towards the defence of the sub-continent. The British and Gurkha units would gradually 'waste away' and the Commonwealth officers would be replaced by Indians.[1] There would then be a new all-India army which might in the long-term pave the way to a re-unification of the sub-continent.

Both in this paper relating to external defence, and in a second paper written about the same time on 'India's Mongol Frontier', General Tuker stressed the importance of the northern and north-eastern frontiers in the defence of India – he was convinced that China, not Russia, would become the main threat to the sub-continent. This frontier, especially the Himalayan section, had for centuries been regarded as impregnable, but with the coming

[1] Used in the old sense, i.e. officers from both Hindustan and Pakistan.

of air power its strength had decreased and its importance increased; and with the development of nuclear weapons its importance had become even greater. The vital area was the Tibetan plateau, which would be the base for any attempt to conquer eastern India, and it was therefore India's 'prime interest to prevent the military occupation by China of the Tibetan plateau'. China had always claimed Tibet, her influence at Lhasa was greatly increasing, and moreover pro-Chinese Tibetans were infiltrating into Assam, Sikkim and Bhutan. 'There is no doubt that as British influence and power withdraws from India, so will Tibet . . . lean more and more towards China.' Rather than see a Chinese occupation of Tibet, India should be prepared to occupy the plateau herself, for an invasion of India by various routes through Tibet would be quite practicable with modern equipment. The old caravan route from Lhasa through Sikkim, and the 'Diwangiri' route could both be easily made passable for modern transport. For the same reasons it would be essential for India to keep the friendship and even active co-operation, of the peoples of this frontier from Nepal to the Naga Hills, and particularly the peoples of Nepal. The presence of a large Gurkha contingent in the external defence force would help in this, attaching Nepal to the Indian, rather than to the Chinese, interest. 'There is every reason why Nepal should insist that as she holds a great part of the Indian frontier, she should therefore be consulted in India's defence and be allowed to contribute her share.'

Turning to the other frontier, Tuker suggested that from the point of view of wider strategy there would be a certain advantage for Hindustan in having a strong Islamic 'strip' between her and Russian communism. Once the initial period of suspicion between the two successor states had ended Hindustan might be expected to welcome a strong Pakistan helping to protect her from dangers to the north, and allied to other Muslim countries from north Africa to Afghanistan, and even Islamic Malaya and Indonesia. She could concentrate on solving all her many social and economic problems sheltered from the two greatest threats to her security, Russia and China, by a strong and friendly buffer state.[1]

Because internal peace was a necessary prerequisite to successful external defence, Tuker put considerable emphasis in his defence paper on the necessity for classing the Indian army in good time, that is, dividing it into Hindu and Muslim units. He was convinced that communalism would infect the army sooner or later, and that after the British withdrawal it would break up. To prevent this, it would be necessary to separate the Hindus and Muslims in the mixed units well in advance of the date of independence, and site the resulting classed units well away from areas of communal tension, but in positions from which they could easily deal with any trouble which might arise before partition, and with any collision between the two new states after partition. Yet in his view the classing of the army was not merely a device for dealing with the communal problem, but a preliminary to securing the proper defence of the external frontiers, and he would have considered it advisable whether India were partitioned or not.

[1] It should be remembered that in 1945 before the communal rioting of 1946–7 and the post-independence clashes between India and Pakistan this theory would not have seemed as optimistic as it now appears.

Tuker had first considered the advisability of classing at least part of the army for purely military reasons. His experience as chairman of the frontier committee set up in 1944 'to examine and report on the problem of the defence of the North-West Frontier of India, in view of the urgent need to reduce the regular forces employed in the tribal areas', had convinced him that the north-west frontier had in the past absorbed far too many of the resources of the army. In fact frontier military policy had 'led to our being organized, trained and equipped to produce forces mainly for operations in the tribal areas'. The report concluded that the presence of British and Hindu troops was a constant source of irritation to the tribesmen and provoked incidents which then, of course, had to be put down at considerable expense in men and materials: on the other hand if Muslim troops only were stationed in tribal areas the frontier could be kept peaceful at much less cost, and with fewer troops. If only Muslim troops were in future to be used on the north-west frontier, the army would have to be classed to a certain extent: moreover, administratively, class units had considerable advantages – it was easier to recruit for them than for mixed regiments, and easier to feed and clothe them. Nevertheless, a proposal to divide the army on communal lines was bound to be unpopular with many of the British officers of the Indian army whose emotional attachment to the service was such that even to contemplate its division caused them the 'greatest grief'. As an officer of the Gurkha brigade, in which the question of classing did not arise, Tuker was less affected by such sentiment, than were, for example, Field Marshal Auchinleck and Lord Ismay, who moreover disagreed strongly with Tuker on the question of communalism in the army.

General Tuker first drew up his plan towards the end of 1945 as an academic exercise, but when the parliamentary delegation visited India in January 1946, the members spent a day with him, and read and discussed his plan. They were still hoping though to preserve the unity of India and were not prepared to consider seriously any plan based on partition. Tuker later wrote: 'I do not think I impressed any one of them in the slightest.' However, when the cabinet mission visited India the following March Tuker received an urgent telegram from the C.G.S., Sir Arthur Smith, asking him to send as soon as possible his thoughts on the military implications of Pakistan. So he sent his plan along to Delhi, but 'the only use that G.H.Q. and the C. in C. put this paper to was to send a note to the Viceroy (Wavell) to point out how very difficult it would be to defend a partitioned India, whereas [the] paper . . . very definitely points out how far easier it would be to defend a partitioned India than an integrated India filled with discord, provided that one set to work to set up the defence structure in good time . . .' Tuker also had a discussion with Sir Stafford Cripps in New Delhi, during which he stated that in his (Tuker's) opinion India must be partitioned, and if partition came there must be a neutral force to prevent the otherwise inevitable collision on the new frontier between Hindustan and Pakistan. He asked that the Gurkha brigade should be secretly earmarked for this neutral force. However, 'I don't think he was impressed as he was confident that India would be one piece when we left', and indeed in its report the cabinet mission came out strongly against the division of the forces, saying:

'The case for a united defence is even stronger. The Indian Armed Forces have been built up as a whole for the defence of India as a whole, and to break them in two would inflict a deadly blow on the long traditions and high degree of efficiency of the Indian Army and would entail the gravest dangers . . . The two sections of the suggested Pakistan contain the most vulnerable frontiers in India and for a successful defence in depth the area of Pakistan would be insufficient.'

Throughout the rest of 1946 and 1947, whenever he visited Delhi, and in correspondence, Tuker continued to press his views, and especially his conviction of the necessity of classing the Indian army, on the commander-in-chief, Field Marshal Auchinleck, but without any success. His last attempt was made on June 2, 1947, when he asked Lord Ismay to persuade the viceroy (Mountbatten) to accept an impartial force, mainly of Gurkhas, to be made ready at once against the date of partition, to take the collision which was imminent in the Punjab. Ismay replied that Nehru would never agree to such a proposal. Events however were taking over. Already at a meeting of the defence committee on April 25th the decision to divide the army had been made in principle, although it had been decided that no plans for separation should be made until the political decision had been announced. Once the announcement had been made plans were eventually drawn up and the division was carried out smoothly. But collision in the Punjab was not avoided. Whether the Indian leaders could have been persuaded to accept a neutral force stationed along the Punjab boundary, and whether Tuker's Gurkhas could have succeeded in controlling the situation there had they been sent in time, is entirely a matter of opinion. Tuker believed the answer to both questions to have been 'yes': others disagree.

K. N. Chaudhuri argues elsewhere [1] that economic considerations played little part in the political division of India: strategic considerations played even less. Even in military circles at this time, little interest was being shown in strategy, in so far as it related to the external defence of the sub-continent, and such discussion as there was tended to be backward, rather than forward, looking. In the political conditions of 1946–7 there was no chance of a plan for the army being considered solely on its strategic merits. Tuker's plan for the defence of the northern frontiers and for the maintenance of internal security after the British withdrawal went by default rather than by opposition: it was never seriously considered. That was his complaint.[2]

[1] Below, pp. 312–13.

[2] This plan of Tuker's was only one of several which he drew up at various times to cover various eventualities, one of which, to restore order in eastern command in the event of a complete breakdown of law and order, has been mentioned above, p. 137. Another was for the defence of India after the British withdrawal based on a phased withdrawal which would have left the British only on the frontiers. Another zoned the whole command and allocated particular units to particular zones, ready to step in and take over in the event of collapse. And there were others; but as the situation developed from 1945 to 1947, the plan discussed here proved relevant, and, at least, one would have thought, worth discussing.

NEHRU, THE INDIAN NATIONAL CONGRESS AND THE PARTITION OF INDIA, 1935–47

by B. R. NANDA*

I

During the twelve years covered by this volume, Jawaharlal Nehru was one of the foremost leaders of the Indian National Congress, a member of its executive (the working committee) and presided at three of its annual sessions. He exercised a considerable influence on the politics of the organization, but he did not by any means dictate them. In spite of the allegations of its political opponents at the time, the Congress organization was not monolithic, but collective in its leadership. No one individual, not even Gandhi, could bend the Congress to his will without carrying conviction to its leadership and educating its rank and file. The Congress working committee included members who diverged widely in temperament and political convictions, who argued, differed and even quarrelled but finally made up under the compulsion of events or the benign influence of Gandhi.

Nehru's views on the communal problem were clearly thought out and strongly held, but they cannot be explained except with reference to the changing pattern of Indian politics, the pressures operating within and on the Congress and the state of almost continual conflict between the Congress and the government. Nehru did not see the communal problem and the challenge of the Muslim League as a thing apart; the communal issue seemed to him one aspect of the total situation with which nationalist India had to reckon. In this essay an attempt has, therefore, been made to interpret the attitudes and actions of Nehru – and the Congress leadership – to the challenge of Muslim separatism in the context of not only the Congress-Muslim League equation, but of the Congress-Government equation; the latter influenced, aggravated and distorted the former.

II

When the Government of India Bill was being piloted through the house of commons during the winter of 1934–5, Jawaharlal Nehru was in jail and writing his autobiography. 'It is an illusion to imagine', he wrote in this book which was as much a personal chronicle as a political manifesto, 'that a dominant imperialist Power will give up its superior position and privileges unless effective pressure amounting to coercion is exercised.'[1] He quoted with approval the words of Reinhold Niebuhr: 'Since reason is always to some degree the servant of necessity in a social situation, social justice cannot be resolved by moral or rational suasion alone.'[2] In a country without a democratic constitution, 'constitutional' activity had little meaning: it was

* Director, Nehru Memorial Museum and Library, New Delhi.

[1] Jawaharlal Nehru, *An Autobiography* (1958 edition), p. 544. [2] *Ibid.*

synonymous with what was 'legal' which in practice meant the will of the all-powerful executive. Nehru did not therefore set much store by the Government of India Act 1935: it was hedged with too many 'safeguards', checks and balances: it was as if a motor vehicle was to be set in motion in low gear with the brakes on. In the federal legislature, the princely states were to be allotted nearly one-third of the total seats; in the absence of elective bodies, the states' representatives were to be nominees of the princes. Apart from this built-in conservatism of the federal legislature, its powers were severely circumscribed: matters relating to the military, the services and the interest charges, for example, were outside its purview. In the provinces, a wider field had been permitted to ministers responsible to elected legislatures, but even there the governors were invested with overriding and preventive authority in financial and other matters.

These limitations led Nehru to describe the Act of 1935 as 'a Charter of Slavery'.[1] In his presidential address to the Lucknow session of the Indian National Congress in March 1936, he declared that the new constitution offered India only responsibility without power, and therefore, deserved to be rejected 'in its entirety'. Sensing the mood of the party, he did not oppose Congress participation in the elections. But he left his audience in no doubt that he did not expect India's salvation through the new constitution. On the other hand, he pinned his hopes on a 'Constituent Assembly elected on adult franchise and a mass basis. . . . That Assembly will not come into existence till at least a semi-revolutionary situation has been created in the country and the actual relationships of power, apart from paper constitutions, are such that the people of India can make their will felt.' When this was to happen he could not predict, but the world seemed to him in 1936 'too much in the grip of dynamic forces today to admit of static conditions in India or elsewhere for long'.[2]

Though Nehru had agreed that the Congress should contest the elections to prevent politically reactionary elements from capturing the new legislatures, the idea of his party holding office under the new constitution seemed unthinkable to him. 'It is always dangerous', he warned 'to assume responsibility without power even in democratic countries; it will be far worse with this undemocratic constitution, hedged in with safeguards and reserved powers and mortgaged funds where we have to follow the rules and regulations of our opponents' making. . . . The big thing for which we stand, will fade into the background and petty issues will absorb our attention and we shall lose ourselves in compromises and communal tangles and disillusion with us will spread over the land.' [3]

Nehru's distrust of the Act of 1935 and of British intentions stemmed not only from the clauses of that Act, but from what he and the Congress had gone through at the hands of the government. The government of India under Lord Willingdon had waged a total war on the Congress, jailed its members by the thousand, sealed its offices, frozen its funds, choked its publicity media, and tried to crush it for once and all.[4] All this could not

[1] J. Nehru, *India and the World* (1936), p. 86.
[2] *Ibid.* [3] *Ibid.* p. 91–2.
[4] For details, see B. R. Nanda, *Mahatma Gandhi* (1958), pp. 332–44.

but leave a bitter taste in Nehru's mouth. Early in 1936 he confessed to Lord Lothian:

'I feel a certain hesitation in meeting people who have been officially associated with the Government of India during the past nightmare years. That period is full of horror to us and it is very difficult for me to understand how any sensitive person could tolerate it, much less give his approval to it. It is not so much the repression and suppression of much that was best in India that I refer to, but the manner of it. There was, and is, in it an indecency and vulgarity that I could hardly have conceived. And the wonder of it is that hardly anyone in England realizes this or has any idea of what is happening in India's mind and heart.' [1]

III

'The real problem before us', Jawaharlal Nehru had told the Lahore conference in December, 1929, 'is the conquest of power; and the withdrawal of the army of occupation and economic control by Britain.' [2] Seven years later, he held the same opinion. He was convinced that the communal problem had been over-rated and over-emphasized both by the government and vested interests in the two countries.[3] He himself was remarkably free from religious passion and prejudice. His father, Pandit Motilal Nehru had defied Hindu orthodoxy, employed Muslim clerks and servants, and avowed his love of Persian classics and Urdu poetry. Both father and son cherished Muslim friends and colleagues. Indeed they were often accused of being objectionably pro-Muslim. A Hindu Mahasabha leader went so far as to describe Jawaharlal Nehru as 'English by education, Muslim by culture and Hindu by an accident of birth'.[4] The fact is that Jawaharlal was a rationalist and a humanist, and did not view cultural conflict in twentieth-century India in the same way as the leaders of communal parties did. The real struggle seemed to him not between Hindu and Muslim cultures, but between these two cultures and the conquering scientific culture of modern civilization. 'I have no doubt personally,' he added, 'that all efforts, Hindu or Muslim, to oppose modern scientific and industrial civilization are doomed to failure and I shall watch this failure without regret.' [5] 'The communalism of today,' he told an English correspondent, 'is essentially political, economic and middle class.' [6] Of this communalism he had a good glimpse in 1928 when he helped his father in drafting the report of the all-parties conference, which came to be known as the Nehru report. He saw how upper-class politicians both Hindu and Muslim, with little contact with the masses, or appreciation of the social and economic issues, wrangled endlessly over the distribution of seats in legislatures and jobs under the government, which in any case could benefit only a tiny minority. It was a crazy political arithmetic in which

[1] Jawaharlal Nehru to Lord Lothian, December 9, 1935.
[2] *Congress Presidential Addresses, 1911–34* (Natesan), 2nd ser. p. 893.
[3] J. Nehru to Lord Lothian, January 17, 1936.
[4] Rafiq Zakaria (Ed.); *A Study of Nehru* (1960), article by N. B. Khare.
[5] J. Nehru, *An autobiography*, p. 470.
[6] J. Nehru to Lord Lothian, January 17, 1936.

majorities in legislatures (such as in the Punjab and Bengal) wanted to be protected, minorities asked for weightages, and rival claims of Muslims, Sikhs, Scheduled Castes and others were irreconcilable. The protagonists of these claims had one eye on the unity conference they were attending and the other on Whitehall or the Viceregal Lodge, the repositories of real power and patronage. This had led Motilal Nehru to lament at the Calcutta Congress in December 1928: 'It is difficult to stand against the foreigner without offering him a united front. It is not easy to offer a united front while the foreigner is in our midst domineering over us.'

Jawaharlal had thought deeply on the causes of the communal deadlock that frustrated the Nehru report and blocked the Round Table conference, and came to the conclusion that the political bargaining and haggling could not take the country far, because 'whatever offer we make, however high our bid might be, there is always a third party which can bid higher and, what is more, give substance to its words. The third and controlling party inevitably plays the dominant role and hands out its gifts to the prize of its choice.' [1] It was only by visualizing a political structure without the British, and an economic structure oriented to the needs of the masses rather than to those of the upper and middle classes, that the communal problem could be lifted out of the grooves in which it had been stuck. This was the reason why Nehru was attracted to the idea of a constituent assembly elected on adult franchise to draw up the constitution of free India. By 1936 he had won over Gandhi and the Congress to this solution of both the political and communal problems. The demand for the constituent assembly figured prominently in the Congress election manifesto.

IV

After the Lucknow Congress, Nehru was intimately concerned with the preparations for election campaign. There was not much time to lose. The Congress working committee constituted a parliamentary board consisting of a number of national leaders and of presidents of all the provincial Congress committees. The parliamentary board met on July 1, 1936 and elected an executive committee of eleven members with Vallabhbhai Patel as president and Rajendra Prasad and G. B. Pant as secretaries. The burden of planning the election campaign and guiding the provincial committees fell on this executive committee.

Though most of the restrictions on its activities had been withdrawn, the Congress organization was still illegal in the whole of North West Frontier Province, and in parts of Bengal. Elsewhere, it was not difficult to see that official sympathy – if not active support – went to parties opposing the Congress. In Nehru's home province, the United Provinces, the governor and high British officials had encouraged the formation of the 'National Agriculturist Party' in which Hindu and Muslim landlords combined to oppose the Congress.[2] In December 1936, the chief secretary to the U.P. government reported to the government of India: 'Though the National

[1] J. Nehru, *An Autobiography*, p. 137.
[2] C. Khaliquzzaman, *Pathway to Pakistan* (1961), p. 153.

Agriculturist Party do not appear to be functioning very effectively . . . they are concentrating on and strengthening their personal influence, relying on friendly visits and the feudal tie. The latter still seems fairly powerful and the Congress are not likely even in districts where their forces are strongest to have a walk-over.' [1]

Nehru was aware of the fact that the Congress was anathema to the official world. In September 1936, he came across a copy of a circular letter from the secretary of the court of wards, Allahabad to all district officers advising them that it was 'essential in the interests of the class which the Court of Wards represents, and of agricultural interests generally to inflict as crushing a defeat as possible on the Congress with its avowed socialistic principles. To this end it is of the utmost importance to avoid to the greatest extent practicable a split in the landlord vote, and a consequent dissipation of the voting power of the elements opposed to the Congress'.[2] It was after reading this letter that Nehru issued a statement to the press on September 18, 1936: 'The real contest is between the two forces – the Congress as representing the will to freedom of the nation, and the British Government of India and its supporters who oppose this urge and try to suppress it. . . . Let this position be clearly understood by our people as it has been understood and acted upon by the Government. For the Government, there is only one principal opponent – the Congress.' This statement was directed not against the Muslim League – which later was to make much play with it – but against the government. It is noteworthy that Nehru had described the contest as between 'two forces', not between 'two parties'. What he was stating was the obvious truth: the Congress represented the main anti-imperialist force in India.

It was in this election that Nehru revealed for the first time his tremendous stamina and ability as a campaigner. During the eight months preceding the elections, he covered over 50,000 miles by railway train, motor car and aeroplane, addressed thousands of meetings and came into direct contact with about ten million people.

His labours and those of his colleagues were well rewarded. The Congress won clear majorities in Bihar, U.P., C.P., Madras and Orissa. In Bombay it came out as the largest party; in Assam and N.W.F.P., it gave a very good account of itself. Nehru's own assessment of election results was given in a letter to Sir Stafford Cripps on February 22, 1937. 'Remarkable as this election victory has been,' Nehru wrote, 'the really significant feature of the election campaign has been the shaking up of the masses. We carried our message not only to the thirty million and odd voters but to the hundreds of millions of non-voters also. The whole campaign and the election itself have been a revelation of the wide-spread anti-imperialist spirit prevailing throughout the country. It has made clear the class cleavages among the people. The big landlord class and other vested interests were ranged against us. They were swept away in the flood, their most determined opponents being

[1] U.P. Government Fortnightly Report on the Political Situation for the first half of December 1936, Government of India Home Department File 18/12/36 Pol.

[2] Circular No. K-70/C.W.886/34 dated July 9, 1936 from Secretary, Court of Wards, U.P. Allahabad to all District Officers in the U.P., except Kumaun.

their own tenants. This class cleavage is very apparent in the comparison between the elections for the Provincial Assemblies (Lower Houses) and the Provincial Councils (Upper Houses). In the former the franchise was low and the electorates were large, the average constituency having as many as forty to sixty thousand voters. In the latter, the franchise was a high property one and the electorate was very small, usually some hundreds. In the Assembly elections we carried all before us and our majorities were prodigious.... In the Council elections we fared badly (though even here we won a few seats). The election made it perfectly clear that the wider the mass appeal, the greater was our success.'

Nehru acknowledged that the Congress had not done so well in Muslim constituencies:

'Partly this is due to our own timidity as we ran few Muslim candidates. The burden of running over a thousand candidates (in the general constituencies) was great and we did not wish to add to it. If we had run more Muslim candidates, I trust we could have had a fair measure of success, especially in the rural areas.... It is true that the Muslim masses are more apathetic. They have been too long fed with communal cries.... Even these Muslim masses are getting out of the rut of communalism and are thinking along economic lines. Equally significant is the change that is coming over the younger generation of Muslims. These young people are definitely cutting themselves away from the old communal ways of thought. On the whole I think that the communal position is definitely brighter. The Hindu communalists have been largely swept away by the Congress and they count for little.[1] The Muslim communal leaders still function, but their position weakens, for they have no reply to the question of poverty, hunger and unemployment and independence that their own people put to them. They can only think in terms of jobs for the upper classes.'

In the light of later history, it may seem that Nehru's optimism was premature, but early in 1937, Nehru had good reasons to hope that the Muslim intelligentsia and masses were acquiring keener consciousness of economic issues: he himself had done much to sharpen this consciousness.

The U.P. government had indeed been alarmed by the impression that Nehru was beginning to make on the Muslim community and even on avowedly loyal elements. Commenting on Nehru's tour of the western districts, which had a sizable Muhammadan population, the U.P. government reported to the government of India in September 1936:

'What the tour makes evident for the first time in this province is the remarkable hold that Mr. Nehru has obtained on the popular imagination. He has in fact become Mr. Gandhi's successor as the popular leader. That the Municipal Board, Cawnpore, constituted with what was regarded as a strong anti-Congress majority, should have taken the lead in presenting him with an address was not perhaps extraordinary in view of Hindu feeling in urban areas; but it is remarkable that the Muslim Chairman of the Meerut District Board, a leader of the National Agriculturist Party, who was justifiably proud of his success in

[1] The Hindu Mahasabha did not win a single seat in the U.P. Legislative Assembly.

routing the Congress party at the local elections, should find it necessary to read an address to the arch-enemy of his party and class. Lawyers and businessmen who would be the first to suffer if Mr. Nehru achieves his objects, which he makes but little attempt to disguise, joined in doing him honour....'[1]

In his 1500-word survey of the election results to Cripps, Nehru did not so much as mention the Muslim League. Evidently in February 1937, Nehru had a low opinion of the League, but his opinion was not different from that Jinnah himself is reported to have expressed a year earlier. According to Khaliquzzaman, Jinnah told him in February 1936 that the Muslim League 'consisted mostly of big landlords, title-holders and selfish people who looked to their class and personal interests more than to communal and national interests and who had always been ready to sacrifice them to suit British policies'.[2] It is true that Jinnah had promised Khaliquzzaman that he would reform the League, of which he had been virtually a permanent president for twenty years. To the average observer in 1937 the composition of the League did not seem to have changed much: the titled gentry, the khan bahadurs, the nawabs and the gallant knights still occupied important positions in it; former Congressmen like Khaliquzzaman, who had recently switched their allegiance to the League, were in a small minority and regarded with a little suspicion by the colleagues as well as by the government. It is true that the League manifesto in 1936 had expressed some progressive views, but so did almost every other party. Neither the composition nor the past history of the League raised hopes of its capacity to pursue a radical course on political and economic issues.

After the elections the question of office acceptance was fiercely debated in the Congress party. It was argued that if the Congress abstained from forming ministries, conservative elements, favoured by the government would step in. Gandhi's opinion seems to have tilted the scales in favour of office acceptance. The Mahatma himself had no ambition to be a legislator or a minister, but he wondered whether with all its limitations, the new constitution could not be used to improve the lot of the people in India's villages: to encourage village industries, ensure a clean water supply, and a cheap and nutritious diet, reduce the burdens on the peasantry, promote the use of home-spun cloth and extend education. Those who opposed office acceptance – and Nehru was one of them – felt that nothing much could be got out of the new constitution, and that the Congress would have to bear the odium for the apparatus of imperialism without securing a real relief to the people. As a compromise between the two opposing groups it was decided by a convention of Congress members of the provincial legislatures, and of the All-India Congress Committee held on March 18, 1937, that the Congress should form ministries provided the leader of the Congress party in the provincial legislatures was satisfied and was able to state publicly that the governor would not use his special powers of interference or set aside the advice of ministers 'in regard to their constitutional activities'. This assurance the

[1] U.P. Government Fortnightly Report on the Political Situation for the first half of September 1936, Government of India Home Department File 18/9/36 Pol.

[2] C. Khaliquzzaman, *op. cit.* p. 141.

governors seemed unwilling to give. Official spokesmen took the line that the governors could not contract themselves out of the terms of an Act of Parliament or instrument or instructions issued to them. The government called upon other parties in the legislature to form *interim* ministries. 'It is clear now,' Patel wrote to Nehru on March 29th, 'that there is going to be no Congress ministry anywhere'.

Not until June 22, 1937 did the viceroy issue the statement which became the basis for acceptance of office by the Congress. The 'assurances' given by the government were not very explicit, but it was evident that much would depend upon the strength and discipline of the Congress parties. The political situation was fraught with a great deal of uncertainty. No one could say in the summer of 1937 how the Congress would hit it off with the British bureaucracy, which until recently had been its arch enemy. The long record of antagonism between the two was not likely to be erased overnight. The Congress approach to office acceptance was, therefore, marked by a measure of caution and reserve. Nehru and his colleagues were apprehensive that in the peculiar conditions of India, 'parliamentary activities' could lead to demoralization and division in a nationalist party. In the 1920s, Motilal Nehru, his tremendous personality and prestige notwithstanding, had been unable to stop the rot in the Swaraj party; some of his adherents had succumbed to official blandishments and communal pressures. Strong and disciplined parties in the provincial legislatures were therefore, a necessity if the Congress was not to lose its character as a militant national party.

It is important to remember this background when reviewing the negotiations between the Congress and the Muslim League in the U.P. for the representation of the latter in the provincial cabinet. The crucial question in these negotiations was not whether the U.P. cabinet should have one or two representatives of the Muslim League,[1] but whether the provincial cabinet, after the induction of the League members, would be able to maintain its cohesion. Nehru's own part in these negotiations was small. Soon after the elections he had one of his rare spells of ill-health which made him less active than usual. He was of course consulted by Abul Kalam Azad (who conducted the negotiations on behalf of the Congress) but the decision did not really rest with Nehru. Indeed G. B. Pant, Rafi Ahmed Kidwai, K. M. Ashraf, P. D. Tandon and other members of the U.P. legislature exercised as much influence, if not more, on the ultimate result of the negotiations. The most important consideration with the provincial Congress leaders, as with Nehru, was that if the Muslim League with its landlord support came into the cabinet, the Congress programme for agrarian reform, particularly the abolition of *zamindari*, would be jeopardized.[2] That this fear was not groundless is proved by the stubborn opposition of the Muslim League to land reform in the U.P. during the years 1937–46.[3]

[1] As suggested in Abul Kalam Azad's *India Wins Freedom* (1959), p. 161.

[2] Ramnarayan Chaudhary, *Nehru in His Own Words* (1964), p. 87.

[3] Sajjad Zaheer, a young left-wing Congress Muslim in 1937, has recorded that he pleaded with Abul Kalam Azad 'against any kind of compromise with the Muslim League, which in our view was a reactionary organization . . . ridden as it was at the time with jaded Muslim landlords and Nawabs . . .'. Quoted from 'Notes on Hindu-Muslim Unity', *Mainstream*, June 17, 1967.

Khaliquzzaman and Nawab Ismail Khan may have honestly felt that they could co-operate with the Congress in 1937; but it is doubtful if they would have been permitted to do so by the League leadership. On April 25, 1937, Khaliquzzaman and his friends were taken to task by the working committee of the U.P. Muslim League parliamentary board for their flirtations with the Congress.[1] Early in May, the committee of the Bombay Provincial Muslim League, with Jinnah in the chair, appealed 'to the Muslim member of the U.P. Legislative Assembly who had been elected on the League ticket not to act in such a way as to cause disunion among Muslims of India by arranging sectional or provincial settlements with the Congress'.[2] 'We shall face the challenge of the Congress', Jinnah declared, 'if they think that the Muslims will accept their policy and programme, because our policy and programmes are different in vital respects.' [3] A couple of days later, Jinnah visited Lucknow to assert his authority over the provincial party. He was reported to have rebuked Leaguers, who 'talked loosely of cooperating with the Congress', and affirmed that 'for the time being they would join hands neither with the Congress nor with the Government, but wait till they had gained strength by organizing the Muslims'.[4]

Such a minatory posture on the part of the League leader was not calculated to reassure Congress leaders that a coalition with the League was workable. Indeed, in the negotiations for an understanding between the League and the Congress in Bombay, the Congress was willing to let Jinnah nominate two members of the provincial cabinet. But his conditions were such as the Congress could not accept. According to K. M. Munshi (with whom Vallabhbhai Patel and Abul Kalam Azad were staying in Poona when Jinnah's terms were received) the 'position would have been that Mr. Jinnah would have dictated the whole policy (of the Bombay cabinet) through one or two of his nominees who would threaten to resign at any moment they chose. . . . Such terms would have imposed the dictatorship of Mr. Jinnah over every Congress Government in the country.' [5]

The Congress could not afford to make its first experiment in ministry-making vulnerable at the very outset. The party position in the U.P. legislature did not suggest any urgent need for or the inevitability of a coalition with the Muslim League.[6] In 1937 it was difficult for it to foresee how the equation

[1] *The Leader*, April 28, 1937.

[2] *Ibid.* May 6, 1937.

[3] *Ibid.*

[4] *Ibid.* May 9–10, 1937.

[5] Interview with the writer, October 18, 1966.

[6] Total strength of U.P. Legislative Assembly was 228, as given below:

General (including 20 seats reserved for Scheduled Castes and 4 for women)	144
Muhammadans	66
Anglo-Indians	1
Europeans	2
Indian Christians	2
Commerce	3
Landholders	6
University	1
Labour	3
Total	228

The state of parties in U.P. Legislative Assembly in 1937 was as follows:

Congress	134
National Agriculturist Party	29
Hindu Sabha	0
Muslim League	26
Liberal	1
Independent Hindus	8
Independent Muslims	24
Independent Christians	2
Europeans and Anglo-Indians	4
Total	228

with the government would work out. For nearly four months (March–June 1937) there seemed little prospect of the Congress being able to form ministries. Indeed in April 1937 – after the introduction of the new constitution – the government of India at the highest level was considering the prosecution of Jawaharlal Nehru for the speeches he had delivered during the election campaign.[1] Even after the formation of the ministries in July, the Congress was not sure how far it would be allowed to carry out its programme, in such matters as release of political prisoners and radical economic reforms. In these circumstances it is not difficult to see why the Congress should have been reluctant to admit the Muslim League (whose leader emphasized fundamental differences in outlook and programmes between the two organizations) into partnership in the U.P. without ensuring that the cohesion of the cabinet would be maintained.

V

Whatever the merits of the coalition controversy in U.P., there is no doubt that the events of 1937 had a tremendous, almost a traumatic effect upon Jinnah. The tide of provincial autonomy had come and gone and left him high and dry. The real tragedy was not the failure of his party to secure two seats on its own terms in the U.P. cabinet; but the collapse like a house of cards of the assumptions on which he had conducted his policies for twenty years. He had pinned his hopes on separate electorates and on organizing Muslims on a separate political platform, on the formation of as many Muslim-majority provinces as possible by 'redrawing provincial boundaries', and on weighted representation for Muslims in provinces where they were in a minority. His 'Fourteen Points' had been practically conceded in the new constitution. But all these safeguards had not yielded the fruits he had hoped from them. In the Muslim-majority provinces where indeed the Muslim League could legitimately have hoped to be voted to office, it had met with an electoral disaster of the first magnitude. In the Sind legislative assembly the League had won three seats, in the Punjab only one, and in the North-West Frontier Province none at all. In Bengal it had won a third of the Muslim (and one-sixth of the total) seats in the legislative assembly, but it did not occupy a commanding position even in that province. Party alignments in Muslim-majority provinces had cut across religion; Sir Sikandar Hyat Khan in the Punjab, Fazlul-Haq in Bengal, and Sir Ghulam Husain Hidayatullah in Sind had not responded to Jinnah's appeal for 'Muslim unity', and seemed to be swayed by personal, and class interests rather than by religious affiliations. The Muslim electorate had failed to vote the League to office in the Muslim-majority provinces; in the Muslim-minority provinces the League's performance was hardly less disappointing. It did not win a single seat in the lower houses of three provinces, Bihar, the Central Provinces and Orissa. Only in two provinces it did well winning 27 out of 64 Muslim seats in the U.P. and 20 out of 29 Muslim seats in Bombay. And it was only in these two provinces that the possibility of a coalition was seriously explored.

[1] Notes in the Home Department, Government of India File 4/10/37 Pol.

In the summer of 1937 Jinnah was faced with the stark fact that his party scarcely figured on the political map of India under the new constitution. While Gandhi and Nehru and the Congress leaders could guide and control six (and later eight) provincial ministries, there was not one ministry he could call his own, or in the formation of which he had a say. And it may have seemed that Jinnah could do little about this situation until the next round of elections. He was however not the man to let history pass him over his head. 'In politics,' he once said, 'one has to play one's game on the chess board.' [1] He made a masterly move calculated to achieve through a propaganda blast what the ballot box had denied him.

The by-election to the Jhansi, Jalaun Hamirpur Muslim seat in the U.P. gave an inkling of the new strategy. In this by-election the Muslim League simply raised the cry of 'religion in danger'. Nehru was shocked by this unabashed exploitation of religious feeling; even the appeal issued by Jinnah in support of the League candidate did not contain a single reference to political and economic issues. Nehru begged Jinnah not to import religious emotion into politics:

'The leaders of the Muslim League have issued many . . . leaflets and appeals. I have read some of these, but in none of them have I found any reference to a political and economic issue. The cry raised is that Islam is in danger, that Non-Muslim organizations have dared to put up candidates against the Muslim League. . . . Mr. Jinnah has capped the sheaf of Muslim League leaflets and statements by his appeal in his capacity as the president of the Muslim League. He appeals in the name of Allah and the Holy Koran for support of the Muslim League candidate. Mr. Jinnah knows well that many eminent Muslims including leaders of the Jamiat-ul-Ulema like Maulana Hussain Ahmed are supporting the Congress candidate. Have they ceased to be Muslims because of this? . . . To exploit the name of God and religion in an election contest is an extraordinary thing . . . even for a humble canvasser. For Mr. Jinnah to do so is inexplicable. I would beg him to consider this aspect of the question . . . It means rousing religious and communal passions in political matters; it means working for the Dark Age in India. Does not Mr. Jinnah realize where this kind of communalism will lead us to ?'[2]

Nehru wrote to Khaliquzzaman, the U.P. League leader who was his fellow-prisoner during the non-co-operation movement, protesting against the electioneering tactics of the League. Khaliquzzaman in his reply deplored these occurrences but explained how candidates had to proclaim themselves 'to be as good and pious Muslims as their opponents . . . and all the religious zeal of the belligerents must be brought into play to carry the electorates with them'.[3] This was an eloquent commentary on the effect of separate electorates on Muslim politics, particularly at election time, and on the difficulty of posing concrete political and economic issues to the electorate. The by-election was a pointer to the new strategy which unfolded itself at the Lucknow session of the All-India Muslim League in October 1937. Not even

[1] *Star of India*, December 31, 1938.
[2] Press statement, Allahabad, June 30, 1937.
[3] C. Khaliquzzaman, *op. cit.* p. 175.

three months had passed since the Congress had formed ministries, but Jinnah was already proclaiming that Muslims could 'not expect any justice or fair play at their hands. The majority community had clearly shown their hand that Hindustan is for the Hindus. The result of the present Congress party policy will be, I venture to say, class bitterness and communal war.' [1] There had not yet been time to circulate 'atrocity stories', but the League leader was warning his co-religionists: 'There are forces which may bully you, tyrannize over you and intimidate you . . . but it is by going through this crucible of fire of persecution which may be levelled against you . . . a nation will emerge worthy of its past glory. . . .' [2] Writing in the British-owned *Pioneer*, a Muslim observer noted the heated atmosphere at the Lucknow meeting of the League. 'The doctrine of aloofness was preached *ad nauseam* in a most unrestricted and irresponsible language. Out of the clouds of circumlocution and confusion arose the cry of Islam in danger. The Muslims were told that they were disunited and about to be crucified by the Hindus. Religious fervour was raised to a degree when it exhibited itself in blind fanaticism. In the name of Muslim solidarity Mr. Jinnah wants to divide India into Muslim India and Hindu India.' [3]

Conscious humility had rarely characterized Jinnah's public utterances, but from the summer of 1937, they acquired a new edge of bitterness. Referring to Nehru in a press statement on 26 July he said: 'What can I say to that busybody President (of the Congress). . . . He seems to carry the responsibility of the whole world on his shoulders and must poke his nose into everything except minding his own business.' [4] Commenting on a statement by Gandhi, he said: 'A more disingenuous statement it would be difficult to find, coming from Gandhi, and it is a pity it comes from one who is a votary of truth.' [5] The Mahatma, Jinnah jeered on another occasion, was the 'oracle of Delphi'.[6] Light had not dawned upon Sewagram. Gandhi was groping in the dark; he had designs to 'sabotage and vassalize the Muslims under the Hindu Raj'.[7] The Congress was trying to 'encircle' and 'annihilate' the Muslim nation. For Muslim nationalists, who did not follow Jinnah's lead, the harshest epithets were reserved. Abul Kalam Azad was denounced as a 'puppet president' of the Congress,[8] Muslims differing with League programme or policies were guilty of the 'grossest treachery' and 'betrayal' and stabbing their co-religionists in the back. Indian Muslims were warned to beware of 'Muslim agents of the Hindus' and 'Muslim agents of the British'. In spite of the not-too-recent discomfiture of his party at the polls, Jinnah was arrogating to himself the right to speak on behalf of the hundred million Muslims of India: 'When I say hundred million I mean that 99 per cent of them are with us – Leaving aside some who are traitors, cranks, supermen or lunatics.' [9]

When Nehru returned after a brief visit to Europe in 1938, he was struck

[1] Jamil-ud-din Ahmad, *Some Recent Speeches and Writings of Mr. Jinnah* (1946), p. 30.
[2] *Ibid.* p. 40.
[3] Dr Mahmudullah Jung in the *Pioneer*, November 7, 1937.
[4] Jamil-ud-din Ahmad, *op. cit.* p. 25.
[5] Jamil-ud-din Ahmad, *op. cit.* p. 122.
[6] *Ibid.* p. 225.
[7] *Ibid.* p. 154.
[8] *Ibid.* p. 428.
[9] *Ibid.* p. 567.

by the similarity between the propaganda methods of the League in India and of the Nazis in Germany: 'The League leaders had begun to echo the Fascist tirade against democracy . . . Nazis were wedded to a negative policy. So was also the League. The League was anti-Hindu, anti-Congress, anti-national. . . . The Nazis raised the cry of hatred against the Jews, the League [had] raised [its] cry against the Hindus.' [1] The denunciation of democracy as a form of government, the right of a racial minority to blackmail and disrupt the state, the claim by sub-national groups to self-determination, the reiteration of wildly exaggerated and usually fictitious 'atrocity stories' – were the common coinage of German propaganda in 1937–8 and to all appearances the Nazis were earning good dividends from this propaganda. If the Sudetan Germans could embarrass the Czech majority and dismember the state of Czechoslovakia, could not the Muslim minority do the same to the Hindus in India? At a meeting of the Sind Muslim League provincial conference in October 1938, Abdulla Haroon, the chairman of the reception committee warned the Hindus that 'if the League's demand was not conceded, Czechoslovakian happenings would find an echo in India as well'.[2] The warning was repeated by Jinnah. S. Wazir Hasan, a former chief justice of Allahabad, who had presided over the 1936 session of the All-India Muslim League, warned Nehru of 'the propaganda of misrepresentation, lies and religious and communal hatred not only between Mussalmans and Hindus, but also between Mussalmans and Mussalmans' which had been started in the Lucknow session of the League.[3]

VI

Nehru was shocked by the propaganda of the League, but he did not take long to realize its explosive possibilities. When riots broke out in Allahabad in April 1938, he rushed to his home-town and helped to restore peace. He urged the U.P. Premier Pant not to spare any official, high or low, who was guilty of partiality in communal riots. Nehru knew that the communal temperature had risen not because of local grievances but through the political heat generated by the League. He tried to remove misunderstanding by opening correspondence with Jinnah; and explaining to him Congress attitudes and policies. Jinnah's response was cold, formal, legalistic. At the same time Nehru wrote to Nawab Muhammad Ismail, the U.P. League leader, at great length to clear doubts on such general questions as the mass contact movement, the national anthem and the national flag which had become the targets of League criticism.[4] The Congress mass-contact movement, he told the nawab, was not directed against the Muslim League; it had never been thought of in terms of Muslims alone, nor was it confined to them. The Congress had worked among the Hindu masses and 'disabled the Hindu Mahasabha politically'; it had done effective and successful work among the Christian masses of the south, the Parsis, the Jews and the Sikhs. The *Bande*

[1] Dorothy Norman, *Nehru The First Sixty Years*, vol. ii, pp. 344–5.
[2] *Star of India*, October 15, 1938.
[3] S. Wazir Hasan to Nehru, February 11, 1938.
[4] Nehru to Nawab Muhammad Ismail Khan, February 4 and 5, 1938.

Mataram song, Nehru recalled, had first become popular during the agitation against the partition of Bengal when it came to be regarded by the British as a symbol of sedition. From 1905 to 1920, the song had been sung at innumerable meetings at some of which Jinnah himself was present. The Congress flag had taken its birth during the days of the Khilafat movement and its colours had been determined to represent the various communities: saffron for Hindus, green for Muslims and white for other minorities. Had not Maulana Muhammad Ali, the Khilafat leader delivered scores of speeches on the 'national flag' as representing the unity of India? As for the Wardha scheme of basic education, it was no diabolical plot against Muslim children; it had been devised by two eminent Muslim educationists, Zakir Husain and K. G. Saiydain, to substitute a co-ordinated training in the use of the hand and eye for a notoriously bookish and volatile learning which village children unlearned after leaving school.

The Congress leaders were distressed by the widening of the communal rift and discussed all aspects of it from the choice of Muslim ministers to that of a national anthem. How far the Congress leadership was prepared to go to soothe Muslim feelings is shown by the fact that a sub-committee went into the question of the national anthem and on its recommendation, it was decided that out of deference to Muslim susceptibilities, only the first two stanzas should be sung on ceremonial occasions.

Not content with making general allegations, the Muslim League brought forward charges of cruelty and tyranny against Congress ministries: the *Pirpur Report* and *Shareef Report* listed these charges in highly coloured language. Some of the allegations in these reports were discussed in provincial legislatures; some were enquired into by British officers and refuted in press communiqués. The Bihar government issued a detailed (and as Professor Coupland described it)[1] a reasoned reply to the *Pirpur Report*. Nevertheless, the charges continued to be repeated against the Congress ministries by Muslim League politicians and newspapers. Nehru vainly appealed to Jinnah to agree to an impartial enquiry. Rajendra Prasad suggested an enquiry by Sir Maurice Gwyer, the chief justice of the federal court: this suggestion was not accepted by Jinnah on the ground that the matter was under his excellency the viceroy's consideration. Later, in December 1939, Jinnah called for a royal commission, a demand which the British government were hardly likely to concede in wartime and for raking up such a controversy.

'It has been our misfortune', Nehru wrote to Jinnah on December 14, 1939, 'that charges are made in a one-sided way and they are never inquired into or disposed of. You will appreciate that it is very easy to make complaints and very unsafe to rely upon them without inquiry.'

While isolated acts of petty tyranny by local officials may have occurred in remote villages and towns in Congress (as well as in non-Congress) provinces, the theory of a concerted tyranny directed against the Muslim community in the Congress provinces in 1937–9 would be difficult to sustain. It is important to recall that during these years nearly half of the members of

[1] R. Coupland, *Indian Politics, 1936–1942* (1944), p. 187.

the I.C.S. were still British.[1] They occupied almost all the key appointments in the secretariat besides holding charge of important districts. Almost all the inspectors-general of police were British,[2] and so were most of the police superintendents. There was a fair sprinkling of Muslims and Christians in the I.C.S. and in the Indian police, and Muslims were well-represented in the middle and lower ranks of the police. It is also a significant fact that there is hardly any evidence in the records of the home department of the government of India to support the theory of a *Hindu raj* in Congress governed provinces. Law and order was of course a provincial subject, but the channels of communication between the viceroy and his colleagues in the executive council on the one hand, and the British governors and chief secretaries on the other, had not dried up.[3] It is impossible to believe that deliberate ill-treatment of the Muslim minority could have gone on unnoticed and unrecorded by the representatives of the *raj* even in their confidential correspondence.

That the Muslim League should have thrown cold water on proposals for holding judicial inquiries into its allegations against the Congress ministries is understandable. The League was not trying to convince the British or the Hindus: its propaganda was meant for 'home consumption', for the Muslim community; in this aim it attained a remarkable success. The spectre of a *Hindu raj* roused the deepest fears of the Muslim intelligentsia; religious emotion was worked up to a high pitch; political and economic issues receded to the background. The effect of this propaganda was felt not only in Hindu majority provinces, but in the Muslim majority provinces where the Muslim League had cut no ice in the 1937 elections.

At the Patna session of the Muslim League (December 1938) a threat of direct action was held out against the Congress and even the soft-spoken Sir Sikandar Hyat Khan, the premier of the Punjab, offered to join this agitation. 'Such an offer', Nehru wrote to Sir Sikandar, 'by a Prime Minister of a provincial government is unusual and if seriously meant, likely to lead to grave consequences.'[4] In adopting this heroic posture, Sir Sikandar may have been swept off his feet by the over-heated atmosphere at Patna, but it is not unlikely that he was acting under the impulse of self-preservation. He was aware of the deep religious feeling which was being roused among his co-religionists and of the fact that with its help the Muslim League could cut the ground from under his feet in the Punjab. Sir Sikandar had therefore no objection to joining in the tirade against the Congress if in return he was left alone in his own province. Similar considerations seem to have influenced

[1] 'In 1938, of the members of the I.C.S. serving in the Provinces, 490 were British and 529 were Indians.' R. Coupland, *Indian Politics, 1936–1942*, pp. 118–19.

[2] Of the eight inspectors-general of police who attended the home minister's conference in May 1939, only one was Indian.

[3] The viceroy in a white paper stated in October 1939 that the Congress ministers had conducted their affairs 'with great success'. For details see Cmd. 6121.

Compliments to the Congress ministers' administrative ability and general impartiality were paid by Sir Harry Haig, governor of the United Provinces, 1934–9, in an article entitled 'The United Provinces and the New Constitution', in the *Asiatic Review*, July 1940, and Lord Erskine, Governor of Madras, in an article entitled 'Madras and the New Constitution' in *Asiatic Review* (January 1941).

[4] J. Nehru to Sir Sikandar Hyat Khan, January 4, 1939.

Fazlul-Haq, the prime minister of Bengal who had been at first unresponsive to Jinnah's overtures.

Nehru and his colleagues in the working committee were distressed by the League's propaganda which was bound to provoke a reaction from Hindu communal groups. As president of the Congress Nehru had tried, and so had Subhas Chandra Bose after him to open negotiations with Jinnah. Neither of them could proceed beyond the preliminary stage. Jinnah insisted that before the dialogue started, the Muslim League must be recognized as the sole authoritative organization of Muslims. This was a novel demand; it had not been raised earlier, when Jinnah had discussed the communal award with Rajendra Prasad who was Congress president in 1935. At that time he had insisted that the agreement with the Congress should also be endorsed by the Hindu Mahasabha.[1] From 1937 onwards, Jinnah branded the Congress as a Hindu organization and denied its right to speak for any other community. The Congress was of course not a homogeneous organization and included in its ranks members of different communities as well as different schools of thought. The divisions in the Congress, however, were not on religious lines. If the Congress was to accept Jinnah's condition and accept the status of a communal body, what was it to do with the hundred thousand Muslim members on its rolls, with the Christians, the Jews, the Sikhs and the Parsis who had served it devotedly for long years? And what was to be done about trade unions, peasant unions, chambers of commerce, employers' associations and others which cut across communal lines, and looked up to the Congress for political leadership?

In retrospect it would seem as if this pre-condition for the recognition of the Muslim League as the one and only organization of Muslims was laid down by Jinnah to avoid coming to the negotiating table. In March 1938 when Nehru had urged the League leader to spell out the demands of the League, all that he could do was to refer Nehru to the 'Fourteen Points' and to an anonymous article in *The Statesman* dated February 12, 1938, another article in *The New Times* of March 1, 1938 and to a statement by M. S. Aney, the Nationalist party leader. The fact is that almost all the political demands of the Muslim community embodied in the 'Fourteen Points' had been practically conceded in the constitution which had come into force in 1937, and Jinnah had no concrete demands to make. This interpretation is supported by the confession of Khaliquzzaman that if the negotiations between the Congress and the League had really got off the ground during the years 1938–9, he (Khaliquzzaman) 'wondered what positive demands we could have then made. The Communal Award had been conceded. There was no demand by the Hindu community for its abrogation after 1936. . . . Both Nawab Ismail Khan and I were at a loss to find any substantial radical demand on the Congress to satisfy us and our community.'

So the interesting fact emerges that during the years 1937–9 while the Congress ministries offered the handiest peg on which the Muslim League could hang its grievances, it had really no political demands to make on the Congress.

[1] Rajendra Prasad, *India Divided* (1946), p. 155.

VII

The brief partnership between the Congress and the government which the installation of Congress ministries in eight provinces had begun, ended with the outbreak of world war in September 1939.

Thanks to the lead given by Nehru, the Indian National Congress had consistently and emphatically expressed its sympathy in favour of the allies and denounced every act of aggression by Japan, Italy and Germany. Nehru who had visited Europe in 1936 and 1938 had reacted strongly against the make-believe policy of the 'appeasement' period. When the war broke out, he was touring China. He hurried back to India and declared that in the conflict between democracy and freedom on the one hand and fascism and aggression on the other, 'our sympathies must inevitably be on the side of the democracy. . . . I should like India to play her full part and throw all her resources into the struggle for a new order.' [1]

The Congress working committee met soon afterwards and offered its co-operation in the struggle against fascism but it was to be 'a co-operation between equals by mutual consent for a cause which both considered to be worthy'. This was in Nehru's view, the only honourable course for the Congress to adopt. How could India hold aloft the banner of freedom and democracy in Czechoslavakia or Poland while she was herself in bondage? Apart from the moral aspect, there was an important and practical consideration. Wars were no longer bouts between professional armies in distant battle-fields; whole nations had to be mobilized as workers or soldiers; unless Britain could release India's energies by treating her as equal partner in a common struggle, it was hardly possible for her to play her full part in the world struggle.

What was required in the autumn of 1939 was a little imagination and a little courage: these qualities were not forthcoming from the government of India headed by Lord Linlithgow and the British government headed by Neville Chamberlain. The viceroy had made the blunder of issuing a declaration of war on behalf of India without any kind of consultation with Indian opinion. He tried to make up for this omission by inviting Indian leaders to meet him, but he had precious little to tell them. During the early weeks of the war, Linlithgow was extraordinarily cautious; he seems to have been lulled into a false sense of security by the 'phoney war'. In his assessment of the political implications of the war, he lagged behind even the India Office. He under-rated the gravity of the international situation and misread the mood of the Congress. The Congress plea for a declaration that after the war Britain would concede Indians 'the right of self-determination by framing their own constitution through a Constituent Assembly', left him cold. Nor was he willing to let the Congress and other political parties have an effective participation in the administration at the centre. It had never been the British policy in the past (he told the secretary of state) 'to expedite in India constitutional changes for their own sake or gratuitously to hurry the handing over of controls to Indian hands'.[2] The continuing discords between

[1] V. P. Menon, *Transfer of Power*, p. 60.

[2] Lord Linlithgow to Lord Zetland, December 28, 1939 quoted in Zetland, '*Essayez*' (1956) p. 277.

the communities he thought, would strengthen Britain's hold on India for many years.[1] Among the minorities and special interests which stood in the way of accepting the Congress demand, the viceroy listed not only 'the great communities of India' but European business interests and the Indian princes.[2] As he went through the interminable negotiations with numerous parties and individuals, it was obvious that he was finding arguments for maintaining the political *status quo*.

'The same old game is played again,' Nehru wrote to Gandhi 'the background is the same, the various epithets are the same and the actors are the same and the results must be the same.'

Having failed to receive a response from the government, the Congress decided to call out its ministries in eight provinces. The suspension of the provincial part of the constitution was a serious step, but to the British officials in Delhi it may not have been entirely unwelcome; unhampered by the politicians they could now concentrate upon beating the Germans.

The Congress had realized at an early stage of the war that it could flare up at any time and envelop India. The old issues had suddenly become outdated. The crisis called for new initiatives. It was this feeling which had led the Congress working committee to invite Jinnah to attend its first meeting after the outbreak of the war in September 1939. Jinnah did not of course avail himself of the invitation, but Nehru wrote to him on October 18th after learning from a common friend that the Muslim League leader seemed to be in a co-operative mood. Nehru made as cordial an overture as he could: 'I entirely agree with you', he wrote, 'that it is a tragedy that the Hindu–Muslim problem had not been settled in a satisfactory way. . . . With your goodwill and commanding position in the Muslim League a solution should not be difficult as people imagine . . . for after all the actual matters under dispute should be and indeed are easily capable of adjustment.' He begged Jinnah to join the Congress in protesting against India being plunged into the war, without her consent. He appealed to Jinnah's patriotism: 'Our dignity and self-respect as Indians has been insulted.' For once Jinnah seemed interested and even cordial, but he did not commit himself to any course of action, and agreed to continue the conversations.

There were good reasons for Jinnah to adopt this posture. The war had created a new situation; the Congress and government were drifting apart but there was still a possibility of a *modus vivendi* between them. It was only when the talks between the government and the Congress broke down that he showed his hand. In December 1939 just when Nehru was preparing to leave for Bombay to meet him, the League leader called upon Indian Muslims to observe December 22nd as a 'Day of Deliverance' from the Congress ministries, 'from tyranny, oppression and injustice during the last two and a half years'. The aggressiveness of this gesture left Nehru gasping, but it took many people including members of the League by surprise. Some observers felt that Jinnah had overshot his bolt, and that his extreme tactics might even cause a split in the League.[3]

[1] See R. J. Moore. 'British Policy and the Indian Problem 1936–40' above, pp. 79–94.

[2] Gwyer and Appadorai, *Speeches and Writings on the Indian Constitution*, vol. ii, p. 492

[3] Report from the U.P. Government to the Government of India, January 5, 1940, Government of India, Home Department File 18/12/39 Pol.

Jinnah's statement on the 'Deliverance Day' was a vitriolic attack on the Congress party; after reading it Nehru could not bring himself to meet the League leader. He began to wonder if there was any common ground between them at all. Nehru's heart was set on political independence and a socialist society, and the instrument of the new order was to be a constituent assembly elected by the people on the basis of adult franchise.

To Jinnah, the proposal for the constituent assembly seemed wholly utopian. 'It is puerile', he said 'to ask the British Government to call a Constituent Assembly of another nation and afterwards to have the honour and privilege of placing the Constitution framed by this supreme assembly of India on the Statute Book of the British Government.' [1] On social and economic problems Jinnah spoke rarely but he had no sympathy with Nehru's radical economics: 'All talk of hunger and poverty', he declared, 'is intended to lead the people to socialistic and communistic ideas for which India is far from prepared.' [2]

VIII

By December 1939 it was clear to Nehru that Jinnah would neither settle with the Congress nor embroil himself with the government. What Nehru did not quite forsee was Jinnah's ability to turn to his advantage the growing rift between the Congress and the government. The observance of the 'Deliverance Day' had created a new gulf between the League and the Congress. Three months later, the Lahore session of the League in March 1940 made the gulf wider. It was at this session that the League resolved that 'no constitutional plan would be workable in this country or acceptable to the Muslims unless it is designed on the following basic principles, viz. that geographically contiguous units are demarcated into regions which should be so constituted, with such territorial readjustments as may be necessary, that the areas in which the Muslims are numerically in the majority as the North Western and Eastern zones of India should be grouped to constitute "Independent States" in which the constituent assemblies are autonomous and sovereign.'

The 'Pakistan resolution', as it came to be known, gave a new twist to the communal problem. All the solutions hitherto thought of – separate electorates, composite cabinets, reservation of posts – suddenly became out of date.

Twenty-seven years after the passage of this resolution and twenty years after the emergence of Pakistan as an independent state, it is difficult to realize that it came as a bomb-shell not only to the Congressmen, but to almost everyone outside the inner circles of the Muslim League.

Nehru's immediate reaction was that 'all the old problems . . . pale into insignificance before the latest stand taken by the Muslim League leaders at Lahore. The whole problem has taken a new complexion and there is no question of settlement or negotiations now.' Nehru was not alone in reacting sharply to the League's new stand. Gandhi described the two-nation theory as 'an untruth', the strongest word in his dictionary. Rajagopalachari called

[1] Jamil-ud-din Ahmad, *op. cit.* p. 126.
[2] *Ibid.* p. 36.

it 'a mediaeval conception' [1]; Abul Kalam Azad described it 'meaningless and absurd'.[2] Sir Sikandar Hyat Khan, [3] premier of the Punjab and Sir Ghulam Husain Hidayatullah,[4] the premier of Sind, rejected the idea of partition of India outright. Khan Abdul Qaiyum, who was later to be a lieutenant of Jinnah, declared that 'the Frontier Province will resist [partition of India] with its blood'.[5] Syed Habibul Rahman, a leader of the Krishak Praja party said the proposal was not only absurd, chimerical and visionary but 'will for ever remain a castle in the air . . . the Indians, both Hindus and Muslims, live in a common Motherland, use the offshoots of a common language and literature, and are proud of the noble heritage of a common Hindu and Muslim culture, developed through centuries of residence in a common land, There is no one among Hindus and Muslims who will be prepared to sacrifice all this in order to accept what is demanded by Mr. Jinnah.' [6]

'For the moment', wrote *The Manchester Guardian*, 'Mr. Jinnah has re-established the reign of chaos in India.' [7]

In the spring of 1940, most serious observers of the Indian scene would have described the Pakistan plan as 'chimerical and impractical', words used by prominent Muslim witnesses before the joint parliamentary committee in August 1933.[8] Even after the Pakistan proposal had been embodied in a resolution of the All-India Muslim League, it was no more than a political phantom. It was left to the spokesmen of the British government to give it body and soul.

We know now that in March 1939, two Muslim League politicians, Khaliquzzaman, and Abdul Rahman Siddiqi met Lieutenant-Colonel Muirhead, the under-secretary of state, and Lord Zetland, the secretary of state for India, and received the impression that if the proposal for a separate Muslim state in the north-west and east of India was put forward the British would 'ultimately concede' it.[9] This impression was conveyed to Jinnah and may have influenced him in formulating the Pakistan demand in 1940. There is also evidence to show that Jinnah took the viceroy into his confidence and mentioned the Pakistan resolution to him several weeks before the League held its Lahore session.[10] In private the viceroy may have described the Pakistan proposal as an extreme and 'preposterous claim', which had been put forward for 'bargaining purposes', but he did more than any other person to lend to it the air of feasibility which was needed before it could gather support even among the Muslims. In his long-awaited public statement of August 8, 1940, the viceroy included a remarkable passage:

> 'It goes without saying that they [His Majesty's Government] could not contemplate the transfer of their present responsibilities for the peace and welfare of India to any system of government whose authority is directly

[1] *The Hindu*, March 27, 1940.
[2] *Ibid.* April 8, 1940.
[3] *The Tribune*, September 11, 1940.
[4] *The Hindu*, April 17, 1940.
[5] *The Tribune*, March 29, 1940.
[6] *The Hindu*, April 4, 1940.
[7] *Manchester Guardian*, April 2, 1940.
[8] A. Yusuf Ali, Ch. Zafarullah and Dr Shuj-ud-Din, cited in Rajendra Pradsad, *India Divided*, p. 207.
[9] C. Khaliquzzaman, *op. cit.* p. 211.
[10] *Ibid.* p. 234.

denied by large and powerful elements in the Indian national life nor could be a party to the coercion of such elements into submission to such a government.'

Evidently this passage had been included out of deference to Jinnah.

It is a curious fact that the Indian National Congress had to agitate for thirty-two years before securing Edwin Montagu's declaration of 1917 about 'responsible government' being the goal of British policy in India. Another twelve years had to elapse before the phrase dominion status was used with reference to India. But it took the Muslim League exactly four and half months to secure an indirect endorsement of a novel – and in the light of Indian constitutional evolution until 1940 – of a drastic doctrine for the solution of Indian constitutional problem.

A further encouragement to the Pakistan proposal came in the speech delivered by Amery, the secretary of state in the house of commons:

'The foremost among these elements stands the great Muslim community, ninety million strong and constituting a majority both in north-western and north-eastern India, but scattered as a minority over the whole sub-continent. In religious and social outlook, in historic tradition and culture, the difference between them and their Hindu fellow countrymen goes as deep, if not deeper than any similar difference in Europe. . . .'

These two statements by the viceroy and the secretary of state were later cited by Jinnah as 'solemn pledges' on the part of the British government endorsing the two-nation theory and Pakistan.[1] The viceroy and the secretary of state could not have been unaware of the implications of the League's demand. But they had their own reasons for not antagonizing the Muslim League. On the very day the August offer was announced by Lord Linlithgow, he had signed a secret letter to the governors informing them of the plans which had been perfected in the home department of the government of India for a knock-out blow at the Congress, 'a declared determination to crush that organization as a whole'.[2] Having written off the Congress, the viceroy and his advisers could hardly resist the temptation of backing up its principal opponent. 'Some British officials', says Hugh Tinker, 'welcomed this [Pakistan] plan as a means of checkmating Congress demands.'[3] Testimony has been borne by at least one League leader to the support received from senior British officers[4]: it is difficult to say how far this support was due to their affinity with the Muslim Leaguers whose loyalty had never been in doubt, and with whom they could meet on friendly terms, and how far to their antipathy to the khadi-clad, vegetarian, jail-going Congressmen who were the avowed enemies of the British *raj*. In 1940 many of these British officers may not have troubled themselves about the merits of the proposal for the partition; it was enough for them that there was little chance of other parties accepting the proposal, that the political deadlock was likely to last indefinitely, and that the only alternative was the continuance of British rule.

1 *Dawn*, March 23, 1946 and Jamil-ud-din Ahmad, *op. cit.* p. 443.
2 B. R. Nanda, *Mahatma Gandhi*, p. 440.
3 Hugh Tinker, *Experiment With Freedom*, p. 24.
4 C. Khaliquzzaman, *op. cit.* p. 257.

IX

The circle of mistrust between the Congress and the government which had begun with Linlithgow's declaration of war in September 1939 was to be completed with the passage of 'Quit India' resolution by the All-India Congress Committee in August 1942. It was borne in upon the Congress leaders during the first two years of the war that the British government, headed by Winston Churchill in Britain and by Linlithgow in India was reluctant to pledge itself to Indian freedom after the war, or to take the Congress and other political parties into effective partnership during the war. All that the Indian National Congress was offered was membership of advisory committees and seats in the viceroy's executive council without effective voice in the administration. This was a passive role which a militant nationalist party with twenty years of struggle behind it, could not accept. It could hardly sit back with folded hands and be a spectator of events while the future of nations was in the melting pot. Pressures began to build up within the Congress for a mass civil disobedience movement. Gandhi resisted these pressures as long as he could and then diverted them into the relatively innocuous channels of 'individual' *satyagraha.* This was conceived as a token protest without seriously embarrassing the war-effort, but nearly 30,000 prominent Congressmen courted imprisonment during the years 1940–1. A certain complication arose at this time because of Gandhi's firm faith in non-violence and his refusal to countenance anything but non-violence even against external aggression. Gandhi's pacifism was not, however, shared by Nehru or indeed the majority in the Congress working committee. On two occasions, after the fall of France and the entry of Japan in the war, when a 'National Government' for vigorously prosecuting the war seemed to be on the cards, Gandhi did not stand in the way of his colleagues and stepped aside to let them co-operate with the government, if honourable terms were forthcoming. In the beginning of 1942, as the Japanese swept everything before them in south-east Asia, and eastern India came perilously close to the theatre of war, a section in the Congress led by Nehru, Azad and Rajagopalachari felt that it was time to mobilize national resources to the utmost for defence against Japan.

The critical war situation had also its impact on the British war cabinet, and resulted in the despatch of Sir Stafford Cripps to India. His 'Draft Declaration' was a great step forward in so far as it recognized India's right after the war to frame a constitution through a constituent assembly. The basic demand of the Congress had been conceded but it was vitiated by certain provisions introduced out of deference to the Muslim League, the Indian princes and perhaps the British Tories. This clause in the draft declaration laid down that any province or provinces which did not acquiesce in the new constitution would be entitled to frame a constitution of their own giving them 'the same full status as the Indian Union'. This clause threatened to convert India into a political chequerboard, containing scores of princely states and independent provinces or groups of provinces which could make short work of India as a political and economic entity. This was indeed a prospect which made every Indian nationalist shudder. Gandhi, who had been specially invited from Wardha to see Cripps, after reading the proposals, advised him to take the first plane home. Nehru's feelings on 'balkanization' were equally strong; in a telegram to Krishna Menon in England he criticized the 'whole conception [of] leading [to] break up India with British forces guarding States interfering [with] freedom [of the] Union, encouraging disruptive tendencies'.

In his press conferences and broadcasts, Cripps defended the provision for non-accession of provinces on the ground that it would, by reassuring Muslims make the drastic step of secession superfluous. 'The door must be left open', Cripps said in one of his broadcasts. 'If you want to persuade a number of people who are inclined to be antagonistic to enter the same room, it is unwise to tell them that once they go in, there is no way out.' [1] Cripps failed to foresee that this approach would have a contrary effect upon the Muslim League. Jinnah welcomed the non-accession clause as a 'recognition given to the principle of partition'. His only grievance was that it was a 'veiled recognition' and not in unequivocal terms.[2] He demanded amendments in the details of the constitution-making process which would ensure beyond doubt the secession of the provinces he claimed for Pakistan. In the event, Cripps succeeded not in weaning Jinnah from his secessionist aims but in encouraging him in the belief that the partition of India would be conceded by Britain, if the League persisted in its campaign.

In its resolution of April 2, 1942, on the Cripps proposals, the Congress working committee criticized the 'novel principle of non-accession for a Province', but affirmed 'nevertheless the Committee cannot think in terms of compelling the people of any territorial unit to remain in an Indian Union against their declared and established will'. As an organization pledged to democratic principles and non-violent methods, the Congress may have felt justified in making such a declaration, but it was an indirect endorsement of the possibility of secession by a territorial unit, which could not but be a source of encouragement to the Muslim League. The immediate effect of the Cripps mission was therefore to give a boost to the movement for Pakistan and to lower the morale of those, particularly Muslims, who had stood against it.

For Jawaharlal Nehru, as for his colleagues in the working committee, the long-term proposals of Sir Stafford Cripps had serious snags, but he was prepared to shelve the constitutional issue and to concentrate on the formation of a national government to resist the Japanese, who were battering at the gates of India. Nehru's mind was full of plans for raising national militias to fight the invader if he got a foothold on Indian soil. No agreement could, however, be reached on the formation of a national government owing to the basic hostility of not only the viceroy, but of prime minister Churchill to bringing the Congress, or as he had frankly described it, 'hostile elements into the defence machine'. While the British government was unwilling to admit the Congress as a partner in the defence against Japan, the Muslim League maintained its hostility to the Congress despite the immediate peril from Japan. When Nehru suggested that the Muslim League would have

[1] Gwyer and Appadorai, *op. cit.* vol. ii, p. 522.
[2] Jamil-ud-din Ahmad, *op. cit.* pp. 418–20.

joined a national government if it had been possible to form one, Jinnah immediately refuted the statement. 'I assert', he said, 'that if the Congress demand [for a national government] had been accepted, it would have been the death-knell of the Musalmans of India.'[1] We know now that there was a school of thought in the Muslim League council which opposed participation in a national government at the centre even during the war lest this participation in a unitary government should prejudice the demand for Pakistan.[2]

In the weeks following the failure of Cripps mission, Gandhi was driven to the conclusion that something had to be done to save India from going the way of Malaya and Burma, by giving to the Indian people a stake in the defence of the country. He became convinced that no solution of the communal problem was possible so long as Hindus and Muslims had a third party – the British – to look up to. These convictions provided the main impulse behind the 'Quit India' resolution which the All-India Congress Committee passed at its Bombay meeting on August 8, 1942. This meeting was preceded by hectic political activity. The Congress leaders felt that their organization faced the greatest crisis of its long history. In this crisis they were prepared to review relations not only with the British government, but with other political parties, particularly the Muslim League. They were clapped into prison immediately after the 'Quit India' resolution was passed, but there is evidence to show that if they had been allowed time to do so, they would have tried to reach an agreement with the League. Testimony to this is borne by Dr Abdul Latif of Hyderabad who had been meeting and corresponding with Nehru and Azad at this time. In a letter dated August 6, 1942, Nehru explained his views on the Pakistan issue to Dr Latif:

'India as it is, contains nearly all the important elements and resources that can make her a strong and more or less self-sufficient nation. To cut her up will be from the economic point of view as well as others, a fatal thing, breaking up that national economic unity and weakening each part.

'All these arguments are reinforced by recent world history, and in fact by the course of the war itself.

'This has shown that small nations have no future before them except hangers-on of larger nations. We do not want India or any part of India to be such a hanger-on or a kind of semi-dependency political or economic, of any other nation. . . . In fact the tendency in the world is for large federations to come into existence. . . .'

The All-India Congress Committee's main resolution of August 8th had pledged the Congress to a federal constitution, 'with the largest autonomy for the federating units and with the residuary powers vesting in these units'. Dr Latif who had talked to Congress leaders during these critical days before their arrest was convinced that they were willing to go to the farthest limit to satisfy political aspirations of the Muslim community and to remove its misgivings. Gandhi had in fact gone so far as to propose that the British should quit India by transferring power exclusively to the All-India Muslim League.

1 Jamil-ud-din Ahmad, *op. cit.* p. 423.

2 C. Khaliquzzaman, *op. cit.* p. 288.

Dr Latif was not an adherent of the Congress; indeed in his correspondence with Nehru, he had started as a sharp critic. But by the summer of 1942 he had realized that the Congress was prepared to concede to the provinces the widest autonomy with a limited centre – 'the substance of Pakistan'. He begged Jinnah to respond to the Congress gestures; the division of India, he argued, would not solve the communal problem but only aggravate it. Jinnah dismissed Latif's correspondence with the Congress leaders as 'contradictory, disingenuous and dubious'. 'Arguments as these', replied Latif, 'only go to confirm the view held by the Congressites that Mr. Jinnah was never serious about a settlement with the Congress. For aught I can say, it is clear to my mind, from my talks with its leaders that the Congress on its part appeared sincerely anxious to settle its differences with the League and with its help and willing co-operation to rally the people of India for the defence of the country by forming an interim popular government'.[1] 'I have reasons to believe', Latif observed later

'that he [Jinnah] and his Working Committee had neither studied nor attempted to grasp the full implications of Pakistan. He has unfortunately lulled himself into the belief that if he could only carve out two small so-called independent states for the Mussalmans in the north-west and north-east, he would have solved for all times, the problems of Indian Muslims.

'The real Muslim problem does not concern so much the Muslims of those parts where they form a majority, and where they can look after themselves in any constitution, as it concerns the Muslim minority from Delhi, Lucknow, Patna towns to Cape Comorin, who would be rendered eternal orphans under Mr. Jinnah's plan. . . . I have found Mr. Jinnah incapable of conceiving the hundred million Muslims in India as an indivisible entity and that we can secure all the advantages of his Pakistan without having to labour under its inevitable disadvantages by setting the scheme against an all-India background.'[2]

Dr Latif's plea to Jinnah to grasp the hand of friendship that the Congress leaders were extending before they were removed from the political scene did not evoke a response. The arrest of the Congress leaders immediately after the meeting of the All-India Congress Committee, mob violence in some parts of the country and the swift and strong repression by the government brought the government-Congress relations to the lowest ebb ever, and created a situation which the Muslim League immediately turned to its advantage.

The Muslim League working committee hastened to denounce the 'Quit India' movement as an attempt to establish 'Hindu Raj' and 'to deal a death-blow to the Muslim goal of Pakistan'. The League's tirade against the Congress was useful to the government of India which had switched its war-publicity machine with its full force against the Congress, so as to represent it as anti-British, anti-national and pro-Axis.

With the Congress outlawed, its leaders in prison, its publicity media silenced, the political stage was clear for the Muslim League. 'The Government have no love for the League,' a Congress leader wrote, 'less for its

[1] Nazir Yar Jung (Ed.) *The Pakistan Issue* (1943), p. 125. [2] *Ibid* pp. 137–8.

leader. For them, the League and its leader are the enemy's enemy, the common enemy being the national forces represented by the Congress.'[1] Engaged in the task of an all-out offensive against the Congress, the British governors and officials were glad to see an ally in the most vociferous opponent of the Congress.

The political gains of the League's new posture were not long in coming. In August 1942, Sir Saadullah Khan formed a League ministry in Assam. A month later, Allah Bakhsh, the premier of Sind (whose sympathy with the Congress was an open secret) renounced his title of Khan Bahadur and O.B.E.; for these offences he was dismissed from his office even though he commanded a majority in the legislative assembly. A League ministry was formed in Sind. In March 1943, Nazimuddin, Jinnah's loyal supporter in Bengal formed a ministry with the help of the European group. In May 1943, the Muslim League was able to form a ministry in the North West Frontier Province, as most of the Congress members were in jail.

'The middle years of the war', a British historian has recently pointed out, 'saw the consolidation of the Muslim League in the Muslim majority provinces.'[2] This consolidation was a direct result of the breach between the Congress and the government and the skill of Jinnah in making political capital out of it. This was not a new technique: he had practised it since the outbreak of war.[3] It was only when the estrangement between the Congress and the government reached its peak that the dividends to the League were the highest in the form of League ministries in provinces which it claimed for Pakistan.

X

As the tide of the war turned against the Axis powers in 1944 there were indications that Indian political deadlock might relax. C. Rajagopalachari, who had been pleading for two years with his colleagues in the Congress party for the 'recognition of the right of separation of certain areas from united India', presented to Jinnah in April 1944 a formula which became the basis of talks between Jinnah and Gandhi in September. Gandhi had been released from prison on grounds of health in May and was persuaded to take the initiative in seeking an understanding with Jinnah on the issue of Pakistan. Gandhi did not accept the two-nation theory, but agreed that after the war a commission should demarcate contiguous districts in the north-west and north-east of India where the Muslim population was in absolute majority and the wishes of the inhabitants of the areas should be ascertained through the votes of the adult population. If the vote went in favour of separation, these areas were to be formed into a separate state as soon as possible after

[1] J. B. Kripalani, 'League and War Effort' in *National Herald*, October 5, 1941.

[2] Hugh Tinker, *op. cit.* p. 30.

[3] V. P. Menon records that in February 1940, Jinnah in the course of an interview with Lord Linlithgow sought the support of the governor Sir George Cunningham in teaching 'a salutary lesson to the Congress' by forming a League ministry in the N.W.F.P., the Congress ministry having resigned a few months earlier. See V. P. Menon, *Transfer of Power*, p. 78.

India was free from foreign domination. However, there was to be a treaty of separation between the successor states in the sub-continent 'for satisfactory administration of Foreign Affairs, Defence, Internal Communications, Customs, Commerce and the like which must necessarily continue to be matters of common interest between the contracting parts'.

That Gandhi should have offered these terms to Jinnah in September 1944, would have been unthinkable four years earlier, when he had described Pakistan as an untruth. Gandhi had not merely recognized the principle of partition, but even suggested a mechanism for it. It is important to note that while Gandhi suggested links between the two states, he did not insist on a central government. He was content to have 'a Board of Representatives of both the States' for certain common purposes and services. He could not, he confessed to Jinnah, envisage the two [successor] states after the partition 'as if there was nothing common between . . . [them] except enmity'. The search for cultural and economic autonomy was legitimate enough, but some safeguards were in Gandhi's view essential to prevent an armaments race and an armed conflict between the two states.

Jinnah rejected Gandhi's offer. The district-wise demarcation of boundaries was unacceptable to him though he was to accept it in 1947. He would have nothing less than the 'full' six provinces for Pakistan, even though in two of them (the Punjab and Bengal) the Muslim majority was marginal, and in one province, Assam, it was non-existent. Jinnah did not see why non-Muslim populations in these provinces should have a voice in determining their own fate: if there was to be a plebiscite or referendum, it was to be confined to Muslims. Nor would Jinnah agree to any common links between India and Pakistan for such matters as foreign affairs, defence or customs. Nor would he agree that 'marriage should precede divorce', that partition should come, if at all, after the British departure and after the two parties had an opportunity to co-exist. While these conversations were no more than a kind of re-education for Gandhi, they brought an accession of political strength to Jinnah. That Gandhi had knocked at his door raised Jinnah's prestige. The fact that the Mahatma had relented so far as to discuss the machinery for the exercise of 'the right of self-determination' by Muslims was a feather in Jinnah's cap.

Two efforts at a short-term solution in 1944–5 met with no more success than Gandhi's attempt at a long-term solution. Early in 1944, the Bhulabhai Desai-Liaqat Ali pact for Congress-League co-operation in an interim government at the centre was published. Liaqat Ali backed out. Desai burnt his fingers in these parleys; the pact was rejected out of hand by Jinnah, but it nevertheless introduced the idea of parity between the Congress and the League in the formation of a national government. At the Simla conference summoned by Lord Wavell in June 1945, this parity was almost taken for granted: by the time the conference ended Jinnah had raised his price by demanding a parity between the Muslim League and all other parties. The Simla conference broke down because Jinnah would not permit the viceroy to nominate to the executive council any Muslim member – not even a non-Congress Muslim Unionist from the Punjab – who did not owe allegiance to the League.

XI

The Simla conference had failed to break the deadlock. But two important events occurred in the wake of the conference which made a new initiative possible. With the surrender of Japan on August 15, 1945, the war came to an end and the Labour party came into power. Lord Wavell went to London, and on return to India announced on September 19th, that the British government was still working in the spirit of the Cripps offer and intended to convene a constitution-making body. Elections to the central and provincial legislatures, which were in any case overdue, were announced. Indian politics were again deeply stirred and entered a period of intense excitement, interminable negotiations and bitter controversy.

In the early months of 1945, the Congress leaders could see the beginnings of a change in the British policy, but they were not yet convinced of the British *bona fides*. This was understandable in view of what they had gone through. Nehru himself had spent 3,251 days in British prisons; his latest term from August 9, 1942 to June 15, 1945 had been the longest. A member of the parliamentary delegation has recorded how the members of the Congress working committee 'all ex-prisoners regarded the British parliamentarians with a suspicious reserve behind a veil of courtesy'. Nehru had been quoted in the British press as having called the delegation 'a huge hoax'; he had not used these words, but neither he nor his colleagues were impressed by the gesture of a goodwill delegation. Indeed, it was not only the Congress leaders, who had lost faith in British sincerity; the veteran Liberal leader Srinivasa Sastri, who was on his death-bed, told Gandhi in January 1946, 'We know nothing can come out of it [the British parliamentary delegation]. Labour or Conservative so far as India is concerned, they are all one and the same'. That this melancholy judgment should have been passed at a time when the transfer of power was about to take place, and by one who had always been a friend of the British connection, showed that the representatives of the British *raj* in India, with whom the Indians came into contact, gave no inkling of an early departure.

The cabinet mission reached Delhi on May 24, 1946. Nearly fifty persons were summoned for exchange of views with the mission. 'It is difficult to understand,' Vallabhbhai Patel wrote to Nehru on 27th March, 'why this procedure has been adopted and what useful purpose can be served by calling such a group again. It looks as if they are pursuing the same old process to which this country is accustomed, and it leads one to believe that the local bureaucracy must be behind it.'

As the negotiations with the cabinet mission proceeded, the Congress distrust of the British diminished, but it never entirely disappeared. It was not a question of the sincerity of Pethick-Lawrence, Cripps, Alexander and Wavell. They seemed anxious to do the right thing, but they were surrounded by men – senior officials – who could hardly be expected to suddenly unlearn the history of the previous three decades. To the sympathy of some of senior British officers with the League, testimony has recently been borne by one of its prominent members.[1] There were, it seemed to Congress leaders, 'English

[1] C. Khaliquzzaman, *op. cit.* p. 333.

mullahs' around the viceroy, who were not sorry to give a parting kick to the party who had been primarily responsible for challenging and liquidating the *raj*, and for wrecking promising British careers in the I.C.S. and the Indian army.

As the negotiations with the cabinet mission got under way, it became evident that the main confrontation was between the Congress and the League. For the first time Jinnah had been brought to the negotiating table, made to stay there, and to spell out his terms. Nehru and his colleagues were naturally cautious in dealing with him. For eight years he had defied all attempts at a direct and fruitful dialogue. In one important respect, the situation had of course changed. The rift between the Congress and the government which had given Jinnah his favourable bargaining position was closing. 'It would not be right to allow any minority, however large and important', Sir Stafford Cripps had declared in July 1945, 'to hold up the attainment of self-government in India, any more than it would be right to force the Muslim majority Provinces into a new constitutional arrangement. . . .' [1] The Churchill–Amery–Linlithgow team which in the early years of the war had been so sympathetic to the League had been substituted by the Attlee–Pethick–Lawrence–Wavell team, which could be expected to take a more objective view of the Indian political situation.

The Muslim League seems to have realized this; from the beginning of 1946 it increasingly stressed the dangers of civil war and issued threats which were calculated to rouse the Muslims, frighten the Hindus and impress the British. In March 1946, Abdur Rab Nishtar, later a League nominee to the interim government declared: 'the real fact is that Mussalmans belong to a martial race and are no believers of the non-violent principles of Mr. Gandhi.' [2] Abdul Qaiyum Khan, the League leader of N.W.F.P., threatened that the people in the tribal areas 'who were all armed' were for Pakistan. Muslims, he said, were for Pakistan. He was asked by many Muslim students and men in uniform as to when the 'marching orders would be given by the Quaid-e-Azam . . . If they [the British] decide there should be one Constituent Assembly, then the Muslims will have no other alternative but to take out the sword and rebel against it.'[3] Sir Firoz Khan Noon, whose loyalty to the British *raj* had never been in doubt, threatened on April 9th: 'I tell you this much. If we find that we have to fight Great Britain for placing us under one Central Government or Hindu Raj, then the havoc which the Muslims will play will put to shame what Chengiz Khan and Halaku did.' Sir Firoz said that if the Hindus and the British did not concede Pakistan, 'the only course left to Muslims was to look to Russia. There was already a great movement in the Punjab, including landlords, in favour of communism'.[4] This menacing posture was a novel one for a political party which had always been careful not to embroil itself with the government and included among its leaders men who had been instruments, if not the pillars of the *raj*.

[1] Gwyer and Appadorai, *op. cit.* vol. ii, p. 566.
[2] *Dawn*, March 26, 1946.
[3] *Indian Annual Register*, January-June 1946, p. 197.
[4] *Ibid.* p. 196.

It was to the accompaniment of this tearing propaganda campaign that the cabinet mission commenced its work in March 1946. From the record of the negotiations, it is obvious that the Congress working committee was subject to three divergent and to some extent, contradictory pulls, which made decisions painfully difficult. In the first place, the Congress was eager to get rid of foreign rule, and to make a constructive response to the gesture of the Labour government in sending a high-powered mission to India. Secondly, the Congress was prepared to make the widest concessions to the minorities, particularly the Muslims, in the future constitution of India by agreeing to a limited centre, residuary powers in the provinces and the maximum constitutional safeguards for protection of religious and cultural rights. These two considerations had, however, to be balanced against another: the Congress wanted to avoid pitfalls which the ingenuity of the Muslim League or the astuteness of the 'English mullahs' operating behind the scenes might devise: it was important not to accept constitutional formulae which would not work, or which would do permanent damage to the future of the country.

The three-month long negotiations in the trying Delhi summer were indeed a great strain on the British ministers. We know that Pethick-Lawrence was exhausted, Cripps became ill and Alexander exasperated. But the strain on Gandhi, Nehru, Azad and Patel was no less serious. They knew they were engaged in not only a battle of wits but of wills with Jinnah. By sheer tenacity and refusal to make any concession, the League leader had built up his position and made the constitutional problem almost intractable. His price for settlement had progressively risen. It had begun with separate electorates in 1916, gone up to 'Fourteen Points' in 1929, to composite ministries in 1937, and finally to the partition of the country in 1940. The six provinces he claimed for his Pakistan included Assam, where the Muslim population was 33 per cent, and the Punjab and Bengal where the Muslim majority was slight indeed. The League's insistence on holding a position which seemed untenable intrigued and exasperated the Congress leaders. They felt that the League was out to achieve its objective by a combination of intransigence and threats of civil war. Why did the League want to include in its homeland dominantly non-Muslim areas? The mental processes of the exponents of partition are illuminated by a letter written on October 7, 1942 by a prominent member of the League council to Jinnah:

'Further, one of the basic principles lying behind the Pakistan idea is that of keeping hostages in Muslim Provinces as against the Muslims in the Hindu Provinces. . . . If we allow millions of Hindus to go out of the orbit of our influence, the security of the Mussalmans in the minority provinces will be greatly minimized . . . complete segregation of the Muslim and Hindu population as at present situated is impossible but there may come a time that it may become feasible. If we allow large territories to go out of our hands in the process of readjustment [of territories] such an exchange of population would be impossible; because the territories which will be left over with us will not be sufficient to receive and maintain large population migrating from the other land . . . There is one other factor which should be taken into account. If the whole of Punjab becomes a part of Pakistan zone, Kashmere and other Punjab native states will have no direct communication left with the non-Muslim provinces. They will naturally desire union with them and shall be forced to ask the Pakistan Union for a right of transit. In that event, the Pakistan Government can fairly claim the same right for Hyderabad and other Muslim estates [*sic*] to establish contact with the Pakistan Union.' [1]

XII

The negotiations with the cabinet mission were conducted by Azad on behalf of the Congress, though Nehru, Patel and Abdul Ghaffar Khan were associated with him. The working committee was continually in session and Gandhi was available for consultations. Nehru was very much in the picture, but it was Gandhi whose scepticism particularly about the grouping of provinces influenced the Congress attitude in the early stages of the negotiations.

Torn between their desire for an early end of British rule and their anxiety about being out-manoeuvred by the Muslim League into a wrong decision, the Congress working committee had many an agonizing reappraisal before it passed its resolution on June 25, 1946 accepting the long-term cabinet plan. In the final decision, Vallabhbhai Patel's influence was probably dominant, but he was able to carry with him his colleagues in the working committee including Nehru. Gandhi's doubts were not entirely resolved, but when the time came for ratification by the All-India Congress Committee, Gandhi threw his weight behind the working committee. The All-India Congress Committee met at Bombay on July 7, 1946. It was at this meeting that Nehru took charge of the Congress presidency from Abul Kalam Azad and delivered a speech which has been described as a 'serious tactical blunder' [2] and even an act of direct sabotage of the cabinet mission plan. This speech is alleged to have wrecked the cabinet mission plan, and the last hope of preserving the unity of the Indian sub-continent. The charge is based on some of the remarks made by Nehru but without reference to the context in which he spoke. Nehru was replying to the attacks made by socialist speakers. One of them, Achyut Patwardhan, had argued that 'the Cabinet Mission Plan foreboded ill both for Congress integrity and the communal problem',[3] and suspected the influence of 'Clive Street European capitalists' in the proposals for grouping of provinces. Another speaker, Aruna Asaf Ali had pointed to the 'traps laid by British imperialists' and called for a mass civil disobedience struggle to throw out the alien rulers.[4] A number of critics had cast doubts on the status and power of the constituent assembly, which was to be convened by the government and could exist only on its sufferance. It was this criticism that Nehru attempted to answer in his speech of July 7th. The oft-quoted sentence from this speech: 'We are not bound by a single thing except that we have decided to go to the Constituent Assembly', was not the

[1] C. Khaliquzzaman, *op. cit.* pp. 425–7.
[2] Michael Brecher, *Nehru A Political Biography*, p. 317.
[3] *Bombay Chronicle*, July 8, 1946. [4] *Ibid.*

most important part of it. The whole tenor of his 6,000-word speech was to justify the acceptance of the cabinet mission plan. 'We cannot forget', he pleaded with his socialist critics, 'that while we have to be revolutionary, we also have to think in terms of statesmanship – not in shouting slogans and escaping responsibility but in terms of facing the big problems. The world looks to you and the Congress for great decisions and it is no use to sit cursing, fuming and fretting. . . .' [1] Nehru refuted the charge that the constituent assembly would be a 'sham', or a nursery game at which Indian politicians would play while the British Government supervised them. This was why he declared that no 'dictation' from the British government would be tolerated.

Three days later, on July 10th, Nehru covered the same ground at a press conference in Bombay. Here again, while he emphasized the sovereign character of the constituent assembly, he affirmed that the Congress was determined to make a success of the constitutional mechanism outlined by the cabinet mission. 'Once the Congress went into the [Constituent] Assembly', Nehru said, 'its main objective would be to see how to make it a success . . . and in so doing the Congress would certainly have to take into consideration the situation created by the Cabinet Statement of May 16.' [2]

'But', he added with some emphasis, 'the Constituent Assembly would never accept any dictation or any other directive from the British Government in regard to its work. The only two factors which limit the sovereignty of the Constituent Assembly are those relating to the minorities and the Indo-British treaty. . . . When the Congress had stated that the Constituent Assembly was a sovereign body, the Cabinet Mission replied, "Yes, more or less subject to two considerations. Firstly, proper arrangement for minorities and the other treaty between India and Britain." I wish the Mission had stated both these matters are not controversial. It is also obvious that the minorities question has to be settled satisfactorily. It is also obvious that if there is any kind of peaceful change-over in India, it is bound to result in some kind of a treaty with Great Britain.' [3]

Clearly, Nehru had no intention to repudiate the framework of the cabinet mission plan. All the available evidence indeed points to his anxiety to arrive at a satisfactory solution of the minority problem, and of Indo-British relations after the withdrawal of British power. In so far as Nehru was outspoken, even provocative in his utterances at Bombay on July 7th and 10th, his words were directed not to the Muslim League, but to the critics of the Congress policy within the Congress organization or to the British government.

On grouping of provinces in the cabinet mission plan, Nehru told the press conference that 'the probability is, from any approach to the question, that there will be no grouping. . . . Section A would decide against grouping. There was but little chance of the N.W.F.P. supporting grouping. . . . Further, there was a good deal of feeling against grouping with the Punjab, in the N.W.F.P. and in Sind for economic and other reasons. . . . Both these provinces were afraid of being swamped by the Punjab.'

[1] *Bombay Chronicle*, July 8, 1946.
[2] *Bombay Chronicle*, 11 July, 1946.
[3] *Ibid.*

This statement has been often cited as a destructive piece of work. In fact Nehru was doing no more than stating the political probabilities as they seemed to him in July 1946: the lack of majority support in the Punjab (which had a non-League coalition ministry), the natural reluctance of even Muslims in Sind to be swamped by the Punjab; the presence of a Congress government in N.W.F.P. with its solid base in the Muslim community, and opposition to the League, to grouping and to Pakistan.

It is arguable that Nehru should have avoided a public discussion of political probabilities which could not but provoke the League. But he was committing neither a breach of faith with the cabinet mission, nor an act of sabotage. Neither in his speech at the All-India Congress Committee nor at the press conference did he intend to wreck the cabinet mission plan. His ideas on how the constituent assembly would function were given in his broadcast on September 7, 1946 after the formation of the interim government. In this he said,

'There has been much heated argument about sections and groupings in the Constituent Assembly. We are perfectly prepared to, and have accepted, the position of formation of groups . . . we do not look upon the Constituent Assembly as an arena for conflict or the forcible imposition of one viewpoint on another. That would not be the way to build up a contented and united India. We seek agreed and integrated solutions with the largest measure of goodwill behind them. We shall go to the Constituent Assembly with the fixed determination of finding a common basis for agreement on all controversial issues.

'And so, in spite of all that has happened and the hard words that have been said . . . we invite even those who differ from us to enter the Constituent Assembly as equals and partners with us with no binding commitments. It may well be that when we meet and face common tasks, our present difficulties will fade away.' [1]

The meeting of the All-India Muslim League Council which was to withdraw acceptance of the cabinet mission plan, had been called by Nawabzada Liaqat Ali Khan, its general secretary, *before* Nehru held the press conference in Bombay. The Nawabzada's statement announcing the meeting referred to 'the grave possibility of the All-India Muslim League not participating in the Constituent Assembly for lack of assurance that the fundamental principles of the Cabinet Mission Scheme will be adhered to'. The League had been sore at not being invited to form the interim government though it had conveyed its acceptance of the cabinet mission plan, while the Congress had not. The Nawabzada charged the viceroy and cabinet ministers with breaking their pledges.[2] 'I ask the Muslims', he said, 'to be prepared and ready. We want peace with honour, but if there is to be war, we should accept the challenge.' Nehru's remarks at Bombay were thus not the initial, or even the primary factor in provoking the League to revoke its earlier resolution. As Pethick-Lawrence told an Indian visitor, '. . . those remarks

[1] Dorothy Norman, *Nehru The First Sixty Years*, vol. ii, p. 251.
[2] *Statesman*, July 1, 1946.

gave Jinnah the excuse he was looking for to get out of the Constituent Assembly and the Cabinet Mission Plan'.[1]

In the resolution which the All-India Muslim League passed on July 29th, countermanding its acceptance of the cabinet mission plan, it asserted that 'of the two major parties, the Muslim League alone has accepted the statements of May 16th and 25th acceding to the spirit and letter of the proposals embodied therein'. This assertion is not borne out by the very terms of the resolution passed by the League's council on June 6, 1946. One of the reasons given in this resolution for the acceptance of the cabinet mission plan was that the League saw in it 'the basis and the foundation of Pakistan . . . [which] are inherent in the Mission plan by virtue of the compulsory grouping of six Muslim provinces in section B and C.' The resolution went on to affirm that the Muslim League agreed 'to co-operate with the constitution-making machinery proposed in the scheme outlined by the Mission in the hope that it would ultimately result in the establishment of complete[ly] sovereign Pakistan.'[2]

Clearly, the League did not consider the cabinet mission plan, with its three-tier structure, as a final compromise between the Congress ideal of a strong and united India and the League objective of two separate sovereign states. On the contrary, the League made no secret of its hopes and plans that the cabinet mission plan would be a stepping stone to an independent Pakistan. In his speech to the Muslim League council on June 5th, Jinnah made no secret of his intentions or tactics. 'Let me tell you', Jinnah told his colleagues, 'that Muslim India will not rest content until we have established full, complete and sovereign Pakistan. . . . The Lahore Resolution [of March 1940] did not mean that when Muslims put forward their demand, it must be accepted at once. . . . It is a big struggle and continued struggle. The first struggle was to get the representative character of the League accepted. That fight they had started and they had won. Acceptance of the Mission's proposal was not the end of their struggle for Pakistan. They should continue their struggle till Pakistan was achieved.'[3]

As for 'groups of provinces', Jinnah told his council, that they 'should have powers on *all* subjects except defence, communications and foreign affairs. But so far as defence was concerned, it would remain in the hands of the British till the new constitution was enforced. They would fight in the Constituent Assembly to restrict "communications" to what was absolutely necessary for defence only.'[4] The cabinet mission plan was thus to be made a prelude to Pakistan in two ways. In the first place, the 'grouping' of provinces in the east and the west was to be made compulsory, the widest powers were to be conferred on the 'groups', and provincial autonomy was practically to cease to exist. In the second place, the central government was to be made as weak and ineffective as possible by the narrowest interpretation of its functions and by denying it any right for taxation. A central government which lived on doles, had no say in trade, industry, communications (except

1 Sudhir Ghosh, *Gandhi's Emissary* (1967), p. 180.
2 Gwyer and Appadorai, *op. cit.* vol. ii, p. 601.
3 *Indian Annual Register*, January-June 1946, vol. i, p. 181.
4 *Ibid.* p. 182.

for defence) and was composed of representatives of antagonistic units in its executive and legislature, could scarcely be expected to prevent the secession of the League's groups of provinces in the north-west and east.[1]

A three-tier constitution such as the cabinet mission had outlined was a delicate mechanism with numerous checks and balances. Unless the two major parties, the Congress and the League entered the constituent assembly with tremendous goodwill and determination to co-operate, it was impossible to draft a workable constitution, much less to enforce it. In retrospect it is clear that the Muslim League's idea of a central government for a sub-continent like India, in mid-twentieth century was completely out-of-date. A weak central government might endanger the security of the country and its economic growth, but was likely to create the ideal conditions in which units could break off. The Congress of course had no intention of letting the League get away with the Pakistan of its own conception with 'full' six provinces, by disguising them as groups of provinces in the first instance. This was the background of the opposition by Gandhi, Nehru, Patel and indeed the entire Congress leadership to the compulsory grouping of provinces. This opposition could have been softened if Jinnah had tried to assure the Hindus of Assam and West Bengal, the Congress Muslims of N.W.F.P. and the Sikhs of the Punjab, that grouping of provinces was a voluntary and constructive association of neighbouring provinces for mutual advantage, and that it would not involve coercion of minorities. By failing to give this assurance, Jinnah sealed the fate of the grouping scheme, and thus of the cabinet mission plan: it is true he thus made sure of Pakistan, but it was to be a Pakistan minus East Punjab, West Bengal, and the major portion of Assam.

XIII

After the rejection of the cabinet mission plan by the Muslim League, events moved fast. The Congress working committee passed a resolution reaffirming its acceptance 'in its entirety' of the cabinet mission plan. The viceroy who had invited both the parties to join an interim government decided to go ahead with the proposal even though the Muslim League refused to come in. Nehru went to see Jinnah but the League leader declined to co-operate in the formation of the interim government.

The formation of the interim government raised the frustration and bitterness of the League to a high pitch. Its leader spoke of 'the Caste Hindu, Fascist Congress and their few individual henchmen of other communities who wanted to be installed in power and authority in the Government of India to dominate and rule over Mussalmans . . . with the aid of British bayonets'.[2] The Congress knew what it was to be in the wilderness; that had been its portion for a quarter of a century. But for the League it was the first occasion when it was on the wong side of the government.

[1] For Muslim League's conception of the functions and resources of the central government, see the 'Terms of the offer made by the Muslim League as a basis of agreement 12 May 1946', reproduced in Gwyer and Appadorai, *op. cit.* vol. ii, pp. 573–4.

[2] *Indian Annual Register*, July-December 1946, p. 226.

The resolution withdrawing the League's acceptance of the cabinet mission proposals had included a threat of 'direct action'. 'This day we bid good-bye to constitutional methods', Jinnah had told the League council on July 29th, 'Today we have also forged a pistol and are in a position to use it.' [1] The League declared August 16th to be direct action day and asked Muslims to observe it all over India. One wonders whether League leaders had thought out the implications of 'direct action'. This was a technique the Congress had employed against the government on a number of occasions, but in each case it had been under the leadership of Gandhi for whom *satyagraha* had been a life-long discipline. No other Congress leader had ventured to launch a mass movement. Evidently League leaders did not realize that 'a direct action movement' required more than angry feelings and strong words.

It is not necessary here to go into the details of the communal riots which began at Calcutta on August 16th with the observance of the direct action day, and spread like a chain-reaction from Calcutta to East Bengal, from East Bengal to Bihar, and from Bihar to the Punjab. Unfortunately the League leaders reacted to the riots with a political rather than a human bias. Even though a League ministry was in office in Calcutta, Jinnah blamed the riots on 'Gandhi, the Viceroy and the British'. Each communal outbreak was cited as a further endorsement of the two nation theory, and of the inevitability of the partition of the country.

Shaken by the Calcutta riots, the viceroy Lord Wavell decided to bring the Muslim League into the interim government where the League members functioned from the outset as an opposition bloc. As one of them put it: 'We are going into the Interim Government to get a foothold to fight for our cherished goal of Pakistan.' [2] This meant disruption of the interim government from within. There was hardly an issue of domestic and foreign policy on which the representatives of the two parties saw eye to eye. An unfortunate result of this antagonism was that the civil service was affected by the communal virus.

By March 1947 when Mountbatten replaced Wavell, the Congress leadership had been sobered by its experience in the interim government as well as by the growing lawlessness in the country. A *modus vivendi* with the League seemed not remote but impossible. Partition of India as demanded by the League was bad enough, but even worse possibilities had begun to loom ahead. In the twilight of the British empire in India, some of the Indian princes were nursing new ambitions. The political department was proceeding on the assumption that British paramountcy over the Indian states would lapse with the withdrawal of British power, and each of the rulers of 562 states would be free to decide his future. The princes of western and central India, under the inspiration of some of the larger states, especially Bhopal, were thinking in terms of leagues of princes. It was the intrigue by the ruler of Bastar, a small state in central India with the Nizam of Hyderabad and the attitude of the political department to it which finally convinced Patel that it was imperative to secure immediate British withdrawal even if it meant acceptance of the partition of India. A similar conclusion was reached by

[1] *Indian Annual Register*, July-December 1946, p. 178.
[2] *Ibid.* p. 79.

Nehru after the frustrating experience of the working of the interim government where he noticed a 'mental alliance' between British officials and the League members.

It has been suggested that Nehru and Patel agreed to the partition of India because they were avid for power. It is important to recall that the decision in favour of partition was not that of Patel and Nehru alone; it was endorsed by the working committee and in the All-India Congress Committee 157 voted for it and only fifteen against it. It was a painful decision taken with a heavy heart, but there seemed no alternative to it at that time. The immediate problem as Nehru saw it was 'to arrest the swift drift to anarchy and chaos'.

In retrospect it appears the Congress acceptance of the partition was not such a sudden development as it may have seemed at the time. It was the culmination of a process which had begun immediately after the passage of the Pakistan resolution by the Lahore session of the All-India Muslim League. Gandhi had opposed the two-nation theory and 'vivisection' of India, but he had nevertheless written as early as April 1940: 'I know no non-violent method of compelling the obedience of eight crores of Muslims to the will of the rest of India, however powerful the majority the rest may represent. The Muslims must have the same right of self-determination that the rest of India has. We are at present a joint family. Any member may claim a division.' [1] This was perhaps an inevitable position for a leader who was committed to non-violence but another leader such as Abraham Lincoln could have insisted that there could be no compromise on the unity of country. Two years later, the Congress working committee in its resolution on the Cripps proposals affirmed that 'it cannot think in terms of compelling the people of any territorial unit to remain in the Indian Union against their declared and established will'.[2] Under the impact of the League propaganda and the political deadlock with the government, the Congress position on the question of partition was gradually softening. In 1944, Gandhi in his talks with Jinnah not only accepted the principle of partition but even discussed the mechanism for the demarcation of boundaries. In 1946 the Congress after much heart searching accepted the cabinet mission plan with its loose three-tier structure, and a central government which was unlikely to have the powers or the resources to maintain the unity of the sub-continent.

The cabinet mission plan proved still-born. The interim government revealed the incompatibility of the two major parties. Henceforth, there were only two options: partition of the country as demanded by the League, or a moratorium on political controversy and conflict for a couple of years to allow tempers to cool and to produce the climate in which a compromise solution could be secured. Unfortunately communal rioting unleashed on the land in August 1946 made it impossible to have a respite. In April 1947 when the situation looked grim, one man still hoped to build bridges of understanding between the communities. Gandhi toured the villages and towns of Bengal and Bihar condemning violence irrespective of who perpetrated it, rehabilitating refugees, restoring confidence and preaching the brotherhood of man. His greatest triumphs in this self-imposed mission lay ahead: in

[1] D. G. Tendulkar, *Mahatma: Life of Mohandas Karamchand Gandhi*, vol. v, pp. 333–4.
[2] Gwyer and Appadorai, *op. cit.* p. 525.

Calcutta in August 1947 and in Delhi in January 1948. But he was convinced that the tension, however serious it might look, was a temporary phase and that the British had no right to impose partition 'on an India temporarily gone mad'.[1] He suggested to Mountbatten that Jinnah should be invited to form a Muslim League government; by this supreme gesture the Mahatma hoped to win over the League leader. One wonders whether this proposal was seriously considered by the viceroy, and whether Nehru, Patel and their colleagues who had the frustrating experience of the interim government would have liked to hand over all power to the League. Jinnah's reaction to Gandhi's proposal has not been recorded, but it is doubtful if it could have been different from what he had said about a similar proposal made by Gandhi in August 1942. 'If they [the Congress] are sincere I should welcome it. If the British Government accepts the solemn declaration of Mr. Gandhi and by an arrangement hands over the government of the country to the Muslim League, I am sure that under Muslim rule non-Muslims would be treated fairly, justly, nay, generously; and further the British will be making full amends to the Muslims by restoring the government of India to them from whom they have taken it.'[2]

The crux of the problem was whether the delay such as Gandhi envisaged could have staved off the partition. The political temperature had risen; it did not suit the Muslim League to have it lowered; for the League it was a case of 'now or never'. Gandhi's plea that there should be 'peace before Pakistan' did not impress the League. In fact the League's argument was that there could be no peace until Pakistan was established; that it was either to be a 'divided or destroyed India'. Having declared their resolve to leave India by June 1948 the British government did not want to and perhaps could not antagonize the Muslim League, or compel it to a particular course of action. Three or four years earlier the British could have exercised a moderating influence on the League; in 1947 the scope for this influence was limited. The sins of Linlithgow were visited on Wavell and Mountbatten.

It is arguable that communal tension or disorder could not have lasted indefinitely. But it is difficult to judge such situations with any degree of confidence when events are moving fast. The mounting tension in 1947 could have touched off a civil war; alternatively it could have been brought to an abrupt end by some unforeseen, and spectacular incident, such as a fast by Gandhi. In the event Mountbatten's judgment that division of the country was the only practical solution in the summer of 1947 was accepted by the three main parties to the decision, the British Government, the Indian National Congress and the All-India Muslim League.

XIV

The final result, the partition of India, was a personal triumph for Jinnah. By arousing deep emotions, by avoiding the details of his demand for Pakistan and by concentrating on a tirade against Hindu *raj*, and Congress tyranny, Jinnah was able to sustain a large consensus in his own community.

[1] Pyarelal, *Mahatma Gandhi: The Last Phase*, vol. ii, p. 208.
[2] Jamil-ud-din Ahmad, *op. cit.* p. 447.

By keeping his cards close to his chest, he was able to keep his following in good order. Such was the magical effect of his insistence on the full six provinces – Pakistan – that large numbers of his adherents in Bengal and the Punjab failed to see the consequences of a division of the country. Even a seasoned politician like Suhrawardy confessed later that he had never expected the partition of Bengal.[1] As for Muslims in the Hindu-majority provinces, they had in any case nothing to gain from the secession of provinces in the east and west; the two nation theory and the theory of hostages were to do them no good at all. Jinnah had played his cards skilfully. From near political eclipse in 1937 he had brought his party to a position where it could decisively influence events. His success was, however, due not only to his skill and tenacity, but to the tension between the Congress and the government which prevailed throughout this period except perhaps for the two years in which the Congress held office in the provinces.

The Government of India Act of 1935 was not the radical measure of constitutional reform it is being made out by some historians. It retained the levers of ultimate authority in British hands; the federal structure, with its communal and princely checks and balances, if it had come into being, could have been capable of sustaining British rule for many years. In 1939 the British hierarchy in India may not have had the optimism of earlier generations of the I.C.S., but the *raj* seemed a solid enough structure. Sir S. P. Sinha, an able and patriotic man, the first Indian to be appointed to the viceroy's executive council, had estimated before the first world war that British rule would last 400 years. Twenty-five years later, on the eve of the second world war, most Britons in India would have confidently predicted a lease of fifty years if not longer for the *raj*. It was the aim of the Indian National Congress to wear down the British reluctance to part with power. The antagonism between Indian nationalism and British rule was inherent in the unnatural relation between the two countries. This antagonism helped the Muslim League in two ways: in securing it at crucial moments the support of certain British politicians and civil servants who were embittered with the Congress, and in ensuring to the League almost the exclusive possession of the political stage when the Congress was not only out of office, but outlawed. The brunt of the struggle for the liberation of India was borne by the Congress. The Muslim League had no lot or part in this struggle, of which the establishment of Pakistan was a by-product. Others forced open the doors through which Jinnah walked to his goal. Nehru has been criticized by latter-day writers for estranging the Muslim League and for driving it to extremist policies. Much of this criticism is due to an inadequate appreciation of Nehru's ideas and attitudes and of the political framework within which he and the Congress party had to function.

Nehru's secularism was not a tactic against the Muslim League, but a deep conviction which he held in his years of office with the same tenacity as in the years of opposition. The 'mass contact movement' was not a conspiracy against the Muslim League, but an integral part of the Congress programme since 1920 for educating the people of all communities in all parts of India on political and economic issues. There were good reasons for stressing mass

[1] C. Khaliquzzaman, *op. cit.* p. 397.

contact in the late thirties – the electorate had expanded from two to ten per cent of the population, and was bound to increase further if the Congress aim of adult franchise was to be realized. The idea that only the Muslim League had the right to approach Muslim masses was a totalitarian doctrine which made nonsense of democracy and political life, as they were commonly understood.

It has already been indicated that the failure of the coalition talks in the U.P. in 1937 was in the circumstances of the time almost inevitable: in the face of Jinnah's minatory posture, the Congress could hardly have hamstrung itself in its very first attempt at ministry-making. It was not the failure of these talks, but the electoral disaster of 1937, which seems to have driven Jinnah – who had his roots in the Victorian age and was trained as a rationalist and constitutionalist in the school of Dadabhai Naoroji and Gokhale – to use the dynamite of religious emotion for blasting his way to political influence and power. The new strategy brought quick results. The cry of religion in danger, the reiteration of 'Congress tyranny' and the spectre of 'Hindu Raj' roused the Muslims, widened the communal gulf and created the climate in which the proposal for the partition of the country could be mooted.

It is difficult even today to contest the validity of the argument of Nehru and his colleagues, that religion is not a satisfactory basis for nationality in the modern world, that multi-religious, multi-lingual and even multi-racial societies should seek a political solution within the framework of a federal structure. This is what has been done under widely divergent conditions by the USSR, USA, Canada and South Africa.

No serious attempt at a compromise solution could, however, be made. From 1937 to 1940, Jinnah refused to start a dialogue with the Congress until it conceded the League's right to be the exclusive representative of the Muslim community. From 1940 onwards, he refused to start a dialogue until the Congress conceded the principle of the partition of India. He did not elaborate the constitutional, economic and even geographic content of his proposal. While the Congress attitude towards the constitutional future of India underwent important changes between 1939 and 1946, Jinnah did not meet the Congress half-way, not even quarter-way. He did not budge an inch from the position he adopted. Every overture was rejected; every concession treated as a bargaining counter for a better deal. Only once, in June 1946, he seemed to agree to a compromise by accepting the cabinet mission plan; but his acceptance (as already explained in this essay) was more apparent than real; in any case it was withdrawn within seven weeks.

If Jinnah's posture had little flexibility, his political style was hardly calculated to assist in a compromise. He heaped ridicule and scorn on all Congress leaders from Gandhi and Nehru downwards. Some critics have suggested that Nehru was on occasions too theoretical, too proud and impatient to deal with Jinnah successfully. It is well to remember that the patience and humility of Gandhi, the cool calculation of Rajagopalachari, the militant radicalism of Subhas Chandra Bose, the sedate realism of Abul Kalam Azad and the gentleness of Rajendra Prasad equally failed to work on the League leader.

THE CONGRESS AND THE PARTITION OF INDIA

by S. R. MEHROTRA*

THE CONGRESS AND THE GOVERNMENT OF INDIA ACT, 1935

The Government of India Act of 1935 provided for the establishment of full responsible government, subject to 'safeguards', in the eleven provinces of British India; it provided also for a federation of India, comprising both provinces and states, with a federal central government and legislature for the management (subject to 'safeguards' similar to those which were to operate in the provinces) of all central subjects except foreign affairs and defence. While the provincial part of the Act was to come into force on April 1, 1937, the federal part of the Act was to become operative only when and if a sufficient number of states (i) to occupy 52 of the 104 seats allotted to the states in the upper house of the federal legislature and (ii) to make up half the total population of all the states, had acceded to the federation.

If the Act of 1935 had been enacted soon after the first world war it would have been hailed as a welcome step along the road to self-government. In the temper of the 1930s the Act received a frigid reception in India. It was condemned by almost all political groups and parties in India, though not always for the same reasons. As was to be expected, the Indian National Congress, with its pronounced nationalist and democratic-socialist outlook, was the most vehement in its denunciation of the Act.[1] The Congress denounced the 'safeguards' as rendering responsible government nugatory. It demanded complete responsibility in the provinces and at the centre. The Congress particularly denounced the excessive weightage given to the states in the proposed federation – 40 per cent in the council of states and $33\frac{1}{3}$ per cent in the federal assembly, whereas the population of the states was only 24 per cent of the total population of India at that time. It denounced also the manner of the states' representation. The Congress wanted the representatives of the states in the federal legislature to be elected by their people and not, as provided for in the Act, nominated by their rulers.

The Congress coupled its condemnation of the Act of 1935 with the far-reaching demand that the future constitution of India should be framed by Indians themselves by means of a 'constituent assembly' elected on the basis of universal adult franchise. But, while the Congress 'rejected' the Act of 1935 and resolved 'not to submit to it both inside and outside the legislature so as to end it',[2] there was an influential section within the Congress which felt that the provincial portion of the Act should be permitted to function. Both the right and the left in the Congress were agreed on the desirability of

* Lecturer in Politics, School of Oriental and African Studies, London.

[1] For the attitude of the Congress to the Act of 1935 see *Indian Annual Register* (1936), vol. i, pp. 248–9; vol. ii, pp. 27–8.

[2] *Ibid.* vol. ii, pp. 27–8.

contesting the elections for the provincial legislatures, but they were divided on the question of 'acceptance of office'. The Congress, at its Faizpur session in December 1936, accordingly, decided to contest the elections to the provincial legislatures due early in 1937, but postponed decision on the controversial issue of 'acceptance of office' till after the elections.

THE ELECTIONS OF 1937

With able leaders, an effective organization and a simple yet attractive programme, the Congress won a notable victory at the polls early in 1937.[1] Of the 1,585 seats in the provincial legislatures the Congress contested 1,161 and won 716.[2] The Congress victory is all the more impressive when it is borne in mind that of the 1,585 seats less than half, 657, were 'general' or open, that is not allotted to a separate, closed elect group such as Muslims, Sikhs, Christians, Europeans, Anglo-Indians and landholders. Of the eleven provinces in British India the Congress secured a clear majority in six and was the largest single party in three others.

By contrast, the Muslim League won only 109 of the 482 seats allotted to the Muslims, securing only 4·8 per cent of the total Muslim votes.[3] It did not win a majority of seats in *any* of the four Muslim-majority provinces. In fact, its performance in certain Muslim-majority provinces was far worse than that in the Muslim-minority provinces.

[1] For the results of the 1937 elections see *Return Showing the Results of Elections in India* (1937), Cmd. 5589.

[2]

Provinces	*Total number of seats in the Legislative Assembly*	*Seats won by the Congress in the elections of 1937*
Assam	108	35
Bengal	250	54
Bihar	152	95
Bombay	175	88
Central Provinces	112	71
Madras	215	159
N.W. Frontier Province	50	19
Orissa	60	36
Punjab	175	18
Sind	60	8
United Provinces	228	133

[3]

Provinces	*Total number of seats allotted to Muslims in the Legislative Assembly*	*Seats won by the Muslim League in the elections of 1937*
Assam	34	9
Bengal	117	39
Bihar	39	—
Bombay	29	20
Central Provinces	14	—
Madras	28	10
N.W. Frontier Province	36	—
Orissa	4	—
Punjab	84	1
Sind	33	3
United Provinces	64	27

But the success of the Congress, though impressive, was by no means unqualified. While the Congress virtually routed the Hindu communalists and reactionary landlords in the Hindu-majority provinces, it failed to do so in the Muslim-majority provinces. Its performance in Bengal and the North-West Frontier Province was not bad, but it cut a rather sorry figure in Sind and the Punjab. Its greatest failure, however, lay with the Muslim electorate. The Congress in 1937 had probably many more Muslims on its rolls than did the Muslim League and some of them were individually quite distinguished, but, except in the North-West Frontier Province, they were not very popular with the Muslim masses in general. The Congress ran only fifty-eight candidates for the 482 separate Muslim seats and won twenty-six. The elections of 1937 showed that Hindu communalism was stronger in the Muslim-majority provinces than in the Hindu-majority provinces and that Muslim communalism was more firmly entrenched in the Hindu-majority provinces than in the Muslim-majority provinces. But, on the whole, the electorate all over India had preferred non-communal parties and individuals to the purely communal parties and individuals. This was a result which could not fail to delight the Congress and encourage its hopes for the future. The Congress, tired of trying to promote an agreement between the various communities of India by means of private parleys and public conferences, had appealed directly to the masses over the heads of communal leaders on the basis of its own political and economic programme and scored a notable triumph. The results of the 1937 elections, besides proving the effectiveness of Congress organization and the popularity of its programme, had apparently vindicated the correctness of its new approach to the solution of the communal problem in India. The leaders of the Congress naturally concluded that if they persisted in their efforts they could without much difficulty wean the masses away from their communal organizations and rally them under the banner of the sole national organization in India. They therefore intensified their campaign of contacting the masses, especially the Muslims. The communal leaders saw in the Congress move a threat to their very existence. They felt that, unless they organized themselves like the Congress and regained their popularity with the masses, they might get up one fine morning to find that the Congress had walked away with their flock.

The spectacular success of the Congress in the elections of 1937 – especially when contrasted with the miserable performance of the Muslim League – was not only galling to the pride of the leaders of the Muslim League, it also disturbed many of their comfortable assumptions. For example, one of the reasons why League leaders had agreed to work the Act of 1935, for what it was worth, was their calculation that they would be able to dominate the Muslim-majority provinces and that the divisions amongst the Hindus would enable 'the solid Muslim bloc', elected on the basis of separate electorates and the 'communal award', to play an effective and even balancing role in the legislatures of the Hindu-majority provinces. The results of the 1937 elections disproved this calculation. They showed that, while the vast majority of the Hindus, especially those in the Hindu-majority provinces, were behind the Congress, only a very small percentage of the Muslims supported the Muslim League, and that, despite their numerous divisions, the Hindus were capable of greater unity in political action than the socially more homogeneous Muslims. In none of the four Muslim-majority provinces was the League in a position to form a ministry. In the legislatures of three Hindu-majority provinces (Bihar, Orissa and the Central Provinces) there was not a single Muslim member elected on the League ticket. In the legislatures of the four other Hindu-majority provinces (Assam, the United Provinces, Bombay and Madras) Muslim League members were in such a minority that they could safely be neglected by the Congress party in the formation of ministries. While Congress leaders occupied the centre of the political stage in India in 1937 and decided the fate of ministries, M. A. Jinnah and his colleagues in the Muslim League were in the political wilderness, sadly learning the lessons of their débâcle and struggling hard to check their small following from defecting to the Congress.

The results of the 1937 elections also underlined the fact that, while the Hindus enjoyed an overwhelming numerical superiority in almost all the provinces in which they were in a majority, the Muslims did not enjoy the same superiority in at least two of the provinces in which they were in a majority, namely the Punjab and Bengal. These provinces accounted for 40 million out of the 80 million Muslims in British India. This meant, according to the calculations of the Muslim communalists, that, while the Hindus would dominate all the Hindu-majority provinces, the Muslims could not be sure of dominating two of the Muslim-majority provinces which they considered to be their mainstays. Unpromising as the situation was in the provinces from the point of view of the Muslim League, it was likely to be far worse in the future federation of India, for there the Muslims had only one-third of the total seats allotted to British India. If the last elections were any indication, the Congress was sure to capture the majority of the non-Muslim seats in British India and, if it succeeded in coercing the princes (the vast majority of whom were Hindus anyway), it would capture most of the seats allotted to the states in the federal legislature.

The lessons of the 1937 elections were clear and unmistakable and the Muslim League did not fail to learn them. The prospect that was starkly obvious to the leaders of the League was this : either they must cease to be the leaders of the League or they must accept a position of permanent inferiority and exclusion from office in the Hindu-majority provinces and the proposed all-India federation. Only in the Muslim-majority provinces was there some chance for the leaders of the League, provided they could make their organization as effective as the Congress, to be able to exercise the kind of power which the leaders of the Congress exercised in India. Not unnaturally, the leaders of the League clutched at this off-chance, but very soon they realized that their ambition could not be fulfilled without detaching the Muslim-majority provinces from the rest of India.

The notable victory of the Congress at the polls strengthened the hands of those Congress leaders who had been in favour of working the provincial part of the 1935 Act. On March 18, 1937 the All-India Congress Committee, meeting at Wardha, permitted, despite the determined opposition of its small but influential left wing, 'the acceptance of offices in provinces where the Congress commands a majority in the legislature, provided . . . the leader of the Congress party in the legislature is satisfied and is able to state publicly that the Governor will not use his special powers of interference or set aside the advice of ministers in regard to their constitutional activities'.[1] Not until June 21, 1937 did the governor-general, Lord Linlithgow, make a public statement which was regarded by the Congress as satisfactory on this point. In July 1937 Congress ministries were formed in six provinces (Bihar, Orissa, the United Provinces, the Central Provinces, Bombay and Madras). Later in the same year the Congress was able to form a ministry in the North-West Frontier Province and in March 1938 in Assam as well. In forming their ministries the leaders of the Congress party in the various provincial legislatures took special care to include a fair proportion of Muslims. The latter were either Congressmen elected on the Congress ticket or independents and pro-Congress Muslim Leaguers who had signed the Congress creed.

The Congress expressed its readiness to co-operate with any other party or group in the provincial legislatures on the basis of its published economic and political programme, but it set its face firmly and definitely against the recently revived proposal of 'communal coalition cabinets',[2] the proposal that the Congress ministries should contain 'an adequate number of Muslims possessing the confidence of their community', which in effect meant that the latter should be either elected by the Muslim legislators or nominated by the Muslim League. The Congress could never be expected to accept this proposal, which it rightly regarded as an extension of the vicious principle of communal representation and a negation of democracy.

THE CONGRESS AND THE MUSLIM LEAGUE

Except for a short and rather unusual period of six years (1915–21) during and after the first world war, when the Muslim League came to be dominated by Muslim Congressmen and temporarily subordinated its creed of communal separatism to the demands of Indian nationalism, its relations with the Congress had never been cordial. The Congress stood for democracy, secularism and a common Indian nationality. The Muslim League existed primarily to safeguard and promote the interests of the Indian Muslims as a separate political entity. In the circumstances created by the basic conflict between the ideologies and objectives of the two organizations there were possibilities

[1] M. Gwyer and A. Appadorai (eds.), *Speeches and Documents on the Indian Constitution, 1921–47* (1957), vol. i, pp. 392–3.

[2] Jinnah's famous Fourteen Points of March 1929 had proposed that 'no cabinet, either central or provincial, should be formed without there being a proportion of at least one-third Muslim ministers'. At the Round Table conference some Muslim delegates had urged that the representation of minorities should be specifically provided for in the constitution. This demand was indirectly rejected by the joint parliamentary committee in criticizing an earlier draft of the instruments of instructions, which seemed to fetter the discretion of governors by making it obligatory that they should select ministers from minority communities and vitiated the principle of joint responsibility of ministers. Nothing was said on the subject in the Act of 1935 and the governors, in the instructions issued to them, were only told 'to appoint those persons (including as far as practicable members of important minority communities) who will best be in a position to command the confidence of the legislature', but in so acting they should 'bear constantly in mind the need for fostering a sense of joint responsibility' among their ministers. See Gwyer and Appadorai, *op. cit.* vol. i, p. 379.

for manoeuvre, but little ground for compromise on essentials. Scores of attempts were made in the twenties and thirties to arrive at a settlement between the Congress and the Muslim League, but they foundered on the rock of mutual incompatibility. The Congress was not prepared to give up its national character; the Muslim League refused to give up its communal character. As the introduction of representative and responsible government proceeded in India, the Muslim League, as the champion of Muslim interests, demanded that the share of the Muslims in the services, elected bodies and cabinets should be fixed by statutory enactment. The Congress, while prepared to concede the substance of this demand in practice and as a matter of temporary political expediency, could never accept it in principle and in perpetuity, because it militated against the Congress objective of a secular, democratic and united Indian nation. There could be no lasting co-operation between the Congress and the League unless either one or the other changed its character. From the point of view of the Congress the price demanded by the League for its temporary co-operation was not only too high, it was also not worth paying for it did not subserve the ultimate purpose of the Congress.

Too much has been made by certain writers, who seem to be more eager to apportion blame than to ascertain facts, of the alleged refusal of the Congress to form coalition ministries with the Muslim League in 1937. It has been said[1] that the Congress, because of the 'intoxication of victory' or its foolish adherence to 'orthodox parliamentarianism', 'socialism' and 'totalitarianism', lost a great opportunity in 1937 of winning over the Muslim League by unceremoniously turning down the latter's offer of coalition.

It is entirely untrue to suggest, as has been done by some latter-day writers, that there was any understanding between the Congress and the League about the elections or the coalition ministries to be formed after the elections of 1937. The slight apparent similarity between the election manifestos of the Congress and the League was not the result of any desire on the part of the two organizations to arrive at an electoral or post-electoral arrangement. On many economic and political issues there was little difference between the right wing of the Congress and the left wing of the Muslim League, and quite a few radical Muslim Leaguers were also members of the Congress. In fact, the election manifestos of almost all political parties in India in 1937 were impeccably progressive. The election manifesto of the Muslim League was meant to conciliate the radical Muslims who considered the League to be conservative and reactionary and who were, therefore, inclined to be pro-Congress. It was drafted also with an eye on the Muslim peasant and middle class voter, for in a good many constituencies the Muslim League candidates were pitted against the khan bahadurs and the khan sahibs. On important issues like the separate electorates, the 'communal award', the safeguards for minorities, the Act of 1935, the idea of a constituent assembly and the abolition of landlordism, the Congress and the League were in complete disagreement and their leaders made no secret of their disagreement. It was significant that Jinnah inaugurated the Muslim League election campaign in Bengal by emphasizing the differences between the Congress and the League. Speaking

[1] See, for example, R. Coupland, *Indian Politics, 1936–1942* (1943), pp. 110–12, 179, and Beni Prasad, *India's Hindu-Muslim Questions* (1946), pp. 61–2.

in Calcutta on January 3, 1937 he remarked: 'Pandit Jawaharlal Nehru is reported to have said in Calcutta that there are only two parties in the country, namely, the Government and the Congress and the others must line up. I refuse to line up with the Congress. There is a third party in this country and that is the Muslims.'[1] In a speech at Dacca on January 8, 1937 he said that 'at present there was a fundamental difference between the League and the Congress'.[2]

In the elections held in January-February 1937 Congress Muslim candidates were pitted against the Muslim League candidates in almost all the provinces.[3] As Muslim seats were on a separate register and the Congress contested only fifty-eight of the total 482 Muslim seats, the elections of 1937 were only partly a Congress-League trial of strength. But the decision of the Congress to contest Muslim seats gave great offence to Jinnah, who publicly warned the Congress early in January 1937 'to leave the Muslims alone'.[4] This sparked off a bitter controversy between Jinnah and Nehru which dragged on for months and served only to widen the gulf that already separated the Congress and the Muslim League and their respective leaders. 'Our policy and programme differ in vital respects from those of the Congress,'[5] asserted the leader of the Muslim League. 'Let us agree to differ',[6] replied the leader of the Congress. 'We shall not bow our head before Anand Bhavan',[7] said Jinnah. 'In the hour of trial when we faced the might of a proud Empire many prominent leaders of the Muslim League sought alliance with the die-hard leaders of the Conservative Party in England, than whom there are no greater enemies of Indian freedom. Are we to submit to them now, we who have refused to submit to the embattled power of that Empire, and who prepare afresh for fresh trials and tribulations in the struggle for independence which has become the life-blood of our activities?'[8] asked Nehru.

In this environment of growing political antagonism and personal invective, it would have been a miracle if the All-India Muslim League had offered to join the Indian National Congress in forming coalition ministries. Actually, the League made no such offer and so there was no question of the Congress accepting or rejecting any offer of the League.

Of the six provinces in which the Congress secured clear majorities, the Muslim League had not a single elected member in three (Bihar, Orissa and the Central Provinces), where the problem of including Leaguers in the ministries simply did not arise. Only in the three other provinces (the United Provinces, Bombay and Madras) had the Muslim Leaguers any members who could be included in the ministries formed by the Congress. But in Bombay and Madras no move was made by either party even to initiate talks for a

[1] *Statesman*, January 4, 1937.
[2] *Ibid.* January 9, 1937.
[3] In the United Provinces, for example, of the fourteen Muslim candidates run by the Congress no less than four were pitted against Muslim Leaguers. See *Leader* and *Pioneer*, February 9–20, 1937. The alleged 'understanding' or 'agreement' between the Congress and the League in the United Provinces does not appear to have gone beyond some informal co-operation between a few Muslim Congressmen and Muslim Leaguers 'with Congress leanings' in the 1937 elections.
[4] *Statesman*, January 4, 1937.
[5] *Leader*, March 15, May 3, 1937.
[6] *Ibid.* May 4, 1937.
[7] *Ibid.* May 12, 1937.
[8] *Ibid.* May 4, 1937.

possible coalition.[1] Only in the United Provinces was some attempt made to negotiate a Congress-League settlement, but it failed. The full story of the negotiations in the United Provinces in 1937 is not yet known and probably never will be known, but the following brief account, based mainly on newspaper reports and other published sources, should suffice for our purposes.

Before the elections of 1937 Jinnah tried, though not with much success, to organize Muslim League parliamentary boards in the various provinces of British India, comprising leaders of all shades of Muslim opinion. The complexion of these parliamentary boards differed from province to province. In Bengal, for example, the provincial Muslim League parliamentary board was dominated by the reactionary landlords – a fact which made it difficult for the local Muslim League to have an electoral agreement with Fazlul Haq's Krishak Praja party. In the United Provinces, on the other hand, the provincial Muslim League parliamentary board was dominated by the progressives – the representatives of the Ahrars, the Jamiat-ul-Ulema, the Momins, the Shia political conference, and the pro-Congress Muslims. It was headed by Choudhry Khaliquzzaman, who was also a Congressman with pronounced socialist leanings and close personal relations with many Congress leaders. But hardly was the Muslim League parliamentary board formed in the United Provinces when differences arose and a few leaders of the Ahrars, the Momins, the Jamait-ul-Ulema and the Shia political conference resigned from it, expressing their dissatisfaction with its proceedings. This process was accelerated during and after the elections and the result was that the position of the few progressive Muslims who still remained on the board became precarious. There were three main elements within the board and they were trying to pull it in different directions. One element favoured an alliance with the National Agriculturalist party – the party of the landlords in the United Provinces – whose leader, the nawab of Chhatari, had formed the interim ministry in the province. The second element, which came increasingly to dominate the proceedings of the board, wanted to pursue a purely communal and anti-Congress policy under the direction of Jinnah and was anxious to unite all the Muslim M.L.A.s. The third element, which was in a minority and consisted of men like Khaliquzzaman, Hafiz Muhammad Ibrahim, Suleman Ansari, Saiduddin Khan and Ali Zaheer, favoured co-operation with the Congress. What was true of the United Provinces Muslim League parliamentary board was also true of the United Provinces Muslim League and its legislature party. In all the three bodies the progressives were fighting a losing battle against the reactionaries composed of the landlords and the pure communalists.

It was in these circumstances that some Muslim League progressives, chief amongst whom was Choudhry Khaliquzzaman, opened negotiations with the local Congress leaders in March-April 1937, offering their co-operation in the legislature on the basis of the Congress programme as laid down by the Congress working committee at its meeting at Wardha on February 28, 1937. Congress leaders reacted favourably to the offer, though some of the

[1] In Bombay some informal soundings about a possible coalition between the Congress and the League appear to have been made, but no reliable information about them is available.

younger socialist Congressmen, especially Muslims, did not conceal their dislike of any parleys with the Muslim Leaguers. The reaction of Khaliquzzaman's more communally-minded associates in the United Provinces Muslim League was positively hostile to any idea of co-operation with the Congress. They openly accused Khaliquzzaman of hatching 'a dreadful plot against both the Muslim League and Mr. Jinnah', of trying to wreck the latter's plan 'to organize the Muslims to stand against the Congress', and of 'hoisting the Congress colour on the Muslim League Parliamentary Board'.[1] They complained to Jinnah, who issued a public statement on April 25th condemning Khaliquzzaman's move.

'I want to make it clear', said Jinnah, 'that it will be useless for any individual or individuals to effectively carry the Muslims behind them if any settlement is arrived at with a particular group or even for the matter of that with a particular province. I say that it is a pity that these roundabout efforts are being made. The only object of it can be to create some differences between Mussalmans. It is no use deciding with those men who are in and out of the Congress and in and out of the Muslim League, one time with one and another time with the other as it suits them. I am sure that the Muslims of the United Provinces will not betray the Mussalmans of India and therefore any effort to settle by individuals which may be advantageous to them for the time being will not carry us anywhere. . . . I only trust that he [Khaliquzzaman] will not enter into any commitments which may be repudiated by the Muslims of all India.' [2]

A stormy meeting of the working committee of the United Provinces Muslim League parliamentary board took place at Lucknow on April 25, 1937 at which Khaliquzzaman and his friends were severely criticized for their flirtations with the Congress and a resolution was passed which said that 'it is not possible for the Muslim League Parliamentary Board or the members elected on its ticket to join the Congress in its policy of wrecking the constitution, but [they] can co-operate with the Congress or any other progressive party in the legislature whose policy and programme are approximately the same as of this Board'.[3] On May 4, 1937 the committee of the Bombay Provincial Muslim League, meeting under the chairmanship of Jinnah, passed a resolution which 'appealed to the Muslim members of the United Provinces Legislative Assembly who had been elected on the League ticket not to act in such a way as to cause disunion among the Muslims of India by arranging sectional or provincial settlements with the Congress'.[4] Speaking at the meeting Jinnah remarked: 'We shall face the challenge of the Congress if they think that the Muslims will accept their policy and programme because our policy and programme are different in vital respects.'[5] A couple of days later Jinnah visited Lucknow and reasserted his authority over the local Muslim League, though his efforts to bring about unity among the different groups of Muslim M.L.A.s did not quite succeed. He was reported to have rebuked those 'who talked loosely of co-operating with the Congress' and to

[1] See, for example, the statement of Syed Muhammad Husain in *Leader*, April 21, 1937.
[2] *Ibid.* April 28–29, 1937.
[3] *Ibid.* April 28, 1937.
[4] *Ibid.* May 6, 1937.
[5] *Ibid.*

have said that 'for the time being they would join hands neither with the Congress nor with the Government, but wait till they had gained strength by organizing the Muslims'.[1] On May 7, 1937 the United Provinces Muslim League parliamentary board reaffirmed, with certain significant alterations and additions (which were indicative of the increasing dominance of the anti-Congress element in the counsels of the board), the earlier resolution of its working committee, dated April 25, 1937, about the possibility of the League's co-operation with other parties in the legislature. The resolution adopted by the board said 'that the Muslim League Party in the legislature cannot and should not join the Congress in its policy and programme of wrecking the constitution, but that co-operation and coalition with the Congress or any other party on the basis of work in the legislature upon a programme that may be agreed upon in conformity with the programme of the Board should be explored, provided the communal award and separate representation in the local self-governing bodies be allowed to stand till an agreed settlement is arrived at between the communities concerned on an all-Indian basis'.[2]

These developments must have indicated to Khaliquzzaman and his friends how far they could hope to carry the local Muslim League party and the All-India Muslim League with them in their efforts to co-operate with the Congress in the United Provinces. Nor should it be forgotten that the Congress had not yet formed ministries in the provinces where it had secured majorities, that the elements within the Congress who were bitterly opposed to the formation of Congress ministries were the strongest in the United Provinces and that the official policy of the Congress about wrecking the constitution of 1935 had remained unchanged.

In the meantime the relations between the Congress and the League had further deteriorated. On March 26, 1937 Jinnah had issued a statement directing the Muslims not to participate in the demonstrations proposed to be organized by the Congress to mark 'the Anti-Constitution Day' on April 1, 1937.[3] The war of words between the leaders of the Congress and those of the Muslim League had continued unabated. League leaders had deprecated the assurances demanded of the governors by Congress leaders as a condition of their accepting office and instead suggested that the latter should give assurances to the minorities in the Congress-majority provinces.

Early in May 1937 the Congress organized conventions of the newly elected legislators at the provincial capitals and at New Delhi which were boycotted by the Muslim League, though a few isolated pro-Congress Muslim Leaguers did take part in them. The leaders of the Muslim League also toyed with the idea of organizing conventions of Muslim or non-Congress M.L.A.s. In mid-May 1937 some nationalist Muslims met in a conference at Allahabad. They criticized the 'separatist' and 'anti-Congress' policy of the Muslim League and advised their co-religionists 'to unconditionally join the Indian National Congress and participate in the struggle for the freedom of the country'.[4] Those who figured prominently at the Allahabad conference included not only the well-known Congress Muslims such as Maulana Abul

[1] *Leader*, May 9–10, 1937.
[2] *Ibid.* May 10, 1937.
[3] *Pioneer*, March 27, 1937.
[4] *Leader*, May 19, 1937.

Kalam Azad and Dr Syed Mahmud and the leaders of the pro-Congress Muslim organizations (Jamiat-ul-Ulema and others), but also Syed Wazir Hasan, who had presided over the last session of the All-Indian Muslim League held at Bombay in April 1936. Early in June 1937 a prominent pro-Congress Muslim who had been elected to the United Provinces legislature on the Muslim League ticket, Hafiz Muhammad Ibrahim, resigned from the Muslim League, complaining of the League's 'anti-national' and 'anti- Congress' policy, and joined the Congress party.[1] Ibrahim's example was followed a few weeks later by four other Muslim M.L.A.s in the United Provinces (two elected on the League ticket – Muhammad Suleman Ansari and Saiduddin Khan – and two as Independents – Abdul Hakim and Aqbal Suhel).[2] When, therefore, the Congress ultimately formed ministries in the six provinces where it had secured clear majorities, its strength in the United Provinces legislature had increased to 139, including seven Muslims (two elected on the Congress ticket and five Muslim M.L.A.s who had recently defected to the Congress).

Congress-League relations in the United Provinces touched a new low in June-July 1937 when the two parties set up rival candidates to contest the Jhansi-Jalaun-Hamirpur Muslim seat in a by-election. The contest became a veritable trial of strength between the Congress and the League who strained all their available resources to win it. Congress leaders were greatly annoyed at the manner in which League leaders conducted their election campaign, particularly the appeals openly made by the latter to the communal feelings of the electorate,[3] and the result was that personal relations even between the few local leaders on both sides who had hitherto managed to remain friends were badly damaged. As against the superior organization and resources of the Congress, the League depended – as Shaukat Ali later confessed[4] – entirely on the cry of 'Allah-o-Akbar', and carried the day.

The defeat of the Congress candidate in a bitterly contested by-election, coming as it did almost on the eve of the formation of the Congress ministry in the United Provinces, could not have been conducive to the success of the negotiations for a 'Congress-League coalition' which had recently been resumed, mainly at the instigation of Khaliquzzaman. A rather slippery politician who had a foot in almost every camp, Khaliquzzaman was torn between his old loyalty to the Congress and his new loyalty to the League, between his attraction to a ministership and his fear of being repudiated by his colleagues in the Muslim League. He persisted in continuing his negotiations with the Congress leaders, but these negotiations ultimately failed on July 28, 1937, not, as has been alleged by some latter-day writers, because the Congress laid down any impossible conditions,[5] but because of Khaliquzzaman's

[1] *Leader*, June 5, 1937.

[2] *Ibid.* July 25, 1937; *Pioneer*, July 24, 1937.

[3] See, for example, Nehru's statement in *Leader*, July 3, 1937, and his letter to Khaliquzzaman in *A Bunch of Old Letters* (1959), pp. 258–60.

[4] *Pioneer*, July 18, 1937.

[5] For the terms offered by Maulana Azad on behalf of the Congress see *Leader*, August 4, 1937. There were only two main conditions laid down by the Congress for a coalition with the League, namely, that the 'Muslim League group in the United Provinces Legislature shall cease to function as a separate group' and that the 'Muslim League Parliamentary

insistence that communal questions should be specifically excluded from the scope of the agreement[1] and that a colleague of his in the Muslim League legislature party – Nawab Muhammad Ismail Khan – who was not acceptable to Congress leaders both on personal and political grounds, should also be included along with him in the ministry.[2] The breakdown of the talks between Khaliquzzaman and the Congress leaders in July 1937, though regretted by some, caused little surprise and elicited few comments at the time. The most significant commentary on the whole episode was provided by Khaliquzzaman himself. 'I am afraid', he said in a statement issued on July 30, 1937, 'I was trying to accomplish the impossible.'[3]

THE SCHISM WIDENS

After the elections of 1937 Jinnah redoubled his efforts to make the Muslim League the sole representative organization of the Muslims so as to enable him – as the leader of the League – to bargain on a level of equality with the leaders of the Congress. There is reason to believe that Jinnah was in 1937 still thinking in terms of reaching an ultimate settlement with the Congress, but he was not sure what this settlement could be or of his ability to get it endorsed by his community. This may well explain why he never really cared

Board in the United Provinces will be dissolved, and no candidates will thereafter be set up by the said Board at any by-election'. As regards the first condition, all that needs to be said is that it is difficult to see how a Congress-League coalition government could function effectively in the United Provinces if the Muslim League group in the local legislature continued to function as a separate group. As regards the second condition, it is necessary to point out that the Congress had already dissolved its own parliamentary board and all that it was asking the League to do was to follow suit, with the sole object of avoiding a confrontation between the Congress and the League in any future by-election. It is significant that none of these two conditions was specifically objected to by Khaliquzzaman in his public statement of July 30, 1937.

[1] See Khaliquzzaman's statement in *Leader*, August 4, 1937.

[2] See the statement of Maulana Ahmad Said in *ibid.* November 10, 1937. Also, A. K. Azad, *India Wins Freedom* (1959), pp. 160–1, and Khaliquzzaman, *Pathway to Pakistan* (1961), pp. 160–3. It seems that the objection of Congress leaders to the inclusion of Nawab Muhammad Ismail Khanin the ministry was due not merely to the fact that he was a nawab. They wanted to have a cabinet of six ministers in the United Provinces, at least one of whom was a Congress Muslim. They were, therefore, unwilling to admit more than one Muslim Leaguer in the cabinet. Khaliquzzaman, on the other hand, demanded that one-third of the members of the cabinet should belong to the Muslim League. As he says in his *Pathway to Pakistan* (p. 160): 'Pandit Pant . . . asked me how many seats in the Cabinet I would demand in case of a coalition between the Congress and League. I replied: Three in nine and two in six, i.e., one-third of the total strength of the Cabinet whatever it may be.' Had Congress leaders conceded Khaliquzzaman's demand, they would have been required either to have no Congress Muslim in the cabinet or to have fifty per cent Muslims in the cabinet. In either case, a precedent would have been created which was not welcome to Congress leaders. As Yakub Hasan, a leading Congress Muslim from Madras, wrote later ('The Hindu-Muslim Situation', *Indian Review*, April 1940, p. 218): 'If the Congress had been short-sighted enough to agree to the proposed arrangement, the Congress-League cabinets would have been today ruling over all the 11 provinces. . . . The two-nation formula that has been propounded lately would not have come before the public as a pet theory of Mr. Jinnah, for it would have already become an accomplished fact and thereby a legitimate demand would have been created for the inclusion of the two-nation principle in the new constitution of India.'

[3] *Leader*, August 4, 1937.

to spell out his conditions for a possible settlement, though he was repeatedly asked by Congress leaders to do so. A vigorous campaign was launched to organize the Muslim League at various levels all over the country. The cry was raised – even before the Congress formed ministries in the six provinces where it had secured clear majorities – that Islam was in danger and that the Congress was trying to divide the Muslims in its bid to establish Hindu *raj* throughout the country. The Muslims were asked to rally under one banner for their survival and an attempt was made to coerce or cajole Muslims of other political persuasions to fall in line with the League. The decision of the Congress to accept office was represented as a crowning piece of Hindu hypocrisy and the result of a sinister understanding between the Congress and the British government. The formation of a Congress ministry in the predominantly Muslim North-West Frontier Province later in the year was treated as an insult to the Muslims and as a warning that very soon the Congress would capture governments even in the remaining Muslim-majority provinces. Governors were denounced for not using their special powers to nominate Muslim ministers who were truly representative of their community in the Congress-governed provinces. The League, which had earlier condemned the scheme of federation embodied in the Act of 1935 as being not democratic enough, now changed its ground and condemned the Act as being detrimental to the interests of the Muslims in particular, for it meant their subjugation to the vast Hindu majority, propped up by British bayonets. Pressure began to be secretly exercised on Muslim states, especially Hyderabad, to stay out of the proposed federation.[1] The League skilfully exploited every act of omission or commission by Congress governments to build up the image of the Congress in the eyes of the Muslims as that of a party of the tyrannical Hindu majority bent upon oppressing the Muslims, denying them their due rights and privileges and destroying their religion and culture.

Jinnah steadily succeeded in achieving his objective of making the League the most powerful organization of the Muslims, but in the very process of doing so he ruined all chances of reaching an amicable settlement with the Congress. The more he tried to rally the Muslims under the banner of the League by appealing to their communal hopes and fears, the more he had to succumb to and identify himself with those communal hopes and fears, thus abandoning his old role of 'the ambassador of Hindu-Muslim unity'. Congress leaders, too, were embittered by what they considered to be a systematic and malicious campaign of vilification against the Congress launched by the Muslim League. Efforts were none the less made by Congress leaders in 1937–8 to open negotiations with Jinnah, but they failed to make any headway. Having consolidated his position to a considerable extent, Jinnah now insisted that before negotiations could begin the Muslim League should be recognized as the one and only organization that represented the entire Muslim community in India and that the Congress should speak only on behalf of the Hindus. The Congress refused to accept Jinnah's condition, for it would have meant its committing suicide as a national organization. As Rajendra Prasad rightly pointed out, it 'would be denying its past, falsifying

[1] See Marquess of Zetland, '*Essayez*'*; the Memoirs of Lawrence, Second Marquess of Zetland* (1965), pp. 254–5.

its history, and betraying its future'.[1] Lacking any common ground or common approach, staking exaggerated claims and working at cross-purposes in an increasingly unpropitious atmosphere, the Congress and the League steadily became two absolutes between whom no compromise was possible.

As long as Congress ministries remained in office, the League derived and extended its power by resistance to and negation of Congress rule, but when Congress ministries resigned in October 1939 over the war issue, negation alone left the League static. For this reason as well as any other, Jinnah and his associates had inevitably to evolve a positive procedure. The circumstances, too, were favourable: the Congress was out of office, the government was engaged in war and was in search of friends, the federation was shelved, and there was a clear prospect of the transfer of power at the end of the war. In March 1940, at its Lahore session, the All-India Muslim League formally demanded the partition of India and the creation of a separate independent Muslim state.

THE EMERGENCE OF THE DEMAND FOR PAKISTAN

The demand as such was neither new nor sudden. The idea of 'Pakistan' or a separate homeland for the Indian Muslim had been floating in the imagination of many educated Muslims for quite a long time. It was born of the feeling entertained and sedulously propagated by certain Muslim intellectuals that their community formed a distinct cultural and political entity, different from the other Indian communities, especially the Hindus. It was encouraged and fortified by the sentiment of pan-Islamism, the grant of separate electorates and the fear that in a united India the Muslims would inevitably be placed under the domination of the Hindus, who outnumbered them by three to one. It received its real strength and substance, however, from the fact that there were certain regions in India, particularly in the north-west and the north-east, where the Muslims formed a majority of the population and which they thought they must dominate. But for this accident of geography, the idea of Pakistan – even if it were born – would never have materialized. If the Muslim population in India had been more evenly distributed throughout the sub-continent, it would have been a minority everywhere which could have neither dreamt nor been in a position to dominate – as a community – any region.

The myth of the inevitability of Pakistan has already grown and historians have, as is their wont, been of late busy proving and perpetuating it. They have traced the idea of Pakistan back to Sir Syed Ahmad Khan in the nineteenth century, to Shah Waliullah and Shah Abdul Aziz in the eighteenth century, and even to Mohammad bin Qasim, the first Muslim invader of India early in the eighth century. They have attributed its emergence to the ancient and allegedly incurable religious and cultural schism between the Hindu and the Muslim, to the British policy of divide and rule (which later took the form of 'divide and quit'), to the working of the inexorable logic of the separate electorates conceded to the Muslims in 1909, to the theory of

[1] Cited in V. P. Menon, *The Transfer of Power in India* (1957), p. 57.

'two nations', to the determination of the Muslims in India not to submit to the Hindu majority and instead secure a homeland for themselves, and to the lapses on the part of the Hindu and Congress leaders.

These theories are often illuminating. But, while they may explain the historical phenomenon of Muslim separatism in India, they do not really explain the emergence of Pakistan as a geographical and political phenomenon. Muslim separatism in India had a long history, but it was not the only separatism that afflicted India. It had created many complications in the past and it could create many more in the future. It might have even led to a civil war. But Muslim separatism in itself could not have led to Pakistan, unless there were Muslim-majority regions in India which could be easily separated from the rest of India. The Muslim desire for a separate homeland of their own could not, even if it had arisen, have found fulfilment in the manner in which it ultimately did unless there were clearly demarcable regions in which the Muslims were in a majority and which they could turn into their own separate homeland. Further, even the existence of well-defined and easily separable Muslim-majority provinces and the Muslim desire to dominate them as a community would not necessarily have led to the partition of India. For, without great difficulty, some form of loose all-India federation could have taken cognizance of both these facts. After all, the Muslims were dominant in the Muslim-majority provinces – this dominance could have been made more effective by making some territorial and other adjustments – and the strong sense of Muslim solidarity militated against the idea of the division of India. But it was the alliance of Muslim separatism with the Muslim will to power which proved decisive. It was the determination of the All-India Muslim League, the carrier of the ideology of Muslim separatism in India, to dominate the Muslim-majority provinces which led directly and inevitably to the partition of India and the creation of Pakistan. The fact of Jinnah's leadership has relevance in this context only in so far as he became both the architect and the symbol of the alliance between Muslim separatism and the Muslim will to rule the Muslim-majority provinces. In their reckless pursuit of power the leaders of the League not only divided India, they also divided the so-called Muslim nation in whose name they had claimed a separate homeland. History offers few better examples of poetic justice than this.

As long as constitutional reforms in India were limited to the introduction of representative institutions, the Muslims as a minority community felt their position fully safeguarded by separate electorates. But no sooner did the prospect of responsible government in India appear on the horizon after the first world war than the Muslims began to fear for their own future in a state in which, under any system of popular election, they would be in a position of perpetual subordination to the Hindu majority. There was, however, one redeeming feature in the grim prospect that awaited them. The Muslims were not in a minority in all the provinces. In Bengal, the Punjab, Sind and the North-West Frontier Province they actually formed a majority of the population. If, therefore, the powers of the central government could be reduced to the minimum and the provinces given the utmost autonomy, there was a chance that the four Muslim-majority provinces could provide some sort of a balance to the seven Hindu-majority provinces in British India. As for the

Muslim minority in the Hindu-majority provinces, its position could be safeguarded by statutory enactment or by the threat that whatever treatment was meted out to it would be given also to the Hindu minority in the Muslim-majority provinces. Early in the 1920s Muslim opinion began to veer round to this simple solution of the political and communal problem in the country as their only hope of security in a future self-governing India. Some Muslims began to think in terms of a loose federation, with a weak centre for minimum common purposes and written safeguards for the minorities, and of fully autonomous provinces, vested with the residuary powers, so as to enable the Muslims to play an effective role at the centre and to dominate at least the four provinces in which they formed a majority of the population.

This Muslim solution of the Indian political and communal problem was put forward publicly – probably for the first time – by Maulana Hasrat Mohani in his presidential address to the Muslim League session held at Ahmedabad towards the end of December 1921.[1] With slight variations of emphasis or detail, it formed the substance of the various demands put forward in the twenties and thirties by most of the prominent Muslim organizations and leaders on behalf of their community. Attempts were being made concurrently to provide with an adequate rationale the Muslim demand to dominate the provinces where the Muslims were in a majority. The Indian Muslims, it was urged, were a 'nation' by themselves, totally different from the other 'nations' in India, and as such entitled to exercise their right of self-determination and to establish a homeland for themselves where they could work out their destiny according to their own ideas of Islamic culture and polity. While some, such as Muhammad Iqbal[2] in 1930, favoured 'the creation of a Muslim India [with-] in India', others, such as Rahmat Ali[3] in 1933, advocated the total separation of 'Muslim India' from the rest of India and the creation of a new Muslim state ('Pakistan'). The results of the 1937 elections came as a great shock and surprise to the communally-minded Muslims. They showed that the Muslims were weak, divided and disorganized. They had no strong and effective all-India organization like the Congress. They were a negligible quantity in the Hindu-majority provinces. Even in the Muslim-majority provinces their position was far from being invulnerable. In two of the Muslim-majority provinces – Bengal and the Punjab – they had no effective majorities and were dependent on the support or sufferance of the non-Muslims. While the separate electorates, which they had so far regarded as their Magna Carta, precluded them from influencing the results of the elections in the non-Muslim constituencies, the Congress could, if it tried and as the 1937 elections proved, influence the results of the elections in the Muslim constituencies. The proposed all-India federation, instead of offsetting, as many Muslim leaders had hoped it would, the vast Hindu majority in India as a whole, was likely to reinforce it. The writing on the wall was clear. And it read: Muslims as a community could not be sure of dominating even the Muslim-majority provinces in India. 'The creation of a Muslim India [with-] in India' was impossible.

[1] See *Indian Annual Register*, 1922, vol. i, Appendices, pp. 71–2; also S. R. Mehrotra, *India and the Commonwealth* (1965), pp. 197–8. [2] Gwyer and Appadorai, *op. cit.* vol. ii, p. 437.
[3] See Choudhary Rahmat Ali, *Pakistan: The Fatherland of the Pak Nation* (1947), p. 225.

Soon after the elections – on May 28, 1937 – Iqbal was writing to Jinnah: '. . . the enforcement and development of the Shariat of Islam is impossible in this country without a free Muslim State or States . . . it is necessary to redistribute the country and to provide one or more Muslim States with absolute majorities. Don't you think that the time for such a demand has already arrived?'[1] On June 21, 1937 – almost a month before Congress ministries were actually formed in six provinces – we again find Iqbal writing to Jinnah that 'the idea of a single Indian federation' was 'completely hopeless' and that Muslim leaders 'ought at present to ignore Muslim-minority provinces' and instead concentrate on the creation of 'a separate federation of Muslim [-majority] provinces' in the north-west and the north-east.[2] Iqbal once again urged upon Jinnah the need for making known publicly the new objective of the Muslims. But Jinnah was no visionary like Iqbal and apparently decided to wait until the Muslims were 'sufficiently organized and disciplined'.[3] As a practical politician he knew that before demanding the creation of 'a separate federation of Muslim [-majority] provinces' he should have a strong and united Muslim party, preferably in control of the governments in the Muslim-majority provinces and some definite prospect of British withdrawal from India.

But, while Jinnah held his hand, others did not hesitate to show theirs. It was not long before an increasing number of Muslim politicians and publicists got busy with their scissors, cutting and rearranging the map of India according to their individual fancy.[4] Some of them were separationists pure and simple, others were separationists-cum-confederationists. The idea of a 'Muslim India' – within or without India – proved to be a catch-all. It made a tremendous appeal to the hopes and fears of the Muslims. The desire to have undisputed sway over the Muslim-majority provinces, the prospect of undisturbed place and power, the attraction of a separate homeland and an Islamic state, probably forming part of a future Pan-Islamic federation, fear of Hindu competition and domination, anxiety about the preservation of their communal way of life, and annoyance with the Congress made a steadily growing number of thinking Muslims favour the idea of a separation of 'Muslim India' from 'Hindu India'. While most of them took up the idea enthusiastically, at least a few accepted it rather regretfully as offering an easy and perhaps the only practicable solution to the chronic and extremely intractable Hindu-Muslim problem.

Still very weak and inchoate, the Muslim League in 1937–8 was probably not in a position to commit itself definitely on the issue, but it could not afford to postpone its commitment for long. The British government had its plan of establishing an all-India federation embodied in the Act of 1935. The Congress had countered it with its own plan of a 'constituent assembly'. The Muslim League, while opposing both the British and the Congress plans, had in 1937 virtually no alternative plan of its own. Hitherto, it had at least nominally subscribed to the idea of a loose federation for India, but the

1 *Letters of Iqbal to Jinnah* (1956), pp. 17–19.

2 *Ibid.* pp. 23–4.

3 *Ibid.*

4 For some well-known schemes see Coupland, *op. cit.* pp. 199–206 and Gwyer and Appadorai, *op. cit.* vol. ii, pp. 444–65.

results of the 1937 elections, by indicating what the position of the Muslims and of the Muslim League – even with separate electorates and the reservation of seats – was likely to be in the proposed federation, had forced it to reconsider its stand. There was a growing realization in Muslim League circles that the League's earlier adherence to the idea of an all-India federation as such, however qualified, had been a mistake. This was accompanied by an increasing apprehension – not entirely unfounded – that the Congress might ultimately agree to work the federal part of the 1935 Act. The League, therefore, became more firmly and unitedly opposed to the federation envisaged by the Act of 1935 than the Congress.

But mere opposition to the British plan of an all-India federation – and to the Congress plan of a 'constituent assembly' – was not sufficient. The Muslim League had to put forward an alternative plan of its own. Already the League rank and file were pressing for it and a good many Muslim Abbés Sieyes were busy trying to fill in the gap.

At its annual session held at Lucknow in October 1937 the Muslim League officially proclaimed its 'emphatic' disapproval of the federal scheme of the 1935 Act as being 'detrimental to the interests . . . of the Muslims in particular'.[1] While, in redefining its creed at this session as 'the establishment in India of full independence in the form of a federation of free democratic states, in which the rights and interests of the Muslims and other minorities are adequately and effectively safeguarded in the constitution',[2] the League apparently reiterated its continued adherence to the idea of a federation as such, the proceedings of the Lucknow session left no doubt as to the direction in which the current of League politics was set. Jinnah and other prominent speakers at the session breathed fire and sword against the Congress and the Hindus. They accused the British of aiding the Congress in its design of establishing Hindu *raj* and perpetrating 'atrocities' on the Muslims. They denied that India was a nation and talked of establishing 'Muslim *raj*' in opposition to 'Hindu *raj*'. Reviewing the Lucknow session of the League, a competent Muslim observer – Dr Mahmudulla Jung – wrote: 'The doctrine of aloofness was preached *ad nauseam* in a most unrestricted and irresponsible language. Out of the clouds of circumlocution and confusion arose the cry of Islam in danger. The Muslims were told that they were disunited and were about to be crucified by the Hindus. Religious fervour was raised to a degree where it exhibited itself in blind fanaticism. . . . In the name of Muslim solidarity Mr. Jinnah wants to divide India into Muslim India and Hindu India.'[3] Nehru's comment on the Muslim League annual session of 1937 was equally significant: 'The League and its supporters stand clearly and definitely today for the division of India, even on the political and economic planes, into religious groups. Whatever it may be, it is the antithesis of the nationalist idea of the unity of India. It is a reduction to absurdity of modern life and its problems. It is mediaevalism in exelsis.'[4]

A clearer picture of the aims and intentions of the Muslim League emerged

[1] *Leader*, October 20, 1937. The question of an alternative to federation was discussed at this session but no definite conclusion was reached.

[2] *Ibid.* October 19, 1937.

[3] *Pioneer*, November 7, 1937.

[4] *Ibid.* October 19, 1937.

at the Sind Provincial Muslim League conference held at Karachi in the second week of October 1938. The conference was presided over by Jinnah and attended by many prominent Muslim leaders from all over India. Speaking at the conference, Shaukat Ali remarked: 'If the Congress will not allow the Muslim League to have ministries in the four provinces where the Muslims are in a majority, vagabonds like me will run amuck.'[1] Jinnah accused the Congress of trying 'to destroy the Muslim League, divide the Muslims and dominate them', and he added in warning: 'This will result in India being divided.'[2] The chairman of the reception committee of the conference, Sir Abdulla Haroon, hinted at the possibility of 'an independent federation of Muslim States'.[3] Fazlul Haq, the premier of Bengal, was greeted with 'a wild burst of cheering' by the audience when he remarked: 'If Mohammad bin Qasim, an eight year old lad, with 18 soldiers could conquer Sindh, then surely nine crores of Muslims can conquer the whole of India.'[4] Sheikh Abdul Majid threatened 'that if the Congress did not concede Muslim rights Muslims would have no alternative but to fall back upon the Pakistan scheme' and that 'nothing would prevent Muslims, from Karachi to Calcutta, to march to their own self-determination'.[5]

The most significant episode of the conference was the tabling of a long resolution which, after cataloguing all the possible sins of the Congress and the Hindus, said:

'The Sindh Provincial Muslim League Conference considers it absolutely essential in the interests of an abiding peace of the vast Indian continent and in the interests of unhampered cultural development, the economic and social betterment and political self-determination of the two nations, known as Hindus and Muslims, that India may be divided into federations, namely, the federation of Muslim States and the federation of non-Muslim States.

'This Conference therefore recommends to the All-India Muslim League to devise a scheme of constitution under which Muslim-majority provinces Muslim Indian States and areas inhabited by a majority of Muslims may attain full independence in the form of a federation of their own with permission to admit any other Muslim State beyond the Indian frontiers to join the Federation and with such safeguards for non-Muslim minorities as may be conceded to the Muslim minorities in the non-Muslim Federation of India.' [6]

At the subjects committee stage of the proceedings of the conference, however, this particular portion of the resolution was altered to read as follows:

'This Conference considers it absolutely essential, in the interests of an abiding peace of the vast Indian continent and in the interests of unhampered cultural development, the economic and social betterment and political self-determination of the two nations, known as Hindus and Muslims, to recommend to the All-India Muslim League to review and revise the entire

[1] *Leader*, October 11, 1938. [2] *Ibid.*

[3] *Times of India*, October 10, 1938.

[4] *Ibid.* October 11, 1938.

[5] *Statesman*, October 12, 1938.

[6] *Ibid.* October 11, 1938. See also *Times of India*, October 5 and 10, 1938.

conception of what should be the suitable constitution for India which will secure honourable and legitimate status to them.' [1]

We do not precisely know the reasons which prompted this alteration. Probably some League leaders felt that the resolution as originally tabled was too explicit and premature. A remark made by Jinnah at the conference is highly significant in this connection. 'The Government', he said, 'is still in the hands of the British. Let us not forget it. You must see ahead and work for that ideal which you think will arise 25 years hence.'[2]

In December 1938 the annual session of the All-India Muslim League, held at Patna, reiterated its opposition to the scheme of an all-India federation embodied in the 1935 Act and authorized its president, Jinnah, to adopt such courses as might be necessary with a view to exploring a suitable alternative to the aforesaid scheme which would safeguard the interests of the Muslims.[3] The idea of the physical division of India was discussed at almost every gathering of Muslim Leaguers during 1939. On March 26, 1939 the working committee of the Muslim League appointed a committee, headed by Jinnah, to examine and report on the various draft schemes 'already expounded by those who are fully versed in the constitutional developments of India and other countries and those that may be submitted hereafter to the President and report to the Working Committee their conclusions at an early date'.[4] The committee appointed by the working committee of the Muslim League presumably examined the 'several schemes in the field including that of dividing the country into Muslim and Hindu India',[5] but there is no evidence to suggest that its year-long deliberations enabled it to reach any final decision and to recommend a particular scheme of its own to the Muslim League working committee. Opinion in the committee – as in Muslim League circles generally – was apparently divided on three main questions: What areas should form part of 'Muslim India'? Should 'Muslim India' be completely separate and independent? Should there be a transfer of population between 'Muslim India' and 'Hindu India'? This division of opinion probably accounts for the vagueness and imprecision of the famous resolution passed by the All-India Muslim League at its annual session in Lahore on March 23, 1940, which affirmed 'that no constitutional plan would be workable in this country or acceptable to the Muslims unless it is designed on the following basic

[1] *Pioneer*, October 15, 1938.

[2] *Statesman*, October 14, 1938. Similarly in early 1937 Jinnah had sarcastically wished Nehru 'long life' in order to be able to realize his dream of political independence for India in his own lifetime (*Leader*, May 3, 1937). These remarks lead us to conclude that in 1937–8 Jinnah still believed that the British had no intention of withdrawing from India in the near future. It was the assurance given by the British government after the outbreak of the war—especially that contained in the viceroy's statement of January 10, 1940—that India would be granted dominion status as soon as possible after the war, which probably convinced Jinnah that the transfer of power could not be far off. In his presidential address to the Lahore session of the Muslim League in March 1940 Jinnah made a pointed reference to 'the termination of the British regime, which is implicit in the recent declaration of His Majesty's Government' (*Leader*, March 24, 1940). This fact has some relevance to the timing of the Muslim League's demand for Pakistan.

[3] *Statesman*, December 29, 1938.

[4] *Pioneer*, March 28, 1939.

[5] *Indian Annual Register* (1939), vol. i, p. 374.

principles, viz. that geographically contiguous units are demarcated into regions which should be so constituted, with such territorial readjustments as may be necessary, that the areas in which the Muslims are numerically in a majority as in the North-Western and Eastern zones of India should be grouped to constitute "Independent States" in which the constituent units shall be autonomous and sovereign'.[1]

The usual arguments, with which we have become familiar, were urged in favour of the resolution adopted by the League at Lahore in March 1940: that the Muslims must dominate the areas in which they were in a majority and that this dominance could not be assured in a united India with its 'hostile' and 'tyrannical' Hindu majority, that India was not one nation, that the Muslims of India constituted a separate nation and were as such entitled to a separate homeland of their own where they could work out their destiny according to their cherished ideals, and that western democracy was not suited to Indian conditions. Whatever the views of other League leaders, there can be no doubt that Jinnah had now crossed the Rubicon and that what he demanded was the partition of India pure and simple and the creation of a separate, sovereign Muslim state, popularly known as Pakistan. With him at least the demand for Pakistan was neither a bluff nor a bargaining counter, but a solemn and irrevocable decision.

THE CONGRESS AND THE MUSLIM LEAGUE'S DEMAND FOR PAKISTAN

The Muslim League's demand for Pakistan was open – and in fact subjected – to many obvious criticisms. It was a grave blow to the ideal of a united India which generations of Indians had cherished and laboured for. The vivisection of India was an outrageous idea to all those who had become accustomed to the geographical, political, economic and cultural unity of the country. It was considered to be retrograde, impracticable and dangerous. If religion were to be acknowledged as the criterion of nationality and each nationality allowed to have a separate homeland for itself, it would mean the Balkanization of India. If the non-Muslims were to continue staying – as most League leaders assured they would – in the areas claimed for Pakistan, how would those areas be different in political composition and power from what they were at present and in what sense would they become Islamic? If Hindus and Muslims were two separate and antagonistic nations in India, how would they become one peaceful nation in Pakistan? Similarly, if democracy was not suited to India, how would it become suited to Pakistan? The division of India would not improve the position of the minorities. It would in fact worsen their position by converting them into hostages. Smaller minorities would be subjected to the domination of bigger majorities. Instead of solving, the creation of Pakistan would perpetrate and even aggravate communal differences. It would not bring peace but the sword. The Muslims in India would raise the cry of oppression at the hands of the Hindus and the Hindus in Pakistan would raise a similar cry, and there would be retaliatory wars. Instead of peace and harmony there would be aggression of one state against

[1] Gwyer and Appadorai, *op. cit.* vol. ii, p. 443.

the other and the sub-continent would for ever remain exposed to third-party intervention. The creation of Pakistan would be detrimental even to the best interests of the Muslims, for it would permanently divide and weaken them.

These and similar other weighty objections were raised against the Muslim League demand for Pakistan by the leaders of almost all the other political parties and groups in the country, but they failed to make any impact on Jinnah and his followers. To Congressmen the idea of Pakistan was particularly distasteful, for it threatened to undo the effort the Congress had been making for over half a century. In the same week of March 1940 in which Jinnah put forward the demand for Pakistan on the basis of the 'two nations' theory at the Lahore session of the Muslim League, another – and a more learned and devout – Muslim, Maulana Abul Kalam Azad, reiterated the creed of Indian nationalism at the Ramgarh session of the Congress:

'It was India's historic destiny that many human races and cultures and religions should flow to her, finding a home in her hospitable soil, and many a caravan should find rest here. . . . One of the last of these caravans, following the footsteps of its predecessors, was that of the followers of Islam. This came here and settled here for good. This led to a meeting of the culture-currents of two different races. Like the Ganga and Jumna, they flowed for a while through separate courses, but nature's immutable law brought them together and joined them in a *sangam*. This fusion was a notable event in history. . . . Eleven hundred years of common history have enriched India with our common achievements. Our languages, our poetry, our literature, our culture, our art, our dress, our manners and customs, the innumerable happenings of our daily life, everything bears the stamp of our joint endeavour. This joint wealth is the heritage of our common nationality and we do not want to leave it and go back to the time when this joint life had not begun. . . . The cast has now been moulded and destiny has set its seal upon it. Whether we like it or not, we have now become an Indian nation, united and indivisible. No fantasy or artificial scheming to separate and divide can break this unity. We must accept the logic of fact and history and engage ourselves in the fashioning of our future destiny.'[1]

Gandhi called the 'two nations' theory 'an untruth' and wrote: 'The vast majority of Muslims of India are converts to Islam or are the descendants of converts. They did not become a separate nation as soon as they became converts. A Bengali Muslim speaks the same tongue that a Bengali Hindu does, eats the same food and has the same amusements as his Hindu neighbour. They dress alike. I have often found it difficult to distinguish by outward sign between a Bengali Hindu and a Bengali Muslim. The same phenomenon is observable more or less in the south among the poor, who constitute the masses of India. . . . Hindus and Muslims of India are not two nations. Those whom God has made one, man will never be able to divide.'[2]

But, while Congressmen flatly refused to countenance the 'two nations' theory and the proposed partition of India and continued nourishing the hope

[1] *Leader*, March 21, 1940.

[2] D. G. Tendulkar, *Mahatma* (1952), vol. v, pp. 334–5.

that League leaders would finally turn back from the brink, they also made it clear that they would not use coercion to resist the demand for Pakistan. 'Unless the rest of India', wrote Gandhi in April 1940, 'wishes to engage in internal fratricide, the others will have to submit to the Muslim dictation, if the Muslims will resort to it. I know no non-violent method of compelling the obedience of eight crores of Muslims to the will of the rest of India, however powerful a majority the rest may represent. The Muslims must have the same right of self-determination that the rest of India has. We are at present a joint family. Any member may claim a division.'[1] Again in the same month he wrote: 'As a man of non-violence, I cannot forcibly resist the proposed partition if the Muslims of India really insist upon it. But I never can be a willing party to the vivisection. . . . For it means the undoing of centuries of work done by numberless Hindus and Muslims to live together as one nation. Partition means a patent untruth. My whole soul rebels against the idea that Hinduism and Islam represent two antagonistic cultures and doctrines. . . . But that is my belief. I cannot thrust it down the throats of the Muslims who think that they are a different nation. I refuse, however, to believe that the eight crores of Muslims will say that they have nothing in common with their Hindu and other brethren. Their mind can only be known by a referendum made to them duly on that clear issue. The contemplated constituent assembly can easily decide the question.'[2]

The Congress did not formally express its attitude to the demand for Pakistan until April 1942 – and then, too, indirectly – but there is reason to believe that Gandhi's views, quoted above, were shared by a great majority in the Congress. As a nationalist organization, which had unfortunately failed to secure the confidence of the Muslim community, wedded to democracy and non-violence, the Congress could not afford to resist the demand for Pakistan by force, especially while it was still engaged in fighting the British for the political freedom of India. The Congress, however, could not accept the 'two nations' theory. It could not be a willing party to the division of India. But, if the Muslims were really insistent upon Pakistan, they could have it. Let them send their representatives to the proposed constituent assembly with a clear mandate and let these representatives settle the issue.

Jinnah, however, insisted that the Congress should first concede the principle underlying the demand for Pakistan. Probably he was just biding his time for he was as yet not sure of securing a decisive verdict in favour of Pakistan from his own community.

The annoyance and distress caused in Congress circles by the Lahore resolution of the League was not unmixed with a certain amount of relief, especially at the thought that League leaders had at last given up their frivolous demands and shown their real hand and that this had cleared the air. Nehru, for example, was reported to have remarked that, instead of feeling sorry at the Muslim League's new demand, 'he was pleased, not because he liked it – on the contrary he considered it to be the most insane suggestion – but because it very much simplified the problem. They were now able to get rid of the demands about proportionate representation in legislatures, services, cabinets, etc. . . . [He] asserted that if people wanted such things, as

[1] D. G. Tendulkar, *Mahatma* (1952) vol. v, pp. 333–4. [2] *Ibid.* pp. 336–7.

suggested by the Muslim League at Lahore, then one thing was clear, they and people like him could not live together in India. He would be prepared to face all consequences of it but he would not be prepared to live with such people.'[1]

Having more or less resigned themselves to the distasteful possibility of the partition of India, if the vast majority of the Muslims insisted upon it, Congress leaders decided to concentrate almost all their attention on securing the political freedom of India as early as possible and on preserving the political unity of as large a part of the country as possible. They could not coerce the Muslim League into giving up its demand, but they could not also allow the Muslim League to coerce them into giving up their own cherished ideals. Their fight for the independence and unity of India was to continue with unabated vigour and they were not to enter into any temporary or patchwork settlement with either the Muslim League or the British government which was likely to damage their ultimate objective. As often in the past, Gandhi gave clear expression to this new mood of Congressmen in a series of articles in the *Harijan*.

'The British', he wrote in the *Harijan* of May 4, 1940, 'can retain their hold on India only by a policy of "divide and rule". A living unity between the Muslims and Hindus is fraught with danger to their rule. It would mean an end to it. Therefore, it seems to me that a true solution will come with the end of the rule, potentially, if not in fact. What can be done under the threat of Pakistan? If it is not a threat but a desirable goal, why should it be prevented? If it is undesirable and is meant only for the Muslims to get more under its shadow, any solution would be an unjust solution. It would be worse than no solution. I, therefore, am entirely for waiting till the menace is gone. The whole world is in the throes of a new birth. Anything done for a temporary gain would be tantamount to an abortion.

'I cannot think in terms of narrow Hinduism or narrow Islam. I am wholly uninterested in a patchwork solution. India is a big country, a big nation composed of different cultures, which are tending to blend with one another, each complementing the rest. If I must wait for the completion of the process, I must wait. It may not be completed in my day. I should love to die in the faith that it must come in the fullness of time. I should be happy to think that I had done nothing to hamper the process. Subject to this condition, I would do anything to bring about harmony. My life is made up of compromises, but they have been compromises that have brought me nearer the goal. Pakistan cannot be worse than the foreign domination. I have lived under the latter, though not willingly. If God so desires it, I may have to become a helpless witness to the undoing of my dream. But I do not believe that the Muslims want to dismember India.

'The partition proposal has altered the face of the Hindu-Musllm problem. I have called it an untruth. There can be no compromise with it. At the same

[1] *Leader*, April 15, 1940. On another occasion Nehru was reported to have remarked: 'Many knots of the Hindu-Muslim problem had been merged into one knot, which could not be unravelled by ordinary methods, but would need an operation . . . he would say one thing very frankly that he had begun to consider them [Muslim Leaguers] and people like himself, as separate nations.' *Leader*, April 16, 1940.

time I have said that, if the eight crores of Muslims desire it, no power on earth can prevent it, notwithstanding opposition, violent or non-violent. It cannot come by honourable compromise.'[1]

Again, in another issue of the *Harijan*, dated June 15, 1940, Gandhi underlined the difficulty of achieving a common measure of agreement between parties which did not have a common ground or a common approach and asserted that the Congress could not afford to betray its trust just for the sake of achieving such an agreement. He wrote: '. . . if the Congress loses hope and faith and comes to the conclusion that it must surrender its original position for the purpose of getting a common measure of agreement, it will cease to be the power it is. Today it is the sheet-anchor of India's hope and faith. It will be well for it, if it refuses to move away from its moorings, whether it is in a minority or a majority.'[2]

The reaction of Congress leaders to Jinnah's demand for Pakistan must have convinced him that, though Congress leaders might not willingly concede it – at least not on principle – they would not forcibly resist it, and that all that he really needed to do in order to achieve his objective was to produce evidence of overwhelming support for the demand among the Muslims and to persuade the British government to agree to it. This he could easily do. The cry of Pakistan swept the Muslims off their feet. That it should have been popular with the Muslims of the Muslim-majority provinces is easily understandable, but the extent to which Muslim Leaguers were able to delude themselves and their co-religionists in the Hindu-majority provinces into believing that Pakistan was good for them, is one of the most astonishing phenomena of modern times – a phenomenon which students of mass psychology might study with benefit. It was, however, not until the elections of 1945–6 that Jinnah could effectively establish his claim that the vast majority of the Muslims supported the demand for Pakistan.

British attitude to the demand for Pakistan had, of necessity, to be equivocal. Though few Britons ever believed that India could be governed as 'one and indivisible' by their brown successors, the prospect of the partition of India could not be pleasing to those who took pride in the creation of the administrative and political unity of the sub-continent as being one of the greatest of British imperial achievements. On the other hand, as the viceroy publicly affirmed on August 8, 1940, the British government 'could not contemplate the transfer of their present responsibilities for the peace and welfare of India to any system of government whose authority is directly denied by large and powerful elements in India's national life'.[3] It had not been British policy in the past 'to expedite in India constitutional changes for their own sake, or gratuitously to hurry the handing over of controls to Indian hands'[4] and the British government saw no reason to alter that policy at a moment when it was 'engaged in a battle for existence'. Faced with conflicting claims and lacking a plan of its own, the British government adopted the not uncongenial attitude of giving its ear to all and its mind to none. To

[1] Cited in *Statesman*, May 5, 1940.
[2] *Ibid.* June 16, 1940.
[3] Gwyer and Appadorai, *op. cit.* vol. ii, p. 505.
[4] Lord Linlithgow to Lord Zetland, December 28, 1939, cited in Zetland, *op. cit.* p. 277.

many Britons in India, who found the Congress either incomprehensible or irritating, the demand for Pakistan appeared to be a condign punishment to the Congress for its impudence in asking the British to quit India. They regarded the partition of India as inevitable and not entirely unwelcome. Commenting upon the Lahore resolution of the Muslim League, the *Statesman* of Calcutta wrote on March 26, 1940:

'Partition, we have to recognize, is becoming a live issue. If India receives Dominion Status partition seems the inevitable result in view of the attitude which the Muslim community appears disposed to adopt. If that really represents their position neither the Congress nor the Hindu Mahasabha would be able to hold them. There would probably be fighting, but in any case there would be partition. The situation would be further complicated by other facts. The Congress resolution repudiates association with Great Britain and aims at severing economic links, and the most vocal section of the Congress, the Leftists, demand a new economic orientation and affiliation with Soviet economy, while the Rightists are in economics purely reactionary and talk of reversion to the spinning wheel, and village economy to replace national industry. The Muslims on the other hand propose that their independent Northern and Eastern federation shall be permanently allied with Great Britain and free from fads either about the spinning wheel or the dictatorship of the proletariat. Actually at the back of their minds is probably the intention of making an easy meal of the other half of India, while it is busy with the quarrel between the spinners and the Marxists, and establishing an Islamic empire to be a glory of the modern world.'[1]

TOWARDS PARTITION

The story of the various efforts made to solve the Indian problem during and after the war is long and complicated, but for the purposes of this paper it can be easily told. While the Muslim League examined every proposal from its own point of view, namely, whether or not it led directly and speedily to the creation of Pakistan, the Congress examined the same proposal from its own point of view, namely whether or not it ensured the freedom and the maximum possible unity of India. The Congress did not regret the shelving of the federal part of the 1935 Act for it had never regarded it as capable of leading to the emergence of a united and free India. The Congress turned down the long-term proposals of the Cripps mission of 1942 for similar reasons. In its resolution dated April 2, 1942 the working committee of the Congress said:

'The complete ignoring of ninety millions of people in the Indian States, and their treatment as commodities at the disposal of their rulers, is a negation both of democracy and self-determination. While the representation of an Indian State in the constitution-making body is fixed on a population basis, the people of the State have no voice in choosing those representatives, nor are they to be consulted at any stage while decisions vitally affecting them are being taken. Such States may in many ways become barriers to the

[1] *Statesman*, March 26, 1940.

growth of Indian freedom, enclaves where foreign authority still prevails, and where the possibility of maintaining foreign armed forces has been stated to be a likely contingency and a perpetual menace to the freedom of the people of the States as well as the rest of India.

'The acceptance beforehand of the novel principle of non-accession for a Province is also a severe blow to the conception of Indian unity and an apple of discord likely to generate growing trouble in the Provinces, and which may well lead to further difficulties in the way of the Indian States merging themselves into an Indian Union. Congress has been wedded to Indian freedom and unity and any break of that unity especially in the modern world when people's minds inevitably think in terms of ever larger federations would be injurious to all concerned and exceedingly painful to contemplate. *Nevertheless, the Committee cannot think in terms of compelling the people of any territorial unit to remain in an Indian Union against their declared and established will. While recognising this principle, the Committee feel that every effort should be made to create a common and co-operative national life. Acceptance of this principle inevitably involves that no changes should be made which would result in fresh problems being created and compulsion being exercised on other substantial groups within that area.* Each territorial unit should have the fullest possible autonomy within the Union consistently with a strong national state.

'The proposal now made on the part of the British War Cabinet encourages and will lead to attempts at separation at the very inception of the Union and thus create great friction just when the utmost co-operation and goodwill are most needed. This proposal has been presumably made to meet the communal demand, but it will have other consequences also and lead politically reactionary and obscurantist groups among the different communities to create trouble and divert public attention from the vital issues before the country.'[1]

A careful perusal of this resolution would reveal that, while the Congress working committee rejected the long-term proposals of the Cripps mission because it feared that they might lead to the disintegration of India, it had implicitly conceded (in the italicised portion of the statement) the Muslim League's demand for Pakistan, provided, first, that a common centre was maintained, and second, that the non-Muslim-majority areas in Assam, Bengal and the Punjab were not to be compelled to join Pakistan. Had the Muslim League been willing to accept Pakistan in association with the rest of India it could have easily struck a bargain with the Congress in 1942. But obviously it was not willing to do so.

During his talks with Jinnah in 1944 Gandhi further spelled out the terms of the Congress offer. Gandhi wrote to Jinnah on September 24, 1944:

'I proceed on the assumption that India is not to be regarded as two or more nations, but as one family consisting of many members of whom the Muslims living in the north-west zones, i.e., Baluchistan, Sindh, the North-West Frontier Province, and that part of the Punjab where they are in absolute majority over all the other elements, and in parts of Bengal and Assam where

[1] Gwyer and Appadorai, *op. cit.* vol. ii, p. 525. Italics added.

they are in absolute majority, desire to live in separation from the rest of India.

'Differing from you on the general basis, I can yet recommend to the Congress and the country the acceptance of the claim for separation contained in the Muslim League Resolution of Lahore, 1940, on my basis and on the following terms:

'(*a*) The areas should be demarcated by a commission approved by the Congress and the League. The wishes of the inhabitants of the areas demarcated should be ascertained through the votes of the adult population of the areas or through some equivalent method.

'(*b*) If the vote is in favour of separation, it shall be agreed that these areas shall form a separate State as soon as possible after India is free from foreign domination and can, therefore, be constituted into two sovereign independent States.

'(*c*) There shall be a Treaty of Separation which should also provide for the efficient and satisfactory administration of Foreign Affairs, Defence, Internal Communications, Customs, Commerce and the like, which must necessarily continue to be matters of common interest between the contracting parties.

'(*d*) The Treaty shall also contain terms for safeguarding the rights of minorities in the two States.'[1]

Jinnah rejected Gandhi's proposals as being 'fundamentally opposed to the Lahore Resolution' and insisted that the Muslims of India should be recognized as a nation, with an inherent right of self-determination which they alone were entitled to exercise; that Pakistan should comprise six provinces, namely, Sind, Baluchistan, the North-West Frontier Province, the Punjab, Bengal and Assam, subject only to minor territorial adjustments; and that vital matters like foreign affairs, defence, internal communications, customs and commerce, 'which are the life-blood of any State, cannot be delegated to any Central authority or Government'.[2]

The Gandhi-Jinnah talks (July-October 1944) – and the correspondence which punctuated the talks and was later made public – brought into full relief the differences between the Congress and the Muslim League and to that limited extent they served an extremely useful purpose. It was now clear to Congress leaders – and to the public at large – that Jinnah's three main demands were, in fact, the recognition of the 'two nations' theory as a condition precedent to the discussion of the details of any possible settlement; the inclusion, almost in their entirety, of six existing provinces within the proposed state of Pakistan; and the creation of two completely independent sovereign states with no connection between them, except probably by treaty.

Having known Jinnah's mind, Congress leaders began to think out their own line of action for the future. It was generally felt that they could not yield to Jinnah on his first two demands and that any further concession they could make would have to be on his third demand.

As regards Jinnah's first demand – the recognition of the 'two nations'

[1] Gwyer and Appadorai, *op. cit.* vol. ii, pp. 549–50. [2] *Ibid.* pp. 550–1.

theory – there was absolute unanimity in Congress circles that it should not and could not be conceded. It ran counter to the creed of the Congress and to the facts of Indian life. It was mischievous and potentially dangerous. It would give Pakistan a handle to interfere in the affairs of India, undermine the basis of India's existence and encourage other groups and communities in the country to emulate the Muslim League. The future state of independent India could not stand on the theory of disintegration and, whatever its enemies might say, the Congress had no ambition to establish a Hindu state.

As regards Jinnah's second demand – the inclusion in Pakistan of almost the entire area covered by six existing provinces – Congress leaders became determined that if Jinnah had Pakistan it should not be Pakistan with those districts of Assam and Bengal and of the Punjab in which the population was predominantly non-Muslim. They decided to hoist Jinnah with his own petard. Every argument that could be used in favour of Pakistan could equally be used in favour of the exclusion of the non-Muslim areas from Pakistan. Moreover, Jinnah had already compromised his position on this point. The Lahore resolution of the Muslim League had spoken only of the demarcation of 'geographically contiguous units' and admitted the necessity of 'territorial readjustments'.[1] The non-Muslim majority districts of Assam and Bengal and of the Punjab were equally contiguous to the rest of India and with popular feeling there being strong against their inclusion within Pakistan, the Congress was in a formidable bargaining position *vis-à-vis* the Muslim League.

As regards Jinnah's third demand, namely, the total separation of Pakistan from the rest of India and the elimination of a common centre in any form, the Congress had already gone a long way in meeting it. In fact, Gandhi in his talks and correspondence with Jinnah in 1944 had studiously avoided mentioning the term 'central government' and had instead suggested 'a Board of Representatives of both the States' or any other 'authority acceptable to both the parties' whose effectiveness would largely or solely depend upon mutual goodwill.[2] But Jinnah had insisted 'first on complete partition as between two nations, and then an agreement between them as on Foreign Affairs, etc. He would not agree to anything simultaneous.'[3] Congress leaders, therefore, did not need to make any further material concession in order to meet Jinnah's third demand in full. All that they were now required to do was to reconcile themselves – and their followers – to the painful prospect of the complete separation of Pakistan from the rest of India. It was, however, by no means any easy task. For over half a century the Congress had cherished the dream of a united India and struggled, according to its lights, to realize that dream. For the Congress, to accept the partition of India was to accept the destruction of its dream and the failure of its struggle. Nor was the feeling for Indian unity confined to Congressmen. As the cabinet mission noted in 1946, there was 'an almost universal desire, outside the supporters of the Muslim League, for the unity of India'.[4] If the idea of Pakistan was repugnant to the Hindus because, as Muhammad Ali once said, they worshipped the map of India, it was equally repugnant to those Muslims who realized that

[1] Gwyer and Appadorai, *op. cit.* vol. ii, p. 443.
[2] *Ibid.* pp. 554–5.
[3] *Ibid.*
[4] *Ibid.* p. 577.

it meant the vivisection of their community. The partition of India was not only painful to contemplate, it was also fraught with grave risks. The Muslim League's demand for Pakistan had given a dangerous encouragement to the forces of communal, cultural, linguistic and political separatism in India. Already demands were being made for a separate homeland for the Sikhs ('Khalistan') and Dravidians ('Dravidistan') and for the creation of linguistic provinces such as Andhra and Maharashtra. Some of the princes were known to be dreaming of independence. Congress leaders therefore had to walk warily. They had to ensure that the establishment of Pakistan would not lead to the disintegration of the rest of India. They had to consolidate the forces working for Indian unity and to contain the menacing forces of separatism – both old and incipient – in India. They were fortunate in being aided in their difficult task by the accidents of time and circumstance. The Pakistan issue came to overshadow every other issue in the country. The very extremism of the Muslim League annoyed and alienated many moderate groups and parties in India and drove them closer to the Congress. The new viceroy, Lord Wavell, was a believer in the geographical unity of India. The Labour government, which came to power in Britain in July 1945, was not entirely unsympathetic to the aims and aspirations of the Congress. The elections of 1945–6 in India simplified the political scene by virtually eliminating the minor parties and leaving the Congress and the Muslim League as the two real contenders for power in India.[1] While the triumph of the Muslim League in the elections loaded the dice heavily in favour of Pakistan, the far more impressive triumph of the Congress in the elections held out a fair hope that the Congress would be able to hold together the rest of India even after the creation of Pakistan and to thwart the Muslim League's design to include the predominantly non-Muslim areas of Assam and Bengal and of the Punjab within Pakistan.

Having failed to settle their dispute in 1944, the Congress and the League naturally awaited the reaction of the British government. It was not, however, until mid-1945 – with the end of the war already in sight – that the British government felt able and willing to make a positive reaction. Rather unexpectedly, instead of acting as an arbitrator, the British government decided to act as a peacemaker. But it was too late for peacemaking in India in 1945. Not all the king's horses and all the king's men could now reconcile the Congress and the League. Congress leaders knew that Jinnah was determined to have a fully sovereign independent Pakistan and they, on their part, were equally determined that such a Pakistan should be confined to the Muslim-majority areas alone, that is, it should exclude those districts of Assam and Bengal and of the Punjab in which the population was predominantly non-Muslim. Jinnah knew that the Congress – through Gandhi – had already

[1] In the elections to the central legislature the Congress secured 91 per cent of the votes cast in non-Muslim constituencies and won 57 seats; the Muslim League secured 86 per cent of the votes cast in Muslim constituencies and won 30 seats. In the elections to the provincial legislatures the Congress increased its strength to 930 seats; it gained an absolute majority in 8 provinces (including Assam and the N.W. Frontier Province) and constituted the second largest party in the remaining 3. The Muslim League won 427 of the 507 Muslim seats, but it could form ministries only in Bengal and Sind. See *Indian Annual Register* (1946), vol. i, pp. 229–31.

offered him, what he had contemptuously described as, 'a maimed, mutilated and moth-eaten Pakistan'[1] and all that he was interested in knowing was whether the British government could offer him anything better. Neither party was willing to accept any temporary settlement which might prejudice its ultimate objective. Undeterred by the fiasco of the Simla conference (June-July 1945), the British government sent out to India early in 1946 a special mission of cabinet ministers to make yet another attempt at peacemaking, but it met with no better success. The cabinet mission frankly told Jinnah that if he wanted a separate and fully independent sovereign state he would have to be satisfied with the smaller Pakistan offered to him by Gandhi in 1944, for, in the mission's view, there was no justification for including within such a state those districts of the Punjab and of Assam and Bengal in which the population was predominantly non-Muslim.[2] The cabinet mission also tried to demolish Jinnah's case for the partition of India by arguing that, apart from providing no acceptable solution for the communal problem, there were 'weighty administrative, economic and military considerations' against it.[3] But the mission 'were greatly impressed by the very genuine and acute anxiety of the Muslims lest they should find themselves subjected to a perpetual Hindu-majority rule' and they were led to believe that this feeling had become so strong and widespread amongst the Muslims that it could not be allayed by mere paper safeguards.[4] They therefore proceeded, despite continuing objections from the Congress and the League, to recommend certain complicated and 'purposely vague'[5] proposals of their own[6] which offered the League the temptation of securing a bigger Pakistan, provided it was willing to try and work for some time the constitution of an 'Indian Union', and at the same time offered the Congress the temptation of preserving at least a semblance of Indian unity, provided it was willing to run the risk of India being divided not only into two but three or more parts in the future. Not unnaturally, both the Congress and the League at first showed interest in the proposals of the cabinet mission and then shied away from them.

Though the cabinet mission's long-term proposals of May 16, 1946 were drowned in a welter of conflicting alarms and interpretations, their short-term proposals – for the establishment of a constituent assembly and the interim central government – were duly implemented. The League at first stayed away from both the constituent assembly and the interim central government and resorted to 'direct action' to secure Pakistan. Later, realizing the risks of continued abstention, the League entered the interim central government and turned it into another battlefront of 'the holy war'. Meanwhile, in the prevailing atmosphere of uncertainty and fear, mounting communal passions burst out into spasmodic rioting which threatened to develop into civil war. Lord Wavell was apparently so disgusted at the sight of riotous

[1] Jamil-ud-din Ahmad, *Some Recent Speeches and Writings of Mr. Jinnah* (1947), vol. ii, p. 578.

[2] Gwyer and Appadorai, *op. cit.* vol. ii, p. 578.

[3] *Ibid.* p. 579. [4] *Ibid.* p. 578.

[5] The description is that of Sir Stafford Cripps (July 18, 1946). See H. C. Deb., vol. 425, col. 1397.

[6] For the text of the proposals, dated May 16, 1946, see Gwyer and Appadorai, *op. cit.* vol. ii, pp. 577–84.

mobs and squabbling politicians in India that, soldier as he was, he advised the British government either to allow him to re-establish British authority in India or to march out of the country and let the Indians stew in their own juice. This advice cost the viceroy his recall in February 1947.

PARTITION AND INDEPENDENCE

Lord Mountbatten did not, like Lord Wavell and the cabinet mission, attempt to erect matchwood dams against the Indian political torrent. He squarely faced the realities of Indian politics and persuaded the politicians in India to do the same. The partition of India was carried out with exemplary speed and smoothness, amidst circumstances which would have deterred a lesser man.

On February 20, 1947 the British prime minister, Clement Attlee, had announced His Majesty's Government's 'definite intention to take the necessary steps to effect the transfer of power into responsible Indian hands by a date not later than June 1948'[1] and clearly hinted at the possibility of partition. On March 8, 1947 the Congress working committee had passed a resolution welcoming Attlee's announcement and implicitly recognizing the necessity of partition.[2] In April 1947 Nehru publicly stated what had in fact been the view of the Congress at least ever since 1944. 'The Muslim League', he said, 'can have Pakistan if they want but on the condition that they do not take away other parts of India which do not wish to join Pakistan.'[3] But the first partition plan which Mountbatten's staff produced in May 1947 in accordance with the instructions of the British cabinet was so wrong-headed that Nehru angrily rejected it.[4] It provided for the transfer of power to the provinces or to such confederations of provinces as the latter might decide to form. As Nehru rightly pointed out to Mountbatten, the plan 'would encourage disruptive tendencies everywhere and chaos and weakness'.[5] It is difficult to believe that in May 1947 a group of British civil servants and statesmen could have seriously put forward a plan which would have encouraged units to cut adrift from the union and the princely states to stand out and might have easily led to the total disintegration of India. Jinnah fought hard against another feature of the plan, namely the proposed division of Bengal and the Punjab, but ultimately reconciled himself to the inevitable. Almost as a consolation prize he was allowed to have the predominantly Muslim district of Sylhet in Assam for Pakistan. Jinnah also demanded a 800-mile corridor to link East and West Pakistan, but, in the face of firm Congress opposition, he did not press the issue.

In the framing of the second plan – better known as the June 3rd or the Mountbatten plan – a distinguished Indian civil servant, V. P. Menon, appears to have played a crucial role.[6] It was accepted by all the parties concerned and finally became the basis of the Indian Independence Act, 1947.

[1] Gwyer and Appadorai, *op. cit.* vol. ii, pp. 667–9. [2] *Ibid.* pp. 669–70.

[3] Michael Brecher, *Nehru: A Political Biography* (1959), p. 345.

[4] V. P. Menon, *op. cit.* p. 361 and Alan Campbell-Johnson, *Mission with Mountbatten* (1951), p. 89. [5] V. P. Menon, *op. cit.* pp. 406–7.

[6] *Ibid.* pp. 357–67. For the text of the plan see Gwyer and Appadorai, *op. cit.* vol. ii, pp. 670–5.

It provided for the transfer of power to India and Pakistan on the basis of dominion status, without disturbing constitutional continuity. In a certain sense this particular arrangement supported the claim of Indian leaders that the Union of India was the rightful successor to the British *raj* and that Pakistan was merely the secession of a few provinces and parts of provinces from British India. This proved to be of some importance for the subsequent international status of the Indian Union: the United Nations recognized this claim.[1] Jinnah's 'two nations' theory found no mention either in the June 3rd plan or in the Indian Independence Act and Congress leaders could legitimately claim that, far from vindicating the 'two nations' theory, the partition of India was really in accordance with the view which they had consistently adopted towards the demand for Pakistan, namely, that India was not to be regarded as two or more nations, but as one family consisting of many members of whom the Muslims living in certain areas desired to live in separation from the rest of India.

Congress leaders were extremely critical of the declaration made by the British government that paramountcy was to lapse on August 15, 1947 and the rulers of the Indian states were to become technically and legally independent, because they felt that it posed a grave threat to the stability and integrity of India, for all but a dozen of the six hundred-odd states were contiguous to Indian territory. They argued that paramountcy came into being as a fact and not by agreement and that on the British withdrawal the successor authority must inherit the fact along with the rest of the context. They insisted that no state should be allowed to declare independence, and that the princes must make up their minds to accede to India or Pakistan, taking into account their geographical situation, before August 15, 1947.[2] Jinnah, on the other hand, insisted that the rulers had absolute freedom of decision.[3] By their firm and tactful handling of the situation, Congress leaders were able to persuade nearly all the rulers to accede to the Dominion of India. The notable exceptions were Hyderbad, Kashmir and Junagarh; these also later acceded to the Dominion of India, but the circumstances under which this happened do not fall within the scope of this paper.

In agreeing to the partition of India, Congress leaders chose the lesser evil. Partition was bad, but the alternatives to partition in 1947 were worse. Continued slavery, civil war, chaos and the fragmentation of India – these were the only alternatives to partition in 1947. Nor was partition, in the judgment of many Congress leaders, an unmixed evil. India was at long last free. The unity of at least two-thirds of India had been preserved. The Congress had not compromised its ideals of secularism, democracy and a common Indian nationality. In fact, it had ensured that these ideals would find freer play in the Indian Union of the future. Some Congress leaders also hoped that partition would be transitory and that, instead of permanently barring, it might even clear the way to a real reunion. 'The division', said Maulana Azad, 'is only on the map of the country and not in the hearts of the people, and I am sure it is going to be a short-lived partition.'[4] Nehru remarked: 'The united

[1] See V. P. Menon *op. cit.* pp. 406–7.
[2] See, for example, Nehru's statement in *Leader*, June 16, 1947.
[3] See *Leader*, June 18, 1947.
[4] *Ibid.* June 16, 1947.

India that we have laboured for was not one of compulsion and coercion but a free and willing association of free people. It may be that in this way we shall reach that united India sooner than otherwise and then she will have a stronger and more secure foundation.'[1] Doubts and fears about the future were expressed by certain other Congress leaders, but these were submerged in the intense agony and ecstasy of the hour.

Most foreign observers applauded the wisdom of all the parties concerned in reaching a settlement. There were, however, two notable exceptions. The newspapers of northern and southern Ireland compared the proposed partition of India with the partition of their country, warning that Ireland had been materially and spiritually weakened by the division, which time had done nothing to heal.[2] From neighbouring Burma came a more ominous warning. 'A divided India', remarked Aung San, 'augers ill not only for the Indian people but also for all Asia and world peace.'[3]

[1] Gwyer and Appadorai, *op. cit.* vol. ii, p. 682.
[2] *Leader*, June 6, 1947.
[3] *Ibid.* June 7, 1947.

GANDHI DURING PARTITION: A CASE STUDY IN THE NATURE OF SATYAGRAHA

by D. G. DALTON*

An appreciation of Gandhi's achievement at any given point in time requires, first, a close examination of that point in time. His peculiar genius becomes evident not in terms of an abstract political philosophy, but rather within the historical context of a series of challenges and responses. The main concern of this paper is with one segment of this series. The challenge is seen here in the chronic communal violence and lawlessness that prevailed in Calcutta during the year preceding partition; that is the 'Great Calcutta Killing' and its aftermath. The response occurs with Gandhi's *satyagraha* in the city, beginning at the time of independence and culminating in his Calcutta fast of early September 1947. The paper is thus divided into two sections: the first attempts to reconstruct the atmosphere of India's largest city in its year of unprecedented turmoil, and to convey the extent to which the processes of orderly government had been undermined by forces of anarchy. The second section analyses Gandhi's Calcutta *satyagraha.* It examines his response to the crisis there, and the manner in which the city responded to him. It concludes with an analysis of the main dynamics of Gandhi's approach.

One purpose of this reconstruction and analysis is to suggest a subject of study fruitful for students of political sociology and political theory. The concern of the former would be with the social and psychological dynamics of the conflict area under analysis, while the latter might assess the significance of the subject in terms of the theoretical problem of conflict resolution. A notable point at which these two disciplines may meet is with an examination of Gandhi's style. The aspect of style, which will be developed in this paper at some length, is suggested by W. H. Morris-Jones when he writes of the 'languages' or 'idioms' of contemporary Indian politics; that is, India's 'modern', 'traditional', and 'saintly' styles of political behaviour.[1] Although Morris-Jones is concerned with 'behaviour and accounts of behaviour', his insights are broadly applicable to Indian political and social thought as well: especially to an analysis of the myths, symbols, imagery, attitudes and beliefs that dynamized Gandhi's technique of *satyagraha.*

THE GREAT CALCUTTA KILLING: ITS BACKGROUND AND AFTERMATH[2]

'The problem of communal strife which is vexing the whole of India can be studied in an intensified and concentrated manner in this focal

* Lecturer in Politics, School of Oriental and African Studies, London.

[1] W. H. Morris Jones, *The Government and Politics of India* (1964), pp. 52–61.

[2] [Editors' note: cf. M. D. Wainwright, 'Keeping the Peace in India 1946–47 . . .', above pp. 127–141.]

city.' – Sir Frederick Burrows, governor of Bengal, in a broadcast to the people of Calcutta, May 1947.

'Calcutta, once the most lively if never the most comfortable city of India, is becoming almost unbearable to its inhabitants. Under the blight of communalism, it is from dusk onwards a city of the dead. Even by day, life is at a low ebb. . . . Shadowed by past calamity, not daring to turn their eyes from the morbid present to a future without hope, [its citizens] drag out meaningless lives, thankful only from day to day that these are still safe from the goonda and the housebreaker. They ask themselves if such terrible conditions are to be permanent and find no answer. If Calcutta passes two 'quiet' days in succession, hope revives – to fall again as the third day brings news of fresh outrages.[1]

This is *The Statesman*, Calcutta's leading newspaper, writing in May 1947, no longer with indignation but in despair. In such an atmosphere of quiet agony all of Calcutta had acquiesced by mid-1947. Only six months before, *The Statesman*, long proud of its independent critical stance and crusading spirit, was alive with attacks on the government of Bengal and exhortations to the citizenry. But these had been gradually replaced by the standard front-page entry: 'A Government Press Note reports that the number of casualties as a result of yesterday's communal disturbances in Calcutta were . . .'. 'The Terror', as it was commonly called, lasted a full year, from August 1946 until independence. Three factors determined its character and fostered its growth: communalism, *goondaism*, and political extremism. Not until these three coalesced was the nature of Calcutta's atmosphere radically transformed; together they wrought (in the words of *The Statesman* after the worst of the Great Calcutta Killing had passed) 'the transference of this dread social phenomenon [of communal violence] into another dimension'.[2] Communalism and *goondaism* had long existed in Calcutta, as throughout India, the latter always ready for the circumstances that would allow exploitation of the former. However, not until political extremism had gained its head was the new dimension added. Political extremism of a kind had of course appeared in India early in the twentieth century, first among Bengali terrorists then later in Gandhi's non-co-operation campaigns. But a decisive change in the political climate came with the events of 1946: the national elections, the Great Calcutta Killing, and its aftermath. Independence combined with the prospect of either a Congress or League *raj* now seemed imminent and the ensuing struggle for power soon consumed the political leadership. In this particular context, there came to flourish a peculiarly virulent form of political extremism with an awesome irresistibility. This was the crucial catalyst. With its entry, Calcutta was plunged into bitter irrationality and intense party rivalry, and events took on the familiar overtones described in that classic text on political extremism, the civil war in Corcyra.[3]

[1] *The Statesman* (Calcutta), May 20, 1947, p. 4. [2] *Ibid.* August 21, 1946, p. 4.

[3] 'Civil war broke out in city after city, and in places where the violence occurred late the knowledge of what had happened previously in other places caused still new extravagances of fanatical zeal, expressed by an elaboration in the methods of seizing power and by unheard-of atrocities in revenge. To fit in with the change of events, words, too, had to

'When the Ganges is in flood', Gandhi remarked in May 1947, 'the water is turbid. The dirt comes to the surface.' [1] The troubled waters of Calcutta began to swell in November 1945. Nine months later, the dirt did indeed come to the surface. The November riots in Calcutta were not communal in nature; rather, they signalled the manner in which the *goonda* element would capitalize on political demonstrations, and the subsequent effect that this would have on the city. On Tuesday, November 21st, the Indian National Army officers' trial had been resumed in Delhi. A procession of 500 students demonstrated in Calcutta, responding to an appeal from their political leaders, to observe this as 'I.N.A. Day'. The procession entered a prohibited area, clashed with the police, and a student was killed. By the next day , the *goondas* had injected into the fracas that adrenalin component which Calcutta was soon to know so well: that Wednesday 'mob violence swept the city'. At the same time, another feature of future patterns appeared: a municipal strike 'put the city into chaos'. *The Statesman* described it as 'The Paralysed City':

'Dazed citizens of Calcutta who up to Wednesday morning were going quietly about their business have lately lived through a fantastic nightmare. . . . They seek to penetrate the cloud of rumour to find out what is happening and why and what prospects there are of an end of this anarchic confusion which has already led to so much tragedy. . . . Lives have been lost, hatred created, business suspended, movement interfered with and discomfort caused to everybody in circumstances which are still largely obscure'.[2]

The phrases used here are to recur again and again until finally abandoned the following year as clichés: 'paralysed city', 'dazed citizens', 'fantastic nightmare', 'anarchic confusion', 'lives lost', 'hatred created', 'so much tragedy'. Surrounding all this is an air of bewilderment, a search for causes and reasons in the midst of 'circumstances which are still obscure'. Of the February riots, soon to come, Sir Francis Tuker wrote, 'There was fear about, and fear in India means trouble.' [3] The fear was there in November, and its full meaning became clear in the next year. Indeed, this element of fear, beginning with uneasy anxieties over the destructiveness of anarchy, and growing by the following summer into an endemic wave of terror, characterizes above all else the phenomenon of communalism in Calcutta. As we shall see, it was precisely the nature and force of this fear that Gandhi understood, confronted, and overcame.

change their usual meanings. What used to be described as a thoughtless act of aggression was now regarded as the courage one would expect to find in a party member; to think of the future and wait was merely another way of saying one was a coward; any act of moderation was just an attempt to disguise one's unmanly character. . . . Thus neither side had any use for conscientious motives; more interest was shown in those who could produce attractive arguments to justify some disgraceful action. As for the citizens who held moderate views, they were destroyed by both the extreme parties. . . . Society had become divided into two ideologically hostile camps, and each side viewed the other with suspicion.'

Thucydides, *History of the Peloponnesian War*, bk. III.

[1] Gandhi, as quoted in D. G. Tendulkar, *Mahatma* (1953), vol. vii, p. 475.

[2] *The Statesman*, November 24, 1945, p. 4.

[3] Sir Francis Tuker, *While Memory Serves* (1950), p. 102.

February set the pattern of disturbances for the new year. Early in the year, increased communal tension was noted by Tuker, then G.O.C. in C., eastern command. Large-scale rioting, though, was not anticipated. On Monday, February 11th, students demonstrated as they had in November, in protest against the I.N.A. trials. The protest, however, was significantly different in this instance: an ex-Muslim officer of the I.N.A. had been court-martialled, and given seven years R.I. The demonstrators were therefore mostly Muslim, protesting against the severity of the punishment; Hindu officers, they added, had recently escaped with much lighter sentences.[1] All Muslim shops in Calcutta were closed, and 2,000 Muslims, carrying League flags, demonstrated. Once again, the demonstrations quickly deteriorated into 'mob violence', with more casualties and over a longer period than the November riots.[2] 'It is an awful warning,' *The Statesman* commented, 'but to more than established authority.'[3] Leaders of the Congress and the Muslim League significantly interpreted this warning in different ways. Congressmen like Maulana Azad, Sarat Chandra Bose, and Surendra Mohan Ghosh vied with one another in issuing blanket condemnations of the riots. For them it showed only that 'the goonda and irresponsible elements of this city have gained the upper hand'. H. S. Suhrawardy, however, then a prominent Leaguer in Bengal and soon to become its chief minister, had taken an active part in the initial demonstrations, and enthused over them. Although he criticized the violence, for him the riot 'was a warning that, once the Muslim public was aroused, it would need all the forces of Government to restrain it.... The reason for our success is the sincerity of purpose behind all this agitation'.[4] Suhrawardy's reaction forebode ill for the next of Calcutta's communal riots, when the responsibility was to fall on him, as chief minister, for maintaining law and order.[5]

For Sir Francis Tuker, the February riots had a special significance: they 'set a match to the fuse which detonated the charges with such fearful violence months later not only in Calcutta and Eastern Bengal, but far afield in Bihar and into the United Provinces at Garhmukteswar and finally into the Punjab'.[6] With hindsight, it is easy to plot such a chain of events. Even without hindsight, though, the ominous aspects of the riots were clear to perceptive observers like R. G. Casey who noted their significance shortly

[1] Sir Francis Tuker, *While Memory Serves* (1950), p. 100.

[2] *The Statesman*, February 13–15, 1946. The rioting lasted four days; 42 killed and 380 injured.

[3] *Ibid.* February 15, 1946, p. 4.

[4] *Ibid.* February 13, 1946, p. 7.

[5] It may be noted that the largest riots of February occurred not in Calcutta, but in Bombay (*The Times of India*, February 22–24, 1946). Indeed, during the months of late 1945 and early 1946. Bombay's incidence of large-scale rioting became the highest in India. Significantly, these riots were non-communal in nature, and therefore the situation in Bombay did not deteriorate on the Calcutta model. These riots did, however, drive home the realization of the terrifying scale that could be reached. Thus, when Gandhi commented on them he struck precisely the note of anxiety that was in the air, and the press throughout India commented on his words: 'A combination between Hindus and Muslims and others for the purpose of violent action [as had happened in Bombay] is unholy and will lead and probably is a preparation for mutual violence—bad for India and the world.' (*Times of India*, February 25, 1946, p. 7).

[6] Tuker, *op. cit.* p. 108.

after his expiration of office, as governor of Bengal, in February.[1] Casey's successor, Sir Frederick Burrows, arrived in the wake of the February riots to assume an 'onerous appointment', (in Tuker's view) 'that we would none of us have touched with the proverbial bargepole, and [we] admired the sense of public duty that brought him from gentle England to turbulent Bengal'.[2] For a time, it seemed that Burrows had imposed some of this gentleness on the turbulence around him. India, particularly Bombay and Ahmedabad, experienced rioting, but Calcutta was relatively calm.

A national political crisis now emerged, though, which was to affect Calcutta directly. At the end of July, the council of the All-India Muslim League met in Bombay and revoked their earlier acceptance of the cabinet mission plan. 'The time has now come,' the council resolved, 'for the Muslim nation to resort to direct action to achieve Pakistan . . . The Council calls upon the Muslim nation to stand to a man behind their sole representative, the All-India Muslim League, and be ready for every sacrifice.'[3] Sacrifices were indeed to be made. August 16th was subsequently fixed by the council for the observance of 'Direct Action Day' throughout India. Muslims were urged to stage 'a hartal on that day, to hold public meetings and other demonstrations'. Another 'Day' was thus designated for political demonstrations; but this day India was not soon to forget.

While the League was making decisions in Bombay that would, in less than three weeks' time, transform Calcutta, Bengal was preoccupied with quite another matter. On the same day (July 29th) that the direct action resolution had been passed, a one-day general strike of transport, industrial and government employees 'completely paralysed' Calcutta. The general strike coincided with the postal strike (of 16,000 employees) that had been in progress throughout Bengal since July 21st. This was in turn followed by still another strike, of the Imperial Bank employees, which further belaboured the city.[4] The strike of last November had coincided with the riots; now larger strikes preceded far greater rioting. This is not surprising, since the effect of each of these strikes was to quicken the forces of unrest and disorder in the city.

Once the postal strike was resolved, on August 7th, Calcutta could turn again to the national scene, which the Congress now dominated. By August 14th, Nehru had accepted the viceroy's invitation to form an interim government, and had written to Jinnah asking for his co-operation. The latter replied that 'the situation remains as it was and we are where we were'; and, after meeting with Nehru in Bombay on August 15th, Jinnah told the press, 'There will be no more meetings between me and Pandit Nehru.'[5] The stage was thus set for August 16th: Jinnah adamantly pledged to direct action, Nehru engrossed in the formation of his interim government, with the viceroy hoping for a reconciliation. And Gandhi, in Sevagram, was pondering, 'I have never had the chance to test my non-violence in the face of communal riots . . . the chance will still come to me . . .'.[6]

Gandhi's remark might be thought prophetic; and in a general sense it

[1] R. G. Casey, *An Australian in India* (1947), p. 38.
[2] Tuker, *op. cit.* p. 114.
[3] *The Statesman*, July 31, 1946, p. 1.
[4] *Ibid.* July 31–August 2, 1946.
[5] *Ibid.* August 13–16, 1946.
[6] Gandhi, quoted in *The Times of India*, August 5, 1946, p. 5.

undoubtedly was, for no one was more aware than Gandhi of the troubles ahead. The remark was not a prophesy, though, of what would happen in Calcutta on direct action day. No Indian political leader foresaw that event. Indeed, most of them do not appear to have had the slightest inkling of the scale on which the Calcutta riots would occur. The Indian press was a shade more foresighted. Among the major English-language papers, mild warnings of the consequences of direct action appeared in *The Times of India* and *The Statesman;* and *The Leader* singled out Calcutta, on the day before the tragedy as the most likely trouble spot, although this comment, as noted below, hardly foresaw the scale or intensity of the rioting.[1] One insight into the peculiar context of the political situation in Calcutta occurred in *The Times of India* on August 7th. After observing that the Congress had tended to dismiss the very real dangers of direct action, the writer wondered whether the League ministries, in Bengal and Sind, would resign, since the direct action would be directed against them. If they did not resign, 'quite an interesting situation will have been created by Leaguers breaking the law in Sind and Bengal, where the League may be in charge of the maintenance of law.'[2] The remark did anticipate the dilemma which the League ministry in Bengal faced.

Suhrawardy attempted (like the League minister in Sind) to overcome this dilemma by declaring August 16th a public holiday. This, the chief minister declared, would 'minimize chances of conflict', and was preferable to 'stopping business by means of stone-throwing, intimidation, and dragging people out of buses and cars and burning the vehicles'.[3] The Congress opposition immediately pounced on this remark as a confession of the government's inability to maintain order, or much worse (from the Congress point of view) the use of government to further narrow party ends. It is likely that the chief minister thought that the government could walk the tightrope by having peaceful demonstrations on behalf of the League which would not degenerate into uncontrollable rioting. This was a major blunder. What is certain, however, is that neither the government nor the opposition nor the press anticipated the magnitude of the tragedy. While the Congress did attack Suhrawardy, and *The Leader* reinforced this censure on the day before the riots, both concentrated their criticism on the chief minister's unwarranted use of government power to achieve party aims. Neither focused its criticism on what was later to form the crux of the indictment. Suhrawardy's failure to take adequate preventive measures. This was simply because neither the opposition nor the press had guessed what 'adequate' might involve. The statement issued by the government of Bengal on the riots, six months after their occurrence, cannot be gainsaid: 'What was not foreseen and what took everybody by surprise including the participants was the intensity of the hatred let loose and the savagery with which both sides killed.'[4] The chief minister, the governor, and the police should have taken stronger precautions at the beginning and then acted with more dispatch as the disturbances gained ground. Suhrawardy in particular was appallingly negligent, perhaps in the

[1] *The Leader* (Allahabad), August 16, 1946, p. 4.
[2] *The Times of India*, August 7, 1946, p. 6. ('Candidus').
[3] *The Statesman*, August 15, 1946, p. 6.
[4] *Ibid.* February 23, 1947, p. 11.

early stage of the killing even deliberately provocative. Yet, it is hardly realistic to place all the blame on the government, or on any single party to the conflict. Seen in this light, two points may initially be made on the killing: first, it was precisely the total unexpectedness of the calamity that produced its aftermath of shock, terror, and vengeance. Second, the search for scapegoats which followed only obfuscated (given the political atmosphere of the time) the real lessons that might have been grasped at once. In this connection, one of the most salutary and refreshing features of Gandhi's approach was his insistence that everyone was in some measure responsible for the continuing violence, and therefore every citizen had it in his power to exercise some degree of control over it. Unfortunately, another year passed, after the killing, before Calcutta came to appreciate this basic truth.

It could be argued that the real tragedy of the Great Calcutta Killing[1] came not with the massacre itself, but rather with the character of the response to it, especially among India's politicians. Consumed with the political demands of forming an interim government, and oblivious to what might have happened in Calcutta, Pandit Nehru, when asked by the press (on early reports of the riots) whether Calcutta's disturbances would affect his plans, replied, 'Our programme will certainly not be upset because a few persons misbehave in Calcutta.'[2] Once the scale of this 'misbehaviour' struck the Congress, though, no time was lost in placing the responsibility 'for all that has happened' on the League ministry.[3] Simultaneously, Jinnah was saying, 'I cannot believe that any Muslim Leaguer would have taken part in using any violence'.[4] Thus, the dog-fight was on. 'There is no indication that the Calcutta riots have induced a calmer frame of mind,' wrote *The Times* of London correspondent; rather, 'recriminatory and, indeed, vitriolic' comments prevail among all circles in India.[5] Liaqat Ali Khan, then general secretary of the League, attributed the killing solely to 'the Hindu elements whose actions plunged Calcutta into these orgies of violence and slaughter'. Liaqat agreed that a 'bitterness' now 'sweeps India as never before, and the inevitable bloodshed . . . will continue to be caused'; but, for him, the exclusive cause was 'the communal arrogance and the spirit of violence fostered by the Congress'. The Congress contemplates another 'Hindu raj' but 'a hundred million Muslims will resist it'.[6] *The Statesman*, since the killing, had pressed the 'leader of the Muslim League' for an 'apology'. From Mr Jinnah came word that the main 'responsibility' for Calcutta must rest with 'the Viceroy, Mr Gandhi, and the Congress'; for 'it was an organized plot to discredit the Muslim League on the part of the Hindus'.[7] *The Statesman* did not press further.

[1] The Great Killing began on the morning of August 16, 1946 and lasted until August 20th. Approximately 4,000 were killed and 11,000 injured. The most graphic account occurs in Tuker's *While Memory Serves*.

[2] Nehru, quoted in *The Statesman*, August 18, 1946, p. 1.

[3] Maulana Azad quoted in *The Statesman*, August 20, 1946, p. 1. The indictment was repeated by Sarat Chandra Bose, leader of the opposition in the central assembly of Bengal.

[4] Jinnah, quoted in *The Statesman*, August 18, 1946, p. 1.

[5] *The Times* of London, August 26, 1946, p. 5.

[6] Liaqat Ali Khan, quoted in *The Statesman*, August 28, 1946, pp. 1, 5.

[7] Jinnah, quoted in *The Statesman*, September, 5, 1946, p.1.

In this atmosphere, the question of which side started the riots on that morning of August 16th could hardly be judged impartially by the parties involved. However, this did not deter the Congress and the League from pursuing their respective 'investigations' into the matter. The Congress working committee discovered that first blood was drawn by Muslims carrying 'big bamboo sticks, swords, spears, daggers and axes which they brandished' before unarmed Hindus.[1] The working committee of the Bengal Muslim League, however, found that 'peaceful Muslim processions almost everywhere had to face a barrage of brickbats, stones, and missiles'.[2] The *Modern Review* (Calcutta) replied with 'photographic evidence' of the Muslim aggressors on that morning, and concluded that the riots started when 'their Fuehrer had declared a Jehad, and thousands of gangsters had been imported to reinforce them'.[3] On this hysterical exchange, the most acute comment came from Arthur Moore: 'For any given man-made catastrophe, all participating parties bear some responsibility. In party politics the procedure considered correct and honourable is for each component to blame the others and entirely exonerate himself. . . . We have produced a situation in which civil war is an obvious possibility. . . . I have a deep sense of terrible disasters impending.' [4]

As early as April 1946, Gandhi had criticized 'loose talk of civil war', but by late August such talk was widely accepted. In the press commentary on the killing, no term was more often applied than 'civil war'. 'What befell India's largest city last week', summed up *The Statesman*, 'was no mere communal riot. . . . It was three days of concentrated, unprecedented Indian civil war.' [5] Ten days after the killing, *The Times* of London correspondent reported: 'To put it bluntly, far too many thinking Indians are resigned to the prospect of civil war in the near future. . . . Was Calcutta the first battle of a civil war, and is this country threatened with massacres carried out with ruthless fanaticism by the baser elements of the communities?' [6] Such were the doubts and fears emanating from Calcutta, and Arthur Moore's 'deep sense of terrible disasters impending' was widely shared. For Gandhi, the killing was an 'ocular demonstration' of the fruits of direct action; for many other Indians, it was an ocular demonstration of the reality of the abyss beyond. 'One principal lesson of the tragedy', editorialized *The Times* immediately after the killing, 'lies in its illustration of the perilously narrow margin which today divides order from anarchy in India.' [7] After August 16th, anarchy and civil war of the worst form were no longer abstractions in India; they had become spectres which overshadowed all else by the end of the year. It is above all in this sense – in terms of a 'psychosis of fear' – that the Great Calcutta Killing marks the watershed of events in a study of partition. 'Would that the violence of Calcutta were sterilized', exclaimed

[1] *The Statesman*, Spetember 1, 1946, p. 1.

[2] *Ibid.* September 7, 1946, p. 5.

[3] *The Modern Review*, edited by K. Chatterji (Calcutta), September, 1946, p. 171.

[4] Arthur Moore, in a letter to the editor from Delhi, dated August 22, 1946. *The Statesman*, August 27, 1946, p. 4.

[5] *The Statesman*, August 23, 1946, p. 2.

[6] *The Times* of London, August 26, 1946, p. 5.

[7] *Ibid.* August 20, 1946, p. 5.

Gandhi, when he heard of the killing, 'and did not become a signal for its spread all over'.[1] But this was not to be. The grim chain reaction immediately began in which India was soon convulsed: Dacca, Noakhali, Bihar, and the Punjab.

'By the end of 1946 India was drifting rapidly to chaos. The real power had passed from British hands; senior officials, anxious about their future, were conscious that they were caretakers under notice and were disheartened; Ministers, paralyzed by the communal situation, seemed unable to come to grips with the problems of administration; and the unparallel communal riots in Calcutta, together with serious disorder in many parts of India, made it clear that nobody was in effective control.' [2]

Of this situation, Calcutta was an inextricable part, acting from within India upon it, and in turn reacting to the anxiety and disorder from without.

The agony that Calcutta experienced in the year after the Great Killing is indescribable. Communal fear and hatred pervaded the city. Many sought to escape, either fleeing from the city or withdrawing into armed communal camps within it. The first major riot of the year occurred in late March. A series of stray incidents quickly escalated into large-scale mob violence and troops were called in to restore order.[3] After March, rioting became chronic, persisting, in Governor Burrows words, in 'a stream, . . . now ebbing, now flowing, but never completely ceasing for more than a few days.' [4] The government had clearly lost control, for despite the fact that Suhrawardy now took maximum precautions,[5] 'so far has the position now deteriorated that the public has come to realize that its only protection is, in the last resort, India's armed force.' [6] The once effective Calcutta police had itself become undermined and demoralized by communalism,[7] and the Hindu majority regarded the League ministry with intense suspicion. 'We have come to a stage', Suhrawardy admitted, 'when nobody, not even the Government, can guarantee that there will not be arson, stabbing or looting.' [8] At the national level, Mountbatten had induced Gandhi and Jinnah to sign, on April 15th, a joint appeal for peace, deploring the recent acts of 'lawlessness and violence.' All communities were urged 'to refrain from violence in any form.'[9] This appeal had little affect on India, and certainly no influence on Calcutta. Gandhi sensed this, and on a visit to the city in early May, threatened a 'fast unto death'.[10] On the prospect of Gandhi fasting, *The Statesman* commented:

[1] Gandhi, quoted in *The Statesman*, August 27, 1946, p. 5.

[2] Percival Griffiths, *Modern India* (1957), p. 85.

[3] The riots lasted from March 26th to April 1st, 73 were killed and 481 injured. See *The Statesman*.

[4] Governor Burrows, quoted in *The Statesman*, May 28, 1947, p. 7.

[5] For example, on 'Pakistan Day', March 23, 1947, Suhrawardy banned all processions, demonstrations and public meetings in Bengal, and enforced this ban stringently with troops. *The Statesman*, March 21 and 22, 1947.

[6] *The Statesman*, April 10, 1947, p. 4.

[7] See Tuker on this point, *op. cit.* pp. 234, 412.

[8] *The Statesman*, April 9, 1947, p. 1.

[9] *Ibid.* April 16, 1947, p. 1.

[10] *Ibid.* May 10, 1947, p. 1.

'It is with regret that many will learn that Mr. Gandhi has again spoken of a fast, more than once hinted at, to reinforce the joint appeal . . . We think, however, that all those who are close to him should do their best to dissuade him . . . The contemplated fast could not be expected to influence Muslims generally, whether aggressors or (as both communities tend to believe of themselves when involved) acting on the defensive. In such circumstances, if Mr. Gandhi started a fast, he would presumably continue to the end. As Hindus saw his life ebbing away, their own bitterness would greatly increase and the outcome would be in every way disastrous.

'Like many others, we have never been able fully to understand these Gandhian fasts. The appeal they make is primarily to the emotions, to the heart. But also, perhaps, they are intended to appeal to the head. If one man greatly admired is so strongly convinced of the rightness of the cause he advocates that he is prepared to sacrifice his life for it, then, his opponents may come to think there must be more to be said for it than they concede; and so they start to consider their own position afresh – although, we think, under compulsion. But with communal disputes it is different. That they are primarily emotional is true; but once feelings are aroused to fever-pitch, there is no more possibility of subduing them by appeal to some other nobler emotion than of curing a rabid dog of his madness by talking gently. As for the intellectual factor, that is wholly absent. It should be plain, we think, that fasts, by whoever undertaken, can have little effect in such conditions. We trust that Mr. Gandhi will see that his duty is not to use this last weapon . . .'[1]

THE CALCUTTA SATYAGRAHA: EXPLANATION AND ANALYSIS

> 'Is the Satyagraha of my conception a weapon of the weak or really that of the strong? I must either realize the latter or lay down my life in the attempt to attain it. That is my quest.' – Gandhi, December 1946.

Gandhi arrived in Calcutta on August 9th. The previous month had seen the city's worst communal riots of the year. The most notable feature of these disturbances was the flash panic that had instantly consumed the population. 'Lurking in the back of most minds is the possibility of a sudden new conflagration on last August's scale. Monday's events started panic which may not be quickly allayed.'[2] Many urged the enactment of martial law. No longer, moreover, could Suhrawardy serve as scapegoat: on July 3rd, a West Bengal cabinet had been formed of which Dr P. C. Ghosh of the Congress became chief minister. Now he, with Suhrawardy (who remained *de jure* chief minister of Bengal until August 14th), bore responsibility for communal violence. When, therefore, it became obvious that the Congress, like the League, was unable to curb the riots, the open attacks by the press and others on the League ministry were superseded by more sweeping indictments of the very process of democratic government itself.[3] This breakdown in civil

[1] *The Statesman*, May 12, 1947, p. 6.
[2] *Ibid.* July 9, 1947, p. 4.
[3] *Ibid.* August 4, 1947, p. 4.

authority meant in fact an almost total reliance on the military. In early August, the announcement came that 'the military forces in Calcutta will soon be strengthened considerably'.[1] This increase of troops was immediately reinforced by the governor's application of the 'Disturbed Areas Ordinance' to the whole of Bengal. The ordinance gave utmost powers to magistrates and the police in their enforcement of a prohibition on public assemblies or the carrying of weapons.[2] The civil government, therefore, had gone about as far as it could go, short of acquiescence to martial law. Yet, only a week before independence, severe communal rioting again broke out, when, on the day before Gandhi arrived in Calcutta, a crowd of over three hundred had stopped a train, selected twelve of its passengers, and wantonly slaughtered them in full public view. This incident, which ignited many others, is a prime example of the impotence of government when the citizenry, in fear and vengeance, turn to support forces of anarchy.

Gandhi had announced that he would spend independence day in Noakhali, but after a day spent in Calcutta, 'listening to the woes of the city', his departure for Noakhali was postponed. At his prayer meeting, on the evening of August 10th, Gandhi told a vast crowd that his 'head hung in shame at this recital of man's barbarism' in Calcutta. This was madness, and his aim was to effect a return to sanity. He refused to write off Calcutta's riots as simply a manifestation of *goondaism*. All citizens of Calcutta were responsible for the widespread violence, all must 'turn the searchlight inwards' and see that 'wide open *goondaism* was a reflection of the subtle *goondaism* they were harbouring within'. He had decided to delay his departure, and work here for peace, because (as he pointedly said) 'the argument of his Muslim friends had gone home'. Then he promised that he would make an extensive tour of the riot areas, and this brought huge crowds the next day, 'Hindus and Muslims, including women, who told him their grievances'.[3] Two weeks before, *The Statesman* had commented, 'The need now is not so much of political reassurance as of psycho-therapy, could that be practised on a mass scale.'[4] The therapist had arrived, and his genius was such that he, above all Indian leaders, knew intuitively how it could be practised on a mass scale.

On August 11th, Suhrawardy returned to Calcutta from Karachi, and went immediately to see Gandhi at his Sodepur ashram. He implored Gandhi to stay in Calcutta, at least until after independence. Suhrawardy had made a similar plea three months earlier, when Gandhi had last visited the city. Gandhi's reply at that time was that he would remain if Suhrawardy would enlist him as 'his private secretary'; they could then work together as a team against communalism. The chief minister had dismissed the suggestion as 'madness'.[5] Now, however, Gandhi had an even more extraordinary proposal. He suggested to Suhrawardy that they both move into a deserted Muslim

[1] *The Statesman*, August 5, 1947, p. 1. This followed Lord Mountbatten's visit to Calcutta at the end of July during which he expressed his 'grave concern at the disturbed conditions in the city'. It will be recalled, moreover, that in this seminar, Lord Spens remarked that he had himself urged the central government to increase military forces in Calcutta at this time.

[2] *Ibid.* August 7, 1947, p. 1.

[3] *Ibid.* August 11–12, 1947, p. 1.

[4] *Ibid.* July 31, 1947, p. 6.

[5] The incident is related in N. K. Bose, *My Days with Gandhi* (1953), p. 232.

bustee, in one of the worst-affected localities of the city, and live there together, for whatever period was required, until peace was restored to Calcutta. 'It would be best', Gandhi thought, 'to live unprotected by the police or the military.' 'In brotherly fashion' they would approach the people, reason with them, and foster a return to sanity. Suhrawardy considered the proposal, and after twenty-four hours gave his unqualified acceptance. 'In view of the fact', he told the press, 'that an insensate orgy of violence has started and the feeling of revenge, instead of subsiding, is increasing, I have decided to accept Mr. Gandhi's offer.' [1] The year since the killing had humbled Suhrawardy. The irrepressible Calcutta riots had blackened his ministry; and the League itself had partly withdrawn its favour, as suggested by his defeat by Nazimuddin, the week before, in the election for party leader of East Bengal. Gandhi, however, was not concerned with Suhrawardy's political status in the League, but rather with what the chief minister meant to the Muslims and Hindus of Calcutta. When Gandhi wrote to Patel of his Calcutta 'experiment', the Sardar, with characteristic humour replied, 'So you have got detained in Calcutta and that too in a quarter which is a veritable shambles and a notorious den of gangsters and hooligans. And in what choice company too!' [2] For Gandhi's purpose, Suhrawardy was indeed 'choice company'. No individual could have better disarmed Muslim suspicion and also attracted the hostilities of the Hindus, drawing them into the 'experiment' where they could be neutralized non-violently.

Hostile Hindu elements were present in full force when Gandhi and Suhrawardy arrived at the deserted 'Hydari Mansion' in Belliaghatta, the afternoon of August 13th. The original crowd of two hundred swelled in size, and eventually broke into the house, hurling stones, smashing doors and windows. Gandhi confronted them. Why had he now 'come to the rescue of the Muslims' when it was the Hindus who had suffered? How could he, a Hindu, associate himself with the man who was responsible for the slaughter of countless Hindus a year ago? Gandhi replied with the simple argument that he had used, as a reformer, all his public life: 'How can I, who am a Hindu by birth, a Hindu by creed and a Hindu of Hindus in my way of living be an "enemy" of Hindus?' [3] This reasoning had the desired effect and the crowd eventually dispersed. For almost three weeks after this initial outburst, Calcutta not only remained calm, but on independence day became the scene of unprecedented communal fraternization. All India was astounded at the sudden transformation.

How far Gandhi's experiment and personal example influenced the independence day metamorphosis in Calcutta is impossible to determine precisely. At the least, Gandhi was 'a lightning conductor for unpleasant verbal storms', whose experiment offered 'an object lesson in the neighbourliness which is the only true answer to communal fury'.[4] At most, he was, in the words of the new governor of West Bengal, Rajagopalachari, 'the magician' who performed the 'Calcutta miracle'.[5] Perhaps the truth lies

[1] *The Statesman*, August 13, 1947, p. 1.
[2] Sardar Patel quoted in Pyarelal, *Mahatma Gandhi, The Last Phase* (1958), vol. ii, p. 365.
[3] *Ibid.* p. 367. [4] Comment in *The Statesman*, August 15, 1947, p. 6 (Leader).
[5] Rajagoplachari in *The Statesman*, August 19, 1947, p. 5.

somewhere between these two points. Gandhi's experiment in Belliaghatta did provide, on the eve of independence, 'a place of pilgrimage for thousands of Calcutta's citizens. Both Hindus and Muslims came in a constant stream [on August 14th] . . . and placed their grievances before Mr. Gandhi and sought his advice.' [1] The experiment, therefore, acted as a remarkable catharsis at the critical moment of independence, and its effect continued in the days immediately after. Throughout August, unprecedented crowds gathered at Gandhi's evening prayer meetings, and rejoiced together in an astounding upsurge of communal harmony. Gandhi did not, it should be noted, suppress or eliminate the atmosphere of extreme tension present in the city since the killing; indeed, he watched as it burst into a form of social hysteria. What Gandhi did was to act, at this point, as one of several forces [2] which served to release desirable social energies, and thereby precipitate an explosion of communal goodwill rather than of violence. When, however, the city's tensions and anxieties once again sought violent expression, Gandhi abandoned his milder cathartic techniques and applied instead an extreme form of social control. For the fast was the ultimate weapon of *satyagraha*, employed only when all other means had failed. As it was then used by Gandhi in Calcutta, the fast marked the final and climactic stage of his *satyagraha*, an intense method of conflict-resolution through non-violent action. In this sense, the fast may be seen as an 'escalation' of non-violent conflict, the culmination of a process in which power is increasingly applied to achieve selected ends.

THE FAST: SEPTEMBER 1–4, 1947

As the end of August approached, Calcutta's political leaders and its press enthused over 'the miracle of communal harmony in India's largest city.' [3] The announcement of the boundary award had not caused further disturbances, and the *Id* festivities had been marked by more scenes of 'unforgettable communal friendliness.' [4] Glowing tributes to Gandhi flowed in from the highest political sources, including Lord Mountbatten [5] and the Muslim League. Gandhi's[6] prayer meetings held on the Calcutta maidan

[1] *The Statesman*, August 15, 1947, p. 1.

[2] Sir Francis Tuker gives several other reasons for the explosion of communal goodwill at the moment of independence. He terms Gandhi's influence 'considerable'. *While Memory Serves*, pp. 415, 421–2.

[3] Comment by *The Statesman*, August 28, 1947, p. 4.

[4] *Ibid.* August 19, 1947, p. 1.

[5] On August 26th, Mountbatten wired Gandhi in Calcutta: 'My Dear Gandhiji, In the Punjab we have 55 thousand soldiers and large scale rioting on our hands. In Bengal our forces consist of one man, and there is no rioting. As a serving officer, as well as an administrator, may I be allowed to pay my tribute to the One Man Boundary Force, not forgetting his Second in Command, Mr. Suhrawardy.' (Gandhi, *Correspondence with the Government, 1944–47* (1959), p. 277.)

[6] On August 24, 1947, The Muslim League party in the Indian constituent assembly passed a resolution expressing its 'deep sense of appreciation of the services rendered by Mr. Gandhi to the cause of restoration of peace and goodwill between the communities in Calcutta' (*The Statesman*, August 25, 1947, p. 1). The press throughout India acclaimed Gandhi's achievement in exalted terms: see, *The Mail* (Madras), August 20, 1947, p. 4; *The Leader* (Allahabad) August 20, 1947, p. 4; and *The Times of India*, September 3, 1947, p. 4.

(especially the one held for the celebration of *Id*) seemed to demonstrate the complete success of his 'experiment'. Congress leaders urged him to leave for the Punjab and plans for his departure on September 2nd were accordingly made. Nehru had referred to the Punjab riots, which were now being reported daily in Calcutta, as constituting a 'grave crisis', and General Rees warned in Lahore that 'the spirit of retaliation is abroad in the land'.[1] On September 1st, the Calcutta press described the Punjab as being in the throes of 'primitive blind vengeance' and torn by a 'veritable civil war'.[2] Hideous tales of mutual violence wrecked by Sikhs and Muslims there proliferated throughout Bengal. Reports of restiveness, especially among the Sikhs of Calcutta, now appeared. As the old fears once more emerged in the city, it seemed to many inevitable that, despite the recent 'miracle', the urge to retaliate would again prevail.

The fact that the recrudescence of violence in Calcutta actually began at Gandhi's Belliaghatta *bustee*, indicates the extent to which his experiment had become the magnet for communal tensions. Late in the evening of Sunday, August 31st, a crowd converged on Hydari mansion, carrying an injured Hindu, allegedly knifed by a Muslim. They demanded that Gandhi call for retaliation. Not only did his attempts to quiet them fail, but he was almost seriously wounded when the crowd attacked his party. The police soon restored order, but Gandhi's detailed statement of the incident to the press indicates the extent to which he himself was severely shaken by it. The disturbance here triggered an outburst of violence the next day throughout the city; by evening fifty people had been killed and over three hundred injured in uncontrollable rioting. Troops immediately came in, but since the demands of the United Provinces and Punjab had drastically reduced the military resources available to Bengal, the situation, in Tuker's view, was far more critical than it had been in July or August. Major General Ranking, area commander, 'acted at once with all the troops at his disposal, calling in Gurkhas' as well; yet even this, the military realized, was inadequate, and Ranking 'pressed the government to impose martial law'.[3]

Gandhi toured the affected areas, and then wrote to Sardar Patel, 'What was regarded as the "Calcutta Miracle" has proved to be a nine days' wonder. I am pondering what my duty is in the circumstances.'[4] When Rajagopalachari came to visit him on the evening of September 1st, Gandhi had already made his decision. He proposed a fast. 'Can one fast against the goondas?' Rajaji asked. 'I want to touch the hearts of those who are behind the goondas,' Gandhi replied. 'The hearts of the goondas may or may not be touched. It would be enough for my purpose if they realize that society at large has no sympathy with their aims or methods and that the peace-loving element is determined to assert itself or perish in the attempt.' Rajaji urged him to 'wait and watch a little', but Gandhi was adamant. 'The fast has to be now or never. It will be too late afterwards. The minority community cannot be left in a perilous condition. My fast has to be preventive

[1] Nehru and Rees reported in *The Statesman*, August 29, 1947, pp. 1, 5–6.

[2] *The Statesman*, September 1, 1947, p. 5.

[3] Tuker, *op. cit.* p. 426.

[4] Gandhi to Patel, Calcutta, September 1, 1947, in M. K. Gandhi, *Letters to Sardar Patel* (1957), pp. 225–6. Also, Pyarelal, *op. cit.* p. 406.

if it is to be of any good. I know I shall be able to tackle the Punjab if I can control Calcutta. But if I falter now, the conflagration may spread.' [1]

'The weapon which has hitherto proved infallible for me is fasting,' Gandhi announced in his public statement that evening. 'To put in an appearance before a yelling crowd does not always work. It certainly did not last night. What my word in person cannot do, my fast may. It may touch the hearts of all the warring elements in the Punjab if it does in Calcutta. I, therefore, begin fasting from 8:15 tonight to end only if and when sanity returns to Calcutta.' [2] The focus throughout the country was at once on Gandhi. *The Times of India* commented, 'More than his life – the peace of India – is at stake.' [3] Indian political leaders responded with alarm and exhortation. On the first day of the fast, however, it was clear that the city's communal antagonists, inflamed by *goondaism*, had not yet felt the impact of Gandhi's move. Looting and rioting persisted as the casualties mounted.

But on September 3rd, the second day of the fast, quiet came to Calcutta. Gandhi cautiously observed that 'The leaven has begun to work.' [4] The positive effects of his action on the city were plain: a deputation from the Calcutta bar association came to pledge their assistance; and they were followed by a large mixed procession of Hindus and Muslims, who promised to reconcile their differences; then, peace demonstrations of students, political workers and government officials of both communities, paraded through the city to Hydari mansion. Gandhi told them all to 'go out together to patrol the troubled areas and relieve the police of its arduous duties'. Meanwhile, the police force itself, European and Indian, had commenced a twenty-four hour fast in sympathy while remaining on duty. This show of civic sympathy was precisely what Gandhi wanted; of less interest to him were the public broadcasts with which provincial and national Congress leaders bombarded the city.

By September 4th, the third and last day of the fast, the mass therapy had progressed still further. Scores of members of Hindu 'resistance groups', formed since direct action day, surrendered to Gandhi a small arsenal of weapons, and admitted to him their complicity in the communal violence. They were followed by a large gang of *goondas* who offered to 'submit to whatever penalty you may impose, only that you should now end your fast'. To both groups, Gandhi replied, 'My penalty for you is that you should go immediately among the Muslims and assure them full protection. The minute I am convinced that real change of heart has taken place, I will give up the fast.' [5] 'The function of my fast,' Gandhi explained, 'is not to paralyze us or render us inactive,' but 'to release our energies. . . .' [6] Release them he did: not only was Calcutta without a single incident on this day, it was mobbed with processions to Hydari mansion clamouring for an end to the fast.

Earlier *The Statesman* had argued (in the May editorial quoted at length above) against a fast under these circumstances. The leader admitted that

[1] Pyarelal, *op. cit.* p. 407.
[2] Gandhi in *The Statesman*, September 2, 1947, p. 10.
[3] *The Times of India*, September 3, 1947, p. 4.
[4] Pyarelal, *op. cit.* p. 412.
[5] *Ibid.* p. 421.
[6] *Ibid.* p. 420.

'we have never been able fully to understand these Gandhian fasts', and then proceded to demonstrate this lack of understanding. It began with all the wrong assumptions: 'the contemplated fast could not be expected to influence Muslims generally', and since 'Hindu bitterness would greatly increase the outcome would be in every way disastrous'. Then it went on to point out that the appeal of the fast is 'primarily to the emotions, to the heart', although it is also 'intended to appeal to the head'. It is conceivable, the leader admitted, that in some instances this appeal might work, 'But with communal disputes it is different . . . once feelings are aroused to fever-pitch, there is no more possibility of subduing them by appeal to some other nobler emotion than of curing a rabid dog of his madness by talking gently. As for the intellectual factor, that is wholly absent.' This argument is worth repeating, not only for its suggestion of an almost fatalistic acceptance of the 'mad dog' forces of communalism, even among the most intelligent observers, but also because it reflects their confident scepticism of the efficacy of an essentially non-rational effort. At the crux of this effort was the will of one extraordinary individual, a will which he directed at the 'rabid dogs' of Calcutta, not merely by talking gently, but through the potent force of non-violent action; and this summoned a power so considerable that it persuaded even *The Statesman* to reconsider its position:

'On the ethics of fasting as a political instrument we have over many years failed to concur with India's most renowned practitioner of it, expressing our views frankly. But never in a long career has Mahatma Gandhi,[1] in our eyes, fasted in a simpler, worthier cause than this, nor one more calculated for immediate effective appeal to the public conscience. We cordially wish him unqualified success. . . .' [2]

Now, all Calcutta was wishing him 'unqualified success'. But for Gandhi, the right time to break the fast had still not come. At 6 p.m. on September 4th, what he regarded as a decisive breakthrough occurred. Gandhi was visited by another deputation: they included N. C. Chatterjee and Debendranath Mukherjee, the president and secretary, respectively, of the Bengal Mahasabha; R. K. Jaidka, a prominent Hindu Punjabi businessman; Sardar N. Singh Talib, the Sikh editor of the influential Sikh daily, *Desh Darpan;* Dr G. Jilani of the Muslim League; Dr A. R. Choudhury and M. Rahaman of the Pakistan Seamen's Union, and the ever-present Suhrawardy. As Suhrawardy escorted them in to Gandhi, the deputation joined Rajagopalachari, Acharya Kripalani, and P. C. Ghosh, who were already at his bedside. Gandhi, of course, appreciated that among these men were represented the most powerful interests in the city, and, after

[1] The shift, in this *The Statesman* leader, from the use of 'Mr.' to 'Mahatma' is not coincidental; an editorial of September 1st, had announced it as part of the paper's future policy. The change was made in response to numerous requests from readers, one of whom wrote (letter to editor, September 1, 1947, p. 4): 'I have always had great respect for Mr. Gandhi, but could not make up my mind to speak of him as Mahatma. However, seeing the wonders he has done in Calcutta I have no hesitation now in doing so. I hope that you will take the same view and in future write Mahatma Gandhi and not Mr. Gandhi.'

[2] *The Statesman*, September 3, 1947, p. 4.

listening to their pleas for ending the fast, he demanded of them two promises: first, that communal violence would not recur in Calcutta; second, that if it did recur, they would 'not live to report failure', but would lay down their lives to maintain order. If these pledges were given and broken then he vowed that he would begin an irrevocable fast until death. The deputation withdrew to another room, conferred, and emerged with a joint agreement: 'We the undersigned promise to Gandhiji that now that peace and quiet have been restored in Calcutta once again, we shall never allow communal strife in the city and shall strive unto death to prevent it.' [1] Gandhi immediately broke the fast; it had lasted seventy-three hours. On September 7th, he left for Delhi. Communal violence, during this critical period surrounding partition, did not return to Calcutta.

'Gandhiji has achieved many things,' said Rajagopalachari afterwards, 'but in my considered opinion, there has been nothing, not even independence, which is so truly wonderful as his victory over evil in Calcutta.' [2] Perhaps even more representative of the city's sentiments was the acting mayor's comment on Gandhi's departure that 'Calcutta has been spared the horrors of a strife which easily might have been as bad or worse than former disturbances.' [3] This was the judgment of the moment, not only by Congressmen, but by the press and political leaders of both communities. But it was not only the judgment of the moment; it has been confirmed by sober reflection as well, nowhere expressed better than by E. W. R. Lumby in his account of the fast:

> 'His triumph was complete, and the peace that he brought was destined to endure. A League newspaper, acknowledging the debt Calcutta Muslims owed him, said, "he was ready to die so that they might live peacefully". He had in fact worked a miracle, perhaps the greatest of modern times.' [4]

ANALYSIS

'In this, the last year of his life, Gandhi's influence was transcendent. By the people of India he was treated with the awe given to the great prophets and religious teachers of the past. Indeed he was already numbered with them. It was his preaching of the doctrine of non-violence more than any other single factor that stood between India and bloodshed on a frightful scale. . . .' [5]

[1] Quoted in Pyarelal, *op. cit.* p. 423.

[2] Quoted in *The Statesman*, September 6, 1947, p. 1. [3] *Ibid.* September 7, 1947, p. 1.

[4] E. W. R. Lumby, *The Transfer of Power in India, 1945–1947* (1954), p. 193. For further specific comment on Gandhi's achievement in the Calcutta *satyagraha*, and especially the September fast, see V. P. Menon, *The Transfer of Power in India* (1957), p. 434; also, Lord Pethwick-Lawrence *et al.*, *Mahatma Gandhi* (London: Odhams Press, 1949), pp. 297–8; Tuker, *op. cit.* p. 426. Extensive accounts of the fast itself are in Pyarelal, *op. cit.* N. K. Bose, *op. cit.* D. G. Tendulkar, *op. cit.* vols. vii, viii, and Manubehn Gandhi, *The Miracle of Calcutta* (Navajivan, 1959). General comment on the extent of Gandhi's influence during the partition period occurs in Nicholas Mansergh, *Survey of British Commonwealth Affairs, 1939–1952* (1958), p. 222, and his *The Commonwealth and The Nations* (1958), p. 142; Penderel Moon, *Divide and Quit* (1961), p. 249; Wilfred Russell, *Indian Summer* (1951), p. 26; and Percival Spear, *India, A Modern History* (1961), p. 424.

[5] Nicholas Mansergh, *The Commonwealth and The Nations*, p. 142.

The aim of this analysis is to examine, 'in this, the last year of his life', the nature and scope of Gandhi's influence; or, more specifically, some of the main sources and dynamics of his power, and the manner in which he used this power, within the context of the Calcutta *satyagraha*. The scope of Gandhi's influence at this time may best be described as 'popular', rather than as political in the strict sense. Nicholas Mansergh observes of Gandhi that 'As his inclinations seemed to lead him to withdraw more and more from the narrow political issues of the hour and to devote his efforts to the noble work of pacification, so his reputation grew. . . .' [1] While it is true that Gandhi's popular influence increased at this time, his withdrawal from politics was accompanied by a sharp decrease in influence within the higher political circles, where the decisions on partition were being made. His decline, here, had begun at least as early as September 1944, with his failure to reach a compromise in his talks with Jinnah. Deeply aware of this decline, and profoundly discouraged with the political trend of events, he wrote in October 1946, 'I know that mine is today a voice in the wilderness.' [2] As the 'vivisection of India' became imminent, his own sense of impotence increased: this, while, as Nicholas Mansergh rightly asserts, Gandhi's influence 'more than any other single factor stood between India and bloodshed on a frightful scale'. This apparent paradox itself illuminates, among other things, the peculiar nature of Gandhi's power, and the extent to which it was, particularly in this last phase, trans-political in character. This is evident especially in the Calcutta *satyagraha*. In this instance, at least three main dynamics of Gandhi's power emerge: his past experience with the communal problem, the style which he developed in dealing with it, and his theory of fasting, which he increasingly applied to its resolution. The last of these is especially noteworthy, since it exemplifies both his stylistic achievement as well as elements of his social thought, that is, his ideas on society and on means of social control.

'My South African experiences had convinced me', Gandhi recollected in his *Autobiography* in 1927, 'that it would be on the question of Hindu-Muslim unity that my Ahimsa would be put to its severest test, and that the question presented the widest field for my experiments in Ahimsa. The conviction is still there.' [3] This conviction had, throughout Gandhi's life, much to sustain it. In September 1924, for example, communal violence reached a high peak and Gandhi decided to fast, his first major fast on behalf of communal unity. 'The recent events', he announced from the home of a Muslim friend in Delhi, 'have proved unbearable for me. My helplessness is still more unbearable. My religion teaches me that whenever there is distress which one cannot remove, one must fast and pray. . . . I am therefore imposing upon myself a fast of twenty-one days commencing from today.' [4] Like the Calcutta fast, undertaken twenty-three years later for the same purpose, this one was begun in a Muslim home and Muslim friends cared for him; these elements of his style, then, had already taken shape. The 1942

[1] Nicholas Mansergh, *The Commonwealth and The Nations*, p. 142.
[2] Gandhi, *Harijan*, October 6, 1946, p. 338.
[3] Gandhi, *Autobiography* (1957), p. 441.
[4] Gandhi, *Speeches and Writings of Mahatma Gandhi*, 4th ed. (Madras, 1938), p. 999.

fast, however, represents only one high point in his consistent concern for communal harmony. Whatever mistakes Gandhi may have made in his later dealings with the League, no Indian leader gave greater attention, over a longer period, to the fundamental problems of Hindu–Muslim relations. For three decades, during his career in the Congress, he emphasized Hindu–Muslim unity as among 'the three pillars of Swaraj'; and, at the end of this long career, when communal violence suddenly gained its head, Gandhi acted intuitively to meet the emergency. He turned first to Bengal. After the Great Calcutta Killing, he realized that an alternate form of 'direct action' was necessary; and, when the first report of the Noakhali atrocities reached him in October 1946, he knew that this action demanded, above all, his physical presence in the disturbed areas. With this decision to wage *satyagraha* against large-scale communal rioting, that series of developments in method began which culminated a year later in the Calcutta 'experiment'.

While, therefore, the Congress working committee were passing resolutions in Delhi, finding 'it hard to express adequately their feelings of horror and pain at the present happenings in East Bengal', Gandhi was heading for the Noakhali villages.[1] Had it not been for the precedent of the Calcutta killing, the early reports of casualties in Noakhali would have seemed incredible (5,000 killed and 50,000 injured). Gandhi arrived there, after a brief stop-over in Calcutta, in early November. The next four months were spent in a relentless effort to restore confidence among the Hindu minority. He moved slowly through the area toward his destination of Srirampur, a remote village where he spent six weeks organizing the *satyagraha*. Then came his renowned 'a village a day pilgrimage': a walking tour of seven weeks in which he covered 116 miles and 47 villages. During this time, Gandhi was receiving reports of the Hindu retaliation in Bihar. This eventually prompted his departure from Bengal, arriving at Patna in early March. Here it was the Muslim minority that he sought out and consoled, while the Hindus now bore the brunt of his censure. The technique, however, was substantially the same in Bengal and Bihar: a tour of the devastated villages, visiting the afflicted homes and families; then the inevitable prayer meeting, with its ingenious admixture of the traditional and the contemporary; and finally the delegation of responsibility to one individual or group in the village that order might be preserved. Occasionally, as at Srirampur, Gandhi would remain for a prolonged period in one of the most remote and ravaged of the villages, until his persuasiveness and sheer courage stabilized the area. Fundamentally, this was the programme of action that directed the Calcutta *satyagraha*.

While Gandhi was touring the villages of Bihar, Nehru was preoccupied with running his inter-Asian relations conference in Delhi. Gandhi had been persuaded to attend, so he left Bihar at the end of March to address the closing session. During the summer in Delhi, recurrent reports of disturbances in Bengal and Bihar unnerved Gandhi, and the summer was subsequently broken with visits to Calcutta and Patna. Then, at the end of July, he travelled throughout Kashmir, leaving there in early August for Calcutta *en route* to Noakhali. Gandhi came to Calcutta, then, as a revered leader who

[1] [Editors' note: cf. Wainwright, above, p. 134–5.]

had courageously fought communalism, first, on behalf of the Hindus in Noakhali and then in defence of the Muslims in Bihar. His reputation had indeed grown, and for good reason; among India's leaders he was unique in having gone to the villages and struggled there in the interests of both communities. Moreover, as both Hindus and Muslims turned increasingly to him with trust, Gandhi's own confidence in his mission increased. Only days before the Calcutta killing, he had said, 'I have never had the chance to test my non-violence in the face of communal riots.' Now, this had been tested. The results were successful; not as dramatic, perhaps, as the Calcutta fast, but the work in Noakhali and Bihar did give him the opportunity to sharpen his methods, which soon were to find their proving ground in Calcutta.

Gandhi's style, abundantly manifest in his ingenious use of traditional Indian language, images, and symbols, goes further than any other single factor to explain the source and dynamics of his power. This style had been cultivated since his early South African experience. The attention given to it is most evident in his use of words, like *satyagraha*, *swaraj*, *sarvodaya*, *ahimsa* and *harijan*. These were terms which Gandhi either coined or re-interpreted. Language, though, represents only one element of his style: other components, often less obvious, contributed equally to the way in which he communicated with the Indian people. In his last phase, his style had, after a lifetime of public contact, become largely instinctive; and for this reason, his power over the Indian people reached its zenith.

Gandhi's 'experiment' at Hydari mansion marks the most imaginative of his stylistic achievements in this period. The richness of symbolism here shows everywhere the touch of the master. For at Hydari mansion appeared the microcosm on which the whole should be patterned: Gandhi, the 'Hindu of Hindus', moving into a house owned by a Muslim widow, cared for throughout by a volunteer squad of Muslim friends and admirers, and receiving daily an endless stream of Muslim devotees into his 'confessional' (men and women, the latter, he always proudly said, never observing purdah in his presence). Then there was his companion, Suhrawardy, the last Muslim for whom any Calcutta Hindu would have felt 'brotherly love'. Yet, here was Gandhi, saying often and unrepentantly of this notoriously untrustworthy Muslim politician, 'I trust him, he is my friend.' [1] All this Gandhi could do because he was Gandhi. But there were reasons why this man came to be seen as the Mahatma; and his sense of style, now fully developed, was not the least of these reasons.

Another example of Gandhi's style appears with his use of a device tested in Noakhali and Bihar and further developed in Calcutta: the prayer meeting. In this last phase, almost all Gandhi's major moves and decisions, often of political import, were first announced, not at press conferences, party conventions, or political assemblies, but in prayer meetings. These meetings had two parts: the first consisting of a reading from religious texts followed

[1] Suhrawardy, moreover, not only behaved like Gandhi's trusted comrade during the experiment, but, to the astonishment of his Hindu antagonists, he admitted what he had heretofore denied vehemently: that he should bear the largest responsibility for the Calcutta Killing.

by hymns and prayers; the second, that of Gandhi's personal 'post-prayer message', which he said should 'be regarded and listened to as an integral part of the prayer'.[1] The first part served to set an example of tolerance: verses from the Koran and the Bible were read along with those from Hindu texts – unless, that is, a member of the audiences objected. In that case, Gandhi would omit the prayers, and, with consummate skill, take as his text for the 'post-prayer message' the very example of intolerance that the objector had shown. The manoeuvre often resulted in the audience itself castigating the objector, and insisting that the prayers be read after all.[2] At the huge gatherings in Calcutta, the emphasis in Gandhi's post-prayer message was often on the need for social discipline; and Gandhi used the meeting itself as a testing ground for the maintenance of discipline, censuring the crowd's restiveness or praising their orderliness. After the meetings, Hindus and Muslims could mingle together in an atmosphere of trust; and although the attendance in Calcutta generally numbered in the hundreds of thousands, no incident of communal violence occurred at Gandhi's prayer meetings. Rather, they provided the opportunity for a needed release of anxiety, and display of friendship.

The prayer meeting and its associated psychological effects, date far back into the history of organized religion. Gandhi's genius, in this as in other instances, was to adapt a traditional concept and experience to his own use, in this case for the resolution of communal conflict. The most brilliant example of this adaptation appears in his theory and practice of fasting, which is both illustrative of his stylistic achievement, and suggestive of some of the main assumptions underlying his conception of *satyagraha*. 'Satyagraha', he wrote, 'has been designed as an effective substitute for violence,' [3] that is, to wage non-violent conflict in a way that will resolve a conflict situation. The fast became, in Gandhi's hands, the most potent of all ways: 'an integral part of the satyagraha armoury, . . . the greatest and most effective weapon in its armoury.' [4] Gandhi repeatedly use the term 'weapon' when describing the technique: 'a fiery weapon', 'an infallible weapon'.[5] The term is employed to convey the idea of waging non-violent conflict. The course of this conflict should be carefully plotted by the *satyagrahi*, and the fast should come only as 'a last resort when all other avenues of redress have been explored and have failed'.[6]

Beyond this consideration, two special conditions should be attached to the fast: first, it must be used in a constructive sense, to reform an individual, to gain his repentance for a wrong committed, to awaken his conscience and induce a re-examination of his position. Its general aim, therefore, is 'to evoke the best in [the wrong doer]. Self-suffering is an appeal to his better

[1] Gandhi, *Delhi Diary* (1948), p. 302.

[2] The technique of the prayer meeting, developed in Calcutta, was perfected by Gandhi in Delhi (September 1947–January 1948). For his use of the 'objector' in the audience see, for example, *Delhi Diary*, pp. 27, 29–32, 38, 45–8.

[3] Gandhi, *Harijan*, September 9, 1933, p. 4.

[4] *Harijan*, July 26, 1942, p. 248. A convenient collection of Gandhi's thoughts on fasting is Gandhi, *Fasting in Satyagraha* (Ahmedabad, 1965).

[5] *Harijan*, October 13, 1940, and *Harijan*, April 21, 1946, p. 93.

[6] *Harijan*, April 21, 1946.

nature, as retaliation is to his baser. Fasting under proper circumstances is such an appeal *par excellence*.' [1] The second condition attached by Gandhi to the fast reveals his understanding of its dynamics. He says that a *satyagrahi* should always fast against a 'lover'; that is, one who shares, however unconsciously, an underlying sympathy and respect for his aim. This condition is significant for at least two reasons. On the one hand, it indicates Gandhi's awareness of the fast's inherent limitation. He concedes that 'You cannot fast against a tyrant.' [2] On the other hand, with this condition may be seen Gandhi's insight into the real source of the fast's power: in his case the overwhelming sympathy of the Indian people, manifest in the fact that Gandhi's fasts worked best when waged against his own countrymen, Hindus and Muslims.

All these requirements and conditions that Gandhi attached to fasting in *satyagraha* were fulfilled in the Calcutta fast except the last, and this was only partially met. The Calcutta *goondas* were not tyrants, but even Gandhi did not assume that they were sympathetic to his cause. Rajagopalachari's first objection (noted above) when Gandhi proposed the Calcutta fast came with the question 'Can one fast against the goondas?' Gandhi replied that the *goondas* could be overcome by a determined effort by society at large to keep the peace. It is this emphasis upon social responsibility that lies at the heart of Gandhi's conception of *satyagraha:* since society, he reasoned, is responsible for the existence of *goondaism* in the first instance, then it both bears the moral responsibility for curing this disease of the body politic as well as the power to do so. Neglect of this responsibility is tantamount to moral cowardice.

'Goondas do not drop from the sky, nor do they spring from the earth like evil spirits. They are the product of social disorganization, and society is therefore responsible for their existence. In other words, they should be looked upon as a symptom of corruption in our body politic.' [3]

This was Gandhi in 1940; when in 1946, he was confronted with the Bihar riots, he again unequivocally placed the responsibility where it belonged: 'I deprecate the habit of procuring a moral alibi for ourselves by blaming it all on the goondas. We always put the blame on the goondas. But it is we who are responsible for their creation as well as encouragement.' [4] Gandhi argued these simple truths because he was intensely involved in the problems posed by communal violence and desperately sought their resolution through *satyagraha*. For those more removed from the heat of the struggle, it was easier to sidestep the implications of Gandhi's arguments. After Sarvepalli Radhakrishnan had visited Gandhi during the Calcutta fast, he commented to the press: 'I have told Mahatmaji not to confuse between goonda activities and communal violence. What had happened in Calcutta during the last few days was absolutely the work of goondas and nothing else.' [5] From Gandhi

[1] *Harijan*, July 26, 1942.
[2] *Young India*, May 1, 1924.
[3] *Harijan*, September 15, 1940, p. 285.
[4] *Harijan*, November 17, 1947, p. 402.
[5] Radhakrishanan, quoted in *The Statesman*, September 5, 1947, p. 8.

came a reasoned restatement of earlier views which again steadfastly refused to dodge the crucial question of social responsibility, and the subsequent issue of the right method of social control:

'The conflagration has been caused not by the *goondas* but by those who have *become goondas*. It is we who make *goondas*. Without our sympathy and passive support, the goondas would have no legs to stand upon. . . . During one year of past anarchy, it is understandable how these elements in society have gained respectability. But the war between Pakistanis and those for Undivided India has ended. It is time for peace-loving citizens to assert themselves and isolate *goondaism*. Non-violent non-co-operation is a universal remedy. Good is self-existent, evil is not. It is like a parasite living on and around good. It will die of itself when the support that good gives is withdrawn. The heart of the anti-social elements may or may not be changed; it will be enough if they are made to feel that the better elements of society are asserting themselves in the interests of peace and in the interests of normality.' [1]

Gandhi's hopes for communal harmony rested, in the last analysis, not with government or law enforcement agencies, but with the 'better elements of society' willing to assert themselves 'in the interests of peace and normality'. The Calcutta fast, he stressed, was 'meant to activize the better, peace-loving and wise elements in society', for only these could forge lasting bonds of communal friendship. In the days immediately after the Calcutta fast, and before his departure for Delhi, Gandhi met with numerous civic groups in an attempt to consolidate, through them, the salutary results of the *satyagraha*. Private citizens, businessmen, students, volunteer groups, and other social agencies were formed into 'Peace Brigades' and assigned to patrol affected areas of the city. These civic forces alone, Gandhi believed, could strengthen the fabric of their society, after a year of incessant violence had left it in shreds. If there was a 'miracle' in Calcutta, then it occurred when one man's thirty-day *satyagraha* restored to over two million people the will and sense of responsibility needed to mend their strife-torn city.

[1] *Harijan*, September 14, 1947, pp. 317, 323–4.

ASPECTS OF THE DEVELOPMENT OF MUSLIM LEAGUE POLICY, 1937–47

by Z. H. ZAIDI*

'The feeling among Muslims here is . . . that Gandhi will support the demand of unitary Govt. If this is done, our Muslim provinces will be like clay in the hand of the potter. The Hindu majority in the centre & the Hindu Govt. will make short work of the Punjab & Sindh. Of course the Sikhs will support it.'

Shafaat Ahmad Khan to Jinnah, 1931.

'As a community, the Moslems were extremely anxious about their future. It is true that they were in a clear majority in certain provinces. At the provincial level they had therefore no fears in these areas. They were, however, a minority in India as a whole and were troubled by the fear that their position and status in independent India would not be secure.

'In a country so vast as India and with people so diverse in language, customs and geographical conditions. a unitary government was obviously most unsuitable. Decentralization of power in a federal government would also help to allay the fears of the minorities.'

Maulana Abul Kalam Azad, *India Wins Freedom* (1960).

INTRODUCTION

The experience of contesting the elections of 1936–37 and forming ministries under conditions of responsible government revealed the inner dynamics of Indian politics. It brought to the surface both majority and minority attitudes in a new and striking way. The most significant of these was the Congress tendency towards a one-party polity in India that assumed the submersion of other Indian parties. Another was the emergent unity of Muslim India. In the experiences of those years Jinnah learned lessons in practical politics that a theoretical approach never could have taught him. He and the Muslim League went into the elections as idealists; they emerged from the aftermath as political realists. The change could hardly have been more significant for India and the shape of her independent future.

SEARCH FOR UNITY

Prior to the elections of 1937, Muslim politics were chaotic, in a state of desperate disorganization, with interests in conflict in all levels, provincial, local and personal. No Muslim organization appeared capable of overcoming the differences that divided the Muslim body politic. Such organizations as Jamiat-ul-Ulema-i-Hind, All-India Muslim Conference and the All-India Muslim League had been deliberative bodies. Their spheres of activities, in the past had been limited to annual meetings and discussions. Since the non-co-operation days the Jamiat had been in oblivion and was not sufficiently

* Lecturer in the History of Islam in India, School of Oriental and African Studies, London.

organized. It continued to plough its lonely furrow [1] until the time when it unconditionally joined the Congress in 1937. The All-India Muslim Conference (originally the All-Parties Muslim Conference organized under the leadership of Aga Khan in 1928), had been inactive. Its executive board under the chairmanship of Abdoola Haroon, after holding a few meetings in the early months of 1936, decided to withdraw from the election campaign. While abstaining from specifically mentioning any particular parties, the conference, winding up its offices, asked the electors to support those candidates who stood by the communal award and pledged themselves to safeguard the religious and cultural rights of the Muslims and were committed to the working of the provincial constitution.[2] Like other Muslim organizations, the Muslim League, during the last few years had been in a moribund condition. In 1933, with a total income of Rs. 1318.11.6 its annual expenditure showed a deficit of some 564 rupees.[3] Out of the total of 300 members on its council ninety-two were under notice to pay arrears of membership.[4] After the second session of the Round Table conference, Jinnah had stayed in England. During his absence the Muslim League had 'lived on paper'.

But the Muslim League was older than other Muslim organizations. It had played a part in the past in organizing the Muslim community on an all-India basis. Its lack of success in becoming a dynamic organization was mainly because its leadership in the past had been composed of 'careerists' – professional politicians who lacked mass political appeal and some of whom felt no particular dedication to their cause. Convenience rather than conviction, governed their politics. Though the Muslim League was the only Muslim organization in the field to fight elections on an all-India basis, it had to set its own house in order before it could start organizing the machinery for a national effort.

Jinnah had returned to India in 1935 and started reviving the dormant Muslim League. At its 24th annual session held at Bombay in April 1936, while condemning the federal scheme embodied in the Government of India Act of 1935 as 'most reactionary, retrograde, injurious and fatal' and 'totally unacceptable', the League decided to utilize the provincial part of the Act for 'what it was worth' and authorized Jinnah to form a central parliamentary board. The board was to consist of not less than thirty-five members and was empowered to affiliate provincial boards in the various provinces to contest the elections on the ticket of the Muslim League.[5]

Jinnah received certain assurances of help. Maulana Ahmad Saeed, secretary of the Jamiat-ul-Ulema-i-Hind wrote: 'Unless you visit a good number of important towns in different provinces, it is very difficult to form representative local boards on proper lines. . . . I would request you with all the force at my command to start on a tour and visit certain important centres of political activity. . . . We have not yet started work in earnest. The continuous publicity of the aims and objects of the League and its present

[1] *Star of India*, April 6, 1936. [2] *Ibid.* April 26, and September 29, 1936.

[3] *Annual Report of the All India Muslim League for the years 1932 and 1933*, p. 10. Presenting the annual report for 1935, Sir Yaqub Hasan also referred to the 'financial bankruptcy' of the League. See *Star of India*, April 13, 1936.

[4] Asaf Ali to Sardar Abdur Rab Nishtar, May 1, 1933, *Nishtar Collection.*

[5] *Star of India*, April 13, 1936.

policy is essential for educating the public and the press alike. An Urdu Daily, at least a Bi-weekly, wholly devoted to the Cause of the League is badly needed.... I have already written to the members of the Jamiat-ul-Ulema-i-Hind to make effective speeches in support of the Muslim League in public meetings and appeal to the Moslem voters to reserve their votes for the candidates of the League only.' Mazhar Ali Khan, general secretary of Majlis-i-Ahrar-i-Islam Hind, temporarily joined hands with the League. Even the secretary of the Unionist party, Ahmad Yar Khan Daultana, who called himself one of the 'ardent jinhites' tried to bring about a settlement and submitted to Jinnah a list of members to be elected on the League council adding: 'All these are your men against the whole world.' After the failure of the League-Unionist negotiations, Ahmad Yar Khan Daultana once again approached Jinnah: 'You have millions of admirers in this world but I can assure you that few will come up to my standard of devoted loyalty and profound admiration.' He assured Jinnah that like himself, Sikandar Hyat Khan was also 'a great admirer of your leadership, statesmanship and your other unique qualities. I feel it will be very unfortunate if there is any hostility between two parties in which you and Sir Mohammad Iqbal are on one side and Sir Sikandar and myself on the other. I am writing to Sir Sikandar to have a talk with you and to try to come to a working settlement. Let us have minor difference of opinion but it should be far from hostility or ill-will to each other.'

It was on May 21, 1936, that Jinnah announced the personnel of the central parliamentary board consisting of fifty-six members.[1] (Bengal 8, Punjab 11, Sind 4, North West Frontier Province 4, Madras 4, United Provinces 9, Bihar 5, Central Provinces 2, Delhi 1, Assam 2, Bombay 6). Jinnah had encountered difficulties in nominating the members of the board. Provincial leaders representing different Muslim parties had already formulated programmes and embarked upon their election campaigns. Jinnah was late in the field and had, perforce, to depend on those leaders who were still unattached to any provincial parties or those whom he could persuade to merge their organizations with the Muslim League.[2] It is difficult now to be sure whether all the fifty-six members nominated on the said board had been previously consulted by Jinnah and had agreed to serve on the board for there were many absentees from the first meeting of the board held at Lahore on June 8, 1936.[3] Some of them, being the organizers and leaders of provincial parties, were torn by their provincial loyalties, their chances of domination in the provincial politics and their reluctance to come under the dictation of a central board. Leaders like Fazlul Haq (Krishak Praja Samity, Bengal), Syed Abdul Aziz (United Party, Bihar), Sheikh Abdul Majid Sindhi (Azad Party, Sind), Syed Rauf Shah (Muslim Parliamentary Party, Central Provinces), Maulana Zafar Ali Khan (Majlis-i-Ittehad-i-Millat, Punjab), Nawab of Chattari, Sir Muhammad Yusuf, Liaqat Ali Khan (National Agriculturist Party, United Provinces), though originally nominated on the board had organized their respective parties to fight the elections under the auspices of their own organizations.

[1] *Star of India*, May 23, 1936.
[2] *Civil and Military Gazette*, May 23, 1936.
[3] *Ibid.* June 9, 1936. Also see *Star of India*, June 10, 1936.

Though some of these local Muslim parties did not merge themselves with the Muslim League until after the elections, in many respects their programmes and policies were not at variance with those of the League. The unwillingness of some of the leaders of provincial parties to serve on the Muslim League parliamentary board was therefore mainly due to their fear of the domination of rival groups. Apparently these organizations would have been prepared to join the League if they had been given a freer hand in provincial politics. Till such freedom was promised, personal, local and mainly vested interests kept them away.

In Bengal, for instance, there was a clash between the United Muslim party and the Krishak Praja Samity. Early in 1936 Muslim Bengal was in revolt against the Calcutta corporation, mainly over the question of a reasonable communal ratio in services of the corporation which had led to a wholesale resignation of the Muslim councillors including Fazlul Haq the mayor.[1] New elections for the corporation were held and these were boycotted by the Muslims of Calcutta. The boycott brought together the Muslim leaders who had already been busy in forming a united group of Muslims of Bengal to fight the provincial elections. On May 24, 1936, the United Muslim party of Bengal was formed.[2] The party included conservatives like the nawab of Dacca, progressives like Nooruddin representing the New Muslim Majlis (formed in 1932), and members of the Khilafat committee like Maulana Akram Khan. Efforts were made to persuade Fazlul Haq and his Krishak party to join the United Muslim party. Though initially willing to come to some settlement, Fazlul Haq backed out at the last moment.[3] On August 17, 1936, Jinnah arrived in Bengal at the joint invitation of three groups – United Muslim party, Krishak Praja Samity and the Presidency Muslim League – to bring the contending groups together under the Muslim League.[4] Apparently an agreement between all the parties was arrived at. A provincial Muslim League parliamentary board was set up.[5] Fazlul Haq and his party, however, repudiated the agreement[6] as Fazlul Haq demanded that the members of the provincial parliamentary board should also sign the pledge of his party. Personal and provincial rivalries rather than the differences with the Muslim League lay behind the trouble.

Similarly in Bihar the differences between the United party and the Ahrar party were largely of a personal nature between the leaders of the two parties. The tug-of-war behind these two parties for domination in the provincial sphere continued and did not let them sink their differences so as to come within the domain of the Muslim League.[7] Nevertheless the programme of both organizations was similar to that of the League. In fact the United party was more emphatic and vocal than the League in demanding recognition of and safeguards for the rights of the Muslims as a distinct political entity, the communal award and the fourteen points of Jinnah.[8]

[1] *Star of India*, January 6 and 20, 1936.
[2] *Ibid.* May 25, 1936.
[3] *Ibid.* June 16 and 17, 1936.
[4] *Ibid.* August 10, 11 and 21, 1936.
[5] *Ibid.* August 25, 1936.
[6] *Ibid.* September 1, 1936.
[7] *Ibid.* June 6 and 7, 1936.
[8] *Ibid.* October 7, 1936. The Ahrar party and the Independent party included similar items in their programme. *Ibid.* June 24, and October 7, 1936.

A Muslim League parliamentary board had been formed in the Central Provinces with Siddique Ali Khan as president and M. Y. Shariff and S. A. Rauf Shah as vice-presidents.[1] Soon, Rauf Shah and thirteen other members resigned. They formed a new party called the Muslim Parliamentary party. There was no difference about the policy of the Muslim League and its objectives between the two groups; the split occurred over the question of the nomination of candidates for election.[2] The story repeated itself in Madras, where Abdul Hakim formed the Madras Presidency Muslim Progressive party, though the aims of the party were in keeping with the Muslim League programme.[3]

In Sind, as in other provinces, the Muslim leaders were divided. There were three parties, (1) the Sind United party formed on the lines of the Unionist party of the Punjab under the leadership of Abdoola Haroon, (2) the Azad party organized by Sheikh Abdul Majid Sindhi and (3) the Muslim Political party of Sir Ghulam Hussain. Personal bickerings of the leaders and the question of the distribution of offices kept them apart.[4]

JINNAH'S OUTLOOK IN 1936

It was against this division in the Muslim ranks that Jinnah raised his voice and tried to lift Muslim politics from the provincial and local to an all-India level. He believed that as long as the Muslims were divided and disorganized, as long as they continued to follow disparate paths having provincial groups with no wider unity and cohesion – there could be no chance of a settlement with the Congress. For these splinter organizations had no public sanction behind them. Only a united Muslim party would have the authority and sanction to speak powerfully. If 'the entire Muslims of India were politically organized and if they remain united', said Jinnah, 'then they will be forging sanctions behind them in order to play their part in the decisions of all-India questions'.[5]

In organizing the Muslims under the banner of the Muslim League, Jinnah did not believe that he was diminishing the chances of Hindu–Muslim co-operation. He had been a nationalist and had been called the 'ambassador of Hindu–Muslim unity', and according to Nehru, had been 'largely responsible in the past for bringing the Moslem League nearer to the Congress'.[6] He still believed that without Hindu–Muslim unity, without united efforts on the part of the two major communities, India's drive towards freedom could not succeed. United action, a common platform and mutual trust and confidence were needed to solve the political tangle and bring India nearer to its cherished goal of freedom. Referring to his part at the Round Table conference, he said in March 1936, 'I displeased the Muslims, I displeased my Hindu friends because of the 'famous' 14 Points. I displeased the Princes because I was deadly against their under-hand activities and I displeased the

[1] *Star of India*, November 14, 1936.
[2] *Ibid.* December 4, 1936 and January 6, 1937.
[3] *Ibid.* June 4, August 12, October 8 and November 10, 1936.
[4] *Ibid.* June 15, August 26 and December 24, 1936.
[5] *Ibid.* August 21, 1936.
[6] Jawaharlal Nehru, *An Autobiography* (1945 edition), p. 67.

British Parliament because . . . I rebelled against it and said that it was all a fraud. . . . But whatever I have done, let me assure you there has been no change in me, not the slightest, since the day when I joined the Indian National Congress. It might be I have been wrong on some occasions. But it has never been done in a partisan spirit. My sole and only object has been the welfare of my country.' Jinnah was anxious for communal co-operation and understanding. 'I will not and I cannot give it up. It may give me up, but I will not.' [1]

In fact the League as early as January 1935 had expressed its readiness 'to co-operate with any community or party with a view to secure such future constitution for India as would satisfy the people'. Jinnah continued his efforts to bring unity and solidarity among the Muslims. But this was never without advocating co-operation with their sister communities. In fact he gave out that the Muslim League would be prepared to co-operate with all progressive parties in the country especially the Congress. About two weeks after the Muslim League session held at Bombay, Jinnah in a statement on April 27, 1936 made this clear, 'Hindus cannot take Muslims seriously and that the Congress does not take us seriously because so far we Muslims have not proved ourselves worthy of alliance and that until we are ready to take a proper place in the national life of the country, there cannot be a whole-hearted and real settlement.' His advice to Muslims was that 'they should first organize themselves and deserve before they desired'. For he believed that 'if Muslims would speak with one voice, a settlement between Hindus and Muslims would come quicker'. Justifying the move of organizing the Muslims and putting their affairs in order, he explained that it did not mean that the Muslims 'should not stand as firmly by national interest. In fact, they should prove that their patriotism is unsullied and that their love of India and her progress is no less than that of any other community in the country.' [2]

Jinnah did not, at this stage, regard the separate electorates or the communal award as an ideal arrangement. They were a temporary measure, and could be replaced by something better. But until such an arrangement could be made, they must remain. 'So long as the separate electorates existed', he said on July 24, 1936, 'the separate organization of Mussalmans was an inevitable corollary. But that did not mean that such a position was an ideal one or that he was satisfied with it.' [3]

Throughout 1936 and the beginning of 1937 Jinnah continued to speak for Hindu–Muslim co-operation. He realized that there had been differences in the past but he believed that those differences were not incapable of solution for he was still looking at the Indian political scene as an idealist. 'If out of 80 million Indian Muslims', declared Jinnah on October 20, 1936, 'I can produce a patriotic and liberal-minded nationalist block, who will be able to march hand in hand with the progressive elements in other communities, I will have rendered great service to my community.' [4]

Perhaps because of his earnest desire for co-operation with the Congress,

[1] *Civil and Military Gazette*, March 3, 1936.
[2] *Ibid.* April 28, 1936.
[3] *Star of India*, July 29, 1936.
[4] *Civil and Military Gazette*, October 20, 1936.

Jinnah had got Wazir Hassan, a liberal known for his nationalist views elected as president of the Bombay session of the League. This was explained to Wazir Hassan in a letter written to him just after his election: 'Raja Saheb of Salimpur was very anxious for his election as President of the Annual Session of the League and came to Delhi twice during the last two weeks. Mr. Shaukat Ali, in his usual way, had been canvassing for him. But Mr. Jinnah with great tact managed the whole thing in a marvellous way and you were elected without having recourse to voting. Mr. Jinnah came from Lahore only for this meeting yesterday in the morning and returned to Lahore last night.'

When Jinnah embarked on rallying the Muslims on the League platform and asked them to stand by its policy, he was far from running the Muslim League as a counter to the Congress. For him the memories of the Lucknow pact were still fresh. He regarded it as a 'landmark in the political history of India'. There were differences between the Muslims and the Hindus but if the two communities had been able to compose their differences once, there was no need for despair. It was for this reason that the League was endeavouring by systematic organization to produce the best material among the Muslims. At a public meeting on January 7, 1937, Jinnah was still prepared to say, 'Hindus and Muslims could join hands and form one party' provided they could evolve a common programme of work both inside and outside the legislatures.[1]

Jinnah wanted to make the Muslim League a popular organization built not on the support of a few at the top but one which had a wider appeal for the masses. He was conscious of the charges often levelled against the League that it had been a party of 'toadies' and rich landlords. He was aware that the organization though open to all, had been able to attract only a minority of the Muslim community. He knew that so far it had failed to evoke any general enthusiasm from the Muslim intelligentsia, and that it lacked mass contact. It could not, he held, effectively and authoritatively speak for the Muslims of India until it had a wider basis of support. This, he believed, was essential in order to lay the real foundation of Hindu–Muslim unity. 'The masses should be persuaded and educated in that direction so that lasting unity could be attained.' [2]

MUSLIM LEAGUE PROGRAMME AND ELECTION MANIFESTO

The main feature of the Muslim League programme was to maintain the solidarity of the Muslims as an all-India community and to save them from breaking up into provincial parties and groups. The election was to be fought – and this is an important point – not essentially between the Congress and the Muslim League (as some of the members of the Muslim League continued to be the members of the Congress) but between the Muslim League and the

[1] *Star of India*, January 9, 1937. Addressing a meeting of students of Calcutta University, Jinnah said, 'Remember India cannot make any progress and India's salvation lies in the unity of all communities especially the Hindus and Muslims . . .. It is up to you all, whether as Hindus and Muslims, or Parsees or Christians, it is up to you neither as a Hindu nor as a Muslim but as an Indian to find the solution . . .', *Star of India*, August 24, 1936.

[2] *Ibid.* July 29, 1936.

local Muslim parties. The issue was whether local interests should be subordinated to the all-India interests of the community or vice versa.[1]

The manifesto which was adopted on June 9, 1936, while maintaining that the position of Muslims should be protected and safe-guarded in any future political constitutional structure, argued that such a demand did not 'savour of communalism'. For it was not only 'natural, but essential for securing a stable national government by ensuring whole-hearted and willing co-operation of the minorities who must be made to feel that they can rely upon the majority with a complete sense of confidence and security'. The manifesto asked for the replacement of the present provincial constitution and the proposed central constitution by 'democratic full self-government'. In the meantime the representatives of the Muslim League were to 'utilize the legislatures in order to extract maximum benefit out of the constitution for the uplift of the people in various spheres of national life'. The need for a new social order with a view to ameliorating the condition of the poor and backward Muslims was also stressed.

The League adopted the following programme:

1. To protect the religious rights of the Mussalmans. In all matters of purely religious character, due weight shall be given to the opinions of Jamiat-ul-Ulema-i-Hind and the Mujtahids.
2. To make every effort to secure the repeal of all repressive laws.
3. To resist all measures which are detrimental to the interest of India, which encroach upon the fundamental liberties of the people and lead to economic exploitation of the country.
4. To reduce heavy cost of administrative machinery, central and provincial, and allocate substantial funds for nation-building departments.
5. To nationalize the Indian army and reduce the military expenditure.
6. To encourage development of industries, including cottage industries.
7. To regulate currency, exchange and prices in the interest of economic development of the country.
8. To stand for the social, educational and economic uplift of the rural population.
9. To sponsor measures for the relief of agricultural indebtedness.
10. To make elementary education free and compulsory.
11. To protect and promote Urdu language and script.
12. To devise measures for the amelioration of the general conditions of Muslims.
13. To take steps to reduce the heavy burden of taxation.
14. To create a healthy public opinion and general political consciousness throughout the country.[2]

ELECTIONS

The Muslim League had hardly been adequately reorganized when it fought the elections. With few or no provincial and district branches, with limited financial and propaganda resources, it gathered itself together to go into the

[1] *Civil and Military Gazette*, June 11, 1936.
[2] *Ibid.* June 12, 1936. Also see *Star of India*, June 12, 1936.

election campaign. The League was fighting the elections for the first time on an all-India basis. While other organizations had come into the field much earlier, it had taken steps to formulate a programme only in the middle of 1936. With some six months to organize the election machinery and confronted as it was with warring elements, local jealousies and rivalries, it could hardly be expected that the League would make much headway. In the event it won 109 seats out of a total of 482 reserved for Muslims. However, it had not contested all the seats; Jinnah claimed that the Muslim League had won sixty to seventy per cent of the seats contested by the League candidates.[1] For instance, in the Punjab, the Muslim League put up only seven candidates and won two seats,[2] in the United Provinces it contested thirty-five seats and won twenty-nine, in Madras ten out of eleven Muslim League nominees were elected.[3] In Bihar, Orissa, North West Frontier Province and Sind, no Muslim League candidates were set up.[4] In Assam, the League won nine out of a total of thirty-four reserved seats, in Bengal thirty-nine out of one hundred and seventeen, in Bombay, twenty out of twenty-nine seats.[5]

Of the 1,585, seats, the Congress won 716 (about 44 per cent of the total). Of the Muslim seats it only secured twenty-six (5·4 per cent of the total).[6]

On the basis of the election results, neither the Muslim League could be regarded as the sole representative body of the Indian Muslims nor did the Congress have the right to speak for all Indians, especially the Indian Muslims. In fact the results show that the Congress had very little hold on Muslims. It could not even find a sufficient number of Muslims to contest all the reserved seats on its ticket. No Muslim was returned on a Congress ticket from Muslim constituencies in Bengal, Sind, Punjab, Assam, United Provinces, Bombay, Central Provinces and Orissa. The Congress success was mainly limited to the Frontier Province, though it won a few seats in Madras and Bihar. The *Madras Mail*, commenting on the election results, wrote that more than the success of the Congress party, the election results had 'demonstrated the development of the cleavage between the Hindu and Muslim communities. The inability of a single Congress Muslim to secure election in the United Provinces by a Muslim Constituency and the failure of the majority of the Congress Muslims in other provinces cannot be disregarded.' The paper added that the ballot box had proved that 'the belief that the Congress party is a predominantly Hindu party out to serve the Hindu community is widely held among Muslims'.[7]

Thus the election results of 1937 showed that while the Congress had a great hold on the non-Muslim electorate, its hold on Muslims was negligible.[8]

[1] Jamil-ud-din Ahmad, *Speeches and Writings of Mr. Jinnah* (1964), vol. i, p. 26, hereafter referred to as *Speeches and Writings of Jinnah.*

[2] *Star of India*, December 2, 1936. Also see *Civil and Military Gazette*, April 4, 1937.

[3] *Ibid.* March 2, 1937.

[4] *Ibid.*

[5] Figures based on *Return showing the Results of Elections in India* (1937), Cmd. 5589. These figures do not seem to be correct. It was reported by *Civil and Military Gazette* of April 4, 1937 that the Muslim League won fifty seats in Bengal.

[6] The Congress contested only fifty-eight Muslim seats.

[7] *Madras Mail* quoted in *Star of India*, March 12, 1937.

[8] *Civil and Military Gazette*, April 4, 1937.

The results had confirmed the general Muslim aversion to coming within the fold of the Congress. They had failed to vindicate the Congress approach towards solving the communal problem through an economic programme and had clearly indicated that a change of approach was needed. Moreover if the Congress leaders thought that those who did not side with the Muslim League were with the Congress, it was a miscalculation on their part, and if they evaluated the Muslim League as it stood at the time of elections, they did not bother to take into account the idea it represented. Nehru's own admission that the Congress lacked success with regard to Muslim seats [1] ought to have served as an eye-opener. It was because of this failure that Nehru asked the Congress provincial committees to concentrate on the enrolment of Muslim members to the Congress [2] and set up a separate department in the A.I.C.C. secretariat to deal exclusively with Muslim questions.[3] Thus instead of coming to terms with the Muslim League, the Congress decided to approach the Muslims over their heads. In this they met with dismal failure.

JINNAH-NEHRU CLEAVAGE

In view of Jinnah's earlier statements regarding the need for a Hindu–Muslim compromise, a settlement between the two parties should not have been difficult. But Jinnah's offers did not meet with any response from Nehru. Nehru had recently returned to India 'full of communistic and Marxian ideas' as Pattabhi Sitaramayya expressed it.[4] He was ardently committed to a socialistic programme and thought that it was the answer to all the problems which afflicted the body politic of India. To him the urgent problems of the country were 'the appalling poverty, unemployment and indebtedness of peasantry'.[5] Consequently communal questions had no importance. To deny, as Nehru did, that there was a communal problem and to say that the question before the country was an economic one, which once solved, would cause the communal problem automatically to disappear was all very virtuous but hardly practical politics.[6] Nehru did not stop there; he attacked those who talked about a communal settlement as being 'political reactionaries' who had 'sided with the British Imperialism in vital matters'.[7] He banged the door on such persons, 'With them there can be no co-operation, for that would mean co-operation with reaction.' [8] Jinnah had earlier clarified the position of the Muslims, declaring that there were no 'religious or communal motives which actuated them as a minority community to ask for certain safeguards from the Hindus before marching with them along the road to freedom'.[9] But Nehru kept on harping on the same theme. On June 1, 1936, he said at Amritsar, 'the communal question was the creation of a third party', and as such it was of no vital importance.[10] Nehru's approach, which *Justice*

[1] *Star of India*, March 20, 1937.
[2] *Pioneer*, April 2, 1937.
[3] *Star of India*, April 2, 1937.
[4] Pattabhi Sitaramayya, *The History of the Indian National Congress* (1947), vol. ii, p. 11.
[5] Congress resolution, *Star of India*, April 16, 1936.
[6] *Civil and Military Gazette*, May 17, 1936.
[7] *Star of India*, April 13, 1936.
[8] *Ibid.*
[9] *Civil and Military Gazette*, March 7, 1936.
[10] *Ibid.* June 2, 1936.

characterized as 'impracticable idealism'[1] did not even please his close associates. Rajendra Prasad warned Nehru, 'We have got many difficulties and problems which baffle solution. The country has not yet found a solution of the Hindu–Muslim problem in spite of the greatest efforts.' In such circumstances, asked Rajendra Prasad, 'is it practical politics to say that all our communal and international differences will vanish in no time if we can concentrate our attention on economic problems and solve them on Socialistic lines?'[2] Undeterred by criticism and though finding 'himself one against the world', Nehru carried on the crusade.

Nehru's attitude pained Jinnah, whose offers of co-operation were spurned. On January 5, 1937, Jinnah, while inaugurating the Muslim League election campaign, had commented 'Mr. Nehru is reported to have said that there are only two parties in India – the Government and the Congress – and others must line up. I refuse to line up with the Congress. I refuse to accept this proposition. There is a third party in this country and this is Muslim India.' Jinnah did not stop there. He stressed the desirability of acknowledging the fears which the Muslims entertained as regards their safeguards in a future constitution. Were that done, he offered co-operation. 'We are willing as equal partners to come to a settlement with our sister communities in the interest of India.'[3] But the reference to the existence of Muslim India as a distinct party did not please Nehru who called such ideas 'medieval and out of date'. The present contest, replied Nehru, 'lies between Imperialism and Nationalism. All third parties and middle and undecided groups have no real importance. . . . They have consequently no great strength and they function only in election and the like and fade away at other times. Thus in the final analysis, there are only two forces in India today – British Imperialism and the Congress – representing Indian Nationalism.' Referring to the Muslim League, Nehru said that it did not stand for independence and only functioned in the 'higher regions of the upper middle classes.' As for Jinnah's offer of co-operation, Nehru made it clear that there could be 'no pacts and compromises between handfuls of the upper class' and the Congress.[4] This was a painful rebuff to Jinnah. It was also a challenge to show that the Muslim League had not come to function in election time and fade away later.

Despite the bickerings which the elections caused between the two organizations, Jinnah reiterated his desire for co-operation. On February 28, 1937, he extended an invitation, 'We are free and ready to co-operate with any group or party if the basic principles are determined by common consent.'[5] 'We can enter into no alliances with other groups', came the reply from Nehru.[6] 'The Congress cannot include the League as the Congress is for wrecking the Constitution, while the Muslim League is prepared to work it', explained Rajendra Prasad.[7] Jinnah pleaded that there were no serious differences between the Congress and the Muslim League except that the latter stood for the safeguarding of the rights of Muslims.[8] Jinnah had only stated

[1] *Justice*, quoted in *Star of India*, April 16, 1936.
[2] *Civil and Military Gazette*, June 2, 1936.
[3] *Star of India*, January 4, 1937.
[4] *Ibid.* January 12, 1937.
[5] *Ibid.* March 2, 1937.
[6] *Ibid.* March 4, 1937.
[7] *Ibid.* March 3, 1937.
[8] *Ibid.* March 15, 1937.

what Nehru admitted later when he wrote to Nawab Ismail Khan, 'I do not quite know what our differences are in politics. I had imagined that they were not very great.'[1] When, on March 18, 1937, the Congress decided to accept office, Jinnah thought that the two organizations had come 'within the domain of constitutional activities' and that it would now be 'easier for the All-India Muslim League to co-operate with other progressive parties'. He, therefore, suggested that the two organizations should try to remove the causes which stood in the way of forming a 'united front'.[2]

But the Congress, it seems was determined not to have anything to do with the League. Its leaders, jubilant over the recent success, assumed a dictatorial attitude. On March 19, 1937, the all-India convention of legislators met at Delhi under the presidentship of Nehru to formulate a programme for a conference in connection with the framing of the future constitution for India. Yaqub Hasan, perhaps impressed by the recent offers of Jinnah, moved a resolution to invite all non-Congress members of provincial legislatures to this conference. Nehru ridiculed the suggestion, 'How could Congressmen', said Nehru, 'invite the co-operating semi-Imperialist groups and permit them to have a say in the matter of framing the future Constitution? It was a dangerous thing to revert to an all party attitude. The constitution should be drafted by the strong right of the masses, not by quill pens placed above their ears.'[3]

The intentions of Nehru seemed clear. No party other than the Congress was to be tolerated. If the Congress accepted any offers of co-operation from the Muslim League except on its own terms, it would thereby strengthen the chances of the Muslim League of remaining in the political field. Only by ignoring the Muslim League completely, could the Congress succeed as the only party in the political scene. The Muslim League was therefore, offered the opportunity to terminate its own existence. This was what the Congress attempted to do in the United Provinces.

THE COALITION CONTROVERSY

Pending the clarification sought for by the Congress regarding the special powers of the governors, interim ministries had been formed in the provinces. Though various legislatures had met, the U.P. legislature had not been called. Pandit Govind Ballabh Pant issued letters to all the members of the assembly for a meeting to be held at Allahabad. He suggested that the Congress with other groups should elect a speaker and declare the legislature in session.[4] Negotiations also started between Khaliquzzaman and the leaders of the Congress on the possibility of a coalition. Earlier the Muslim League had issued instructions prohibiting negotiations with any group or party except through the leader and subject to ratification by the party.[5] Brisk activity in the Congress camp to wean away members from the Muslim League, prompted Jinnah to issue a statement that it was 'no use encouraging an individual Mussalman to come into the fold of the Congress for the sake of

[1] Nehru to Nawab Ismail Khan, November 10, 1937, *Nehru-Jinnah Correspondence*.
[2] *Star of India*, March 21, 1937.
[3] *Ibid.* March 22, 1937.
[4] *Ibid.* April 17, 1937.
[5] *Ibid.* March 2 and 16, 1937.

a prize'.[1] For about a month Jinnah had been in the dark as regards developments in the United Provinces. He had asked Khaliquzzaman in vain to let him know the situation. Having waited for three weeks for a clarification, Jinnah on April 25, 1937, issued a public statement:

'I understand that there is a move to invite to a meeting members of the Congress Party in the United Provinces to be held on May 2 and 3. Some Muslim Members who have been elected on the Muslim League ticket in the United Provinces are also holding a conference in the United Provinces. I am entirely in the dark as to what the object of this move is. But I want to make it clear that it will be useless for any individual or individuals effectively to carry Muslims behind them if any settlement is arrived at with a particular group or even for that matter the whole province. I say it is a pity that these roundabout efforts are being made. The only object of it can be to create some differences among Mussalmans. It is no use dealing with those men who are in and out of the Congress and in and out of the League, one time out of the one and another time of the other as it suits them. I am sure that the Muslims of the United Provinces will not betray the Mussalmans of India and, therefore, any effort at a settlement by individuals such as may be advantageous to them for the time being will not carry anywhere . . . I can only trust that he [Khaliquzzaman] will not enter into any commitments which may be repudiated not only by the Muslims of his province but by the Muslims of India. This method of dealing with individuals or groups can only result in isolating and dividing the Muslims, group by group or province by province and destroying the united front.'[2]

Khaliquzzaman deprecated Jinnah's statement and issued a rejoinder. He said that Jinnah had been 'carried away by half-truths that have been conveyed to him from interested quarters'.[3] It was, however, not until the meeting of the U.P. parliamentary board held on May 7th, *under the presidentship of Jinnah*, when Khaliquzzaman gave a resumé of his negotiations that Jinnah was appraised of the correct situation. Khaliquzzaman was then unanimously authorized to continue the negotiations with a view to finding out a common programme of work in the legislature. He was also asked to find out whether a Congress-League alliance as suggested by the leader of the Congress party in the U.P. assembly would be of a permanent nature. Khaliquzzaman was, however, to make it clear that while the Muslim League party in the United Provinces would welcome the fullest co-operation with the Congress on all matters affecting U.P., it would not be prepared to merge itself in Congress. The Board adopted the following resolution:

'The Muslim League Party in the legislature cannot and should not join the Congress in its policy and programme of wrecking the constitution, but that co-operation and coalition with the Congress or any other party on the basis of work in the legislature upon a programme that may be agreed upon in conformity with the programme of the Board should be explored, provided

[1] *Star of India*, March 2 and 16, 1937.
[2] *Ibid.* April 27, 1937. Also see *Civil and Military Gazette*, April 27, 1937.
[3] *The Times of India*, April 27, 1937.

that Communal Award and separate representation in the local self-governing bodies be allowed to stand *till an agreed settlement is arrived at between the communities concerned on an all-India basis*.'[1]

Negotiations which had already started earlier reached a hopeful stage in middle July 1937 when Azad and Pant were reported to have had talks with Khaliquzzaman.[2] The *Leaaer* reported that the Muslim League representatives might be included in the ministry.[3] Later Nehru also reached Lucknow to participate in the negotiations. On July 28, 1937, these negotiations came to an end, not only because of Khaliquzzaman's insistence on excluding communal matters from the scope of the agreement, but also, as Khaliquzzaman stated, because of the 'unfairness of the conditions' dictated by Azad,[4] which besides others, included one that the members of the Muslim League group in the U.P. assembly would 'cease to function as a separate group' and would become part of the Congress party.[5]

MUSLIM REACTION TO CONGRESS MINISTRIES

Probably, what Jinnah visualized as a first step towards a major settlement was the creation of coalition ministries in the provinces. His later statements show the bitterness and frustration which the Congress attitude caused. In his presidential address at the 1937 session of the Muslim League, held at Lucknow, Jinnah showed his indignation: 'Wherever they [Congress] are in majority,' complained Jinnah, 'and wherever it suited them, they refused to co-operate with the Muslim League Parties and demanded unconditional surrender and signing of their pledges.' [6] Recalling his earlier efforts at co-operation, Jinnah said, 'No settlement with [the] majority community is possible, as no Hindu leader speaking with any authority shows any concern or genuine desire for it. Honourable settlements can only be achieved between equals, and unless the two parties learn to respect and fear each other, there is no solid ground for any settlement. Offers of peace by the weaker party always mean confessions of weakness, and an invitation to aggression. *Appeals to patriotism, justice and fair-play and for good-will fall flat. . . . Politics means power and not relying on cries of justice or fair-play or goodwill.*' [7]

There is little doubt but that this signifies an important change in Jinnah's approach to the Indian political scene. The League had been badly mauled in the tough political in-fighting associated with the forming of ministries. Without a strong base and mass support the League could not bring any

[1] *Pioneer*, May 8, 1937. Italics not in the original.

[2] *Leader*, July 17, 1937.

[3] *Ibid.* July 18, 1937.

[4] *Ibid.* August 4, 1937.

[5] *Leader*, August 4, 1937.

[6] *Speeches and Writings of Jinnah*, vol. i, p. 29. On August 5, 1937, Raja of Mahmudabad had issued the following statement: 'The Muslim League is always willing to collaborate with any party which stands for progress. The point was made clear in its election manifesto. It has collaborated with the Congress in the troubled political history of these provinces in the past and is ready to march shoulder to shoulder with any political organization even now. But when any organization, in the intoxication of success, asks the League to commit suicide at the steps of Anand Bhawan, the Muslim community has to put its foot down.' *Leader*, August 8, 1937.

[7] *Speeches and Writings of Jinnah*, vol. i, p. 30. Italics not in the original.

real pressure to bear at the bargaining table. Goodwill and the desire, alone, for co-operation were not enough. From now onwards the Muslim League changed its tactics. It laid more stress on strengthening and acquiring that power within the Muslim ranks which could give it self-reliance and the power to deal with the Congress on terms of equality.

The Muslim League session held at Lucknow in October 1937 was itself a striking proof of its rapidly-growing strength. Provincial leaders who had fought elections on the tickets of their organizations and had showed reluctance to merge their parties with the Muslim League joined the League. Fazlul Haq's Praja party came within the fold of the League. Many Muslim leaders from Sind, Frontier, Madras, Assam, Central Provinces merged their parties with the Muslim League. The Unionist group in the Punjab led by Sikandar Hyat Khan joined the League. Immediately after his return from Lucknow, Sikandar wrote to Jinnah: 'You will be glad to learn that enrolment of the League members is going apace and we hope to be able to set up district Leagues throughout the province in a short space of time. I have instructed all the Muslim Unionist members to start enrolling Muslims in their ilaqas and I am receiving very promising and satisfactory reports from the various parts of the province. On the whole, the development at Lucknow which brought about the solidarity of the Muslims throughout India has been welcomed by the Muslim masses. . . .' The Lucknow session gave fresh strength to the League and the unity which Jinnah aspired to have was partly achieved within about a year of his launching the programme.[1]

An economic, social and educational programme was also evolved to bring the organization into touch with the masses. This included the encouragement of cottage industries, use of 'swadeshi' articles, organization of a volunteer corps for social service, ameliorating the conditions of factory workers, abolition of usury, reduction of rural and urban indebtedness, rural uplift, the introduction of compulsory primary education and the re-organization of secondary and university education.[2]

Steps were also taken to reorganize the League. Provincial and district branches of the League were to be reshaped. The League membership fee was reduced to two annas. The council of the Muslim League was to consist of 465 members elected by provincial branches and no one was to be elected on the said council without being a member of the primary League, district or tehsil.[3] It was also proposed that the Muslim League central office be shifted to Bombay but the proposal was dropped.[4]

Jinnah's call for unity amongst Muslims and his plans to reorganize his community appeared to Nehru as a 'fascist development' and 'an attempt to consolidate vested interests by a group of privileged people'.[5] However, the *Madras Mail* commented differently, 'To ignore the portent of Mr. Jinnah's call to Muslims to organize would be the uppermost folly. For that call is a challenge to all, the Government, the majority community and all thinking men who wish India well.' [6]

[1] *Pioneer*, October 15 and 17, 1937.
[2] *Ibid.* October 19, 1937.
[3] *Star of India*, October 18, 1937.
[4] *Pioneer*, October 19, 1937.
[5] *Leader*, October 20, 1937.
[6] *Madras Mail* quoted in *Star of India*, October 20, 1937.

The installation of Congress ministries in various provinces and the exclusion of the Muslim League made the Muslims generally bitter. It 'marked the beginning of a reaction among the bulk of politically minded Muslims against the idea of a "Congress Majority" which was presently to make the League a more powerful force throughout Muslim India than it had ever been before'.[1] The exposition by the League of the weaknesses of the Congress rule through such reports as the 'Pirpur Report' and the 'Shareef Report' further strengthened the League's hold on the Muslims. These reports though by no means objective and neutral left a lasting impression on the Muslim mind of the 'injustices' of the Congress. According to Humayun Kabir, not a Leaguer himself, the dissatisfaction which the Congress rule had aroused amongst Muslims could not have continued unless there had been discontent and a real sense of injury behind it. 'The ground may have been imaginary but the discontent was real.'[2] Even the Jamiat-ul-Ulema-i-Hind, in view of this general dissatisfaction, asked the Congress to appoint a committee to investigate the complaints. It particularly objected to certain features of the Wardha scheme. The Jamiat warned the Congress that a civil disobedience movement would be started if the entire scheme were enforced.[3]

The fear that the Muslims would remain a permanent minority subjected to a majority rule was confirmed. The 'Pirpur Report' explained this with added emphasis. It demonstrated that, unlike the situation in Britain, where majorities and minorities change, 'in India we have a permanent Hindu majority and the other communities are condemned to the position of perpetual minority'.[4] The parliamentary system said the 'Shareef Report' as practised in the provinces had proved to be worse than the system already in vogue before the introduction of provincial autonomy.[5] In coming years, the League's approach to the constitutional issue underwent a change. Weightages in the legislatures and the safeguards provided by the constitution were no longer regarded as meaningful.

TOWARDS PAKISTAN

The Sind Provincial Muslim League conference held at Karachi during the second week of October 1938 foreshadowed the trend of Muslim thinking. Abdoola Haroon, chairman of the reception committee, speaking on October 9, 1938 said: 'We have nearly arrived at the parting of the ways and unless this problem [the minority problem] is solved to the satisfaction of all, it will be impossible for anybody to save India from being divided into Hindu India and Muslim India both placed under separate federations.'[6] Haroon warned that India could never present a united front as long as the majority community was determined 'to annihilate the individuality of minorities. I warn the majority community that if it does not concede our demands,

[1] R. Coupland, *Report on the Constitutional Problem in India*, part ii, *Indian Politics* (1943), p. 112.

[2] Humayun Kabir, *Muslim Politics 1906–42*, p. 14.

[3] *The Times of India*, March 7, 1939.

[4] *Pioneer*, December 24, 1938.

[5] *Ibid.* March 28, 1939.

[6] *Star of India*, October 10, 1938.

Czechoslovakian happenings would find an echo in India as well.'[1] The following resolution was tabled by Sheikh Abdul Majid Sindhi:

'The Sind Provincial Muslim League Conference, considers it absolutely essential in the interests of an abiding peace of the vast Indian Continent and in the interests of unhampered cultural development, the economic and social betterment and political self-determination of the two Nations, known as Hindus and Muslims, that India may be divided into two Federations, viz.: the Federation of Muslim States and the Federation of non-Muslim States.

'This Conference therefore recommends to the All-India Muslim League to devise a scheme of Constitution under which Muslim majority provinces, Muslim native States and areas inhabited by a majority of Muslims may attain full independence in the form of a federation of their own with admission to any other Muslim State beyond the Indian Frontiers to join the Federation and with such safeguards for non-Muslim minorities as may be conceded to the Muslim minorities in the non-Muslim Federation of India.'[2]

This resolution, however, was not passed at the conference. Instead another resolution asking the council of the Muslim League to review, for the sake of 'political self-determination of the two nations known as Hindus and Muslims' the question of a future constitution for 'India which will secure honourable and legitimate status due to them . . . and to devise a scheme of Constitution under which Muslims may attain full independence' was passed.[3] Thus for the first time the Muslims and Hindus were defined by the Muslim League as two nations and the claim for political self-determination of the two nations was put forward. In the following years, the Muslim League leaders kept on talking of a physical division of India. They, however, were not clear whether such a division would entail complete separation with nothing in common between the two federations. The evidence suggests that the possibility of some sort of a common centre was visualized. Sheikh Abdul Majid Sindhi who had moved the original resolution for the creation of two federations was inclined to keep the possibility of a common though limited centre open. The centre was to administer certain specified subjects such as foreign affairs, defence, safeguards for minorities and the settlement of disputes between the two federations.[4] Nawabzada Liaqat Ali Khan, in his presidential address at the Meerut Divisional Muslim League conference, held on March 25, 1939, gave the same indications when he said: 'Whatever scheme is finally adopted, it is obvious that if the Hindus and Muslims cannot live amicably in any other way, they may be allowed to do so by dividing the country in a suitable manner. . . . If this is done, a limited and specific Federation would not only be easy but desirable.'[5]

Slowly but surely, the Muslim leaders came to realize that the safeguards provided by the Act of 1935 were no longer adequate to protect their interests.

[1] *Star of India*, October 15, 1938. Jinnah also spoke in the same tone, *ibid.* October 12, 1938. [2] *Ibid.* October 11, 1938.

[3] Resolution of the All-India Muslim League quote in Khalid Bin Sayeed, *Pakistan The Formative Phase*, pp. 115–16.

[4] Sheikh Abdul Majid's interview, the *Daily Jung* (Karachi), March 23, 1965.

[5] *The Times of India*, March 27, 1939.

They spoke in a mood of desperation and gave a timely warning of the trends that had been taking shape in their thinking. And yet, it seems, they were not seriously contemplating a division of India. When they talked about it, they apparently employed the threat as a counter for bargaining and settlement.

An opportunity for such a settlement came towards the end of November 1939. After the declaration of the war, the viceroy had suspended the federal scheme to which the Muslim League had shown its determined opposition in previous years. However, the suspension of the scheme was not enough and the League in a resolution of September 18, 1939, asked for its complete abandonment and urged upon the government the need of revising and reviewing the entire constitutional problem *de novo*.[1] In November, the viceroy had conversations with Gandhi, Rajendra Prasad and Jinnah, seeking the co-operation of the Congress and Muslim League. He asked the leaders to have consultations among themselves to formulate a programme for co-operation in provincial and central governments.[2] It was reported that in his talks with the Congress leaders, Jinnah in order to reach some settlement, asked for the formation of coalition ministries in the provinces on the condition that the Muslim ministries appointed should enjoy the confidence of a certain proportion of the Muslim members in a legislature.[3] But the Congress leaders seemed to be in no mood to discuss the formation of coalitions in the provinces, nor ready to evolve a programme for the centre unless the government first complied with their demand to clarify the war aims and had made a declaration of independence.[4] The talks, however, produced no results and the communal problem remained unsolved as, according to Nehru, 'the British Government had deliberately put this problem to the fore . . .'.[5]

The Congress approach to the solution of this problem was made clear by Gandhi in a statement issued on November 8, 1939. While maintaining that the minorities were entitled to full protection he wrote that the question could be solved only through a constituent assembly. 'Britain has hitherto held power . . . . by playing the Minorities against the so-called majority and has thus made an agreed solution among the component parts well-nigh impossible. . . . So long as Britain considers her mission to bear this burden so long will she continue to feel the necessity of holding India as dependency.'[6] Gandhi, however, failed to state how a solution would be evolved after the British had left, when all the previous attempts at a settlement had failed. The constituent assembly of the Congress would have been confronted with the same issues and problems which kept the leaders divided. Thus the last chance of agreement, before the Muslim League passed its famous resolution at Lahore, was lost. The Congress interpreted communal questions as 'irrelevant issues' and reiterated its demand for a constituent assembly, which alone in its opinion, was an 'adequate instrument for solving the communal and other difficulties'.[7]

[1] Gwyer and Appadorai, *Speeches and Documents on the Indian Constitution, 1921–47* (1957), vol. ii, pp. 488–90.
[2] *Pioneer*, November 6, 1939.
[3] *Ibid.* November 4 and 5, 1939.
[4] *Ibid.* November 6, 1939.
[5] *Ibid.* November 7, 1939.
[6] Gwyer and Appadorai, *op. cit.* vol. ii, pp. 495–6.
[7] Congress resolution, November 19–23, 1939, *ibid.* pp. 496–7.

The Congress blinded by its own political ideology looked at the communal problem merely as a British creation, rather than as a fundamental problem of Indian politics, and, as representatives of the majority community, failed to understand the true nature of minority fears. Merely a few safeguards provided in the constitution could not win the co-operation of the Muslims, for a strongly entrenched government can always get round and nullify safeguards, however elaborately built in. The Congress rule in many ways, implicitly and explicitly, smacked of Hindu rule. The Muslim League was not prepared to leave their security to an uncertain future in the hands of a party which had done very little to win their confidence and which had arrogated to itself all political power and authority.

While the Congress insisted that a constituent assembly would be the answer to the communal problem, the Muslim League, having rejected the federal scheme, resolved that partition was the only practical solution of the problem. In March 1939, the Muslim League had appointed a small committee to look into various constitutional schemes.[1] Since the only commonly known proposals were those of Muhammad Iqbal and Rahmat Ali, it was not until August 1939 that the Muslim League could begin to consider fully elaborate plans. These were the three schemes prepared by Sayyid Abdul Latif, Sikandar Hyat Khan and a joint scheme of Sayyid Zafrul Hasan and Muhammad Afzal Husain Qadri.[2] Even then it was only after the last efforts at settlement had failed that the Muslim League adopted the Lahore resolution, commonly known as the Pakistan resolution. Jinnah in his presidential address at the Muslim League session held at Lahore during the last week of March 1940, put the claim for a separate homeland for the Muslims. He declared that the Muslims stood for the freedom of India. 'But it must be freedom for all India and not freedom for one section. . . .' The inauguration of provincial autonomy, he said, had convinced them that placed as they were, any constitution for India would mean a permanent 'Hindu majority government'. 'The Musalmans are not a minority. The Musalmans are a nation by any definition.' And nations must have 'their homelands, their territory and their state. We wish to live in peace and harmony with our neighbours as a free and independent people. We wish our people to develop to the fullest our spiritual, cultural, economic, social and political life in a way that we think best and in consonance with our own ideal and according to the genius of our people.' The only way, according to Jinnah, to secure such a development was to have an independent state for the Muslims.[3] On March 23, 1940 at Lahore the Muslim League resolved that 'no constitutional plan would be workable in this country or acceptable to the Muslims unless it is designed on the following basic principles, viz. that geographically contiguous units are demarcated into regions which should be so constituted, with such territorial readjustments as may be necessary, and the areas in which the Muslims are numerically in a majority, as in the North-Western and Eastern zones

[1] *The Times of India*, March 27, 1939.

[2] Liaqat Ali Khan to an official of the League, August 10, 1939 (copy with the author). For details of the schemes see Gwyer and Appadorai, *op. cit.* vol. ii, pp. 444–65.

[3] *Speeches and Writings of Jinnah*, vol. i, pp. 143–62.

of India, should be grouped to constitute "Independent States" in which the constituent units shall be autonomous and sovereign.' [1]

In coming years Pakistan became the goal of the Muslim League. Its policy and programme were formulated to achieve that objective. At the annual session of the League held in April 1941 at Madras, its constitution was amended and the Lahore resolution in a slightly amended form was adopted as one of the aims and objects of the All-India Muslim League.[2] Thus Pakistan became the national manifesto and the national ideal of the Muslims. It was the symbol of Muslim nationalism and their ultimate destiny. Jinnah's strategy and tactics were centred round the realization of the goal. He pursued the objective with zeal and in return received the complete loyalty and devotion of his followers.

II

CRIPPS MISSION

The increasing difficulties of the war and the exigencies created by it led the British government to adopt a fresh approach to solving the Indian political deadlock. Accordingly, in March 1942, Sir Stafford Cripps arrived in India with a set of proposals. These related to both long-term and short-term plans. The long-term proposition promised India the status of a dominion, the setting up of a constitution-making body to frame a single constitution for the Indian Union after the end of the war. The long-term proposal, apparently to placate the Muslim League, also gave an option to any province to refuse to join the proposed Indian Union, if it so desired. The non-acceding provinces could then form their own union with 'complete self-government'.[3]

Both the Congress and the Muslim League rejected the proposals. The Muslim League read in the non-acceding clause the possibility of the creation of Pakistan by 'implication by providing for the establishment of two or more independent Unions in India'. But such a provision was 'purely illusory' as the creation of Pakistan was 'relegated only to the realm of remote possibility'.[4] The Congress was indignant at the inclusion of the states as constituent units in the proposed union and over the 'novel principle of non-accession for a Province'. The working committee of the Congress in its resolution of April 2, 1942, however, recorded that it 'cannot think in terms of compelling the people of any territorial unit to remain in an Indian Union against their declared and established will. While recognizing this principle, the Committee feel that every effort should be made to create a common and co-operative national life. Acceptance of this principle inevitably involves that no changes should be made which would result in fresh problems being created and compulsion being exercised on other substantial groups within that area. *Each territorial unit should have the fullest possible autonomy within the Union consistently* with a strong national state.' [5]

This dubious and well-guarded resolution of the Congress did not mean that the Congress was willing to allow any unit to opt out of the Indian

[1] Gwyer and Appadorai, *op. cit.* vol. ii, pp. 443–4.
[2] Khalid Bin Sayeed, *op. cit.* p. 124.
[3] Gwyer and Appadorai, *op. cit.* vol. ii, pp. 520–4.
[4] *Ibid.* pp. 526–8. [5] *Ibid.* pp. 524–6.

Union. Such an acceptance would have amounted to nullifying the Congress stand for Indian unity. The utmost the resolution conceded was the 'fullest possible autonomy' (Congress reserving the right to itself to define and interpret this in future according to its own convenience). This too was made less meaningful by the corresponding clause 'within the Union consistently with a strong national state'. Probably, in accepting the principle of non-compulsion, the Congress was motivated by the wish to form a national government at the centre, and believed that the rejection of the non-accession clause outright would minimize the chances of negotiating with Cripps. Apparently Azad had this in mind when he pointed out to Cripps that 'the main purpose of his [Cripps] mission should be the settlement of political issues, that other issues like the Communal question and the question of the States would not be relevant at that stage and they were cases to be settled by Indians themselves'.[1]

The Congress working committee in the resolution under discussion had also expressed its view that the non-accession clause would lead to 'attempts at separation at the very inception of the Union and thus create great friction just when the utmost co-operation and goodwill are most needed'. Yet the Congress failed to strive for that 'co-operation and goodwill'. Later, when such a move was made to secure them, Congress brusquely denounced it.

In the last week of April 1942, the Madras Congress Legislature party, headed by Rajagopalachari, perhaps inspired by the Congress's implied though reluctant acceptance of the non-accession clause, and eager to bring about an understanding between the government and the Congress passed two resolutions:

'It is absolutely and urgently necessary in the best interests of the country at this hour of peril to do all that the Congress can possibly do to remove every obstacle in the way of establishment of a National administration to face the present situation; and therefore, in as much as the Moslem League has insisted on the recognition of the right of separation of certain areas from united India upon the ascertainment of the wishes of the people of such areas as a condition precedent for a united national action at this moment of grave national danger, this party is of opinion, and recommends to A.I.C.C. that to sacrifice the chances of the formation of a National Government at this grave crisis for the doubtful advantage of maintaining a controversy over the unity of India is a most unwise policy, and that it has become necessary to choose the lesser evil and acknowledge the Moslem League's claim for separation should the same be persisted in when the time comes for framing a Constitution for India, and thereby remove all doubts and fears in this regard, and to invite the Moslem League for a consultation for the purpose of arriving at an agreement and securing the installation of a National Government to meet the present emergency.'

The second resolution called upon the A.I.C.C. to permit the Madras Legislature party to form a coalition with the Muslim League in order to 'facilitate united and effective action . . .'.[2]

[1] *The Statesman*, April 30, 1942.

[2] *Ibid.* April 25, 1942. See also *Civil and Military Gazette*, April 24, 1942.

A close look at Rajagopalachari's resolution about Pakistan would reveal that the Madras Legislature party had only admitted the existence of the demand for Pakistan. They had not approved of it, nor did they concede it. All they attempted to do was to get the Congress to be more realistic and thereby seek the co-operation of the Muslim League by merely recognizing the fact that such a demand did exist.[1] Thus the recognition of the principle of separation was not opposed to the policy enunciated by the Congress working committee on April 2nd. On the other hand the framers of the Madras resolution were as anxious as the Congress working committee to safeguard and maintain the unity of India. But they were of the opinion that 'to sacrifice the chances of the formation of a National Government for the doubtful advantage of maintaining a controversy over the unity of India' was an unwise policy. It would lead to greater friction and would minimize all future chances of co-operation. The only apparent difference between the resolution passed by the Congress working committee and that embodied in the Madras resolution was that whereas the working committee had seemingly conceded the principle of self-determination to any territorial unit which wished to enforce it, the Madras resolution made a specific reference to the Muslim League's demand for separation. Nowhere did the Madras resolution accept the demand as being that of the Muslims as a whole. This was consistent with the reiterated Congress stand that the demand came from the Muslim League alone and that the Muslims as a whole were opposed to it. Besides, the Madras resolution did not give a blank cheque to the Muslim League. The secession of the areas from the Indian Union was to be put to a test and was conditional upon the 'ascertainment of the wishes of the people', if after the war they still insisted on separation.[2]

The Madras Legislature party, by recognizing the principle of separation strove to win the goodwill of the Muslim League and thus create an atmosphere of co-operation. In fact it attempted to do what Maulana Muhammad Ali as president of the Congress had said was the situation in 1929: 'In India political unity can be achieved not so much by annihilating smaller units that may appear to conflict with the ultimate scheme of unity, but by recognizing their force and inevitableness.'[3]

But this the Congress was not now prepared to do. Naturally, Rajagopalachari's resolutions brought forth severe criticism from various Congress quarters.[4] Black flags awaited Rajagopalachari at Allahabad where the Congress committee was meeting. Undeterred by the criticism and opposition, the Madras leader moved the two resolutions at the meeting of the A.I.C.C. held on April 29, 1942. Both the resolutions were lost. The first, acknowledging the Muslim League's claim for separation, was rejected by 120 votes against 15. Had the matter been left there, perhaps the difficulties which arose between Gandhi and Jinnah in 1944 in connection with the

[1] *Civil and Military Gazette*, April 25, 1942. [2] *Ibid.* April 26, 1942.

[3] Afzal Iqbal (ed.), *Select Writings and Speeches of Maulana Mohamed Ali* (1963), vol. ii, p. 127.

[4] Bhim Sen Sachar, leader of the Congress party in the Punjab assembly, Krian Sanker Roy, leader of the Bengal Congress Parliamentary party, Dr Gidwani, president of the Sind provincial Congress committee and many other leaders denounced the move. For details see *Civil and Military Gazette*, April 25, 26, 28 and 30, 1942.

acceptance of the Pakistan formula, might still have been overcome. But Jagat Narain's counter-resolution sealed the fate of any amicable settlement. Jagat Narain's resolution, passed by 92 against 17, stated that 'any proposal to disintegrate India by giving liberty to any component state or territorial unit to secede from the Indian Union or Federation will be detrimental to the best interests of the people of the different states and provinces and the country as a whole and the Congress, therefore, cannot agree to any such proposal'.[1] After rejecting Rajagopalachari's resolution, there was hardly any need to pass the counter-resolution of Jagat Narain. Despite Nehru's assertion that Jagat Narain's resolution was not contrary to the resolution passed by the working committee of the Congress, the resolution was to create another complication; so long as the resolution was on the statutes of the Congress, the basis of any fresh negotiations, as made by Gandhi in 1944 was closed. Rajagopalachari had evidently foreseen this when he pleaded that the Congress should not accept Jagat Narain's resolution. He prophetically warned: 'The house might throw out his own resolution but let it not pass the other resolution. *It would tie the Congress up*. It was a most dangerous proposition.'[2] Rajagopalachari's view that the freedom of India could not be achieved without a settlement with the Muslim League had thus found no response. In sheer disgust, Rajagopalachari tendered his resignation.

III

THE MUSLIM LEAGUE ORGANIZATION AND PROGRAMME

During the coming years, the Muslim League grew from strength to strength. The Quit India movement of the Congress when the principal leaders of the Congress were behind prison bars, virtually left the political field open to Jinnah. He utilized the situation to the fullest advantage in building up the League as a powerful party. An effective and extensive propaganda was carried out in favour of Pakistan. Muslim separation was no longer the ideal of the 'reactionaries'; it became the creed and ideology of the progressives, the intellectuals, the business community, the middle class and the masses. The 'first five year plan' of the Muslim League, as Jinnah put it, referring to the revival and re-organization of the League, was completed in 1941. During this period, Jinnah had succeeded in organizing the League from one end of the country to the other. 'Muslim India', claimed Jinnah, 'was never so well organized nor so alive and politically conscious as today.' The Muslim League had 'established a flag, a platform displaying and demonstrating the complete unity of the entire body of Muslims' and had defined its goal.[3]

As pointed out earlier, it was after the Lucknow session that the League had undertaken the work of re-organization seriously. Its machinery was geared to accelerate its activities throughout the length and breadth of the country. Provincial organizing committees were constituted for the enrolment of members. Each province was divided into divisions (Bombay for instance

[1] *Civil and Military Gazette*, May 3, 1942. Also see *The Statesman*, April 27, 1942.
[2] *Ibid.* Italics not in the original.
[3] *Speeches and Writings of Jinnah*, vol. i, pp. 249–53.

was divided into four divisions, northern, central, southern and the city of Bombay). Divisions were sub-divided into districts (northern division of Bombay comprised Ahmedabad, Kaira, Panchmahal, Broach, Surat and Thana), big cities were divided into wards (the city of Bombay had eight wards). Branches of the League in a ward or an area within a district were called primary Muslim Leagues. To become a member, it was necessary to belong to a primary League and no one could be a member of more than one primary Muslim League. Representatives of primary Leagues formed the district Muslim League and were in charge of the affairs of the League within a particular district. A primary Muslim League was entitled to elect one member for the district Muslim League for every hundred members that were on its rolls. The district Muslim Leagues elected members at their annual general meetings. Such elected members formed the provincial Muslim League; the number to be elected by each district was fixed. Detailed rules for enrolment of members, conduct of meetings, election of office bearers, maintenance of accounts, etc., were also framed.

Full details of membership of the League in various provinces are not available. However, it is possible to have some idea of the growing strength of the League. By the end of 1938, the Madras provincial Muslim League claimed to have 183 primary Leagues with a total of 43,920 members. In 1940, it had 330 primary Leagues with 88,833 members. By 1941 though the number of primary Leagues had dropped down to 302, it had a total membership of 112,078. In the Central Provinces, 23,000 members had been enrolled by September 1938; during 1943, 33,541 new members were enrolled. In 1939, a deputation of the Muslim majority provinces undertook a tour of the United Provinces. They covered about 3,924 miles and addressed sixty-four meetings. The secretary of the deputation reported that the membership of the League in each district of the province ranged between eight to ten thousands. Abul Hashim, the secretary of the Bengal provincial Muslim League in his annual report submitted in 1944, asserted that the League had become a 'revolutionary' and 'mass movement' and had penetrated into rural Bengal. Abul Hashim claimed that in 1944, 550,000 members had been enrolled in Bengal (Barisal had 160,000 members, Dacca, 105,000 and Tippera 52,000). The figure of membership according to the secretary 'exceeded the number ever scored by any organization in the province not excluding the Congress'. This was 'apart from the vast allegiance of the large Muslim population to the League'. Likewise, the president of the Sind provincial Muslim League in his report of May 13, 1944, claimed that 300,000 members representing about twenty-five per cent of the adult male Muslim population of Sind had been enrolled in the Muslim League.

To educate and build up Muslim public opinion in favour of the League, district and provincial conferences were held from time to time. In order to keep in touch with the districts and to explain the League creed, central and provincial leaders worked out a programme of extensive touring. These tours besides going a long way towards educating public opinion in matters of political importance also afforded opportunities for useful constructive work. Wide publicity of the proceedings of the meetings was made through Muslim newspapers and by distributing leaflets.

A separate information, publicity and propaganda department was created. The department collected information about the existing newspapers in various languages to publicize the League's activities. Contact was established with news agencies which were classified as 'Sympathetic, Neutral and Opposition'. A number of propagandists, preachers and speakers were trained. While on publicity work they were to take into account the audience which was classified into educated, literates, uneducated, urban, rural, industrial, trade and tribal groups, etc. The distinct needs and sentiments and the appropriate ways of approach to the above grouping was taken into consideration. The people engaged in publicity work were classified as organizers, workers, followers, inactive sympathizers, neutrals, inactive oppositionists and hostiles. Paid propagandists were also appointed and some of the whole-time workers lived at party houses. A committee of writers was appointed to produce suitable literature on social, political, educational and other matters. A number of pamphlets commonly known as *Pakistan Literature Series* and *Home Study Series* were produced. Tracts and brochures were issued by the central office of the League. Reading rooms and libraries were supplied with Muslim League literature. Popular songs were written and even the services of professional musicians were acquired for reciting the songs.

Jinnah realized that the propaganda machinery of the Muslim League should be backed by a good press in order to widen and sustain political consciousness. Though Muslims produced a few Urdu papers, they had no English daily. The only Muslim papers in English were the *Morning News* and *Star of India*, both of Calcutta, and *Dawn* which was a weekly with a limited circulation. Jinnah decided to convert *Dawn* into a daily. He worked out the details of the investment and equipment needed, with the help of some business magnates. Underlining the need, he wrote in May 1942 to Ispahani, 'There is a very strong feeling and you will get an immediate support and what is more necessary is to consider that it [an English daily] is undoubtedly essential for our cause.' [1]

After overcoming initial difficulties of investment, type, paper and staff, Jinnah succeeded in making *Dawn* a daily. On October 3, 1942, he again wrote to Ispahani, 'Once more I am very thankful to you for the help and the interest that you are taking in establishing and launching this venture. I hope to see the paper become a really first class English daily which will be [the] genuine, real and true voice of Muslim India, and I think, so far, everything is in our favour. It is a thing which Muslim India never had and if we are able to achieve what we desire, this may give a lead to other Provinces as the reading public is now growing and is very anxious to know the news and views of Muslim India.' [2]

Muslim national guards were also organized. They were provided with uniforms. As the secretary of the League explained, 'the uniform was intended to give them a uniformity of dress and only the preliminaries of the military formation parade were sought to be taught to facilitate the regulation of their movements'. The main purpose of enlisting and training the national guards was 'to create in them a spirit of service and sacrifice and to make them a

[1] Account based on M.A.H. Ispahani's unpublished manuscript.
[2] *Ibid.*

disciplined body of enthusiastic selfless workers for the social, economic and political uplift of the masses'. The district Leagues were asked to recruit as many young men as possible 'to teach them a code of morals, to engage them in beneficial activities like the spread of literacy and keep them attached to the League by providing for them healthy sports and games . . .'. The national guards on different occasions performed 'excellent services'.

Having achieved organizational success and unity within the Muslim ranks, and refounded *Dawn* as a mouthpiece for their views, Jinnah embarked upon his second 'five year plan', which included the planning and building up of what he called 'the departments of national life of Muslim India'. In this he laid increased emphasis on the educational, social and economic uplift of the Muslims.[1]

The areas claimed for Pakistan were mainly agricultural, and were industrially backward, far behind many of the other provinces. Economically the Muslims had lagged behind their sister community. Jinnah therefore encouraged Muslims to enter business and to establish heavy industries, which would open new vistas for workers and labourers, and new prospects of employment to educated youth.[2] As Jinnah said while addressing the Baluchistan Muslim League conference on July 4, 1943, 'So long as a nation is weak economically, it cannot hope to win the battle of life.'[3]

At the next Muslim League session, held at Karachi in December 1943, it was accordingly decided to appoint a planning committee. The function of this committee was to examine the condition of India, particularly of 'the Pakistan areas', with a view to preparing the Muslim League 'to participate in the national developments in the directions of commercial and agricultural expansion, and industrialization, and be ready for a gigantic and co-ordinated drive in the field of economic reconstruction, and in the post-war reconstruction'. The committee consisted of technicians, economists, men of commerce and practical business men.[4]

Some business and industrial magnates were already associated with the League and were members of its council. If Congress had its Tatas and Birlas, the League had its Ispahanis and Adamjees. By personal persuasion and drive, Jinnah now encouraged them to take part in the economic development of Muslim India. From the middle of 1943 onwards, Jinnah untiringly devoted his attention to the establishment of a federation of Muslim chambers of commerce with a view to encouraging commercial and industrial enterprises. Nurur Rehman, the secretary of the Calcutta Muslim chamber of commerce was appointed as the organizing secretary of the federation. Finally, the federation was established towards the end of 1944. Jinnah kept in close touch with the programme of the federation and finding that not much work had been done by the federation, he wrote to Ispahani on April 5, 1945, 'Have you been sleeping over the Federation of Muslim Chambers of Commerce and is it merely to remain a paper scheme? I am very much disappointed indeed that so much delay has been caused in holding even

[1] *Speeches and Writings of Jinnah*, vol. i, pp. 249–53.
[2] *Ibid.* vol. ii, pp. 7, 17, 28–9.
[3] *Ibid.* vol. i, p. 522.
[4] Jinnah to Abdur Rab Nishtar, April 12, 1944, *Nishtar Collection.*

your first meeting. We are losing a very valuable time and a golden opportunity. Every week that passes is now not only creating a sense of frustration and despair amongst those who have worked and are willing and ready to work, but in the rapid developments that are taking place, Muslim India will unfortunately find itself as usual with the motto "Too Late".'

When the first meeting of the federation took place on April 24, 1945 and practical steps were taken to step up the programme of the federation, Jinnah was pleased but he warned the organizers of the importance of the enterprise. He again wrote to Ispahani on May 6, 1945, 'I hope that you people realize the urgency and the importance of Muslim India making every effort to make up the leeway. What we want is selfless workers and deeds and not mere words and thoughts and speeches.'

Jinnah kept on initiating other economic enterprises. Realizing the importance of banking, he encouraged the creation of the Muslim Commercial Bank, which was eventually incorporated in Calcutta in July 1947 with an authorized capital of three crores of rupees. Similarly, the Muhammadi Steamship Company was launched with the help of the Habibs.

Even during the hectic months of political turmoil of 1946, Jinnah found time to initiate the idea of an airline owned and operated by Muslims. He himself backed the project with personal financial participation and purchased a share of Rs. 25,000 in the airline, Orient Airways, which was registered in 1946. Even poor Muslims were encouraged to have shares in the company as the value of the share was made as low as rupees five.[1]

In 1944 an education committee was also appointed to 'examine the system of education in vogue in India, taking into consideration the existing conditions and problems as well as those which are likely to arise after the war; to make such recommendations as are necessary for the preservation, fostering and promotion of Islamic traditions, culture and ideals; and general well-being of the Muslims; and to suggest ways and means for implementing the recommendations in various parts of India'. The committee appointed various other sub-committees, the primary and secondary education committee, the women's education committee, the teachers' training committee, the higher education committee, and science education committee.

A statement containing a brief outline of the objectives and methods for promoting education amongst Muslims was issued to elicit public opinion. A detailed questionnaire was also prepared and circulated amongst educationalists throughout India. Facts and figures were collected from central and provincial departments of education.

The committee received a large number of recommendations and memoranda from the educationalists on different aspects of education. The sub-committee for primary and secondary education made a survey of various schools and submitted a number of proposals. An outline for a new scheme of education for the primary and secondary schools was prepared. The other sub-committees also submitted draft schemes for improvement of education. The sub-committee for scientific and technical education prepared a plan for promoting scientific, technical and vocational education at all stages. Schemes for Muslim polytechnic schools were also drafted.

[1] Account based on M. A. H. Ispahani's unpublished manuscript.

IV

ELECTIONS OF 1945–6

With a strong press, a well built political organization claiming the loyalty of almost every Muslim, with a more vigorous social and economic programme, the Muslim League had become a people's party. The elections of 1945–6, after the failure of the Simla conference, offered the opportunity to the League to support its demand for a separate state with the verdict of the Muslim electorate. The Muslim League fought the elections on the issue of Pakistan.[1] Jinnah challenged the Congress to set up Muslim candidates on Congress tickets and prove their claim that they represented a united India. 'If the Muslim verdict is against Pakistan,' Jinnah cried, 'I will stand down.'[2] Jinnah's prediction that the 'final counting of the votes' would be the verdict on the Pakistan issue, proved true. The Muslim League won all thirty Muslim seats in the central legislative assembly, the nationalist Muslims 'forfeiting their deposits in many cases'.[3] In the provincial elections held in February 1946, the success of the League was equally impressive. It won 439 out of a total of 494 seats (88·8%).[4] As in the elections of 1937, very few Muslim seats were won by the Congress. Thus 'Jinnah's claim to speak for the Muslims had been triumphantly vindicated'.[5]

After the elections, Jinnah was in a much stronger position to demand Pakistan. The Muslims had given a clear mandate. The Muslim League, during the last few years had aroused the passions of the Muslims to such a high pitch on this issue and had committed itself so unequivocably to the demand that it could not now back away from it. At a Muslim League convention held on April 9, 1946, to which the elected members of provincial and central legislatures were invited, the League re-affirmed its faith in Pakistan. The convention passed the following resolution:

'This Convention of the Muslim League Legislators of India, Central and Provincial, after careful consideration, hereby declares that the Muslim Nation will never submit to any constitution for a United India and will never participate in any single constitution-making machinery set up for the purpose, and that any formula devised by the British Government for transferring power from the British to the peoples of India, which does not conform to the following just and equitable principles, calculated to maintain internal peace and tranquillity in the country, will not contribute to the solution of the Indian problem:

1 *Speeches and Writings of Jinnah*, vol. ii, p. 202.
2 *Ibid.* p. 219.
3 V. P. Menon, *The Transfer of Power in India* (1957), p. 226.
4 Jamil-ud-din Ahmad, *Final Phase of Struggle for Pakistan* (1964), p. 26. Seats won by the Muslim League were as follows: Assam 31 out of 34, Bengal 113 out of 119, Punjab 79 out of 86, Bihar 34 out of 40, U.P. 55 out of 66, Bombay 30 out of 30, Orissa 4 out of 4, Central Provinces 13 out of 14 (the remaining member later joined the League), Madras 29 out of 29, Sind 28 out of 34 (later in the second general election held in December 1946, the League won 33 out of 34 seats), N.W. Frontier Province 17 out of 38.
5 Penderel Moon, *Divide and Quit*, quoted in Jamil-ud-din Ahmad, *op. cit.* p. 27.

'1. That the zones comprising Bengal and Assam in the north-east and the Punjab, North-West Frontier Province, Sind and Baluchistan in the north-west of India, namely Pakistan zones, where the Muslims are in a dominant majority, be constituted into a sovereign independent State and that an unequivocal undertaking be given to implement the establishment of Pakistan without delay;

'2. That two separate constitution-making bodies be set up by the peoples of Pakistan and Hindustan for the purpose of framing their respective constitutions;

'3. That the minorities in Pakistan and Hindustan be provided with safeguards on the lines of the All-India Muslim League Resolution passed on March 23, 1940 at Lahore;

'4. That the acceptance of the Muslim League demand for Pakistan and its implementation without delay are the *sine qua non* for Muslim League co-operation and participation in the formation of an interim Government at the Centre.'

This convention further declared that any attempt to impose a constitu
on a united India basis or to force any interim arrangement, at the c
contrary to the Muslim League demand, would leave the Muslims no
tive but to resist such imposition by all possible means for their sur
national existence.[1]

CABINET MISSION

With this determined and clearly defined goal of a sovereign Pakistan before it, it was unlikely that the Muslim League would accept the cabinet mission plan of May 16, 1946. The plan offered a three-tiered constitution. This envisaged autonomous provinces, groupings of such provinces as were willing to take certain subjects to be administered in common, and a union empowered to deal with defence, foreign affairs and communications. However, the compulsory grouping of the provinces into three sections, (A) consisting of six Hindu majority provinces, (B) including Punjab, North West Frontier Province and Sind, and (C) consisting of Bengal and Assam was a compromise between a sovereign Pakistan and a united India. Confronted with the choice of having nothing or accepting a plan which had the germ of Pakistan, the Muslim League on June 6, 1946, reiterated that 'the attainment of the goal of a complete sovereign Pakistan still remains the unalterable objective of the Muslims in India'. Nevertheless 'prompted by its earnest desire for a peaceful solution' of the Indian constitutional problem, the Muslim League accepted the plan.[2]

The mission had made it abundantly clear that each of the sections would be empowered to frame the constitution for the provinces within its group irrespective of whether they attended the constitution framing assembly or not. The opting out clause was only operative after the constitution including the union constitution had been framed and the right of a province to

[1] Choudhry Khaliquzzaman, *Pathway to Pakistan* (1961), pp. 340–1.
[2] Gwyer and Appadorai, *op. cit.* vol. **ii**, pp. 600–2.

secede was not automatic but was subject to the agreement and consideration of revising machinery.[1] Despite the interpretations which the Congress put on certain clauses, its working committee on June 25th, decided to join the proposed constituent assembly.[2]

However, a few weeks later the plan was wrecked. Nehru took over as the new president of the Congress and he issued statements which his biographer Brecher calls 'the most fiery and provocative statements in his forty years of public life'.[3] Nehru said, 'So far as I can see it is not a question of our accepting any plan, long or short. It is only a question of our agreement to go into the Constituent Assembly. That is all. And nothing more than that. We will remain in that Assembly so long as we think it is good to India and we will come out when we think it is injuring our cause. When India is free India will do just what she likes. It is quite absurd and foolish to lay down now what she is going to do a few years hence.' [4] This and other statements [5] led directly to the Muslim League's withdrawal of its acceptance of the cabinet mission plan.[6] The League indeed had gone a long way in accepting the plan, for it fell far short of its demands. As Jinnah said, 'The League, throughout the negotiations, was moved by a sense of fair play and sacrificed the full sovereign state of Pakistan at the altar of the Congress for securing the independence of the whole of India.' [7] Nehru's statements, according to Azad, 'were one of those unfortunate events which change the course of history'.[8]

After the League's withdrawal of acceptance, the League decided to resort to direct action to achieve Pakistan. The later endorsement by the Congress of its having accepted the plan in its entirety failed to dispel the League's misgivings. The League, however, joined the interim government but boycotted the constituent assembly. The stalemate continued. The political atmosphere was contaminated by increasing communal riots. Peace makers seemed to be at their wits' end and further negotiations produced no results. With the British prime minister's announcement of February 20, 1947, about the British government's intention 'to effect the transfer of power into responsible Indian hands' and the assumption of office by Lord Mountbatten, things moved faster. The June 3rd plan and its acceptance by the Congress and the Muslim League finally broke the deadlock by conceding the means of creating a sovereign independent Pakistan.

On August 14, 1947, Pakistan came into being. The Muslim League had come to the end of its journey. Its achievement was truly epoch-making. If one remembers the weak, disorganized League of 1935, with its small

[1] 'Note of discussion between Secretary of State and Sir Stafford Cripps on one side and Nawab Mohammed Ismail Khan, Nawabzada Liaquat Ali Khan and Sardar Abdur Rab Nishtar on behalf of Muslim League,' May 16, 1946, *Nishtar Collection.*

[2] Gwyer and Appadorai, *op. cit.* vol. ii, pp. 610–11.

[3] Michael Brecher, *Jawaharlal Nehru: A Political Biography* (1959), p. 316.

[4] *Civil and Military Gazette*, July 9, 1946.

[5] For Nehru's statement of 10 July 1946, see Gwyer and Appadorai, *op. cit.* vol. ii, pp. 612–15.

[6] [Editors' note: for this episode cf. B. R. Nanda, 'Nehru, the Indian National Congress and the Partition of India', above pp. 178–82, and, A. G. Noorani, 'The Cabinet Mission and its Aftermath', above, pp. 108–10.]

[7] *Speeches and Writings of Jinnah*, vol. ii, p. 309.

[8] Maulana Abul Kalam Azad, *India Wins Freedom* (1959), pp. 154–5.

membership and extremely limited appeal, one is filled with wonder at the revolution in Muslim politics which the party had brought about in a decade. The phenomenon can be explained neither in terms of charismatic leadership, nor as a feat of propaganda and organization, nor even as a response to the appeal to religious emotion. For to the last a considerable section of the religious leaders (the *ulema*) remained with the Congress. The idea of Pakistan appealed to some of the deepest yearnings in the heart of the ordinary Indian Muslim. Jinnah had explained this urge even before the demand for Pakistan was made:

'Muslims have made it clear more than once that besides the question of religion, culture, language and personal laws, there is another question of life and death for them and that their future destiny and fate are dependent upon their securing definitely their political rights, their due share in the national life, the Government and the administration of the country.'[1]

[1] Quoted in Khalid Bin Sayeed, *op. cit.* p. 194.

THE PERSONALITY OF JINNAH AND HIS POLITICAL STRATEGY

by KHALID B. SAYEED*

There are two central themes in this paper. First we shall try to see whether Jinnah's political strategy flowed out of certain desires and objectives which can only be brought to light by a study of his personality. The second theme is an analysis of his strategy. The overall strategy that he followed provides a fascinating study in itself. He was a superb tactician and the various moves that he made were all parts of a master plan, the supreme objective of which was the accumulation and concentration of enormous power in his hands – an objective which he could rationalize in terms of the well-being and social goals of the Muslim nation and Pakistan. A study of this kind may possibly improve our understanding of the political developments that took place during the thirties and forties leading to the establishment of Pakistan.

A study of Jinnah's personality should tell us about his early upbringing, the influence of his parents in moulding his character, his education, his desires and ambitions, his characteristics, and his capabilities. Finally, it should tell us how he transformed his private motives into public purposes. Some of these components of a personality have been reduced into a general formula by Lasswell which may be stated as follows: $p\zeta\ d\zeta\ r = P$. In this formula, p stands for private motives; d equals displacement on to a public object; r signifies rationalization in terms of public interest; P equals the political man and ζ equals transformed into.[1]

We know very little about his father and his family except that he came from a Khoja family and his father was a hide merchant. About the Khojas, the *Bombay Gazetteer* states:

'The Khojah enjoys a good business reputation. A Parsi would rather trust a Khojah than a Meman. A keen jealous spirit of competition is the chief trait in the Khojah character. The Khojah is a good hater. *Vedmen Khojo*, *Dikhmen sojo:* For hate a Khojah, for pain a boil. The Khojah expresses his contempt for an upstart rival by the term *Tre penjyo* A three-twenty-fiver that is a man who fancies himself wealthy because he owns three times twenty-five rupees. Though called *Tundas* that is beliefless epicures the Khojahs have agreat regard for their religion the tenets of which they observe faithfully. They are neat, clean, sober, thrifty, ambitious, and in trade enterprising and cool and resourceful.'[2]

There is no doubt that Jinnah possessed in abundant measure all the qualities that the *Bombay Gazetteer* credits his community with. He was neat, clean,

* Professor of Political Studies, Queen's University, Kingston, Ontario.

[1] Harold D. Lasswell, *Psychopathology and Politics* (1960), pp. 75–6.

[2] *Gazetteer of the Bombay Presidency*, vol. ix, part ii, 'Gujarat Population, Musalmans and Parsis' (1899), p. 44.

sober, thrifty, ambitious, and in his profession and politics, enterprising, cool and resourceful.

Drawing his information from the correspondent of *The Manchester Guardian*, Edwin S. Montagu, secretary of state for India, 1917–22, recorded: 'In Bombay, there was only one man – Jinnah. At the root of Jinnah's activities is ambition.'[1] Similarly, from all accounts he had complete confidence in his ability and judgment and was extremely domineering in his attitude towards others. Lord Casey, at one time governor of Bengal, wrote: 'He is dogmatic and sure of himself; I would believe that it does not ever occur to him that he might be wrong.'[2] Jinnah is reported to have said to a rival politician, 'You try to find out what will please people and you then act accordingly. My way of action is quite different. I first decide what is right and I do it. The people come around me and the opposition vanishes.'[3] Some of these attitudes and postures were interpreted differently by his admirers and adversaries. His flashes of anger, his bitter sarcasm and righteous indignation in the law courts, have become legendary. A private secretary to the viceroy told me, 'Jinnah was deliberately rude to gain a point or gain better consideration of his views from the viceroy.' Lord Mountbatten is reported to have remarked, 'I have never been treated in all my life like this.'

However, it may be pointed out that with all his supreme confidence in himself and his overbearing nature, there was a strong streak of hardheaded realism in Jinnah which shaped and influenced his political behaviour. He was not a revolutionary or a fanatic who not having any doubts in the righteousness of his cause or ideology or the eventual success of his methods took up a position of all or nothing. He was always aware of the limitations of his strategy and waited for the right opportunity to extract the best bargain from a given situation. Some people have characterized the entire political strategy of Jinnah as amounting to no more than pitching his demands higher and higher or adopting a negative attitude. Montagu once asked Jinnah: 'What I should like to put to you is that it has been your role in politics always to accentuate and increase your demands, as what is given you is increased in itself?'[4] Nehru, giving his estimate of Jinnah to Mountbatten, said: 'The secret of his success – and it had been tremendous, if only for its emotional intensity – was in his capacity to take up a permanently negative attitude.'[5] But it must be said that particularly during the twenties Jinnah in all his negotiations either with the British or with the Congress was always trying to bring about a workable compromise. In other words, there were two Jinnahs – the Jinnah of the twenties and the Jinnah of the late thirties and of the forties. During the twenties Jinnah's object was to reach a Hindu-Muslim settlement on the basis of an acceptable compromise. Later, in the late thirties and forties, when this approach had failed, he adopted a seemingly rigid attitude and negotiated from a position of considerable strength which was based on the political power that he had mobilized.

[1] E. S. Montagu, *An Indian Diary*, edited by Venetia Montagu (1930), p. 67.
[2] R. G. Casey, *An Australian in India* (1947), p. 63.
[3] H. Bolitho, *Jinnah Creator of Pakistan* (1954), p. 87.
[4] *Joint Select Committee on the Government of India Bill.* vol. ii: *Minutes of Evidence* (H.M.S.O., 1919), p. 219.
[5] A. Campbell-Johnson, *Mission With Mountbatten* (1953), p. 44.

In 1917, one sees him trying to persuade Montagu, the secretary of state for India, to release the Ali brothers. Montagu wrote: 'He assured me that he had not meant to threaten, but only to tell us, as was his duty, the consequences that were likely to occur with the growing feeling and belief that they were innocent men.'[1] The evidence that Jinnah presented to the joint select committee on the Government of India Bill in 1919 displays a knowledge of constitutional law and parliamentary institutions which has seldom been equalled by any Hindu or Muslim scholar or political leader.[2] In 1920, Jinnah bitterly opposed the civil disobedience movement in support of the Khilafat question launched by Gandhi. But in 1922, as the secretary of the Malaviya conference, he had drafted a resolution urging the desirability of holding a Round Table conference 'under conditions acceptable to Mr. Gandhi and the Government, the idea being to put a stop to certain activities on both sides.'[3] There were meetings of the All-India Muslim League when neither the conservative faction led by Sir Muhammad Shafi nor the progressive faction led by Maulana Azad and others would participate in the deliberations and it was only Jinnah who kept the meeting going and tried to bring about a compromise between the two forces. In the council meeting of the All-India Muslim League in 1934, Asaf Ali, pointed out:

'It was this hope and Mr. Jinnah's return to the League, which made it possible for the Speaker and his friends to come and see a change of spirit in the League. . . . Mr. Jinnah commanded the respect of all since he wanted India to walk along the path of progress.'[4]

When he appeared before Montagu and Chelmsford in 1917, Montagu recorded his impressions as follows:

'I was rather tired and I funked him. Chelmsford tried to argue with him, and was tied up into knots. Jinnah is a very clever man, and it is, of course, an outrage that such a man should have no chance of running the affairs of his own country.'[5]

During the twenties and early thirties, Jinnah genuinely believed that through a process of mutual accommodation and adjustment of claims and demands, Hindus and Muslims could come to an understanding and thus facilitate the advancement of their country towards responsible self-government. His opposition to separate electorates is too well known to need any documentation. But when he found that Muslim fears of being swamped by the Hindu majority both in the Muslim minority as well as the Muslim majority provinces were genuine, he agreed to advocate their cause. This was not because he had changed his point of view but because he thought that a concession to the Muslim demand would lead to a settlement. It is also well known that in 1919, before the joint select committee on the Government of

[1] Montagu, *op. cit.* p. 143.

[2] *Joint Select Committee on the Government of India Bill.* vol. ii: *Minutes of Evidence*, pp. 208–30. The evidence was given both by Jinnah and Hasan, but nearly all the questions were put to and answered by Jinnah.

[3] *The Indian Annual Register 1922* vol. i, p. 277.

[4] *The Indian Annual Register 1934* vol. i, p. 318.

[5] Montagu, *op. cit.* pp. 57–8.

India Bill, he declared, 'Nothing will please me more when that day comes' when all distinctions between Hindus and Muslims would have disappeared.[1] In the all-parties conference in 1925, Jinnah said: 'I have not come to say what Mussalmans want. We have come to sit with you as co-workers. Let us put our heads together not as Hindus or Mahomedans but as Indians.'[2] It seems that he did not believe at that time that political leaders in India should merely function as spokesmen of their respective communities or parties. In other words, enlightened and responsible leadership demanded that the leaders would put their heads together and like a body of detached and dispassionate experts would do everything possible to resolve the Hindu-Muslim conflict. As experts, they were expected to solve constitutional maladies in the way physicians tackled physical maladies. Just as physicians did not become spokesmen of patients, political leaders, according to this point of view, were not charged with a mandate to carry out the wishes of their communities. According to Nehru, 'He suggested once privately that only matriculates should be taken into the Congress.'[3] In December 1928, before the all-parties national convention, he pleaded for the adoption of what he regarded as moderate proposals under which Muslims would be given one-third representation in the central legislature and that 'residuary powers' would be vested in the provinces. These proposals were not only rejected, but Jinnah's representative capacity as a spokesman of the Muslims was questioned. This has been interpreted as another great mistake that the Congress leaders made. It is reported that Jinnah took this to heart. 'He had tears in his eyes as he said, 'Jamshed, this is the parting of the ways.'[4]

POLITICAL DISAPPOINTMENTS AND PERSONAL FAILURE

So far as Jinnah was concerned, this turned out to be a tragic turning point in his life. He had found that his whole method of trying to bring about a constitutional settlement by playing the role of a mediator or a political broker had broken down. This method could work in law courts or in legislative assemblies. But the whole atmosphere of Indian politics had changed as a result of the emergence of mass politics and people were beginning to believe that only national civil disobedience movements could produce results. During 1928–9, he was not only faced with this failure in his political life, but also with a traumatic experience involving first separation from his wife and later her death in 1929. His wife was younger than he was by over twenty years and by origin a Parsi who had come from an extremely wealthy family. Her parents had opposed the marriage. They had overcome this opposition because they were in love. When she died in February 1929, they had already been separated and attempts at reconciliation had failed. Thus, Jinnah must have felt that he had not only been rebuffed in politics, but failure also stared him in the face in his personal life. It is also possible that he also felt that he might have been partly instrumental in bringing unhappiness and early death

[1] *Joint Select Committee on the Government of India Bill.* vol. ii: *Minutes of Evidence*, p. 225.

[2] *The Indian Quarterly Register 1925.* vol. i; January–June 1925, p. 67.

[3] J. Nehru, *An Autobiography* (1958), p. 68.

[4] Bolitho, *op. cit.* p. 95.

to somebody whom he loved dearly. Kanji Dwarkadas, who was a friend of both Jinnah and his wife, Ruttie Jinnah, wrote: 'Something I saw had snapped in him.' Jinnah took her death 'as a failure and personal defeat in his life'. 'He never recovered from his loneliness, and this loneliness added to the bitterness of his life; and I must add that this bitterness, born out of this personal loss and disappointment travelled into his political life.'[1]

Psychological explanations of why and how great men strive for power have recently gained considerable currency and intellectual respectability. Nathan Leites and Harold D. Lasswell have pioneered these studies. Lasswell has pointed out:

'Our key hypothesis about the power seeker is that he pursues power as a means of compensation against deprivation. Power is expected to overcome low estimates of the self, by changing either the traits of the self or the environment in which it functions.'[2]

Following this line of thinking, Alexander L. George and Juliette L. George wrote their famous book, *Woodrow Wilson and Colonel House A Personality Study*. They tried to show how Wilson was so completely dominated by his father during his childhood that he sought compensation from this deprivation through his ceaseless struggle for the acquisition of political power. 'Throughout his life his relationships with others seemed shaped by an inner command never again to bend his will to another man's.'[3] Jinnah is also reported to have said that you could break him but never bend him. Like Jinnah, Wilson also had a 'single-track mind'. But there is no evidence to suggest that Jinnah's deprivation arose as a result of his personality being suppressed and dominated by his father. However, as we have seen, the deprivation that Jinnah suffered was his traumatic experience arising out of the failure of his marriage and the death of his young wife. Lasswell has cited cases 'in which a severe deprivation relatively late in life has led to furious concentration upon power'. The untimely death of his beloved wife and above all the shock that his wife had not loved him transformed Joseph II of Austria into the grim figure of his later days. Another case is that of John Bright, whom Jinnah admired often quoting his famous prophecy regarding the disintegration of the Indian empire into several states, who was so grief-striken by the death of his first wife that he was persuaded by Richard Cobden to immerse himself completely in the struggle for the repeal of the Corn Laws.[4]

Jinnah even during his early political life followed his own line of thinking and action. Again, to go back to his evidence before the joint select committee, he told Montagu that he had openly disagreed with the Congress, the Muslim League, and that some of his views were at variance with those of the Home Rule League. After the political disappointments that he had suffered during the twenties and particularly in 1928, his political loneliness was even greater. Describing his role in the Round Table conference, Lord Templewood

[1] K. Dwarkadas, *Ruttie Jinnah. The Story of a Great Friendship* (n.d.), pp. 57 and 58.
[2] Harold D. Lasswell, *Power and Personality* (1962), p. 39.
[3] Alexander L. George and Juliette L. George, *Woodrow Wilson and Colonel House A Personality Study* (1964), p. 11.
[4] Harold D. Lasswell, *Power and Personality*, p. 51.

wrote: 'He never seemed to wish to work with anyone.'[1] *The Manchester Guardian* said:

'Mr. Jinnah's position at the R.T.C. was unique. The Hindus thought he was a Muslim communalist, the Muslims took him to be a pro-Hindu, the princes deemed him to be too democratic. The Britishers considered him a rabid extremist – with the result that he was everywhere but no where. None wanted him.'[2]

The sense of helplessness that he suffered from and the low estimates that he had formed of himself at that time were best described by Jinnah himself:

'At that time there was no pride in me and I used to beg from the Congress . . . I began to feel that neither could I help India, nor change the Hindu mentality, nor could I make the Musalmans realize their precarious position. I felt so disappointed and so depressed that I decided to settle down in London. Not that I did not love India; but I felt utterly helpless. I kept in touch with India. At the end of four years I found that the Musalmans were in the greatest danger. I made up my mind to come back to India, as I could not do any good from London. Having no sanction behind me I was in the position of a beggar and received the treatment that a beggar deserved.'[3]

Thus, rejected by his peers and deeply hurt by what had happened to his marriage and the death of his wife, the first reaction of Jinnah was to withdraw from Indian politics and settle down in Britain where he bought a home and decided to set up his law practice there. One may say that during 1929–35 Jinnah went through an agonizing reappraisal of his role in Indian politics. S. M. Ikram has written that during a visit to Oxford in 1932, Jinnah bitterly asked,

'But what is to be done? The Hindus are shortsighted and I think, incorrigible. The Muslim camp is full of those spineless people, who whatever they may say to me, will consult the Deputy Commissioner about what they should do! Where is, between these two groups, any place for a man like me?'[4]

Lord Hailey told the author that when Jinnah had started practising in Britain during the early thirties he wanted very much to become a member of the judicial committee of the privy council. Even in 1934, when the leaders of the various factions in the Muslim League withdrew in favour of Jinnah who was offered the presidentship, Jinnah still decided to return to England. He was urged to stay in the country 'at this critical hour'. Jinnah assured his followers that he would be promoting the interests of the country in England and that he could come back to India any time his presence was needed. It was only towards the end of 1935 that he returned to India to organize the Muslim League for the forthcoming provincial elections.

From this period onwards, one could see that he had decided to embark on a course radically different from that he had followed in his earlier life.

[1] Viscount Templewood, *Nine Troubled Years* (1954), p. 52.
[2] Cited in Joachim Alva, *Leaders of India* (1943), p. 82.
[3] Jamil-ud-din Ahmad, ed., *Speeches and Writings of Mr. Jinnah* 6th ed. (1960), vol. i, pp. 38–9.
[4] A. H. Albiruni, *Makers of Pakistan and Modern Muslim India* (1950), p. 209.

He would not go before committees or conferences to plead with them for the acceptance of his demands or suggestions. Jinnah thought that his will and character were so strong that neither disappointments in public life nor personal grief could overwhelm him. Political life had always fascinated him and by immersing himself in it with greater passion, rewards like power and glory and above all opportunities of service to his people, would crown his efforts. The Muslim community had also been looking for a great saviour and they regarded it as their religious duty to follow a leader who was prepared to unite the community and bring earthly glory to Islam. Thus, there took place a congruence between the personal needs and ambition of a leader like Jinnah and the needs of the Muslim community. Jinnah had a domineering personality and nearly always had a point of view different from that of other Indian leaders. Since he could not get along with others, he needed an organization which he could dominate and through which he could put forward his point of view. In the dominant role that he played in the Muslim League movement after 1937, he found an outlet for the political talents and qualities of leadership that he possessed. In the warmth and affection that the Muslims displayed towards him, he could overcome his loneliness and personal tragedy.

POLITICAL STRATEGY

As we have suggested earlier, Jinnah must have realized from as early as 1920 onwards that the constitutional way in politics, or the role of mediation, in a country which was in the throes of mass politics launched by Gandhi were becoming increasingly ineffective and impotent. Later, during 1928–9, we have seen how he was faced with certain acute crises in his life both of a personal and political nature. During 1929–34, there took place in Jinnah's thinking what we have characterized as an agonizing reappraisal of the entire situation in India and the new role that he could play in it. One can detect a marked change in Jinnah's speeches to the annual sessions of the Muslim League in 1937 and 1938. Jinnah laid bare his conception of politics when he declared, 'Politics means power and not relying only on cries of justice or fair-play or goodwill'.[1] It seems his thinking had also been influenced by the kind of power politics that was unfolding itself on the international stage for in his presidential address in 1937, he referred to the tragedies that countries like Abyssina, China, Palestine, and Spain were facing. One could see how far he had moved from his early days of skilful mediation and compromise-making.

'Honourable settlement can only be achieved between equals, and unless the two parties learn to respect and fear each other, there is no solid ground for any settlement. Offers of peace by the weaker party always means confession of weakness, and an invitation to aggression. Appeals to patriotism, justice and fair-play and for goodwill fall flat. It does not require political wisdom to realize that all safeguards and settlements would be a scrap of paper, unless they are backed up by power.'[2]

[1] *The Indian Annual Register 1937*, vol. i, p. 317.
[2] Jamil-ud-din Ahmad, *op. cit.* vol. i, p. 30.

If Jinnah's conception of politics was one in which an honourable settlement could only be achieved between two equal parties who respected and feared each other, it was obvious that in order that the Congress and the British should fear the Muslim League, the Muslim League should become an organized party with massive support in the cities and the countryside. But this was not enough for a leader could, by making certain wrong tactical moves, throw away the advantage that he had acquired. Secondly, a leader by antagonizing too many forces could find himself faced with a situation when his newly acquired strength was still inadequate to face the forces arrayed against him and his organization. Therefore, a political strategy had to be devised. Jinnah gave some hints regarding the need for such a grand strategy. In the annual session of the Muslim League in 1938, referring to the fact that a few Muslims in the past had thought of promoting Muslim interests through an alliance with British imperialism and how they had been disillusioned, he declared:

'I say the Muslim League is not going to be an ally of anyone, but would be the ally of even the devil if need be in the interests of Muslims.'
A pin-drop silence suddenly appeared to seize the House at this stage.
Mr. Jinnah paused for a moment and then continued; 'It is not because we are in love with imperialism; but in politics one has to play one's game as on the chess-board.'[1]

One could see the sort of moves that flowed out of the chess-board-like strategy that Jinnah had suggested in his speech. The fact that he actually followed such a strategy was also confirmed by the series of tactical moves that he later made. In this strategy, the first step that he had to take was to revitalize and reorganize the Muslim League. Since it would take time before the Muslim League could emerge as an organization as strong as the Congress, he should not be in a hurry to reach a settlement. Secondly, he should not only strengthen his position and that of the organization, but also try to weaken the position of his opponents by drawing maximum advantage from the wrong moves they made. Thirdly, he should mislead his opponents and induce them to make wrong moves as a result of which they would weaken themselves and strengthen his position. Above all, he should never allow himself to be embroiled in a conflict or struggle out of which he and his organization would emerge weaker. Jinnah knew that he must avoid a head-on clash with the British government, particularly during the war.

A successful pursuit of this broad strategy depended upon Jinnah's assessment of the existing situation as well as his short-term and long-term views of the future of Indian politics. It was apparent to him that the Muslim middle classes and particularly the intelligentsia were fearful and jealous of their Hindu counterparts who were ahead of them in business, industry and other professions. For example, the Muslim middle classes in Bengal resented the monopolistic position that the Hindu middle classes had enjoyed in business, in law, and in other professions. In the U.P. and Bihar, on the other hand, Muslims were keen to preserve the favourable position that they enjoyed in government services. It was clear that these classes would support

[1] Jamil-ud-din Ahmad, *op. cit.* vol. i, p. 78.

an organization like the Muslim League which would articulate and promote their interests either by capturing political power in Muslim majority provinces or protesting against alleged injustices meted out to Muslims by Congress governments in Hindu majority provinces.

Another set of circumstances that favoured Jinnah and the Muslim League was the Congress mistake in not only refusing to include Muslim League representatives in Congress cabinets in Hindu majority provinces but also the Congress unwillingness to co-operate with a Muslim leader like Fazlul Haq who emerged as the premier of Bengal. It has been reported that Fazlul Haq 'pleaded and pleaded in vain for active co-operation or even tacit support' and thus was 'forced into the arms of the Moslem League'.[1]

It also became clear to Jinnah that the provincial Congress organizations were filled with Hindu leaders who were so steeped in Hindu culture and traditions that they were not far-sighted and broadminded in tackling issues and problems which were of a sensitive nature to Muslims. The installation of Congress ministries led to increasing alienation of Muslims both in the urban and rural areas. This enabled the Muslim League to mobilize Muslim support.

The problem for Jinnah was not merely that of making full use of favourable circumstances, but also one of overcoming several obstacles. He knew that the British did not support him and in fact during the early thirties on several occasions they had tried to weaken his influence in Indian politics. Particularly in an area like the Punjab they were in no mood to allow an urban politician like Jinnah to disturb the countryside from where the British had drawn a major portion of their army. In order to maintain support in these areas, the British had relied heavily on the influence of the landed gentry and the power of the deputy commissioner. As stated earlier, in 1932 Jinnah complained of those 'spineless' Muslim leaders who would consult the deputy commissioner before extending their support to him. The British had given support to Unionist leaders like Sir Fazl-i-Husain to consolidate their position in the Punjab. Instead of dividing the people of Punjab into rival groups of Hindus, Muslims and Sikhs, the British had viewed with favour the emergence of the Unionist party which had brought within its fold Hindu, Muslim and Sikh peasants and landowners belonging to the Jat and Rajput tribes. Punjabi soldiers, who constituted half of the British Indian army, came from these rural classes. Thus, one could see that the British disliked the idea of these classes being drawn into the maelstrom of either Indian agitational politics or the purely communal pull of the Muslim League. When Jinnah started reorganizing the Muslim League in early 1935, Fazl-i-Husain sent word to him that he should keep 'his finger out of the Punjab pie'.[2] The pro-British Aga Khan, leader of the Khoja community in India, lent his financial support to the Unionist party and not to Jinnah's Muslim League.

It is well known that the Muslim League's performance in Punjab in the provincial elections of 1937 was extremely poor. But Jinnah succeeded in making the best of these adverse circumstances. Sir Sikandar Hyat, the

[1] H. Alexander, *India Since Cripps* (1944), p. 52.
[2] Azim Husain, *Fazl-i-Husain* (1946), p. 309.

Unionist premier, joined the Muslim League and a pact known as the Sikandar-Jinnah pact was concluded between the two parties. When Sir Muhammad Iqbal complained that this alliance had damaged the prestige of the League in the Punjab, Jinnah is reported to have assured Iqbal that while agreeing with his objective of building Muslim solidarity, he had to devise the best possible means in the short-run to achieve the long-term objective. Jinnah wrote: 'I want to pull them [Muslims] up step by step and before making them run I want to be sure that they are capable of standing on their own legs.'[1]

It was clear that after the installation of Congress ministries in 1937, in Jinnah's eyes the greatest adversary of the Muslim League was the Congress. He knew that the Muslim League by itself could not oppose the Congress. Therefore, he thought of building a broad front consisting of the Muslim League and other minorities. This thinking was reflected in some of the resolutions that the Muslim League passed in 1937 and 1938. In one of the resolutions it was pointed out that the object of the Muslim League was the establishment of a federal polity in India consisting of free democratic states 'in which the rights and interests of the Musalmans and other minorities are adequately and effectively safeguarded in the constitution'.[2]

It seems Jinnah was more or less certain that the Congress, having emerged as a well-organized and strong party in the provincial elections and having been installed in office in seven provinces, were in no mood to come to a settlement with the Muslim League. To Jinnah, such a settlement could only be arrived at if the Congress were to recognize the Muslim League as the sole representative organization of the Muslims. Any status accorded to the League which was less than that would not have been acceptable to Jinnah because, as we have seen, in his strategy an honourable or workable settlement could only be arrived at between two organizations which were equal and feared each other. Jinnah also knew that the Congress were not likely to accept such a demand because it would reduce Congress to the position of a completely Hindu organization. The strategy that Jinnah pursued was simple and clear. He attacked the Congress where it hurt them most, namely, by describing the policy and actions of the Congress provincial governments as deliberately designed to persecute and oppress the Muslim minority. A number of letters were exchanged between Congress leaders like Gandhi, Nehru, Subhas Chandra Bose, Rajendra Prasad, on the one hand, and Jinnah on the other. Congress leaders denied Muslim League charges of Congress persecution. The Muslim League published several reports and pamphlets giving details regarding the glaring injustices to which Muslims were subjected during Congress rule. The Congress suggested that they would be prepared to have these charges investigated by a British chief justice, but this offer was not accepted by Jinnah. Jinnah was again in a very strong position because given the communal atmosphere of Indian politics, a large number of Muslims genuinely believed that the Congress governments had persecuted the Muslim minority. It was well known that in spite of sincere attempts by leaders like

[1] *Dawn*, December 25, 1955.

[2] *Resolutions of the All India Muslim League from October, 1935 to December, 1938* (n.d.), p. 4.

Nehru; the Congress had not been able to eliminate communalists from its ranks. Even leaders like Tilak and Gandhi in their attempts to mobilize mass support had appealed to Hindu sentiments and traditions. Nehru himself had deplored this method of political mobilization, but he thought that such an approach was understandable in view of the fact that it was a quick way, of reaching the heart of the people'.[1] However, in all this controversy, Jinnah's aims were clear. He wanted to discredit the Congress claim that it represented both Hindus and Muslims. Secondly, he wished the Congress to recognize the Muslim League claim of being the sole spokesman of Indian Muslims. Jinnah was not interested in a settlement at that time because the Muslim League had not yet reached the organizational strength to establish his claim. In a letter to Nehru, he said: 'We shall have to wait and depend upon our inherent strength which will determine the measure of importance or distinction that it possesses.'[2]

Jinnah took full advantage of the Congress decision to resign office after the outbreak of the war. He called upon the Muslims to celebrate what he designated as the 'Deliverance Day' on December 22, 1939. This was supposed to be deliverance from 'tyranny, oppression and injustice during the last two and a half years'. Jinnah was bitterly criticized even by Muslim leaders for this action. But it fitted into the broad pattern of strategy that he had devised. Congress resignations and later the imprisonment of Congress leaders provided full opportunity to Jinnah to build his prestige and that of the League. Later, in 1945, while commenting upon these developments following the outbreak of the war, he said:

'There was going to be a deal between Mr. Gandhi and Lord Linlithgow. Providence helped us. The war which nobody welcomes proved to be a blessing in disguise. Meanwhile we did some spade work and then we were sufficiently strong not to be ignored completely.'[3]

In his dealings with the British, Jinnah trod a wary path. Congress were openly hostile to the British war effort and they had also resigned office. Under such circumstances, Jinnah could have easily made one of two tactical mistakes. First, he could have antagonized the British by trying to extract too many concessions from them or he could have adopted the opposite course of wholehearted co-operation with the British including acceptance of office at the centre. Without a Jinnah, most of the Muslim League leaders would not have been able to resist the latter temptation. Jinnah avoided both these alternatives and followed a course of action in which without giving his full co-operation to the British, he was successful in extracting certain real concessions from them. He knew that the British, having lost the support of the Congress, would have been reluctant to alienate Muslim public opinion as well. The viceroy's declaration of August 8, 1940 stated that the British government 'could not contemplate the transfer of their present responsibilities for the peace and welfare of India to any system of government whose

[1] Nehru, *op. cit.* p. 72.
[2] S. S. Peerzada, *Leader's Correspondence With Mr. Jinnah* (1944), p. 132.
[3] Jamil-ud-din Ahmad, ed., *Speeches and Writings of Mr. Jinnah*, 2nd ed. (1964), vol. ii, p. 245.

authority is directly denied by large and powerful elements in India's national life. Nor could they be parties to the coercion of such elements into submission to such a Government.' This was perhaps one of the greatest triumphs that Jinnah had achieved through his brilliant strategy. The British, through this assurance, had given him the power to veto all constitutional advance or a settlement which the Muslim League did not approve. This meant that he could bide his time, build his organization, and eventually force the Congress to accept his demand that the Muslim League was the sole representative organization of the Muslims.

On March 23, 1940, the famous Lahore resolution, which became known as the Pakistan resolution, was passed. It was somewhat vague. It spoke of more than one sovereign state and referred in a very general way to territorial adjustments. Jinnah was criticized for not giving a clear picture of all the details of his Pakistan scheme. But, again, it seems that Jinnah knew what he was doing. In 1940, with the war going on his main object was to mobilize and maximize his support among the Muslims. The Muslim League organization had penetrated the Muslim majority provinces of Bengal and the Punjab. Now, inspired by this ideal of a separate Muslim state, a Muslim peasant or a city dweller in areas like the Punjab and Bengal could hold his head high even though his cash was low and material possessions meagre as compared to the more prosperous Hindus. During 1936 to 1938, Jinnah was looking for support in Punjab and Bengal. He had entered into a pact with the Unionist premier in the Punjab who had trounced the Muslim League in the provincial elections. But now the situation had altered so much that the powerful Sir Sikandar Hyat said 'that unless he walked warily and kept on the right side of Jinnah he would be swept away by a wave of fanaticism'.[1]

It was clear that Jinnah's position was growing from strength to strength. The tactics that he pursued were designed to build his image as a strong and powerful leader of the Muslims whose will and decisions would not be defied by any Muslim leader however powerful he might be. This was well demonstrated in July 1941 by the way he demanded from the premiers of the Punjab, Bengal and Assam that they should resign from the national defence council which had been set up by the British government to help the war effort. Jinnah knew that the viceroy had made a tactical mistake by inviting them as representatives of the Muslim community without obtaining his prior approval. The three premiers were under the impression that they had been invited to represent their provinces and had already indicated their willingness to join the national defence council. When Jinnah confronted Sir Sikandar Hyat with a text of the message that the viceroy had sent to him through the governor of Bombay and which indicated that he had been invited as the representative of the Muslim community, the Punjab premier had no choice except to tender his resignation. The Bengal premier, Fazlul Haq, was at first resentful and defiant, but later he had to resign as well. He complained that Jinnah had known of their selection at least a day before the names were published but did not care to indicate his disapproval immediately. 'He kept waiting and watching till our names were published and then he came out

[1] P. Moon, *Divide and Quit* (1962), p. 38.

with his thunder that he had decided to take disciplinary action against us.' He 'took us unawares as if he was anxious to make a public exhibition of his authority'.[1]

In 1942, during the negotiations regarding the Cripps proposals, Jinnah was satisfied with the modest tactical gains that the League had achieved in the sense that the possibility of Pakistan was recognized by implication in the proposals and that the Muslim League had emerged as a principal political force. But a greater triumph was that achieved during the Gandhi-Jinnah talks in 1944 when the two leaders representing the two main political forces in the country met to reach a settlement on the issue of Pakistan. One could see that through these talks Jinnah achieved two of his main demands, namely, that he was the most important leader of the Muslims of India and, secondly, that a settlement between the Congress and the League involved discussion of the Pakistan issue. Jinnah knew from the very beginning that Gandhi had not come to the talks as a representative fully authorized by the Congress to negotiate on their behalf. He also knew that Gandhi was not likely to concede his demand for a sovereign Pakistan for the formula of Rajagopalachari, on the basis of which talks were being held, referred to the possibility of a confederal arrangement between Muslim provinces and the rest of India. In addition, the formula made it clear that the whole of Punjab and Bengal would not be included within the Muslim state and a commission would be appointed for demarcating contiguous districts in the north-west and east of India wherein the Muslim population constituted an absolute majority. Jinnah during the talks opposed all these proposals. Why did Jinnah agree to hold these talks when he knew that there was no guarantee that a settlement reached between the two leaders would be accepted by the Congress or supported by the British government who were not a party to these talks? The only explanation is that Jinnah agreed to meet Gandhi and conduct these negotiations because he thought this would improve the position of the Muslim League and also enhance his prestige.

In the Simla conference which was held during June-July 1945 Jinnah again took a strong position even though the viceroy's proposals had conceded parity of representation in the executive council between the Muslim and caste Hindu members. One could see the enormous strength that Muslims had acquired under Jinnah's leadership. In December 1928, Jinnah had pleaded in vain before the all-parties convention to accord no more than one-third representation in the central legislature to the Muslims. The Simla conference failed because Jinnah would not agree to a non-League Muslim being included in the executive council. Jinnah wanted to impress upon all the Muslim leaders that they were not likely to get any prize offices by remaining outside the Muslim League.

In the protracted negotiations that took place both before and after the cabinet mission plan was announced on May 16, 1946, one could see that there was a sharp and bitter clash between the Congress strategists and Jinnah. It may be said to the credit of Jinnah that he was alone on the League side to match his wits against a number of first-rate minds on the British as well as the Congress side. The Congress leaders felt that the time had come to

[1] *The Statesman* (weekly overseas edition), September 18, 1941.

offer a stiff resistance to Jinnah's demands. The cabinet mission, after considering the diametrically opposed proposals of the Congress and the League – the former demanding a fairly strong centre and the latter demanding Pakistan including the entire provinces of the Punjab and Bengal – announced their own plan. The cabinet mission plan turned down the plan for a sovereign Pakistan, but provided for the compulsory grouping of the six Muslim majority provinces in sections B and C. The Muslim League thought that the basis and foundation of Pakistan had been conceded and that later the Muslim League would have an opportunity to demand secession of provinces or groups from the union. It seems that Jinnah was again bargaining very shrewdly. The cabinet mission probably felt that since they had rejected the League's Pakistan scheme, the League should be placated by providing for the compulsory grouping of provinces. They made another major concession to the League in their proposal regarding the formation of the interim government. In the statement issued by the cabinet mission and the viceroy on June 16, 1946 regarding the formation of the interim government, the names of those leaders who were being invited to join the government were also announced. From this announcement, it was clear that all Muslim members were from the Muslim League. Moreover, paragraph 8 of the statement said:

'In the event of the two major parties or either of them proving unwilling to join in the setting up of a Coalition Government on the above lines, it is the intention of the Viceroy to proceed with the formation of an Interim Government which will be as representative as possible of those willing to accept the statement of May 16th.[1]'

When the Congress turned down the interim government plan on the plea that they had a right to include a Muslim in their quota, Jinnah believed that the viceroy was committed to invite the Muslim League, which had accepted both the cabinet mission plan and the interim government plan, to join the interim government.

The viceroy was in a very difficult position because he did not want to precipitate a crisis by excluding the Congress from the interim government. Therefore, he decided to continue his negotiations with the Congress. Later, he changed his position regarding the formation of the interim government in the sense that he wrote to Jinnah saying: 'It will not be open to either the Congress or the Muslim League to object to the names submitted by the other party, provided they are accepted by the Viceroy.'[2] Jinnah was indignant that the viceroy had gone back on his commitment. The contention of the Muslim League was that the Congress had not only not accepted the interim government plan announced on June 16th, but that they had also accepted the cabinet mission plan of May 16th, with so many qualifications and reservations that such an acceptance amounted to an open rejection of the plan. Azad in a letter to the viceroy wrote: 'While adhering to our views, we accept your proposals and are prepared to work them with a view to achieve our objective.'[3] Nehru had attacked the entire grouping plan and had

[1] M. Gwyer and A. Appadorai, eds. *Speeches and Documents on the Indian Constitution 1921–47* (1957), vol. ii, p. 603.

[2] *Ibid.* vol. ii, p. 641.

[3] *Ibid.* vol. ii, p. 602.

asserted that the Congress would enter the constituent assembly 'completely unfettered by agreement and free to meet all situations as they arise'. Azad in his book, commenting on this statement, wrote: 'It was not correct to say that Congress was free to modify the Plan as it pleased.'[1] To Jinnah, this was gross betrayal and surrender on the part of the British government because of their fear of the Congress capability to start a civil disobedience movement. On July 29, 1946 the council of the All-India Muslim League withdrew its acceptance of the cabinet mission proposals and its resolution stated that since Muslims had failed to find a peaceful solution 'by compromise and constitutional means' and since 'power politics and not justice and fair-play are the deciding factors in Indian affairs', the Muslim League was convinced 'the time has come for the Muslim Nation to resort to direct action'.[2] Again, one could see how different the Jinnah of the forties was compared with the Jinnah of the late twenties when, after his proposals were rejected in December 1928, he was so dejected that he decided to settle down in Britain. In July 1946, he was prepared to settle a political issue by means of power and direct action. He had mobilized political support, had transformed the Muslim League into a powerful organization and was demanding that Muslims, a minority, should be treated as a community equal to the Hindu majority. When the viceroy went back on his assurance, he thought the time had come to demonstrate the power that he had created.

'If there is not sufficient power, create that power. If we do that, the Mission and the British Government may be rescued, released and freed from being cowed down by the threats of the Congress that they would launch a struggle and start non-co-operation. Let us also say that.'[3]

The League's threat to resort to direct action worsened the communal situation. Riots in Calcutta and Noakhali were followed by riots in Bihar. There was a tragic pattern in all this in the sense that if a particular community suffered more in a riot, it would be followed by retaliatory action by that community in areas where it was in majority. This would have eventually engulfed the whole sub-continent in a civil war. The viceroy and the Congress both made efforts to persuade the Muslim League to join the interim government. Gandhi, after his talks with Jinnah, signed a statement which said: 'The Congress does not challenge but accepts that the Muslim League now is the authoritative representative of an overwhelming majority of the Muslims of India.'[4] Nehru and other Congress members of the interim government were very unhappy with this statement, but were prepared to accept its substance provided that all the ministers of the interim government would agree to work as a team and never invoke the intervention of the governor-general. Jinnah was prepared to discuss the latter statement but would not commit himself to it. The Muslim League entered the interim government in October 1946. As compared to the portfolios of finance and commerce that the League now obtained, the Congress controlled portfolios like defence, external affairs,

[1] A. K. Azad, *Indian Wins Feeedom* (1960), p. 155.
[2] Gwyer and Appadorai, *op. cit.* vol. ii, pp. 620–1.
[3] M. Ashraf, ed., *Cabinet Mission and After* (1946), p. 291.
[4] Gwyer and Appadorai, *op. cit.* vol. ii, p. 648.

and home. The Congress probably felt that having denied to the League key portfolios like home and defence, the League members would not be able to pose much of a problem. But the League's control of finance gave it such a strategic advantage that it could virtually paralyse the working of the government. It was also clear that the Muslim League had entered the government fully determined to wage their struggle for Pakistan from within the government. Nehru wanted to be accepted by the League members as the *de facto* prime minister and wished the government itself to work as a cabinet. Jinnah dismissed such attempts with his brutal sarcasm. When told that the viceroy himself had referred to the interim government as a cabinet, Jinnah's rejoinder was: 'And the Viceroy saw no real objection if it pleased Pandit Nehru when they assumed office. Little things please little minds and you cannot turn a donkey into an elephant by calling it an elephant.'[1]

Many people have speculated from time to time that if the Congress had agreed to work the cabinet mission plan, partition might have been avoided. But such speculations do not take into account the personality of Jinnah and the consistent strategy that he had followed in strengthening the Muslim League and resorting to every possible device to weaken his opponents. There are others, of course, who would argue that the long uninterrupted stream of Muslim separatism was so strong that it could never allow itself to be merged into the Indian river. However, what the author has tried to show in this paper is that Jinnah possessed such a domineering personality that he would never allow himself and his community to be dominated by Congress leaders. One of the members of the Muslim League working committee told the author that if the cabinet mission plan had been accepted, Jinnah would have followed his own prepared plans which were designed to strengthen the autonomy of the Muslim majority provinces and build an all-India front against the Hindus with the help of the Scheduled Castes and other minorities.

It has often been argued that what Jinnah had once described as a moth-eaten and truncated Pakistan was the one which he finally obtained in 1947. It has been suggested that he could have got this Pakistan in 1944 after reaching a satisfactory settlement with Gandhi. We have indicated why such a settlement could not have been arrived at in 1944 when the British were not a party to the Gandhi-Jinnah talks. In addition, it is extremely doubtful whether Jinnah's representative position at that time had been amply demonstrated to induce his opponents to concede his demands. We have also suggested that Jinnah's strategy was to take the offensive and ask for more than he would eventually get. Therefore, it could be argued that Jinnah might not have got what he eventually obtained had he not bargained for more. Jinnah also knew that shrewd moves by themselves could not produce results. According to him, the amount of power that a political party possessed played a crucial role in inducing its adversaries to concede the demands of that party. Therefore, one could say that since Jinnah did not possess sufficient power during the early forties, he could not have obtained his Pakistan.

Why did Jinnah not settle for a common governor-generalship? Pakistanis have complained that Mountbatten after August 14, 1947 had become excessively pro-India and anti-Pakistan. Exaggerated as these accusations may

[1] Jamil-ud-din Ahmad, *op. cit.* vol. ii, p. 375.

sound, there was an element of truth in them. Sir George Cunningham in his diary reports:

'MESSERVY came up from 'PINDI for a talk; just back from England. He was in DELHI two days ago and was surprised to find MOUNTBATTEN directing the military operations in KASHMIR. M.B. is daily becoming more and more anathema to our Muslims, and it certainly seems as if he could see nothing except through Hindu eyes.' (November 7, 1947).[1]

The suspicion that Jinnah had towards Mountbatten after he became governor-general was of an earlier origin. Again, to quote Cunningham's diary regarding communal massacres:

'JINNAH says this was known in June 1947; that MOUNTBATTEN was aware of it and decided in July to round up all the leaders, but put it off and off, and finally said he would do it simultaneously with the publication of the Border Commission Report; so he was able to play out time until after the 15th Aug. and thus did nothing. JINNAH says he has documentary proof that the Report was in MOUNTBATTEN's hands by 7th Aug. and could have been published then if M.B. had not held it up. JINNAH very bitter about the whole thing.' (February 9, 1948).[2]

It is well known that Jinnah and Mountbatten did not get along well. Secondly, Jinnah might have been suspicious that if he were to allow a common governor-generalship, there might be some difficulties in the future for Pakistan to establish its separate and complete sovereignty. In passing, it may be noted that the Labour government had considered the idea of retaining certain common links between India and Pakistan and the structure of the Austro-Hungarian dual monarchy united by the link of the Habsburg Crown had been discussed as a possibility for the sub-continent.[3] I may also point out that it was suggested to a British political scientist by a leading member of the Labour government that he should study the structure of the Austro-Hungarian empire and particularly constitutions of international bodies under the League of Nations when he was appointed as an adviser to Lord Mountbatten. However, soon after his arrival, the British political scientist found that the idea had disappeared and he was never consulted very much as an adviser. Thus, a number of such considerations might have influenced Jinnah's mind when he calculated the risks of a common governor-generalship.

It has been reported to the author that even though Jinnah was horrified by the slaughter and carnage that followed the partition of the country, yet there were moments when he found the experience of having established a separate state thrilling. However, like other great figures in history, he had paid his price for the power and glory that he struggled for. We have already noted the personal tragedy that he had suffered and the political disappointments that he had encountered in the late twenties. We have argued that Jinnah sought power as a means of compensation for the deprivations that

[1] Sir George Cunningham's Diary—1947, p. 23.
[2] *Ibid.* p. 34.
[3] H. N. Brailsford, *Subject India* (1943), p. 91.

he had suffered. But we have suggested that the mere possession of a strong will and the desire for power could not have made him the Qaid-i-Azam. We have pointed out the congruence that existed between his needs and characteristics and the needs of his people. A society when it is faced with a desperate situation surrenders itself to the leadership of desperate and domineering men. It is only during periods of doubt and despair that men turn to leaders with a mission. Such men have been characterized as 'crowd compellers'. These are 'men who can conceive a great idea, mould a crowd big enough to carry it into effect and force the crowd to do it'.[1] In Max Weber's terminology, these are charismatic leaders.[2]

However Jinnah's leadership cannot be explained away only in such terms. One can understand the greatness of a Gandhi or Churchill for they possessed on an elevated plane the inherent qualities of their respective races. But Jinnah was so different from his people. The Muslims of India by reputation and by nature are warm-hearted people. And it continues to be an enigma how these people followed a leader who was so austere and so remote from them. One explanation is, and it is not a complete one, that this power-conscious man promised to them the political power which the Qur'an had promised to them and which their forbears had wielded in India.

[1] Harold D. Lasswell and Abraham Kaplan, *Power and Society A Frameword for Political Inquiry* (1963), p. 154.

[2] Reinhard Bendix, *Max Weber An Intellectual Portrait* (1962), pp. 298–303.

ECONOMIC PROBLEMS AND INDIAN INDEPENDENCE

by K. N. CHAUDHURI*

This paper is an attempt to survey the economic alignment of the principal political parties in India and to trace the interaction between economic events and public affairs in the crucial years between 1930 and 1947. A word may be said at the beginning about the nature of an enquiry of this kind and its possible usefulness. To those familiar with the period it is a commonplace knowledge that much of the public discussion on economic conditions and plans for economic development did not get beyond the paper on which they were written. A statement of policy was often confused with positive action, while those who clamoured for swift and drastic reforms realized when responsibility and office came to them that Indian society had unseen complexity, reflected in the intractability of its economic problems. If the student of historical ideas is faced with certain methodological difficulties, these in turn are multiplied when the subject is economic history. For economic activities do not lend themselves to easy and tangible analysis as might, for example, constitutional issues, and vital policy decisions have to be formulated on the basis of conjectures, current economic theories, and the influence of extraneous events. Economic ideologies, nevertheless, do play a positive part in the process of history and an examination of those in India during the period under review not only demonstrates their close relationship to the developments after independence had been achieved in 1947, but it also reveals in a striking manner the long continuity and the historical origin of these ideas.

Discussion of economic affairs had always been part of the Indian political scene since the early days of the British rule. The year 1930 was one of economic distress for India brought about by the world depression and much of the economic thinking of the leading political parties was shaped and influenced by the conditions arising out of it. But exactly a hundred years ago a similar event had also led to some astonishingly powerful analysis of India's economic structure. Throughout the second half of the nineteenth century economic issues and matters of policy remained at the forefront of public consciousness slowly gathering intensity. In fact the main stream of Indian nationalism derived its motivating force from two complementary directions. There were in the first place, the concrete political objectives and secondly, there was, no less important, the desire to control and direct the country's social and economic welfare. By the late 1920s the nationalists had reached a turning point. Their increasing sense of political power combined with the catastrophic economic events brought sharply into focus the fact that the long preparation

* Lecturer in the Economic History of Asia, School of Oriental and African Studies, London.

for political education must be matched by a definite programme of economic policy. One fact, however, needs to be noted here. As long as the economic ideas of the Indian nationalists remained vague and nebulous, dominated by the classical view of India's economic past in the nineteenth century, there also remained a certain degree of agreement among all shades of opinion. Even in the mid-1930s when communal differences had driven the Hindus and Muslims, the Congress and the Muslim League, wide apart, the party spokesmen generously borrowed from each other's economic programmes. At this stage the main difference of opinion was still with the government of India and the British interests in India. Jinnah attacked the Ottawa agreement with as much vehemence as did the Congress members. But no sooner did the Congress leaders attempt to formulate a concrete plan of economic advancement when pressure of ideology split the nationalists on horizontal lines. Thus, so far as economic matters were concerned, there seemed to emerge four main groups, the government, the Congress right, Congress left and finally the Muslims.[1]

As we have already stated, the conditions created by the great depression of 1930 were primarily responsible for the mounting urgency of economic action. While nearly all agricultural countries suffered from the slump, the duration and intensity of the deflationary forces in India continued almost until the outbreak of the war. The index of wholesale prices (taking the year 1929 as base) fell by 18 points in 1930, by 32 points in 1931, reaching its lowest level in 1933 when the index stood at 61·7. In 1938 it was still at 67·6.[2] The recovery which had followed in the economy of the industrialized countries since 1935 was largely absent from India, and the drastic fall in prices had a most serious effect on agricultural incomes. Peasants faced with fixed debt charges and rent and revenue demands found the burden intolerable, and there were signs that at the prevailing level of prices they were unable to recover their costs of cultivation. The problem of the agriculturists, particularly in relation to the payment of government revenue, was debated at all levels. Gandhi himself, writing in *Young India* in 1931, produced tables showing the index number of prices in India since 1880 and demonstrated that a fifty per cent drop in the prices of staples had taken place from 1915. He assured the peasants of the United Provinces that he had discussed the question with the viceroy and suggested drastic remission of revenue payments. But at the same time he warned them against listening to any advice that they should not pay any rents at all to the zamindars. 'Congressmen cannot,' he wrote, 'we do not seek to injure the Zamindars. We aim not at destruction of property. We aim only at its lawful use.' All this, as we shall see, was in line with Gandhi's social ideas. But what was new was the fact that he attempted to assign a positive role to the Congress; for in the same article he said that the Congress was trying and would try to investigate the peasant's complaints of harsh treatment by landlords, would plead with the latter and even advise legal relief where such became imperative.[3] Ultimately,

[1] Cf. *Parliamentary Papers* (1940), vol. 10.

[2] P. S. Lokanathan, *India's Post-war Reconstruction and its International Aspects* (1946), p. 1.

[3] *Young India*, May 28, 1931, published in *Towards Non-violent Socialism* (1951).

the government adjusted the revenue demand to the fall in agricultural prices.[1] But the nationalist opposition to the government's taxation policy continued. For example in 1935 in the legislative assembly during a debate on Dr Ziauddin's amendment motion for a review of taxation policy, Sardar Mangal Singh demanded that land revenue should be graduated according to the peasants' ability to pay. Speaking on behalf of the government, Sir James Grigg declared that such a proposal would not be feasible in entirety, for in land revenue there was a considerable element of rent and he announced that the government would remain neutral on the amendment motion. Other speakers such as Shri Prakash and Dr P. N. Banerji complained of the inactivity of the authorities in taking steps to relieve the distress of the people during the depression and claimed that the government raised taxes not for 'nation-building' purposes but for maintaining the expensive bureaucracy and the unnecessarily large army.[2]

If the nationalists were often irresponsible in criticizing in detail the various omissions in the government's policy, Congress itself was accused of being instrumental in causing the decline in India's export trade. While analysing India's foreign trade figures in January 1931, *The Statesman* declared in a leader that the essence of the lesson to be drawn from the declining trade figures was that no country could go deliberately to work to destroy the trade of those from whom it buys without harming in an even greater degree its own business and that the greatest sufferer from the boycott and the political agitation had been India.[3] That the decline in India's balance of trade in merchandise was severe there is no doubt. But whether it was the effectiveness of the Congress action alone that was responsible for it was another matter. For the total value of India's exports in 1928–9 had been Rs. 381 crores; in 1929–30 it was 361 crores and by the following year it had dropped to 257. The lowest level was reached in 1931–2 when the figure was 181 crores. The fall in the value of the imports was equally drastic, the total figure declining by almost a half over the same years. Since India was at this time a debtor country, the external accounts were balanced by a heavy export of gold. The government, however, maintained the exchange rate at 1s 6d per rupee and came under repeated criticism that it was doing nothing to lessen the rigour of deflationary forces working in the economy by way of external trade. In fact the weight of opinion of the Indian economists seemed to be that the government of India in not devaluing the rupee failed to use one useful, and in many cases a more effective, instrument of securing equilibrium by a more active monetary and currency policy.[4] Nehru himself turned this issue into political propaganda in his presidential address at Faizpur in December 1936 when he declared that 'industry cannot expand properly because of the economic and financial policy of the Government . . .', and he went to say that 'the currency ratio continues in spite of persistent Indian protests; gold has been pouring out of India continuously now for five years

[1] Cf. W. C. Neale, *Economic Change in Rural India* (1962).

[2] Legislative Assembly Debates, February 14, 1935, printed in *Indian Annual Register* (1935), vol. i, p. 132.

[3] *The Statesman*, January 11, 1931.

[4] Lokanathan, *op. cit.* p. 3.

at a prodigious rate, though all India vehemently opposes this outflow. And the new Act tells us that we may do nothing which the Viceroy or the Governor might consider as an unfair discrimination against British trade or commercial interests. The old order may yield place to the new, but British interests are safe and secure.'[1] The world depression of 1930 and its consequent effects were largely an economic phenomenon, but in the heat of partisan feelings generated by political turmoils this fact was often forgotten or ignored. Even the Indian chambers of commerce commented in April 1937 that India's foreign trade was being adversely affected by economic nationalism on the one hand and Empire policies on the other.[2]

Were the nationalists justified in ascribing to the government an almost complete absence of an overall economic policy? On the whole it seems that they were right. In this context it is useful to remember that the need for effective state action in the national economic life had not yet become a political doctrine even in the highly complex industrialized countries of the west. In many ways the position of the government of India in this respect was more advanced than that of the British government. But the thinking of the government was still dominated by the traditional method of action which can be described as an *ad hoc* method. Policies were devised and steps taken according to each new situation. Harassed by the onerous task of political repression, afraid of revolutionary outbreaks, and continually attacked in what it considered to be its main duty, the maintenance of law and order, the government seemed to have abandoned any plan it may have had of an integrated economic programme for India as a whole. Furthermore, the traditional obsession with a balanced annual budget always raised the problem of financing the construction of social overhead facilities.[3] In 1931 for instance *The Statesman* declared that half the defects that had been found in the Montagu reforms were not so much due to that experiment in government as to the fact that there had never been the money to make the reforms effective on the nation-building side.[4] The Act of 1935 transferred the responsibility for industrial developments to provincial governments, a change that was not likely to step up India's industrial progress. In a review of the government's industrial policy, issued by the department of industries and labour in October 1936, it was pointed out that the central government could now assist the economic position of industries only through its tariff policy, and that, although the provinces had in theory almost unlimited powers to assist industries, in reality 'their financial resources, their technical equipment and the difficulty of dealing with industries of all-India importance on a provincial scale contributed to confine their activities largely to the less organized form of industries'.[5]

From time to time through the viceroy's speeches the government expressed the desire to improve the economic condition of the people.[6] But it was not

[1] Presidential Address, Faizpur Congress, December 1936, printed in Dorothy Norman, *Nehru: The first sixty years* (1965), vol. i, p. 471.

[2] *Indian Annual Register* (1937), vol. i.

[3] Cf. M. D. Morris, 'Toward a Reinterpretation of Nineteenth Century Indian Economic History', *The Journal of Econ. Hist.* vol. xxii (1963).

[4] *Indian Annual Register* (1936), vol. ii, p. 378.

[5] *The Statesman*, January 11, 1931.

[6] Lord Linlithgow's speech, June 20, 1937.

until the outbreak of the war that the government found the will to take positive measures of some kind. As early as 1934 G. D. Birla, the industrial and business magnate, had asked the question why it was that with her wide resources including supplies of idle labour India could not raise her standard of living to a reasonable level. To him the answer was simple. 'We cannot improve our lot', he wrote, 'until we decide to take mass action, well thought out, well planned, as part of a scheme of co-ordination launched with the necessary authority to make it a success. Government intervention thus becomes necessary . . . the Government knows the evil of drifting without a plan. But it would not think of taking planned action. Probably the apathy on the part of the Government is due to the fact that the head of every department in the Secretariat has a five year plan of ruling and then retiring . . . the one object of the men in authority in New Delhi is to maintain law and order and balance budgets and of the Clive Street Burra Sahib to retire leaving things as he found them . . . the result is that whatever we achieve, we achieve in a haphazard fashion.'[1] Sir George Schuster writing a foreword to Birla's book in 1950 declared candidly that though he and the author were critics of each other in the old days, they agreed on one fundamental issue which was 'first that India could only advance to true welfare by increasing her production and secondly that the great national effort required to achieve this objective could only be inspired by a National Government'.

If the feeling expressed by Sir George Schuster was general among the British administrators and officials during this period, it provides an explanation for the relative inactivity of the government as compared with the quite remarkable outburst of thinking on economic development on the part of the Congress leaders. This was undoubtedly a self-conscious process engendered by the increasing sense of power which the Congress party came to feel as a result of its identification with a mass political movement. If in many ways the Congress began to assume the role of an unofficial opposition party, it also came to realize that not only was the government most vulnerable to criticism on the economic front but the effectiveness of its own popular appeal and claims to control the political destiny of India depended to a considerable extent on the formulation of a comprehensive programme which promised to deal with the outstanding economic problems of the day. As early as May 1929, the All-India Congress Committee had passed a resolution declaring that 'in order to remove the poverty and misery of the Indian people and to ameliorate the condition of the masses, it is essential to make revolutionary changes in the present economic and social structure of society and to remove gross inequalities'.[2] From this broad enunciation of a general principle the Congress progressed in seven years to the election manifesto of 1936 and finally to the national planning committee. Dominated by its middle-class outlook and wholly nationalistic in sentiment, the Congress had hitherto been cautious towards adoption of any revolutionary proposals for economic reform. Nehru later expressed the view that the resolution of 1929 indicated an approval of socialistic theories, but apart from this general approval and

1 G. D. Birla, A Plea for Planning, printed in *A Path to Prosperity* (1950).

2 *Report National Planning Committee* (1949), p. 35.

some further advances in subsequent resolutions, the Congress did not in any way accept socialism.[1]

The pace nevertheless quickened from now on. Gandhi had long been busy laying the ideological foundation of the party, but from the early thirties Nehru's ideas began to come to the fore-front. The difference in the temperament and outlook of the two leaders was partly responsible for imparting a divided image to the Congress. In fact there were now three discernible divisions in the party. Gandhi and his followers came first, followed by Nehru and the idealists, and in the background were the conservatives. Gandhi's economic and social ideas were not methodically worked out. But one fact is clear: in spite of his unusual views and his opposition to western system of values, the Mahatma always preserved a sense of sanity. His intensely individualistic approach to social questions always gave him a loophole for escape, and he openly adopted the slogan of each man according to his needs.[2] Gandhi, however, was not always fortunate in finding any great intellectual qualities among his followers, some of whom went to bizarre lengths in propounding the most grotesque advocacy of a return to the state of nature. Gandhi's basic ideas were simple. His hostility to industrialization sprang from a conviction that it disturbed social harmony and was based on the principle of exploitation. Socialism on the other hand was a 'beautiful word' because it implied human equality.[3] But any attempt to force equality on the people was not to be thought of. When Jayaprakash Narayan once stated that the Congress Socialist party was advancing a new programme, that of labour and peasant organization as the foundation of a revolutionary mass movement, Gandhi expressed dread of the language used. 'I have organized both,' he commented, 'but not perhaps in the way Shri Jayaprakash has in mind.'[4] Along with his dislike of the possible use of violence as a means of achieving social revolution, went his famous theory of social trusteeship. In 1934 when a section of the Congress party under the lead given by Nehru was moving towards a radical position on social and economic questions, Gandhi gave an interview to the *Madras Mail* during which he is not only supposed to have apologized for Nehru's conduct but also defended the big zamindari system. As Nehru noted with dismay in his *Autobiography*, the system appeared to be sinking of its own weight, 'and yet Gandhiji was in favour of it and talked of trusteeship and the like'.[5] Gandhi himself later stated that at the root of his doctrine of equal distribution of wealth must lie that of the trusteeship of the wealthy for the superfluous wealth possessed by them. According to this 'the rich man will be left in possession of his property for his personal needs and will act as a trustee for the remainder to be used for society.' In this argument he assumed honesty on the part of the trustee.[6] Gandhi's adherence to the principle of individual moral sanctions was absolute and was the starting point of all his assumptions.

If Gandhi's views on social organization and individual conduct were deeply ingrained in the minds of the Congress rank and file, Nehru and other avowed left-wing leaders attempted systematically from 1930 onwards to

[1] *Report National Planning Committee* (1949), p. 36.
[2] *Harijan*, August 25, 1940.
[3] *Ibid.* July 23, 1947.
[4] *Ibid.* January 16, 1940.
[5] Dorothy Norman, *op. cit.* vol. i, p. 327.
[6] *Harijan*, August 25, 1940.

associate the Congress with a radical stand of the western type. In this Nehru was profoundly influenced by the Marxist theory of historical determinism, although typically his humanist outlook caused him to reject formal communist theories. What was happening in India he saw as the part of a world historical development the main feature of which was the decline of capitalism and its corollary the disappearance of economic imperialism. However he interpreted the latter concept in a way different from that of the orthodox Marxists in so much as he associated the working-classes in England with this process, whereas Lenin had argued that investment in empires had the direct consequence of holding down the rates of wages at home.[1] The conviction in Nehru's mind that India's problem, though peculiar in one sense, was also the problem common to the whole world had, as we shall see later, important consequences on the political developments in India. For it led him to the view that the real problem of the world was primarily economic and not political. 'We agitators', stated Nehru, 'are accused of upsetting the State. But the truth is that no agitator has such superhuman powers as to be able to do that. The agitator, though he may temporarily direct the events, merely gives expression to the existing grievances. In India those grievances are agrarian.' He went on to state that the zamindari system was both anachronism and autocracy and that what the world, including India, needed primarily and fundamentally was a plan of social and political foundations laid upon economic justice.[2] To these ideas Nehru returned again and again, and his analysis of India's economic weaknesses was accompanied by the plea for the necessity for positive action. As he expressed it, 'I feel that in these days of economic breakdown of the capitalist order, it is essential for us to lay down a clear economic policy for the national movement'.[3] Gaining of political independence was not enough by itself, the people must be given economic freedom which will inevitably mean that vested interests in India will have to give up their special position and many of their privileges.[4] In a press conference given in London in February 1936 Nehru said that 'we should organize on the socialist basis and have large scale agriculture, co-operative or collective big machine industries . . .'.[5] So far as Nehru was concerned socialist principles and methods of economic development were the only ones that promised to bring about a solution to India's vast economic problems.

How did the Congress party react to this pressure for socialism from one of its most influential members? Nehru himself had expressed hope in 1929 when he was chosen president of the Trade Union Congress, that he might form a link between the labour movement and the National Congress in inducing the latter to become more socialistic and proletarian. If the Congress was to become a revolutionary party representing the masses in India it was clearly imperative to bring in both the organized labour and the peasantry. Nehru and other prominent Congressmen must have seen this and one cannot escape the conclusion that this ulterior political motive was perhaps at the root of the emphasis that Congress came to place on the reform of the

1 *Whither India* (1933); Dorothy Norman, *op. cit.* vol. i, p. 310.
2 *Indian Annual Register* (1933), vol. ii, p. 52.
3 Dorothy Norman, *op. cit.* p. 297.
4 *Ibid.* p. 433.
5 *Ibid.* p. 415.

land system, nationalization, state control, and expropriation. These ideas, however, did not gain currency within the Congress without struggle and resistance from the conservative members. The first Congress resolution dealing with the principles of economic reform was passed at Karachi in August 1931. Since it became the basis for all further resolutions on the subject it may be useful to quote the relevant clauses in full. It was stated that:

(2) (*a*) The organization of economic life must conform to the principle of justice, to the end that it may secure a decent standard of living.

(*b*) The state shall safeguard the interests of industrial workers and shall secure for them, by suitable legislation and in other ways, a living wage, healthy conditions of work, limited hours of labour, suitable machinery for the settlement of disputes between employers and workmen, and protection against the economic consequences of old age, sickness and unemployment.

(3) Labour to be freed from serfdom and conditions bordering on serfdom.

(6) Peasants and workers shall have the right to form unions to protect their interests.

(7) The system of land tenure and revenue and rent shall be reformed and an equitable adjustment made of the burden on agricultural land, immediately giving relief to the smaller peasantry, by a substantial reduction of agricultural rent and revenue now paid by them, and in case of uneconomic holdings, exempting them from rent so long as necessary, with such relief as may be just and necessary to holders of small estates affected by such exemption or reduction in rent, and to the same end imposing a graded tax on net incomes from land above a reasonable minimum.

(12) The State shall protect indigenous cloth; and for this purpose pursue the policy of exclusion of foreign cloth and foreign yarn from the country and adopt such other measures as may be found necessary. The State shall also protect other indigenous industries when necessary against foreign competition.

(14) Currency and exchange shall be regulated in the national interest.

(15) The State shall own or control key industries and services, mineral resources, railways, shipping, and other means of public transport.

(16) Relief of agricultural indebtedness and control of usury, direct and indirect.[1]

Nehru's comment on the economic content of the resolution was that it was only a very short step in the direction of socialism. In fact a capitalist state, according to him, could easily have adopted everything contained in the resolution.[2] The resolution in its entirety was clearly a compromise which respected the views of the conservative members and attempted to incorporate some of the new, albeit somewhat unrealistic, ideas of the progressives. But henceforth the Congress party, whatever may have been the misgivings of the right-wing group, was increasingly committed to these principles under the

[1] *Report National Planning Committee*, pp. 26–9.
[2] *Autobiography*, Dorothy Norman, *op. cit.* p. 248.

twin pressure of its own desire to find a mass appeal and the growing feeling of social ferment in the country of which the growth of the leftist opinion within the Congress was perhaps one of the indications.[1] The formation of the Congress Socialist party of 1934 under the leadership of Jayaprakash Narayan, the numerous socialist conferences in the provinces, and the attempt to organize the peasantry alarmed both the government and the big business elements in the country. Furthermore, Gandhi had now unexpectedly declared his intention of retiring from politics and was engrossed in his village industries association. The government clearly did not believe that the latter merely fulfilled an economic function and when pressed in the legislative assembly early in January 1935 Sir Henry Craik admitted that the government could not rule out the possibility that the association was aimed at creating revolution which was to proceed from the villages.[2] In an administrative report issued by the U.P. government it was pointed out that the most important development in the province during the year 1935 was the growth of the Congress Socialist party, the policy of which was declared to be 'to wreck the reforms to organize the peasants and workers in one corporate mass to overthrow the forces of capitalism and to work for the cancellation of peasants' debts and elimination of landlords and talukdars'. The socialist influence, according to the report, apparently was resulting in an increasing preference on the part of the Congressmen for work among the rural rather than among the urban population.[3] The importance of recruiting the support of the workers and peasants was stressed by Nehru in a Congress pamphlet on labour and peasant organization issued in 1937, and it was because this was now being widely recognized that, he added, all manner of strange people who never had anything to do with the peasantry before were to be found talking in terms of economic programmes.[4] Even the political reactionaries, while expressing fear and hatred of communistic ideas, were beginning to pay lip-service to the prevalent fashion, the most ludicrous example of which was to be seen in a speech of Sir Phiroze Sethna in the council of state given in September 1936. 'A carefully adjusted, socialistic principle,' he said, 'without trying to destroy private property, without showing any unfairness and hostility to capitalism, without seeking to foment class struggle, and to do away with capitalism altogether might not be open to any objection.'[5]

In terms of policy decisions the year 1936 was a busy one for the Congress party. Its agrarian programme issued at the Lucknow session in April was followed by the election manifesto in August and the Faizpur session in December confirmed once again the main heads of the party's rural policy. In his presidential address at these two sessions Nehru offered what was perhaps the most eloquent and comprehensive example of his historical theories and doctrinal beliefs. In his Lucknow speech, after outlining the historical role of the Congress party in the last fifteen years seen against the background of domestic and international politics, Nehru went on to plead the necessity of socialism in India. It was, he declared, not only an economic

[1] Cf. Michael Brecher, *Nehru: A Political Biography* (1959).
[2] *Indian Annual Register* (1935), vol. i, p. 105.
[3] *Ibid.* (1936), vol. i, p. 489.
[4] *Ibid.* (1937), vol. i, pp. 227–8.
[5] Council of State, September 28, 1936, *Indian Annual Register* (1936), vol. ii, p. 68.

doctrine which could end the poverty, vast unemployment, the degradation and the subjection of the Indian people, and bring a new civilization radically different from the present capitalistic order, but in was also a vital creed in which he believed with all his head and heart. Aware of the fact that much of his personal enthusiasm for socialization was not shared by fellow Congressmen, he assured the delegates that he had no intention of forcing this issue on the Congress if it was likely to jeopardize the struggle for independence. But he himself regarded the Congress programme of hand-spinning and village industries as merely a transition stage in India's vital problems, which would inevitably have to make way for rapid large-scale industrialization.[1] There was soon active proof that Nehru's views and plan of popular action were not acceptable to the 'old Guard'. Gandhi had written to Agatha Harrison on April 30th that though Jawaharlal was extreme in the presentation of his methods he was sober in action. He was hopeful that Nehru would not precipitate a conflict of classes and accept the decisions of the majority of his colleagues.[2] On June 29th seven senior members of the working committee which included Rajendra Prasad, Rajagopalachari, Patel, and Kripalani wrote to Nehru offering their resignation as they considered that 'the preaching and emphasizing of socialism particularly at this stage by the President and other socialist members of the working committee while the Congress has not adopted it is prejudicial to the best interests of the country and to the success of the national struggle for freedom . . .'. Nehru was unpleasantly surprised and hurt and it was his turn to threaten resignation. Ultimately, the situation was retrieved through Gandhi's intervention. 'Why should you not allow your humour to play upon the meetings of the W.C.? Why should it be so difficult for you to get on with those with whom you have worked without a jar for years? If they are guilty of intolerance, you have more than your share of it. The country should not be made to suffer for your mutual intolerance,' thus the Mahatma wrote to Nehru.[3]

The result of these stresses within the Congress party meant that its attitude to the question of economic organization and in particular the land problem remained moderate and indecisive. The agrarian programme passed by the Lucknow Congress laid down that 'the most important and urgent problem of the country is the appalling poverty, unemployment and indebtedness of the peasantry fundamentally due to antiquated and repressive land tenure and revenue systems and intensified in recent years by the great slump in prices of agricultural produce. The final solution of this problem inevitably involves the removal of British imperialistic exploitation, a thorough change of the land tenure and revenue systems and a recognition by the State of its duty to provide work for the rural unemployed masses.' A definite agrarian programme was postponed for the time being on the ground that rural conditions and the systems of land tenure varied from province to province and hence the provincial Congress committees and peasant organizations needed to be consulted. The main points on which the latter were asked to make recommendations were the safeguarding of the peasants' interests where there were intermediaries between the state and themselves, the relief

[1] Dorothy Norman, *op. cit.* p. 435. [2] *Ibid.* p. 453.
[3] *Ibid.* pp. 455–60.

of rural indebtedness, and the reduction in rent and revenue demands.[1] It will be seen that nothing was said about the ownership of land, the abolition of the zamindari system or the collectivization of agriculture. Congress thinking on land problem appears to have been still dominated by political considerations and its insistence that the revenue system was solely responsible for the rural backwardness completely ignored other aspects of agricultural economics.[2] The election manifesto provided a further re-statement of the principles already announced at the Karachi and Lucknow sessions. It promised to the peasants tenurial reforms, reduction in rent and revenue demands, and a possible moratorium on debts; to the industrial workers promises were made to 'secure to them a decent standard of living, hours of work, and conditions of labour'.[3]

We have hitherto confined our attention to the Congress views on economic questions. Before we go on to discuss the agrarian legislations carried out by most of the provincial governments between 1938 and 1940, it may be convenient to review briefly the Muslim standpoint. In 1936, the Congress for the first time made an attempt formally to relate the communal problem to the economic ones. In the election manifesto the Congress sounded a warning that 'the whole communal problem in spite of its importance, has nothing to do with the major problems of India – poverty and unemployment. It is not a religious problem and it affects only a handful of people at the top. The peasantry, the workers, the traders, and merchants and the lower middle-class of all communities are in no way touched by it and their burden remains.' The superficial similarity between the Congress economic programmes and those of the Muslim League at the time of the elections of 1936 and the subsequent absence of any great interest in economic matters on the part of the prominent Muslim leaders would seem to confirm the Congress claims. This is to a certain extent a misleading impression. Just as the Congress interest in economics can be shown to have been a mixture of political motives as well as the desire to draw up a plan for a free and independent India, so the Muslim nationalism appears to have had an economic foundation. In the case of the Congress party the force of economic nationalism was primarily directed against the British; in the case of the Muslims it was directed against the Hindus. W. Cantwell Smith in his book *Modern Islam in India* (London, 1946) has forcefully argued that the Muslim separatism was in many cases strengthened and heightened by a sense of economic grievances felt against the Hindus. He has shown these as operating both among the Muslim middle and lower classes. Among the latter when the natural cleavage of economic interests, as for example between peasants and landlords and debtors and money-lenders, also coincided with communal divisions, the communal feelings expressed themselves in violent disturbances, while among the former the lack of widespread economic opportunities resulted in a spasmodic feeling of suspicion and bitterness.[4] This analysis of the Muslim mind has been endorsed by other writers both British and

[1] *Indian Annual Register* (1936), vol. i, p. 250.
[2] Cf. Neale, *op. cit.*
[3] *Indian Annual Register* (1936), vol. ii, pp. 189–91.
[4] W. Cantwell Smith, *Modern Islam in India* (1946), pp. 176–7.

Muslim. Lord Casey (then R. G. Casey) writing of his experiences as governor of Bengal during the war remarked that he believed the principal motive behind the demand for Pakistan to be economic, the expression of an urge on the part of the Muslims to advance themselves economically in the world and to get away from being the hewers of wood and drawers of water for the caste Hindus.[1] Jinnah himself had stated in his presidential address to the Muslim League in October 1937 that 'the Mussalmans all over India are numerically in a minority and weak, educationally backward, and economically nowhere'.[2] The most clear expression of the Muslim feeling of separatism was put forward by Jamil-ud-din Ahmad, a Muslim lecturer in the University of Aligarh, who wrote, 'The chief argument for the Western brand of nationalism is that economic questions know no distinction of Muslim and Hindu. This again is a superficial and false view to take. The economic principles and even economic needs and interests of Muslims and Hindus are different. The various trades, professions, calling and services have become divided on the lines of Muslims and Hindus.... The large majority of Muslims consists of peasants, labourers, petty traders, or men in services.... Muslims are heavily in debt. The Hindus command all positions of power... trade, commerce, industry and high posts. They are also bankers and money-lenders. Naturally, the economic interests of Hindus and Muslims conflict at every point.' [3] It may be argued that just as the Congress often over-stressed its case against British imperialism and the theory of economic exploitation (in the context of the conditions in the 1930s), so the Muslims were exaggerating their case against Hindu capitalists and landlords. Nevertheless, Muslim fears were genuine, and Congress leaders such as Nehru were ignoring the reality when they labelled these as medieval. When Dr S. A. Latif sent a proposal to Nehru for an exchange of population between Hindu and Muslim 'territorial zones', Nehru described it as fantastic. In reply, Dr Latif wrote prophetically, 'You will have to move towards it, even as you move towards a fatality... the spectre of Pakistan alone will stare you in the face tomorrow, if today you fail to use your opportunities to frame a constitution for the country agreeable to all.' [4]

It is not easy to discover the positive side to the Muslim approach to economic questions. The Muslim League has been described as conservative and even reactionary, supported financially by big Muslim landlords.[5] Jinnah certainly appears to have held orthodox and conservative economic views, and disliked any doctrinaire treatment of the economic problems. During his speech to the annual session of the Muslim League in 1937 he declared that all the talk (presumably Congress) of hunger and poverty... is 'intended to lead the people towards socialistic and communistic ideas for which India is far from prepared'.[6] Other leaders such as Maulana Mohani held socialism and nationalism to be inconsistent, while the Raja of Mahmudabad identified socialism, when shorn of its bad points, with the

[1] R. G. Casey, *An Australian in India* (1947), p. 76.
[2] *Speeches and Writings of Mr. Jinnah* (ed. Jamil-ud-din Ahmad), vol. i, p. 28.
[3] Jamil-ud-din Ahmad, *Is India One Nation?* (1941 ?).
[4] S. A. Latif, *The Pakistan Issue* (1943).
[5] Cantwell Smith, *op. cit.* p. 249.
[6] *Ibid.* p. 250.

teachings of Islam. He criticized Lenin for having failed to incorporate the principles of Islam into his programme.[1] Apart from the question of ideological convictions, the Muslim League was in a difficult position. As a party claiming exlusively to represent a particular religious community in India, the League found it difficult to frame a distinctive economic programme and hence could only appeal for efforts to improve the general economic conditions of the Muslims in India. It is conceivable that the leaders of the Muslim League agreed with the Congress that the fundamental economic problems were the same in India for the Hindus and Muslims alike, but in view of their political considerations any public admission of this fact would have amounted to a confession of weakness in the Muslim demand for political separatism. However, even Jinnah could not wholly ignore the current fashion for laying down economic policies and later to a certain extent modified his apparent preference for maintaining the economic *status quo*. In 1943, for example, he gave a warning to the 'landlords and capitalists' who had flourished at the expense of the people by a vicious and wicked system that they would be wise to adjust themselves to the new and modern conditions of life.[2] Again, two years later in an interview, he expressed the view that under modern conditions it was essential for the state to control and manage the essential key industries and certain public utilities, but what was a key industry, he added characteristically, was for the law-makers to say.[3] It must be pointed out that not all Muslims in India agreed with the communal views of the Muslim League or its leader. The land policy of the Krishak Praja Party in Bengal was little different from the policy of the left-wing elements in the Congress, even though its identification with the peasantry and opposition to the permanent settlement served to work against the interests of the predominantly Hindu landowners of Bengal. In fact, the conflict between the League and the K.P.P. in this province has been attributed to the latter's advocacy of radical measures on land questions and the League's dislike of anything that looked like expropriation.[4] There was also the Azad Muslim Party which was vehemently opposed to the idea of a separate Islamic state and one of its leaders Maulavi Abdul Majid stated quite categorically that 'the economic prosperity of the people did not depend on differences of religious convictions but was determined by the vagaries of the present economic system . . . the question of the economic welfare of the Indian people and of Muslims in particular was closely related to the question of independence'.[5] It may be open to question whether moderate Muslim opinions such as these were of any significance in the increasingly violent feelings of communal tension, but a survey of the material available certainly points to a situation of great complexity in which economic, ideological, and political cross-currents, all played their part.

Some of the problems created by the conflicts of interest in Indian society on communal or economic lines can be studied from the debates of the provincial legislative councils on agrarian reforms. The stream of legislation that followed the formation of nationalist governments in the provinces in

[1] *The Statesman*, October 15–18, 1937. [2] *Leader*, April 26, 1943.
[3] *Speeches and Writings of Mr Jinnah*, p. 431. [4] Humayun Kabir, *Muslim Politics* (1944).
[5] *Indian Annual Register* (1940), vol. ii, p 263.

1937 was the expression of the mounting public concern at the deteriorating conditions of the peasantry during the previous decade. As we have already seen, the main Congress attack on the British government in India and its election pledges in 1936 were based on the question of land reform. In the event, however, neither the provincial ministries nor the representatives of the peasants considered the work undertaken as adequate or satisfactory, and the measures were criticized by the landowners, peasants, or the communalists, according to the critics' particular view-point. A thorough reform of the land and revenue system in India was hardly possible under the political conditions prevailing at that time, and in most cases the actual legislation was the outcome of compromise. Only in two provinces, Madras and Orissa, did the Congress governments attempt to initiate radical reforms. In Madras, under the chairmanship of T. Prakasam, the revenue minister, a committee of the legislature recommended that in all areas of the permanent settlement in the province the ryot and not the zamindar should be declared the owner of the soil and the level of rents should be restored to that in 1802.[1] But in spite of extensive discussions in the assembly the government was unable to draft a bill by the time the Congress high command had decided to resign. In Orissa, the Congress efforts were equally abortive. It is true that Biswanath Das, the chief minister, succeeded in passing a bill that drastically reduced the zamindari rents, resulting in many in a reduction of income amounting to fifty to sixty per cent, but the governor-general's assent was withheld and the bill did not become law.[2]

These failures were balanced by the solid achievements gained in the United Provinces, Bihar, and Bombay. The U.P. Tenancy Act of 1939 was perhaps the most comprehensive and ambitious, but here again the Act really was a step forward in the same direction as the previous legislation. It would be tedious to examine the provisions of the Act in detail, most of which were of a technical nature, and it is sufficient for our purpose to note that it provided greater security and freedom in the use of land by the tenants, restricted the rights of owners over private domain (*sir*), and introduced certain new principles in the fixation of rents for the hereditary tenants. In Bihar the tenancy legislation included a general reduction in rents on an average of about twenty-five per cent, strengthening of the peasants' right to transfer land, and it drastically reduced the landlords' power to recover arrears of rent.[3] In most cases the tenancy reforms were accompanied by legislation on peasants indebtedness and attempts were made to provide relief by reducing the legal rates of interest, by regulating the business of the money-lenders and in some cases by cancellation or reduction of interest on debts incurred before a certain date.[4] The Congress efforts to secure agrarian changes were fully matched by those in provinces where a predominantly Muslim ministry was in power. The Bengal Tenancy (Amendment) Bill brought in by Fazlul-Haq was very similar to the Congress bill in Bihar, while in the Punjab the government of Sir Sikandar Hyat Khan passed a

[1] R. Coupland, *The Constitutional Problem in India* (1945), part ii, pp. 137–8.
[2] *Ibid.*
[3] Neale, *op. cit.* p. 117, Rajendra Prasad, *Autobiography* (1957), p. 454.
[4] Coupland, *op. cit.* p. 140.

whole series of Acts which strengthened and carried forward the provisions of the Punjab Alienation of Land Act 1900 and greatly added to the restrictions already imposed on the mortgaging and alienation of land for agricultural indebtedness.

Useful as these measures were, they naturally did not entirely satisfy the various parties concerned. Although most of the provincial ministries were bound by the electoral promises made to the peasants, it was not possible to adopt a revolutionary solution to the problem of 'landlordism' owing to the presence of a large number of landowners in the provincial legislative assemblies.[1] In U.P. the passage of the Tenancy Bill was interminably delayed by the opposition of the landlords.[2] In Bihar, the Congress openly negotiated with the zamindars for a compromise and the chief minister Shri Krishna Sinha assured the latter in the assembly that it was not the policy of the government to cause the least harm to the zamindars who, he said, played an important part in the economic system of the country.[3] The Congress–zamindar agreement in Bihar was severely criticized by the *Kisan Sabhas* in the province, and under the leadership of Swami Sahajanand large scale peasant disturbances took place. In many ways, the previous Congress agitations in favour of land reforms had aroused the hopes of the peasantry to exaggerated lengths which the Congress ministers now found difficult to fulfil with the consequence that they were now denounced as bitterly as the landlords. Although the demonstrations and agitations by the peasants in Bihar and U.P. did not get out of hand, in these years the Congress had an important object lesson in the dangers of using economic and social discontent in general as the basis for organizing political action.[4] While the peasantry on the one hand remained dissatisfied, the landlords were equally antagonized. During the landholders' conference in December 1938, the Maharaja of Dharbhanga declared that it was the duty of the landlords to strengthen the hands of the government and to co-operate with those who had made no secret of their disapproval of the violent and revolutionary methods, for the Congress left-wing, he went on to say, are openly 'fomenting class hatred, violence and unrest . . .'.[5] In Bengal during the reading of the Tenancy Bill the landholders' group staged a walk-out under the direction of Maharaja Santosh and threatened to appeal to the British parliament for the vindication of the permanent settlement which they considered as the bulwark of the economic structure of Bengal.[6]

A different source of opposition to the agrarian legislations came from the misrepresentations made by the communalists. The most violent denunciation of Congress motives was perhaps to be seen in the writings of Jamil-ud-din Ahmad. 'Congressmen', he wrote, 'feel no scruple or shame in opposing the Tenancy Bill of the Bengal Government because most of the landlords there are Hindus and the peasants Muslims. But in the U.P. they insist on an ill-conceived and crooked tenancy law to persecute the landlords, no matter whether it would do real good to peasants or not, for the Muslims have some share in the land ownership. . . . But in Bihar, where Hindu landlords are

[1] Coupland, *op. cit.* p. 140.
[2] Rajendra Prasad, *op. cit.* p. 459.
[3] *Indian Annual Register* (1938), vol. ii, p. 398.
[4] Coupland, *op. cit.* part ii, p. 126.
[5] *Indian Annual Register* (1938), vol. ii, p. 398.
[6] *Ibid.* (1938), vol. i, p. 163.

strong, the Congress readily entered into a compromise with them over the tenancy question.' These allegations were made in spite of the fact that the leader of the Congress party had declared in the Bengal legislative council that his party was not prepared to oppose the passage of the tenancy bill, even though it was only a half-hearted measure and did not go far enough to improve the conditions of the cultivators.[1] In U.P. the Muslim members of the legislative assembly also alleged that the Congress rural development schemes were only meant to strengthen the latter's party organization.[2] It must be pointed out that the behaviour of the Congress members and the extreme Hindu leaders in the Punjab were similar when the government attempted to introduce legislation controlling the money-lenders and these bills were declared 'black bills', and violently attacked in the legislature and Congress newspapers. On July 16, 1938 Sir G. C. Narang stated that the trading and money-lending classes should understand that they could not expect anything from the government which was bent on destroying credit in trade and industry and setting back the clock of political advancement. In reply, Sir Sikandar Hyat Khan vigorously denied that the bills were either a class or communal measure. They were intended to apply equally to all classes and communities, to banias as well as to Pathans.[3] These charges and counter-charges perhaps illustrate more than anything else how in those days in India even issues that needed to be judged on independent criterion could be distorted by a fusion of nationalist and communal feelings.

The outbreak of the war in the autumn of 1939 brought far-reaching changes to the Indian economy which was subjected to unusual stresses during the next five years. Its immediate effect was a spectacular rise in the prices of food-grains and other essential commodities, although the pattern of this increase was uneven. There was also a great improvement in the volume of industrial production and the level of employment and wages. But with the growing demands made on the economy as the war efforts intensified, the country was gradually faced with serious shortages of both consumer goods and food supplies, which reached its most disastrous climax in the Bengal famine of 1943. Although inflation in India generally led to an increase of money incomes, the effects of the price rise were injurious to large sections of the community which had failed to secure a share in the adjustment in the national income. In the early years of the war, however, after the experience of the world depression, there was much public satisfaction at the new turn of events. It was contended that as India was an agricultural country, the rise in the agricultural prices was generally beneficial to the people. In the council of state in March 1940, one speaker even moved a resolution expressing concern at the government's price control policy and demanded that no action should be taken to arrest what he described as a normal rise in the price of agricultural produce. In reply, Sir Ramaswamy Mudalier, the commerce member, stated that the government could hardly base its price control policy on any consideration of buying loyalty by allowing prices to go up.[4] Eventually, as the public came to realize that the

[1] Jamil-ud-din Ahmad, *op. cit.* [2] *Indian Annual Register* (1938), vol. i, p. 186.
[3] Coupland, *op. cit.* part ii, pp. 53–4; *Indian Annual Register* (1938), vol. ii, p. 196.
[4] Council of State, *Debates*, March 4, 1940.

financing of India's contribution to the war involved both a drain on her real resources and an inflationary spiral, the government was once again criticized for not adopting positive measures earlier on. It was pointed out that it was not until 1943 that the government appointed a foodgrain policy committee and took measures to introduce price fixation, rationing, and control of supplies. Furthermore, it was alleged that where a country was already at the lowest level of subsistence, the need for a big production drive was urgent and if the government had undertaken an intensified programme to increase production and implemented the recommendations of the Grady mission from the United States the conditions of India would have been different.[1] The view that the inflationary conditions in India were the result of the official policy of allowing the money supplies to expand against sterling balances held to India's credit in London was rejected by G. D. Birla who wrote an article in which he expressed the view that no amount of currency deflation or curtailment of prices or freezing of income would solve the problem of scarcity. The only solution was to produce more food and more cloth and other consumption goods. To the question whether production could be increased, he replied that it 'could be increased and enormously if government were capable of inspiring, planning and mobilizing the country's mind and capacity'.[2]

Whatever may have been the shortcomings of the government in dealing with the economic problems during those difficult days, there is little doubt that the war brought fundamental changes in its attitude and approach to economic questions. The increased sense of purpose and direction on the part of the government expressed itself in two directions. There was in the first place much discussion on the post-war reconstruction of India's economy and secondly much greater emphasis was now put on the role of the state and the need for central planning. The idea of planning was not new to India. Professional economists had been discussing it for years and here again the Congress had taken the lead in formulating a definite policy in regard to planning. Since the government's attitude to planning during the war years was in effect an acceptance of the ideas first put forward by the Congress, it may be permissible to digress here for a moment and review briefly the latter's stand-point on planning. In 1938 under the initiative of Subhas Chandra Bose, the Congress president for that year, a resolution was passed at the conference of provincial ministers of industries held in Delhi that 'the problem of poverty and unemployment, of National Defence and of the economic regeneration in general cannot be solved without industrialization. As a step towards such industrialization a comprehensive scheme of National Planning should be formulated.' This scheme was to provide 'for the development of heavy key industries, medium scale industries and cottage industries, keeping in view our national requirements, the resources of the country, as also the peculiar circumstances prevailing in the country'.[3] Eventually, a national planning committee was set up under the chairmanship of Nehru who took the most active part in its work, and the report of the committee was published in twenty-six volumes. The main emphasis of the committee

[1] Lokanathan, *op. cit.* p. 38. [2] Quoted in above, p. 29.

[3] *Report National Planning Committee*, p. 5.

was placed in giving overall direction to economic development in general. As Nehru stated in a memorandum in February 1940, 'It is important to bear in mind that the outlook governing a planned scheme is different from the outlook of an unplanned private economy. It is this outlook which must be kept in view in drawing up the plan, so that all the different sections of the plan may be integral and co-ordinated parts of the full programme. Such control as may be necessary to bring this about will have to be taken by the State.' [1] The necessity for the state control of defence and other key industries was reiterated and the committee took some trouble to point out, in order to reassure the Gandhians, that the promotion of large-scale industries would not mean a discontinuation of the cottage industries in the rural areas.

Nehru himself did not regard the work done by the national planning committee as anything but modest. It was essentially an academic exercise in preparation for the days when Indians could hope to control their own economic destiny, and with the outbreak of the war and the Congress involvement in other serious political issues the national planning committee languished into inactivity. However, the government itself now began to take interest in the prospect of planning India's economic future after the war. In his budget speech in 1941 Sir Jeremy Raisman, the finance member, declared that the steadily increasing industrial efforts now made in India were likely to place her among the industrial nations of the world. 'The expansion in the demand for the products of Indian industry,' he continued, 'and the organized efforts which Government are making to increase the supply of trained workers must create an enhanced productive power which will be available in the period after the war, to improve the standard of life in India and to help to lessen the dependence of its growing population upon agriculture and secondary employment.' [2] Addressing the associated chamber of commerce in December, the viceroy himself gave an assurance that not only was the government prepared to grant some form of protection to the specific industries started under the stimulus of the war but the question of post-war economy with special reference to industrial development was being closely studied.[3] The upshot of these discussions was that the government set up an inter-departmental committee for investigating the problems of post-war reconstruction, and in March 1943 this was enlarged to a committee of the viceroy's council, known as the reconstruction committee of the council. Finally, in 1944 the government created a department of planning and development under Sir Ardeshir Dalal with powers to co-ordinate and centrally direct the plans prepared by the various government departments.

The government's interest in planning appears to have been greatly stimulated by the publication of a plan for the economic development of India which was prepared by eight prominent Bombay industrialists and published in January 1944. The main objective of the plan was to double the *per capita* income in a period of about fifteen years, which was to be achieved by raising the output from agriculture by 130 per cent, from industry by 500 per cent and from services by 200 per cent. It also dealt with broad lines of development in respect of agriculture, transport, industry, education,

[1] *Report National Planning Committee*, p. 140.
[2] *Indian Annual Register* (1941), vol. i, pp. 164–5. [3] *Ibid.* (1941), vol. ii, p. 287.

housing, and public health.[1] Although the government expressed reservations about the plan, particularly in regard to the methods to be followed, the part played by the state and private enterprise, and its financial practicability, its own statement of post-war development policy published in 1944 went far to recognize the 'need for planning for the whole of India and the exercise of far more initiative by the State than hitherto in matters of social reform and economic development'.[2] The report went on to state that, since the ultimate object of all planning must be to raise the standard of living, it was essential to increase the purchasing-power of the people by improved efficiency and productivity of labour on the one hand and a simultaneous development and re-organization of agriculture, industries, and services on the other. The recommendations of the report on specific measures to be adopted to transform India's war-time economy to conditions of peace were confirmed by the government's statement of industrial policy issued in 1945. The need for such a statement arose from the fact that it was felt that 'the general economic policy pursued by the Government of India under their own constitutional powers exercises a profound influence over industrial development'. Secondly, it was recognized that the progress of planning made it abundantly clear that certain industries must be taken over under central control in the interests of co-ordinated development. The fundamental objects of industrialization were declared to be threefold; to increase national wealth by the maximum exploitation of the country's resources, to make the country better prepared for defence, and finally to provide a high and stable level of employment.[3] It will be seen that by 1945 there was little difference between the views of the government and those of the Congress on planning, although the government clearly hesitated to lay down any specific targets or adopt a doctrinaire approach to economic planning. However, the political implications of planning by the government were raised both by the European group and the Muslim League during the debates on post-war economic development in March 1945. Alarmed by its possible consequences on constitutional development, the latter had demanded that the financial provisions under the head 'post-war planning and development' in the budget should be reduced to one rupee, and Sir Ardeshir Dalal felt it necessary to assure the League members that the whole idea of planning was without prejudice to the idea of Pakistan, although he himself did not personally believe in Pakistan.[4]

We now come to the last point in our inquiry, namely the economic implications of the partition of India. It is necessary at the outset to stress the fact that the actual process of the partition was carried through purely as a constitutional and political issue. It will be wrong to state that there was no discussion at all of the economic implications, but there is little evidence to suggest that economic considerations played anything but a marginal role in the political division of India. Campbell-Johnson, for example, mentions only two occasions when the question of the economic viability of Pakistan

[1] *Plan for Economic Development of India* (1944).
[2] *Reconstruction Committee of Council: Post-war Development Policy* (1944).
[3] *Statement of Industrial Policy* (1945).
[4] *Indian Annual Register* (1945), vol. i, pp. 174–5.

was discussed by the viceroy's advisers only to reach the conclusion that the western part of Pakistan, i.e. the Punjab, *may be* a practicable proposition.[1] Nevertheless, with the emergence of the demand for Pakistan following the Lahore resolution of the Muslim League in 1940 the economic aspects of a possible partitioned India were considered from time to time. Most of the discussion turned on the question whether an independent Islamic state comprising those provinces of India where the Muslims were in a majority would have the necessary financial and natural resources to stand on its own. Arguments were advanced for or against the idea of Pakistan from both sides according to their respective political convictions, although on the balance there seemed to be a general consensus of opinion even among impartial observers that an independent Pakistan would be at a serious economic disadvantage compared with India, though the latter also could not hope to escape from the injurious effects of the proposed partition. Such was the view of Nehru in 1942 when in a letter to Dr Latif he pointed out that a united India contained nearly all the important elements and resources which could make her a strong and more or less self-sufficient nation, and that 'to cut her up would be from the economic point of view – a fatal thing, breaking up that natural economic unity and weakening each part'[2] Jinnah himself resorted to the same type of arguments when it was his turn to defend the unity of the Punjab and Bengal against the Hindu demand for a partition of these provinces. 'If such a process were to be adopted', he said in April 1947, 'it will strike at the root of the administrative, economic, and political life of the provinces which have for nearly a century developed and been built up on that basis.'[3] The similarity in the arguments of the two leaders who held such diametrically opposite views on other matters demonstrates that economic considerations were very small counters in the political bargaining that brought about the partition.

One of the main difficulties in assessing the economic consequences of a divided India was the fact that no one knew with certainty what was to be the exact territorial demarcation of Pakistan. The Muslim League had demanded that Pakistan should be composed of two zones, 'North-West and North-East, comprising six provinces, namely Sindh, Baluchistan, North-West Frontier Province, the Punjab, Bengal and Assam, subject to territorial adjustments that may be agreed upon'. However, it may be doubted whether Jinnah or other Muslim leaders ever entertained serious hopes of securing Pakistan on this territorial basis, and this together with the fact that even the demand for Pakistan was not generally conceded may explain why the League's economic programmes and plans remained vague and indefinite. But there were signs that Muslim economic nationalism was daily becoming more aggressive and self-confident. Demands were made in the central legislative assembly that the government should not recognize trade unions unless they were communal or sectional, that a quota should be fixed for Muslims and other minorities in the selection of grades in the services, and that representatives of the Muslim League should be associated with 'the officials and

[1] A. Campbell-Johnson, *Mission with Mountbatten* (1951).
[2] Latif, *op. cit.*
[3] *Leader*, May 1, 1947.

capitalists at every stage in the planning and execution of schemes of production and distribution'.[1] While generally exhorting the Muslims to improve their economic conditions and participate more in the commerce and industries, Jinnah had stated categorically in April 1941 that the aim of the Muslim League was to establish a completely independent state in the north west and eastern zones of India with full control of finance, defence, foreign affairs, communications, customs, currency and exchanges.[2] Nor was he to be deterred by arguments of the financial unsoundness of Pakistan. In 1941, a Muslim writer, Reazul Karim, arguing against the idea of Pakistan, had stated, 'If it comes into being the only question we will have to consider is what will be its economic effect upon the demand of Pakistan. . . . Do you want Pakistan at any cost, for the benefit of the Moslims? If you want it at any cost, then no ground is necessary for its support. But if you want it for the benefit of the Moslims, then certainly its economic aspect should be considered. . . . If it is proved sound economically and financially, then its acceptance might have some meaning.' [3] The answer to this type of question appears to have been given by Jinnah in an interview to the correspondents of the *New York Times* in 1942 when he remarked that 'if we are willing to live sensibly and poorly so long as we have freedom, why should the Hindus object? . . . The economy will take care of itself in time.' [4] There were also other, more positive justifications for the economic prospects of Pakistan. The agricultural products of the western zones it was pointed out, were not only enough for the requirements of these areas but also provided surpluses for the rest of India. In Bengal the export crops such as cotton, jute, and tea would create the basis of a prosperous economy, and in all these discussions it was automatically assumed that Calcutta with its port facilities and industrial areas would be included in Pakistan.[5] In 1943, the Muslim League authorized the president to appoint a planning committee to prepare a comprehensive scheme for economic advancement which would include state industrialization in Pakistan zones, introduction of free primary education, reform of the land system, stabilization of rent, security of tenure and improvement in the condition of labour and agriculture.[6] Characteristically, Jinnah stated that the aim of his planning committee would be to examine the problems in practical terms and 'not plan out schemes of hundred thousand crores depending upon the release of Mr. Gandhi and the establishment of a National Government'.[7]

The financial and economic viability of Pakistan was examined among others by Sir Reginald Coupland, R. Casey, and the Sapru committee on constitutional proposals. Sir Reginald calculated that on the basis of the main heads of revenue and expenditure for 1938–9, the western zone of Pakistan with no alteration in the provincial boundaries would have a small surplus of about 2,97 lakhs of rupees. But his estimates of expenditure excluded defence which he held to be the crux of the financial problem for

[1] *Leader*, March 26, 1941; *Indian Annual Register* (1943), vol. i, pp. 167, 287.
[2] *Leader*, March 16, 1941.
[3] Reazul Karim, *Pakistan Examined* (1941).
[4] Quoted in *Constitutional Proposals of the Sapru Committee* (1945), Appendix III, p. xix.
[5] Ikbal Ali Shah, *A Plan for India*, p. 39; East Pakistan Renaissance Society, *East Pakistan: its population, delimitations and Economics* (1944).
[6] *Indian Annual Register* (1943), vol. ii, pp. 293–4; (1944), vol. i, p. 211.
[7] *Ibid.*

Pakistan. So far as the financial prospects of the north-east were concerned, the outlook was more speculative and depended on whether Calcutta and the industrial sectors of western Bengal would be included within Pakistan.[1] Very similar were the views of the Sapru sub-committee which was asked to examine the economic and financial problems arising out of the partition of India. The opinion of Sir Homi Mody and Dr John Matthai (to which the third member of the committee, N. R. Sarkar, dissented) was that judged solely by the test of ability to maintain existing standards of living and to meet budgetary requirements on a pre-war basis but excluding provision for defence, the partition would be workable on economic grounds. But they warned that if provision had to be made for future economic development and for measures of adequate defence both 'Hindustan' and Pakistan would suffer unless there was some considerable economic co-operation between the two countries. Even with this latter reservation, Sir Homi Mody stated, he would be prepared to recommend, if the Muslim League insisted on a division, only on a 'district-wise' Pakistan. The grounds on which N. R. Sarkar based his dissent from the others are now familiar. In the first place, there was the disparity in the mineral and other resources necessary for development of industries between India and Pakistan. The Pakistan areas had very little reserves of coal and practically no iron ores. The actual industrial resources were equally meagre. Although Pakistan produced forty per cent of the total raw cotton of undivided India, only 15 cotton mills were located there against 857 in India, while most of its jute was exported and processed through Calcutta which possessed all the jute mills in Bengal (111). Furthermore, even if it was possible to introduce some form of modern industry, he argued, the limited size of the domestic market would prove a serious obstacle to efficient production. He concluded his report with the remarks: 'If in order to make Pakistan economically feasible, we have to give away the rich districts of Bengal then one might as well propose to add even more territories to Pakistan, in order to make it even more rich and self-sufficient. Pakistan on the basis of contiguous districts is the only logical basis on the principle of religious division. But then it would be extremely poor, barely able to maintain the existing deplorable standards of living, while the cost of defence would present a formidable problem to its exchequer.'[2] Ultimately, none of these considerations had any effect on the proposal to partition India, and the actual financial and economic problems such as the division of the assets and liabilities of the government of India, the separation of the currency and banking systems, or trade and customs across the frontiers, were settled by a series of agreements between the two governments which, without raising any questions of sovereign rights, partially restored the economic unity which India had enjoyed before August 15, 1947. Although the immediate economic dislocation caused by the partition was large and in some cases catastrophic, subsequent events proved that neither of the two countries in spite of their political differences could exist without some measure of economic and commercial co-operation.

[1] Coupland, *op. cit.* part iii, p. 91–6.
[2] *Constitutional Proposals* . . ., pp. 143–5; Appendix III.

PERSPECTIVES AND REFLECTIONS

THE BACKGROUND OF THE PARTITION OF THE INDO-PAKISTAN SUB-CONTINENT

by MUMTAZ HASAN

Before independence, when the Muslims were struggling for Pakistan, a number of European and American voices were heard against the Pakistan movement. The British government was officially opposed to the partition of the sub-continent, and it was a refreshing exception to find a man like Beverly Nichols supporting the idea. Since independence, the same kind of attitude has persisted even in well-informed and well-meaning quarters. The argument is that most of the Muslims in the sub-continent are local converts and are of the same race as the non-Muslims. The outsiders have been comparatively few, and form no more than a fraction of the total Muslim population. Thus, the race being largely the same, why should there be two countries instead of one? I have always found it difficult to understand this argument, particularly when it emanates from European and American quarters.

Let us take the Europe of today. According to experts, there is a basic racial unity in the European sub-continent. 'The racial characteristic of the Europe of today', says Professor Dixon of Harvard, 'is the dominance of the Alpine and Palae-Alpine types. Except for portions of Southern Scandinavia, the Western Baltic lands and shores of the North Sea, the British Isles and the Iberian Peninsula, Corsica, Sardinia, Sicily and Southern Italy, together with small areas in West Central France and South Eastern Russia, the whole continent is dominated by brachycephalic types, which are themselves central, whereas the dolichocephalic types are mainly marginal'. Let us add to this the fact that the civilization and culture of Europe as a whole has a Graeco-Roman foundation. There is also a common background of historical experience in the shape of the Roman empire, the spread of Christianity, the crusades, the renaissance and the reformation. The development of the fine arts also has an all-European basis. For example, even now Russian music, ballet and theatre, in spite of their communist environment, are a part of European culture. So are Goethe, Shakespeare, Dante, Voltaire, Victor Hugo, Ibsen, Dostoevsky, Tolstoy, Pasternak and even Sholokov. So too are the musicians, men like Beethoven, Mozart and Leopardi; the artists, such as Leonardo da Vinci, Michelangelo, Rubens, and Titian; the philosophers, such as Socrates, Plato, Kant, Rousseau, Schopenhauer, Nietschze and Bergson, and the scientists, like Newton, Einstein, Max Planck, Madame Curie, Pavlov and Heisenberg. The Europeans have the same classics, the same Greek and Latin sources of inspiration, the same scientific outlook, the same way of living, and the same approach to the basic problems of life. And yet there are more than twenty countries in Europe, which are most of the time uneasy in each other's company. Similarly in South America, we find a common religion and language as well as largely common ethnic characteristics, and yet there are so many different countries in the area with their own political ambitions and aspirations. On the other hand, in the United States, which is pre-eminently a melting-pot of nationalities, where populations have migrated from all parts of Europe and the rest of the world, and where a new world outlook is developing, the old national groups still persist and are likely to continue for some time before they are assimilated fully into the American system.

The explanation for the existing multiplicity and diversity of states in the western world may partly lie in the existence of separate linguistic groups (we may even say perhaps, in this context, that American English is different from English English, Canadian French from French French, and Swiss German from German German) even though there are, on the other hand, also some conspicuously multi-lingual states like Canada, Switzerland, and the USSR. The more important reason seems to be the geographical divisions introduced by mountains and rivers and the impact of historical accident on the group consciousness of various units of population which now receive inspiration mainly from the highly emotional idea of 'the glory of the Fatherland' and their military and economic superiority over other national groups which helps them to establish political hegemony over them.

We have seen how, in spite of a large measure of racial and cultural unity, the western world is divided into so many independent states whose friendliness towards each other cannot always be taken for granted. Is there anything very strange, then, in the existence of two independent states in the Indo-Pakistan sub-continent? Let us look into the matter a little more closely.

In the first place, is it a fact, let us ask, that Pakistan and India are racially of the same stock? Let us also ask whether the sub-continent is inhabited by one race? I am afraid that the answer to both questions is in the negative. Even as far back as the Indus Valley civilization, the answer was in the negative. The human remains discovered during the excavations at Mohenjodaro, as Sewell and Guha tell us,[1] disclose the existence of at least four racial types, the proto-Australoid, the Mediterranean, the Mongolian branch of the Alpine stock and the Alpine. This was the position in pre-historic times. As we all know, in course of time, many ethnic groups, such as the Aryans, the Scythians, the Kushans, the Huns and the Semite migrated to this sub-continent, peacefully or otherwise. This racial diversity, according to Professor Dixon, lies at the root of the caste system in India. His analysis of the data available led him to the conclusion 'that caste groups do differ from each other racially, and that the social status of the caste usually bears a direct relation to the racial composition of its members'.[2]

So much for ethnic unity. As regards language, according to Mario Pei, 'India has thirty-three major tongues along with a host of minor tongues and dialects'.[3] At present, while Pakistan shares some languages with India – notably Bengali, Panjabi and Urdu – there is a growing gulf between the two countries. Urdu, which developed as a result of Hindu-Muslim contact in the days of Muslim rule and which was the *lingua franca* of the larger part of

1 Sir John Marshall, *Mohenjodaro and the Indus Civilization* (1931), pp. 599 ff.
2 Roland B. Dixon, *The Racial History of Man* (1923), p. 269.
3 Mario Pei, *The Story of Language* (1952), p. 288.

the sub-continent before independence, has in India been officially replaced by highly sanskritized Hindi, which cannot be understood by the people of Pakistan. Similarly the Bengali language in East Pakistan has shown a different trend from the Bengali of West Bengal and Calcutta, both in form and content. At the official level, English is the only contact language between the two countries.

The next question to consider is whether the sub-continent was at anytime a political unit in the true sense of the word. Starting from about 500 B.C. which represents the dawn of recorded history in the sub-continent, we find that before the advent of the Muslims, the sub-continent, as a whole, was hardly ever consolidated into a single political and administrative unit, except, perhaps, for a few years under Ashoka. With the Muslim conquest, the larger part of the sub-continent was brought under centralized control and during the reign of Alauddin Khalji in the fourteenth century, Malik Kafoor, a famous general, also subdued almost the entire region of south India. Subsequently disintegration set in and it was not till the Mughals came to power that India was again ruled by a strong hand at the centre. After the death of Aurangzeb in 1707, the provincial governors gradually became independent, even though some semblance of allegiance to the Mughal throne was maintained for some time in certain cases. In any case, the sub-continent was far from being politically united when the British took over. Indeed, the lack of political unity was one of the main reasons for the success of the new rulers.

The British, who ruled the larger part of the sub-continent for two hundred years and the whole of it for a century, consolidated the administration of the sub-continent with the help of roads, railways, posts and telegraphs and improved inland water transport. Towards the end, air communications were also established within the country. Incidentally, Burma was also a part of British India until it was separated from India in 1937, ten years before the sub-continent itself was partitioned. Burma had never been part of India, and its inclusion in the British Indian dominions gave the whole British administration an artificial complexion. Moreover, the British were always regarded as foreign rulers and their consolidation of the sub-continent was based on considerations of their own administrative convenience rather than any process of inner political evolution. The consolidation did not grow from within; it was imposed from without. Nevertheless, when in the latter half of the nineteenth century the British government began to think of the devolution of political power to the people of the country and constitutional reforms began by instalments, the Hindu intellectuals of the time were quick to take advantage of the British consolidation of the sub-continent. Having come into contact with European ideas of nationalism and democracy, these politically conscious intellectuals, who were the main force behind the newly formed Indian National Congress, which the British Indian government under Lord Dufferin had themselves promoted and fostered, saw a rare opportunity before them, and in the name of democratic freedom began to claim India for the Indians, which in effect came to mean: for the majority community. The majority of the Muslims, who regarded themselves as a distinct and separate community, did not take kindly to this nationalistic but impracticable view of a future Indian democracy which did not include adequate safeguards for them as a separate people. As the British government desired to associate the people with the administration in increasing measure, particularly in the shape of the Montagu-Chelmsford reforms of 1919 and the establishment of provincial autonomy in 1937, the scramble for power and position in the political and administrative set-up of the country became more and more bitter and the relations between the Hindus and Muslims deteriorated progressively. Communal riots became so common that the period from 1913 onwards, with a brief interval for the Lucknow pact and the non-co-operation movement of 1921, can best be described as one of continued civil war. The Simon commission counted 112 major communal riots in the sub-continent in the five years 1923–27. The subsequent period was, if anything, worse than this. Under these conditions the Muslim political leaders, who had been active since the foundation of the All-India Muslim League at Dacca in 1906, concentrated their attention on devising safeguards for their people against the dominance of the Hindu majority in a democratic India. The Minto-Morley reforms of 1909 had conceded separate electorates to Muslims but this was only the beginning of the solution.

Subsequent events were, however, not encouraging. The partition of Bengal in 1905, which Lord Curzon undertook as an administrative measure, and the consequent establishment of a new province of Eastern Bengal and Assam, which incidentally was a province with a Muslim majority, was violently opposed by the Hindus. Its annulment, which was announced by King George V at the Delhi Durbar of 1911, was an occasion of deep frustration for the Muslims and great jubilation for the Hindus. Notwithstanding these adverse developments, Muhammad Ali Jinnah, who was at the time was president of the All-India Muslim League though still a member of the Indian National Congress and dedicated to the cause of a united India, negotiated the Lucknow pact with the Indian National Congress. The pact confirmed and extended the principle of separate electorates for the Muslims in the central and provincial legislatures with reservation of seats, but this could be achieved only at the expense of their majority in the crucial provinces of the Punjab and Bengal. The Muslims regarded this as too high a price to pay as the pact gave them no effective voice either in the minority provinces or in the Punjab and Bengal where they were in a majority. The atmosphere of goodwill built up by the pact was short-lived and there was a renewal of communal tension after the Montagu-Chelmsford reforms of 1919 transferred power to the elected representatives of the people.

The non-co-operation movement, which brought the Hindus and Muslims nearer each other than at any time before and as a result of which the Hindus, under the leadership of Mahatma Gandhi, all but succeeded in destroying the Muslims as a political entity, was followed by the severely communal movements of *shuddhi* and *sanghtan*, which aimed at the wholesale conversion of the Muslims or their expulsion from the sub-continent. The Muslim reaction to this took the form of the *tabligh* and *tanzeem* movements, which sought to promote Muslim missionary activity and the political solidarity of the Muslim community. It is significant that the leaders of both these movements were some of the former leaders of Hindu-Muslim unity, namely Swami Shardhanand, Dr Moonje and Pandit Malaviya on the one hand and Dr Saifuddin Kitchlu on the other. The foundation of the aggressive anti-Muslim Rashtriya Sewak Sangh in 1925 and the increase in the activities of the militant All-India Hindu Mahasabha increased the fears of the Muslims still further. There were numerous attempts by Muslim leaders, including Jinnah's famous 'Fourteen Points', to arrive at some solution which might provide satisfactory safeguards to the Muslim community. No such solution was forthcoming, as none was acceptable to the Hindus.

The Nehru report, which represented the thinking of the Hindu-dominated Nehru committee about the future constitution of the sub-continent, recommended a unitary form of government and repudiated the principles of separate electorates and weightage for the Muslims in the provinces in which they were in a minority. This report was followed by the publication of the report of the Simon commission which represented British thinking about future constitutional reforms. From the Muslim point of view, this report also went against them, particularly on the issues of their adequate representation in the Punjab and Bengal assemblies, and on raising the status of the Frontier and Baluchistan provinces. The report was followed by two Round Table conferences in London, at which political leaders from the sub-continent were invited and asked to agree on a scheme for the future, particularly on the issue of representation for various communities. No settlement, however, was reached at these conferences, with the result that the British prime minister, Ramsay MacDonald, had to give his own award on the issue. The award, while conceding the continuance of separate electorates, maintained the previous position in regard to the majority provinces of the Punjab and Bengal where the Muslim majority was not allowed to be reflected in the legislature. All this added to the disappointment of the Muslims.

In the rapidly changing world around them, the Muslims, who were poorer and less educated than the Hindus and had little influence in the administration, were pre-occupied with the idea of preserving themselves as a political and social entity in the sub-continent. They could not, however, think of anything except the somewhat negative approach implied in the demand for safeguards. This led them nowhere, and their frustration increased. It was left to Iqbal to realize that the Muslims needed a state of their own in order to be able to live their life as a people in their own way. This idea of an independent Muslim state now seems to us to have been the obvious solution, but, strange as it may seem, it appeared as a revolutionary idea at the time.

It is hardly possible to understand the political struggle without taking note of two factors which are of basic importance: the economic position of the Muslims and their status as a distinct and separate cultural entity. I have dealt with the subject at length elsewhere, and would content myself with a brief resumé of the position on the present occasion.

Let us take up the economic factor first. The Muslims ruled the sub-continent for more than a thousand years and while their administration was moderate and considerate (had it been otherwise, it could not have continued for a thousand years) their own position as rulers was one of undisputed advantage. They had hardly any economic problem to worry about. When, however, their political power declined and the East India Company supplanted them as rulers, they suffered loss of wealth and social status along with the loss of their political position. The British, who had taken power from them, had no particular reason to trust them. On the contrary, they began to take early steps to make sure that the Muslims were reduced to a position of helplessness. In Bengal, for instance, after Lord Clive took the Diwani from the Emperor Shah Alam in 1765, the Muslims, who held a majority of posts in the revenue and judicial departments and in the military, lost these avenues of employment. Again, their educational system suffered because the East India Company discontinued the grants given by Muslim kings and nobles to Muslim educational institutions. In 1793, Lord Cornwallis, the governor-general of India, introduced the permanent settlement of Bengal which, in the words of James O'Kinealy, 'elevated the Hindu collectors, who up to that time had but unimportant posts, to the position of landlords, gave them a proprietary right in the soil, and allowed them to accumulate wealth which would have gone to the Muslims under their own rule'. On the other hand, the old Muslim zamindars, formerly the lords of all they surveyed, were reduced to poverty and destitution. Sir William Hunter has given us a picture of the misfortune that had overtaken the once powerful Muslim community in India. In 1837, when Persian was replaced by English in the company's offices, the prospects of employment for Muslims diminished still further. The British policy was to cultivate and trust the Hindu and to leave the Muslim to his fate. Lord Ellenborough as governor-general, wrote to the Duke of Wellington in 1842, urging patronage of the Hindus who, according to him, were nine-tenths of the population, rather than trying to appease the Muslims, who were only one-tenth and could not be reconciled to the British power. 'It seems to me most unwise', said he, 'when we are sure of the hostility of one-tenth, not to secure the enthusiastic support of the nine-tenths which are faithful.'

The events of 1857 made the Muslim position still worse. Notwithstanding the fact that Hindus and Muslims were jointly responsible for the uprising and the first mutineer, Mangal Panday, whose name became a generic apellation for all mutineers, was a Hindu, the British thought the Muslims were at the root of the trouble. 'Tell these rascally Musalmans', said Lieutenant Roberts (later Field Marshal Lord Roberts), 'that by the grace of God we shall still be Masters of India.' This kind of feeling led to further persecution of these Muslims. In 1871, after the Crown had taken over the administration, a survey of employment conducted by E. C. Bailey, a secretary to the government, was summed up by him by saying that there was scarcely a government office in Calcutta at that time in which a Muslim could hope for 'any post above the rank of porter, messenger, filler of ink-pots and mender of pens'.

The educational movement of Syed Ahmad Khan aroused the Muslims to a sense of their degradation as a community and helped them to some extent to participate in government administration and economic activity. The Hindus, however, were so far ahead in the race that there was no hope of catching up with them in the ordinary way. On the other hand, the Muslims were growing in population and poverty. From about 18 million in 1850 or thereabouts, they had grown to about 50 million by the turn of the century. In a famous speech in 1907, Iqbal described the abject poverty of the Muslim people. As time went on there was some improvement in the position, particularly after the British government had agreed to a reservation of posts in the services for Muslims. The relative position of Hindus and Muslims, however, continued to be that of 'haves' and 'have-nots' down to the partition. The economic disparity between the two peoples, the almost complete absence of industries in the Pakistan areas (which was hardly noted by any European observer except Professor Coupland[1]) and the lack of any prospects of economic well-being among the Muslims in the face of the Hindu monopoly of the economy were major contributory factors in the demand for partition.

On March 23, 1940, the Muslim League adopted the Pakistan resolution at its Lahore session, and thenceforward Pakistan became the accepted goal of the Muslims of the sub-continent. Nevertheless, in 1946, the Muslims, in the interest of peaceful political evolution, agreed, under Jinnah's leadership, to accept the cabinet mission plan which envisaged an undivided India with a group system that would have allowed some freedom for economic development for the Pakistan areas in the Indus and the Ganges-Brahmaputra basins. It was, however, precisely this feature of the plan which provoked Hindu opposition. The plan, therefore, did not go forward. It was the last of an innumerable series of attempts to find a solution to the Hindu-Muslim problem in an undivided India. It failed because the Hindus failed to inspire any confidence among the Muslims and indeed, succeeded only in giving the impression that they wanted to damage, if not altogether destroy the political, cultural and economic position of the Muslim community. Outbreaks of communal violence did nothing to allay these fears. There was no question any more of Hindus and Muslims living together; they had to part and part they did.

More important than the economic aspect of the Hindu-Muslim relationship is the cultural aspect. Indeed, it is the most fundamental line of cleavage between Hindus and Muslims. In order to understand the significance of this cleavage, it is necessary to bear in mind the revolutionary impact of the Islamic movement on men and peoples. Those who accept Islam, have their whole personality transformed, with a clear break with the past and a complete change of direction. Islam, with its distinct moral values and approach to the problems of life, binds its adherents into a compact ideological community. History gives us more than one example of a people who started their career by a campaign of destruction against Muslim countries and Muslim culture and ended up by becoming devout adherents of Islam. The Saljuqs and the Mongols are two such examples. 'Just as in the case of the Saljuqs' says Professor Hitti, speaking of the Il-Khans, 'the religion of the Moslems had conquered where their arms had failed. Less than half a century after Hulagu's merciless attempt at the destruction of Islamic culture, his great-grandson Ghazan, as a devout Moslem, was consecrating much time and energy to the revivification of that same culture.'[2]

[1] R. Coupland, *The Future of India* (1944), pp. 78–9.
[2] Philip K. Hitti, *History of the Arabs* (1951), p. 488.

The fact that a large number of Muslims in Pakistan and the rest of the sub-continent are descendants of Hindu converts to Islam is irrelevent, for once a man becomes a Muslim, his whole outlook on life becomes different. His loyalty and allegiance and his whole attitude to life and the universe is completely changed. As an example of the dynamic impact of Islam, we may mention Iqbal himself, who was a Kashmiri Brahmin of the Sapru caste by origin and who has become the greatest exponent of Muslim thought in modern times.

The problem of culture in the sub-continent is not as simple as it is sometimes made out to be. In the course of a thousand years of Muslim rule contacts developed between the ruler and the ruled, particularly after the first five centuries of Turkish sway, and a semblance of a common culture emerged. This culture, which was shared by the upper strata of Hindu and Muslim society, had inevitably a Muslim bias. It was based on the Persian language and literature, in which both Hindus and Muslims acquired proficiency and produced poets, writers and scholars of eminence. We have, for example, Tekchand Bahar, the great lexicographer of the Persian language and Chandar Bhan Brahman the famous poet, and a whole host of Hindu scholars of Persian. The Mughal school of painting produced some outstanding Hindu artists like Manohar and Bachitter, while the old classical Hindu music was supplemented and improved by eminent Muslims like Amir Khusro, Sultan Hussain Sharci and Mian Tan Sen. Again, the Bhakti movement with its emphasis on monotheism was a product of Islam's impact on Hinduism, and produced such great men as Guru Nanak, Kabir and Chaitanya. Social contacts in the upper layers of Hindu and Muslim society were frequent and intimate, culminating in Akbar's marriages with a number of Hindu princesses and similar other matrimonial alliances. The Hindus filled a large number of civil and military offices, including some of the highest. Todar Mal Khatri, who was the revenue minister of Sher Shah Suri before he became imperial chancellor under Akbar, Hemu the grocer, the commander-in-chief of the Suri forces at the second battle of Panipat, and Man Singh, one of the highest ranking generals of the Mughal army, are three out of many examples. The judicial system aimed at even-handed justice to Hindus and Muslims alike. Kings and emperors were personally accessible to any one who cared to knock at their door for justice. Trade and industry was largely in the hands of the Hindus, who were free to exercise their religion. In the lower strata of society, they were free even to maintain, as they did, a social boycott of the Muslims throughout the period of Muslim rule. The Muslim rulers had settled down in the country and had severed their connections with their ancestral territories of origin, but the Hindus never really accepted them as their own. They were still 'malechas', the low and the impure; or 'jabans', the hateful foreigners, as Bankim Chatterjee calls them.

The Muslim rulers generally maintained an atmosphere of peace and tranquillity which encouraged friendly relations between Hindus and Muslims. It must be admitted, however, that, as was inevitable, the relationship between ruler and ruled was not always a balanced one. Moreover, there is no doubt that with all the concessions they enjoyed, the Hindus were a subject people. The relationship between a ruling people and a ruled population can never be a healthy one and is bound to leave a trail of bitterness behind it. You cannot expect gratitude from the people you rule. It was hardly surprising, therefore, to find that as soon as the Muslim power declined and the British established their authority over the sub-continent, the Hindus lost no time in turning their back on their former rulers and in ingratiating themselves with the new power in the land. Soon the last vestiges of the old Hindu-Muslim culture disappeared.

The Urdu language, which has a foundation of Sanskrit (most basic verbs are of Sanskrit origin) and a super-structure of Persian and which developed as a result of Hindu-Muslim contact under Muslim rule, is a particular case in point. Some of the great poets and writers of this language have been Hindus like Daya Shankar Nasim, author of the classic poem *Gulzar-i-Nasim* or *Gul Bakavali*, Rattan Nath Sarshar, author of another classic, the prose romance of the *Fasana-i-Azad* and a number of other well-known works, Prem Chand, the greatest short story writer of the language, Ufaq Lakhnavi, Barq Dehlavi, and Naubat Rai Nazar Lakhnavi, all front rank poets and writers, Brij Narain Chakbast Lakhnavi, outstanding poet, writer and critic, Lala Sri Ram, author of the monumental *Khumkhana-i-Javed*, the best known biographical dictionary of Urdu poets and writers, Pyare Lal Ashob, a pioneer of the Urdu language in the Punjab, Ram Babu Saksena, author of the best known history of Urdu literature, Daya Narain Nigam, editor of one of the foremost Urdu literary magazines, the *Zamanah*; Suraj Narain Mihr, one of the best known writers of children's poems; Talok Chand Mahrum and Labhu Ram Josh Malsiani, both poets of high rank (the latter an authority on the Urdu language); Durga Sahai Saroor, a leader of the transition from the neo-classical to the modern Urdu school of poetry, Professor Firaq Gorakhpuri, an outstanding exponent of the new ghazal, Anand Narain Mulla, a polished and versatile poet and writer, Pandit Brij Mohan Dattatrya Kaifi, famous scholar, poet and writer, and a number of others. Even in our own generation, we have had men of the stature of Hari Chand Akhtar, a master of the Urdu ghazal, Rajinder Singh Bedi and Balwant Singh, two of the best short story writers of Urdu, Arsh Malsiani, Jagan Nath Azad, Dwarka Dass Shula and Munawwar Lakhnavi, who rank with the best poets of their generation, Malik Ram a scholar of great eminence and an authority on Ghalib, and a great many others. Indeed, no account of Urdu language and literature would be worth the paper it was written on if the Hindu contribution were to be omitted from it. And yet Urdu became an early victim of the Hindu hostility towards the Muslims. The Hindus began to promote Hindi as against Urdu and some of the most acrimonious controversies of the late nineteenth and early twentieth centuries centred round the Urdu-Hindi problem. Indeed, the French scholar, Garcin de Tassey, was moved by these controversies to remark that the Hindu wanted to do away with every thing that reminded them of Muslim rule.

In the new environment in which the two communities found themselves under the British *raj*, with the old common culture disappearing, both the Hindus and the Muslims were thrown back on themselves, and there was a revival of culture on both sides. When they were not concentrating on their own culture, the Hindus and Muslims could live together in an atmosphere of social and cultural amity, but with the revival of Hindu and Muslim culture which took place in the latter half of the eighteenth and the first half of the nineteenth century, the differences were seen to be obvious and fundamental. Let us take the Hindu and Muslim views on some of the important problems of life. The Hindu view of ultimate reality is flexible, while the Muslim view is not. You may believe in one God or in a million gods or no god at all and yet you can be a Hindu. A Muslim, however, can remain a Muslim only if he believes in one God and one alone. Let us take the influence of the incidence of birth on the social status of the human individual. Despite legislation against the caste system in India, the Hindu generally continues to be loyal to the caste in which he is born. If he is a Shudra, he has to be a good Shudra, and not aspire any higher. As Ambedkar tells us, the caste Hindu does not expect the Shudra to aspire even to listening to the sacred Vedas; if he does, he may have molten lead poured into his ears. Good conduct may enable him to be born in a higher caste in the next life. On the other hand, a bad Shudra may descend to the body of a lower animal when born again. Islam, on the other hand, recognizes no caste system. A man may be born in any station in life; he is entitled to rise to the highest rung of the social ladder on his merits. The slave kings of India and the mamelukes of Egypt are remarkable examples of men born in slavery or descended from slaves rising to the highest positions of power. Again, coming to habits of eating and drinking, Hindus and Muslims do not eat or drink together, except when they have been Europeanized. A good Hindu would not let a Muslim touch his glass or his eating utensils. Again, rightly or wrongly, the Muslim is fond of eating the cow and, rightly or wrongly, the Hindu regards it as a sacred animal entitled to protection. The Hindu loves music, which forms an integral part of his devotional activities. The Muslim may love music, but does not like to have it presented to him when he is at prayer. That is why we have had so much blood-shed over cow-slaughter and music before mosques. In the field of literature, the Hindu sources of inspiration lie largely in Sanskrit and its dialects, while the Muslim turns to Persian and Arabic. Mario Pei makes an acute observation when he points out that Gandhi, the Hindu leader, derived his title of 'Mahatma' from Sanskrit, while Jinnah, the leader of the Muslims, had his popular name of 'Quaid-e-Azam' from Arabic. Before independence, the Indian National Congress adopted *Bande Mataram* as the national song of India, without regard to the fact that this song, which occurs in Bankim Chandra Chatterjee's *Anandamath* is written as a battle cry against the foreigner, including the Muslims.

Added to all this is the fact that the process of history which forms the main explanation of the separate existence of so many states in the western world, has produced persons in the sub-continent in the course of a thousand years or so of Muslim rule who have come to be regarded as heroes by the Muslims and villains by the Hindus and vice versa. Shivaji and Aurangzeb are two well-known examples. Their quarrel was political, but in the nineteenth century, the Hindu nationalists gave it a deeply communal colour and made Shivaji a national hero of the Hindus. To this the Muslims re-acted by making Aurangzeb a hero of Islam.

It is sometimes suggested that the sub-continent forms one geographical unit. While it is true that the sea and the Himalayas provide a geographical boundary, the inherent geographical unity of the sub-continent is far from obvious. Indeed, it would appear that the area south of the Vindhiachals which is technically a peninsula, with its separate physiography, terrain and climate, has hardly any connection with the rest of the sub-continent. In the same way, the Indus basin and the Ganges-Brahmaputra basin, which broadly represent West and East Pakistan respectively, are self-contained geographical (and economic) units, distinct from all others. Similarly, Rajputana is a separate arid zone. The diversity in natural geography in the sub-continent has resulted in a variety of climate, with a variety of related features, such as fauna and flora. As a matter of interest, the sub-continent has areas of the heaviest and the lowest rainfalls in the world, namely Cherapunji and the desert areas around Khairpur respectively. Similarly, we have in the sub-continent what has so far been regarded as the hottest place on earth, namely Jacobabad, while, at the same time, we have some extremely cold places in the Himalayan regions. In the circumstances, it must take a great deal of courage on the part of anyone to assert the geographical unity of the sub-continent.

Again, it has been said that the separation of East and West Pakistan by a thousand miles of Indian territory makes Pakistan an unusual geographical phenomenon. At first sight this may appear to be so, but a little reflection would place this phenomenon at least on the same footing as the USA and Alaska, not to mention Hawaii.

Let us try to sum up. We have seen that there is no racial or linguistic unity between India and Pakistan. We have also seen that the revival of Muslim culture on the one hand and of Hindu culture, on the other, has disclosed the existence of an unbridgeable gulf between the Hindus and the Muslims. With cultural outlooks so divergent, it was, to say the least, difficult for two peoples to live together and devote their combined efforts to a joint purpose. We have seen the growth of economic disparity between Hindus and Muslims under British rule, a disparity which could not have been remedied in an undivided India with the Hindus holding a monopoly of economic power. We have had a glimpse of the political process which caused ceaseless controversy and growing bitterness between the two peoples. We have seen that the sub-continent was never really a political unit (nor is it a geographical unit). Whatever political unity was achieved from time to time was imposed from without by strong and alien rulers.

Our study of the past makes it clear that history charted different courses for the Hindus and the Muslims in the sub-continent. It could not have been otherwise. What divided them was so much stronger than what was common between them. The question before the Muslims was whether they should live as free and independent people, preserving their religion and their culture for themselves, or should let themselves be merged into the caste system of Hindu India, with its inhuman limitations. But Islam is too vital a force to suffer such a fate. The result, therefore, was the partition of the sub-continent. This was inevitable. There were historical forces working themselves to their logical conclusion. The Hindus, with rare exceptions like G. K. Gokhale and C. R. Das, did not understand these forces, and were, therefore, not amenable to the obvious solution until it was wrested from their hands. The Muslims on the other hand, were fortunate enough to produce two great men, Iqbal and Jinnah, at the critical stage of their history – the one a man of vision and the other a man of action. The man of vision could discern the inner process of history behind the outward events and give voice to the latent aspirations of his people in clear and unambiguous terms. The man of action gave concrete shape to the visionary's dream and led the movement which gave the Muslims of the sub-continent an independent state of their own.

Pakistan represents the struggle of Muslim culture to survive in this part of the world. 'The construction of a polity on national lines,' said Iqbal, 'if it means the displacement of the Islamic principle of solidarity is simply unthinkable to a Muslim.'[1] He demanded the formation of a consolidated Muslim state in the best interests of Islam and India. That, for him, as well as for Jinnah was the only way to peace in the sub-continent, provided, of course, that the Hindu showed understanding of the position. Let us hope that, in spite of all that has happened, a proper understanding of the meaning of Pakistan will dawn on those who are still somewhat confused about it. It is only through such an understanding on the part of the Indian rulers and the world at large that a permanent solution of the problems of the Indo-Pakistan sub-continent can be found.

[1] Shamloo, *Speeches and Statements of Iqbal* (Lahore, 1948), p. 9. (Presidential address to the Allahabad Session of the All-India Muslim League, 1930).

FACTORS LEADING TO THE PARTITION OF BRITISH INDIA

by M. A. H. ISPAHANI*

The question is often posed as to what factors operated to bring about the partition of British India and who was responsible for it. I propose to discuss the question in its historical perspective. Pakistan's dramatic emergence as a separate, sovereign state, contrary to the prevailing notions of territorial nationality, leads some to think that it was the outcome of an emotional urge and lacks the rationale of an historical process. To take this view is to misread history. To make a correct appraisal of the phenomenon, one has to delve deep into the socio-political factors and forces which culminated in the disappearance of an illusory unity – a unity maintained by force of arms of the British rulers, a unity artificially forged for British administrative convenience – and the emergence of separate independent states in the sub-continent.

The Indian attitude towards Muslims and Pakistan is a product of the religious, psychological and philosophical conditioning of Hindu society. It is well known that Hinduism is more a social system than a spiritual doctrine or creed. Its distinctive features are its rigid, unalterable caste system, its insularity and its intolerance of other faiths. It refused to co-exist with Buddhism, which it practically banished from India. It also showed no spirit of toleration or accommodation to Islam, but Islam could not be extirpated from the sub-continent. In the whole history of Hindu–Muslim relationships, one fact stands out prominently – there never was a merger of Hindu and Muslim societies. Two social systems, two cultures, two civilizations have existed since the Muslims first stepped on the soil of the sub-continent. While there could be no fusion, there could have been a workable partnership between the two peoples, but it was rendered impossible by certain features and tendencies inherent in the Hindu social system and Hindu nationalism.

As early as A.D. 1001, the world-renowned savant Al-Beruni, who had accompanied Sultan Mahmud Ghaznavi to India made the following observation regarding the Hindu attitude towards the Muslims in his book, *Kitab-ul-Hind:* 'All their fanaticism is directed against those who do not belong to them – against all foreigners. They call them Malechha, i.e. impure and forbid having any connection with them, be it by inter-marriage or by any other kind of relationship, or by sitting, eating or drinking with them, because thereby they would be polluted. They consider as impure anything which touches the fire and water of a foreigner, and no household can exist without these two elements. They are not allowed to receive anybody who

* Member of the Muslim League Working Committee until 1947, and after independence Pakistan ambassador to U.S.A., 1947–52, High Commissioner in U.K. 1952–4, etc.

does not belong to them even if he wished it or is inclined to their religion. This renders connection between them quite impossible and constitutes the widest gulf between them and us.' This relationship has existed since the Muslims first set foot on the soil of the sub-continent. The two societies – Hindu and Muslim – like two streams, sometimes touched, but never merged, each following its separate course.

A distinguished British observer and writer, Sir Valentine Chirol, who made a special study of Indian conditions also came to the conclusion that India was neither a country nor a nation. In his book, *Indian Unrest*, he observes: 'India has never approached to political unity any more than Europe has, except under the compulsion of a conqueror. For India and Europe are thus far alike that they are both geographically self-contained continents, but inhabited by a great variety of nations whose different racial and religious affinities, whose different customs and traditions, tend to divide them. . . . We too often forget that caste has driven into the Indian society lines of far deeper cleavage than any class distinctions that have survived in Europe.' Even a Hindu historian, K. M. Panikkar, in his book *A Survey of Indian History* supports the view that ever since the advent of Islam in India, Hindus and Muslims have existed as two different nations. He says: 'The main social result of the introduction of Islam as a religion into India was the division of society on a vertical basis. Before the tenth century, Hindu society was divided horizontally and neither Buddhism nor Jainism affected the division. They were not unassimilable elements and fitted in easily with the existing divisions. Islam, on the other hand, split Indian society into two sections from top to bottom and what has now come to be known, in the phraseology of today as two separate nations, came into being from the beginning. At all stages, they were different and hardly any social communications or intermingling existed between them.'

The Muslims ruled over the major part of the sub-continent for well-nigh eight hundred years. And then, as happens to all ruling races, decay and decline set in. The empire fell into disarray. Into the disrupted situation of the sub-continent, a new element was introduced by the rise of the British. They originally came as traders but succeeded, partly by their own clever manoeuvring and largely through the perfidy of some local elements, in establishing themselves as a political power. The process of Muslim decline and downfall was completed by the unsuccessful war of independence of 1857, which saw the final break-up of the last vestiges of Muslim authority. The Muslims found themselves in the throes of a great catastrophe. They had to contend with two inimical forces – the new conquering British power which treated them with feelings of wrath and revenge, and the Hindu majority community which had made common cause with the British to reduce the Muslims to the position of a subjected and degraded minority. This is illustrated by Lord Clive's secret deals with Hindu bankers like Rai Durlabh and Jagat Seth in putting an end to Muslim power in Bengal. It is further corroborated by the Hindu historian, K. M. Panikkar who says: 'An alliance was struck between the head of European baniadom, the English company and the Marwari merchants who commanded the wealth of Bengal.'

That the Hindus had resolved to build up their nationalism on their own lines under the aegis of the British is well-illustrated by the writings of the famous Bengali novelist, Bankim Chandra Chatterjee. In his novel *Anandamath* (Abbey of Bliss) the rebellion of the sanyasis (Hindu ascetics) against Muslim rule in Bengal in the seventies of the eighteenth century is depicted as a national movement and the ascetic marauders are represented as champions of a kind of religious nationalism whose rallying point was God in the form of the Mother. The Muslims are painted as the villains and the British hailed as the friends and benefactors. The book unmistakably shows that it was the set policy of the Hindus to strengthen British rule and Hindu nationalism was directed against the Muslims rather than the British. The following extract from the song 'Bande Mataram' which was sung by sanyasi marauders shows the kind of inspiration Bankim Chatterjee's writings provided for Hindu nationalism:

> Mother, to thee I bow
> Who hath said thou art weak in thy lands
> When the swords flash out in twice seventy million hands
> And seventy million voices roar
> Thy dreadful name from shore to shore?
> With many strengths who are mighty and stored,
> To thee I call, Mother and Lord!

'Bande Mataram', it may be recalled, was the anthem of the Hindu nationalist movement in British India and continues to be the national song of India.

In Bengal, a Hindu leader, Nabagopal Mitra, organized an annual gathering called the Hindu Mela. As the historian R. C. Majumdar states, Nabagopal held that 'the chief criterion of nationalism in unity. This unity according to him, is brought about, sustained and promoted in different peoples by different means and in different principles . . .'.[1] He maintained that the basis of national unity in India has been the Hindu religion. He said that Hindu nationality is not confined to Bengal. It embraces all of Hindu name and Hindu faith throughout the length and breadth of Hindustan; neither geographical position nor the language is counted a disability. 'The Hindus', he said, 'are destined to be a religious nation.'[2] Another Hindu leader Rajnarain Bose, in the course of a lecture in 1872, said 'I see in my mind the noble and puissant Hindu nation rousing herself after sleep and rushing headlong towards progress with divine prowess. I see this rejuvenated nation again illumining the world by her knowledge, spirituality and culture and the glory of the Hindu nation again spreading over the whole world.'[3] In other parts of India, the Hindu nationalist movement was spearheaded by the Arya Samaj, a militant religious movement. As R. C. Majumdar says, 'The young Arya Samajists openly declared that they were waiting for the day when they would settle their account both with Moslems and the Britishers.'[4]

One of the earliest manifestations of Hindu nationalism to the detriment of the Muslims after the events of 1857 was the agitation launched by certain

[1] R. C. Majundar, *History of the Freedom Movement* (1962), vol. i, p. 331.
[2] *Ibid.* p. 332. [3] *Ibid.* pp. 332, 333.
[4] *Ibid.* p. 335.

Hindu leaders of the United Provinces in 1867 to get Urdu replaced by Hindi in government offices and law courts. Syed Ahmad Khan, a man of broad views and sympathies who had boldly championed the cause of Indians in general in his famous pamphlet 'Causes of the Indian Revolt', who had worked for the general advancement of all Indians and who regarded Hindus and Muslims as the 'two eyes of a beautiful bride', was so moved by this pernicious and divisive move that he had to revise his views and attitude. He told a senior British officer: 'It was now impossible for the Hindus and Muslims to progress as a single nation and for anyone to work for both simultaneously. I am convinced that both these nations will not join wholeheartedly in anything. At present there is no open hostility between the two nations, but on account of the so-called "educated" people it will increase immensely in future. He who lives will see.' [1] A dark prophecy but one which proved literally true.

The Anglo-Hindu alliance and the British patronage of the Hindus were manifested in the manner of establishment of the Indian National Congress. In 1885, a retired British civilian officer, Allan Octavian Hume, with the blessings of the viceroy and other dignitaries, founded the Congress. Its sessions used to be attended by provincial governors, it had five Englishmen as presidents of its annual sessions from 1888 to 1910 and its leaders were the first choice for prize jobs in the government. From the beginning the Congress showed its hand as a body interested in establishing Hindu domination over the entire sub-continent. It started by demanding appointments even to non-convenated posts on the basis of competition alone, the object being to secure more and more posts of power and responsibility for the Hindu majority community who were clearly in a more advantageous position. Its second demand was the introduction of the elective system, pure and simple, in the governor-general's council and the provincial councils which, in the peculiar socio-economic conditions of a heterogeneous country like India, would undoubtedly work in favour of the Hindu majority and to the detriment of the Muslims.

Fortunately for them, Syed Ahmad Khan who had already made herculean efforts for the social uplift and educational advancement of the Muslims, came forward to give them a correct and wise lead in the political sphere. By cogent reasoning he convinced them that the best course for them was to keep aloof from the agitation launched by the Hindus through the Congress and concentrate their efforts on acquiring education and on building their social and economic life. In the circumstances then prevailing, this was the soundest policy for the Muslims. The famous Aligarh College founded by him became the symbol of the movement for a Muslim renaissance in the sub-continent. He proved by citing facts and figures that the introduction of the system of parliamentary election, pure and simple, would result in the establishment of Hindu rule, and he exposed the real aim of the Congress as follows: 'The object of the Congress is to have the British Government in name in India but the internal Government of the country should pass into their hands. They do not openly mention their own name, but they know well that the Muslims are not fit to run the administration, hence the internal

[1] Altaf Husain Hali, *Hayat-e-Javed* (1957), pp. 193, 194.

Government will come into their hands.'[1] In one of his speeches Syed Ahmad Khan frankly spoke of Hindus and Muslims as two separate nations who could not share power in the same country. He said: 'The proposals of the Congress are exceedingly inexpedient for a country which is inhabited by two different nations. . . . Now suppose that all the English were to leave India, then who would be the rulers of India? Is it possible that under these circumstances two nations – Hindu and Mussulman – should sit on the same throne and remain equal in power? Most certainly not. It is necessary that one of them should conquer the other and thrust it down. To hope that both would remain equal is to desire the impossible and the inconceivable. At the same time, it should be realized that though they are less numerous than the Hindus in India, the Muslims should not be looked down upon and considered weak. Probably they would be sufficient to defend themselves.'[2]

The apprehensions of the Muslims were further intensified by many other developments besides the demands of the Congress and the agitation against Urdu. Towards the closing years of the nineteenth century, the movement for the prevention of cow slaughter, sponsored largely by those who were also leaders of the Congress, led to violent clashes. B. G. Tilak, a prominent Congress leader, organized the *ganpati* festival and started annual fairs in celebration of the birthday and coronation of Shivaji, the Maratha bandit chief, who was represented as a national hero. Tilak founded cow protection societies which conducted a virulent propaganda calculated to rouse chauvinistic feelings among the Hindus. The remarks of the well-known historian, Reginald Coupland, in this connection are noteworthy: 'The first extremists were out and out Hindus. . . . It was mainly in fact a religious movement at the outset and as such it was necessarily anti-Moslem. One of its champions, for example, founded a society which sought to inhibit Moslems from killing the sacred cow. And when the movement developed its political side, there too, it was clear the Moslems had no place. This was particularly shown when B. G. Tilak, a Brahmin of Maharashtra, who headed the extremists in Western India, started a cult of Shivaji, the famous Maratha rebel against Moslem rule. Moslems to him were Malechhas or foreigners. Evidently the political set-up of free India he dreamed of and fought for, would reflect the period when the Marathas were in the ascendant.'[3]

As time passed, the Hindu ambition of establishing their hegemony over the entire sub-continent under the protection of British arms became more and more evident. As a result, the Muslims became conscious of their independent destiny and realized the need for a separate political course which Syed Ahmad Khan had envisaged for them. This found expression in articulate consciousness of their social and cultural identity and separate political entity which led to the demand for separate electorates. When the proposal for the introduction of elective bodies was in the offing in 1906, the Muslim leaders' deputation, organized by Nawab Mohsinul Mulk and headed by the Aga Khan, put forward this demand before the viceroy, Lord Minto. They adduced such cogent reasons and arguments in favour of the demand

[1] Mohammed Amin Zubeiri, *Siasat-i-Milli* (1941), p. 25.
[2] Imamuddin, *Majmooa-e-lectures-o-speeches Sir Syed* (1901).
[3] R. Coupland, *India a Restatement* (1945), pp. 94, 95.

that it had to be conceded. The institution of separate electorates was vehemently opposed by the Hindus, for they realized that it clearly meant recognition of the separate entity of the Muslims which would militate against the establishment of Hindu domination under cover of Indian nationalism.

Similarly, the Hindus also carried on a raging and tearing campaign against the partition of Bengal and the creation of the province of Eastern Bengal with a Muslim majority which rectified an ancient wrong and afforded an opportunity to the Muslims to improve their down-trodden condition. It was a purely Hindu communal movement but the Congress championed and supported it in the name of Indian nationalism. The Hindus resorted to methods of terrorism and lawlessness and inflamed religious passions in the name of the goddess Kali. The British authorities repeatedly assured the Muslims that partition was 'a settled fact'. But for reasons of their own, they annulled the partition in 1911, when the agitation had almost petered out, thus sacrificing their pledged word at the altar of expediency. The Hindus enjoyed a majority in almost all the provinces then existing and in India as a whole, but they could not tolerate the Muslims being in a majority in one province.

Through the sincere and untiring efforts of M. A. Jinnah the Congress and the Muslim League were brought close to each other. Their political creeds became approximately the same and in 1916 at Lucknow, the two bodies jointly sponsored a scheme, popularly known as the Lucknow pact, which laid down the mode and quantum of representation of the Muslims in the legislative bodies on the basis of separate electorates and provided for a half-way house on the road to full self-government. In the dismal history of Hindu–Muslim relations this was the only bright spot. But the Congress of 1916, which had recognized the identity and rights of the Muslims, underwent a transformation under the influence of the Gandhian ideas of *ahimsa*, *satyagraha* and *ram raj* a few years later and the spirit of the Lucknow pact did not survive. Never again did the Congress show the capacity to accommodate the just claims of the Muslims and the other minority elements.

From 1920, commenced the Gandhian era of Congress politics. The Muslims were greatly agitated over the hostile attitude of the British government towards the caliphate, and Ottoman Turkey after the first world war. Gandhi took advantage of the Muslims' anti-British sentiment and enlisted their co-operation ostensibly by associating himself with the demand for restoration of the temporal power of the caliph. In reality, he wanted, with their support, to achieve the swaraj of his conception. It was initially on the strength of the fund of over one crore of rupees raised by the Muslims that Gandhi and other Congress leaders toured India and canvassed support for the non-co-operation movement. In the exuberance of their sincerity and enthusiasm the Ali brothers raised Gandhi to the 'gaddi' of national leadership – a mistake committed in all genuineness, which they were to regret later. Smaller in numbers and poorer in material wealth, the Muslims not only supplied the bulk of the fund but filled the jails and were foremost in renouncing titles and relinquishing government jobs. Gandhi, supported by the Ali brothers, launched a full-scale attack on the Muslim university at

Aligarh, calling upon its governing body to sever all connections with the government and the students to give up their studies. Aligarh proved to be the test case. It provided the clue to the motives which actuated the Hindu leaders. While the Ali brothers and their followers were prepared to go to the length of sacrificing Aligarh, for which their love could not have been doubted, Gandhi and other Hindu leaders were careful not to touch the Hindu university at Benares.

What with the general levelling up in their ranks, their unbounded energy, boldness and sacrifice, the Muslims were becoming a power in the land, and Gandhi and other Hindu leaders grew alarmed. Taking shelter behind an incident of violence committed at a police station at Chauri Chaura in Gorakpur district, Gandhi called off the movement just at a moment when British authority seemed unnerved. A fearful reaction set in. The right-wing Hindu leader, Pandit Malaviya, had talks with the viceroy, Lord Reading, as a result of which there were six meetings between him and Gandhi. The latter disclaimed all responsibility for the strong tone of the Ali brothers' speeches, even though they were his staunch supporters. As Kanji Dwarkadas says: 'Lord Reading expressed his resentment at the violent speeches made by the Ali brothers and Gandhiji said that he was travelling all the time and had no time to look into newspapers and therefore, he was not able to read what the Ali brothers had said! Reading showed him extracts from Ali brothers' speeches and Gandhiji agreed to get an apology from the Ali brothers for having preached violence.'[1] *shuddi* and *sanghtan* movements were started to overawe and convert the poor Muslims. The façade of unity broke down. Hindu–Muslim riots became the order of the day.

It was during the non-co-operation movement that Gandhi stated his position as a Hindu in the following words: 'It will be seen that for me there are not politics but religion. They subserve religion. The politician in me has never dominated a single decision of mine, and if I take part in politics it is only because politics encircle us today like the coil of a snake from which one cannot get out, no matter how much one tries. In order to wrestle with this snake I have been experimenting with myself and my friends in politics by introducing religion into politics. . . . I call myself a Sanatani Hindu because firstly, I believe in the Vedas, the Upanishads, the Puranas and all that goes by the name of Hindu scriptures and, therefore, in Avatars [God-incarnate] and re-birth, Secondly, I believe in Varanashrama Dharma [law of caste system] in its Vedic forms. Thirdly, I believe in the protection of the cow as an article of faith, and fourthly, I do not disbelieve in idol worship.'[2] And yet Gandhi and other Congress leaders used to blame the Muslims for introducing religion into politics. To remove Hindu apprehensions created by his outward fraternization with the Muslims, Gandhi said: 'It has been whispered that by being so much with the Musalman friends I make myself unfit to know the Hindu mind. The Hindu mind is myself. Surely I do not live amidst Hindus to know the Hindu mind when every fibre of my being is Hindu?'[3] These confessions of Gandhi are an eloquent commentary on

[1] Kanji Dwarkadas, *India's Fight for Freedom* (1966), p. 167.
[2] Jamil-ud-din Ahmad, *Speeches and Writings of Mr. Jinnah* (1943), pp. 458, 459.
[3] *Ibid.* p. 459.

the nationalism and 'secularism' by which he and his followers in the Congress were never tired of swearing.

After the failure of the non-co-operation movement, several earnest attempts were made by the Muslim leaders, especially by Jinnah and Muhammad Ali, to bring about a Hindu–Muslim settlement and accord regarding the future constitution which was the *sine qua non* for the attainment of real freedom for all the elements composing the Indian population. Gandhi sometimes showed concern for Hindu–Muslim unity but he and the Congress leaders never came out with any concrete proposals to achieve unity and concord. It was always the Muslim leaders who took the initiative but their efforts were invariably frustrated. In March 1927, prominent and influential Muslim leaders met under the presidentship of Jinnah at Delhi and put forward certain proposals, popularly known as the Delhi proposals, for a Hindu–Muslim settlement which stipulated the constitution of Sind as a separate autonomous province, the introduction of reforms in the North West Frontier Province and Baluchistan, the reservation of seats for Muslims on a population basis in the Punjab and Bengal, and the allocation of one-third of the seats in the central legislature for the Muslims. Upon the acceptance of these terms the Muslim leaders were prepared to give up their cherished right of separate electorates in favour of a joint electorate. These proposals were first welcomed by the Congress in 1927 but later they were sabotaged under the influence of Gandhi and Motilal Nehru in 1928. The committee headed by Pandit Motilal recommended the scheme of a highly centripetal constitution which, in practice, meant a Hindu-dominated government for the whole sub-continent. It also completely negatived the Delhi proposals. Jinnah's earnest and reasoned pleadings to secure modifications of the Nehru committee's recommendations on the lines of the Delhi proposals fell on deaf ears at the Calcutta all-parties convention of 1928 which shut the door on Hindu–Muslim understanding and co-operation. There was no appreciation whatever of the great sacrifice the Muslims were making in offering to give up separate electorates for the sake of a settlement. Jinnah was deeply dismayed at the attitude of the Hindu leaders and he called it the 'parting of the ways'. Muhammad Ali, who was an ex-president of the Congress and had given of his best to build it up into a powerful organization, was hooted down at the convention. He walked out, never to return. Little did the Congress leaders realize that, in the course of time, they would have to yield much more than the modest proposals put forward by Jinnah. Muslim India was deeply agitated and, though there were different schools of thought among them, detailed proposals known as the 'Fourteen Points' were formulated by Jinnah representing the consensus of opinion among all sections of the Muslims, barring the few Congress Muslims. They postulated a recognition of the Muslims as a distinct social and cultural entity whereupon they would be willing to co-operate in a scheme of a common government for the whole of India. While Hindus would be a majority in seven provinces, Muslims would have a similar position in five provinces, thus creating a balance of power. Due importance was to be given to provincial autonomy, the centre confining itself to subjects of common interest, so that the Muslims, as the less numerous and economically weaker community, could, at least, develop their lives accordingly to their genius and traditions in the Muslim-majority provinces. The most important point was the vesting of residuary powers in the provinces which, according to the canons of political science, implied the right of secession of a province from the federation in case of repression by the centre. The proposals provided for some form of organic unity of the sub-continent, but the Congress and the Hindu leaders showed no willingness to compromise on the basis of the proposals.

Another opportunity for reaching a Hindu–Muslim settlement arose at the Round Table conference in London in 1930 and 1931 but the Hindu leaders failed to grasp it. I will let a prominent Hindu leader speak on this point. Sir Chimanlal Setalvad of Bombay who attended the conference as a delegate, says in his book *Recollections and Reflections:*

'After we reached London well in advance for the Round Table Conference, it was arranged that some representatives of Hindus and of Muslims should meet to consider the question of a communal settlement. Sapru, Sastri, myself, Jayakar, Moonje and Ambedkar were deputed for this meeting and the Agha Khan, Jinnah and one other gentleman represented the Muslims. . . . When we first met, I put the question to the Agha Khan, whether if we arrived at a satisfactory settlement on other points he would agree to joint electorates. He said, "if you satisfy our demands on all other matters we would agree to joint electorates, with reservation of seats for Muslims." I put a further question, "If we come to a settlement on all matters including joint electorates, will the Muslim delegates support the national demand at the Conference?" His answer was characteristic. He said, "In that event you lead and we follow.' "[1]

Sir Chimanlal then states that Sapru, Sastri and himself would have agreed immediately to those demands, but they 'were seriously disappointed in the attitude of Jayakar and Moonje.'[2] He laments that 'a great opportunity was thus lost'.[3] The Aga Khan too in his *Memoirs* refers to these discussions as follows: 'In his memoirs, Sir Chimanlal Setalvad has referred to these offers of mine and his evidence at least stands firmly on record that if the first Round Table Conference did not achieve all that was expected of it, and if, ultimately, not only was "Dominion Status" not brought about, but India had to be partitioned, some at least of the beginnings of these momentous happenings are to be found in the Hindu delegation's refusal to accept my offer.'[4]

At the second Round Table conference in 1931, it was Gandhi's turn to frustrate all efforts for a Hindu–Muslim settlement. He first insulted the Muslim leaders, the depressed class leader Dr Ambedkar and other Indian delegates by claiming that he alone represented the Muslims and the depressed classes and that all the other Indian delegates represented no vital interests. He told the Muslim delegates that he would agree to their proposals on two conditions – the Muslims should not support the Scheduled Castes' demand for any kind of separate electorate or special treatment and the Muslims

[1] Sir Chimanlal Setalvad, *Recollections and Reflections* (1946), p. 358.
[2] *Ibid.* [3] *Ibid.*
[4] The Aga Khan, *Memoirs* (1954), p. 218.

should agree that they would fight for the freedom of India. The Muslims could never accept such humiliating conditions. They could not deny to the poor depressed classes what they themselves desired, and love of freedom was not Gandhi's monopoly. He had previously maintained that Hindu–Muslim agreement was essential for the attainment of swaraj. But addressing the minorities committee of the Round Table conference he said: 'The solution of the communal tangle can be the crown of Swaraj constitution and not its foundation. Our differences have hardened if they have not arisen by reason of the foreign domination. I have not a shadow of doubt that the iceberg of communal differences will melt under the warmth of the sun of freedom.'[1] This kind of argument provoked even the then prime minister, Ramsay MacDonald, who was otherwise known for his pro-Congress sympathies. Pointedly addressing Gandhi he said: 'Be honest and face the facts. The communal problem is a problem of fact. Does the problem exist in India or does it not exist? I do not answer. I leave you honestly to answer it for yourselves and to yourselves. Then, if the communal problem does exist, how can it be discussed with a view to settlement either in India or here? At the foundation of any progress towards the setting up of an Indian constitution, lies the problem of community representation, community rights, community protection and so on. . . .'[2] A prominent Hindu leader Kanji Dwarkadas blames Gandhi and other Hindu leaders for the failure of the efforts to produce a Hindu–Muslim settlement: 'The Communal and Depressed Classes problems would have been settled in London at the R.T.C. but Gandhiji was under the influence of Hindu Communalists – Pandit Malaviya, Jayakar and G. D. Birla.'[3] We might also note here what the Aga Khan who led the Muslim delegation has to say about the negotiations on the Hindu–Muslim question. The discussions between the Muslim delegates and Gandhi were held at the Ritz hotel suite of the Aga Khan who refers to Gandhi's cold response to his sentimental gesture as follows:

'I opened it [the discussion] by saying to Mahatmaji that, were he now to show himself a real father to India's Muslims, they would respond by helping him to the utmost of their ability, in his struggle for India's independence. Mahatmaji turned to face me. "I cannot in truth say," he observed, "that I have any feeling of paternal love for Muslims. But if you put the matter on grounds of political necessity, I am ready to discuss it in a co-operative spirit. I cannot indulge in any form of sentiment." This was a cold douche at the outset, and the chilly effect of it pervaded the rest of our conversation. I felt that, whereas I had given prompt and ready evidence of a genuine emotional attachment and kinship, there had been no similar response from the Mahatma.'[4]

With regard to the trend of the discussion the Aga Khan says:

'The Mahatma sought to impose a first and fundamental condition: that the Muslims should, before they asked for any guarantees for themselves, accept Congress's interpretation of Swaraj – Self-Government – as their goal. To

[1] Jamil-ud-din Ahmad, *op. cit.* pp. 462, 463.
[2] *Ibid.* p. 463.
[3] Kanji Dwarkadas, *op. cit.* p. 404.
[4] The Aga Khan, *op. cit.* p. 227.

which Mr. Jinnah very rightly answered that, since the Mahatma was not imposing this condition on the other Hindu members of the various delegations attending the Round Table, why should he impose it on the Muslims? Here was another heavy handicap.' [1]

In spite of Hindu opposition the Muslims managed to secure some rights in the Government of India Act of 1935. Separate electorates were retained; Sind was separated from Bombay and constituted into a separate province; reforms were introduced in the N.W.F.P.; seats were reserved for Muslims in the ratio of 49 per cent in the Punjab and 48 per cent in Bengal, although on a population basis they were entitled to 56 and 55 per cent respectively. The Hindus, however, violently opposed the concession of these rights to the Muslims. The Congress adopted a curious attitude of neutrality on this question, although in practice it meant opposition, for the Congress stood for 'combating the Act' and the withdrawal of the new constitution of which the communal award was but a part.

Actuated by an earnest desire to bring about a League–Congress understanding with a view to accelerating constitutional progress, Jinnah again entered into negotiations with the Congress president, Rajendra Prasad in 1935. He suggested that the communal award should be accepted till the communities agreed upon a substitute and they should continue their efforts to achieve a constitution to the full satisfaction of the people. He made it clear that if the Congress and other Hindu leaders could put forward a formula on the basis of joint electorates which would better safeguard Muslim interests, the League would consider it. But no such formula was offered and the Jinnah–Prasad talks proved unfruitful.

The manner in which the Congress was inducted into office in the provinces again illustrates the Anglo–Hindu alliance at the expense of the Muslims and their legitimate rights. During the election campaign in 1937, there existed a sort of unofficial understanding between the League and the Congress candidates to lend moral support to one another. Jinnah expressed sentiments of goodwill towards the Congress, emphasized the need for friendly co-operation between the League and the Congress and declared, 'Ours is a movement which carries the olive branch to every community.' The unexpectedly large success of the Congress in the Hindu constituencies in the Hindu-majority provinces, however, had an upsetting effect on the Congress leaders' mental balance. The Congress president, Subhas Chandra Bose, talked of 'party dictatorship' and opposed the idea of co-operation with other parties. Nehru declared in a militant tone that there were only two parties in the country – the Congress and the government – and others must line up. He derided the talk of Muslim rights as 'nonsense' and condemned the efforts to bring about a settlement between the Muslims and Hindus as 'medieval'.

The Congress talked of 'combating' and 'wrecking' the Government of India Act but it also decided to permit the formation of Congress ministries if assurances were given that the governors would not use their special powers against ministers 'in regard to their constitutional activities'. This

[1] The Aga Khan, *op. cit.* p. 229.

tortuous and disingenuous decision was designed to coerce the governors into surrendering their constitutional obligations, especially with regard to the safeguarding of the interests of the minorities, so that a totalitarian Hindu rule might be established in the majority of provinces and eventually over the whole of India. The governors could not possibly give the kind of assurances demanded by the Congress with the result that the Congress refused to form ministries. This was an attempt at blackmailing. The new viceroy, Lord Linlithgow, issued a statement which, though not yielding any constitutional ground, appealed to the Indian people to count on him 'to strive untiringly for the full and final establishment in India of the principles of parliamentary government'. The result was, in Jinnah's words, 'Hastily the constitutional guardians of minority and other rights jettisoned their trust and amidst much mutual appreciation of each other's statesmanship the Congress and the British Government came into political alliance.' [1]

The instrument of instructions in the Act enjoined inclusion of minority representatives in the cabinet. The Congress refused to include such Muslims as enjoyed the confidence of the Muslim members of the assemblies. Instead it enticed away a stray Muslim Leaguer or an independent Muslim member to sign the Congress pledge in exchange for a ministership and the governors meekly acquiesced in the nefarious process. In the United Provinces, the Congress leaders entered into negotiations with Choudhry Khaliquzzaman, leader of the Muslim League party in the assembly, over the head of the president and executive of the All-India Muslim League and laid down terms and conditions for the inclusion of League members in the cabinet which, if accepted, would have resulted in the virtual dissolution of the Muslim League in the province. Khaliquzzaman almost succumbed to the Congress pressure and was prepared for a sell-out, but Muslim public opinion which by this time had become vocal and assertive and the note of warning sounded by Jinnah averted the danger of the merger of the U.P. Muslim League parliamentary party in the Congress. On that occasion Khaliquzzaman had led us almost to the brink of disaster and Jinnah our national hero and leader saved us.

The Congress high command adopted a similar attitude in Bombay. As Kanji Dwarkadas discloses:

'Kher, the chief Minister-designate, before forming the Ministry, saw Jinnah. He requested Jinnah to give him two members of his Muslim League to join the Ministry. Jinnah readily agreed and offered his and Muslim League's fullest co-operation to the Congress Ministry. But what happened? Kher told me the whole story and later Jinnah confirmed it. The High Command, Sardar Patel in particular, took Kher to task for having approached Jinnah. The High Command wanted no truck with Jinnah. So, Kher's request for two Muslim Leaguers in the Ministry was turned into a demand by the Congress that the Muslim Leaguers must resign from the Muslim League and join the Congress and then only would they be taken as Ministers. This was a humiliating condition for the Muslim League to accept. Jinnah rightly resented it. He therefore, summarily rejected the Congress suggestion.

[1] Jamil-ud-din Ahmad, *op. cit.* p. 115.

He wanted to co-operate with the Congress Ministry but not by liquidating and sabotaging his own party.' [1]

The narrowness of outlook displayed by the Congress leadership is criticized by a distinguished Hindu scholar, Beni Prasad:

'Orthodox Parliamentarism led the Congress leaders to forget that the one-party theory, even if true of political agitation, was not, in the absence of an accomplished revolution, applicable to Ministerial office. The change from extra-constitutional action to governmental responsibility to which the Congress assented in 1937 was a change of scale and methods of the profoundest significance and called for a fresh evaluation and rearrangement of political forces. The country was passing through a crisis, and crises have usually been surmounted even in England through coalitions, for instance in 1915, 1931 and 1940. . . . The majority principle is at bottom not an ethical maxim but a rule of expediency and has always to be so interpreted as to command minority affirmation. Orthodox parliamentarism, however, carried the day and excluded the Muslim League from a share in power.' [2]

Another well-known Hindu historian, R. C. Majumdar, is very critical of the Congress attitude: 'To sacrifice collaboration with the Muslim League in the name of ideals which did not at all correspond with existing facts was an extremely unwise – almost fatal – step for which India had to pay very dear. . . . The Muslims now fully realized that as a separate community they had no political prospects in future. The Congress ultimatum was the signal for the parting of ways which, by inevitable stages, led to the foundation of Pakistan.' [3]

So far as the Muslims were concerned, the two years of Congress rule represented a nightmare of harassment, persecution, suppression and discrimination in the various fields – administrative, social, cultural, political, economic and educational. The Congress launched upon a campaign of Muslim contact with the advantage of governmental authority, thinking it could ride rough-shod over the Muslim League and force them into submission. Even the ordinary Congress volunteers, leave alone the leaders, behaved as if Hindu *raj* had been established. The well-known historian, Sir Reginald Coupland, who had studied the situation in the Congress-governed provinces remarks: 'It was not only the Working Committee's control of the Congress Ministries that showed that "a Congress Raj" had been established in their provinces. It was betrayed by the conduct and bearing of Congressmen, both in the performance of public duties as individuals at the outset of the regime . . . Many of them behaved as if they were a ruling caste, as if they owned the country.' The Congress ministries also devised a clever method to undermine the culture and education of the Muslims. A scheme of education known as the Wardha scheme was prepared under the guidance of Gandhi. Its whole trend was to impress on the mind of Muslim children the inferiority of Muslim culture and promote the revival and supremacy of the primitive Hindu culture of vedic times.

[1] Kanji Dwarkadas, *op. cit.* pp. 466, 467.

[2] Quoted in Abdul Waheed Khan's book, *India Wins Freedom—the Other Side* (1961), p. 86.

[3] R. C. Majumdar, *op. cit.* pp. 563, 565.

The coming into power of the Congress ministries signalized an alarming increase in the number of Hindu–Muslim riots. It was the oppressive and discriminating policy of the Congress governments that led to frequent riots. The Muslims resented injustice and discriminatory treatment in the matter of civil liberties, economic measures and employment and educational opportunities. Their constitutional protest and agitation was dubbed as 'communalism' and was sought to be ruthlessly put down. In certain parts of the country, unspeakable atrocities were perpetrated on the Muslims but the Congress governments took no steps to bring the offenders to book. Even the administration of justice was interfered with to shield the perpetrators of these atrocities.

The experience of the working of elected legislatures and a limited measure of responsible government in the provinces was leading Muslim thinkers and politicians to realize more clearly the menace which the Hindu majority's attitude posed for the Muslims and the other minorities. The idea of a separate federation of Muslim-majority provinces was gaining popularity. Allama Iqbal had already, in 1930, suggested the creation of a Muslim state in north-west India. He said: 'I would like to see the Punjab, N.W.F.P., Sind and Baluchistan amalgamated into a single state. Self-government within the British Empire or without the British Empire, the formation of a consolidated North-West Indian Muslim State appears to me to be the final destiny of the Muslims of at least North-West India.' [1]

In January 1940, Jinnah contributed an article to the British paper *Time and Tide* in which, after giving a graphic review of the working of the provincial part of the Government of India Act of 1935 and the injustice it entailed on the Muslims and the minorities, he laid down two propositions: (1) the British people must realize that unqualified western democracy was totally unsuited for India and attempts to impose it must cease, (2) in India it must be accepted that 'party' government was not suitable and all governments, central or provincial, must be governments that represented all sections of the people. In conclusion, he asserted that there were in India two nations which must both share in its governance. In this connection the remarks of the historian Reginald Coupland are noteworthy: (1) 'The doubts so persistently expressed by British statesmen in the past as to the possibility of successfully transplanting the British system of parliamentary government had been justified; (2) the chief reason why the domestic political situation in India had deteriorated to a point which would have seemed almost inconceivable a few years earlier was the manifest purpose of the Congress to take over the heritage of the British Raj.' [2]

All overtures made over a period of twenty-five years by Muslim leaders for a compromise plan which, while preserving some form of union of the subcontinent, would allow full opportunity to the Muslims to maintain their identity and develop according to their genius and ideals, failed to elicit any response from the Hindu majority. Muslim feeling, therefore, crossed the line and a clear-cut partition remained the only alternative. In March 1940, presiding over the Lahore session of the All-India Muslim League,

[1] Shamloo, *Speeches and Statements of Iqbal* (1948), p. 12.

[2] R. Coupland, *op. cit.* p. 191.

Jinnah gave forceful expression to Muslim sentiments and ideas. He observed:

'The problem in India is not of an inter-communal character but manifestly an international one.... It is extremely difficult to appreciate why our Hindu friends fail to understand the real nature of Islam and Hinduism. They are not religions in the strict sense of the word, but are, in fact different and distinct social orders, and it is a dream that the Hindus and Muslims can ever evolve a common nationality ... The Muslims and Hindus belong to two different religions, philosophies, social customs, literatures ... To yoke together two such nations under a single state, one as a numerical minority and the other as a majority, must lead to growing discontent and final destruction of any fabric that may be built up for the government of such a state ... Mussulmans are a nation according to any definition of a nation and they must have their homelands, their territory and their state.' [1]

The lead having been given so clearly by the Qaid-e-Azam, the All-India Muslim League adopted on March 23, 1940 the resolution which stated *inter alia* that 'geographically contiguous units are demarcated into regions which should be so constituted with such territorial readjustments as may be necessary, that the areas in which the Muslims are numerically in a majority as in the North-Western and Eastern zones of India should be grouped to constitute "Independent States" in which the units shall be autonomous and sovereign.' [2] The plan for partition was further clarified in the resolution passed at the convention of 470 Muslim members of the central and provincial legislatures at Delhi in April 1946, which laid down that 'the zones comprising Bengal and Assam in the North East and the Punjab, N.W.F.P., Sind and Baluchistan in the North West of India where the Muslims are in a dominant majority, be constituted into a sovereign, independent state' [3] and 'two separate constitution-making bodies be set up by the peoples of Pakistan and Hindustan for the purpose of framing their respective constitutions'.[4]

In 1942, when the war was not going too well for Britain and her allies, the British government made an attempt to come to terms with the Indian political parties so as to secure their co-operation in the prosecution of the war effort. Sir Stafford Cripps, one of the British cabinet ministers, was sent to India to negotiate with the parties on the basis of a declaration. In his very first interview with Jinnah Cripps declared: 'I have changed my opinion in the last eighteen months particularly during the last six months. I do not hold my old views. The Cabinet of Britain too hold my view. We appreciate the Muslim case. I give you the assurance that I recognize that so far as the Mussalmans are concerned I recognize no body and no party among them other than the League and its President. Many persons and organizations have pressed me to recognize them and I have point blank refused.' The

[1] Jamil-ud-din Ahmad, *op. cit.* pp. 153–5.

[2] Resolutions of All-India Muslim League, December 1938 to March 1940 published by its Central Office, pp. 47, 48.

[3] Resolutions of All-India Muslim League, January 1944 to December 1946, published by its Central Office, Delhi, pp. 46, 47.

[4] *Ibid.*

declaration boiled down to (*a*) the immediate setting up of a national government at the centre, (*b*) the creation of machinery after the conclusion of the war, to frame a constitution for the proposed Indian union with the proviso that in the event of its not accepting the framed constitution a province would have the right to stand out and such a province or provinces would have the right to form its own or their own separate union, which means that the possibility of formation of more than one union was visualized. This declaration meant that the so-called unity of India was after all not sacrosanct, and the foundations of division were laid, though vaguely. The Congress had an excellent chance of achieving a transfer of power in terms of the declaration by reaching an understanding with the Muslim League but they spurned the British offer, for they wanted a monopoly of power and nothing less. They were not willing to recognize the provinces' right of non-accession. Jawaharlal Nehru stated in an article in the *New York Times* of July 19, 1942: 'Now they [the British] have tried to introduce the idea of partitioning India not only into two but possibly many separate parts. This was one of the reasons which led to bitter resentment of the Cripps' proposals. The All-India Congress could not agree to this.' [1]

After rejecting the Cripps' proposal and the Congress prepared itself for a show-down with the government at a critical time when the war was not going too well with the allies. Gandhi called the Cripps proposal a 'post-dated cheque on a crashing bank', which meant that the Congress considered a Japanese victory over the British to be imminent and believed that their dream of Hindu *raj* stood a better chance of realization when the British had been pushed out of India by the Japanese. It was this calculation which led them to launch the 'Quit India' movement in August 1942, but in the scheme of things they had in mind there was no place for the Muslims except that of a subjugated minority.

The Muslim League working committee met at Bombay in August 1942, to consider the serious situation arising out of the arrest and incarceration of Gandhi and other Congress leaders and to determine the Muslim attitude. Propaganda had been set afoot that the Congress meant to be fair and honest with the Muslims and to give them the type of independence they were seeking and therefore this was the opportunity for the Muslim League to join hands with the Congress to gain independence for the peoples of the sub-continent. Some members of the League working committee, including myself, held the view that this was an opportune moment to co-operate with the Congress and that we should not let slip the opportunity to achieve freedom from the British for both Hindus and Muslims. It did not take us long to realize that our leader, the Qaid-e-Azam, who was gifted with an uncanny foresight and power of anticipation, did not share our view for he knew the mind and designs of the Congress leaders better than we did. In his usual cool and dispassionate fashion he sponsored the view that the interests of the Muslim nation called for a policy of avoiding both the Congress and British traps and for a cautious neutral position and to utilize the opportunity to infuse drive and teeth into the Muslim League organization.

Jinnah's opinion, clearly and convincingly expressed, prevailed in the

[1] Jamil-ud-din Ahmad, *op. cit.*, p. 470.

working committee. When my friend the Raja Saheb of Mahmudabad and I called on the Qaid-e-Azam on the first Sunday morning after the termination of the working committee meetings, he produced two articles – one written by Gandhi in the *Harijan* and the other a statement by Nehru which appeared in the *Bombay Chronicle* of August 23, 1942 – both of them having been written a few days before the arrest of the Congress leaders. These articles proved beyond doubt that all the inspired talk which had filled the air with the blessings of the Congress leaders outside prison and influential big Hindu businessmen had no meaning and was a clever trap to throw the Muslim League off balance and to involve it in trouble similar to that of Congress, which, due to the arrest and imprisonment of its top leaders, had become a ship that had lost its rudder and was caught in a storm in mid-ocean. It was clear that the Hindu or Congress attitude *vis-à-vis* the Muslims had not undergone any change and Muslims, in their thinking, were to remain a minority and enjoy such rights as would be conceded to minorities in an all-India 'democracy'.

It did not take long to get enough proof from happenings around us that the decision taken under the sole guidance of our leader was the correct one. Had he not successfully pleaded with the working committee to ignore the crafty approaches of the Congress second line leaders outside jail and other Hindu leaders and utilize the opportunity afforded us to build and strengthen the Muslim League, the Muslim nation would have suffered a set back from which it would not have recovered in time to demand and obtain its freedom.

In September 1944 at Bombay Gandhi entered into negotiations with the Qaid-e-Azam on the question of Pakistan. Their meetings lasted from September 9 to September 26, 1944. Gandhi laid down the following conditions to which the Muslim League was required to agree before the question of the separation of certain areas could be taken up: (1) the immediate grant of independence to India as one single national unit; (2) the immediate formation of a provisional interim government responsible to the existing central assembly or a newly elected one (naturally with a 75 per cent Hindu majority); (3) the provisional government to frame the constitution of India or to set up an authority to frame the constitution after withdrawal of British power; (4) this government to draft the treaty and agreements as regards administration of matters of common concern such as foreign affairs, defence, communications, customs, commerce and the like which would be matters for efficient and satisfactory administration under a central authority; (5) the provisional government to set up a commission to demarcate continuous districts having an absolute Muslim majority. After all these conditions had been complied with, the demarcated areas would be permitted to decide through a plebiscite of *all* their inhabitants whether they wished to form a separate state. But in any case all matters of vital importance were to be administered by a central authority with a Hindu majority. Gandhi was pleased to call this scheme a partition or division between brothers. The Qaid-e-Azam naturally declared, 'This is not independence. It is a form of provincial autonomy subject always in the most vital matters to an overwhelmingly Hindu federal authority.' [1]

[1] *Jinnah-Gandhi Talks* published by Central Office of All-India Muslim League (1944), p. 76.

Perhaps Gandhi realized that his offer did not amount to acceptance of the sovereign Pakistan demanded by the Muslims, for, he said, after the breakdown of his talks with the Qaid-e-Azam: 'Where there is an obvious Muslim majority they should have the fullest right to constitute themselves into a separate state. But if it means utterly independent sovereignty, so that there is nothing common between the two, I hold it to be an impossible proposition. Then it means a fight to the knife.' [1] Here was the apostle of peace and non-violence threatening the Muslims with a fight to the knife if they insisted on claiming their share in freedom.

The British government made another move in June 1945, to enlist the co-operation of the political parties so as to create an impression on the outside world that India was making a voluntary contribution to the war effort and was sympathetic to Britain's aspirations. It was announced that the viceroy's executive council would be reconstituted within the framework of the existing constitution (Government of India Act 1919) so as to contain equal proportions of caste Hindus and Muslims, and that this would be without prejudice to the essential form of the future permanent constitution or constitutions for India. The viceroy, Lord Wavell, convened a conference of party leaders at Simla to consider the proposal and arrive at an agreement. The Congress, instead of reaching an understanding with the Muslim League on the basis of parity, denied the latter's right to represent the Muslims and insisted on claiming seats out of the Muslim quota. Thus another opportunity for a smooth transfer of power by mutual consent was lost due to Congress's incorrigible tendency to grab power to the detriment of other elements.

Both the British and the Hindus were strongly opposed to the emergence of Pakistan. In May 1946, the British cabinet mission after consultations with the Congress and the Muslim League leaders put forward a compromise plan for a three-tier constitution – provinces, groups of provinces and a union centre confined to three subjects namely defence, foreign affairs and communications. The constituent assembly was to split up into three sections – (A) consisting of Hindu-majority provinces, (B) the Punjab, N.W.F.P., Baluchistan and Sind, (C) Bengal and Assam. The sections were to settle the provincial constitutions and also to decide whether a group was to be formed and, if so, to frame the group constitution with the stipulation that a province could by a vote of its legislature opt out of the group after the first general elections had been held under the new constitution. At the next stage the three sections were to reassemble as a constituent assembly to frame the constitution of the union centre for the three aforementioned subjects with the proviso that any question raising a major communal issue would require for its decision a majority of the representatives of the two major communities and any province could by a majority vote of its legislature call for a reconsideration of the terms of the constitution after an initial period of ten years and ten-yearly intervals thereafter, which carried by implication the right of secession from the union.

I remember the tense scene when the sealed envelope containing the cabinet mission's scheme was handed to the Qaid-e-Azam's secretary. The

[1] *Jinnah-Gandhi Talks*, *op. cit.* p. 61.

Qaid read the contents once and glanced through them a second time and thereafter the Muslim League working committee met and studied with care every line and every word of the communication. The consensus of opinion was that the mission had placed us on the horns of a dilemma for we had been given the option of accepting what the mission offered, in which we were clearly told no change of a major nature could be made, or of rejecting their proposal *in toto* and thereby drawing upon ourselves the responsibility for the failure of the mission and with it the consequences which might follow.

Just before the final session of the working committee terminated, it was agreed that the proposal might be accepted, although it did not go far enough to meet our demands and aspirations, but it was left to the president to take the final decision. That was not the first occasion when the brunt of responsibility was thrown on the president by his working committee. A suitable reply was drafted and signed and a short while thereafter the Qaid had dinner and repaired to bed.

I saw him the next morning immediately after breakfast. He appeared more rested and cheerful, for it seemed as if a load had been taken off his mind. He told me, 'I have thought much in bed and have prayed for guidance, because the decision I was called upon to make would mar or make the destiny of our nation. Now that the die has been cast and the decision made and communicated to Pethick-Lawrence, I feel as carefree as does a student after he has finished his last examination paper.' The day had not yet passed when he began to worry again. It appeared that on reconsideration he would rather have rejected the proposal but it was too late. All that we could do was to hope that the Congress working committee would either reject the proposal or ask for such amendments or put such interpretations on it as would vitiate their acceptance of it.

The period of suspense, however, was not unbearably long, for news came through that the Congress had not unreservedly accepted the plan. The report of the acceptance with reservations by the Congress made the air of Simla more refreshing and bracing for us. The Qaid was pleased, for the blame would now fall on the Congress and the Muslim League would be able to extricate itself from a difficult situation.

In contrast to the Congress, the Muslim League's acceptance of the plan was forthright. It was an honest attempt by the Qaid to arrive at an amicable and peaceful settlement with the Congress without sacrificing essential Muslim interests. In accepting the plan, the League was actuated by the following considerations: (1) The Muslim majority in sections B and C comprising six undivided provinces could frame both provincial and group constitutions with regard to all but three subjects and the framing of these constitutions was to precede that of the union constitution; (2) the provision relating to major communal issues could be used to safeguard Muslim interests in the union assembly and prevent the union centre from encroaching upon the autonomy of the provinces and the groups; (3) the Muslim majority in sections B and C would be in a position to negotiate with the Hindu majority in section A to ensure safeguards for minorities on reciprocal basis; (4) the whole constitution would be open to revision at the end of ten years and at ten-yearly intervals which meant by implication that the provinces and groups would have freedom to opt out of the union.

It speaks volumes for the Qaid-e-Azam's power of reasoning and the confidence he enjoyed that he was able to persuade the nation's representatives to accept a plan which apparently amounted to rejection of the demand for a sovereign Pakistan. Lord Pethick-Lawrence paid a tribute to Jinnah's courage and statesmanship in obtaining the Muslim League council's approval for the plan.

The Muslim League accepted the cabinet mission's plan, as it met the substance of the demand for Pakistan and kept the way open for the emergence of a sovereign Pakistan in case the union centre functioned to the detriment of the Muslim provinces. The Congress, from the beginning, adopted a dubious attitude. While professing to accept the plan, it twisted it by misinterpreting the grouping scheme to mean that a province could, in the first instance, decide whether or not it would belong to a group and also frame its own constitution. The Congress president, Nehru, went a step further and declared in a militant tone that it was not a question of the Congress agreeing to any plan, long or short, adding, 'We are not bound by a single thing except that we have decided for the moment to go into the Constituent Assembly', and further, 'What we do there, we are entirely and absolutely free to determine'.[1] Nehru's assertions were naturally regarded as a clear breach of faith on the part of the Congress, being an outright repudiation of the terms and conditions on which the compromise plan of the cabinet mission rested and was supposed to be worked by the two main parties. Leonard Mosley in his book *The Last Days of the British Raj* (p. 27) observes: 'It was a compromise plan which obviously could not afterwards be altered in favour of one side or the other. In the circumstances, Nehru's remarks were a direct act of sabotage.' Another British writer, Penderel Moon, in his book *Divide and Quit* takes the same view: 'Gandhi by persuading the Working Committee to reject the interim government had knocked down half of it. Nehru proceeded to demolish the rest of it.' This view is shared by thinking Indians, too. The well-known historian R. C. Majumdar criticizes Nehru as follows: 'Unfortunately, at this critical moment, when a peaceful settlement of India's future was almost within sight it was upset by some indiscreet utterances of Pandit Jawaharlal Nehru. In 1937, his outright rejection of Jinnah's offer of Congress-League Coalition Ministry ruined the last chance of Hindu–Muslim settlement. His observations in 1946 destroyed the last chance – though a remote one – of a free, united India'.[2]

Even a close friend and colleague of Nehru, Maulana Azad, about whose loyalty to the Hindu Congress it could be said that he was 'more loyal than the King', in his book *India Wins Freedom* characterizes Nehru's stand as 'one of those unfortunate events which changed the course of history'.[3] Referring to Nehru's utterances repudiating the basic terms of the cabinet mission's plan, Maulana Abul Kalam Azad says: 'I must place on record

[1] V. P. Menon, *The Transfer of Power in India* (1957), p. 280.
[2] R. C. Majumdar, *op. cit.* vol. 3, p. 770.
[3] Abul Kalam Azad, *India Wins Freedom* (1959), pp. 154, 155.

that Jawaharlal's statement was wrong. It was not correct to say that the Congress was free to modify the Plan as it pleased.' [1,2]

The Congress party in Assam was encouraged by the Congress high command to refuse to join section C from the very beginning. The Assam premier, Gopinath Bardoloi submitted a memorandum to the Congress working committee opposing the grouping of Assam and Bengal. According to Azad, Gandhi 'gave his support to Bardoloi' and 'to the interpretation suggested by the leaders from Assam'. Bardoloi got the Assam provincial assembly to pass a resolution giving a mandate not only to the Congress members but also the Muslim representatives elected by a separate bloc of Muslim members to have nothing to do with the 'C' group from the very beginning.

It was at this stage that the Muslim League felt constrained to withdraw its acceptance of the cabinet mission's plan in view of its deliberate mutilation by the Congress and the British government's failure to bring the Congress to the path of reason. The strong reaction of the Muslim League seemed to jolt even Congress circles, for the Congress working committee stated that while they did not approve of all the proposals contained in the cabinet mission's plan, they accepted the scheme in its entirety. They, however, immediately qualified the acceptance by asserting that provincial autonomy was a basic provision and each province had the right to decide whether to form or join a group or not. This was in reality a reiteration of their previous stand and was no acceptance at all.

I may here make a brief reference to another episode, the formation of a one-party interim government in September 1946, which was another ill-advised action on the part of Attlee's government. The situation which was already tense owing to the Congress repudiation of the basic terms and conditions of the cabinet mission's plan was further aggravated by the viceroy's invitation to the Congress president Nehru to make proposals for the formation of an interim government, and the Muslim League was by-passed. This was contrary to all solemn assurances and pledges given to the Muslims by successive British governments. The Congress had never really accepted the long-term plan of the cabinet mission and the League's subsequent withdrawal of its earlier acceptance was a natural sequel to the Congress's rejection of the plan. If there was a commitment to form an interim government as representative as possible of those who had accepted the statement of May 16th it had been flagrantly broken when the viceroy had refused to proceed with the formation of the interim government according to the cabinet mission's own proposal of June 16th which the League had unreservedly accepted. The procedure which the viceroy had now been directed to follow in inviting one of the parties to make proposals for an interim government was wrong and without sanction, because the viceroy was not a constitutional governor-general as in the self-governing dominions: the interim government was only the executive council under the Government of India Act of 1919 and it was not responsible to the legislature.

[1] Abul Kalam Azad, *India Wins Freedom* (1959), pp. 154, 155.

[2] [Editors note: cf. B. R. Nanda, 'Nehru, the Indian National Congress and the Partition of India', above, pp. 178–82 and A. G. Noorani, 'The Cabinet Mission and its Aftermath,' above, pp. 108–10.]

It was clearly the viceroy's duty to form the executive council and he was not entitled to pass on the initiative to the leader of one political party, thus seriously prejudicing the rights and interests of other political elements who had an equal claim for representation on the council. A one-party government, however, was installed, but it created a very tense situation. The Muslims registered their protest by observing a 'black-flag' day throughout India. There were serious disturbances in Calcutta. Lord Wavell flew post-haste to Calcutta and what he saw there seemed to convince him of the futility of carrying on with a one-party government. On his return to New Delhi he sent for Gandhi and Nehru and impressed on them the imperative need of making a clear declaration of Congress willingness to abide by the procedure relating to the grouping of provinces laid down in the May 16th statement, but the Congress leaders now firmly in the saddle rejected the viceroy's suggestion.

Wavell, however, was alive to the importance of enlisting the Muslim League's co-operation. He invited the Qaid-e-Azam for consultations, which took place at Delhi from September 16th onwards. As a result of assurances given by the viceroy, the Muslim League working committee decided to accept his offer of five seats in the interim government. The League's entry into the interim government when the odds were against us was a strategic triumph. The Qaid-e-Azam succeeded in putting the League into the interim government in its own right and without any commitment to join the constituent assembly in the way the Congress wanted it to join and without recognizing Nehru's leadership of the so-called cabinet. The League was certainly not opposed to the transfer of more power to Indian hands. But if the position claimed by Nehru for himself and the interim government were recognized it would have meant pre-judging the constitutional issue in a sense favourable to Congress designs, namely a unitary government for the whole of India responsible to a legislature dominated by the Hindu majority. The League had to guard against this danger, for it would have militated against the principle of Pakistan.

The Qaid-e-Azam told us that he had extracted the last ounce of concession from the viceroy in difficult circumstances and the League's representatives were going in as 'watch-dogs' of Muslim interests. Their function was to safeguard vital Muslim interests and prevent the Congress from manipulating things in such a way as to thwart the establishment of Pakistan. When the horizon appeared dark, the Qaid again rose to heights of diplomacy and regained the initiative which paved the way for Pakistan's emergence as a sovereign state. He saved the whole of India from the disaster which had loomed large with the formation of a one-party government at the centre.

The British government made an effort to iron out the differences between the Congress and Muslim League at a conference of their representatives at London in December 1946, but the effort failed again due to Congress intransigence. I, along with Begum Shah Nawaz, had been deputed by the Qaid-e-Azam to project the case for Pakistan in the USA. At the conclusion of our tour I received a call to meet the Qaid-e-Azam in London. There he told me that His Majesty's government had tried to pressure him into accepting the cabinet mission's plan as interpreted by the Congress, but he did not yield any ground and stood firm. His hands, he said, had been further strengthened by a consolidation of the Muslim position, particularly the League's cent per cent victory in the Sind elections, the news of which he had just received. The statement issued by the British government at the end of the conference upheld the Muslim League's viewpoint that provinces could opt out of the groups only after the first general elections under the new constitution and the decisions in the sections should, in the absence of agreement to the contrary, be taken by a simple majority vote of the representatives in the sections. The Congress, instead of gracefully accepting the position now clarified beyond all doubt by the British government, again resorted to pettifogging. Its resolution stated that, while it was prepared to advise action in accordance with the interpretation of the British government in regard to the procedure to be followed in the sections, this must not involve any compulsion of a province, adding that in the event of any attempt at such compulsion, a province or part of a province had the right to take such action as may be deemed necessary to give effect to the wishes of the people concerned. This again was a misinterpretation, for there was no question of compulsion of any province, much less of part of a province, which was nowhere mentioned in the cabinet mission's plan, the provinces being free to opt out of their groups after the first general elections, which was a sufficient safeguard for the freedom of provinces.

In view of the Congress' persistent refusal to honour the terms of the plan the British government declared on February 20, 1947, that the plan could not be successfully implemented except on the basis indicated by them and if a constitution were framed by a constituent assembly in which a large section of the Indian population were not represented they could not contemplate forcing such a constitution on any unwilling parts of the country. The plan, therefore, collapsed due to the obduracy of the Congress, and the way for the emergence of Pakistan was thrown wide open. Penderel Moon, aptly remarks that it was almost as if a 'curse' had been laid on Nehru and his colleagues, causing them 'to act in such a way as to bring about exactly the opposite result to that which they intended. They passionately desired to preserve the unity of India they consistently acted so as to make its partition certain'.[1]

When the British and the Hindu leaders found that the Muslims were invincibly determined to resist the imposition of a united India by all possible means, they worked together to concede Pakistan on such terms and to create such conditions as would make it well nigh impossible for Pakistan to consolidate itself as a separate state. The partition plan drawn up by Lord Mountbatten in May 1947 may be said to be an Anglo-Hindu plan, for it was the result of consultations between Mountbatten, Jawaharlal Nehru and a Hindu officer, V. P. Menon.[2]

The way Mountbatten set about persuading the Congress leaders to agree to partition shows his ulterior motives. According to Leonard Mosley's *The Last Days of the British Raj*, the viceroy tried to persuade Sardar Vallabhbhai Patel as follows: 'Think of the peace if the Muslims could be

[1] Penderel Moon, *op. cit.* p. 14.

[2] V. P. Menon, *op. cit.* pp. 365, 366.

banished once and for all to their own (very small and unworkable) country. No opposition to Congress plans. No cunning campaign against the owners of the Congress money-bags. A free India under a one-party regime, free to carry out its plans without interference'.[1] Mountbatten advocated partition not out of any sense of fairplay or regard for the legitimacy of the Muslim claim to a share in freedom but because of his eagerness to help the Congress build up a mighty Hindu state which would through its strength, one day absorb the remaining areas.

In May 1947, the viceroy was in Simla where Nehru was staying as his guest. He showed Nehru [2] (but not the Qaid-e-Azam) the plan he had sent to London through Lord Ismay for His Majesty's government's approval. As V. P. Menon says, 'On the night of 10 May Lord Mountbatten showed Nehru the plan he had received from London. Nehru turned it down most vehemently and made it clear that the Congress would in no circumstances accept it.' The plan envisaged demission of authority to provinces or such confederations of provinces as might decide to group themselves in the interim period before the actual transfer of power. Nehru immediately turned it down, because he was particularly opposed to the provinces initially becoming independent. There were then secret discussions between Mountbatten, Nehru and V. P. Menon,[3] who was acting more as a partisan of the Congress than as a government servant. As a result of these talks, certain heads of agreement were formulated on the basis of which a new draft plan for partition was drawn up and approved by His Majesty's government. It was released to the public on June 3, 1947. Though it conceded outright partition and the creation of two sovereign states, the plan was weighted in favour of Hindu India, as it deprived Pakistan of vital areas in the Punjab and Bengal and placed it at a serious disadvantage in the matter of the setting up of a state structure and administrative machinery from scratch.

As late as May 31, 1947, Gandhi had thundered at the Muslims in the following words: 'Even if the whole of India burns we shall not concede Pakistan, no, not if the Muslims demand it at the point of the sword.' [4] By June 4th, he was telling a different story and on June 7th, he had no hesitation in advising the Congress to approve of the partition plan. Acharya Kripalani, the then Congress president, persuaded the Hindu bankers and traders of Sind to migrate, because, as the Congress would have them believe, it would not be long before they would be able to return triumphantly to their homes. The remarks of an American writer, Selig S. Harrison in this connection are pertinent. I quote him:

'The prevailing Hindu view that the new Moslem state would be short-lived was expressed by the Congress President at the time of Partition, Acharya J. B. Kripalani, "A strong, economically successful India", he said, "can win back the seceding children to its lap. The freedom we have achieved cannot be complete without the unity of India." It was deeply exasperating to most

[1] Leonard Mosley, *The Last Days of the British Raj* (1962), p. 101.
[2] See V. P. Menon, *op. cit.* p. 361.
[3] *Ibid.* p. 365.
[4] Ian Stephens, *Pakistan* (1963), p. 10.

Hindus that a Moslem state should be created in part of the motherland envisaged in the ancient Hindu scriptures, and it was deeply frustrating that at the very moment, when Hindus were to rule over the Moslems for the first time in their history, so many of the Moslems should escape their appointed fate.' [1]

The trouble with the Hindu leaders was that they lived in a world of make-believe and adopted an arrogant and domineering attitude towards the Muslims, as if the latter were a subject race who should live at the sufferance of the Hindu majority. They did not correctly gauge the Muslim mind and always miscalculated the strength of Muslim feeling and determination. As is evident from the facts I have narrated, the Hindu leaders always started by opposing even the moderate demands of the Muslims. By the time they came round to recognize these demands, the Muslims had moved a step forward. The Congress contemptuously rejected Jinnah's modest proposals in 1928, spurned his offer of co-operation in 1937 and 1939 and sabotaged the compromise plan for a united India in 1946, but after each and every refusal and rejection it had to yield more ground. As Kanji Dwarkadas remarks: 'This arrogance and lack of political foresight in July 1937, was repeated time and again during the next ten years, culminating, at last in the division of the country into India and Pakistan. . . . If only the Congress had come to terms with Jinnah and his Muslim League we would have had a different story of India during the last twenty-eight years.' [2]

Another prominent Hindu leader Sir Chimanlal Setalvad holds the Congress responsible for the division of the sub-continent. In his book *Recollections and Reflections* he says: 'The real parentage of the Pakistan movement can be traced to the Congress who, by the wrong way in which they handled the communal question and by their behaviour when they were in power, created the great distrust in the minds of the Muslim community which has driven them to advocate Pakistan.' [3]

Even when they agreed to partition, the Congress leaders did so with mental reservations, feeling confident that Pakistan would prove unworkable and would eventually be absorbed in India. G. D. Birla wrote a pamphlet on Pakistan's non-viability. He was considered by the Congress high command to be a great financial brain and economic expert. His views on such matters had almost the sancity of law in the eyes of the Congress leaders. The reservations with which the Congress leaders accepted the partition plan are evident from their utterances. Maulana Azad said in his speech on the partition plan at the meeting of the All-India Congress Committee, 'I am sure it is going to be a short-lived partition'. Gandhi declared that he was sure a time would come when the division would be undone. The All-India Congress Committee in accepting the partition plan entered the following caveat: 'Geography and the mountains and the seas fashioned India as she is and no human agency can change that shape or come in the way of her final destiny. . . . The All-India Congress Committee earnestly trusts that when the present

[1] Selig S. Harrison, *Foreign Affairs*, January 1965.
[2] Kanji Dwarkadas, *op. cit.* p. 473.
[3] Sir Chimanlal Setalvad, *op. cit.* p. 414.

passions have subsided, India's problems would be viewed in their proper perspective and the false doctrine of two nations would be discredited and discarded by all.' [1] As late as 1960, Nehru, in the course of a conversation with Leonard Mosley, revealed his mind as follows:[2] 'The truth is that we were tired men and we were getting on in years too. Few of us could stand the prospect of going to prison again – and if we stood out for a united India as we wished it, prison obviously awaited us. We saw the fires burning in the Punjab and heard everyday of the killings. The plan for partition offered a way out and we took it. . . . We expected that partition would be temporary, that Pakistan was bound to come back to us.' That these expectations and designs did not materialize is due to two factors – one, the leadership of the Qaid-e-Azam whose resourcefulness the Congress leaders always underestimated and two, the peculiar trait in the Muslim character which brings into play his best talents and energies in moments of the greatest stress, strain and danger.

THE ECONOMIC BASIS OF PAKISTAN

Throughout the movement for the creation of Pakistan two main objections were raised against it. First, Pakistan would not be economically viable. Secondly, it would not be able to defend itself against external attacks. I recall that these points were stressed also by the British cabinet ministers during their discussions with my friend the Raja Saheb of Mahmudabad and myself in 1946. Both objections have been disproved. Pakistan's economy has survived all stresses and strains and even onslaughts.

It would not be out of place if I gave a short background of the economic conditions prevailing in pre-independence India in so far they related to the Muslims.

The economic situation in pre-independence India was one of the factors which influenced the Muslims to seek their deliverance and security in the shape of a separate homeland and state. Business and industry were overwhelmingly the monopoly of the Hindu bania and the British merchant and industrialist. The British had a substantial share in big industry, particularly in jute, cotton, tea, mining, engineering and collieries. Their share in the raw cotton and textile industry too was substantial. Most of the industries and almost the entire internal trade, from money-lending to the buying and selling of all types of produce – raw and finished – were in the hands of the Hindus. Muslims only subsisted on the crumbs which were swept off these monopolists' tables. They were largely producers of jute, cotton, and foodgrains which crops were purchased from them at exploitation rates by the wealthy industrialists and banias whose profits, as a result of their operations, swelled each year.

As there are exceptions to every rule, so there were a few exceptions to the British and Hindu monopoly of business and industry. Here and there was established an industry owned by a Muslim. There were also some Memons, Khojas and Bohras who competed with the Hindu bania in the field of the retail sale of grains, cloth, hardware, etc., and held their ground

[1] V. P. Menon, *op. cit.* p. 384.

[2] Leonard Mosley, *op. cit.* p. 248.

well. But these were exceptions and did not change the general pattern of India's economy. The Muslims generally were poor and were denied opportunities and assistance to improve their lot. As I have said, they were forced by adverse circumstances to eke out their existence by being hewers of wood and drawers of water or by finding employment in the lower echelons of business or government service.

This was the condition of the Muslims while British power still held sway over the sub-continent, while he could still look up to British justice for the redress of his grievances, while he still had some hope of improving his lot. Every thinking Muslim knew full well that with the withdrawal of the British and with the transfer of power to the majority, which was 3 : 1 Hindu, his fate would be sealed. The attitude of the Hindu businessman and employer towards the Muslims is well brought out by a retired British civilian officer, Penderel Moon, who speaks with long experience of Indian conditions. In his book *Divide and Quit*, he says:

'They [the Hindus] might say the Muslims were their brothers but would in fact treat them as less than step-brothers. A few leaders might be sincere in their intentions, but the ingrained exclusiveness of most of the high-caste Hindus was bound to assert itself, so that at most only a few hand-picked Muslims would be embraced as brothers and the rest relegated to the position of outcastes. An excellent illustration of what treatment Muslims might expect from the Hindus, if the latter had a free choice, was afforded in the Punjab. In that province, most of the commercial, industrial and banking establishments were controlled by the Hindus. In none of them was any Muslim employed except in a menial capacity as a coolie or a watchman or as an artisan. Well-paid posts and positions of profit were not open to outsiders but were filled on the basis of family, caste and other similar connections according to the deeply embedded habits and traditions of Hindu society. That society was not going to change its nature overnight at the pious wish of a Gandhi or a Nehru. Hindu professions were widely different from Hindu practice as all Muslims knew. Jinnah's distrust of them was both genuine and well-founded.'

I state here some facts and figures which are revealing. On the eve of partition there existed in India 111 jute mills comprising about 69,000 looms. Of these, only one mill of 500 looms and one of 150 looms were owned by Muslims, namely, Adamjee and Ispahani, respectively. Against all these mills which were located in and around Calcutta, there was not a single unit installed in the region which is today East Pakistan, which was treated merely as an agricultural slum. Today in East Pakistan we have thirty-one jute mills with 22,797 looms which work double-shift, as compared with India's single-shift. In West Pakistan, two jute mills with 679 looms are in commission and two mills with 750 looms are under erection.

Turning to cotton in the western region, the picture is no different. There were two textile mills, one at Okara owned by Birla and the other at Lyallpur owned by Lala Shri Ram, in the region which now constitutes West Pakistan. In our eastern part there were three or four small mills, and these too were owned by Hindus. The rest of the mills, about 400 of them, were located in the neighbouring country – India. The bulk of the cotton produced in the former Punjab, Bahawalpur and Sind was ginned by Hindus and a few foreign firms and shipped principally for consumption in Bombay and Ahmedabad. Today we have 128 cotton mills, our largest unit being of 100,000 spindles.

The tea industry which was and even now is a big foreign exchange earner also did not present a happier picture for the Muslims. Except for Waliur Rahman, Nawab Musharraf Hussain of Jalpaiguri, and a couple of nonentity garden-owners who were Muslims, almost the entire industry, producing in 1947, 561,740,000 lb., was owned and directed by Britons and Hindus. In other industries such as mining, engineering, cement manufacture, the position of the Muslims was even more pathetic.

Another important business which attracted the attention of the Europeans, Parsees and Hindus was the airlines. These three communities among them owned several airlines in India. The Muslims who constituted twenty-five per cent of the population of the sub-continent did not own or float a single company. When they managed to whip up the required capital from the poor and the rich of the community, the Orient Airways Ltd. was floated, but in its very organizing state it was almost strangled by the vested interests in civil aviation before it eventually got permission to operate on the Calcutta/Rangoon route. It was a small airline with only three Dakotas to start off with. Today the same Muslim company has blossomed into the Pakistan International Airlines which by comparison is a big undertaking, flying the most modern and expensive aircraft and considered to be one of the efficient and up-to-date airlines of the world. Here again, we have seen that the Muslim, if given the opportunity, can render a good account of himself in any business undertaking. It is worth mentioning that the entire staff of the P.I.A. – pilots, engineers, technicians, ground staff, as well as direction and management, are entirely Muslim, which again belies the propaganda in pre-independence India that the Muslims were incapable of doing important jobs.

The economic position of the Muslims is also aptly summed up by Mr Justice Mohammad Munir, who was a member of the boundary commission for the Punjab, as follows:

'The function of the Commission was to separate the contiguous Muslim and non-Muslim majority areas and not to divide property or trade or business assets or to separate the intellectually developed from backward areas. In fact, in the figures relied on by the non-Muslims, there lay the strongest argument for the partition of the country. Almost for a century the Muslims had been exploited by the non-Muslims. The wealth of the non-Muslims in Lahore represented the sweat and labour of the Muslims, and it was with a view to doing away with this inequitable position that the Musalman demanded a State where undominated by the Hindu he could improve his lot and enjoy a position of economic independence.' [1]

In view of these conditions, the conviction grew among the Muslims that, with the passing of power into the hands of the Hindus, they would be crushed beyond repair, that they would, in the course of a few years, be reduced to

[1] 'Days to Remember' by Mr Justice Munir, published in *Pakistan Times*, June 22, 23, 24, 1964.

the position and status of the depressed classes and even worse. Without doubt, this would have happened. One has only to look at the state of the Muslims in India today to realize what fate would have befallen the rest of the Muslims of the sub-continent had a united India been forced upon us.

On the other hand, let us look at the condition of the Muslims in Pakistan. Having achieved a homeland of their own, they received all the encouragement and opportunity to pull themselves up by the bootstraps and they did. Today one finds an army of industrialists – big and small – in our country. The performance of some of the big Pakistani industrialists compares favourably with that of the well-known giants of India such as Tata, Birla, Dalmia and Mafatlal. Count the number of industries pulsating with vigour in all parts of our land. Study the commercial part of our life. Where only a few Muslims of prominence existed in this field in pre-partition days, we have today hundreds, nay thousands, in this field. Turn to banking, financing, broking, insurance, internal buying and selling, the same picture reveals itself. In pre-independence India, the notion had been sedulously spread that the Muslims were incapable of handling banking and insurance. It was a vicious circle. On the one hand the Muslims were denied opportunities to participate in these careers and, on the other, they were branded as unfit, so that the Hindu monopoly continued. There used to be only one Muslim bank in pre-partition India – the Habib Bank – which was small in size as compared with countless Hindu and foreign banks operating in the sub-continent. Another Muslim bank, the Muslim Commercial Bank, was founded on the eve of partition, i.e. July 9, 1947, and was preparing to start operations. The position in Pakistan is entirely different. The Muslims have more than proved their mettle in the field of banking. Today there are sixteen Pakistani scheduled banks manned and run by Pakistanis.

The position in the world of insurance in pre-partition India was no better. The Eastern Federal Union Insurance Co., the Habib Insurance Co., the Muslim Insurance Co., all small concerns, were the only Muslim companies operating in the sub-continent. All three were smaller than the smallest non-Muslim companies and their field of operation was very limited. The rest of the insurance companies – and the smallest of them was much larger than the three mentioned – were either owned and directed by non-Muslims or were foreign concerns. Compare that picture with the one which obtains in Pakistan today. There are now forty-three Pakistani insurance companies.

The difference becomes so palpably clear that it is unbelievable. Banking and insurance have proved to be fields which have provided prosperous careers for ever-increasing numbers of Muslim youths.

The Hindu bania and the foreigner are no longer in a position to monopolize our economic life, and this is the fruit of the freedom which we won in the form of our separate state. Muslims, having been afforded the opportunity, have fully availed themselves of it and proved their worth. They have also given the lie to the notion that had been spread by hostile elements that Pakistan would not prove to be economically viable. Need I say anything more?

A CASE STUDY OF THE SOCIAL RELATIONS BETWEEN THE MUSLIMS AND THE HINDUS, 1935–47

by I. H. QURESHI*

The purpose of this paper is to record my personal impressions of the changes in the social relations of the Hindus and the Muslims that took place between 1935 and 1947. It should be remembered that by the year 1935 the idea of the establishment of a separate state where the Muslims would be in a majority had already been mooted but it had not evoked much discussion or response. It was around 1935 that the demand for Pakistan began to gather support and developed a momentum which led to its establishment in 1947. This change in the Muslim outlook could not have happened without accompanying changes in the social and economic relationship between the two major communities of the subcontinent. A description of these changes by an eye-witness who can recall certain events and developments may possess some value for the historian. It may be mentioned that apart from the records of the political activities in support of and against partition and the communal riots which became such a feature of life in the twenties and even more so in the thirties, there is little on record to give a student of this period any information about the changing pattern of inter-communal relations. Obviously, therefore, the writer of this paper has to depend mostly upon his own impressions. These impressions are not scientific in the sense of studies based upon surveys and assiduously collected data and, therefore, their validity may rightly be challenged. Indeed such scientific accuracy is not claimed. Nevertheless, being based upon first hand knowledge and experience this paper may not be devoid of all value.

Autobiographical material which would throw light upon this aspect of the question is extremely scarce. For the relations between the two communities during an earlier period we have an extremely good record in Nirad C. Chaudhuri's well known book *The Autobiography of an Unknown Indian* (1951), but it does not even come up to 1935 so far as the theme of this paper is concerned. I have not come across any study of a similar nature by a sensitive and observant Indian or Pakistani regarding the years 1935 to 1947. In presenting an attempted description of inter-communal relations during this period, I have to rely only on my own impressions. A number of undocumented illustrations could have been given to illustrate the points made, but even if facts had been mentioned profusely they could not have added much in the way of providing a fully scientific basis for these observations. For this reason there is no justification for transgressing the limits of space that should be imposed on a paper.

* Vice-Chancellor, University of Karachi.

It must be also admitted at the very start that within my own limited experience, even during a period of growingly strained relationship, a number of facts could be found which might point in directions different from those indicated in this paper. However, I have chosen only such happenings as, in my opinion, indicated the general trend and to which the greater volume of happenings corresponded.

I have dealt with some of the psychological factors formulating Muslim attitudes in an earlier and fuller work (*The Muslim Community of the Indo Pakistan Subcontinent*, The Hague 1962) and do not intend to repeat all that has been said in greater detail there. Two points, however, must be mentioned. The Muslims in the subcontinent have always been anxious to preserve their separate identity. This has made them highly sensitive to any real or even imagined danger to their religion or culture. And then, a certain amount of revivalism is quite a common phenomenon in all resurgent nationalisms. Most of the manifestations of ill-will, leading sometimes to riots and ugly incidents, were basically the result of revivalist feelings amongst the Hindus and the anxiety of the Muslims to preserve their identity. Relations were less strained when the two antagonisms did not have much impact upon each other and did not affect the masses to the extent of inciting them to violence. Here also the question of volume is involved. Small manifestations of Hindu revivalism would not have produced the same results as did larger attempts that embraced broader aspects of life. On the other hand if the Muslims had not been prone to look upon everything indigenous but not adopted by them to be a source of extreme danger to themselves, feelings would not have been exacerbated to such an extent as to make it difficult for the two communities to work harmoniously.

After the post of non-co-operation intensification of Hindu-Muslim antagonism which expressed itself in movements like *shuddhi*, *sangathan*, *tabligh* and *tanzim* and gave a high crop of riots, the situation was showing some signs of improvement around the year 1935, which was partly due to the fact that the Muslims themselves were not quite clear in their minds regarding their future destiny in the subcontinent. Politically conscious majority opinion still thought that the best way would be to find a *modus vivendi* with the majority community and to form a unit of a multi-national state. As this was considered to be the desideratum by the enlightened Muslims, they were not in favour of augmenting or keeping alive inter-communal friction in any manner. It was, however, difficult to press demands for effective safeguards and substantial autonomy without, in one way or another, creating in the Hindu mind misgivings of their intentions and, what was even more important, of their complete identification with Indian nationalism. The average enlightened Hindu looked upon all such demands as essentially anti-national narrow-minded, based on prejudice and inevitably resulting in a weak state.

These feelings, however, were not very much on the surface, so far as social relations were concerned. The friction of the twenties had not died out. The economic and social repercussions of that friction were still visible, but it was at least felt seriously by a small number of thinking men and women that effort should be made to achieve harmony and friction should be removed so far as possible. This attitude, with the hind-sight that we possess today, seems to have been a form of escapism for the well-intentioned because one does not find any efforts of a positive nature to bring about greater harmony. Either people pretended that the problem did not exist or they thought that it was best left untouched or did not consider it polite or pleasant to bring it up on social occasions. It must be remembered that the intermingling of the two communities at the social level was meagre and confined to the more sophisticated westernized people who would meet one another in clubs. Club life was not popular amongst the Indians at that time and only an infinitesimal part of the huge population cultivated it. Relations at such urbane levels were still pleasant because of the general desire not to throw bricks in otherwise placid waters. This, however, did not mean that the people who met at such levels had no strong political opinions or that personal intimacy removed present or potential political hostility. It only meant that relations had not deteriorated to an extent that would have made social contacts impossible.

Indeed there was little on the horizon that would make feelings immediately exacerbated. The elections to the provincial legislatures in 1937 were fought, generally speaking, in an atmosphere of understanding. At that time, as is generally known, there was no friction between the stated aims of the Indian National Congress and the Muslim League. The scene, however, changed with the formation of the Congress ministries in many provinces. It is not intended to discuss here the policies of the Congress governments, nor is this paper the proper place to discuss the rights and wrongs of the Muslim feelings against the various Congress governments. What the formation of the Congress governments brought out in the open had been lying somewhat dormant below the surface. With substantial power being transferred into the hands of the people of the subcontinent, the innate tendencies could not but assert themselves. The resurgent nationalism of the Hindus started asserting itself in many ways which it considered to be legitimate. If there was to be a common Indian nation, it had to have a common language. This common language should have its roots in the Indian past and also perhaps in the common substance of Sanskritic origin in the field of vocabulary. This also applied to the script. Such a language could be Hindi and not Urdu and because words are impregnated with history, culture and religion, therefore, the general culture of India inevitably was to be Hindu. It had to express and interpret the ideals of the majority through its traditions, *mores*, history and ideals. To the average Hindu citizen and politician it seemed only natural that it should be so. He felt puzzled that such a simple proposition was not accepted without opposition. And he could not, perhaps, be blamed, because the sophistication needed for sustaining a multi-cultural society is rare in even more politically developed societies. This attitude filled the average Muslim with alarm and he resented all attempts at Hinduizing the language, the culture and education.

It seems that this was a natural development and it is doubtful whether it could have been prevented. Even if the Congress had exercised the utmost wisdom, it might have adopted the policy of going slow, but, to my mind, it could not have resisted popular pressures for any length of time. Similarly

Muslim resistance to this process would also have ultimately come to the surface, even if the assertion of Hindu national instincts had been slow and cautious. Perhaps this resistance would have developed gradually. In the beginning it could have been less violent. Nevertheless at some stage or the other, the injury to deep-rooted Muslim feelings would have resulted in discontent and frustration. The year 1937 is rightly considered to be a turning point in the history of the subcontinent. Its importance was magnified because of the lack of experience and foresight on the part of Congress leadership, but it would have remained a turning point in any case as fairly effective authority was transferred for the first time to the representatives of the people. Such transfer could not but raise their inner conflicts and psychological antagonism to the political level. There is the possibility that in case of a more gradual change Muslim sensitivities would have been dulled to a certain extent and perhaps if the possibility of lengthening the process had existed and been utilized, the Muslims might have made adjustments to the new order.

However, all this is mere speculation. Long nurtured ideas do not die so slowly and have an inconvenient habit of making themselves felt time and again. In any case because these antagonisms came to the surface and resulted in widespread and frequent communal riots, feelings were exacerbated and social relations now came to be affected because people's minds were greatly exercised not only by what was happening but also by the possibilities of what might happen in a not too distant future.

The writer of this paper was away from the subcontinent from June 1937 to September 1939 when considerable intensification of ill-will took place. Perhaps the fact that he had remained away for two years from the scene gave him a vantage point. He could compare the conditions that he had left behind in 1937 with those that he found prevailing when he came back in 1939. Even though he had remained in touch with the happenings in the subcontinent through newspapers and correspondence he was amazed at the change that he witnessed on his return. The atmosphere was now surcharged with emotion and even in social gatherings statements were made which showed the extent of estrangement that had taken place. The Pakistan resolution was not adopted by the Muslim League until 1940 but the idea of Pakistan had caught the imagination of the Muslims like wild fire. They had come to believe firmly that they could not accept a common destiny with the majority community. The majority community in its turn had been exasperated to an extent that any suggestions that parting company as friends might be the solution of an otherwise extremely difficult question was looked upon as treason to the ideal of united nationalism.

In view of this exasperation it could not be expected that there would be any attempt at understanding the point of view of the minority. There were a few exceptions here and there among the Hindus who saw some justification in the Muslim desire for separation, but such Hindus were extremely few. Their number sank into insignificance even when compared with that of the Congress-minded Muslims who still believed in a united nationalism and therefore, were called nationalist Muslims. The writer can look back with satisfaction and gratitude to the friendship which was extended to him by a number of his Hindu friends and even more by Hindu students who came into direct contact with him. What is being written hereafter is being done with the fullest consciousness of their kindness. The majority of these friends and students, indeed all of them, were quite firmly convinced that the Muslim attitude was not only deplorable but criminal, but they did not permit this feeling to affect their personal relations with me. On the other hand they never ventured to discuss the question of Pakistan with me, nor for that, did they get any encouragement from me. For the purpose of maintaining my social relations with Hindu friends, colleagues and students and not poisoning them by a discussion of my political convictions or theirs, I also scrupulously avoided any discussion of Hindu Muslim relations with them. Political questions were invariably discussed by the Muslims amongst themselves and also by the Hindus with the members of their own community. Thus practically dialogue on the question of Pakistan ceased at the personal level. Only the press and the political leaders went on discussing the merits of the Muslim case or tearing it to pieces. There was more talking at each other than talking to one another.

In a situation like this it was quite obvious that positive efforts had to be made to maintain any relations. Indeed the worst of escapism was practised by everyone concerned in the sense that it was thought that the discussion of unpleasant topics must be avoided if relations were not to be poisoned. I do not blame either others or myself for this attitude because the Hindu and Muslim points of view were now clearly defined and there was almost a total acceptance of the views of the leaders of either side on these points. Besides the atmosphere was so greatly charged with emotions that it would have been impossible to carry on a discussion objectively or with restraint. Arguments would have carried no weight in the face of convictions held as strongly as religion itself.

This was the general pattern. There were, however, occasional outbursts in private meetings which did little to improve the situation. I remember several such occasions quite distinctly and my counterparts in the other community having to deal with Muslim colleagues and students might perhaps recall similar instances. In a weekly seminar held for the purpose of discussing the developments in the second world war a student blurted out without any provocation that the treatment meted out to the Jews in Nazi Germany was fully justified in view of 'their anti-national activities'. Up to now this remark, however deplorable, would not have created the ill-will that the sentence following it did. He added, 'If the minorities in India are not careful they will have to be dealt with precisely in the same manner'. There was no occasion for a remark like that and yet in a way it was quite natural because the Hindu mind was so much exercised by the likely role of the minorities, especially the Muslim minority, in a future independent India that the student's action was almost entirely involuntary. As an isolated instance it could have been dismissed as irresponsible behaviour of a student, but unfortunately it reflected a good deal of common thinking. I had to stop counter remarks by any of the Muslim students who formed a small proportion of the seminar. I simply ruled the remark out as irrelevant to the discussion.

I found a distinct decline in what was markedly a liberal atmosphere among the honours and postgraduate students. Up to the year 1937 liberalism was very much in fashion. I think that most of it was sincere so far as the university community was concerned. There was a certain amount of schizophrenic tendency to keep liberalism and communal bias in water tight compartments, but, by far and large, liberalism was not openly questioned. From 1939 onwards I found that the attitudes were less liberal and there was a somewhat open adherence to the doctrine of intolerance for the purpose of national good. An incident would perhaps illustrate this point. I was informally discussing with a small number of students the desirability of basing domestic and foreign policies of a free country on the principles of fairplay and justice. We were not discussing any particular problem, nor was this really a profound discussion of social or political ethics. My surprise was therefore extreme when a student said rather excitedly 'What is justice?' and then he went on to add 'Is it just on Mr Jinnah's part to demand Pakistan?' I responded mildly by saying that I was not prepared to discuss the justice or otherwise of Pakistan on that occasion but I said that I hoped that in principle it would be accepted that the only method of securing good and orderly government at home and peace abroad is an adherence to the principles of justice. The student then said, 'One gets a little tired of this word "justice", particularly when so many unpleasant demands are put forward in its name. In any case justice is so difficult to define that it cannot be accepted as a principle any longer in statecraft or international relations and even if it were accepted it would be difficult to determine where justice lay.' This, to my mind, was not an entirely indefensible remark, however morally deplorable it might be. I conceded that it might be difficult in certain circumstances to determine where justice lay but I said that if one came face to face with a situation where justice was not difficult to define one should not shirk its consequences. 'When anyone comes face to face with justice', said I 'let him not turn his face away from it.' The next remark was, in my opinion, extremely revealing. He said, 'In certain instances where national interests are at stake, it is a patriotic citizen's duty to turn his face away from justice.' I was completely stunned. Such sentiments would have been impossible before 1935. This is by no means the most outstanding example of lack of liberalism, but coming from a comparatively intelligent, mild and decent young man it reflected a tendency that was frightening.

Such instances out of incidents witnessed by me – and they could be multiplied – would reveal that, in spite of excellent personal relations existing between the teachers and the students, social relations had a tendency to run into difficulties and the superficial pleasantness and the artificially cultivated smoothness of discussion could not truly hide – even in the academic atmosphere of a university – the fissures that had taken place underneath. As a matter of fact there had not been much commingling of ideas. Persons who were less willing to exercise caution and restraint in their actions and expressions of opinion were far too many even to permit a superficial avoidance of the unpleasant. So far as the Muslims were concerned they also tended to withdraw even more into themselves. They also scarcely could say anything which was perfectly honest and sincere – apart from the general banalities – which would not injure the feelings of others. Gradually the sole communication, so far as the Muslims were concerned, could exist between them and the non-Hindu minorities, where differences could be discussed in a somewhat dispassionate manner.

With the growing bitterness in the dialogue between the Indian National Congress and the Muslim League and particularly after the enunciation of June 3rd plan, relations became extremely strained. This could be felt even in normal academic and official work. The university community could not escape from the effects of the poisoned atmosphere of the city of Delhi or for for that matter of the subcontinent as a whole.

What was happening in the city was now a nightmare. Many quarters in the old city could be easily fortified by placing strong gates on the narrow streets providing ingress and egress. Very soon began a feverish collection of arms. A good deal of material from army disposals after the war surreptitiously found its way into the black market. The fortified *mohallas* (as the quarters were called) developed into arsenals. One could see that an undeclared and unofficial civil war was in the offing. It became the practice to organize parties of able-bodied inhabitants into groups who manned strategic places. At night the house tops began to bristle with armed men. This seems to have been a country-wide phenomenon and ultimately resulted in mass killings in many areas. The details of these pogroms are available in the newspapers and need not be repeated here. The killings were ghastly. A large number of innocent men, woman and children were murdered. Feelings were inflamed by every story of rioting and killing that appeared in the press. It did not take long in cities like Delhi for groups to indulge in street stabbing. It became dangerous even to pass through the main thoroughfares of the city. People seldom ventured out at night; most of the killing was done in broad daylight. Stabbings were invariably cowardly because some one would emerge out of a narrow lane stabbing the victim from behind and disappear, once again, into the labyrinths of the narrow streets of the localities. These killers were sheltered by the inhabitants and could not be traced.

Under such circumstances the meagre social relations which had survived among the members of the two communities came practically to an end. Even the economic relations between the two communities were disrupted. In this the Muslims were the main sufferers. Delhi had a long tradition of Muslim craftsmen working for dealers in traditional materials. For instance, the makers of gold and silver thread laces (*gota*) were given materials by the dealers and their products were bought for wholesale and retail sales. The dealers stopped supplying materials or purchasing manufactured articles resulting in great economic distress to the craftsmen. The same catastrophe befell the manufacturers of gold and silver leaf which was used in fairly large quantities for decorating sweets and dishes. A similar situation developed in handicrafts relating to brass and copper, brocades, ivory and certain decorative arts.

Then began a war of nerves and the nights were full of full-throated war cries raised by hundreds of men in one locality or another. Soon after Sikh and Hindu refugees started congregating in Delhi. Throughout this period militant organizations like the Rashtrya Svem Seva Sangh were active. The Muslims had participated in the inhuman acts of stabbing and the blame for this can be apportioned to both the communities equally. The Muslims, however, did not have an organization like the Rashtrya Svem Seva Sangh. Soon, with the help of the rations dealers, more or less full lists of Muslims living in exposed and undefended localities were compiled. It was known almost with full accuracy how many persons were living in a locality and for that matter in a house. The rations trade was almost entirely in the hands of the Hindus. In such localities it became common for Muslims to find that their houses had been marked in the night with the inverted Hindu swastikas for pogroms which were being secretly organized.

Delhi became a prison for the Muslims. Trains were searched and Muslims were killed in cold blood. Buses and cars met with no better fate. The most ghastly killing took place when the Grand Trunk Express going to Hyberabad and Madras was stopped and every Muslim man, woman and child was slaughtered. News now started pouring in from the surrounding villages and townships of large scale killings. The Muslims could not help noticing the coincidence that the Sikh deputy commissioner who was now always surrounded by leaders of the Rashtrya Svem Seva Sangh would visit a village one day and the very next day its Muslim population would be exterminated. I had known him earlier. He was sociable and had visited me in my house once or twice quite informally. He had admired my collection of Mughul miniatures. After my house had been looted, rumour has it that they found their way to his house.

I lived on the campus of the university. In close proximity was Jawaharnagar which was a Rashtrya Svem Seva Sangh stronghold. The camps of the refugees were also quite near. The arrival of the refugees naturally raised a wave of sympathy for them. I tried my best to accommodate and help refugee students because it would have been inhuman not to try to mitigate human suffering. The feelings of the Hindus and the Sikhs were greatly embittered for which no blame could attach to them. Soon after armed Sikhs and others were seen roaming in and around the campus. As I had been elected to the constituent assembly on the Muslim League ticket, I was now an enemy for all but my own circle of friends and students. My movements were watched, throughout the day and the night some agent of the Rashtrya Svem Seva Sangh was posted at a vantage point to keep an eye on all those who came to see me. A student whom I knew to be a Rashtrya Svem Seva Sangh member came a little too often to see me. Some Muslim friends pointed it out to me that I was in a precarious situation, but there was little I could do. There was a small Muslim community on the campus and if I had left, their morale would have collapsed.

At last the inevitable happened. The Muslim inhabitants of Timarpur, which was within a mile of the campus, were attacked. Stabbings around the campus became common. One day a Muslim recluse living in a deserted mosque nearby was killed. Next day the male members of my family went to the nearest mosque to offer Friday prayers but found it locked and deserted. About a mile away from the campus were located fruit orchards which extended for miles. As the fruit trade had been a Muslim monopoly, the orchards were peopled by Muslims who worked there. By Friday afternoon Muslim refugees from these orchards began to pour towards the university because many had been murdered. That night was full of terror for us. We could hear screams of men, women and children who were intermittently being killed in their homes. Next morning the campus was attacked. There was no loss of life, but all Muslim houses were looted, one by one. Muslim students and teachers were evacuated with difficulty. We escaped in our car. Women hastily put on Hindu caste marks on their foreheads and put on Hindu clothes. I took them to the Pakistan High Commission. The streets were littered with dead bodies. My nine year old son looked up and said simply, 'Father, are you afraid?' I said truthfully "No". I had no emotions at that time. Our house was looted soon after.

I lost all I had except the clothes on our bodies and the money in the bank. I did not mind that, but the loss of my personal library containing some rare manuscripts, and miniatures, quite a few of them heirlooms, was difficult to bear. I had two of my own books, one in manuscript and the other in typescript ready for the press, both of which were irretrievably lost.

Next day I put my family into the Old Fort, where the Muslim refugees from the city had congregated, and plunged into rescue work. There were many memorable incidents, but the most significant of these was that I brought Dr Zakir Husain, later president of India, from his house at the Jamia near Okhla at that time several miles out of Delhi and we two went and saw Gandhi. We did not have to tell him much because his workers were reporting events fully and truly. There was no effort to hide the truth from him. I said to him that only he could stop the carnage. For a moment he grew thoughtful and promised simply, 'I will put in my best in the effort'. And I think he did keep his promise. Otherwise he would not have been assassinated.

DACCA UNIVERSITY AND THE PAKISTAN MOVEMENT

by MAHMUD HUSAIN*

Speaking of Aligarh the Aga Khan in his *Memoirs* observes: 'surely it may be claimed that the independent sovereign nation of Pakistan was born in the Muslim University of Aligarh.' The part which Aligarh played in the Pakistan movement was undoubtedly conspicuous, but what Aligarh did for the movement in the sub-continent as a whole, the University of Dacca did for it in East Bengal and Assam. As one who was associated with the Dacca University from 1933 till after partition, the present writer had an opportunity of watching from close quarters its contribution towards the coming of Pakistan.

It may be worthwhile recalling the special circumstances which led to the establishment of the University of Dacca. When the first partition of Bengal was annulled in 1911, one of the promises made to conciliate the Muslims was the establishment of a university at Dacca. Though not visualized as a denominational institution, it was expected that it would, because of its location, help the cause of the education of the Muslims of East Bengal. Before, however, this unitary and residential university could be established, the first world war came and it could be brought into existence only in 1921.

Thus Dacca University was established primarily for the Muslims of East Bengal and, therefore, came to be sarcastically called the 'Mecca University' by the Hindus. But actually the majority of its students were Hindus right up to later thirties and, of course, the vast majority (90 per cent) of its teachers, even at the time of partition, were Hindus. It was but natural that the condition should be such, because Bengal Muslims had resisted much too long the 'encroachment', so they thought, of western education on the precincts of their traditional culture. They were drawn towards western education only slowly and began to benefit from it much later than even the Muslims of other parts of the sub-continent. It was, therefore, not unexpected that at Dacca teachers should be drawn from the Hindu community. But as East Bengal was and is predominantly Muslim, and as the stigma of western education had begun to lose its bitter sting when Muslims realized how they were losing their control over the political, economic, social and even cultural fields in the country, the number of Muslim students, after the establishment of the Dacca University started increasing. Even Muslim girls started coming in, although their numbers were extremely small up to 1947. By virtue of the fact that an increasing number of Muslim students were getting educated here, that this small city and this small university had enough residential accommodation for a large number of Muslim students and that this university started getting representation in the Bengal legislative assembly, this institution

* Dean of the Faculty of Arts, University of Karachi, since 1957: Reader and Professor of History at Dacca University 1933–48.

became the moulder of new Muslim consciousness, a producer of Muslim leaders in political, economic and literary fields, and the shaper of Muslim thoughts and ideals. Had not this university been established, it would have been difficult for the Muslim League to get a large body of workers and students and teachers drawn from different parts of East Bengal to work day and night for the Pakistan movement. If Islamia College of Calcutta is to be regarded as a centre for the Muslim students of Calcutta and West Bengal, Dacca University and its two Muslim residential Halls, Salimullah Muslim Hall and Fazlul Haq Muslim Hall should be regarded as the centres that provided East Bengal with a devoted band of workers and leaders. If we study the background of the first legislative assembly of Bengal after the Act of 1935 came into operation, we see that most of the Muslim members elected from East Bengal were educated and trained in the University of Dacca. Some of them would never have seen any university because quite a few had come from comparatively poor homes. Let us not forget that the Hindus had formed the richer class of Bengal ever since Cornwallis had introduced the 'Permanent Settlement' and the British government had followed a policy of withholding support from the old education system and of changing the system of administration and judicature. The Hindus had an active and influential middle class. The Muslims of Bengal had hardly any such class. The struggles between the Hindus and Muslims for supremacy in the political field may, from this point of view, be considered as a struggle between the haves and the have-nots, between those who tried to mould the education and cultural pattern of the country according to the Hindu ideas and those who wanted to shake off their decadence and regenerate the spirit of the defeated and suppressed and suffering Muslims and regain an honourable place in all fields.

Dacca University helped in creating that social equilibrium amongst the Muslims of East Bengal which a society can attain only when there is in it a flourishing middle class. The majority of Muslim government servants in Bengal were provided by the Dacca University. The learned professions, teaching, medicine, engineering, law etc., received their quota and many of the former students turned towards business. Thus a vacuum was filled which in its turn made Muslim nationalism take root. This was not unusual. The middle class has been in the history of the modern period the chief protagonist of the idea of the nation and the nation state, and this was what happened in East Bengal.

Dacca University provided the young Muslims of East Bengal with the opportunity of intellectual regeneration. In the late twenties and early thirties this regeneration took the form of revolt against old traditions and complete modernization. It was in Dacca University that 'Muslim Sahitya Samaj' (Muslim Literary Society) was formed with university teachers such as Abul Hossain (later on an M.L.A.) and Qazi Motahar Hossain as leading geniuses. This movement, however, could not last long but it shocked the Muslim community by its radical ideas and modernizing zeal. It was almost an anti-religious movement. This shock at least compelled the Muslims of Bengal to think about their own traditions and values and reconsider their efficacy and significance in the light of the life that was emerging in the sub-continent.

This movement lost its force because of the orthodoxy of the Muslims of the city of Dacca and also because of the bitter communal feelings that had started disturbing and even disrupting the normal life of the province. In moulding the political opinion of the Muslim youth of Bengal, an old student of the University of Dacca, Altaf Husain, played a leading part. During the thirties he contributed under the pseudonym 'Ainul Mulk' a column to *The Statesman* of Calcutta entitled 'Through Muslim Eyes' which exercised great influence. As soon as the League became an active force Altaf Husain gave his support to it through his column. By 1937 Muslim nationalism had gained ascendancy. The election and the resultant formation of the cabinet under the Government of India Act, 1935, reinforced this feeling. Even then Dacca University did not become a stronghold of the Muslim League till the Lahore resolution was passed in 1940. It was the idea of Pakistan which brought about a tremendous change in the attitude and activities of young men and women getting trained in this university. Even Fazlul Haq, an extremely popular figure, had to experience black flags in almost every city of East Bengal when he left the Muslim League and formed a coalition government with the Mahasabha and Congress, the so-called Shayma Prasad-Haq ministry (1941).

1940 to 1947 may thus be regarded as the most active, fruitful and significant period in so far as the contribution of the Dacca University to the Pakistan movement is concerned. In the first place, the Muslim League found a stronghold among the students of this University. When Gandhi started his 'Quit India' movement, the Hindu students boycotted their studies for a short while, picketted at the gates of the university and held meetings. The Muslim students did not participate in the movement. They continued to attend classes though they did not hold any meeting in opposition to the Congress. They did not do so obviously because the Muslim League did not want to start a conflict between the supporters of the Congress and the League.

Secondly, Fazlur Rahman, a former student of the university helped the founding and publication of a fortnightly periodical called *Pakistan* which started coming out in Dacca from July 1942. Several younger Muslim members of the staff worked for the journal which was all a labour of love.

Thirdly, this was the most fruitful period for those writers who were not only supporters of the Pakistan movement, but were also inspired by the idea of having Muslim culture as the generating and governing principle moulding the attitude of life of Muslim writers. The 'East Pakistan Literary Association' was formed in September 1942 and in January 1943 it held an all-Bengal literary conference with astonishing success. The founders of this association wanted writers to draw inspiration from their own traditions, concentrate their attention on the life of the Muslims, and write in a language which was spoken and used by the Muslims of Bengal. They also wanted a revaluation of the Muslim writers of the past. From 1943 to 1946, this organization retained its dominance. It used to hold an annual conference each year and thus a reassessment of Bengali literature was initiated. Even an eminent Hindu scholar wrote a new history of Bengali literature called 'Islamic Literature' (*Islami Bangla Sahitya* by Sukumar Sen). Previously, there had been an attempt on the part of Hindu scholars to play down the importance of Muslim writers and present Bengali literature in such a fashion that a reader of such histories would regard Bengali literature as basically the creation of the Hindu mind. But the movement started by this organization led to a completely new valuation of the past and a new search for manuscripts by Muslim writers. It was soon discovered first that the best writers of early and middle Bengali literature were Muslims and, second, that in the nineteenth and twentieth centuries, the different socio-cultural conditions of the Hindus and the Muslims of this province led to the creation of two different literary traditions. The dominance of the Hindus in the Bengali literature of these two centuries was a well-known fact, but this dominance was not allowed to make the young Muslim writers forget the importance of their own traditions, and the necessity of concentrating their attention on their own society, culture and traditions. In short, this literary association provided writers and thinkers of Bengal with the metaphysical and cultural basis of their own independent identity. The fortnightly *Pakistan* became the mouthpiece of this association. Thus the political and cultural movement united and a new consciousness and pride in their own achievements and glory became a possibility.

Along with these movements and political activities must be mentioned another contribution of the students and political workers produced by Dacca University. Among the most important activities were, firstly, the participation of student League workers in the election of 1946 and in the referendum of 1947. The elections of 1946 were crucial for the success of the movement. It is no exaggeration to state that the League which, unlike the Congress, had no whole-time workers or had hardly any, could not have done so well at the election but for the work put in by the Muslim students, among whom the students of the University of Dacca were by far the most prominent. It is an interesting phenomenon that students and teachers are an important factor in electioneering in the rural areas of East Pakistan to this day – something that cannot be said of the rural areas of West Pakistan where the most influential factor in determining the course of elections is the ex-service man. The importance of the elections for Pakistan is not far to seek.

Bengal was the only Muslim-majority province with a Muslim League ministry on the eve of partition, which repudiated the claim of its opponents that the Muslims of the majority provinces were unconcerned with the movement for Pakistan.

The second occasion when the students of Dacca played a decisive political role was at the time of the referendum on which depended the fate of Sylhet. The question posed to the people of Sylhet was whether they wished to join East Pakistan or continue to remain with Assam. There was a strong Hindu minority in Sylhet and many Muslims were supposed to be under the influence of the *ulama* of Deoband. Had not the students of Dacca gone to Sylhet and propagated the ideal of Pakistan, had they not moved from house to house in the villages, it is doubtful whether the Muslim League would have won the referendum because the Congress was being actively helped by Muslim religious leaders like Maulana Husain Ahmad Madani and other members of the Jamiyat-i-Ulema-i-Hind. From among the university teachers Maulana Azad of the Urdu department and Maulana Margoob Ahmad Taufiq of Islamic Studies were sent by their colleagues to help and inspire the students and counteract the propaganda of the Jamiyat. From outside the university, the one politician who worked hardest in this campaign was Maulana Bhasani, the leader of the National Awami party. The Maulana's influence amongst the students of East Pakistan to this day has something to do with the close association established between him and the students during the Sylhet campaign.

REFLECTIONS ON SOME OF THE CAUSES OF THE PARTITION OF THE INDO-PAKISTAN SUB-CONTINENT

by ABDUL QAIYUM KHAN*

I

For most of the period with which this volume is concerned I was a member of the Indian National Congress. I was a very active member of the Red Shirt movement led by Khan Abdul Ghaffar Khan in the North West Frontier Province, and this movement was an active and live part of the Congress. In 1937, I was elected to the Indian central assembly on the Congress ticket in place of Dr Khan Sahib who had become the first chief minister of a Congress ministry in the N.W.F.P. that year. Later on, I became the deputy leader of the Congress party in the central assembly, and for some time acted as its leader in the absence of Bhulabhai Desai.

When the central assembly was dissolved in 1945, I resigned from the Congress party and joined the Muslim League party. I took a very active part in the N.W.F.P. in a mass movement to wean the Pathans away from the Congress. I was a very active worker during the referendum which preceded partition and in which the province, once the strong-hold of the Indian National Congress, voted overwhelmingly in favour of Pakistan.

I was the first to be arrested by the then chief minister, Dr Khan Sahib, for taking part in the pro-Pakistan movement. Thereafter thousands of Muslim League national guards, workers, students, and others were also arrested. While we were still in jail, Lord Mountbatten, then viceroy of India, visited Peshawar, where a mammoth demonstration in favour of Pakistan was held by the Pathans. As a result, the British government agreed to a referendum in an area where ninety-five per cent of the population was Muslim.

When Pakistan was established, I became, on August 21, 1947, the first chief minister of a Muslim League government in the N.W.F.P. and held that office until 1953.

The above statement of facts is necessary, to show that I was in a position to know the working of the mind of the Congress high command, and at the same time left the party in time to take a very active part in the struggle for the achievement of Pakistan under the leadership of Qaid-e-Azam Muhammad Ali Jinnah.

II

The system of parliamentary government which the British had introduced into India meant the rule of the majority party. While in Britain and other

* Formerly chief minister of the North West Frontier Province (1947–53). Member of the Indian National Congress until 1945 when he joined the Muslim League.

democratic countries majorities are alterable, in India it meant the rule of a permanent and unalterable Hindu majority. The Muslims who constituted about twenty-five per cent of the population could never expect to become a majority or to have an effective share in the government of the country.

When the Congress ministries were first set up in 1937 in the Hindu majority provinces, it soon became obvious that there was not much difference between the Congress and the Hindu Mahasabha. While I found some sincere leaders among the top echelons of the Congress, who wished to give a square deal to the Muslims, and who were for a genuine national integration on secular lines, yet the vast majority of those who counted in the hierarchy were Mahasabhaites at heart. But the Mahasabha was more honest in openly proclaiming that India was a Hindu *rashtrya,* or state, and that Muslims would have to adopt Hindu ways of life, if they wished to stay on in India. The Mahasabha not only preached this, but practised it. On the other hand, the majority of Congress Hindus, while paying lip service to secularism, also practised what the Mahasabha preached.

During the Congress ministries, the majority lost all restraint and came out in the open with their policy of re-establishing Hindu culture. Had they acted with some restraint, accepted the co-operation of the Muslim League as a separate entity and not adopted Hindu revivalism in such an open and unabashed manner, the course of events would possibly have taken a different turn.

The ministries began by replacing the Urdu language, which was not only the language of the Muslims but also of a large number of Hindus in the Punjab, Delhi, the United Provinces, Bihar and parts of the Central Provinces, with a sankritized Hindi, which was Greek to most Muslims and even to Urdu-speaking Hindus. *Bande Mataram*, which Muslims considered idolatrous, was adopted as the national song of India. A scheme of education was introduced which tried to revive the old vedic culture of the Hindus. Muslim schoolboys were obliged to salute the Congress flag, sing *Bande Mataram* with folded hands, wear khadhar clothes and the Gandhi cap, and worship Gandhi's portrait. Restrictions were placed on the slaughter of cows, an animal which Muslims use as food. Cow sacrifice, on the occasion of the *Id* festival, was prevented in villages, Muslim butchers were assaulted, pork was thrown in mosques. Muslim prayers were disturbed by the playing of loud music before the mosques, Muslim shops were boycotted, and Muslims were attacked irrespective of sex and age. The *shuddhi* movement was organized to convert Muslims to Hinduism, and started making headway in remote villages where the Muslims were a mere handful. The *sangathan* movement and the *rashtriya savak sangh* movement, which were militant Hindu organizations, aimed at the annihilation of the Muslims. The Hindu masses and the Sikhs were taught to re-read Indian history. They were reminded that for about eight centuries the Muslims had ruled the sub-continent, and they were doled out stories of atrocities, imaginary and real, and told that Islam had disturbed their caste system and had succeeded in converting many millions of Hindus. The depressed caste Hindu, who was untouchable, on conversion to Islam could rub shoulders with the higher castes of Hindus.

In the higher ranks of the Indian National Congress, there were some

Hindus who were genuinely nationalist, who believed in tolerance and were working for a secular integrated state by extending just accommodation to the Muslims, but such leaders were few. The majority of the Congress leadership, though careful to pay lip service to Congress ideology and all that Congress stood for, in fact thought and acted like the Mahasabha. After all, they had to win elections and could not afford to flout the vast majority of Hindu opinion, which was out to set up a Hindu state, and to revive the glories of the old Hindu past and ancient Hindu culture.

As a result of the Congress ministries the Muslims began to organize the Muslim League on solid foundations, and no longer content to ask for safeguards from the majority, in March 1940 came out in the open with a demand for Pakistan.

It would not be out of place to mention a significant incident which happened in the province of Sind before partition. There arose a dispute between the Hindus and Muslims over the ownership of a building at Sukkur in Upper Sind called 'Manzil Gah'. The Hindus claimed that it was a temple and the Muslims persisted that it was a mosque. Riots broke out in which some people were killed. A pro-Congress ministry headed by Allah Bakhsh held office in Sind at that time, and the working committee of the Congress deputed me to go to Sukkur and to submit a report after an on-the-spot enquiry. What I saw and heard in Sind was an eye-opener. The Muslims constituted seventy-five per cent of the population, but they were mainly occupied in menial and low paid jobs. Hindu landlords were extorting rack rents from the Muslim peasantry, while the Muslim landlords were in debt to Hindu banias. Caste Hindus dominated all the higher services, monopolized trade and commerce and also whatever industry there was in Sind. The provincial Congress committee and the local Hindu Mahasabha were presided over by two Hindu brothers who lived under the same roof.

In my report to the working committee, I strongly advocated a radical change in Congress policy in Sind. I told them that the Sind Congress and the local Mahasabha were interchangeable, and that unless the Congress took up the cause of the Muslim majority and rescued them from their economic slavery to the Hindus, the future of the Congress in Sind was dark indeed. I suggested that the soil was fertile enough for the Muslim League to dominate Sind. Nothing was done by the Congress, and Sind was one of the first provinces to stand out for Pakistan, and it offered its provincial capital Karachi as the seat of the central government of Pakistan after partition.

III

The North West Frontier Province was a stronghold of the National Congress. This province, which is inhabited by Pathans, has a tribal belt where many war-like tribes reside. This tribal belt is sandwiched between the province proper and Afghanistan, and stretches from Gilgit and Chitral in the north right down to the Arabian Sea. Beyond the Quetta division this belt borders on Baluchistan, a large land-mass sparsely populated, in which the various Pathan and Baluchi tribes reside.

The Frontier Pathans were eager to be free and shake off the British yoke. Here Khan Abdul Ghaffar Khan, about 1930, started the *khudai khidmatgar* (or, servants of God) movement, which, at first, aimed at eradicating various social evils which hindered the economic progress of the Pathans. But soon it became a purely political movement, the sole aim of which was to achieve freedom for the Pathans. As the Indian National Congress had similar aims, there developed an affinity of ideas and aims between the Congress and the *khudai khidmatgars*. Mahatma Gandhi and Khan Abdul Ghaffar Khan met several times. The British suspected the movement, which they called the Red Shirt movement, as they feared that it would have repercussions in the tribal belt, where the people had fought and could fight the British. The Pathans of the tribal belt were born fighters, and many were the battles fought between the British and the tribes, who were far from subdued even when the British resorted to aerial bombing, supported as they were by the vast resources of Indian imperialism.

To save the movement from being annihilated by the British, Abdul Ghaffar Khan joined the Congress and became a devoted follower of Mahatma Gandhi. He adopted his cult of non-violence, and the Congress began to finance the movement liberally. As the Muslim League was hardly a live organization at the time, the Red Shirts almost captured the province. Abdul Ghaffar Khan went round the entire area preaching the benefits of joining the Congress, as it alone was likely to bring about 'swaraj' or 'home rule'. He came to be lovingly called the 'Frontier Gandhi'. He made frequent visits to Wardha or wherever Gandhi happened to be. He set up an 'ashram' or 'camp' at a place called Sadaryab on the banks of a tributary of the Kabul River in the Charsadda sub-division of Peshawar district. To this repaired all the Hindu leaders and Congress workers to pay homage to the frontier Gandhi. Various camps were frequently held where people were told what the Congress stood for, and given training on the lines of propaganda which they were to adopt in their campaign. In this ashram, the meetings were always preceded by prayers when Abdul Ghaffar Khan would sit on a wooden raised platform or 'takhat' and with closed eyes listen to recitations from Hindu, Sikh and Muslim scriptures.

The Congress held the province in its grip. It had the majority in the provincial legislature and twice it was inducted into office, with Dr Khan Sahib, the brother of the frontier Gandhi, as chief minister. In fact Khan Sahib held this office when the Pakistan flag was unfurled in Peshawar on August 14, 1947 and Pakistan was proclaimed by the then British governor Sir George Cunningham.

However, the various events which happened in the Hindu majority provinces when the Congress ministries had been installed opened the eyes of the Pathans. And the slaughter of the Muslims in Bihar, along with the communal riots in other parts of India, were further eye-openers. Pathan volunteers who were sent as relief workers into Bihar came back entirely disillusioned after witnessing the harrowing details of the treatment meted out to the Muslims. They opened their ears, and began to listen to the call of the Qaid-e-Azam. The Muslim League became a live organization and for the first time started a mass movement to wean away the Pathans from the

Congress. A network of Muslim League organizations was set up throughout the province and workers and volunteers carried the message of Pakistan into every nook and corner of the province.

In November 1946, there was a by-election for the provincial assembly from the Mardan constituency. Dr Khan Sahib was still holding the office of chief minister. His brother was doing his best to fight back the onslaught of the Muslim League, backed by all the prestige and financial resources of the Congress. Red Shirt national guards in their thousands armed with sten-guns, rifles and other arms, conveniently sanctioned by the Congress ministry, were parading all over the province in large formations. Such was the state of affairs when the Muslim League put up a candidate against the Congress candidate. This area was considered to be the stronghold of the Congress and the Red Shirts, and Dr Khan Sahib stated in his campaign speeches that the result of this by-election would indicate whether the Pathans wanted to join India or Pakistan. I was among many others who went from village to village on foot canvassing individuals and addressing public meetings on behalf of the Muslim League.

The by-election was held. For the first time the Red Shirt volunteers found themselves outnumbered by the Muslim League national guards in their green uniforms. Thousands had come across from the tribal areas to take part on behalf of the Muslim League. The message of Pakistan had spread like wild fire throughout the province.

The counting was going on in the district magistrate courts. The compound was swarming with the Red Shirt national guards who occupied the lawns and were confident of victory. I and some other colleagues were sitting in a room in a nearby tea shop waiting for the result. Soon after lunch, I noticed that the Red Shirts had started discarding their uniforms and were putting on their ordinary clothes. They started melting away and soon the lawn was empty. They had had word from inside that they had lost and the Muslim League had won the by-election. Then the crowds swarmed on to the lawns and the thousands of Muslim League national guards in their green uniforms, carrying the green flag with star and crescent, occupied the lawns vacated by the Red Shirts. Shouts of 'Pakistan Zindabad', 'Long Live Pakistan', 'Qaid-e-Azam Zindabad' and 'Long Live Qaid-e-Azam' rent the air. A huge procession marched through the city firing wildly in the air in the traditional Pathan way to celebrate their victory.

This victory in the by-election was an indication of the complete change in public opinion in the province in favour of the Pakistan ideal. The Muslim League organization had now become very active. Its workers were drawn from amongst the students and youth of the province. They carried the message of the Qaid-e-Azam to every town, village and hamlet. The Congress on the other hand was fighting hard to retain its hold on the province. The Khan brothers were advocating the union of the province with united India.

In early 1947, I was arrested at Mardan along with two or three colleagues and was sent to prison. Thousands of students, workers, national guards and others courted arrest. The situation became so tense that Lord Mountbatten, the viceroy, came to Peshawar to see things for himself. He was greeted on arrival by a mammoth Muslim League demonstration, which, waving the green banners of the League, made a full-throated public demand for Pakistan. Shortly after, we were summoned to New Delhi and even though it was obvious that the tide had turned in favour of Pakistan, the Congress insisted that there should be a referendum in the province. Meanwhile, the Qaid-e-Azam came to Peshawar where he received one of his greatest receptions. In view of the fact that a referendum was about to take place, he called off the League's civil disobedience campaign. We were all released and got busy with mass contact. On the eve of the referendum Jinnah issued an appeal to the people of the province expressing his appreciation of their sufferings and sacrifices and calling for the referendum to be carried out peacefully. The people volted overwhelmingly in favour of Pakistan: the Congress party was able to poll only a few votes.

All the Muslim majority areas, one by one, gave their verdict in favour of Pakistan. The Congress assumed that every Hindu majority area would opt for India or Hindustan, and though insisting on referenda in Sylhet and the Frontier Province, the mere thought of having similar referenda in Hindu majority areas seems never to have crossed their minds. The Congress was fighting hard not to yield an inch of territory, and insisted on partition of the Punjab and Bengal, which in all fairness should have gone completely to Pakistan. And while demanding that the Hindu majority areas contiguous to India should be carved out of these two provinces, they refused to extend this principle of contiguity to the state of Jammu and Kashmir where from seventy-five to eighty per cent of the population was Muslim. Had this been done, or had a plebiscite been held in Jammu and Kashmir, as was done in Sylhet and the Frontier Province, the Kashmir question could have been amicably solved according to the wishes of the people of the state, and all the recurring tensions would have been avoided. India and Pakistan then could have more effectively devoted themselves to solving problems of chronic food shortage, illiteracy, poverty, disease and overpopulation in both their countries.

IV

It will not be out of place to refer to the communal disturbances which immediately preceded the partition and also followed in its wake. I do not propose to write about the disturbances in the sub-continent as a whole, or about the mass movement of people from one dominion to the other, but confine myself to what happened in the Frontier Province. Here the minorities, Hindus and Sikhs, constituted from five to seven per cent of the population. They migrated *en masse* to India. The Christian minority and the depressed class of Hindus were not affected and they have continued to live in peace in this region. Similarly, Hindus and Sikhs in Swat state and the tribal area of Tirah were not affected. They are still there as their ancestors have been for generations.

The Hindus and Sikhs in the six districts of the provinces held a complete monopoly over trade and commerce. They owned the bulk of the urban immovable property and also large tracts of land which they cultivated through their Muslim tenants. They were well represented in government service and the professions and were financially much better off than their

Muslim neighbours. Moreover the relations between the majority and minority community were quite cordial in the province. The Muslim League and the provincial government were anxious to retain all the Hindus and Sikhs as their departure would create a great vacuum in the services and professions and on the economic side it would have almost paralysed the economic life of the province. To inspire confidence in the minority and with a view to urge upon them the necessity of staying on, I requested the British governor, Sir George Cunningham, to tour the province and grant interviews to the Hindu *panchayats* (representative committees) with a view to induce them to stay on. The governor went out on tour and did as we had requested. However, we were reliably informed that all our efforts in this connection were being undone by the Indian deputy high commissioner, who, after meeting the same *panchayats*, advised them to move *en masse* to India, at the same time assuring them that Pakistan would collapse soon like a house of cards, and that it would not be long before they would return to their homelands as victors, and regain all that they would have to leave behind.

Thereafter a clamour arose from the minority for facilities to move to India. Special trains were arranged for them. The entire forty-eight miles of the railway line within the province between Peshawar and Attock Bridge on the River Indus on both sides were guarded by local police, frontier constabulary and additional police so that the trains could pass peacefully through. I used to be present at the railway station to see off the trains. They were thus moved out safely without there being a single incident on the way. While seeing them off, I was deeply touched by this great human tragedy: the sight of friends departing with their families and their moveables, from a land where they had lived for generations and to which they were devoted. There were personal friends with whom I had worked as a colleague and co-worker for many years, and between whom and myself there was deep mutual attachment.

There were some clashes in Bannu, parts of the Hazara district and Peshawar city, but the number of casualties was small as the provincial government took strong and effective measures to protect the minorities. During my tenure of office as chief minister, the police had to open fire in some places on Muslims, namely in Bannu city and Mardan, who were bent on looting Sikhs and Hindus. After partition things settled down.

Perhaps it would be appropriate to refer to a Hindu gentleman who with his family refused to go and still lives in Peshawar as a contented citizen. When riots broke out in Peshawar city, his house was in a disturbed area. I was busy trying to restore order, moving about with the forces of law and order from place to place. I thought of him, as he is a very old friend of the family. I told him that I would like to send some armed police to guard his house. His reply was characteristic of him. He said that he would rather die with his family, but would on no account accept police protection. He added that he was quite capable of looking after himself as this was his house and country. He resolutely stayed on and nothing happened. He has now moved away from his old house on the outskirts of the city to a spacious bungalow at the foot of the Khyber Hills. There were decent God-fearing people on both sides of the partition line.

SOME MEMORIES

by RAJA OF MAHMUDABAD*

All we have gained then by our unbelief
Is a life of doubt diversified by faith,
For one of faith diversified by doubt:
We called the chess-board white—we call it black.

Bishop's Blougram's Apology by Robert Browning.

My involvement with the movements for national independence in India was a deeply personal involvement and a lifelong one. It is therefore perhaps apt to start on a personal note. My estate of Mahmudabad, one of the large holdings in north India, had been handed down to me by my forefathers. My father, the late Maharaja Muhammad Ali Muhammad Khan, throughout his life actively participated in various political and cultural movements in the country. One of his major interests had been the advancement and improvement of Indian education. This was reflected both in his long and close association with the movement for the elevation of the Aligargh College to the status of a national Muslim university, and in his material and moral support of the Hindu University at Benares. In politics, his view of nationalism was similarly wide and this made him acceptable to both the mainstreams of Indian nationalism. He was one of the important leaders of the Muslim League in his time and twice presided over its sessions. At the same time he took an active interest and participated in the deliberations of the Indian National Congress.

I would not merely be fulfilling a filial duty in saying that my father was known for his high sense of charity, his public spiritedness, his loyalty to his friends and his deep love of freedom. Among his friends he counted several well-known British, Hindu and Muslim names. Sir Harcourt Butler was more of a brother than a dignitary-friend. My father always addressed him as 'Bhai Sahib' – an eloquent phrase which includes in itself sentiments of mutual love, respect and trust. From among the Hindus, in fact from among all other Indians with the exception of Muhammad Ali Jinnah, Motilal Nehru was more a member of our family than a friendly visitor. I distinctly remember that in our house in Lucknow a room was reserved for him and no other guests were allowed to stay there. From the day I learnt to speak, I addressed him as uncle and received from him a rare degree of affection and love which not many people are capable of giving. Here I should like to recall one episode which illustrates the qualities of Motilal Nehru and his status in our family. But first a short digression is in order.

From my childhood I had shown somewhat Tolstoyan inclinations of detesting the class to which I belonged and what it stood for. This may perhaps have been due to the love I bore for my mother, who came from a learned

* Closely associated with Jinnah and the Muslim League from 1936: youngest member of the All-Indian Muslim League Working Committee.

and respectable family, but one of moderate means. Her family had produced notable scholars and reformers such as 'Allama Ghulam Hussain Kintoori, Maulana Hamid Husain – author of 'Abaqatal Anwar, and Justice Maulana Karamat Husain – founder of the first Muslim girls' college in the United Provinces. Her marriage to my father had been the result of my grandmother's great desire of marrying someone from à Syed family. The early realization that this matrimonial alliance in no way affected the modest and even tenor of my mother's own family brought home to me the fact that principles need not be the monopoly of the learned rich: grace and dignity after all are taught by the heart and not by the dancing instructor. My maternal uncles continued to live as they used to, unmoved and uninfluenced by their new connection with the aristocracy; even my mother, now a maharani, with an income which must have seemed immense to her, did not give up the simple values ingrained in her by her parents. It was not surprising, therefore, that I did not feel at ease in the feudal society into which I had been born.

Coming back to the earlier reference to Motilal Nehru: partly under my mother's influence and partly because right from my childhood my eyes saw 'khaddar' clad nationalists in our house, I could never bring myself to wearing the expensive and flamboyant clothes prescribed by the traditions of our family and class. Instead I began putting on the homespun, which of course, was intensely distasteful to my father who, it is interesting to note, never raised an eyebrow at seeing practically all his nationalist friends in similar apparel. One day, when Motilal was staying with us, I put on a new coarse 'khaddar' dress and was rather pleased with myself when, all of a sudden my father walked in, looked at me with disapproval and pointed towards my clothes. Stunned by his reaction I stood there with my head hanging down and at a loss to think of an answer. At this moment, uncle Motilal appeared and looking at my terrified expression and at my father's angry face, and divining the situation, said, 'Baita, if you want to wear "khaddar", you should wear it as I do.' By this he meant that I should use the fine quality stuff which he wore. Now it was my father's turn to find himself in a predicament, for soon a gift of several bails of fine spun 'khaddar' arrived from Motilal and my father could raise no further objections to my wearing it. If I were to sum up my impressions of Motilal, I would say that here was a man who would not be out of place in the seat of authority. He had the manner and the polish of a man both born to authority and the right to exercise it.

Motilal Nehru was not the only person who had left a deep impact on my youthful years. Mrs Sarojini Naidu and Rajkumari Amrit Kaur were like sisters to my father and I always called them by the Urdu equivalent of the English, 'aunt' – phupi. Another frequent visitor and a friend of the family was Dr Ansari.

Brought up in this atmosphere and amid such people, the first serious words which reached my ear were not very complimentary to the British. From my childhood I heard my Indian tutors and nurse-maids telling stories about the mutiny and of British repression and Indian suffering. The gentleman who taught me to read the Quran related to me what he had heard from his father who had fought the British during the mutiny in Muftiganj in Lucknow. My conversations with him did not endear the British to me. In fact at this time, a general anti-British feeling simmered under the surface amongst all of us, particularly among those who had witnessed or heard about the terrible deeds of 1857. One extreme instance of this is the way in which a disease was wished to the British instead of the person who suffered from it. The phrase in general use which I first heard from my eighty-year-old nurse when I complained of headache was: 'Baita dard tumhain kyun ho, angrez bandon ke ho' (My son, why should you have pain, may God give it to the British).

Some of my personal experiences added to such hearsay. During Sir John Simon's tour of India in 1927, my father was a vehement opponent of the Simon commission and had helped the Lucknow Congress party in its demonstrations and protests against Simon's visit to Lucknow. When Simon was being entertained at a tea party by the taluqdars of Oudh, kites were flown from various points in the city and were then cut in such a way that they dropped at the place of the feast. They carried on them the words 'Simon go back.' The administration was furious and part of the brunt of their anger was borne by us. Long before the party was due to start a party of policemen arrived, surrounded our house and searched it so thoroughly that even my room was not spared. This left a very bad impression on my mind although later apologies were made to my father by the deputy commissioner of Lucknow and the home member.

Next year something happened which shocked me personally to an even greater extent. The all-parties conference was meeting in Lucknow and nearly all the leaders were staying in our house. I was then attending La Martiniére College, and one morning in the history class our teacher, who was an Anglo-Indian, interrupted the usual lecture and referred to the conference and called its leaders 'swines'. Without a moment's thought I stood up in my seat and said, 'My father is also a nationalist'. Then, throwing my book at him I walked out of the room. I might add that the principal, who himself was an Englishman, but a different kind of a person, saved me from rustication. A few days later I was to learn that the history teacher was asked to leave. A great majority of my classmates were Anglo-Indians and did not conceal their contempt for us Indians either. We were called, 'Niggers and Blackies'. We could then not do much, but I definitely remember that our reaction to this was: all right a day will come when we shall have our revenge.

I was also deeply pained by the attitude of some of our class towards the British administrators. Sometimes I saw the scions of distinguished families having to take off their shoes before entering the deputy commissioner's office. Both my head and my heart revolted at this show of cringing sycophancy. My reaction to all this can perhaps be best expressed by recalling that about this time I began collecting photographs of the nationalist leaders and treasured them as my most valuable possessions. When I heard of the Kakori incident I applauded the men responsible for it. Bhagat Singh was another 'terrorist' who then appealed to me and his photograph occupied a prominent place in my room.

Ever since my younger days the conduct of Britain's relations with her empire has been a fascinating source of study for me – in particular British conduct and institutions in India. The air of patronage introduced by the new system of administration created an hierarchy of its own and replaced the prevailing currents of court intrigue and sycophancy which marked the decaying Indian society. I, and many of my countrymen, were impressed as well as puzzled by the frank and open discussion of the actions and policies of British administrators by those who watched over British interests on the one hand and the system of patronage on the other. In my opinion, the greatest single factor which impressed many Indians with its sense of fair play and justice, its high sense of responsibliity and its seriousness of purpose, was the impeachment of Warren Hastings. British good intentions were proved, and above all it reflected the inherent strength of British democracy and the principle that those who exercise power are accountable for the way in which they exercise it. However, we found a marked contrast between the principle of patronage created and encouraged by the British in India and the principle of responsibility to parliament which was respected and practised in Britain. For some reason the Englishman, born and bred in an open society, was content to establish and sustain a closed society in India. Improvement came with painful slowness: in small halting instalments.

The system of patronage built into the British Indian administrative machine often went too far and even survived the coming of the 'great' reforms of 1935, as the following illustrates. In 1936, soon after I had joined the Muslim League, I was summoned to lunch with his excellency, the governor of the United Provinces. In those days to enter Government House was an honour coveted by all but given to few. But to me the atmosphere of solemn formalities was nothing new. My initiation into the complex system of official protocol had been made complete during my father's life by his close personal relations with the higher reaches of the administration. I was the only guest and therefore serious conversation began right away.

My host informed me that he knew that I had joined the Muslim League and asked me if I was fully aware of the possible consequences of my action. I pleaded ignorance but pointed out that participation in public life was a perfectly normal thing to do. My host assumed an added air of authority and adjusted himself more firmly in his chair. For the first time in my life I realized that an invitation to a meal is not necessarily an act of hospitality. He again asked me if I knew that my estate was a gift from the British sovereign, adding after I had nodded in assent, that I held it at his pleasure. He continued that he was willing to give me time to reconsider my position and to dissociate myself from one whom he called 'the arch enemy of the British Raj'. After a few minutes of conversation I realized that this 'arch enemy' was none other than M. A. Jinnah. On my asking what I was expected to do, he ordered that I should join the National Agriculturist party and made it clear that the British government had no intention of letting the activities of Jinnah and his party continue and that I would have to watch my steps in future. But I told him in reply that I was already committed to Jinnah having given him my word that I would stand by him and that it was impossible for me to break my promise. Later we ate in silence broken only by the formal phrases. I came home half-dazed by the governor's strange behaviour and felt disgust for a system which hindered a person's choice of parties.

II

M. A. Jinnah had had very close relations with the Mahmudabad family since his youth. My father signed his marriage contract on Jinnah's behalf; while Maulana Muhammad Hasan Najafi signed for Mrs Jinnah. The ring which Jinnah gave to his wife on the wedding day was my father's gift. The Jinnahs spent their honeymoon at Nainital in our house.

My first meeting with Jinnah took place in 1923 when I went to Delhi with my father and met him at the Maiden's hotel. I was then only nine but two memories still cling to my mind: I was introduced to Jinnah by my father as 'Your uncle Jinnah' and I was impressed by Mrs Jinnah's beauty. She gave me Rs. 500 to buy toys which at that time was a great deal of money.

Our second meeting took place in 1925 or 1926 at Butler Palace in Lucknow. I had just returned from school when my father took me to meet him and we sat talking on the terrace. He was dressed in a Chinese silk suit with a rather high collar to his shirt. He called me to his side and asked me about my studies. Then came the question, 'What are you, a Muslim first or an Indian first?' Although I hardly understood the implications of the question at that age, I replied 'I am a Muslim first and then an Indian.' To this he said in a loud voice, 'My boy, no, you are an Indian first and then a Muslim.' I stood there with downcast eyes and tears welled up. I thought I had made him cross. Jinnah patted me and was probably going to say something when my father asked me to go and play as they were going to have a serious conversation.

The venue of our next meeting was London where in 1933 I met him at his Hampstead house and had lunch with him. I was accompanied by my cousin and brother-in-law, a younger brother of the Raja of Pirpur. Most of the conversation related to family and property matters as Jinnah was one of the trustees of the Mahmudabad estate. But I remember my brother-in-law asking him when he was finally coming back to India, and Jinnah replying 'Probably before long'. He looked happy and relaxed, and showed me round his house and it was here that I met Dina, his daughter, for the first time. After a few days, at a dinner at the Berkeley Hotel I told him that he must come back to India. To which again he replied, 'I will be coming very soon'.

In March, April 1936, I was asked by Jinnah to come to Delhi to see him. I stayed at the Maiden's hotel for a week and met him once or twice. On one of these occasions Jinnah asked me to accompany him to the home of a friend who was also a friend of my father. We walked over to the Western Court where Deep Narayan Singh, a nationalist leader had a suite. I was introduced to him and they started talking about politics. Jinnah then asked me about my plans and whether I was prepared to join him in politics. I told him that I intended joining the Shantiniketan and that Sir Rabindranath Tagore had already agreed to take me in. Then came the moment which changed the later course of my life. Deep Narayan interrupted me and said, 'No, you should enter politics and stand by the side of your uncle. That would be the best form of education for you. By joining him you will be putting yourself in the hands of a great Indian patriot and nationalist. 'Before we parted company I had decided that I would be prepared to stand by him.

From this date onwards my association with Jinnah became close indeed, except for a short period to which I will come later. I made it a practice to go and stay with him in Bombay or Delhi for about three months every year. All that I had was at the disposal of the League. When I joined I hardly realized that before long the League and the Congress would be poles apart. For I still thought that the two organizations were like two parts of the same army fighting a common enemy on two fronts. With all my nationalistic tendencies and my association with the Congress and other progressive political workers and leaders some of whom I personally knew and admired, I might have joined the Congress. But my enthusiasm cooled down when to my great disappointment I found that instead of trying to understand the League policies, Jawaharlal Nehru showed nothing but contempt for the Muslim League and its leader to whom I had given undivided loyalty. The more Nehru spoke contemptuously and violently about the League and Jinnah, the more I disliked the Congress. This feeling was shared by a large number of the Muslims I knew who, but for this, would have shown less antipathy to the Congress. There was a general feeling that Nehru and Jinnah were talking at each other and that there was not much substance to this personal political dialogue.

III

The results of the general election startled the Muslims into an awareness that the Muslim League's failure to attract more Muslim voters was manifestly the result of Muslim political disunity. When they saw the solid Congress successes in several provinces they realized that in order to win a similar success, at least in the Muslim majority provinces, two things were essential: a closing of their ranks and a re-organization of the Muslim League. It was widely felt that the time had come to develop the League into a broad-based mass organization which could effectively safeguard Muslim rights and interests. We in the United Provinces felt that the next session of the League should be held at Lucknow and accordingly invited the League to do so. For us it was a happy coincidence that the League was holding its session in the same town where in 1916 another session had met under Jinnah. Another coincidence was that the chairman of the reception committee of the 1916 session had been my father, and now in 1937 this honour fell on me. Little did we realize then that the closing words of my welcome address – 'we are here not to follow history but create it' – were to prove true.

The closing of the ranks became immediately obvious in the number of the Muslim leaders who assembled at the Lucknow session. Several provincial leaders, who had fought the last elections at the head of small independent groups and won some seats in almost every province, now joined the Muslim League, thus bringing it much strength. The chief ministers of Assam, Bengal, and the Punjab attended and offered their loyalty and co-operation. Apart from a few 'Nationalist Muslims', there were hardly any Muslim leaders of note who remained outside the League.

In terms of organization and structure a new chapter opened in the history of the League after October 1937. Branches of the League were opened even in the remotest village; paid workers were employed; speakers were trained; the recruitment campaign was accelerated, funds were collected; and membership fee was brought down from four to two annas a year. An uncommonly large number of leaders of different levels toured the whole country to carry the message to the common man. This message was simple enough to appeal even to those people who could not or did not understand the implications of joining a political party. The appeal was for unity, for once unity came other things could then be expected to follow.

The Congress was in office for over two years. The general impression prevalent amongst the Muslims was not at all favourable to the Congress régime. Irrespective of whether all the instances quoted by the League were true or not, the general feeling among the Muslims of all classes was that Hindu *raj* had arrived. I shall here refer to only one aspect. Whereas there is always a spirit of selfrighteousness inherent in any majority community, anywhere in the world, in assimilating and absorbing minority communities, the apprehensions created by the Wardha scheme of education in Muslim minds has generally been underestimated. Certain features of the scheme, for example the emphasis on manual work, were basically sound, but these were overshadowed by its general spirit of indoctrination. We know that a system of education can be used to inculcate in the minds of youth certain doctrines and ideas which may run counter to their cultural traditions and values. Any scheme based on the ideology of one political party or one leader is viewed by the minorities and other groups as an attempt to unduly influence the thoughts of every one in the mould of the ruling party. ('An-nasu 'Ala Deeni Mulookihim' 'The mass of the people generally followed the path of their rulers.') In a country such as India, where the Hindus, Muslims, Sikhs, Christians had to live together, it was absolutely essential to have a system of education which allowed complete freedom of thought, expression and discussions, so that the teacher, whether of one denomination or another, could seek the truth and teach it. This was impossible under the Wardha scheme, for it was meant to proclaim the political creed of one party as the truth. There was no room in it for any other ideals and it was bound to emphasize the superiority of one political philosophy or conviction over others, thus encouraging intolerance instead of understanding.

What added to Muslim anxiety was the uncertain future of Urdu under the scheme. The scheme made Hindustani a compulsory subject, but it soon became evident that Hindustani, at least to Gandhi's mind, was something quite different from Urdu. It must be remembered that for the Muslims, Urdu was not merely a medium of communication or thinking, but a vital part of their culture. By imposing Hindustani, the Wardha scheme was in fact asking the Muslims to give up a language which had been one of the common bonds between the Hindus and the Muslims in favour of one yet to be created.

Instead of understanding the Muslim mind, the Congress tried to solve the problem by recruiting more and more Muslims to its fold. There may be nothing wrong in a political party trying to enrol members from various communities, but in fact the Muslim mass contact campaign brought a bad name to the Congress ministries. The campaign was run by Congress workers while the Congress was in office, which conveyed to the Muslim mind that this enrolment was being carried out, not by the Congress party, but by the provincial governments. Like those of the Congress, many of the League workers were also mercenaries, but unlike the Congress workers they did not carry the stigma of belonging to the ruling party. This actually turned out to be one of the factors responsible for the failure of the campaign and added to Hindu-Muslim bitterness.

Perhaps the Congress did not realize that office brings its own disadvantages. The party in power is more exposed to criticism of every kind by those who are in opposition, without always being able to justify its policies. In this respect the League worked from a point of vantage, and Jinnah, supreme tactician that he was, fully used this advantage.

As pointed out earlier, it was at the Lucknow session that steps had been taken to convert the League into a mass organization. The results were astounding and membership jumped from a little more than half a million in 1937 to over a million in 1941. But in mass nationalist movements figures of membership are no index to a party's following. It is absurd to say that in 1941 only a million Muslims supported the League, for we all know that by this date the League had succeeded in winning the sympathy of an overwhelming majority of the Muslims. A major factor in this growth was the new ideal which the League had put before the people in 1940. The idea of a separate Muslim state in India stirred the imagination of the Muslims as nothing else had done before.

But the League had to pay a price for this swift success. In the new momentum which the League now gained, several elements aligned themselves with it. Their influence was not entirely wholesome. Some of these were conservative in opinion and hindered the activities of the progressive element, thus making the League out as less radical than it actually was. Several members of the landed and moneyed classes also came in and lent support to the conservative thinking in the party. Then there were those who seemed more anxious to gain power and influence than to put in long constructive effort.

A different kind of infiltration took place with the coming of the conservative religious element for whom time had not moved since the Khilafat days. They had no conception of running a modern political movement on sophisticated lines. Their thinking was limited to the contemplation of an Islamic state, and they interpreted to the masses the League ideals in terms to which they were accustomed. There was yet another smaller group of some university teachers, which stood for greater emphasis on Islam in League politics. During 1941–5, I myself came under its influence and was one of the founder members of the Islamic Jamaat. We advocated that Pakistan should be an Islamic state. I must confess that I was very enthusiastic about it and in my speeches I constantly propagated my ideas.

My advocacy of an Islamic state brought me into conflict with Jinnah. He thoroughly disapproved of my ideas and dissuaded me from expressing them publicly from the League platform lest the people might be led to believe that Jinnah shared my view and that he was asking me to convey such ideas to the public. As I was convinced that I was right and did not want to compromise Jinnah's position, I decided to cut myself away and for nearly two years kept my distance from him, apart from seeing him during the working committee meetings and on other formal occasions. It was not easy to take this decision as my associations with Jinnah had been very close in the past. Now that I look back I realize how wrong I had been.

It is perhaps not fully realized that the Muslim League between 1937–47 was the first purely political movement of the Indian Muslims. Not only were Sir Syed Ahmad Khan's efforts concentrated on the educational and cultural improvement of the Muslims, but he went further and actually discouraged them from active political participation. The first Muslim mass movement was that of the Khilafat and it was predominantly religious in character though the politicians ran it. It was only after the re-birth of the League in 1937 that the Muslim masses awoke to political consciousness. Three factors helped to develop and sharpen this consciousness. One was the Congress attitude of indifference and, at times, hostility. Another was the leadership which, under Jinnah, broke new ground and fashioned new political strategy. Still another was the part played by religious appeal in the heightening of this consciousness. The leadership at the top was generally secular-minded and trained in modern political methods, but on the lower levels and especially among the field workers propaganda on religious lines was the general practice.

Long life and maturity are as important to a nationalist political movement as they are to a human being. In less than ten years the revived Muslim League had to reorganize itself; to spread the message among the masses; to provide an ultimate objective, to fight for this objective and to achieve it. The speed at which things moved in India during these ten years made the achievement of the goal more important, almost imperative, than the purification of the organization itself. And the Congress, with its long life and experience, also found it impossible to divest itself of the communal-minded elements within its fold. Consequences for India were grave. Despite the best intentions of the leaders on both sides certain uncontrollable forces were let loose which thrived on religious frenzy. And for a time goodwill and amity disappeared from India. I can well recall the general sense of gloom and despondency that pervaded the two newly-created nation states; instead of the joy and expectancy which should have been ours after these years of struggle there were only premonitions of impending conflicts and a promise of future struggle.

But that is another story: a story which the sons of the sons of those who fought for freedom may live to write another day. For the present this is all that I have to say.

However, in the years to come,

> 'If you're still living, never say never.
> What is certain isn't certain.
> Things will not stay as they are . . . and
> Never becomes Before The Day Is Out.'
>
> *In Praise of Dialectics*, Bertolt Brecht

MUSLIM POLITICS, 1942–7[1]

by HUMAYUN KABIR*

The story of Muslim politics in India between 1942 and 1947 can be briefly told. After the arrest of the Congress leaders in August 1942, political activity in India came almost to a standstill. There were ministries functioning in some of the provinces but not one of them could be regarded as a Muslim League ministry. Fazlul Haq had broken away from the Muslim League and formed an alliance with the Krishak Praja party, a section of the Congress and the Hindu Mahasabha. Together they constituted the Progressive coalition party and ruled Bengal. In the Punjab, Sir Sikandar Hyat Khan owed nominal allegiance to M. A. Jinnah but by and large he followed the policies of the Unionist party established by Sir Mian Fazl-i Husain and Chaudhuri Chhotu Ram as a joint front of rural interests against the Congress, the League and the urban intelligentsia. Sind and the Frontier had never been League strongholds and as for the other provinces, the League was at best a minority group in opposition. All the ministries in office were however engrossed with the war effort and after the subsidence of the August upheaval, political activity was intermittent, sporadic and unco-ordinated.

Soon after followed two tragic events which changed the complexion of Indian politics. The sudden death of Sir Sikandar Hyat Khan and the ghastly murder of Umar Allah Bakhsh removed two of Jinnah's strongest opponents. Sir Sikandar was a force for sobriety and moderation and had successfully resisted Jinnah's attempts to capture the mind of the Muslim masses in the Punjab. His successor, Khizr Hyat Khan broadly followed his policies but lacked Sir Sikandar's experience and standing. Sir Sikandar had kept the bureaucracy under strict control and did not allow the civil servants, whether British or Indian, to meddle with politics. After Sir Sikandar's death, some members of the Indian civil service began to show an undue preference for the politics of the Muslim League. It has sometimes been said that the Muslim members of the Indian civil service did more to strengthen the League than any politician excepting Jinnah. This may be an exaggeration, but there is little doubt that these officers did play a role in securing government support for the Muslim League in many devious ways. Their motives were often mixed. Some smarted from a sense of inferiority *vis-à-vis* some of their British and Hindu colleagues. Others felt that a Muslim state like Pakistan would mean their domination, as most of them regarded themselves as intellectually and morally superior to the politicians. Khizr Hyat Khan did his best to check these tendencies but he was only partially successful.

The murder of Allah Bakhsh had more serious consequences. The mystery

[1] This essay was originally written in December 1947 based on my impressions and memory without reference to documents.

* Prominent Indian politician. Active in Bengal politics before partition: acted as secretary to A. K. Azad. Died 1969.

of his death was never cleared up. Many thought that his murder was due to a personal vendetta. Some attributed it to Allah Bakhsh's strong measures against the Hurs. Others thought that communal elements in Sind were disturbed by his growing strength and popularity. Nothing certain can be said as investigations were carried out in a half-hearted manner even before the partition of the country. After the establishment of Pakistan, the matter gradually went out of the public mind. His assassination was in any case a great loss to the national forces of India. He had emerged as a bold and able leader from a Muslim majority province and many thought that he had the making of an all-India leader who could have challenged Jinnah. The death in quick succession of Sir Sikandar Hyat Khan and Allah Bakhsh left the field open to Jinnah. As once before in the thirties, fate again seemed to favour him.

The one other man who could have challenged Jinnah's leadership was Fazlul Haq. He was a skilful politician and an orator of rare quality. He was also a warm-hearted man whose spontaneous generosity won him friends among men of all communities. He never lost his mass following but certain defects in his character prevented him from achieving all-India leadership. He was fickle and changed sides easily. He was generous in his munificence to the poor but he was not very particular about the way in which he collected funds for distribution among his protegés. He was fighting against the growing intransigence of the Muslim intelligentsia and only the highest standards of intellectual and moral integrity would have enabled him to win back their allegiance. While his popularity never diminished, his support declined sharply, and early in 1943, the British governor of Bengal was able to play on his weakness in order to remove him from office. When this happened, his weaknesses were shown up and he could not stage a come-back.

The role of the British in this period was frankly partisan. When the Congress refused to co-operate with the British war effort, the authorities decided that the power and influence of the Congress must be curbed at any cost. They did not like Jinnah who often criticized the British in sharper language than any used by the Congress. Not only so, he even insulted British dignitaries, but with their unflinching sense of realism and their determination to protect British interests at any cost, the British authorities in India did not allow any personal considerations to stand in their way of utilizing Jinnah and the League against the Congress. When in August 1942, the Congress passed the Quit India resolution, the British were confirmed in their view that no co-operation with the Congress was possible and the League must be encouraged to become its rival on the all-India scene.

The transformation in the fortunes of the League between 1942 and 1947 is remarkable. So long as the Congress ministries were in office, the League had hardly any influence on the course of events. It had no doubt made complaints against the alleged injustices committed by the ministries, but even the British authorities did not take these allegations seriously. When Congress ministries resigned, the League organized a deliverance day and for the first time in its history, it received almost open support from the government. There is no doubt that these celebrations did increase the prestige of the League among the Muslim masses. The British also started treating

Jinnah on terms of equality with Gandhi and the result was that Jinnah's prestige increased rapidly. The Congress leaders could not make up their mind about Jinnah and at times treated him in a cavalier fashion. The sweeping victory of the Congress in 1937 had led many Congress leaders to believe that the League could be fought on a purely economic programme. This was the essence of Jawaharlal Nehru's movement for mass contact among the Muslims but it overlooked the fact that however important economic factors may be, men are not governed by economic considerations alone. The only result of this movement was to harden the attitude of the leaders of the League who resented the Congress attempt to wean away the Muslim masses from their influence. Until 1937, many of Jinnah's demands were consistent with Indian nationalism, but even his legitimate claims were either ignored or treated casually. This infuriated him and turned him from a critic to an enemy of the Congress.

After the resignation of the Congress ministries in 1939, the British made a number of efforts in 1940, 1941 and 1942 to come to terms with the Congress, but Congress rejected all of them. It is true that the League also rejected these moves but the British did not pay the same attention to the League rejection. They rightly held that the League's rejections were formal rather than substantial. While the Congress refusal to co-operate with the British appeared to them to be based on a fundamental divergence of views, they held and rightly that the League response was purely tactical. Jinnah knew that the British would not part with power unless the Congress was a party and hence he waited till the Congress had taken a decision and then announced the same decision but for different reasons.

It was not realized at the time that the Cripps offer of 1942 was perhaps the last opportunity for a united and free India. If the Congress had accepted the Cripps offer, and at one stage it was almost at the point of doing so, there is little doubt that the League would have followed. If a composite government had been formed in 1942 and worked to defend India against the danger of invasion, it is more than probable that many of the differences between the Congress and the League would have been toned down if not eradicated. Co-operation in a common endeavour would have forged bonds of agreement and friendship among some of the major participants. Three years of fellowship in a common government would have overcome their initial suspicion and distrust. It is also true that both Congress and the League could have accepted the offer without undue injury to their position and status. The Cripps formula provided for a united India but at the same time gave the provinces the opportunity to opt out if they so desired. The likelihood is that the experience of common endeavour against an external threat would have created common understanding and ruled out the possibility of opting out at the end of war.

This was, however, not to be. As the Congress moved further away from the British, the British depended more and more on the Muslim League as a counterpoise to the Congress. Early in 1943 Fazlul Haq's ministry was dismissed in Bengal and after a few months replaced by a Muslim League ministry. In the North West Frontier Province, a Muslim League ministry was for the first time formed. Sind and the Punjab also came increasingly under the domination of the League. The British authorities made no secret of their preference for the League, but political life in the country was at an ebb. Jinnah had built up his politics mainly on the basis of opposition to the Congress. With the Congress out of the picture, his attacks lost their force for he seemed to be a man fighting the air. Also, the incarceration of the Congress leaders increased their popularity among the masses. Muslims who had been critical of some of the actions of the Congress ministers gradually lost their sense of bitterness and remembered the many progressive measures that they had initiated. Inflationary pressures began to grow and life became more difficult for the ordinary man. There was large-scale employment but while incomes increased, there was no corresponding increase in the supply of consumer goods. More and more of the national resources were being diverted to purely military purposes, as India was sustaining the entire war effort in south and south-east Asia. She was also largely responsible for maintaining supplies in western Asia and northern Africa.

With manpower drawn away to the battlefields and factories and with greater emphasis on articles needed for the war effort, the condition of life of the ordinary man began to deteriorate. The cracks showed first in Bengal where these all-India tendencies were reinforced by a scorched earth policy intended to deny resources to the Japanese in case they entered India. Withdrawal of rice from some of the border districts had begun in early 1942. The October cyclone and floods also destroyed stocks on a large scale. By the middle of 1943, the food situation in Bengal had assumed alarming proportions. The Bengal famine of 1943–4 was a terrible experience and even according to the most conservative estimates resulted in the death of about two million people. The League ministry in Bengal could not cope with the situation and resentment against the ministry rapidly grew. Jinnah's exhortations about Hindu machinations against a League ministry had little impact on the public mind. There was therefore little regret when the ministry was thrown out of power in spite of the support it had received from the British governor.

It was not, however, in Bengal alone that the League was losing ground. Jinnah saw in Sir Sikandar Hyat Khan's death an opportunity of establishing his strangle-hold on the Punjab. As mentioned earlier, he was helped by a number of officials who from behind the scenes tried to weaken the position of Khizr Hyat Khan. The Punjab premier was a comparatively young man but showed both skill and courage in dealing with Jinnah's attempts to capture the Punjab. He tried hard to avoid an open break but at the same time he took measures to ensure that the Unionist party remained in office and power. Jinnah mounted pressure and ultimately decided to go to Lahore personally in order to replace Khizr Hyat Khan by a more amenable person. At first, it seemed he would succeed. He received a tremendous ovation on his appearance in Lahore but the longer he stayed, the weaker became his hold on the Punjab politicians. His constant attacks against Khizr Hyat Khan were interspersed with equally violent attacks against the Congress. Many who had been sympathetic to Jinnah were alienated by his unseemly attack on an absent foe.

Jinnah also overplayed his hand in some other matters. He had once declared that if Gandhi wrote to him for a settlement, he would take the initiative and he dared the British government to withhold such correspondence from him. Gandhi took him at his word and wrote to him. The British government informed Jinnah of the fact but did not forward the letter to him. Instead of fulfilling his threat that he would in that case take the initiative in forcing the government to come to a settlement, Jinnah publicly complained that Gandhi was trying to embarrass him by creating a conflict with the government. This episode had a rather serious effect in the Punjab and the Frontier. People of these areas place a great stress on the sanctity of one's word. Jinnah appeared to them to be a man of straw who would eat his words in order to avoid a clash with the government.

Within a few months, Jinnah's popularity in the Punjab had diminished greatly. The first meeting he addressed in Lahore was attended by over a hundred thousand people. In two months' time, his audience dwindled to a few hundreds. His negotiations with Khizr Hyat Khan also failed. While the Punjab chief minister paid the courtesy due to Jinnah, he refused to accept the terms Jinnah wanted to impose. Ultimately, the League leader left for Kashmir without achieving his end.

The fortunes of the League seemed very low throughout India in the first half of 1944 but events took a dramatic turn after the release of Mahatma Gandhi in the summer. Soon after he came out, he expressed a desire to negotiate with Jinnah for a settlement of the communal question. This was a move in keeping with Gandhi's character but politically it was another instance of the many Himalayan blunders he made. After the incarceration of the Congress leaders, the Muslim League had steadily lost ground and Jinnah had suffered in personal prestige through his clashes with Fazlul Haq and Khizr Hyat Khan. Nationalist forces among the Muslims were everywhere becoming stronger when Gandhi's decision to deal with Jinnah on equal terms transformed the scene. Once again, Jinnah was held up before the Muslim masses as the one leader with whom the Congress was anxious to come to terms.

It was perhaps inevitable that the Gandhi–Jinnah talks failed. As on previous occasions, there was general agreement on principles but disagreement on minor details. The reaction on the public mind was striking. Congressmen in or outside the jail disapproved of Gandhi's move but very few of them were in a position to criticize Gandhi publicly. Muslim League circles were jubilant and felt that they had at last succeeded in making the Congress accept Jinnah as an equal. This led to a series of discussions between Liaqat Ali Khan and Bhulabhai Desai. Desai, the leader of the Congress party in the central assembly, was a constitutional lawyer of great eminence. His approach was essentially that of a lawyer and as such he did not feel at home in mass movements. An extremely able and patriotic man, he was able to convince Liaqat Ali Khan of his *bona fides*. In the sequel, they were able to draw a plan for co-operation between the Congress and the Muslim League based on a coalition government at the centre. Desai, showed his plan to Gandhi and secured his support. Liaqat Ali Khan was however unable to get Jinnah's approval. This attempt at a solution thus died a premature death.

By this time the war was coming to a close. The British were now sure of victory. The effort had however been too great and had strained Britain's resources in men and materials almost to the breaking point. In addition, there was a general war weariness throughout the British Isles. Lord Wavell who became the viceroy and governor-general of India soon after the Bengal famine was not only a great military leader but also a statesman of high order. He realized before most British leaders that it would be difficult to maintain the *status quo* at the end of war. As one who had been involved in the war effort from the very beginning, he knew the temper of the British soldier and realized that the induction of large number of civilians into the British army had changed its character. He also realized that proper administration in India would become almost impossible without the willing co-operation of the Indian people. He therefore initiated moves for an Indo-British settlement and was able to persuade Churchill to agree to the release of the Congress leaders. They were at first let out one by one but after a series of discussions in London, Wavell announced in June 1945 a general release of all the members of the Congress working committee. Soon after, he convened a conference at Simla to which he invited leaders of all important political parties in the country. This conference dealt with two problems. One was the transfer of power from Britain to India and the other centred round the sharing of power among Indians themselves. On the first question there was general agreement and all sections of Indian opinion accepted the Wavell formula for the transfer of power in two stages. The first would be the constitution of a government at New Delhi composed only of Indians and exercising the powers but not enjoying the legal status of a cabinet. This was to be followed by a constituent assembly at the end of the war when Indians would frame for themselves their own constitution.

Difficulties arose over the second problem of the sharing of power among Indians. Wavell framed his proposals for the purpose largely on the Desai-Liaqat Ali formula. This provided for equal representation of Congress and League on the viceroy's executive council with some seats added to represent the other minorities. The scheme was generally acceptable but difficulties arose over the League's claim to nominate all the Muslim members of the proposed government. The Congress was prepared to concede to the League a quota out of all proportion to its place in Indian national life or the proportion of Muslims to the total Indian population. Congress also agreed that the League would be free to nominate whomever it liked in its own quota and demanded the same right for itself. The League at first insisted that the Congress should nominate only Hindus but later conceded that the Congress might nominate whomever it liked so long as no Muslim was included in the Congress panel. This dictation the Congress was not willing to accept. Maulana Abul Kalam Azad at one stage went so far as to suggest that the League should accept the Congress right to nominate whomever it liked but in practice Congress would not nominate a Muslim. Even this Jinnah was not willing to concede and demanded that the Congress should explicitly declare that it had no right to nominate a Muslim.

It is not yet known why Wavell did not push forward his scheme in spite of Jinnah. The likelihood is that if he had appointed a central government according to his formula, some of the more moderate elements in the Muslim League would have challenged Jinnah's leadership and accepted the offer. Jinnah himself may have relented as he was a realist and knew when his bluff was called. It is likely that the Churchill government was not willing to disappoint Jinnah who had proved an extremely useful ally in the past. It is known that the Conservative party of England had at that time a special liking for the Muslim League and did everything possible to strengthen it *vis-à-vis* the Congress. Whatever be the reason, Wavell's plan did not succeed but it had given a tremendous boost to the Muslim League and again built up Jinnah as the Muslim League counterpart of Gandhi.

Soon after the Simla conference, general elections were held in Britain and the Conservative government suffered a crushing defeat. For the first time in British history, a Labour government was returned with an absolute majority. Earlier Labour governments had been in office but not in power. Clement Attlee was the first Labour prime minister who had effective power and could shape policies as he liked. He carried out far-reaching reforms within the country but even more important, he took revolutionary decisions in respect of overseas territories under British occupation. Attlee had often declared that he would work for the liberation of India and events proved that he was sincere in his professions.

Soon after his assumption of power, Attlee directed that fresh elections should be held throughout India. He also declared that after the elections, popular governments would be formed in the provinces and at the centre and he would take further measures for solving the constitutional tangle. He also appointed a parliamentary delegation which came to India in the winter months of 1945–6 and toured the country extensively. The delegation held detailed discussions with all sections of political opinion in the country and reported that it would be in the best interests of Britain to transfer power to India without further delay. If this was not done expeditiously, the mounting resistance in India would in any case attain its objective but in the process Britain would lose the goodwill of the people. The delegation also noted that discontent was no longer confined only to the political sections of India. The hardships and shortages of war had spread disaffection throughout the countryside.

Even more serious from the British point of view was the return of a million or more Indian soldiers recruited during the war who were coming back to the country with a new political consciousness. They had been told throughout the war that they were fighting for the preservation of democracy. It was natural that they should wish to see the same democracy practised in their own country. Also they had become accustomed to a somewhat higher standard of life and were not prepared to accept the miserable conditions which obtained in most Indian villages. An equally important factor was their resentment at the discrimination in emoluments, treatment and standard of life between themselves and soldiers coming from Britain or the dominions. They resented this the more as the war had proved that they were as good as soldiers of any country and they no longer accepted the myth of western superiority. If Britain was fighting for democracy, the Indian soldiers argued that there should be equality of treatment among soldiers of the Commonwealth without regard to their country of origin, complexion or creed.

The elections resulted in an overwhelming victory of the Congress in all general seats and an equally overwhelming victory of the Muslim League in seats reserved for Muslims. That Congress and League would win in their respective areas of influence was not in question. The magnitude of their victory was however surprising even to their own supporters. The League has never before secured a majority in Bengal, the Punjab or Sind. In Bengal, the League won over ninety per cent of the Muslim seats while Congress victory in the general seats was equally impressive. A national figure like Syama Prasad Mookerjee, who was president of the all-India Hindu Mahasabha, not only lost but forfeited his deposit. A similar fate overtook many of the stalwarts of the Krishak Praja party which in 1937 had defeated the League. It was only in the Frontier that the League could not secure a majority of Muslim seats. With this single exception, polarization of forces in India seemed complete.

When the election results were out and the governments were being formed in different states, it was clear that Congress ministries would come into power in all the provinces of India excepting four. Bengal and Sind formed League ministries immediately. In the Frontier, the Congress again came into office. In the Punjab, though the League had won the largest number of Muslim seats, it could not form a government as Congressmen entered into a coalition with the Unionist party. Khizr Hyat Khan again became the chief minister, but his position was much weaker than it had been when he had fought Jinnah barely two years ago. The Ahrar party and other splinter groups in the Punjab were almost wiped out.

Attlee sent a cabinet mission under the leadership of Lord Pethick-Lawrence to discuss the future set-up in India. The other members were Sir Stafford Cripps and A. V. Alexander. The mission held detailed discussions with all political parties and in the end presented a plan which was a skilful combination of the largest measure of autonomy for the provinces with a unified centre in charge of foreign affairs, defence and communications. The cabinet mission thought that this formula would meet the Congress demand for preserving the unity of India while it conceded the League's claim for the fullest autonomy for the areas where Muslims constituted a majority. There was also provision for zonal co-operation among provinces bound by common ties through an intermediate body with certain prescribed powers. If Congress and the League had accepted the plan without mental reservation and worked it honestly, it might have offered a solution to the tangled Indian problem.

The solution offered by the mission had striking similarities with the scheme prepared by Maulana Azad, then Congress president, who had released to the press a summary of his views in April 1946. The mission must have taken note of his proposal but it depended primarily on the study prepared by Professor Coupland some years before. The idea of zonal combinations interposed between the union and the state units was essentially his and might have succeeded if, instead of three zones proposed by him, the mission had provided for four such zones. The states in the south could easily have formed the fourth zone and in that case, the four zones would have been more or less equal in terms of population, resources and prospects.

One has to admit with regret that neither the Congress nor the League gave a fair chance to the cabinet mission plan. Both accepted the long-term arrangements but interpreted them according to their own lights. What was even more surprising was that when the mission issued certain clarifications, these were not accepted and a demand was made that the plan should be submitted to lawyers in order to find out what was the real intention of the mission. To this the mission very rightly rejoined that no one could know its intentions better than the members of the mission.

A purely legalistic approach never solves large political problems. This was perhaps the major defect in the situation, for lawyers were in command in both the Congress and the League. They looked at all questions in a purely legalistic way with the result that the scope for compromise and accommodation was greatly reduced. Lawyers have great respect for the written word and want to write down everything in unequivocal terms. Power on the other hand cannot be transferred by legal documents. It can be secured only through the exercise of power. The fact that neither Jinnah, nor Nehru nor Patel nor Azad had at any time exercised effective administrative power was at least in part responsible for their failure to grasp the substance instead of straining after the shadow.

Even though the long-term plan was accepted by the Congress and the League, they were in sharp disagreement about the interim arrangement. Lord Wavell was a sincere and well-intentioned man, but lacked diplomatic skill and finesse. He was confused by the endless arguments of the leaders of the Congress and the League. Even the Labour government felt perplexed but in the meantime an event occurred in Bombay which acted as a sharp reminder that things could not wait. This was the naval mutiny in which a section of the Indian naval forces rose in revolt and there were cases of exchange of fire between British and Indian personnel. With their hard-headed realism and acute political sense, the British government realized that it would be dangerous to keep power in exclusively British hands and Indians must be associated with government as early as possible.

The naval mutiny was bad enough, but there were other events which were also causing great concern to the government. Trouble began in the Punjab soon after the formation of the Congress–Unionist coalition ministry and Khizr Hyat Khan had the greatest difficulty in keeping the province under control. Whatever chance there was of things settling down was completely destroyed by the Calcutta riots of August 1946. This arose directly out of Congress/League differences. Soon after Congress accepted the cabinet mission plan, Maulana Azad's term as president of the Congress came to an end. Pandit Nehru who succeeded him made a most unfortunate statement in one of his first press conferences as president. He said that Congress had agreed to join the constituent assembly but accepted nothing else. Once the assembly met, Congress would be free to ask for any changes in the cabinet mission plan that it considered necessary.

Jinnah immediately protested that this was against the spirit of the cabinet mission plan which both the Congress and the League had ostensibly accepted. He further declared that if the Congress could go back on its word even while the British were in India, what guarantee would there be that its assurances would be honoured after the British had left? He accordingly advised the League to reject the cabinet mission plan in the light of the Congress decision. The League decided to hold protests throughout India on August 16th. It was called direct action day to indicate that the League would no longer be content to agitate through legal constitutional means alone. Sober sections in the League leadership pointed to the dangers of such demonstration in the inflamed atmosphere of the day, but the League went on with its preparation and August 16, 1946 broke upon India as one of the darkest days in its history. There was widespread killing in Calcutta and literally hundreds of men, women and children lost their lives in communal frenzy. The fate of the cabinet mission plan was in fact sealed on August 16th even though this was not realized at the time.

An offer was made to Nehru to form an interim government in which he would serve as the vice-chairman of the executive council and be second only to the viceroy. He accepted the offer and immediately asked Jinnah to join the council. The League leader declined as was to be expected in the light of what had happened. Nehru then formed the government without the League and the interim government came into office on September 2, 1946. Nehru took charge of external affairs while Patel became the home member. There were non-Congress men also in the government of whom the most prominent were Sardar Baldev Singh and Dr John Matthai.

The first task of the government was to help in the restoration of law and order and create a sense of security in the country. It was however almost a hopeless task. Not only did the Muslim League stay outside but it also engaged in active opposition to the government. Sporadic riots took place in different parts of the country and the League fomented trouble in the most unlikely spots. Unrest spread over into the Indian states as well. Kashmir, Hyderabad and Travancore were all in turmoil and in the background loomed the danger of communal conflagration throughout the country.

Lord Wavell was most unhappy at this outcome of his efforts to transfer power to Indian hands in a united India. He felt that without participation of the League, the government would remain unrepresentative of a large section of the people. What made the situation even more serious was that political and communal divisions had coincided to threaten the fabric of national life. This had affected the services as well. Fortunately, the defence forces were yet free from the communal virus but all other sections of the people in government and outside were badly affected. Men and women who retained their balance and sanity were like tiny islands in a vast ocean of hatred and fury.

Apart from Wavell's own attempts, other well-wishers of India were also anxious to bring about an understanding between the Congress and the League. Once in the seat of power, the Congress realized that effective administration demanded the willing co-operation of all sections of the people. While it did enjoy the support of a vast majority of Indians, the sullen hostility of the Muslim League and its followers was a factor which could not be overlooked. Denied power, the League felt frustrated. Since a majority of its leading men had always been supporters of the government, they felt baffled and unhappy at being forced into opposition. With their longer experience of administrative power, they also realized that if they remained out of office for long, they would lose their support among the people. There was therefore a mood for discussion and conciliation in both the Congress and the League camps when the nawab of Bhopal took the initiative in attempting a settlement.

In early October 1946, it appeared that these attempts had succeeded. Differences between the Congress and the League were greatly pared down and a stage came when Jinnah agreed to enter the government as a colleague of Nehru. He also agreed that other important members of the Muslim League would join the government with him. It seemed that India would at last have a really powerful government with the ablest members of the Congress and the League serving as an informal cabinet. The fates however willed otherwise. On several earlier occasions, agreement had seemed in sight and yet there was a break-down at the last moment over some trivial issue. The second Round Table conference in 1931 had failed over the question of one seat in the Punjab. The Cripps proposals in 1942 had failed because of a disagreement about the nomenclature and functions of the Indian defence member of the executive council. The failure in October 1946 arose out of a still more trivial reason.

John Matthai, Jagjivan Ram and C. H. Bhabha were at the time members of the interim government as representatives of the minorities and the scheduled castes. Differences arose regarding the method of their replacement if any of them resigned or died. Jinnah insisted that a representative of the minorities or the scheduled castes should be included in the executive council only with the concurrence of the League. Congress agreed that there should be consultation but would not accept Jinnah's claim that the member chosen should be acceptable to him or his successor. The talks broke down over this issue. It did not occur to the leaders of either the Congress or the League that the contingency might never arise. Though John Matthai was comparatively old, both Jagjivan Ram and C. H. Bhabha were much younger than the Congress or the League leaders. There was no reason why they should resign or die simply in order to give the Congress and the League an opportunity to quarrel.

The breakdown of the talks led to further bitterness. Discontent was pervasive. Frequent outbreaks of communal frenzy disturbed the countryside. Nehru visited the Frontier Province and for the first time in his life faced public hostility on a wide scale. Wavell kept on insisting that the League should be brought into the government in order to restore normalcy. In a mood of exasperation, Nehru agreed and Wavell immediately issued invitations to the League to join the government. Jinnah accepted with alacrity but in order to express his anger and disapproval did not himself join the government. He also kept out some of his ablest and most trusted lieutenants. Liaqat Ali Khan was the only representative of the League who could claim all-India standing and he was sent merely to serve as the rallying point for the others. The other nominees of the League could hardly be regarded as all-India figures. One of them was a representative of the scheduled castes who enjoyed the confidence of neither his own community nor the Muslims.

The story of the interim government need not be told in detail. It is enough to say here that the coalition government did not prove a success. On certain issues and at certain moments of crisis, some of its members acted in unison. Thus some League members of the executive council gave Nehru unstinted support when he tried to control the riotous situation in Bihar. The situation nevertheless continued to deteriorate. Attlee made one more attempt at a settlement between the Congress and the League and invited Nehru, Jinnah and some others to London but discussions there proved of no avail. The interim government dragged on but the constituent assembly which was to frame the constitution of free India could not meet because of continued opposition between the Congress and the League. After Nehru, Jinnah and others returned from London, it was clear that the Congress and the League could not come to terms. The Congress decided to go ahead with the framing of the constitution with or without the League.

The constituent assembly met for the first time in December 1946. It formulated the principles on which the constitution should be framed but in the prevailing atmosphere it was difficult if not impossible to carry on with constructive work. The constant sniping by the League from within came to a head when the budget for 1947–8 was presented. Liaqat Ali Khan adopted some of the Congress resolutions in a literal sense but in the process of framing specific proposals gave them a twist which turned socialist recipes into penal measures against Hindu moneyed classes. His proposals were opposed by some of his colleagues and led to an uproar in the assembly. Ultimately, the budget was modified but Liaqat Ali Khan had put the Congress in a very awkward position as it had to modify or go back on some of its earlier professions.

The situation came to a breaking point in the early months of 1947 when the Punjab completely got out of hand. The coalition ministry headed by Khizr Hyat Khan had faced difficulties from the very beginning. After the Muslim League got into the central government, its difficulties increased manyfold. Till then, the sympathizers of the Muslim League in the services had been under some restraint, but once there were Muslim League members in the viceroy's executive council, their daring knew no bounds. Law and order broke down on an extensive scale and riots took place in both eastern and western Punjab. It seemed as if the administration was coming to a standstill. It was at this stage that Attlee announced that regardless of what the Indian political leaders did, the British would withdraw from India by June 1948. Attlee's reading was that once the Indian leaders were faced with the reality of British withdrawal, they would come to terms with one another. This may have happened if Wavell had continued and the plan which he had framed had been carried out. Briefly this was a proposal for British withdrawal from India stage by stage, so that Indian leaders would get the time needed to adjust gradually to their new position of power and responsibility.

Attlee did not approve of Wavell's proposal as he was anxious that there should be immediate transfer of power to Indian hands. He therefore suggested that Wavell might canvas the possibility of a settlement on the basis of a divided India. Wavell was dead against any proposal to divide the country, as in his view it would make the defence of India extremely difficult if not impossible. Since his point of view was not acceptable, Wavell was dismissed and was replaced by Earl Mountbatten.

Mountbatten came to India in the later half of March 1947. He was determined to find a solution of the Indian problem with the least possible delay. He also at first tried for a solution on the basis of a united India but when he found that the League insisted on the creation of Pakistan, he began to explore the possibility of a solution on that basis. To his surprise he found that some of the Congress leaders had resiled from their earlier position of unqualified opposition to the idea of partition. The situation had changed dramatically within five years. At the time of the Cripps mission in 1942, Congress was adamant against partition. The League demanded partition but more as a bargaining counter than as an unchangeable claim. In fact, Jinnah's almost open readiness to accept the Cripps proposals provided the Congress did so first was a virtual admission that for him the claim for partition was only a bid to raise the stakes. Even when the cabinet mission came in 1946, Jinnah had ultimately accepted the plan which was based on the unity of India. In March 1947, the situation was totally different. Jinnah was now confident that with a little more pressure he would win his point. The Congress on the other hand had become hesitant and lost something of its militant confidence. Its attitude seemed to be that while united India was certainly desirable, immediate independence of the major part of India was preferable to a postponement of the independence of the whole of India.

Mountbatten was a man of quick decisions. Once he saw that Congress was more likely to yield than the League, he framed his proposals for freedom on the basis of two states. He also suggested that the two new states should be dominions as it would be easier to transfer power to Indian hands in a dominion than to an independent state unconnected with the Commonwealth. This meant a sharp departure from the stand which both the Congress and the League had taken for years. Congress had declared in 1929 that it would not be content with dominion status but would work for an independent republic outside the Commonwealth. The League had also since 1940 spoken of an independent Pakistan though it had never stated its position so unequivocally as the Congress. In order to sugarcoat the bitter pill, Mountbatten advanced the date of independence considerably. Against Attlee's offer of independence in June 1948, he suggested that independence should be proclaimed by August 1947.

The Congress was anxious to get rid of the British. The League was anxious to get power without the constant fear of Congress hegemony. Attlee was anxious that this vexed question should be settled rapidly and once for all. The Indian people wanted to be free of foreign rule. The British people were tired of war and were in no mood to send soldiers to keep under control an unwilling and hostile territory. When all the parties were thus anxious for an early settlement, it was perhaps not surprising that Mountbatten's formula should be readily accepted. In June 1947, it was accordingly declared that the

British government had decided to withdraw from India and hand over power to the two dominions of India and Pakistan by August 1947.

There followed about eight weeks of hectic activity in carrying out the partition of assets and liabilities. A vast superstructure of government that had been built over almost 200 years was to be dispersed in less than two months. Now that the partition had become a reality, there was for a moment a sense of sadness and even resignation in the minds of some of the major participants. Given the time to think, there might have been a chance of second thoughts. Mountbatten was however determined that there should be no backsliding from the agreement which had been reached after so much effort, anxiety and suffering. He drew up a programme of partition and saw to it that this was carried out without pause or deviation. It was an almost superhuman feat but on August 14, 1947 the task was completed. Jinnah and his colleagues had left for Karachi. In the early hours of August 14th, Pakistan came into existence and the next day the Indian Union was born.

With the partition of the country ended the chapter of Muslim politics which had begun with the establishment of the Muslim League in 1906. The League had fulfilled itself in a Hegelian sense. It had insisted on special rights for Muslims and created a situation where these demands led to a breakup of the Indian polity. Whatever happened in Pakistan, the League's policies and practices had assured that there would never again be a separate political function for the Muslims of India. The League had therefore in a truly dialectical sense negated itself.

EPILOGUE

August 15, 1947, was a day of rejoicing for the Indian people. Vast gatherings turned out to witness the birth of free India. Among the politically conscious, there was however a deep under-current of regret even in the midst of rejoicing. Congressmen who had stood for the freedom of united India grieved that Indian unity was lost. This was specially true of Muslim Congressmen for they felt that all their struggle and suffering for a free united India had failed. Even keener was the sense of sorrow in Gandhi's mind, for no one felt the partition of India more acutely than the Mahatma. He in fact refused to join the celebrations at the national capital and chose to remain in Calcutta where people feared a recurrence of the troubles of August 1946.

When the proposal of partition was first mooted, Gandhi had said that he would oppose it with his life. On more occasions than one, he said that partition would be not only a crime but a sin. Even when other Congress leaders had accepted partition, he did not change his view. He maintained his disapproval but did not take the course of action which many had expected from him. In 1932, he had staked his life to prevent the separation of the scheduled castes from the rest of the Hindu community. In 1947, many hoped that he would even at the last moment pit his enormous strength and prestige against the proposal and avert the division of the country. Why he did not act as he had often said he would remains to this day a mystery. Some say that this was because he lost heart when he found his most trusted lieutenants united against him on this issue. Others say that he was old and tired and did not feel strong enough to launch a struggle on his own. Still others say that he was heart-broken by the way in which Hindus and Muslims had reacted to his life-long endeavour for peace and friendship among all communities. Perhaps, all these factors contributed, but the fact remains that while the majority of Indian political leaders rejoiced, Gandhi remained away from Delhi and brooded in sorrow.

Gandhi had warned again and again that partition would solve no problems but only increase bitterness among the communities. His forebodings turned out to be tragically true. Even before August 14, 1947, there were rumblings of discord and strife in the Punjab. Immediately after independence, violence erupted in different parts of the country and especially in the north-western areas of the sub-continent. Murder, pillage and rapine took place on an unprecedented scale. Millions were uprooted and forced to migrate across the newly created frontiers. Eastern India escaped the holocaust. Perhaps Gandhi's presence in that region was one of the factors for this redeeming feature. Soon the fires spread from the Punjab to Delhi and at one time threatened to overwhelm the newly formed dominions.

In Calcutta itself, there was an outburst of violence on September 1, 1947. Gandhi declared he would fast till the conflict ended and if need be die in order to save Bengal from communal violence. He was strongly backed by Dr Prafulla Chandra Ghosh, the new chief minister of West Bengal, who declared that he considered it an act of non-violence to shoot down a dozen rioters in order to save the lives of millions. Within four days, the situation was brought under control and Gandhi felt sufficiently assured to move to Delhi where the position was becoming critical.

Jinnah had based his demand for Pakistan on his two-nation theory. According to him, Hindus and Muslims differed in ideas and outlook, beliefs, and habits, conduct and modes of behaviour. The tragic events which followed the partition of India proved how wrong he was. Large masses felt, thought and acted in the same way. They exhibited the same senseless hatred and fury and were indistinguishable from one another in their actions and reactions. Equally indistinguishable were the splendid acts of isolated heroism by individuals and groups on both sides of the border who stood up against the raging storm of communal passion and asserted their humanity at the risk of death. The pattern of atrocities on both sides was also tragically similar. Infuriated mobs on either side attacked helpless men and women and showed no regard for the aged or the infant. On either side, small bands of devoted men and women fought against the dehumanizing influence of passion and stood their ground against tremendous odds. In atrocity and cruelty, in suffering and death as well as in nobility and sacrifice, men and women on both sides of the border proclaimed their common nationality.

Gandhi came to Delhi where communal passions were running high. With characteristic courage, he faced the fury of the mob and preached the message of co-operation and friendship. His prayer meetings became a source of strength and solace to countless men and women in the capital and outside. Passions had been so inflamed that some misguided men tried to prevent these meetings, but in spite of opposition, threats and attacks, he continued with them. There had been a murderous attack on him in Calcutta in

September 1947. There were further attacks in Delhi and continuing threats. Nothing however could daunt him and with exemplary courage and patience, he pursued his lone path of understanding and conciliation. There was a stamp of greatness on everything he did from the time he opposed tyranny in South Africa, but perhaps even he had never reached the heights which he achieved in his last six months. A new sweetness and strength welled out of all his words and actions and everyone who came into contact with him came away a purer and better man. The forces of evil were also gathering strength and on January 30, 1948, Gandhi paid the supreme price for his love of his fellowmen. He died a physical death but spiritually he was renewed and joined the band of immortals whose names shine like stars in the firmament of human history.

Gandhi was unhappy till death released him from his suffering and made him a martyr to the cause of human unity and understanding. His assassination had a cathartic effect and throughout India men realized with a shock the depth to which hatred and discord had dragged them. The Indian nation turned back from the brink of the abyss and millions blessed the memory of the man who had made redemption possible.

From all accounts, Jinnah was also an unhappy man after the attainment of Pakistan. Immediately after the achievement of Pakistan, he had declared that religious conflicts must be left behind and men of all communities cooperate for the prosperity and welfare of the land. He had been an ardent nationalist except for the last ten years of his life, and even then he had acted more in anger and sorrow than in a deliberate repudiation of all that he had stood for in his earlier years. Perhaps he had hoped that after the establishment of Pakistan, he could return to his earlier nationalism, but with the background in which Pakistan had been created, this was an impossible hope. In any case, Jinnah was soon disillusioned and it added to his disappointment when he found that the reins were slipping out of his hands. Within a few months of Gandhi's death, he was stricken with mortal illness and in September 1948, he died. Muslim League politics had been one of reaction against Congress policies. Jinnah had built himself up as a counterfoil to Gandhi. When Gandhi disappeared from the Indian political scene, Jinnah lingered for a while but he was like the memory of a shadow bereft of substantial reality.

THE PARTITION OF INDIA IN RETROSPECT

by M. MUJEEB*

I remember a discussion with Dr Iqbal, whom the Jamia Millia had invited to preside over a meeting to be addressed by an eminent Turkish guest, early in 1935. The discussion was frank and informal, and the subject was the destiny of the Indian Muslims. Iqbal had, about five years earlier, expressed the view that Muslims must have territory of their own, a homeland, where they could make the obligatory experiment of living according to the shari'ah. This view was diametrically opposed to the principle on which the Jamia was founded, that Muslims must live and work with non-Muslims for the realization of common ideals of citizenship and culture. The discussion was long and interesting, and entirely free from that bitterness which later marred every exchange of views between nationalist and pro-Muslim League Muslims. To the best of my recollection, Iqbal could find no reasonable ground for rejecting the principle being followed by the Jamia Millia; he only maintained his own point of view, and it also became clear that the Muslims he had in mind were Punjab Muslims who, according to him, were still too weak to stand on their own feet and felt the need of political power to support them socially and economically.

The two points of view presented in the discussion with Iqbal still exist. The territory where Muslims could live in accordance with the shari'ah is now Pakistan, and the Jamia Millia is still where it was, working for the same ends. In November 1946, it had succeeded in bringing together the most eminent leaders of the Congress and the Muslim League on the same platform, and obtained from both an acknowledgement of the value of the religious, cultural and political aims to which it was committed.

This is by way of introduction to the first point I wish to consider, namely whether a partition of the country was necessary to enable the Muslims to live according to the ideals of Islam.

It would be embarrassing to look back to the period of Muslim rule in India. The aspiration to live according to the spiritual ideals of Islam was confined to a small number of individuals; political power was in the hands of a minority, which believed necessarily in expediency rather than moral principle. To illustrate the organic unity of religious and political activity the Muslim has to go back to the days of the Prophet and the first two successors, and to find some ground for rejecting the validity of all that happened subsequently down to his own time. But no historical justification is necessary for the quickening of the religious spirit, and there were several revivalist movements. They were, however, basically theological. The Wahhabis and the Faraizis showed some tendency towards political action, but their leadership had little or no understanding of political ideas or methods. Their sectarian character asserted itself more and more, with the result that they became a

* Vice-Chancellor, Jamia Millia, Delhi.

disintegrating rather than a unifying influence. The Barelvi School, with its bitter condemnation of the Wahhabis, the Ahl-i-Hadith, with their insistence on recourse to the Traditions as the source of guidance and their rejection of the four schools of jurisprudence, the Ahl-i-Qur'an, with their rejection of all other sources of guidance except the Qur'an, were all purely theological in principle and became sectarian in practice. They reduced the teachings of Islam to a set of opinions and the practice of Islam to a search for the most reliable authority on what were essentially matters of detail. Sir Syed Ahmad Khan had a larger view of life than any of the purely religious leaders, and one must be grateful to him for having given commonsense its rightful place in religious thought. Dr Iqbal was a great poet and thinker, but he did not lead what is traditionally regarded as a religious life and did not aspire to religious leadership. Maulana Azad's real contribution to a reconstruction of the Islamic ideal of an active political life inspired by the highest spiritual and moral values lies unobserved in a few paragraphs of his *Tarjum al-Quran.*

The most recent among the religious movements are the Jama'at-i-Islami and the Tablighi Jama'at. In the literature of the Jama'at-i-Islami we find categorical assertions of the superiority of the shari'ah of Islam over all other principles and forms of social and political organization, but its real appeal derives from a rhetorical denunciation of western civilization. The Jama'at-i-Islami has also evolved a concept of the Islamic state, of which any Muslim anywhere can be a citizen, and which will be the best governed because only Muslims of acknowledged piety and integrity will be entitled to hold office and to be elected to its consultative bodies. The Tablighi Jama'at, founded by the late Maulana Ilyas, aims at making those who know something about the beliefs and practices of Islam teach those who know little or nothing about them. It is the only movement that is not theological and aggressive. It has brought all classes of people together in a common realization that they are members of a community, and this membership can have meaning and value if the beliefs and practices on which their community life is based are understood and observed by all.

Since we are trying to analyse the reasons which led to the partition, the material question in this context is whether any expressions of religiosity among Muslims encountered opposition from the non-Muslims or were hampered by the fact of the Muslims being a minority. The answer is that all opposition which Muslim religious movements have had to face has come from the Muslims themselves. Disputes arising from Hindu objections to cow-sacrifice and Muslim objections to music before mosques have generally been engineered by mischief-makers and their effects have been local and temporary. On the other hand, sufis and their graves have been venerated by Hindus. I remember that shortly after the orgy of violence in Bihar I visited the grave of a sufi on the banks of the Ganges. The Muslims living in the *dargah* had fled and the place looked desolate. But soon a group of Hindu women appeared. They performed circumambulations and prostrations, as if nothing had happened that affected their sentiments of veneration for the tomb of a Muslim saint.

But even if there was full freedom for the realization of the spiritual and ethical ideals of Islam, Muslims could still aspire to the creation of an Islamic state as something ideally necessary, and demand territory where this state could be established. My own belief is that the concept of an Islamic state should be present in the mind of every Muslim and should serve as a guide and a corrective in his political conduct. I do not remember that this belief was shared by the prominent men and women of Uttar Pradesh in the Muslim League camp. They were just not the type of persons who would undertake the intellectual task of analysing the concept of an Islamic state. Their allegiance to it was rhetorical; they did not care to be intelligent or serious. The usual answer given to me when I put questions about the political structure of the Islamic state was that this was a matter to be thought about when we had Pakistan. But draft constitutions of the Islamic state were also drawn up. One such constitution was sent to me for scrutiny. I found that the person or persons who had drawn it up had no knowledge of even the elements of political science and the working of governments. This was inevitable. Those who were thinking of creating an Islamic state did not realize that they were creating in a vacuum something which grows out of established political and social ideas and habits, that it must be the culmination of efforts directed to a particular end and not the starting-point of a religious and political adventure.

The absence of habits, tendencies, institutions that could serve as a foundation for the ethics if not the political structure of the Islamic state was a serious shortcoming. It could have been somewhat compensated by a revival of faith. I observed nothing of this kind among the people I knew. Prominent men in the Muslim League of Uttar Pradesh took to praying at least in public when the inconsistency of representing Islam and neglecting even the elementary obligations was made a point of attack by critics, but prayer and fasting are social forms the mere observance of which is no indication of religious zeal. If religious sentiment had been genuine, charitable institutions, orphanages, schools and colleges financed by Muslims would have benefited. To the best of my knowledge none of them obtained any financial support or, if the League was too poor to afford this, even moral support from the Muslim League. On the contrary, the theological seminary of Deoband was disowned for political reasons, and the Jamia Millia was regarded with suspicion or disfavour because it associated itself with basic education and persisted in professing admiration and reverence for Mahatma Gandhi (who, as we know, was the one man who saved the Muslims jettisoned by the Muslim League). If, in November 1946, M. A. Jinnah agreed to attend the silver jubilee function of the Jamia Millia, it was due more to the tact and persuasive power of Dr Zakir Husain than to any change in the attitude of the League.

So much for the religious aspect of the demand for Pakistan. Could we reasonably consider this demand, and the two-nation theory on which it was based, the symptom of an awakened and vigorous political consciousness? Specifically, was there an awareness of needs of Muslims which could be fulfilled only through common political action by Muslims? Were there any positive and general aims that could be regarded as the logical consequence of particular aims already realized?

I shall discuss this question with reference only to Uttar Pradesh and Delhi, because, as already indicated, I happen to have personal knowledge of the Muslim League leadership of these areas.

There were needs that could be regarded as the particular needs of the Muslim population of these areas. The number of Muslim cultivators was nowhere large or concentrated except in Mewat, to the west of Delhi. The Tablighi Jama'at of Maulana Ilyas did considerable work of education and reform among the Mewatis or Meos, who were known to be a hardy and lawless people. The political leadership did nothing constructive, but entered the field in the years immediately before the partition to exploit the newly awakened religious consciousness of the Meos and create conflicts with their neighbours which could only lead to their ruin. In the rural areas of Uttar Pradesh there were large numbers of small landlords whom spendthrift habits had reduced to poverty. They needed to be rehabilitated through co-operative enterprises of banking, seed procurement, irrigation, etc. These small landlords were also in need of education in disciplined living, which could be imparted best by a body like the Muslim League, which had both a religious and a political character. Instead, the frustration and despair of this class was exploited for political ends which could not possibly bring its members any benefit and which, on the contrary, placed their lives and properties in danger because of the passions roused by the propaganda of the League.

In the cities, the artisan classes stood in great need of education and organization. The Muslim community would not have had to regard itself as economically backward in the twentieth century if its leadership had spent in educating its artisans half the effort it wasted in persuading Muslims of the upper classes to take to English education. Muslim craftsmanship enjoyed great prestige. It had lost considerable ground because of the competition with machine-made goods, but also recovered somewhat when Europeans set the fashion of preferring hand-made to mass-produced goods. Muslim weavers, embroiderers, tin, silver and gold smiths, workers in ceramics, shoemakers, to name only the prominent categories, lived and worked within a horizon limited by their lack of education and were severely handicapped by spendthrift habits which kept them on the verge of penury. They were also undependable. But while the educator turned his eyes elsewhere, the preacher never went beyond the occasional sermons he was invited to deliver. The outlook and the habits of the craftsman did not change, and in spite of natural gifts he remained far behind his time and, therefore, economically insecure.

In Uttar Pradesh and Delhi – the situation was different in other parts of the country – the more prosperous merchants dealt mainly in imported goods, and their business depended upon a liberal import policy. But though the risk was obvious, hardly anything was done to establish industries that would support trade. In industry the Muslims would naturally have had to face keen competition, but there was no other way out. There would not, however, have been discrimination against Muslims by Hindu consumers. For a few years, under the influence of the idea that the Muslim consumer should support the Muslim trader, I made it a point to buy what I needed in Muslim shops in Old Delhi. There were good and bad salesmen among the Muslims; the shops of the good salesmen were always crowded, and Muslim customers were an insignificant part of the crowd. But when I tried to propagate my idea in my family circle, I met with a rebuff. The ladies of the family, who did most of the spending, had a very poor opinion of the merchandise offered by Muslim shops and they did not care for the manners of the shopkeepers either.

This is, I believe, sufficient indication that the needs which found political expression were not the needs of the community as a whole but those of a class, which consisted of big and small landlords, and the lawyers, doctors, government servants who belonged to the families of these landlords. Businessmen, unless they belonged to the class, could not be full members; the ulama did not belong to the class. The existence of this class would, of course, be overlooked or even denied when the principle of the equality of all Muslims was under discussion, and it was disintegrated enough to create the illusion that it did not exist. But if I were asked to give the one all-important reason for the upsurge of sentiment which ultimately led to the partition of the country, I would say that it was the reaction of this class to the realities of democracy.[1]

I belong to this class myself. I remember my own reactions when I visited the Uttar Pradesh assembly. It was, I believe, the inaugural session. There were crowds of people in the visitors' galleries and the hall, but hardly a face that was known to me. I was simple-minded enough to ask a man standing next to me where the chief minister was, and I got in reply a reproachful look and the remark, 'Can't you see he is sitting there'? I felt extremely uncomfortable. I could not spot anyone dressed like me, the language spoken around

[1] *'Class' among Indian Muslims of Uttar Pradesh*

Below are given two extracts which are self-explanatory The first is from a speech of Sir Syed Ahmad Khan delivered at a public meeting in Lucknow, after the third session of the Indian National Congress held in Madras in 1887. He severely criticized the solutions of the first Congress about representation in the Councils by election. And the other is from a book, 'The Heavenly Ornaments', which served as a religious and social guide.

(1) 'You will see that it is one of the necessary conditions of sitting at the same table with the Viceroy, that the person concerned should have a high social status in the country. Will the members of noble families in our country like it that a person of lower class or lower status, even if he has taken the B.A. or M.A. degree and possesses the necessary ability, should govern them and dispose of their wealth, property and honour? Never. Not one of them will like it. The seat of the Counsellor of the Government is a place of honour. Government cannot give it to anybody except a man of high social status. Neither can the Viceroy address him as "My Colleague", or "My Honourable Colleague", nor can he be invited to royal levees which are attended by dukes, earls and other men of high rank. So Government can never be blamed if it nominates men of noble families.

'Just think of what happens as a result of competitive examinations in England. You know that there everybody, high or low, whether he is the son of a duke, an earl, a gentleman or a tailor's son, has an equal right to appear for the examination. European officers who take their examination in England and come over here are so remote from us that we have no idea whether they are sons of Lords or Dukes or of tailors and if we are governed by a person of low birth we do not know it. But that is not the case in India. In India, the people of higher social classes would not like a man of low birth, whose origin is known to them, to have authority over their life and property.'

(2) 'Shaikhs, Sayyids, Ansaris, Alawis are equals; the Mughals and Pathans are all one race (*qaum*), and cannot compare with Shaikhs and Sayyids. Weavers, barbers, washermen are not the equals of tailors. There is also a grading on the basis of whether the father or grandfather was converted to Islam.' Thanawi, Maulana Ashraf Ali: *Bihishti Zewar*, Part IV, pp. 9–10. Nur Muhammadi edition, Karachi. Date of publication not given.

me was not the Urdu which I thought was the language of Lucknow, the cultural metropolis of Uttar Pradesh, and there seemed to be no one within sight worth talking to. I left the assembly building with a feeling of mingled panic and disgust. But I was in the fortunate position of not having to go there again; I was a teacher, I kept away from politics and had the leisure to educate myself. What of the sixty-six Muslim members of this assembly, of whom twenty-nine belonged to the Muslim League? They could not follow my example and walk out of the building.[1]

Before the elections in United Provinces under the Act of 1935, the Congress and the Muslim League had formed a kind of alliance against those who were pro-British or not dependable as nationalists, who belonged to no party and hoped to win the election and make a political career on the basis of personal influence. The Muslim League was not very successful, and secured only twenty-nine out of sixty-six seats. The Congress victory was overwhelming, and a ministry could be formed without the assistance of any other party or the independents. The attitude of the Congress leadership to the informal arrangement made with the Muslim League leaders gradually changed and as the negotiations over the appointment of Muslim ministers proceeded, it became more and more obvious that the Congress would dictate the terms of any agreement that was arrived at. I was at home in Lucknow when the draft of the agreement proposed by Maulana Azad on behalf of the Congress was sent to Choudhry Khaliquzzaman. My immediate reaction on reading it was that the Muslim League was being asked to abolish itself. This was an attack not on the persons who wanted to become ministers but on the whole class that had painfully organized itself and was still feeling very shaky. Jawaharlal Nehru made matters still worse by writing to the Muslim League president that there were only two forces in India at that time – British imperialism and Indian nationalism. 'The Muslim League represents a group of Muslims, no doubt highly estimable persons, but functioning in the higher regions of the upper middle classes and having no common contact with the Muslim masses and few with the Muslim lower middle class.'[2] This, as I have already indicated, was my own view of the situation, and knowing Khaliquzzaman and other leaders of the Muslim League as I did, I would have dropped the words 'highly estimable'.

But it was very poor statesmanship that transformed a difference of opinion over a ministerial post or two into a national struggle in which a class felt that it was fighting for its life. It would not have shattered Nehru's prestige if, because of him, the Muslims had got one ministerial post more

[1] The 66 Muslim members of the first Legislative Assembly belonged to the following categories:

Nawabs, rajas, zamindars	21 (including two women)
Khan Bahadurs (persons who had been awarded the second lowest title of honour because they had given some proof of 'loyalty')	12
Advocates (also from zamindar families)	23
No precise category	10
	66

[2] Ram Gopal, *The Indian Muslims*, p. 251.

than they were entitled to; and if Khaliquzzaman had been made a minister the League in Uttar Pradesh would most probably have dissolved of itself. Khaliquzzaman was a very charming person and an eloquent speaker, but he was not a full member of the class because he lacked the requisite property qualification. There would have been resentment against his appointment among those who regarded him as an outsider, and he would either have had to resign or to work against the class which it was his ambition to represent and lead. Nehru and Azad together cleared the way for his becoming the valiant knight of an insulted and injured community.

The conflict between the Muslim League and the Congress might have been on a different level and far less bitter if the Congress governments had not reflected the upsurge of the masses. Most of the new leaders were not known to the Muslims. They were, therefore, not persons but just Hindus, and Nehru, who belonged in every way to the class, had gone and identified himself with them. He had even denied the existence of the culture of which the class was so proud. Nehru's ideas did not impress the class; it was not interested in anything intellectual, except as a matter of occasional conversation, and invariably preferred epigrams to truth. It was not impressed by what Congressmen called their sacrifices, because it regarded suffering as something not required by its code, especially suffering for a cause. The British had obtained dominion over India because of their superior force, and that was generations ago. The Congress had achieved the right to govern not through an exhibition of superior intelligence or power, but through non-violence which, again, did not impress the class because it was something foreign to its traditions. The class, therefore, felt no scruples about saying anything so long as it hurt the Hindus whom the Congress had seated in the high places, or the Hindus in general.

But we must also remember that this class was provided with sufficient excuses for saying ugly things. There was something unbearably upstartish in the conduct of the Congress underlings, who were inclined to talk as if they were both the government and the country. All standards of refinement were reduced to the status of laws without sanctions. Urdu lost its legal position almost overnight, and a language which had no musical values and a large number of words which it seemed incredible the tongue of man had ever spoken was installed in its place. Further, while on the one hand the will of the majority seemed to be an argument which swept everything before it, an attempt was made by the Congress, through a programme of mass contact, to drive a wedge between the class and the Muslim masses. The land reforms that formed an essential part of Congress policy, though intended in fact to benefit the farmer, threatened to deprive the class of its only means of sustenance. It was inevitable that the class should retaliate as vigorously and as viciously as it could.

Those who had witnessed the religious fervour of the Muslims in the early days of the khilafat movement should not have underrated the effects of the appeal to Islam which the class was bound to make. Once the Indian Muslim hears – and rumour is a more powerful incitement than reasoned statement of fact – of any actual or intended act derogatory to Islam, he gets agitated. He has no inclination to verify the truth of any statement made; his mind is submerged in indignation, and his indignation suggests to him that the more aggravating the news, the truer it must be. He has also a predilection for the spectacular. When some Muslims critics of the scheme of basic national education came across the recommendation in the syllabus of basic education that movements to the rhythm of music or elementary dance movements should form part of the physical culture activities in the school, they picked upon it as an indication that in the new schools Muslim girls would be forced to learn dancing. No deductions made from this could be too wild, and basic education stood condemned not only as an attack on Muslim culture but on all ideas of decency. About the same time as the publication of the report on basic education, the chief minister of the Central Provinces (now Madhya Pradesh) introduced a system of schools to be financed or endowed with land by the population that derived benefit from them. These schools were to be called Vidya Mandirs or temples (lit. houses) of knowledge. This scheme of the chief minister had no relationship with national policy or the policy of the Congress governments, but was widely criticized by the Muslims as an attempt to turn schools into temples. These were the major 'atrocities' to which others were added, and the fuse was lighted for the explosion which ultimately split up the common country into India and Pakistan.

The principle on which the country was divided is known as the two-nation theory. This was the final form of the sentiments and taboos which had always kept the Hindus and Muslims apart from each other. Because of the passion with which the theory was advocated by the Muslim League after 1940, it seems to be a creation of Muslim fanaticism, and to show the distance and impossibility of communication between the Muslim classes and the Hindu masses. But India had been declared to consist of two nations by V. D. Savarkar in his presidential address at the annual session of the Hindu Mahasabha in 1937, three years before the Muslim League did so, and again in December 1939, three months before the Muslim League's Pakistan resolution.

It was not enough, however, to collect and magnify instances of Congress atrocities and Hindu fanaticism. The Muslim League was accused with different motives by its supporters as well as its opponents of 'doing' nothing. Since it had no plans for such development as would strengthen the Muslims economically, and organization of itself as a disciplined party was almost impossible, because of the type of people who were its members, the Muslim League had to think of doing something spectacular. It found a very suitable occasion when the Congress ministries resigned in protest at the viceroy's declaration of war against Germany without any reference to them. The Muslim League utilized this opportunity to celebrate deliverance from Hindu *raj*. A religious as well as political colour was given to this celebration and every Muslim who felt aggrieved or irritated or, what was more important, every Muslim who was on the look-out for some form of collective amusement was stimulated to exercise his ingenuity in commemorating the occasion. There was general satisfaction among Muslims over what they had 'done' to express their sentiments, and the next step was to express these very sentiments in oratorical and actual violence.

It is not the purpose of this paper to relate the course of events. In conclusion, it needs only to be said that once the sentiments of the Muslim masses had become involved in the demand for partition, it was not necessary for the Muslim League leadership to define its aims, or to declare what it proposed to do if the demand for Pakistan was conceded. It was certainly beyond the intellectual and moral capacity of the class in United Provinces which rejected the rule of the majority community to plan any alternative. When the catastrophe came, even its own members were left to shift for themselves. Some fled in panic, some crossed over deliberately and, like my own family, unnecessarily; some stayed behind because it was not possible for them to leave, or because they did not want to leave. If today we argue backwards from the partition of India as the solution of the Hindu-Muslim problem, it would appear that either there was no problem at all, or that it required an entirely different approach, if there was to be any solution.

INDIA, 1935–47

by B. SHIVA RAO*

I

Some of the major features of the political situation in India on the eve of the general elections in 1937 deserve mention for a proper understanding of the developments in the period immediately preceding the achievement of freedom in 1947.

The new constitutional set-up after the adoption of the Government of India Act, 1935, was a makeshift arrangement designed to serve a brief transition period. The centre continued to function under the relevant provisions of the 1919 Act, while the provinces were given autonomy in accordance with those of the 1935 constitution. Such an anomalous situation, with full responsible government in the provinces and no responsibility whatsoever at the centre, was bound to generate political friction in increasing measure unless there was full co-operation between the centre and the provinces. The official intention was, according to Sir James Dunnett, at that time the reforms commissioner of the government of India, to bring the federal part of the new constitution into operation, a year or eighteen months after the introduction of provincial autonomy before the end of 1938.

The 1935 constitution had satisfied no political party in India. Early in March, 1936, the working committee of the Congress issued a statement in which it announced that the Congress would enter the new legislatures 'not to co-operate with the Government, but to combat the Act and the policy underlying it, since both are intended to tighten the hold of British Imperialism on India and to continue the exploitation of the Indian people'.

The general policy of the Congress was declared to be 'non-co-operation with the apparatus of British Imperialism, except in so far as circumstances may require variation'.

The Congress goal of 'a genuine democratic State' was outlined, with

'political power transferred to the people as a whole and the government under their effective control. Such a State could only be brought into being only by a Constituent Assembly elected by adult suffrage. But this could only come into existence when the Indian people had developed sufficient power and sanctions to shape their destiny without external interference.'

Congress members of the new legislatures were directed to demand such a constituent assembly immediately after the inauguration of the constitution in 1937 and to back that demand with mass agitation outside.

The Congress was, however, not the only party to express deep dissatisfaction with the new constitution. The Liberals were vigorously critical of its

* Correspondent in Delhi from 1935 of *The Hindu* and *The Manchester Guardian.* Brother of the late Sir Benegal Rau. Had close contacts with Indian nationalist leaders.

limitations and its numerous safeguards, though they coupled their criticism with an appeal to the new ministries to place national interests first in their programmes. Concern was expressed by the Liberals over the possibility of the princes being granted further concessions as an inducement to enter federation. On the other hand, the introduction of certain reforms in the administration of the states they considered to be an essential condition for the states' entry into the all-India federation.

On behalf of the princes conditions were formulated for their entry into federation primarily from the standpoint of their treaty rights and privileges. They were clearly moving away from their own commitments in the first Round Table conference. They had their anxieties about the implications of paramountcy of the Crown and sought the protection of the federal court to 'make it absolutely clear that federation would mean only certain specific powers assigned to it in the legislative field' and nothing beyond them. It would be manifestly unfair in their view that anything entrusted to the Crown during a period of their tutelege should be retained under a federal system evolved on the basis of self-government.

The Hindu-Muslim problem continued of course to baffle the leaders of the two major parties in India, the Congress and the Muslim League; but there was at that stage no support for Pakistan from any representative section of the Muslims. As evidence may be cited the view of a Muslim deputation led by A. Yusuf Ali who told the joint parliamentary committee on the Government of India Bill in 1934 that Pakistan was 'a student's scheme which no responsible people had put forward'. Asked by a member of the committee about the implications of Pakistan, Sir Muhammad Zafrulla Khan's comment was, 'we consider it chimerical and impracticable'.

In India, the British authorities, under the impression that the morale of the Congress had been broken by the prolonged detention of its leaders, seemed to view with little apprehension the outcome of the first general elections in 1937. Many Congress leaders, particularly of the left wing, had no doubt spoken of their plans to 'wreck the Constitution from within'. But the party was torn by internal dissensions at the top and all the principal lieutenants of Mahatma Gandhi had threatened resignation from the working committee (as the party's central executive was called) unless Jawaharlal Nehru, in his capacity as the president, abandoned the policy of preaching socialism as the goal of the Congress.[1]

After a tour of several provinces in 1936, in the course of which I interviewed the leaders of different political groups, including those of the Congress, I recorded my impression that the outcome of the elections in the

[1] In an outspoken letter to Nehru, who was the president of the Congress, Dr Rajendra Prasad, Sardar Patel, C. Rajagopalachari, Acharya Kripalani and other members of the working committee warned him at the end of June, 1936:

'We are of opinion that through your speeches and those of the other socialist colleagues and the acts of other socialists, the Congress organization has been weakened throughout the country without any compensating gain. The effect of your propaganda on the political work immediately before the nation, particularly the programme of election has been very harmful and we feel that in the situation created we cannot shoulder the responsibility of organizing and fighting the coming elections. It is not without much reluctance that we have, therefore, decided to tender our resignation from the Working Committee.'

following year was regarded by Congress leaders with restrained optimism. They expected to win majorities in three or four provinces. In the United Provinces (a key province), the forecast of the officials gave the Congress about seventy seats out of a total of 228, while Congress leaders hoped to win one hundred. (Actually, the Congress secured 135 seats and formed a ministry.)

In the official world of New Delhi and Simla the prevalent impression in the pre-election year was that despite all the criticisms of the shortcomings of the new constitution, moderate elements in the country would capture the seats of power and authority in a majority of the provinces as a result of the elections. It was for this reason that stiff resistance was offered by some senior officials to the proposal that the new viceroy Lord Linlithgow should meet Mahatma Gandhi in the summer of 1936, since an interview might enhance his prestige (as did the Irwin-Gandhi pact in 1931) and improve the prospects of the Congress in the elections.

II

The results of the general elections in the early part of 1937 completely upset all previous calculations and considerably altered the outlook of the different political groups, of the princes and of the British authorities. The Congress emerged as the largest party in seven provinces out of eleven, with a clear majority in six.

In the Punjab the Unionist party – and not the Muslim League – under the leadership of Sir Sikandar Hyat Khan secured a majority, and he formed a cabinet of six ministers consisting of three Muslims, two Hindus and a Sikh. In Bengal Fazlul Haq, the leader of the Praja party, came to the fore with a strong tenants' programme. His plea for the abolition of the permanent settlement and the release of political prisoners and detenus brought him and his party much Congress support before and during the elections.

In one or two provinces, notably the U.P., the success of the Congress party at the polls was due, in great measure, to the solid support of the peasantry. Immediately after the elections, Nehru claimed that the election had proved that the Congress had the complete confidence of the people in the U.P. and said:

'the election has brought a patent fact to the forefront which is this: the masses are hungry and they want bread. Education is starved and the children of the poor classes should be given proper education. The peasantry is crushed by the burden of debt. How to give bread and education and how to relieve the masses from their debt should be the concern of all.'

Suppressed for generations and hard hit by the economic depression of the early thirties, the peasants responded with warmth to the election appeal of the Congress. Their hopes of a better life had been roused by Nehru's personality and his socialist programme. They felt elated that in installing a Congress government in power in the U.P. they had a share. They could go to district officers and even to cabinet ministers with their complaints against landlords and their agents without fear of persecution. Socialists and Communists taking advantage of a Congress ministry in office campaigned in the rural areas, preaching radical doctrines.

The performance in the election of the Muslim League as such was modest; of 482 Muslim seats in all the provincial legislatures, only 109 were captured by League candidates. It is significant that even at that stage, Jinnah's thoughts were not in the direction of a separate state of Pakistan. In a public statement shortly after the elections in 1937 he declared, 'nobody will welcome an honourable settlement between the Hindus and the Muslims more than I, and nobody will be more ready to help it'; and he followed it with a public appeal to Gandhi to tackle this question. The latter's response was prompt but somewhat depressing: 'I wish I could do something, but I am utterly helpless. My faith in unity is bright as ever; only I see no daylight but impenetrable darkness; and in such distress I cry out to God for light.'

The effect of the Congress victories at the polls was noticeable on the princes. Apprehensive of a similar outcome later of the elections for the federal parliament, they stepped up their demands for concessions that were clearly incompatible with any scheme of responsible government. Some of the states, relying on the advice of their legal advisers (like Professor Morgan) considered the safeguards in the constitution to be 'utterly inadequate' and were apprehensive that after their accession to federation they would find themselves 'caught in a trap'. The safeguards in the Act, Professor Morgan had warned them, could not prevent amendments of the constitution on the initiative of India's parliament or of the federal government. An instrument of accession was not a treaty, though 'not even a treaty with a foreign Power could operate to limit the omnipotence of Parliament'. Dominion status having been promised to India, he frankly told the princes, all the safeguards for the rights and interests of the states contained in the Act were destined sooner or later to disappear.

The question has often been discussed, in India and outside, what persuaded Jinnah in the space of three years (between 1937 and 1940) to so change his tactics and his goal as to demand the establishment of a separate state of Pakistan, on the basis of a newly-propounded theory that Hindus and Muslims constituted two separate nations with little in common between them. In 1924 in a debate in the central legislative assembly on Motilal Nehru's proposal for a representative Round Table conference, Jinnah, in supporting the proposal had declared in his speech:

'India is not a nation, we are told. We were a people when the Great War was going on and an appeal was made to India for blood and money. . . . We are a nation when we become a member of the League of Nations to which we have made a substantial contribution. . . . We are not a people nor a nation when we ask you for a substantial advance towards the establishment of responsible government and parliamentary institutions in our own country'.

Later in 1928, in the negotiations over the boycott of the Simon commission, Jinnah asked for a reservation of seats for Muslims in Bengal and the Punjab. Motilal Nehru rejected the demand on the ground that such reservation was justifiable only for minorities and the Muslims were in a majority in these two provinces. Nevertheless, at the first session of the Round Table conference in London two years later. Jinnah supported the national demand for 'a new Dominion of India ready to march along with the other Dominions within the British Commonwealth of Nations'.

The fact, briefly mentioned earlier, needs to be stressed that in 1937 there was singularly little support for the establishment of Pakistan as a sovereign independent state.

What were the forces operating in India in the three years following the general elections of 1937 that gave such vitality to the movement in favour of Pakistan? For an explanation of this phenomenon, one must go to the U.P., a key province so far as Hindu-Muslim relations were concerned. The Muslims, who were only fourteen per cent of the population, had played an important part in the cultural and political development of this region for centuries. Until the general elections, the relations between the Congress and some of the prominent Muslim leaders were generally cordial and even friendly. The Congress party, though confident of challenging the landlords' influential position in the provincial government and the legislature for many years, was not hopeful of securing a definite majority.

Before the elections, the Congress party, working on the asumption that a decisive majority in the U.P. legislature could be ruled out, had virtually agreed to a coalition with the Muslim League. This understanding had facilitated a working arrangement between the two organizations during the elections, so as to avoid contests between their respective candidates in certain constituencies. If the Congress party had adhered to its pre-election intention of forming a coalition ministry, the Hindu-Muslim problem might not have assumed formidable dimensions. But it preferred to exercise the right of forming a party government, since that was held to be the verdict of the electorate. A coalition, it was argued, could not 'wreck the constitution' – the avowed object of a section of the Congress.

But Muslim leaders in the U.P. regarded it as a breach of faith. A series of Muslim by-elections in the U.P. after the general election afforded an opportunity to the two parties to test their relative strength. In the first, the Congress candidate (who had stood in the general elections as a Muslim Leaguer and was returned on that ticket) retained his seat and was taken into the cabinet. Then came Nehru's 'mass contact programme' to win over the Muslim masses to the Congress creed. Muslims even outside the U.P. felt that the League's existence was being threatened; and in the later by-elections, the results showed that Nehru had committed a serious tactical error.

The defeat of the Congress candidates in these by-elections had a visible psychological effect. The stock of the Muslim League rose all over India. Other parties, which had been defeated in the elections, saw in the Muslim League a rallying point for a combined opposition to the Congress. Landlords, in particular, apprehensive of the Congress agrarian programme, naturally turned to the League for indirect assistance and in return gave it support.

The tension between the Congress and the League grew, and sustained propaganda against the Congress government was bound to increase such tension. To add to its difficulties, the Congress in the U.P. reflected, more than elsewhere, left-wing leanings. The premier, Pandit Gobind Ballabh Pant, could not curb, without serious misunderstanding by some of his own supporters, a campaign for a socialist programme. And obviously, the liberty which the left-wingers in the Congress enjoyed could not be denied to Muslim League organizers who made full use of their opportunities for their own programme.

A report was published at this time by the Raja of Pirpur on 'Congress atrocities' in the province. In an interview with Lord Linlithgow, I referred to this document and suggested its scrutiny by a committee with a man like Sir Maurice Gwyer, the chief justice of the federal court, as its chairman. (I had previously discussed the proposal with Dr Rajendra Prasad and obtained his approval for placing it before the viceroy.) Lord Linlithgow's reply was significant: no complaints had reached him from any governor regarding the ill-treatment of Muslims, and the appointment of a committee of enquiry might be a reflection on the governor for his failure to act in the discharge of a special responsibility. The Pirpur report served, nevertheless, a useful propaganda purpose for the Muslim League.

The deterioration in Hindu-Muslim relations in the U.P. attracted attention from outside. The strength of the Congress, it was felt, could be challenged with prospects of ultimate success, on the communal side. As the U.P. had shown itself to be a weak spot among the Congress-governed provinces, to that province turned everyone with a grievance against the Congress.

Princes, even Hindu princes, resentful of agitators demanding popular reforms in the states and stirring up trouble among their people, became markedly sympathetic to the Muslim League. On one occasion the Jam Saheb of Nawanagar (at that time the chancellor of the chamber of princes) told me, in discussing an alliance between the Muslim League and the chamber for the federal elections: 'Why should I not support the League? Mr. Jinnah is willing to tolerate our existence, but Mr. Nehru wants the extinction of the Princes'.

Nehru and Gandhi viewed the developing situation from sharply divergent standpoints. Nehru harped on his favourite theme that the logic of events would 'lead the Congress to Socialism, [as] the only remedy for India's ills'. He was keen on a national convention consisting of all the members of the provincial legislatures elected under the new constitution and of the members of the All-India Congress Committee to frame the new constitution. Gandhi's view of a constituent assembly was that the convention should, instead of frittering away the results of the success at the polls, adopt a programme to be pursued in the legislatures. He said that there was no need for the British to leave India: 'India is a vast country. You and your people can stay comfortably, provided you accommodate yourself to our conditions here'.

I can assert from personal knowledge that Gandhi was anxious for a constructive policy in working the new constitution. In April 1937, on the viceroy's suggestion I interviewed Gandhi to obtain from him a clear statement on the limits he sought for the governors' special responsibilities. That statement, issued from Poona after three days' labour, opened the door for negotiations that ultimately enabled the Congress leaders to form ministries in seven provinces. He told me on that occasion: 'the British are a decent people. It is not difficult to make a fair deal with them.'

Right up to the commencement of the second world war, and even in its early stages, Gandhi was anxious not to embarrass Britain, but on the other hand, to secure if possible an honourable settlement. During this period he was much more with Rajogopalachari and Godbind Ballabh Pant than with Nehru and the left-wing elements in the Congress.

The viceroy had his worries over the receding prospects of federation. Caught in a vortex of opposing forces, with the Congress, the Muslim League and the princes pulling in different directions, he found it increasingly difficult to chalk out a clear policy to ensure the introduction of the federal part of the new constitution as originally scheduled, a year or eighteen months after the inauguration of provincial autonomy. Many among the princely states were moving far away from their previous commitments (to unqualified support of responsible government at the federal centre) in their speeches in the first Round Table conference. The Muslim League, alarmed by the Congress propaganda among the Muslim masses, continued to stress with increasing vehemence the complaints of Muslims in Congress-administered provinces.

III

Meanwhile, in Europe war clouds were gathering ominously in 1938. The Congress working committee adopted a resolution 'following, with great anxiety, events as they (were) developing in Europe'. A major war seemed imminent after Hitler's attack on Poland. Early in September 1939, Britain and France declared war on Germany. On the same day Lord Linlithgow issued a proclamation declaring that India, too, was at war with Germany. This action, taken without consulting the central legislative assembly then in session was greatly resented by the Congress party.

Indian leaders were in a dilemma. For years men like Nehru had seen in the policy of the British government evidence of appeasement of the Axis powers. But they were not prepared to adopt Gandhi's advice of unconditional co-operation without a clear declaration of British post-war policy towards India.

The issue of India's freedom was thus forced into prominence by the second world war. Immediately on the commencement of hostilities, Gandhi made a generous gesture of sympathy for Britain and France, declaring that India's deliverance was not worth having if it followed a defeat of the Allied powers. If his colleagues in the central executive of the Congress had endorsed his policy, there would have been no crisis in India. But they felt that India's active support for the allied cause could not be taken for granted without a clear declaration of Britain's war aims and their application to India. Precious time was lost in an evasion of the real issues on the British side, resulting in a deterioration of the situation in India. Congress ministries, in control of seven provincial governments, were faced with the embarrassing choice of one of two alternatives: either of sending the leaders of the radical sections of their party to prison for conducting anti-war propaganda or of resigning their offices. They chose the latter as on the whole the easier course in order to maintain the unity of the party.

Gandhi, realizing that he could no longer remain a detached adviser of the Congress, assumed control of the movement and by skilful manoeuvering secured some more time for further parleys with the viceroy. He made it abundantly clear that he would not launch a campaign of civil resistance (for which the left-wingers were clamouring) so long as the viceroy was persisting in his efforts to reach a settlement through negotiations. Moreover, Hindu-Muslim tension had become more acute through the occurrence of riots in some parts of the country. At the back of Gandhi's mind was the feeling that, however unsatisfactory might have been Britain's policy towards India, in a war which was forced on her by Germany's aggression, it would be morally wrong to seek advantage from her difficulties in Europe.

I examined, in an article in *The Hindu* in October 1939, the possibilities of establishing, even within the limitations of the 1919 constitution, an executive council which could function more or less as a national government responsive to popular needs though not constitutionally responsible to the legislature. In taking this line, I had positive encouragement from the reforms commissioner, Sir Hawthorne Lewis. Lord Linlithgow seemed interested in the proposals, but had his misgivings, about their practical usefulness. He could work, he told me, with a team of men like Rajagopalachari; but it would be impossible to tackle during the war, periodical crises which Nehru and others of his way of thinking might precipitate. Moreover, warned the viceroy, with Churchill in the cabinet, there would be serious difficulties in securing British approval for my view.

The Congress demand at this time was for a specific declaration that Britain should agree to a constituent assembly, elected on adult suffrage, to frame a constitution for India with complete freedom as its basis. Since the fear had been expressed that it might imply a Hindu majority in perpetual power, the Congress was willing to accept that the constitution must have the support of all important minorities, particularly the Muslims, before British ratification of the scheme.

This, however, failed to evoke a reply from Britain satisfactory from the Congress standpoint. Sir Samuel Hoare declared that India's status at the end of the war would be the same as that of the self-governing dominions. In one respect he went further through an assurance that it would mean the application to India of the statute of Westminster. Its significance lay in the fact that it committed a government which included Churchill to a policy which he had opposed with vigour six years earlier when Baldwin was the premier.

But for Gandhi and the Congress this did not appear to be adequate. They insisted on India's right to frame her own constitution without any outside interference. Independence, they asserted, need not mean hostility to Britain. Through all the twenty years that Gandhi had been the leader of the Congress, he had never faltered in his vision of an Indo-British partnership on a free and voluntary basis. He had told the British government at a plenary session of the Round Table conference in London in 1931:

'If I want freedom for my country, believe me, if I can possibly help it, I do not want that freedom in order that I, belonging to a nation which counts one-fifth of the human race, may exploit any other race upon earth or any single individual. . . . I would love to go away from the shores of the British Isles with the conviction that there was to be an honourable and equal partnership between Great Britain and India.'

In November 1939, came the resignations of Congress ministries from the seven provinces in which it had held office for over two years. The viceroy continued his talks with Gandhi, summoning in addition the Congress president and Jinnah for a joint but unsuccessful discussion of a proposal to expand his executive council within the framework of the 1935 constitution. The Congress main emphasis was on India's post-war status, but the British were unwilling to give any guarantees acceptable to the Congress and go beyond an offer of immediate changes of an interim character.

In January 1940, a statement by the viceroy in Bombay offering India dominion status of the 'Statute of Westminster variety' at the end of the war evoked a prompt response from Gandhi who saw in it 'germs of an honourable settlement'. This hope, however, proved to be short-lived: an interview between the two in Delhi in February ended in failure. The British government was prepared (the viceroy told Gandhi) to examine the entire field of constitutional progress in consultation with representatives of all parties and interests in India at the appropriate time and shorten the transition period to the utmost extent possible. The federal scheme in the 1935 Act he commended as affording the swiftest path to dominion status. The British offer was indicated at that stage as being in two stages: (*a*) an immediate expansion of the executive council; and after the war (*b*) the revival of the federal scheme to expedite the achievement of dominion status.

The vital difference between the Congress demand and the viceroy's offer, as Gandhi visualized it, was that while the latter contemplated the final determination of India's destiny by the British government, the position of the Congress was that the people of India should decide it entirely on their free choice. Gandhi saw no prospect of a peaceful and honourable settlement between Britain and India without the elimination of this fundamental difference: self-determination for India, he argued, would automatically solve the problems of defence, of the minorities, of the princes and of British interests.

Early in March 1940, I made a proposal in *The Hindu* of Madras that a scheme broadly on the lines of the Anglo-Egyptian agreement of 1922 might provide a useful basis for discussion of the Indian problem. It sought a British declaration that India would be free to draft her own constitution at the end of the war with complete freedom as its objective, subject to certain conditions; (1) the constitution to be acceptable to the Muslims and other minorities; (2) a prior agreement between the representatives of Britain and India 'in a spirit of friendly accommodation' – a phrase used in the Anglo-Egyptian agreement – on (*a*) defence, (*b*) British interests, and (*c*) the Indian states. Such a declaration could be coupled with an offer from the viceroy accepting the principle of a provisional national government at the centre, the details of which could be worked out by a conference of the premiers of the eleven provinces.

Gandhi sent a message to me immediately through his secretary, Mahadeo Desai, giving his approval to the formula as an acceptable solution of the

Indian problem. He added that modifications suitable to local conditions could be worked out by a 'Committee of the best Indians and the best Englishmen'. The response from the British side was, however, negative.

The reverses which nearly overwhelmed Britain and her allies in Europe in the summer of 1940 produced profound reactions in India. A section of the Congress, impressed with the need for coming to terms with the British, offered active co-operation in the prosecution of the war through a national government, though radical elements continued to reiterate their demand for a long-range declaration of British policy.

The concept of a separate state of Pakistan began to take shape in a Muslim League resolution at its Lahore session on March 23, 1940. The resolution stated certain basic principles for the framing of a constitution: geographically contiguous units were to be 'demarcated into regions which should be so constituted, with such territorial readjustments as may be necessary, that the areas in which the Muslims are numerically in a majority as in the North-Western and Eastern zones of India should be grouped to constitute "Independent States" in which the constituent units should be autonomous and sovereign'. Secondly, 'adequate, effective and mandatory safeguards were to be specifically provided in the Constitution for minorities in these units and in the regions for the protection of their religious, cultural, economic, political, administrative and other rights and interests in consultation with them'. Reciprocally, in other parts of India where the Muslims were in a minority, safeguards of the same kind were to be inserted in the constitution for their protection and that of other minorities.

The Muslim League's resolution added a proviso to the effect that before the final assumption of authority by the respective regions, transitory arrangements would be necessary for defence, external affairs, communications, customs and such other matters as might be considered necessary.

Jinnah explained in a letter to Gandhi that the contiguous units mentioned in the resolution were:

'Sind, Baluchistan, the North-West Frontier Province and the Punjab in the North-west and Bengal and Assam in the North-East. According to the resolution, these two regions, with necessary territorial adjustments were to be "independent States in which the constituent units shall be autonomous and sovereign".'

Jinnah observed that while Pakistan would consist of the six provinces mentioned above, they would be subject to territorial adjustments that might be agreed upon and the question of demarcating and defining the territories could be taken after the fundamentals had been accepted and machinery for that purpose had been set up by agreement. The two parties concerned (obviously meaning the Congress and the Muslim League) could set up constitution-making bodies to deal with the matter or arrive at an agreement before commencing their respective tasks. What he implied by this statement was that the two parties concerned should arrive at an agreement regarding the boundaries or at least to set up agreed machinery for that purpose before the commencement of settling their respective constitutions.

The resolution was interpreted by Jinnah and by Sir Sikandar Hyat Khan in different ways. The former was clear in his mind that the League resolution implied the establishment of a separate state or states; while Sir Sikandar interpreted it as meaning no more than the concession of maximum autonomy to regions in which the Muslims formed a majority of the population.

Informal efforts were made in private for a settlement between the Congress and a section of the Muslim League led by Sir Sikandar Hyat Khan, the Punjab's premier (who was anxious to avert a partition of the country). Other possibilities were being explored, with Gandhi's knowledge and full approval. He was attracted by the suggestion I had made to him of a war-time federal government especially as I had reasons to believe from personal discussions with Sir V. T. Krishnamachari (Dewan of Baroda) and Sir Mirza Ismail (Dewan of Jaipur) that the progressive princely states would favourably consider such an advance. An executive, consisting of right-wing Congressmen like Rajagopalachari, representatives of the progressive states and Muslims of the type of Sir Sikandar Hyat Khan, appealed to Gandhi as a worthwhile advance for the war period. Sir Sikandar placed before the Congress leaders the following proposal in the spring of 1940:

'His Majesty's Government should make a declaration making it clear that India's status would be that of a self-governing Dominion in accordance with the Statute of Westminster. So far as the framing of the Constitution is concerned, it should be left to Indians themselves to formulate a scheme by mutual agreement. The machinery of the agency to which this task of constitution-framing would be entrusted should be settled by various parties and interests concerned, and the British Government and the Viceroy, if so desired, should be prepared to assist in bringing about a settlement on the question of the machinery.

'For the transition period, which must necessarily elapse before India can assume full responsibility, arrangements should be made for the administration of certain subjects like Defence, External Affairs, etc. The duration of this period, the nature of the arrangements to be made, as also the question of British commercial interests and the Indian States should be settled by negotiations in a Conference of British and Indian representatives.

'So far as Britain is concerned, she should be prepared to confer Dominion status immediately after the war, or even earlier; in fact, as soon as the parties and interests concerned are able to formulate an agreed constitution.'

Gandhi, impressed with the contents of the proposal, indicated to me his personal approval, reserving full assent until after discussions with the other leaders of the Congress.

On the eve of the meeting of the Congress working committee in Delhi in the first week of July, Sir Sikandar Hyat Khan conveyed through me to the Congress leaders a forecast of the proposals that he understood were being formulated by the British cabinet and the viceroy (subsequently described as 'the August 1940 offer'). A Congress–Muslim League settlement, he thought, would probably result in certain improvements in the British proposals: (1) the executive council would be almost completely Indian in personnel, barring one or two subjects; (2) such an executive council would function on the basis of collective responsibility; (3) in the choice of its members the leaders of the Congress and the Muslim League would have a decisive voice.

A section of the Congress working committee was willing to proceed on these lines. A personal meeting between Maulana Azad, the president of the Congress and Sir Sikandar Hyat Khan took place in Delhi; but the negotiations could not proceed in the absence of a positive response from the British side.

Early in August came the announcement of the British government through L. S. Amery, the secretary of state for India. The Congress working committee, while rejecting the offer, was nevertheless willing to reconsider its attitude if a section of the Muslim League led by Sir Sikandar Hyat Khan would come to terms in spite of Jinnah's opposition to such a move. Gandhi's attitude at that stage was one of unwillingness to embarrass the British; but he was reluctantly moving to the conclusion that the British were intent only on exploiting the situation by raising the problem of minorities.

At a critical period following the collapse of France, Gandhi came to the rescue of the government with a timely and effective appeal to the public not to hoard silver or to make a run on banks. When, however, the offer of the Congress of active co-operation in the prosecution of the war through a national government was rejected by the British, he decided, after much deliberation, to start the non-co-operation movement with a twofold intention: to put the claim about India's voluntary war-effort to the test and to provide his followers with an outlet for their long pent-up resentment against the British. The movement was to be restricted to selected individuals, not launched on a mass scale, so as not to embarrass the British while they were engaged in a life-and-death struggle.

While a limited non-co-operation movement was thus in progress, the attempt was renewed once again by Sir Sikandar Hyat Khan to reach a settlement on certain tentative proposals: (1) a representative committee to draft a constitution on the basis of full dominion status; (2) reservations in regard to defence, Indian states, etc. to be agreed to by the representatives of India and Britain for incorporation in the constitution; (3) coalition ministries in the provinces; (4) the re-constitution of the central executive for the interim period to be settled by a conference of the eleven premiers of the provinces; (5) the viceroy to agree to the transfer of all portfolios (with the exception of certain parts of defence) to Indian members of the executive council; (6) such questions as the number of permanent civil servants in the executive, their portfolios, their right to vote or merely to participate in discussions, etc., to be settled by the viceroy in consultation with the eleven premiers; (7) joint deliberations on all subjects by the central executive.

This proposal met with the same unhappy fate as all the previous ones.

IV

Sir Stafford Cripps arrived in New Delhi towards the end of March, 1942, as a member of Churchill's war cabinet, bringing with him proposals for a settlement of the Indian problem.

From the moment of his arrival in New Delhi, Cripps found himself functioning almost in isolation. His previous visit to India was in December 1939, as an unattached member of the house of commons, on an invitation from Nehru and the Congress working committee.[1]

The details of the British cabinet's plan (known subsequently as the Cripps plan) were not known to the members of the government of India before Cripps's arrival, not even to the governors of provinces. The contents were disclosed to the former at a special meeting of the executive council a day after his arrival and later individually to the governors of provinces who were invited to visit Delhi. One of the Indian executive councillors told me what he and his colleagues thought of the proposals: 'We all heaved a sigh of relief when Cripps revealed them to us last night. I said to a colleague next to me, these will never be accepted by the Congress.'

The executive council was resentful that it had not been taken into confidence until almost the commencement of the negotiations. Even later, members of the council saw Cripps only once during the negotiations and collectively again after the final breakdown.

Also, Churchill's announcement in London of the Cripps mission sounded oddly significant: Cripps would discuss the political problem with Indian leaders and the military situation with the viceroy and General Wavell. Press correspondents in New Delhi were briefed to say that the viceroy, far from resenting this arrangement, was 'delighted', because for a few weeks at least he would be free from the pre-occupations of the political problem and could give all his time to the prosecution of the war.

I met Cripps on the day of his arrival in New Delhi. As his first press conference was dispersing, I walked across to his seat and he said in a whisper: 'do you think I will succeed?' 'That depends', I replied, 'on the nature of your proposals. But I am confident the Indian press will give you every help.'

I saw him for a long talk the following night. I told him at the outset about the seriousness of the situation created by the negligence of the authorities in Malaya and Burma after the Japanese occupation in dealing with Indian evacuees and the deep indignation felt all over India. Could he not do something about it at once, because since the Amritsar massacre in 1918, there had not been such racial ill-feeling in India? He made a careful note of the point.

We then turned to the political situation. I pointed out that Japan's entry into the war and especially her spectacular successes in Malaya and Burma had transformed the Indian scene. I discovered early in our talk that Cripps was under the impression that the Congress point of view had not greatly altered during the two years and more that had passed since his first visit to India in 1939. The centre of interest, I said to him, had shifted almost entirely

[1] On that occasion, he and I had a lengthy discussion about a solution of India's problem, I gave him a copy of a note that I had prepared, with Sir B. N. Rau's assistance, on the formation of a constituent assembly to frame India's permanent constitution. He found it interesting and advised me to go to Bombay to ascertain Jinnah's reactions. If they were favourable, I was to meet him again at Wardha, where he would discuss the details with Gandhi and Nehru. Accepting his suggestion, I met Jinnah in Bombay and noted that he was prepared to consider with favour the formation of such a constituent assembly. I went to Wardha according to our agreement and conveyed my impression of Jinnah's attitude to Cripps. That night, I discussed at great length the details of the note with Nehru who struck me as being interested but non-committal.

from the future to the immediate present. 'Give India a National Government now', I said, 'and don't worry about post-war arrangements'.

It was clear he had succeeded only after considerable difficulty, in getting the war cabinet to assent to the proposals associated with his name. They were not entirely his; Amery too had a hand in shaping them. But they were the utmost (he told me) he could get from Churchill: and having gone so far, he was embarrassed to think that the Congress demand was likely to be very different.

'What do you mean by a National Government?' he asked me. I went rapidly, but in some detail, over the provisions of the ninth schedule to the Government of India Act of 1919 and pointed out how, even within the framework of the existing constitution, a great deal could be done to convert in practice the executive council into a cabinet, to enlarge the powers and even the size of the legislature and to make the viceroy the normal constitutional head of the government. With most of what I outlined he seemed to be in agreement. He said, 'my mind has also been working on the same lines'.

Then he referred to defence. 'Be careful', he warned me, 'about touching Defence in war-time.' I told him no Indian defence member would be so foolish as to interfere with the authority or functions of the commander-in-chief. On the other hand, he would be of very great help in getting the best men for the army and relieve the commander-in-chief of many of his burdens. 'There may be serious difficulties', he feared, 'in getting these ideas accepted.'

I also made a passing reference to the princely states and said that the national defence council could be reconstituted on the basis of provinces and states governments' representation, without a non-official element. Another suggestion I made was that in the formation of the executive council the choice need not be limited only to British India but could be extended to the states.

The real obstacle was in regard to defence. Cripps thought there might be serious difficulties in the way of the transfer of defence to an Indian defence member just then, during a critical phase of the war. Would there be interference with the movements of troops, for example? I replied that if a suitable Indian was appointed, there need be no apprehension. He would certainly concern himself with recruiting and do his best to obtain young men of character, courage and enterprise for the defence forces; he would ascertain if there was sufficient equipment for India's defence forces and whether production was receiving adequate attention. In fact, not only would he not hinder the commander-in-chief, but could be of great assistance to him in a variety of ways. I suggested, therefore, that the problem should be looked at differently: how best to secure fullest co-operation between the defence member and the commander-in-chief.

I asked Cripps to look at the problem from another standpoint: what were Indian leaders to tell the country – that while India's youth must be prepared to make sacrifices, even to lay down their lives in this war, the British were not prepared to trust them to the extent of appointing an Indian defence member in spite of assurances that there would be no interference with the authority of the commander-in-chief? The point, I stressed, had a great psychological value at that juncture. The Japanese were making attractive offers of independence to India which a great many foolish people doubtless believed. What would be the strength of an appeal by Indian leaders to their people not to attach any importance to such promises – unless they could say 'we have already achieved almost complete freedom'?

I gave Cripps after our first meeting, a note covering many aspects of the political problem during the previous two years.

An important factor governing India's attitude towards defence at this critical juncture has received singularly little attention. On February 21, 1942, a month before Cripps's arrival in Delhi, General Molesworth, then deputy chief of general staff in India, broadcast to the country:

'Japanese warships are operating in the Bay of Bengal and the Indian Ocean, and we must expect that these activities will be increased. Such activities may affect both our east and west coasts. These activities may include sporadic bombardments of coastal towns coupled with attacks by aircraft carried by surface raiders. The possibility of minor raids and landings on our coasts cannot be excluded. If the threat to Burma develops further, we may have air attacks on North Eastern India from land-based aircraft. Our Eastern Coast line is some 2,000 miles in length and it is far from easy to locate a raider on so vast a sea board.'

Anxieties in India deepened as a result of even franker admissions by the same officer at a press conference of likely developments in the Bay of Bengal. Later still, in an address to the Rotary club of Delhi, he said:

'Everybody in India is asking what are we going to do to keep the Japanese out. From the point of view of the Army in this enormous battle front we shall hold vital places which it is necessary to hold in order to make India safe, but we cannot hold everyone.

'Therefore, what is to be done for the rest of India where we are unable to put troops or air or naval forces?'

'We cannot arm all. On the other hand, we can do a great deal to educate the masses to give the Japanese a great deal of trouble. This must be done by the civil people like you. The army cannot do it. The people can work in bands and give trouble and delay and destroy invasion. It may be there is no proper lead from the top and no proper leadership down below. Still I feel the Japanese invasion can be beaten, if we educate the people on the lines of "They shall not pass". Psychologically it can only be done by the intelligentsia, working definitely shoulder to shoulder to work up the peasant.'

The summarized report of this address, published in *The Statesman* of New Delhi was placed before Gandhi and his secretary and biographer, Mahadeo Desai (who died in detention in the middle of August 1942). Desai, after quoting extensively from the speech commented:

'Even General Molesworth, who knows that he cannot arm our peasants, knows that they can be educated on the lines of "they shall not pass', in other words, non-co-operation. That is in our bones. A few years' suffering, no matter how meagre, has trained us somewhat in the art.'

'All that is needed is the spirit, the will to resist.'

'Spirit pitted against tanks and planes can alone make us worthy of our heritage, which is essentially a spiritual one.'

It was clear from some of his subsequent writings that certain passages in the broadcast had made a profound impression on Gandhi: '(1) We shall hold vital places which it is necessary to hold in order to make India safe, *but we cannot hold everyone.* (2) What is to be done for the rest of India where we are unable to put troops or air or naval forces? (3) *We cannot arm all,* but we can educate the masses to give the Japanese a great deal of trouble. *This must be done by civil people like you.* The army cannot do it.'

According to Cripps's declaration the intention of the British government was 'as far as possible, subject to the reservation of defence, to put power in the hands of Indian leaders'. He explained at a press conference that the object was to 'give the fullest measure of government to the Indian people, consistent with the possibilities of the present Constitution which could not be changed till the end of the war'. In his first broadcast from New Delhi he observed:

'I want to play my part as a member of the War Cabinet in reaching a final settlement of the political difficulties which have long vexed our relationships. Once these questions are resolved, and I hope they may be quickly and satisfactorily resolved, the Indian peoples will be enabled to associate themselves fully and freely not only with Great Britain and the other Dominions but with our great Allies, Russia, China and the United States of America so that together we can assert our determination to preserve the liberty of the peoples of the world.'

On behalf of the Congress, Maulana Azad accepted the position thus outlined by Cripps. He observed:

'We did not ask for any legal changes, but we did ask for definite assurances and conventions which would indicate that the new Government would function as a free government, the members of which act as members of a Cabinet in a constitutional government. In regard to the conduct of the war and connected activities the Commander-in-Chief would have freedom, and he would also act as War Minister.'

The Congress was prepared to consider constitutional progress during the war through 'assurances and conventions', though Cripps himself did not rule out the possibility of minor changes in the constitution, such as the elimination of the provision for three members of the executive council with a minimum qualification of ten years' service under the Crown in India.

Early in April Cripps ran into serious trouble in regard to the arrangements for the administration of the portfolio of defence. At one of my interviews with him, he seemed somewhat agitated. Nehru, at dinner with him the previous night, had taken a tragic view of the negotiations. He urged me to get together Sir Tej Bahadur Sapru, Rajagopalachari and B. N. Rau at once to evolve a formula which might prove acceptable to the Congress leaders on the one side and to the British government on the other. That night, these three, with V. P. Menon and myself sat together into the early hours of the morning to produce the following formula [1]:

'During the critical period which now faces India and before the new Constitution is framed and implemented –

'(*a*) India shall in every possible respect be treated as a free member of the Commonwealth.

His Majesty's Government therefore invite the leaders of the principal sections of the Indian people to undertake the governance of their country and to participate in the counsels of the Commonwealth and of the United Nations in the world war effort.

'(*b*) The members of the Executive Council of the Governor-General will function on the principle of joint responsibility in the manner of a Council of Ministers.

'(*c*) The policies and measures of the Government of Indiain respect to the prosecution of the war will be subject to the decisions of the British War Cabinet. There will be the closest association and co-operation between the Defence Member and the Commander-in-Chief; but this will not affect the authority or responsibility of each in his own sphere.'

Colonel Johnson arrived in Delhi on April 3rd. I saw him at Cochin House very early in the morning of the 5th. He was friendly and cordial and spoke of a settlement of the Indian problem as essential in President Roosevelt's view for success in the war. I gave him, at his request, a fairly complete picture of the Cripps negotiations and mentioned the deadlock in regard to defence. His first remark seemed to open up new possibilities for India: 'we are fighting this war', he said, 'more than the British.' The president he added, was anxious about two points: (1) Would India continue fighting with the allied powers until the end and not seek separate peace with Japan? (2) Would free India give guarantees that she would treat the Muslims and the

[1] This, however, was not the only proposal before Cripps. Mr H. V. Hodson, who later became the reforms commissioner of the government of India, produced a separate draft of his own for administration of the defence department:

'The defence of India is indivisible, every department being responsible for some aspects of it and each department equally responsible to the Governor-General in Council as a whole. Those aspects most directly connected with the active conduct of war will be the concern of one or other of two departments of the new Government, namely, the War and Defence Departments, which will work in close co-operation, both departmentally and through personal consultation between the two members of Council in-charge. The allocation of particular subjects or functions between these two departments will be made by the Governor General after full discussion with his future colleagues, it being understood that while the Commander-in-Chief, as member in-charge of the War Department will exercise those functions and powers necessary to the discharge of his duty as commander of the Allied Forces in or based on India and of the governmental business arising therefrom, the remaining functions of the present Defence Department together with the defence co-ordination functions now discharged by the Governor-General and certain other import defence functions exercised by other departments or still un-allocated, will be allocated to the new Defence Member so as to enable him for his part to discharge his responsibility for sustaining and strengthening the defence of the country.'

untouchables fairly? If he could be convinced on these two points, Johnson said, the president would use his influence with Churchill to give India her freedom. Without any hesitation I replied that on both points Nehru's views would be entirely satisfactory. America, he assured me, was anxious to see China and India occupy dominant places in Asia in the post-war era. The question was whether and how he could help. I said the crisis over defence seemed so serious that his immediate intervention was desirable. His prompt reaction was: could he meet Nehru at once? Johnson was staying at Viceroy's House and an immediate meeting (he thought) might not be possible: why not the next day, he suggested. Delay, I told him, even of a day was unwise. A brief discussion then took place between him and Colonel Herrington who was present throughout our talk. Johnson offered to meet Nehru at 3 p.m. at Cochin House that afternoon.

Directly after the interview, I conveyed to Nehru the substance of my talk with Johnson. He decided without much hesitation to take the risk of meeting him even without the Congress working committee's knowledge or approval. A premature leakage of the Johnson–Nehru meeting greatly complicated matters.

Whether the viceroy or Cripps knew about the meeting before it took place I do not know, though Cripps in the speech he made in the house of commons after his return to London on April 28th, explained that Johnson's first interview with the Congress leaders was arranged in consultation with the viceroy and in accordance with his advice.

To revert to the Cripps negotiations; the resolution of the Congress working committee more or less hostile to the offer was handed over to Cripps on April 2nd; but its publication was delayed at his request and the negotiations continued. Defence (to which the working committee attached the greatest importance) was the main obstacle. On April 4th, the Congress leaders met General Wavell and discussed the situation with him. That evening Gandhi left Delhi for Wardha, disappointed with the working committee's general attitude. In a press conference he referred the correspondents to Nehru and Rajagopalachari regarding the attitude of the Congress toward the Cripps scheme. Pressed to give a message, he somewhat impatiently said, 'I must now live my message of non-violence. What is the use of my speaking when I cannot enforce my message in my own little way?'

Cripps ultimately proposed, on behalf of the British cabinet, the following formula:

(*a*) The Commander-in-Chief should retain a seat in the Viceroy's Executive Council as 'War Member' and should retain his full control over all the war activities of the armed forces in India, subject to the control of His Majesty's Government and the War Cabinet, upon which a representative Indian should sit with equal powers in all matters relating to the defence of India. Membership of the Pacific Council would likewise be offered to a representative India.

(*b*) An Indian representative member would be added to the Viceroy's Executive, who would take over those sections of the Department of Defence which can organizationally be separated immediately from the

Commander-in-Chief's War Department and which are specified under head (i) of the annexure. In addition, this member would take over the Defence Co-ordination Department which is at present directly under the Viceroy, and certain other important functions of the Government of India which do not fall under any of the other existing departments and which are specified under the head (ii) of the annexure.

This formula, if it proved acceptable to the Congress and other 'important bodies of Indian opinion', Cripps suggested, would enable the viceroy 'to embark forthwith upon the task of forming the new National Government in consultation with the leaders of Indian opinion'.

After a long discussion with Nehru on the deadlock in regard to defence, Johnson produced his own formula:

'In amplification of the clause (*e*) of the draft declaration His Majesty's Government make the following proposition upon the subject matter of the Defence of India:

'(*a*) The Defence Department shall be placed in charge of a representative Indian member with the exception of functions to be exercised by the Commander-in-Chief as War Member of the Executive Council.

'(*b*) A War Department will be constituted which will take over such functions of the Defence Department as are not retained by the Defence Member. A list of all the retained functions has been agreed, to which will be added further important responsibilities, including the matters now dealt with by the Defence Co-ordination Department and other vital matters related to the defence of India.'

There was also a useful memorandum on defence as administered in Australia, which I was able to secure from Sir Bertram Stevens, Australia's representative on the eastern supply group council – a war-time organization for ensuring prompt and adequate supplies required for the prosecution of the war in South Asia. Nehru and Azid were grateful for Sir Bertram's elucidation of certain points which had arisen in the discussions with Cripps.

Negotiations continued until April 10, when Azad, in the course of a final letter to Cripps, explained the Congress point of view: 'we cannot accept them [the long-range proposals] as suggested.' At the same time, he added, 'the ultimate decision . . . would be governed by the changes made in the present'. Elaborating this point, he went on:

'the over-riding problem before all of us, and more especially before all Indians, is the defence of the country from aggression and invasion. The future, important as it is, will depend on what happens in the next few months and years. We were, therefore, prepared to do without any assurances for this uncertain future, hoping that through our sacrifices in the defence of our country we would lay the solid and enduring foundations for a free and independent India. We concentrated, therefore, on the present.'

Regarding proposals for the present, the criticism was that they were vague and incomplete:

'except in so far as it was made clear that His Majesty's Government must inevitably bear the full responsibility for the defence of India. These proposals, in effect, asked for participation in the tasks of today with a view to ensure 'the future freedom of India'. Freedom was for an uncertain future, not for the present; and no indication was given in clause (*e*) of what arrangements or governmental and other changes would be made in the present.'

In the final stages of the negotiations, however, the Congress leaders were disappointed with Cripps's explanation. Azad's letter complained:

'You had referred both privately and in the course of public statements to a National Government as a 'Cabinet' consisting of 'ministers'. These words have a certain significance and we had imagined that the new Government would function with full powers as a Cabinet, with the Viceroy acting as a constitutional head. But the new picture that you placed before us was really not very different from the old, the difference being one of degree and not of kind. The new Government could neither be called, except vaguely and inaccurately, nor could it function as a National Government. It would just be the Viceroy and his Executive Council with the Viceroy having all the old powers. We did not ask for any legal changes; but we did ask for definite assurances and conventions which would indicate that the new Government would function as a free Government the members of which act as members of the Cabinet in a constitutional government. In regard to the conduct of the war and connected activities the Commander-in-Chief would have freedom, and he would also act as a war Minister.'

The Congress argument was broadly this: we had asked for assurance from governors five years earlier despite the facts that (*a*) the ministries were responsible to the legislatures; and (*b*) the Congress *alone* would form the cabinets. Those assurances were given by the viceroy with the support of Lord Zetland, the secretary of state for India. But as the centre there was no responsibility to the legislature, the viceroy being supreme; no party majority in the executive, let alone a party cabinet. Therefore, the case in favour of assurances being given in 1942 was immeasurably stronger.

However, during the negotiations, certain members of the executive council had intimate talks with one or two leading members of the Congress working committee and pointed out that the autocracy of the viceroy needed some checks. There was no doubt that Linlithgow had interpreted the constitution in a narrow, illiberal way, almost always to his own advantage, and seriously limited the powers and authority of the executive council.

In the midst of these discussions, I received an oral message from Sri Aurobindo through one of his disciples. I had not seen Aurobindo for twenty-five years nor maintained any contacts with him. The message he sent was to be conveyed to Gandhi and Nehru and briefly implied that there should be no discussions with Cripps of the details of his scheme. He advised the Congress leaders to accept the scheme as it stood, and all would be well with India. Gandhi had already returned to Wardha, but I passed on the message to Nehru and Rajagopalachari.

Right up to the last moment, there was optimism among Congress leaders that there would be a settlement. But misgivings were expressed first on the official side in Delhi.

I saw Cripps twice that week. He was showing signs of weariness because of an early summer. He was also anxious about developments in London. I had suggested to him on an earlier occasion and repeated, in my final talk with him, that he should summon together six or seven of the men he had been seeing separately – not only Congress leaders, but Jinnah, Tej Bahadur Sapru, Rajagopalachari and Ambedkar – and reach a general agreement. He gave me the impression that he had it in his mind. He asked me more than once if the Congress leaders were really keen on a settlement. I told him that while I could not generalize, I was certain that Azad, Nehru, Rajagopalachari and the section they represented were anxious for one.

V

Cripps left Delhi for London on April 12th. Before going he broadcast to India giving the reasons for his failure. The effect was devastating. He blamed the Congress leaders for the breakdown and gave two reasons to account for it: (1) they had demanded an immediate change in the constitution, a point (he said) they raised at the last moment; (2) they had asked for a national government untrammelled by any control by the viceroy or the British government. He interpreted the second point as a system of government 'responsible to no legislature or electorate, incapable of being changed and the majority of whom would be in a position to dominate large minorities'. Such a position the minorities would never accept; nor could the British government consent to a breach of its pledges to them.

Explaining from the Congress point of view the cause of the breakdown, Rajajopalachari said:

'we were proceeding all along under an impression that the National Government to be set up would be a Cabinet functioning as in a constitutional government; that is to say, that the Governor-General would accept the advice of Ministers and that the only reservation was the authority of the Commander-in-Chief and of the British war cabinet, but we were aghast when we were told that all the new Members of Government would only function like the present Executive Council Members and not as ministers in a constitutional government.'

Looking back over that period, I can see many things which made a settlement difficult, almost impossible. The personal factor loomed large. It was clear to me, particularly after seeing the viceroy in the last week of May, that Cripps's technique of seeing the Indian leaders without the viceroy being present had been greatly resented by him.

I wondered, too, especially after Johnson's return to America, whether his intervention did not complicate the situation in two ways. Did Cripps really welcome it, or did he feel embarrassed that Johnson should have come right into the negotiations? Secondly, would Nehru have been quite so firm in his demands if in his many talks with Johnson he had not been encouraged to think that America would insist upon a settlement by agreement? Jinnah's opposition Johnson was from the beginning inclined to regard as only a minor obstacle. If Nehru and the British could come to terms, he told me several times, Jinnah could easily be brought round by the British.

Apart from these leading personalities, the executive council was in no mood to be helpful. I saw, later, a memorandum prepared by some of the Indian members in which they complained in strong language about having been ignored by Cripps throughout the period of the negotiations. They felt that their prestige had been undermined, and Cripps had shown no consideration for the manner in which they had at a critical moment come to the assistance of the viceroy.

Nor was such dissatisfaction confined to the officials alone. European non-officials were given less than half-an-hour for presenting their case to Cripps. At a press conference, Cripps had said that the provisions of a treaty between the Indian constituent assembly and the British government for the protection of racial and religious minorities were not meant to apply to Europeans in India.

Among political parties Cripps made no secret of his view that only the Congress and the Muslim League really mattered. The support of other parties for his scheme would of course be welcome, but was of no essential value. Such an attitude was not complimentary to the Hindu Mahasabha, the Liberals and other groups.

Then there were the princes. Some of them were bitter that the Cripps scheme would not permit the states to form a dominion of their own; and also they could not, after joining the Indian union, retain direct relations with the British government. Two princes saw Cripps by themselves and were told by him in effect: 'the British will quit India after the war; why don't you (Princes) make up with Gandhi and the Congress?'

There were suggestions that Cripps's instructions were altered in the final stages and therefore he could not carry out the promises he had made earlier. Whether this was true or not, no one can say with authority. Johnson asked me shortly after Cripps's departure whether I had heard that Cripps's attitude definitely changed after he had received a cable from London on April 7th.

Discounting all the speculative reports, it is beyond dispute that Cripps did use the terms 'National Government' and 'Cabinet' in the early stages; he had talked of the abolition of the India Office and the removal of the three service members of the executive council. Azad referred in his letter to the 'growing deterioration' of the atmosphere as the negotiations proceeded, Cripps 'explaining away' the earlier promises.

A point of considerable significance needs to be made at this stage: a major reversal of roles occurred between Gandhi and Nehru after the failure of the Cripps mission. From the commencement of the period reviewed in this paper – 1935 – Gandhi was constructive and accommodating in his policies and outlook. He supported the section of the Congress represented by Rajagopalachari which was keen on making the maximum use of the powers conferred on India by the 1935 constitution; in the early stages of the second world war, he was for India's unconditional support of Britain and her allies, consistent with his creed of non-violence; he encouraged more than one effort in 1940 and 1941 designed to establish a transitional war-time federation with the co-operation of Sir Sikandar Hyat Khan and states like Baroda and Jaipur. But from 1941 his faith in the sincerity of British promises and assurances weakened and was practically extinguished by the fate of the Cripps mission.

On the other hand, Nehru, who had no use for the 1935 constitution, except for 'wrecking it from within', saw in the rapid rise of the Nazi and Facist movements in Europe a grave warning to India and the rest of the world. With the allied powers facing a crisis, especially after Japan's entry into the second world war and her spectacular successes in south-east Asia, Nehru's tactics underwent a complete transformation. The failure of the Cripps mission had much less of an impact on him than on Gandhi. The imminence of Japan's attack on India was for him a compelling reason for the need to do fresh thinking on Indo-British relations. In the fateful summer of 1942, it was Nehru, assisted by Azad, who exercised a sobering influence on Gandhi and prevented him from plunging the country into 'anarchy and chaos'. On their insistence, the resolution of the Congress working committee at Allahabad at the end of April underwent modifications for keeping the door open for further negotiations, if possible, with the British government.

Nehru had his own view on the failure of the Cripps negotiations. At a press conference on April 12th (within a few hours of Cripps departure from Delhi) he declared:

'While it was my extreme desire to find a way out and make India function effectively for defence and make the war a popular effort – so great was my desire that some things I have stood for during the last quarter of a century, things which I could never have imagined for a moment I would give up, I now agreed to give up – I am convinced personally that it is impossible for us to agree to the proposals as they eventually emerged from the British Government's mind. I am in complete and whole-hearted agreement with the Congress resolution and the letters of the Congress President.'

After pointing out that Cripps, in his final interview on April 9th, went back completely on his earlier assurances about a national government and the viceroy being only a constitutional head, Nehru declared: 'I was amazed. It might be that he had been pulled up by his senior partner in England or some here.'

About Japan, Nehru was equally explicit:

'The fundamental factor today is distrust or dislike of the British Government. It is not pro-Japanese sentiment. It is anti-British sentiment. That may occasionally lead individuals to pro-Japanese expression of views. This is short-sighted. It is a slave's sentiment, a slave's way of thinking, to imagine that to get rid of one person who is dominating us, we can expect another person to help us and not dominate us later. Free men ought not to think that way. It distresses me that any Indian should talk of the Japanese liberating India.'

Nehru was anxious that regardless of the failure of the Cripps mission, India should continue to maintain the same attitude towards the war. He strongly favoured the adoption of a scorched-earth policy and of guerilla tactics against the Japanese; and in these respects he did not hesitate to hold views different from Gandhi's. He told the same press conference.

'The whole approach was one of lighting a spark in hundreds of millions of minds in India. It was not an easy responsibility for anyone to undertake. Nevertheless, we felt that circumstances demanded it and whatever our grievances with the British Government, whatever the past history of our relations, we could not allow that to come in the way of what we considered duty to our country at present.'

Nehru left New Delhi shortly after Cripps's departure and visited Bengal and Assam before returning to Allahabad in time for the meeting of the working committee at the end of April. This tour made a deep impression on him. He discovered that his point of view did not rouse enthusiasm among his audiences in Bengal and Assam. Thousands of Indian evacuees trekking from Burma over the Assam frontier were full of bitter complaints about the negligence and callousness of British officials in charge of the camps and the racial discrimination displayed between British and Indian evacuees in regard to the arrangements for evacuation.

These reports were also reaching Gandhi at Sewagram. There were complaints of official inconsiderateness towards villagers in East Bengal and Assam who were being compelled, at extremely short notice and with very inadequate compensation, to vacate their villages for military purposes.

Such was the background of the Allahabad meeting of the Congress working committee at the end of April. The reactions of the different Congress leaders were characteristically different. Rajagopalachari, for instance, coming from Madras, reached quick but far-reaching decisions. He was convinced that the British would not resist the Japanese and the people had not the means for effective resistance. Only a national government could save the country; but the British were not willing to part with power. Therefore, power had to be wrested from them. How could it be done? Only, he argued, by coming to terms with Jinnah and the Muslim League. Their demand for Pakistan after the war was the lesser of the two evils, since refusal would mean invasion of India by the Japanese. He put forward this view with great courage, lucidity and persistence at Allahabad and for some weeks later in South India, until finally he resigned from the Congress.

Gandhi, reflecting on the situation, had reacted very differently. He made the suggestion, much-discussed all over the world, of the complete withdrawal of British and allied troops from India. Referring to Britain he said in his paper *Harijan:*

'There is no guarantee that she will be able to protect, during this war, all her vast possessions. They have become a dead weight round her. If she wisely loosens herself from this weight and the Nazis, the Fascists or the Japanese, instead of leaving India alone, choose to subjugate her, they will find that they have to hold more than they can in their iron hoop. Whatever the consequences, therefore, to India, her real safety and Britain's too lie in orderly and timely British withdrawal from India.'

Gandhi saw another advantage in the suggestion he was making:

'The fiction of majority and minority will vanish like the mist before the morning sun of liberty. Truth to tell, there will be neither majority nor minority in the absence of the paralysing British arms. The millions of India would then be an undefined but one mass of humanity. I have no doubt that at that time the natural leaders will have wisdom enough to evolve an honourable solution of their difficulties.'

This statement was interpreted as an invitation to the Japanese to invade India. Gandhi's mind, however, was very clear on the point. In the same issue of *Harijan*, he answered the question:

'If the Japanese really mean what they say and are willing to help to free India from the British yoke, why should we not willingly accept their help? It is folly to suppose that aggressors can ever be benefactors. The Japanese may free India from the British yoke, but only to put in their own instead. I have always maintained that we should not seek any other Power's help to free India from the British yoke. . . .'

Nehru's position was extremely difficult. The Congress working committee was faced with a double crisis. Rajagopalachari was determined to raise the issue of coming to terms with Jinnah on the basis of conceding the principle of Pakistan. These two Congress leaders were agreed on the attitude to be adopted towards the Japanese and on the urgent need for a national government to take charge of India's defences. But their solutions were different. Then, Gandhi raised a number of fundamental issues in the resolution placed before the committee. Nehru realized, particularly after his recent experience in Bengal and Assam, that the Indian people were not willing to accept his lead in regard to the war. Rajagopalachari was pulling one way, Gandhi another. To make matters worse, in the debate in the house of commons on April 28th, both Cripps and Amery repeated the arguments about the impracticability of forming a national government and the charge about Congress wanting party domination in such a government.

I went from New Delhi to Allahabad to report the proceedings for my papers. Before leaving Delhi, I called on Johnson who was most anxious that the Congress leaders should not pass a resolution which would block all further negotiations. Then he said to me: 'draft a declaration which Churchill could make, and the Congress might accept. Show it to Nehru, and if he approves, bring it back to Delhi at once.' His idea was that the draft would then be cabled to Washington and Churchill influenced into making such a declaration, if possible before the end of the proceedings at Allahabad.

I worked on the suggestion and produced the following draft:

'The Congress has not accepted the view that major changes in the Constitution are not possible during the war. Nevertheless, in order to facilitate a settlement it is prepared to agree to a declaration by the British Cabinet on the following lines:

'Indian leaders attach the greatest importance to arrangements for the administration of India in the immediate future. The British Cabinet is willing to go to the farthest limits possible within the framework of the existing Constitution to convert the Executive Council into a National Government in practice.

'For this purpose, the Viceroy is being authorized to invite a small number of representative leaders to examine the Constitution from this standpoint. The Cabinet accepts the view that minor changes in the Act, alterations in the methods of functioning of the Executive Council and in the Central Legislature by resort to rule-making powers, and the establishment of suitable conventions are permissible within the meaning of the formula contained in the last paragraph.

'The Cabinet will accept the decisions of such a body and ask the Viceroy to proceed to the formation of a National Government to replace the present Executive Council. He will discuss with that body the composition and personnel of the National Government which must necessarily include in adequate proportions representatives of the two main political organizations, namely, the Congress and the Muslim League.

'There have been apprehensions expressed in India about the Viceroy's powers of veto. Under the Constitution, he is bound by the decisions of the majority of the Executive Council, unless the adoption of such a course is likely, in his opinion, to imperil the safety or tranquillity of India or any part of India. It is inconceivable that the Viceroy, to borrow the language in which he conveyed a similar assurance to the Congress party in 1937, before it agreed to take office in the provinces, "will act against the advice of the Executive Council, until he has exhausted all methods of convincing the Council that his decision is the right one". He will "do his utmost, before taking a final decision, to persuade his Council of the soundness of the reasons for which he is unable to accept its view".

'In the sphere of defence, it has already been agreed that the Indian Defence Member will take over all such functions as are not assigned to the Commander-in-Chief who as War Member will continue to be a member of the Viceroy's Executive Council. There will naturally be the closest consultation and collaboration between the two. Moreover, the Commander-in-Chief as a member of the Executive Council will be responsible to the Executive Council for all measures and policies originating from his department. The precise allocation of subjects for administration by the Defence and War Members respectively will also be left to the Viceroy and the Conference of leaders for settlement with the Commander-in-Chief invited to take part in the discussions. In the event of disagreement, the matter will be referred to the War Cabinet in London, whose decision will be final.'

Johnson made another request: I was to persuade Nehru to accompany him to Washington for a personal discussion of the Indian problem with President Roosevelt. It would not take, he thought, more than three days for a decision to be reached; and Nehru would be out of India for perhaps two weeks. The arrangements for flying him to Washington and back would be the responsibility of the American mission in New Delhi.

I took my draft to Allahabad, and showed it to Nehru for his approval. He read it carefully and said he had no criticisms to offer. But he was most unwilling to commit himself to it, because many of his colleagues in the working committee did not approve of outside intervention.

I then explained the circumstances under which it had been prepared and the purpose Johnson had in mind in having such a draft. I went on to his second proposal – about Nehru flying to Washington with Johnson for a discussion with the president. On this his mind was made up without any hesitation. He had enough trouble, he indicated to me, over the first interview with Johnson in New Delhi. Some of his colleagues in the working committee had expressed sharp disapproval of his conduct, and he was not going to invite a second rebuff.

The draft remained with me at Allahabad until May 3rd when I returned to Delhi, gave it to Johnson, pointing out the reasons for the delay in my return.

Later, when Nehru arrived in New Delhi on his way to Kulu Valley for a week's holiday, he met Johnson and discussed the draft with him. With Johnson's permission, I consulted Rajagopalachari about the draft and secured his agreement. The last sentence of the draft was Johnson's suggestion.

According to the report of the private proceedings which the police seized from the Congress office at Allahabad in the last week of May and which the government of India published all over the world early in August, the draft of the resolution before the second meeting of the working committee at Wardha (held early in July) was amended in several respects after five days' discussions. Nehru, unable to accept it even in a modified form, produced his own. That was finally rejected by seven votes to four in the committee. After the vote had been taken, Azad appealed to the majority to reconsider Nehru's suggestions which he was willing to amend further to accommodate the majority. The appeal had its effect and the resolution, revised a second time, was adopted by the committee unanimously and later endorsed by the All-India Congress Committee.

From the resolution in the final form, the references to Japan and the possibility of a separate peace with her were omitted. The resolution stated:

'While India has no quarrel with the people of any country, she has repeatedly declared her antipathy to Nazism and Fascism as to imperialism. If India were free she would have determined her own policy and might have kept out of the war, though her sympathies would, in any event, have been with the victims of aggression. If, however, circumstances had led her to join the war, she would have done so as a free country fighting for freedom, and her defence would have been organized on a popular basis with a national army under national control and leadership, and with intimate contacts with the people.'

Non-violent resistance to the aggressor was advocated but on the ground that

'such resistance can only take the form of non-violent non-co-operation as the British Government has prevented the organization of national defence by the people in any other way.'

Gandhi had originally urged the withdrawal of the British and allied armies from India. But in the resolution as adopted the argument was:

'The essential difference between the imperialist and the popular conceptions of defence is demonstrated by the fact that while foreign armies are invited to India for that defence, the vast man-power of India herself is not utilized for the purpose. It is significant and extraordinary that India's inexhaustible manpower should remain untapped, while India develops into a battlefield between foreign armies fighting on her soil or on her frontiers, and her defence is not supposed to be a subject fit for popular control.'

The disapproving reference to scorched-earth and guerilla tactics were dropped from the resolution which simply laid down:

'Not only the interest of India but also Britain's safety and world peace and freedom demand that Britain must abandon her hold on India. It is on the basis of independence alone that India can deal with Britain or other nations.'

Judging from subsequent results, the compromise commended itself neither to Gandhi nor to Nehru. Many features, essential from Gandhi's point of view, had been cut out; while the resolution was very inadequate for Nehru's purposes. It was a compromise intended to prevent a split between the Gandhi and Nehru sections. Rajagopalachari continued to advise his colleagues to accept the principle of Pakistan. Azad and Nehru expressed strong views on the subject, and ultimately the committee adopted a resolution opposing any scheme contemplating the division of India.

Johnson made a final effort from New Delhi to get the president to act. He suggested some modifications in the Cripps plan and added:

'If Churchill and Cripps would approve the proposals generally, then through the Viceroy, at London's direction, Nehru, Jinnah and Rajagopalachari could be brought together here and if necessary taken to London for a final agreement. I can persuade Nehru and Rajagopalachari to attend the meeting. The Viceroy can get Jinnah. Before the meeting I would have G. D. Birla talk with Gandhi.

'Both Congress and Cripps have stated there will be no further approach by either; therefore an outside move must be made if India is to defend herself and not be another France. At this distance I believe no one but the President can move successfully. Nehru writes me today of "fierce feeling against Britain". America alone can save India for the United Nations cause and my suggestion ought not be disposed of on the basis of meddling in the internal affairs of a subject nation. I respectfully urge that saving India concerns America as much as Great Britain. The effort cannot harm. It may be a miracle. I urge immediate consideration and pray for the President's aid. Time is of essence.'

But the president had become cautious and was reluctant to pressurize Churchill further. He replied to Johnson that while he greatly appreciated his earnest efforts,

'an unsuccessful attempt to solve the problem along the lines which you suggest would, if we are to judge by the results of the Cripps Mission, further alienate the Indian leaders and parties from the British and possibly cause disturbances among the various communities. On balance, therefore, I incline to the view that at the present moment the risks involved in an unsuccessful effort to solve the problem outweigh the advantages that might be obtained if a satisfactory solution could be found.'

Johnson returned to Washington later in the summer, a sick man. In a confidential report he said:

'The Viceroy and others in authority were determined at the time of the Cripps Mission that the necessary concessions should not be made and are still of the same opinion; the British are prepared to lose India, as they lost Burma, rather than make any concessions to the Indians in the belief that India will be returned to them after the war with the *status quo ante* prevailing.'

Johnson stated further that he had been reliably informed that the authorities did not propose to attempt any serious defence of India in the event of a Japanese attack, and that he had so stated to Cripps. Cripps naturally refused to believe this, but was prevailed upon by Johnson to confront General Wavell with the allegation. Cripps is reported to have told Johnson later that Wavell had admitted that this was the case.

Johnson maintained that in his opinion neither Churchill, the viceroy nor Wavell desired that the Cripps mission should be a success and that in fact they were determined that it should not be. He believed telegraphic instructions to have been sent solely to prevent the success which Cripps was on the point of attaining. Cripps is said to have admitted that he considered it possible that Churchill had sent him to India with the deliberate intention of destroying his political future.

Roosevelt felt somewhat comforted by a long message from Nehru in which he assured the president:

'The failure of the Cripps Mission has added to the difficulties of the situation and reacted unfavourably on our people. But whatever the difficulties we shall face them with all our courage and will to resist. Though the way of our choice may be closed to us, and we are unable to associate ourselves with the activities of the British authorities in India, still we shall do our utmost not to submit to Japanese or any other aggression and invasion. We, who have struggled for so long for freedom and against an old aggression, would prefer to perish rather than submit to a new invader. Our sympathies, as we have so often declared, are with the forces fighting against fascism and for democracy and freedom. With freedom in our own country those sympathies could have been translated into dynamic action.'

From Chungking, both the Generalissimo and Madame Chiang sent moving appeals for renewed American intervention for a settlement of the Indian problem. The latter said in a message to the president:

'The Cripps Mission's failure has resulted in a deterioration of the position and increased Indian hostile feeling toward Britain. According to Nehru, no real shift in authority was offered and no possibility existed for the establishment of a people's army for defence purpose. Therefore, there was no basis for a compromise.'

Early in May 1942, after a long discussion with Liaqat Ali Khan, general secretary of the Muslim League, I sought an interview with Jinnah but failed to secure a response. In a letter to Gandhi, I said:

'The Working Committee of the Muslim League had adopted a resolution at Nagpur on 25th December, '41, on the defence of India. The operative part of that resolution was as follows:

"The Working Committee once more declare that they are ready and willing as before to shoulder the burden of the defence of the country, singly or in co-operation with other parties on the basis that real share and responsibility is given in the authority of the Government at the Centre and the provinces within the framework of the present constitution, but without prejudice to the major political issues involved in the framing of the further constitution."

I commented on this resolution in my letter:

'I have discussed this with Liaquat Ali Khan. He interprets this offer as containing three main points: (1) All major issues to be postponed until after the war; (2) power to be sought within the framework of the existing constitution; (3) Muslims to have a real share of power at the Centre and in the Provinces.

'Liaquat Ali Khan had elaborated this in his speech in the Legislative Assembly in March last. In that speech he had said that the Muslim League was willing to consider a settlement with the British Government either alone or in combination with the other parties on the above basis. If, however, the Hindus were prepared to concede the principle of Pakistan (leaving details to be worked out after the war) then Jinnah would not limit even the interim arrangements to the existing Constitution but would favour any reasonable adjustments, even if that meant alteration of the Constitution.

'I would respectfully suggest to you that you should meet Jinnah in Bombay and discuss this question with him. You have yourself written more than once in the *Harijan* that if the Muslims want a partition of India, only a civil war can prevent it.'

'A settlement with the Muslim League would enable men of Rajagopalachari's way of thinking to form a National Government both at the Centre and in the Provinces. It will enable such men to resist the enemy by all means available. You too believe in resisting the aggressor but would limit it to non-violent non-co-operation. Each wing may supplement the efforts of the other. Indeed, a situation may arise in parts of India, should the Japanese land in this country, when because of the collapse of armed resistance, non-violent non-co-operation may be the only possible method left to us.'

'I gravely fear that a movement of civil disobedience at this stage will not only introduce confusion in the Congress and outside and hasten a regime of chaos, but directly assist the Japanese. I cannot for a moment believe that the withdrawal of the British from India will impress the Japanese and restrain them from landing in this country.'

'I shudder to think what may be the fate of the country if you should pursue the line that you have been doing in the *Harijan* during the last two or three weeks. Would not the better course be to seek a settlement with Jinnah and the Muslim League so that those who do not and cannot accept your policy of non-violence may be free to adopt a different course but not in antagonism to your own? I am sure that you will not want to force your point of view on the country or even on the Congress at any cost.

'If you succeed in coming to a general understanding with Jinnah, details of the settlement may be left to Nehru and one or two others from the Congress side.'

Gandhi replied promptly to my letter:

'I would go barefoot to Jinnah Saheb if I felt that he would look upon my advance with favour. Why don't you get from him what you have got from the Nawab Saheb [Liaqat Ali Khan]? By a process of exhaustion I have reached the conclusion I am discussing in the columns of *Harijan*.'

I met Nehru in Delhi on May 24th and conveyed to him the substance of my correspondence with Gandhi. He was obviously worried and sad. He decided, after reflecting on the situation for a quiet week in Kulu, to go to Wardha for a frank talk with Gandhi. They had not met for over two months, and much had happened in that interval, including the Allahabad meeting of the Congress working committee. The details of the talk had not at that time been made public; but Gandhi's letter to General Chiang Kai Shek (published in India only in August, 1942, after the arrests of the Congress leaders) seems to have been the immediate outcome. The final passages of the letter reproduced below, revealed the inner working of Gandhi's mind:

'I am anxious to explain to you that my appeal to the British Power to withdraw from India is not meant in any shape or form to weaken India's defence against the Japanese or embarrass you in your struggle. India must not submit to any aggressor or invader and must resist him. I would not be guilty of purchasing the freedom of my country at the cost of your country's freedom. That problem does not arise before me as I am clear that India cannot gain her freedom in this way, and a Japanese combination of either India or China would be equally injurious to the other country and to world peace. That combination must, therefore, be prevented, and I should like India to play her natural and rightful part in this.

'I feel India cannot do so while she is in bondage. India has been a helpless witness of the withdrawals from Malaya, Singapore and Burma. We must learn the lesson from these tragic events and prevent by all means to our disposal a repetition of what befell these unfortunate countries. But unless we are free, we can do nothing to prevent it, and the same process might well occur again, crippling India and China disastrously. I do not want a repetition of this tragic tale of woe.

'Our proferred help has repeatedly been rejected by the British Government, and the recent failure of the Cripps Mission has left a deep wound which is still running. Out of that anguish has come the cry for immediate withdrawal of British power so that India can look after herself and help China to the best of her ability.

'I have told you my faith in non-violence and of my belief in the effectiveness of this method if the whole nation could turn to it. That faith in it is as firm as ever. But I realize that India today as a whole has not that faith and belief, and the Government of free India would be formed from the various elements composing the nation.

'Today the whole of India is impotent and feels frustrated. The Indian Army consists largely of people who have joined up because of economic pressure. They have no feeling of a cause to fight for, and in no sense are they a national army. Those of us who would fight for a cause, for India and China, with armed forces or with non-violence, cannot, under the foreign heel, function as they want to. And yet our people know for certain that India free can play even a decisive part not only on her own behalf, but also on behalf of China and world peace. Many, like me, feel that it is not proper or manly to remain in this helpless state and allow events to overwhelm us when a way to effective action can be opened to us. They feel, therefore, that every possible effort should be made to ensure independence and that freedom of action which is so urgently needed. This is the origin of my appeal to the British power to end immediately the unnatural connection between Britain and India.

'Unless we make that effort, there is grave danger of public feeling in India going into wrong and harmful channels. There is every likelihood of subterranean sympathy for Japan growing simply in order to weaken and oust British authority in India. This feeling may take the place of robust confidence in our ability never to look to outsiders for help in winning our freedom. We have to learn self-reliance and develop the strength to work out our own salvation. This is only possible if we make a determined effort to free ourselves from bondage. That freedom has become a present necessity to enable us to take our due place among the free nations of the world.

'To make it perfectly clear that we want to prevent in every way Japanese aggression, I would personally agree and I am sure the Government of free India would agree that the Allied Powers might, under treaty with us, keep their armed forces in India and use the country as a base for operations against the threatened Japanese attack.

'I need hardly give you my assurance that, as the author of the new move in India, I shall take no hasty action. And whatever action I may recommend will be governed by the consideration that it should not injure China, or encourage Japanese aggression in India or China. I am trying to enlist world opinion in favour of a proposition which to me appears self-proved and which must lead to the strengthening of India's and China's defence. I am also educating public opinion in India and conferring with my colleagues. Needless to say, any movement against the British Government with which I may be connected will be essentially non-violent. I am straining every nerve to avoid a conflict with British authority. But if in the vindication of the freedom, which has become an immediate desideratum, this becomes inevitable, I shall not hesitate to run any risk, however great.

'Very soon you will have completed five years of war against Japanese aggression and invasion and all the sorrow and misery that these have brought to China. My heart goes out to the people of China in deep sympathy and in admiration for their heroic struggle and endless sacrifices in the cause of their country's freedom and integrity against tremendous odds. I am convinced that this heroism and sacrifice cannot be in vain; they must bear fruit. To you, to Madam Chiang and to the great people of China, I send my earnest and sincere wishes of your success. I look forward to the day when a free India and a free China will co-operate together in friendship and brotherhood for their own good and for the good of Asia and the world.'

The points on which Nehru succeeded in getting Gandhi to modify his view-point were:

(1) no action against Britain which might even indirectly assist Japan against China;
(2) a treaty between the Allies and free India permitting the use of India as a base for Allied operations against the Japanese;
(3) avoidance of conflict with British authority, if at all possible.

These, for Nehru, were great gains as from Gandhi they were equally important concessions. The letter to the Generalissimo was actually in print and would have been published but for a last minute appeal from the Generalissimo to hold it back.

The second meeting of the working committee was approaching, and this time the venue was Wardha, to enable Gandhi to attend it. He was going through a mental conflict. An article in *Harijan* of July 12th was entitled 'Our Ordered Anarchy' (written by his English disciple Miraben about conditions in Orissa). Gandhi, it was clear, was now thinking of a mass movement. A settlement with the Muslims was impossible, he was convinced, while the British dominated India: he could not honestly agree to Pakistan. He wrote:

'It is not in my giving. If I felt convinced of the rightness of the demand, I should certainly work for it side by side with the League. But I do not. I would like to be convinced. Nobody has yet told me all its implications.'

Could India keep quiet at this critical juncture? Gandhi said:

'I feel that now is the time for India to play an effective part in the fortunes of the war, if she becomes free from British servitude. I am convinced too that nothing stands in the way of that freedom except British unwillingness to give up India as the happy hunting-ground for the British that she has been for three centuries. If she gives up India, she might as well give up fighting, says the Imperialist.'

India's immediate freedom (but not the withdrawal of British troops) he visualized as a vital necessity. In other words, British dominion over India must end, without thought for the consequences.

He asked:

'Why should not Muslims who believe in Pakistan but also believe in Independent India join such a struggle? If on the other hand they believe in Pakistan through British aid and under British aegis, it is a different story. I have not place in it.'

Free India, he told Edgar Snow, would undoubtedly make common cause with the Allies, adding:

'I cannot say that free India will take part in militarism or choose to go the non-violent way. But I can say without hesitation that if I can turn India to non-violence I will certainly do so. If I succeed in converting 40 crores of people to non-violence it will be a tremendous thing, a wonderful transformation.

'But you won't oppose a militarist effort by civil disobedience? Snow asked.

'I have no such desire, I cannot oppose Free India's will with civil disobedience, it would be wrong.'

At the end of June, the viceroy had announced a further expansion of his executive council, adding more Indians to it, but not giving more power to them. Home and finance continued to be in British hands, and a non-official British businessman was appointed for the first time as the member in charge of the newly constituted portfolio of war transport, including railways. This step had a twofold effect. It meant that the British cabinet was not willing to go as far as Cripps in having a completely Indian personnel for the executive council; and secondly that no settlement would be sought with the Congress.

It is against this background that one must study the July resolution of the Congress working committee. It took the line:

'The freedom of India was necessary not only in the interest of India but also for the safety of the world and for the ending of nazism, fascism, militarism and other forms of imperialism, and the aggression of one nation over another.

'Ever since the outbreak of the world war, the Congress had studiedly pursued a policy of non-embarrassment. Even at the risk of making its satyagraha ineffective, it deliberately gave it a symbolic character, in the hope that this policy would be duly appreciated and that real power would be transferred to popular representatives, so as to enable the nation to make its fullest contribution towards the realization of human freedom throughout the world, which is in danger of being crushed. It had also hoped that negatively nothing would be done which was calculated to tighten Britain's strangle-hold of India.

'These hopes had, however, been dashed to pieces. The abortive Cripps proposals showed in the clearest possible manner that there was no change in the British Government's attitude towards India and that the British hold on India was in no way to be relaxed. In the negotiations with Cripps,

Congress representatives tried their utmost to achieve a minimum, consistent with the national demand, but to no avail. This frustration had resulted in a rapid and widespread increase of ill-will against Britain and a growing satisfaction at the success of Japanese arms.'

'On the withdrawal of British rule in India, responsible men and women of the country will come together to form a Provisional Government, representative of all important sections of the people of India, which will later evolve a scheme whereby a Constituent Assembly can be convened in order to prepare a constitution for the government of India acceptable to all sections of the people. Representatives of free India and representatives of Great Britain will confer together for the adjustment of future relations and for the co-operation of the two countries as allies in the common task of meeting aggression. It is the earnest desire of the Congress to enable India to resist aggression effectively with the people's united will and strength behind it.

'In making the proposal for the withdrawal of British rule from India, the Congress has no desire whatsoever to embarrass Great Britain or the Allied Powers in their prosecution of the war, or in any way to encourage aggression on India or increased pressure on China by the Japanese or any other power associated with the Axis group. Nor does the Congress intend to jeopardize the defensive capacity of the Allied Powers. The Congress is therefore agreeable to the stationing of the armed forces of the Allies in India, should they so desire, in order to ward off and resist Japanese or other aggression, and to protect and help China.

'The proposal of withdrawal of the British Power from India was never intended to mean the physical withdrawal of all Britishers from India.'

'If such withdrawal takes place with goodwill, it would result in establishing a stable provisional Government in India and co-operation between this Government and the United Nations in resisting aggression and helping China.'

'While, therefore, the Congress is impatient to achieve the national purpose, it wishes to take no hasty step and would like to avoid, in so far as is possible, any course of action that might embarrass the United Nations. The Congress would plead with the British Power to accept the very reasonable and just proposal herein made, not only in the interest of India but also that of Britain and of the cause of freedom to which the United Nations proclaim their adherence.'

In comparison with the terms of the Allahabad resolution, this was a great improvement. The approach was fundamentally different. There were no ambiguous references to a free India cherishing no hostile feelings towards the people of Japan. On the other hand, it laid down in strong and clear language that free India would support the war effort. Withdrawal was to be not of British troops – they could use India as a base of operations – but only of British domination.

Azad explained that he contemplated no interval, however brief, between the withdrawal of British rule and the establishment of a national government. The reference to a mass movement both Azad and Nehru agreed to because they did not contemplate it except as a distant possibility. There was Gandhi's assurance that he would avoid a conflict as far as was humanly possible.

The government of India took very little time to come to a decision on the Congress resolution passed at Wardha. A confidential letter of the government's secretary in charge of information and broadcasting (published by the Congress) revealed the official attitude. Analysing the resolution it said that the Congress seemed:

'to envisage the handling over of power to a provisional Congress Government, which shall then itself decide what future arrangements are necessary. Note that British rule is first to be withdrawn; after that a provisional Government is to be formed. What is to happen in the interval? How and by whom is the provisional Government to be formed, and under what constitution will it function?'

'The threat of Civil Disobedience is a direct invitation to the Japanese, but the acceptance of the proposals by the British Government would create a situation which would be an equally open invitation to India's enemies. The proposals for co-operation in the war are negative. A wish is expressed not, "as far as it is possible", to embarrass the war effort or to jeopardize the *defensive* capacity of the United Nations. There is no word of any resolve to fight to total war to the end alongside others.'

I had it on the authority of a member of the executive council that the decision to arrest Congress leaders, after the endorsement of the resolution by the All-India Congress Committee, was actually taken on July 15th. Even the government's official resolution justifying the arrests was drafted between that date and July 20th, final touches only being given just before its issue, immediately after the adoption of the Congress resolution on August 8th. The decision to arrest Congress leaders and the definition of government's policy took no account of the changes in the resolution adopted at Wardha, in comparison with the one passed ten weeks earlier at Allahabad.

Worried by reports from India about the possibility of Gandhi starting a civil disobedience movement, President Roosevelt wrote a letter to him on August 1, 1942, in the course of which he observed:

'I am sure that you will agree that the United States has consistently striven for the supported policies of fair-dealing, of fairplay, and of all related principles looking towards the creations of harmonious relations between nations. Nevertheless, now that war has come as a result of Axis dream of world conquest, we, together with many other nations, are making a supreme effort to defeat those who would deny for ever all hope of freedom throughout the world. I am enclosing a copy of an address of July 23 by Secretary of State made with my complete approval which illustrates the attitude of this Government. I shall hope that our common interest in democracy and righteousness will enable your countrymen and mine to make a common cause against the common enemy.'

Gandhi, Nehru and Azad took a conciliatory line in their statements, both before the commencement of the meeting in Bombay in the first week of

August and during the debates on the main resolution. I saw Nehru on August 5th in Bombay and told him that Gandhi's suggestion about free India negotiating a peace with Japan had been the cause of much misunderstanding abroad, though it had been rejected by the Congress working committee at Allahabad and never repeated since. Nehru promptly authorized me to say in the *Manchester Guardian* that it would be 'a dishonest betrayal of the Allied cause if free India were ever to think of a separate peace with any of the Axis Powers'; that 'the National Government would reaffirm the signature of the representative of the Government of India to the pact of the United Nations'; and further that China was only an example of Japanese aggression. She would have to withdraw from Burma, Malaya, the Dutch East Indies etc. But, added Nehru, India would not fight so that these territories could revert to their old status as imperialist possessions. India would demand the freedom of all such territories.

The resolution, which was passed by an overwhelming majority by the All-India Congress Committee on August 8th, was a carefully worded document. It said that British rule was 'degrading and enfeebling India and making her progressively less capable of defending herself and of contributing to the cause of world freedom'. Therefore its termination was 'a vital and immediate issue on which depend the future of the war and the success of freedom and democracy'.

In order to assure the minorities and particularly the Muslims, who had expressed their fear of a permanent Hindu majority governing India, the Congress accepted the view that the permanent constitution after the war would:

'be a federal one, with the largest measure of autonomy for the federating units, and with the residuary powers vesting in these units. The future relations between India and the allied nations will be adjusted by representatives of all these free countries conferring together for their mutual advantage and for their co-operation in the common task of resisting aggression. Freedom will enable India to resist aggression effectively with the peoples' united will and strength behind it.

'The freedom of India must be the symbol of and prelude to the freedom of all other Asiatic nations under foreign domination. Burma, Malaya, Indo-China, the Dutch Indies, Iran and Iraq must also attain their complete freedom. It must be clearly understood that such of these countries as are under Japanese control now must not subsequently be placed under the rule or control of any other colonial power.'

Viewing the immediate present from this standpoint, the resolution made an earnest appeal to Britain and the United Nations to end 'imperialist and authoritarian government' in India; otherwise, a mass movement based on non-violence was inevitable, adding that the freedom resulting from the success of such a movement would be for all the people in India, not for the Congress alone.

In one respect, the resolution differed from that adopted at Wardha three weeks earlier. The formation of a national government, it was laid down, would follow the declaration of India's freedom, not the withdrawal of British rule. The distinction was made so that no question could arise about a possible interval between these two developments which Gandhi had sometimes declared might be one of chaos.

Nehru declared in his speech that the resolution was not a threat, only an offer of co-operation, but of a free India. Gandhi dwelt at great length in his final speech on the efforts he and the Congress had made to secure a Hindu–Muslim settlement. He endorsed Azad's suggestion that if the British would transfer power to India, the Congress would be willing to impose a self-denying ordinance and keep out of the government.

But neither the resolution nor the speeches had any effect on the decision of the British government. No one in authority studied the implications of the Bombay resolution, or saw that its terms differed from those of the one passed at Wardha. They did not wait for the reports of the speeches, but hastened to carry out the decisions to arrest the leaders.

VI

Roosevelt wrote to General Chiang-Kai-Shek that while he appreciated his anxiety for renewed negotiations with India, he felt:

'that it would be wiser for you and for myself to refrain from taking action of the kind which you had in mind for the time being. . . . I think that you and I can best serve the people of India at this stage by making no open or public appeal or pronouncement but by letting the simple fact be known that we stand ready as friends to heed any appeal for help if that appeal comes from both sides.'

After the imprisonment of the Congress leaders, the American government maintained its interest in India but in a less active form. Cordell Hull pointed out to Lord Halifax that sooner or later there would have to be consideration given to a plan for granting independence to India – a view with which (it seems) Lord Halifax was in 'wholehearted and unreserved agreement'.

Towards the end of 1942, with William Phillips in New Delhi as the president's special envoy in succession to Johnson, Cordell Hull renewed the efforts to get negotiation with India resumed. A note to Phillips indicated 'The President and I and the entire Government earnestly favour freedom for all dependent peoples at the earliest date practicable.' India was mentioned, as receiving 'the President's constant attention'. Chastened, however, by Johnson's earlier experience, Cordell Hull was anxious that it should be made clear to the British government 'that we [the U.S.A.] are not undertaking to speak in any spirit save that of genuine friendship and of the fullest co-operation both during and following the war'. At the same time, Phillips was reminded, 'we have an added interest in the settlement of this matter by reason of its relation to the war'.

Phillips's more cautious approach did not save him from the unfortunate fate of his predecessor. Gandhi's fast early in 1943 compelled him to act, if only to prevent the unfortunate impression that the USA was backing

Britain in regard to India. At long last, he was authorized by Washington to express to Lord Linlithgow the president's great concern about the possible consequences of Gandhi's death. The tragedy, however, did not occur, though Phillips was becoming increasingly diffident about an immediate solution of the Indian problem and finally returned to Washington. In a letter to the president (after his return) analysing the Indian situation, he said:

'India is bound to be an important base for our future operations against Burma and Japan, it would seem to me of highest importance that we should have around us a sympathetic India rather than an indifferent and possibly hostile India. . . . In view of our military position in India we should have a voice in these matters. It is not right for the British to say "this is none of your business" when we alone presumably will have the major part to play in the future struggle with Japan. . . . The peoples of Asia – and I am supported in this opinion by other diplomatic and military observers – cynically regard this war as one between fascists and imperialist powers. A generous British gesture to India would change this undesirable political atmosphere. India itself might then be expected more positively to support our war effort against Japan.'

After the arrests of Gandhi and the Congress leaders in August, 1942, the initiative on the Indian side for resolving the deadlock passed into the hands of a group of men led by Sir Tej Bahadur Sapru. In December 1942 Sapru invited a number of prominent persons in public life to a special meeting at Allahabad. There were present one or two members of the Congress like Rajagopalachari (who had not subscribed to the 'quit India' resolution and were, therefore, out of prison), and spokesmen of the Hindu Mahasabha, the Christian conference, the Trade Union Congress, the Liberal federation, the Akali party and the federation of Indian chambers of commerce.

These persons met on December 12th and 13th, 1942 to consider the situation. No formal resolution was adopted, since the primary object was to explore the possibilities of holding later an all parties' conference; and the members had declared that they had no mandate from their respective organizations to commit themselves to any definite course or policy.

After discussions for two days, Sapru declared that there was a widespread anxiety to reach a solution of the political deadlock and also a basis of agreement likely to prove generally acceptable. The details of such an agreement could not assume final shape until those present at the conference had an opportunity of discussing them with their respective organizations. Therefore, at that stage, an early summoning of an all parties' conference, including therein the two major parties in the country, namely, the Congress and the Muslim League, appeared to be imperative for reaching a settlement.

Sapru also revealed to the conference that Gandhi was earnestly anxious shortly before his arrest to be co-opted in the deliberations of such a conference. Jinnah too had repeatedly declared his willingness to discuss with leaders of other parties the details of a possible solution. In order, however, to ensure the success of the conference Sapru and those associated with him considered it essential that the British government should announce forthwith:

(1) that the provisional government of India, to be formed as a result of a general agreement, would be endowed with full powers and authority over the administration, subject only to the position of the commander-in-chief being duly safeguarded in order to promote the efficient prosecution of the war; and in its relations with Britain and the allies, enjoying the status of a dominion and entitled to all the rights and privileges associated with such status;

(2) the release of Mahatma Gandhi and all Congressmen to enable the representatives of the Congress to participate in the all parties' conference.

These two steps were essential for the creation of a proper atmosphere in which the conference could conduct its deliberations and reach a successful conclusion. The tragic chapter of events of the previous four months, in particular the decision of the Congress to launch a civil disobedience movement, no less than the methods adopted to suppress the disturbances in several parts of the country, must be ended without delay it was felt if bitterness and resentment were to be prevented from assuming dangerous proportions. Sapru concluded the statement in the following terms:

'As men anxious to see India throw all her resources into the war effort we ask the British Government to make this positive contribution towards the success of the All Parties' Conference.'

On his personal responsibility, Sapru sent a cable to the prime minister, Churchill, for a fresh effort. The appeal was couched in the following terms:

'The gravity of the international situation compels some of us who have spent long years in public life in India to make this appeal to you, Prime Minister, to realize the urgent necessity for transforming the entire spirit and outlook of the administration in India. Detailed discussions of the question of the permanent constitution may well wait for more propitious times, until after victory has been achieved in this titanic struggle against the forces which threaten civilization.

'But some stroke for courageous statesmanship is called for without delay in India, at this hour of growing danger to her safety, to enlist her whole-hearted and active co-operation in intensifying the war effort. Millions of men and women are required for the adoption of effective measures designed to protect the civilian population. The heart of India must be touched, to rouse her on a nation-wide scale to the call for service, undistracted by internal and domestic differences.

'Is it not possible for you to declare at this juncture that India will no longer be treated as a Dependency to be ruled from Whitehall, and henceforth her constitutional position and powers will be identical with those of other units in the British Commonwealth? Such a declaration should, we suggest, be accompanied by concrete measures calculated to impress the people that in co-operation with the war effort they are safeguarding their own freedom. These measures are:

'(1) the conversion and expansion of the Central Executive Council into a truly National Government, consisting entirely of non-officials of all recognized parties and communities, and in charge of all portfolios, subject only to responsibility to the Crown;

'(2) the restoration in provinces now ruled autocratically by Governors in accordance with Section 93 of the Government of India Act, of popular governments broadbased on the confidence of different classes and communities; failing this, the establishment of non-official Executive Councils responsible to the Crown, as proposed for the Centre;

'(3) the recognition of India's right to direct representation through men chosen by the National Government in the Imperial War Cabinet (should such a body be set up), in all Allied War Councils, wherever established, and at the Peace Conference;

'(4) Consultation with the National Government, precisely on the same footing and to the same extent as His Majesty's Government consult the Dominion Governments in all matters affecting the Commonwealth as a whole and India in particular.

'These are war measures whose adoption need in no way prejudice the claims or demands of different parties in regard to India's permanent constitution. But knowing intimately the feelings and aspirations of our countrymen as we do, we must express our conviction that nothing less than the inauguration of this policy can resolve the crisis in India. The urgency of immediate action cannot be over-emphasized. We appeal to you in all sincerity but with the greatest emphasis to act, while there is still time for such action, so that India may line up with the other anti-Axis Powers on a footing of absolute equality with them in a common struggle for the freedom of humanity.'

This attempt on the part of Sapru and his associates met with no better fate than all the previous ones.

On January 26, 1943, Phillips asked me to give him a comprehensive note on the Indian problem. In response to his request I drafted one which contained the following passages:

'There is a widespread conviction in India that the British do not mean to part with power. The promise of independence after the war means little and can rouse no enthusiasm unless it is accompanied by as complete a transfer of power *now* as is possible in the middle of a war. Provided there is such a transfer, Congress leaders will be prepared to make large concessions to Muslim League and to other parties in order to secure general agreement. In fact, they have repeatedly declared that the Congress would even agree to the formation of a real National Government without Congress representation therein, under Mr. Jinnah's leadership.

'The first essential, therefore, is a fresh declaration by the British Government. It must of course promise India the right to frame her own Constitution after the war on the basis of self-determination and complete freedom. But immediately it must also concede to India the status and functions of a fully self-governing Dominion, like Australia or Canada. The implications of the offer will have to be elaborated: the disappearance of the India Office in London, transfer of Indian affairs to the Dominions Office, representation of India through men of her own choice in all the Allied Capitals and at the Peace Conference, etc.

'If the transfer of power is complete, there should be responsibility of the Executive to the Indian Legislature. Obviously it cannot be the present Central Legislature. Mr. Rajagopalachari's suggestion is worthy of consideration, namely, to substitute in its place the British Indian part of the federal legislature, elected in the same way. This would mean an Assembly (lower House) of 250 members elected by the provincial Assemblies, and a Council of State (Upper House) of 156 by direct election.

'Will the Muslims agree to responsibility of the Executive to the Legislature? They may, if it be laid down that a vote of no-confidence, to be operative, should have, say, a two-third majority of the Assembly, including therein at least a bare majority of the Muslim members. Responsibility will solve many problems: it will remove the objections stated by Sir Stafford Cripps, reduce the authority of the Governor General to that exercised in the Dominions, and bring into existence a Prime Minister and a Cabinet with collective responsibility.

'Another question is, will the Princes agree to these changes? Their objections may be met in this way: there should be a War Cabinet in India, consisting of certain members of the Indian Government and a representative of the States to deal with all problems connected with the war. Also, the Political Adviser of the Governor-General (who is styled 'Crown Representative' in his relations with the Indian States) should be an Indian, say the Prime Minister of one of the major States with the status of a member of the Indian Cabinet and the right to attend its meetings whenever questions involving the interest of the States arise. Such an arrangement the administration of British India in the hands of the Indian Government, will facilitate joint discussions of all-India concern with representatives of the States, and thus make a change to a federal form of Government after the war.

'Yet another problem is in regard to defence. There is already an Indian Defence Member in addition to the Commander-in-Chief. The constitution, even as it is, does not say that the Commander-in-Chief *shall* be a member of the Executive Council, but only that *if* he is a member his rank and position will be above that of other members! An Indian Defence Member but with far greater powers than are now assigned to him must be an essential part of the scheme. No Government will want to interfere with the discretion and authority of the Commander-in-Chief. What the Congress objects to is the the subordinate role of the Indian Defence Member. Cannot the Australian example (of having General MacArthur) provide a precedent? There is no reason why with strategy and military policy unified, anyone of the United Nations should not send a Supreme Commander-in-Chief for all the Allied forces operating from India. If there were established in India an Allied Council (India being represented thereon), the Commander-in-Chief could be made responsible to such a Council, and there would be little objection from the point of view of India.

'So far as this aspect is concerned, the political settlement will rest on the assumption that the Dominion Government of India will co-operate fully in the war effort, and there is no question of a separate peace with the Axis Powers. Beyond this Britain is not entitled to impose any conditions or to interfere in India's affairs.

'Once there is a settlement on these lines, the Congress, the Muslim League and other parties will come to terms and establish coalitions both at the Centre and in the provinces. Mr. Jinnah will, of course, demand that the British declaration makes one point clear: namely, that the Muslims will have the right of self-determination conceded to them in areas where they are in majority. The Congress and other parties may agree to a compromise such as that the right of self-determination will be exercised, by areas where the Muslims are a substantial majority, say 60 per cent – the right being exercisable by all the voters in such areas, and not by the Muslims alone. Mr. Jinnah is not likely to refuse such a compromise. Even more acceptable from the Congress point of view would be the suggestion that India should work the Constitution for a period of 10 or 15 years and thereafter any area which feels dissatisfied with the provisions may exercise the right of secession in the manner prescribed above. In fact a proposal on these lines was under discussion between Sir Sikandar Hyat Khan and the Congress President in February 1942. I was informed by a common friend that Mr. Jinnah was willing to consider it. But the Cripps offer prevented further discussion.

'This note has discussed the possible contents of a renewed British offer in some detail. Broadly speaking it is a great improvement on the Cripps offer in dealing with the immediate future and goes further than what Nehru and Rajagopalachari were prepared to accept in March last year. Nehru found in April that the Congress rank and file was not willing to agree to all the compromises to which he and Azad had practically committed the party in their talks with Cripps. Since then, there have been civil disobedience and sabotage on the one side, and ruthless repression on the other. Also, the crisis in regard to food is acute. The Government of India and the provincial Governments, as constituted, are incapable of tackling the problem with the necessary drive and imagination. The war situation may be more favourable than a year ago in the sense that there is no danger of an imminent attack on India by the Japanese, and no apprehension of the British inability to defend the country. But the strain on the Government has been extremely heavy during the last few months, bitterness and resentment are dangerously widespread and the British have not today a real friend of influence in the country.

'The British declaration need not go into details such as are given in this note. It must be in general terms, promise *immediately* full Dominion status for all practical purposes, and a permanent Constitution after the war framed by a Constituent Assembly on the basis of self-determination: the only stipulation being that free India will fight with the United Nations and not think of a separate peace.

'Such a declaration, with its implications set out in suitable language will instantly transform the situation.'

'The Cripps proposals involved the principle of self-determination for territorial units. Sikandar Hyat Khan is willing to accept it without modification.

Jinnah, however, insists upon a plebiscite of all Muslims in the area concerned. The question is whether there is a compromise possible between these two points of view.

'So far as the Congress is concerned, whatever be the attitude of the Working Committee and of the A.I.C.C. in the past, it is clear from the latest resolution passed in Bombay on 8th August as well as from the correspondence between Maulana Azad and Nehru and Abdul Latif, that it is willing to make the following concessions:

'(*a*) For the interim period, provided the British agree to the formation of a real National Government, the task for forming such a Government may be entrusted to Mr. Jinnah;

'(*b*) In regard to the permanent constitution, the Congress is prepared to accept the largest measure of autonomy being conceded to the federating units and residuary powers vested in them. If, however, a territorial unit is not satisfied with the basic structure of the new constitution, and desires secession, the federation will not resort to coercion.'

Gandhi's fast and its implications dominated the rest of Phillips's stay in India. On February 10th, he reported to Washington:

'Reluctantly I am coming to the conclusion that the Viceroy, presumably responsive to Churchill, is not in sympathy with any change in Britain's relationship to India. The impression is widespread among Indians that the British Government is determined to preserve the *status quo* in spite of the promises given with regard to post war independence and general assurances contained in the Atlantic Charter.'

Two days later, in a lengthy letter to the president, he observed that the complex political situation in India had become aggravated by Gandhi's fast to capacity. He was embarrassed by the question frequently put to him whether he intended to see Gandhi and the Congress leaders. He, therefore, decided to request the viceroy for permission to call on Gandhi. He explained to Linlithgow:

'My duty was to keep you [President Roosevelt] informed of the situation here and that I could not do this without at least a call upon the leader of the principal party – that I was to see Jinnah, the head of the Muslim League, in Bombay, and Rajagopalachari in Madras, and that a call upon Gandhi as I was passing by would have the advantage of a visit in the ordinary routine.'

Linlithgow, instead of giving a straight answer, explained that Gandhi was to be freed for the duration of the fast and since no member of his government would see him, he had to make a request that Phillips also refrain from doing so. Phillips commented:

'I detected for the first time a suspicion on the Viceroy's part with regard to my motives. He asked me directly what were my intentions, a question which I did not welcome; but when I explained again that I was here to keep you fully informed and not to "intervene", he said 'I see that we understand each other'. He became very friendly, called for drinks, and since then has kept me by personal letters in close touch with developments.'

The results of Gandhi's fast he could not assess, though the general British view in Delhi was that there would be no serious complications, because according to them Gandhi's stock had fallen of late. The position of the American mission in New Delhi, he told the president, was becoming embarrassing. He added:

'Unhappily for me, more and more attention seems to be centred upon this Mission and upon me personally. Every Indian who comes to see me feels that through my influence the present deadlock with the British can be solved. Naturally I am in the picture only because of the popular feeling that the President of the United States alone can bring any influence to bear upon the British Government. I find it very difficult to know what to suggest. I do feel that the Gandhi fast has complicated the situation and made it even more difficult for the British to move, if they had any intention of doing so. But as long as he has no intention of "fasting unto death" he may come out of it without having caused any material change in the situation.'

Giving his personal opinion, Phillips added:

'It would seem wise for Churchill to 'unlock the door' which he could do by convincing the Indian people that the promise of their complete independence after the war is an iron-bound promise. New words and phrases will not, I fear, carry enough weight, and therefore a new approach must be made in order to accomplish results. It must be a willingness on the part of the British Government to transfer as much civil power as possible now, on the understanding that the complete transfer will be made after the war. This would be the invitation to the leaders of the opposing parties to get together, which they cannot do now, not only because the leaders of one party are under arrest but because there is no inducement for them to make the necessary concessions to one another, and in view of the general distrust of British promises.'

Even the princes, he thought, would adopt a different attitude, since the old treaties between them and the British government were (according to the ruler of Nawanagar) obsolete and the princes could not expect to have any greater powers in their states than the king of England himself. Summing up, Phillips said in his letter to the president:

'The entire picture of States and Provinces and the unanimous demand for a new approach on the part of the British Government is a matter of extraordinary interest which I only wish I could convey to you far more satisfactorily than I am doing, but which is almost impossible to present by letter. I feel acutely the fact that public attention is centred upon me in the hope and even expectation that I can do something constructive; and yet here I am, quite unable to do anything but listen to appeals; realizing as I do the importance of not prejudicing my position with the British authorities. At the same time I want to avoid any impression on the part of the Indians that the presence of United States forces and my own presence here indicate that we Americans are strengthening the British hold over India.'

After the termination of Gandhi's fast, Phillips sent another long letter to President Roosevelt in which he observed:

'The general situation as I see it today is as follows:

'From the British viewpoint their position is not unreasonable. They have been in India for 150 years and except for the mutiny in 1857, generally speaking, internal peace has been maintained. They have acquired vast vested interests in the country and fear that their withdrawal from India would jeopardize those interests. The great cities like Bombay, Calcutta and Madras have been built up largely through their initiative. They have guaranteed the regime of the Princes, who control territorially about one-third of the country and one-fourth of the population. They realize that new forces are gathering throughout the world which affect their hold over India and they have therefore gone out of their way – so they believe – to offer freedom to India as soon as there are signs that the Indians themselves can form a secure government. This the Indian leaders have been unable to do and the British feel that they have done all that they can in the circumstances. Behind the door is Churchill, who gives the impression that personally he would prefer not to transfer any power to an Indian Government either before or after the war and that the *status quo* should be maintained.

'The Indians, on the other hand, are caught in the ne widea which is sweeping over the world, of freedom for oppressed peoples. The Atlantic Charter has given encouragement. The British declarations that freedom would be granted to India after the war have brought the picture of Indian independence as never before in the thoughts of the entire Indian intelligentsia. Unfortunately, as the time approaches for ending the war, the struggle for political prestige and power between the parties has increased and this has made it more difficult than ever for the leaders to be willing to reach a compromise agreement. And furthermore, Gandhi and all Congress leaders, not to mention the fifty or sixty thousand Congress supporters, are in jail; and as Congress is the strongest political party, there is no one available to speak for it.

'There is thus a complete deadlock and I should imagine that the Viceroy and Churchill are well satisfied to let the deadlock remain as long as possible. That is, at least, the general impression in most Indian circles.

'The problem, therefore, is, can anything be done to break this deadlock through our help? It seems to me that all we can do is to try to induce the Indian political leaders to meet together and discuss the form of Government which they regard as applicable to India, and thus to show the world that they have sufficient intelligence to tackle the problem. We must not assume that they will adopt the American or British systems. In view of the importance of guaranteeing protection of the minorities, a majority form of Government may not be applicable and a coalition may prove to be the only practical way of guaranteeing internal harmony. We cannot suppose that the British Government can or will transfer power to India by the scratch of a pen at the conclusion of the Peace Conference unless there is an Indian Government fit to receive it. The question remains, therefore, how to induce the leaders to begin now to prepare for their future responsibilities.

'There is, perhaps, a way out of the deadlock which I suggest to you, not because I am sure of its success, but because I think it is worthy of your consideration.

'With the approval and blessing of the British Government, an invitation could be addressed to the leaders of all Indian political groups on behalf of the President of the United States, to meet together to discuss plans for the future. The assembly could be presided over by an American who could exercise influence in harmonizing the endless divisions of caste, religion, race and political views. The Conference might well be under the patronage of the King-Emperor, the President of the United States, the President of the Soviet Union and Chiang-Kai-Shek, in order to bring pressure to bear on Indian politicians. Upon the issuance of the invitations, the King-Emperor could give a fresh assurance of the intention of the British Government of transferring power to India upon a certain date as well as his desire to grant a provisional set-up for the duration. The Conference could be held in any city in India except Delhi.

'American chairmanship would have the advantage, not only of expressing the interest of America in the future independence of India, but would also be a guarantee to the Indians of the British offer of independence. This is an important point because, as I have already said in previous letters, British promises in this regard are no longer believed.

'If either of the principal parties refuse to attend the Conference, it would be notice to all the world that India was not ready for self-government, and I doubt whether a political leader would put himself in such a position. Churchill and Amery may be obstacles; for notwithstanding statements to the contrary, India is governed from London, down to the smallest details.

'Should you approve the general idea and care to consult Churchill, he might reply that since the Congress leaders are in jail, a meeting such as is contemplated is impossible. The answer could be that certain of the leaders, notably Gandhi, might be freed unconditionally in order to attend the Conference. The British may even be searching for a good excuse to release Gandhi, for the struggle between him and the Viceroy is over with honours for both – the Viceroy has maintained his prestige; Gandhi has carried out his protest against the Government by his successful fast and has come back into the limelight.'

A request was made to the viceroy by the Sapru group to permit a deputation to meet Gandhi for a discussion of the Indian problem. The viceroy would not entertain it unless certain conditions were fulfilled. Rajagopalachari commenting on this, remarked (in April 1943):

'The Viceroy has set out what he considers to be his and his Government's duties in this country. Everyone of these things would have been better accomplished if our request had been granted and everyone of these things is farther from accomplishment on account of the refusal. If we had been allowed to discuss the situation with Gandhi and come back to make specific proposals to the Government as well as to various parties in the country,

I repeat everyone of these duties, which His Excellency has defined, would have been brought nearer fulfilment, but passion and prejudice prevents this from being seen.

'The Viceroy's decision in refusing our very modest preliminary request rests on the fallacy of arguing in a circle. He says all parties have not joined in this request; nor has there been a reversal of the Congress policy. But the latter can be accomplished only if we are allowed to go and see Gandhi. It is for this very purpose that we wanted to see him, so as to enable us to approach other parties and to enable a new policy to be adopted by the Congress.

'The Viceroy refers to some of us (trusted friends) having had an opportunity to see Gandhi on the 16th, 17th, 18th and 19th days of his fast. The conversations we had then with him raised in us hopes which induced us to make this request. If on the 18th day of a fast the Viceroy expected that Congress policy would be changed by a word of mouth of Gandhi, I can only say it is extraordinary.'

Phillips, commenting on Linlithgow's statement, told Washington that the leaders who attended the meeting in Bombay were not thinking in terms of negotiating a settlement, but only of request for facilities for ascertaining Gandhi's present position which, if satisfactory, would have opened a way to negotiations between all parties, including the British. It was clear that the viceroy's frame of mind appeared to preclude any possibility of a settlement. His continued refusal to allow mediators access to Gandhi roused suspicions that the authorities had no desire to see the deadlock ended.

Striking a personal note Phillips said that it was doubtful whether the viceroy would respond favourably to his own request to see Gandhi and Nehru. However, he intended to ask the viceroy for such permission before returning at the end of April to Washington for consultation; and without contact with the Congress leaders he could not fulfil the mission entrusted to him.

Meanwhile Phillips had a long interview with Jinnah and made the following report to Washington:

'Yesterday I had a three and three-quarter's hours talk with Jinnah, President of the All-India Muslim League. He insisted that Pakistan was in every way practicable and the only solution of Indian problem. Why should Hindus object he said when they would have as their share three-fourths of India, including most of its wealth? In comparison Pakistan would be poor but would be a block of forty million comprising a State within the British Commonwealth.'

In a final letter, on the eve of his return to Washington in the early part of the summer of 1943, Phillips told the president:

'India is suffering from paralysis, the people are discouraged and there is a feeling of growing hopelessness. The political leaders remain hostile to one another, although they maintain that if the British would open the door to negotiation, they could manage to pull together on a provisional basis for the duration of the war and to prepare for post-war responsibilities. More and more they realize that constitution making is a serious business and will have to be tackled in a more hopeful atmosphere than the present. Meanwhile, there is very little thought given to the war among Indians. India is in a state of inertia, prostration, divided counsels and helplessness, with growing distrust and dislike for the British, and disappointment and disillusion with regard to Americans. Indians say that while they are in sympathy with the aims of the United Nations, they are not to be allowed to share the benefits of such aims, and they feel, therefore, that they have nothing to fight for. Churchill's exclusion of India from the principles of the Atlantic Charter is always referred to in this connection.

'The British are sitting "pretty". They have been completely successful in their policy "keeping the lid on" and in suppressing any movement among the Indians which might be interpreted as a move towards independence. British armies dominate the picture and the fact that large Indian forces have been moved out of the country is a further guarantee of the British power and purpose to dominate the scene, according to their own views. Twenty thousand Congress leaders remain in jail without trial, and the influence, therefore, of the Congress Party is diminishing, while that of the Muslim League is growing.

'The British position becomes clear. There is to be no change, no effort to open the door to negotiation among the leaders, no preparation for the future until after the war, and that date is so uncertain that I believe the Indians generally feel there will be no material changes in their favour even after the war. For it will always be easy to find, in this vast country, plenty of justifications, if one is looking for excuses, to preserve the *status quo* now and in the years to come.

'The British maintain that the present situation is wholly satisfactory for the conduct of the war, and that the country is comparatively quiet, thanks to their energetic measures. Indian indifference and even hostility, they say, will make no difference, for British forces are able to preserve law and order and crush any movement dangerous to the war effort. It is true that comparative quiet prevails throughout the country, but in my opinion, it is a quiet pregnant with disturbing potentialities.'

The political stalemate continued all through 1943 until Gandhi's release from detention in 1944. Towards the end of July of that year I spent four days at Wardha going to Sewagram every day with Rajagopalachari and Bhulabhai Desai. I was also present when Sapru met Gandhi.

I met primarily with the object of placing before Gandhi a suggestion which had been in my mind for some time; namely, that a man like Sapru should analyse Gandhi's recent statements from the standpoint of a constitutional lawyer, in order to make his points the basis of a memorandum, which with suitable modifications would be constitutionally unassailable. When I first put it before Gandhi (before Sapru's arrival) he seemed interested and sympathetically inclined. On the following day in Sapru's presence he himself referred to it with approval. He interpreted it as a suggestion that a number of eminent lawyers like Sapru should draft a memorandum pointing out the reasonableness and practicability of his proposals. Sapru himself was in favour of the suggestion, though he vigorously opposed the idea of a deputation to the viceroy in order to discuss it with him. Gandhi was not particular about a deputation, but he seemed clear in his mind that such a memorandum, drawn up without reference to himself could well be made the rallying point for public opinion of different shades. A movement not confined to the Congress could thus grow round it.

Later, however, when Sapru went to see Gandhi again he seemed to have revised his view, particularly when he found that Sapru, Bhulabhai and Rajagopalachari agreed that responsibility of the executive to the legislature could not be brought about without a change in the existing constitution. Gandhi's immediate reaction to this view was that if the memorandum could support his recent proposals embodied in a letter to the viceroy it would certainly strengthen his hands. If, on the other hand, the memorandum explicitly or otherwise emphasized the difference between Gandhi's proposal and the demands put forward by men like Sapru, it would be hindrance and an obstance.

From the start Rajagopalachari favoured a modification of my suggestion, namely that Gandhi should not only authorize the drawing up of such a memorandum but take the responsibility of supporting it publicly. Gandhi was against this for reasons which he did not explain.

Besides seeing Gandhi daily with Rajagopalachari and Bhulabhai and also with Sapru, I had an interview with him alone just before I left Wardha. I think I understood his point of view. He did not seem optimistic about a settlement with Jinnah, particularly after the interpretation put on the Pakistan demand by *Dawn*. In Gandhi's mind the acceptance of the principle of self-determination for Muslim areas was vitally linked up with the formation of a national government for the interim period. Gandhi wanted Jinnah to associate himself (*a*) with a demand for the immediate declaration of independence to become operative immediately upon termination of war; (*b*) the formation of a real national government except for reservation in regard to defence; (*c*) the release of Congress leaders. I had serious doubts whether Jinnah would agree to any of the three demands.

So far as Gandhi was concerned he was not in favour of two completely separate sovereign and independent states, according to Jinnah's conception. In agreeing to the Rajagopalachari formula he seemed to have relied on the hope contained in the phrases 'common arrangements between the two areas in regard to defence, commerce, communications, etc.,' 'to a common central administration, however loosely knit'.

In any event, Gandhi did not seem at all inclined to commit himself to far-reaching promises in regard to the functions and authority of the interim national government without securing a definite promise of independence after the war. He felt handicapped by the fact that the members of the working committee would not be available to him for consultation before and during his talks with Jinnah.

The Gandhi–Jinnah talks in Bombay produced no positive results. But Gandhi made his own position clear. Modifying in some respects Rajagopalachari's formula for an understanding with the Muslim League, Gandhi wrote to Jinnah on September 24, 1944, offering the following terms:

'The areas should be demarcated by a commission approved by the Congress and the League. The wishes of the inhabitants of the areas demarcated should be ascertained through the votes of the adult population of the areas or through some equivalent method.

'If the vote is in favour of separation it shall be agreed that these areas shall form a separate state as soon as possible after India is free from foreign domination and can, therefore, be constituted into two sovereign independent states.

'There shall be a treaty of separation which should also provide for the efficient and satisfactory administration of foreign affairs, defence, internal communication, customs, commerce and the like, which must necessarily continue to be matters of common interest between the contracting parties.

'The treaty shall also contain terms for safe-guarding the rights of minorities in the two states.

'Immediately on the acceptance of this agreement by the Congress and the League the two shall decide upon a common course of action for the attainment of independence of India.

'The League will, however, be free to remain out of any direct action to which the Congress may resort and in which the League may not be willing to participate.'

Jinnah's response, though inadequate, did not appear to rule out a firm and friendly understanding with the Congress as one of the conditions for the creation of Pakistan. He told a London newspaper correspondent that Pakistan would resist any aggression on India by a foreign power. He visualized, in fact, 'a Monroe doctrine for the whole of Asia'.

On December 31, 1944 – after the breakdown of the Gandhi–Jinnah talks in Bombay – I wrote to Khurshed Ben who was functioning as one of Gandhi's secretaries. I said in my letter:

'I am most distressed by reports about Gandhi's intention to go on a forty days fast. It will do no good to the country from any point of view. Rather than do that, may I suggest that he should seriously apply his mind to the drawing up of the main principles of a new Constitution for India. My mind has been working rather on the following lines. Jinnah wants complete separation, while Gandhi is willing to give self-determination to Muslim majority areas. This issue should be finally settled at the general elections which will be held sooner or later in the various Provinces under the existing Constitution. Before the elections take place, a small Committee sitting with Gandhi's approval should work out the main principles of a Federal Constitution for all India. Under the 1935 Act Indian States have the right to decide in regard to which subjects, they will federate. There are three lists of subjects, the Federal List, the Provincial List and the Concurrent List, in regard to which both the Federal Government and the Provincial Governments have the right to legislate, the latter under certain conditions. In the Federal List there are over forty subjects.

'What I would suggest is that this small drafting committee, with Sapru as the Chairman should draw up a new list of subjects, a very short federal list, say of six or seven subjects which must be federal (like Defence, Foreign

Affairs, Currency, Tariffs etc.) and a concurrent list. There will be no Provincial List according to my plan, all unspecified subjects being left to the Provinces or federating units. Provinces and States will all have to federate in regard to this short list. In regard to the subjects in the concurrent list, it will be open to them to decide if they federate or keep the subjects to themselves. The advantage of this will be that some provinces where the Muslims are not in a majority will want a strong Federal Centre and can federate in regard to a large number of subjects. Muslim provinces can federate only in regard to the minimum federal list and thus enjoy the largest measure of autonomy. There will be provision in respect of the new subjects in course of time.

'So far as the States are concerned, the Drafting Committee should lay down certain minimum requirements of administration to which they should conform before being eligible for admission into the Federation. Gandhi has from time to time laid down some of these minimum. The elective principle must of course be recognized.

'I propose to discuss this with Sir Tej Bahadur Sapru tomorrow. My own suggestion is that, when the Drafting Committee has completed its preliminary task, the principles of the new Constitution on these lines should be popularized. The next general elections for the Provinces and the Centre should not be fought by the Congress on party lines. The only question should be whether the candidate accepts Federation of the type proposed by the Committee (and later approved by Gandhi and a few other leaders) or prefers Pakistan of Jinnah's conception. Candidates should be set up for every constituency including Muslims. The question must be taken up whether Muslims want Federation of this type or Jinnah's Pakistan. All this work needs a great deal of planning and organization and Gandhi should think on those lines and not contemplate a fast.

'I want you to place this letter before him.'

Sapru's comments on Gandhi's attitude at this time are of interest. He wrote to Sir B. N. Rau:

'I had two long interviews with Mahatma Gandhi. He showed me his letter to the Viceroy and discussed the whole situation with me at length. I told him that it was hopeless to establish a national government responsible to the Legislature during the war and that therefore he might accept my formula of a national government consisting of representatives of all parties, who would not be liable to be dismissed by the Legislature during the interim period but would technically be responsible to the Crown: which meant that the power of Parliament and the Secretary of State would continue during the interim period. He entertained this proposal at first as a possible alternative to his formula; but later in the evening he thought that it would not meet his demand by mentioning it as a possible alternative. He was prepared to agree to the principle of self-determination on democratic grounds; but I do not think he would be prepared to go further than the formula of Rajagopalachari.

'He seemed to me to be in dead earnest about a settlement. As you are no doubt aware, it has provoked a great controversy. The Hindu Sabha people and the Sikhs are up in arms. Ultimately the whole matter resolved itself into two questions: (1) was there going to be one Centre or would there be two Centres? Assuming that Jinnah insisted on two Centres, what was going to be the nexus between them? (2) Whether the two Centres would be combined by an Act of Parliament or by a treaty? If by a treaty what would be the means adopted for implementing that treaty? If machinery was set up for implementing it, that machinery must inevitably take the shape of a government. So far as Gandhi's desire to bring about a settlement was concerned, I was in complete sympathy with him and I also realized that without winning over the minorities we could make no advance.'

In 1946, after the visit of the British cabinet mission to India, and its unqualified rejection of Pakistan as impracticable on 'weighty administrative, economic, and military considerations', Jinnah appeared to be of two minds over the demand for a separate Pakistan. In September of that year, after the completion of the elections to the constituent assembly, he raised a number of issues with Sir B. N. Rau, its constitutional adviser, which implied that on an interpretation of the cabinet mission's plan acceptable to him, he might agree to the participation of the League's representatives in the assembly.

Not, in fact, until February 1947, when Attlee made his statement in the house of commons announcing the decision of the British government to hand over power to Indian leaders, not later than June 1948, but on the basis of partition, was the issue lifted out of uncertainty. Nehru, welcomed it as a 'wise and courageous decision', made one final effort to secure the participation of the Muslim League. He declared:

'The moment British rule goes, the responsibility for the governance of India must inevitably rest on her people and their representatives alone. They will have to shoulder that responsibility. Why then should we not accept this responsibility now and work together to find integrated solutions of our problems? No external authority is going to help or hinder us in future.'

The rapidity of the subsequent developments, however, left no time for calm deliberation. The transfer of power was hastened, to occur on August 15, 1947. Unfortunately, in those fateful weeks the need for a treaty between India and Pakistan before the final transfer of power was overlooked – a point conceded by the League's resolution of 1940 and repeated later in 1944 in a different form but firmly by Gandhi. The developments of the last two decades might possibly have been less tragic had some heed been paid to the requirements of a transitional stage before final separation, as suggested by the Muslim League and the scheme had been scrutinized by a team of constitutional experts.

1937–47 IN RETROSPECT: A CIVIL SERVANT'S VIEW

by C. S. VENKATACHAR*

Many years before, when Congress started on the road to mass rebellion under Gandhi's leadership, the Indian Muslims *were not* a nation in the modern sense of the term. But a quarter of a century later, they were on the way to *becoming* one. Had Congress leaders been wiser they need not have become one.

Amaury de Riencourt, *The Soul of India* (1960), p. 343.

There are and there will be differing versions of the causes which led to the partition of India in 1947. This paper sets out some personal impressions of the events of the decade 1937–47. Congress leaders were prisoners of their opinion; the British were hamstrung by their past; the Muslim League gambled on a war of nerves. The three participants had few choices to make; fewer cards to deal.

The author served in the Indian Civil Service from 1922 to 1961. During the years 1933 to 1937 he served as a district officer in the United Provinces and at the headquarters of the provincial government at Lucknow. For the greater part of the period 1941 to 1946, he was commissioner of Allahabad division at Allahabad, Nehru's home town. At the time of partition he was the prime minister of the princely state of Jodhpur.

THE CONGRESS

The year 1937 opened with Congress in a jubilant mood for good reasons. In the preceeding five years, Congress had been in the political wilderness, for the policy of Hoare and Willingdon had been to put down the Congress in the style of Curzon. But the elections had revealed the party's strength in the Hindu majority provinces and Congress had convincingly demonstrated that it held the countryside. In Madras, the Justice party had been routed. In the United Provinces, the party of land-owners, taluqdars, and pro-government loyalists, had been steam-rollered by an unexpected Congress majority.

This jubilation expressed itself in two ways, the significance of which began soon to unfold. Congress victory in the polls had sketched in outline the extent of its nuclear power, though at that time it was not apparent that it would be the maximum extent. Having flattened out the opposition parties, Congress began to reveal its hegemonial character and Jinnah was soon to characterize Congress as the Fascist Grand Council. Nehru impetuously said that there were only two parties, Congress and the British. Jinnah reminded him there was a third, the League.

* Distinguished Indian Civil Servant. Since independence has been secretary to the Ministry of States, secretary to the president of India, High Commissioner in Canada, etc.

No one contemplated the possibility of the *raj* abdicating power in a hurry. Two British writers, Taya and Maurice Zinkin, have recently recorded that Lord Irwin had expressed the view round about 1930 that in twenty-five years time India would willingly become a full member of the Commonwealth, and that Nehru had told a senior Commonwealth diplomat that he did not expect independence before 1970. Before the outbreak of Hitler's war in 1939, Linlithgow was telling Zetland: 'No one can, of course, say what in some remote period of time or in the event of international convulsions of a particular character may be the ultimate relations of India and Great Britain but that there should be any general impression that public opinion at home or His Majesty's Government seriously contemplated evacuation in any measurable period of time seems to be astonishing.' Everybody had the assured feeling that the British were not going away. Congress knew that it had not the strength to displace the British; it had plenty of time to harry them to get out of India. Naturally, Nehru looked ahead to a period of struggle, to 'the basic Congress policy of fighting the new constitution and ending it, to try to prevent the federation from materializing, to stultify the constitution and prepare the ground for the constituent assembly and independence . . . to strengthen the masses and wherever possible, in the narrow sphere of the constitution, to give some relief to them'.

The strength of the British *raj* was in the central government. Towards the end of the nineteenth century, the machinery of the central government had attained a blissful state of 'aloofness, conscious rectitude, confidence in itself but it functioned *in vacuo*'*;* it had acquired a mind above individual minds, adjusting itself and correcting 'particularist antinomies in a serene and elevated solitude'. The British knew by years of experience of governing India that the unity of India, which they had created, rested in this central government, and that unity could not be maintained by an irresponsible central government presiding over democratically governed provinces, the outward pull would be irresistible. They were anxious to establish limited federation under the Government of India Act without delay. In this they were cheated by Hitler in Europe. Time certainly was not on the side of Britain's empire.

The most dangerous of the centrifugal forces was that of Muslim separatism, which was not merely religious in the western sense of the word, but cultural. That powerful springs of separatism lay in the United Provinces, was not apparent either to the administration or to the Congress. The British thought that they had allayed Muslim apprehensions with the communal award and the constitutional safeguards. Where was the cause for any significant movement for Muslim separatism? British officials were very provincial in their affections and in their emotional involvements with their India and Indians. Congress Hindus had somehow established their pretensions to be an all-India force, but Muslim strength lay in its provincial individuality. A British civilian dignitary who was secretary to the governor of the U.P., in 1937 was asking 'What has that fellow Jinnah got to do with U.P. Muslims: who is he in the U.P. any way?'

Congress in office initiated three moves which brought to the surface the latent forces of Muslim separatism. The first has acquired much prominence, since the publication of Maulana Abul Kalam Azad's memoirs in which he details the negotiation with the Muslim League in the formation of the ministry in the U.P. Following Maulana's narrative, the argument is that the genesis of Pakistan lies in the failure of Congress to form a coalition with the Muslim League. Congress in the U.P. was undoubtedly tactless in not taking two Leaguers into the ministry, but its action is understandable and not altogether unjustifiable. One has to follow Nehru's line of thinking in 1937. He had had no understanding with Jinnah on an all-India basis for a coalition with the League. In principle there was no case for such a coalition after the poor showing of the League and the resounding victory of the Congress in the provincial general elections. The formation of ministries was of secondary importance to Nehru. To him the ministries, being the creation of Congress, could be ended at any time. His attention was concentrated on the coming struggle with the British to wrest power at the centre. In this struggle the League Muslims were questionable allies, as they did not share Congress ideology; they were only interested in communal gains.

This was the reasoning part of Nehru. In action he was led by his friend Rafi Ahmed Kidwai, a curious influence in U.P. politics till 1947 and thereafter as Nehru's confidant for several years at the centre. Kidwai could not get elected in the general election from any Muslim constituency but managed to slip through the University Graduates constituency and Nehru would not exclude his nationalist Muslim friend from the U.P. ministry. Nehru's attachment to his friend led by winding and devious steps to the creation of Pakistan, as later his friendship with Sheikh Abdullah led to the Kashmir imbroglio and wars with Pakistan.

Nehru or the Congress could have retrieved the situation. The Muslims of the U.P. had much personal affection for Nehru, whom they considered their friend, an idealist in politics who had been caught in the snare of communalist Hindus. Even today Nehru is entitled to the benefit of the doubt on the ministry question. Where he went wrong was in his failure to realize the extent to which the faith and confidence of the Muslims in the majority party had been shattered. They argued that if this was the attitude of Congress in the limited field of provincial autonomy, how would Muslims fare in the all-vital field of the central government?

The Ministry episode was bad enough. The programme of Muslim mass contact was singularly foolish. Nehru launched this scheme in the U.P. to establish direct contact with the Muslim masses without the mediation of nationalist Muslim organizations. There was opposition to this within the Congress itself. Muslims raised the cry of 'Islam in danger'; they justifiably inferred that Congress was out to wipe them out. Seized with a fear complex Muslims gave mass support to the Muslim League, which in Nehru's opinion was merely a reactionary body for safeguarding the vested interests of the Muslim upper classes and loyalists.

The third move – now only clearly understood in retrospect – was the attack, emanating deep from the Gangetic earth, on Muslim culture. Taking a leaf out of the Congress style of propaganda against British rule, the Muslim League started a virulent campaign of villification against Congress, deliberately distorting facts and producing 'atrocity' reports – the Pirpur report in the U.P., the Sharif report in Bihar and propagandist literature by Muslim intellectuals like Sir Shafaat Ahmad Khan of Allahabad University. Even Fazlul Haq, chief minister of Bengal joined in the chorus. A political dust storm as violent and raging as the dust storms in the Gangetic plain blew over the province. British officials looked upon it with amusement as a familiar recurrent feature of Hindu–Muslim antagonism. The British governor found nothing in the situation to warrant the exercise of his special powers. The upper strata of the Hindus in the cities, who shared with the Muslims the composite Hindu–Muslim culture, had no inkling of the rise of Hindi extremism as an adjunct to politics, so they could not understand what was annoying their Muslim friends.

What had happened was that the countryside had thrown up, as a result of the elections, a distinct type of Hindu political worker. The type, pretty familiar in independent India, was a newcomer in 1937. The type hitherto familiar to the officials was an English-educated middle-class person of a higher caste. The emergent type belonged in greater numbers to the non-English-speaking middle and lower castes, rooted in backward rural society, largely untouched or only partially touched by urban influence, faithful to the traditional Hindu way of life, and attached to 'sanskritization' as opposed to 'westernization'. We are able to see this type in proper perspective, thanks to recent studies by American scholars. This type disliked the westernized English-speaking Indian and had long memories of Muslim tyranny. It had no use for English and Urdu. The Congress government conceded to Hindi equal status with Urdu. The Hindi protagonists threw out hundreds of words derived from Persian and Arabic. Hindi zealots found enthusiastic supporters for their campaign among the Hindu officers of the government.

Muslim intellectuals and the intelligentsia read the danger signals. They remembered that in the last quarter of the nineteenth century a movement had been initiated in Benares, with large popular support, for the replacement of the Urdu language and Persian script with Hindi and Devanagari script. This had given a painful shock to Sir Syed Ahmad Khan who told the commissioner of Benares: 'Now I am convniced that the two communities will not be able to co-operate sincerely in any matter. It is only the beginning. In future I envisage mutual opposition and conflict increasing day by day on account of those who are called educated people. He who lives will see.'

Language rouses deep emotions in a human being. It touches him at several points. The mother tongue is a precious cultural heritage, not just a vehicle of communication. The economic well-being of an individual is dependent on the language he can command. Language again is the medium of approach to his God. Muslim talent and ability had gone into government service. Their economic life was linked with their assured position in administration. Muslims were genuinely alarmed at the sinister implications of Hindi extremism. They felt that their very political future was at stake. They feared that Hindi would be imposed on them.[1] As this conviction

[1] Geoffrey Tyson in *Nehru: Years of Power* (1966) quotes Liaqat Ali as saying that the Muslims in U.P. feated that Hindi would be imposed on them; that was one of the factors in the creation of Pakistan.

The following letter by Tahir Siddiqui, New Delhi, appeared in *The Hindu* of Madras:

rapidly gained ground over Muslim minds, it became one of the prime factors in the creation of Pakistan.

The Muslim voice had by now become shrill, harsh, and strident. Jinnah as a superb tactician, gave a political meaning to the outcry of the U.P. Muslims, in his speech at Lucknow on October 15, 1937: 'The majority community have already showed their hand that Hindustan is for the Hindus.' He used such expressions as 'class bitterness' and 'communal war', foreign to this one-time ambassador of Hindu–Muslim unity. He was gaining the support of the Muslim intelligentsia but no one thought that Hindu–Muslim relations had entered the rapids leading to partition. Partition was still in the womb of time.

Congress leaders were worried. More percipient than Nehru, Gandhi realized the coming danger. He promptly wrote to Jinnah: 'As I read it the whole of your speech is a declaration of war.'

Came the war in Europe in 1939. From 1939 to the failure of the Cripps mission in 1942, Congress politics swayed aimlessly between the alternating phases of Nehrunian and Gandhian moods. Nehru's mood was as usual complex. He had recovered from the intense mental depression reflected in his autobiography and the feeling of loneliness which had led Lord Lothian into thinking that Nehru would withdraw to a life of contemplative solitude. Nehru regained his usual bounce during his visit to Europe in 1938, mentally refreshed by his contact with the British left-wing and by his survey of world forces from Chiang-kai Shek's China to the Spanish republicans at Barcelona. The imperialist war predicted by the Marxists was after all coming – that too very soon. He hated with good reason the viceregal government which had forfeited the moral allegiance of Indians, including the Muslims, who were worried about their own future and cared not a brass-farthing for Britain's future. The Indian government was aware of this. It correctly judged that its war efforts would be supported for reasons of self-interest and not out of any sense of moral duty.

With the war situation in mind, Nehru revised his idea of fighting for power at the centre on the political calculation of 1937–9. There was at that time a feeling among Congressmen that Britain would withdraw her troops from India and would install Congress in power to ensure the loyalty of the Indian army. That apart, Nehru had remarked to an English friend, Edward Thompson, that Britain's cause was just. We now know that he had given Desmond Young, editor of *The Pioneer*, reasonable and moderate terms on which he and the Congress would have been prepared to co-operate with the British government.[1]

'The convocation address of Mr. C. S. Venkatachar at the Madras Institute of Technology on March 15, '67 is an interesting pointer to the students of history. It is evident from his address that had there been no Hindi extremism in U.P., India's unity might not have suffered the tragedy of partition.

'During my visit to Pakistan in November-December, 1966, several leaders of that country including Mr. Firoze Khan Noon, Mr. Mumtaz Daulatana and Chaudhary Khaliquzzaman did not agree with me that a United India would have been a better place to live in for all the communities in the country. All of them talked of Hindi and the threat faced by the Muslim culture in India before 1947. The recent debacle of the Congress in Madras seems to reinforce their point.'

[1] Desmond Young, *Try Anything Twice* (1963), pp. 244–7.

Why did Nehru throw off the substance of power in the provinces, abandon the considerable nuisance value the Congress possessed by being in office in the abnormal situations of war-time, and play directly into the hands of Jinnah? It would be interesting to probe into this question, for which no material is yet available.

Nehru in the plenitude of power, as the undisputed ruler of India showed remarkable self-control and adroitness in managing men and events. As a nationalist leader, his temperamental instability was often his liability. Linlithgow was stupid, but why should Nehru have played into his hands by an act of silliness? This was one of the occasions on which Congress should have shown patience, watched the European horizon, waited upon events, pocketed its pride. Congress in office should have maintained armed neutrality with government. Jinnah was in no position to edge the Congress out of power in the provinces. The British would not lightly have dismissed the provincial Congress governments. If they had, Congress would have strengthened its position.

Instead, Congress started a futile rancorous political dialogue with the viceroy's government, which in its wisdom thought Congress co-operation not essential in the prosecution of war. This dialogue, reinforced with the subtleties of Rajagopalachari, for entering the central government, was fruitless, as Jinnah had set-up a road-block by committing the League to the objective of Pakistan, and on account of the anti-Congress attitude of Linlithgow's government. Congress tactically weakened itself in severing the link with government. What is perhaps less appreciated, is that the public, realistically conscious of the rapidly changing economic situation under war-time conditions, moved away from the impracticalities of the Congress leaders. War brought about wider opportunities for employment in civil administration. Industrial development was stimulated, businessmen made money in the war-economy. Congress which was pressing for the rapid Indianization of the defence services, now began to urge the people not to enlist in a war to which it had refused co-operation. The public, wiser than the Congress, did not listen to it. Whereas there were 400 Indians with the King's commission at the beginning of the war, there were 8,000 at the end, representing about twenty per cent of the total number of Indian army officers. The war-time experience also lessened the preponderance of the so-called martial races. In Nehru's India one daily listened to his favourite word: dynamism. It is surprising that he became insensitive to dynamism in a war-wracked world in which the political and military situation was changing from hour to hour.

There is truth in the observation that the man of insight to lay bare Gandhi's soul has not yet arisen. Gandhi had previously talked of a 'Himalayan blunder' over some minor lapses of a great national leader. By rejecting Cripps's offer he was committing a real 'Himalayan blunder' by making the partition of India inevitable. In fighting the British in August 1942, he was fighting the Muslims by proxy. That was the firm conclusion the Muslims drew. By displacing the British, Congress would overwhelm the Muslims. Henceforth there was no turning away from the Pakistan idea and Jinnah's leadership.

If the consequences of Gandhism irrevocably led to partition, how is it that Nehru did not see his own emerging position as the successor to the *raj?* Already the British government had taken due note of his position and three years later, Mountbatten was to lay on a red-carpet treatment for Nehru at Singapore, as the future prime minister or governor-general of India. In making a final appeal to Nehru to save his plan, Cripps wrote to Nehru: 'Leadership – the sort of leadership you have – can alone accomplish the result.' Political influence and initiative – in both of which the British had become weak – was there for Nehru to pick up; formal possession ofpower was just a matter of time. Nehru hesitated and shied away from seizing the initiative which was his.

Gandhi's anarchism with his distrust of the state and modern civilization 'would have ended not merely in the dissolution of British power but in the dissolution of the Indian State as well and eventually in chaos'. Nehru and the western-educated elites had prevented this from happening by their adherence to an all-India state on the western pattern. His life-long struggle against the British, a deep distrust of Britain's motives, and an intense dislike of the viceregal government, had blunted Nehru's perspectives into the future. That may be one reason why he did not respond to Cripps's appeal. Nehru's failure on this crucial occasion was a contributory cause of the partition of India.

Congress again went into the wilderness for another three years. From June 1945, whatever the British government did was doomed to failure, except walking out of India. However much Congress strained to succeed to an undivided British *raj*, it was equally doomed to failure, for it simply had not the strength to overwhelm the Muslim majority areas, except by wading through a bloody civil war in order to impose unity by its own strength. The political deadlock of 1939, for which Linlithgow and Congress had worked from opposite ends, had now assumed a nightmarish character. It did not appear so to Congress. Nationalist movements develop a peculiar psychology when subjected to repression. With freedom in the air, Congress felt stronger than it was in August 1942. Congress developed a moral certitude that by right it should succeed to an undivided *raj*. This feeling was shared by most Hindus.

What ideas shaped Congress thinking from the Simla conference to the Mountbatten plan? During this period, Gandhi and Nehru were very articulate, so we have considerable documentation. But it would be profitable to bring into focus the position of Sardar Patel whose role is hidden and may never be known in full. He was a man of few words, never articulate. He held in his hands all the levers of the party machinery. He was anti-Muslim. He had his own estimate of Jinnah's strength which, pitted against the Congress, appeared to him weak. Patel thought there was no point in paying a high price to a weak opponent. He communicated to the party a realistic estimate of the political situation. The British were no longer pretending: for good reasons of their own, they were going. The I.N.A. trials demonstrated that army officers were a patriotic element. Patel intervened in the naval mutiny at Bombay and put the left-wingers in their place. He watched with satisfaction the militant mood of the Hindus, in the Congress as well as in such organizations outside the Congress as the Hindu Mahasabha and the R.S.S. He has nothing but contempt for the nationalist Muslims of Azad, reluctantly remitting them money, while being sarcastic about their dubious loyalty. K. M. Munshi's campaign for *Akhand Hindustan*, in answer to Jinnah's Pakistan, had Patel's tacit support. Rajendra Prasad who shared Patel's conservative outlook in the top hierarchy of Congress, published *India Divided*, a skilful argument of the case against Pakistan.

Patel did not, however, rouse fanaticism among the Hindus. The Hindu is not a fanatic in the general sense of the word. Nehru and the westernized elites were welcome to talk in the language of secularism for the benefit of the western world. The traditionalist Hindu better understood Sardar's simple reasoning. The Hindus had lived for seven centuries as second class citizens under the Muslims to whom the Hindus were only *dhimmis* (tolerated unbelievers). Now the wheel had come round. Why should not the Muslims live with the Hindus as equal citizens in a democratic India? All this talk of partition was nonsense. Jinnah had built up his leadership on a bluff, surreptiously supported by the British. Once the British handed over power to Congress whose innate strength they were now recognizing, Jinnah could be dealt with suitably. Patel knew that Gandhi was against partition; this knowledge helped him to tune up the party and its rank and file to any required pitch.

Azad's memoirs have to be read between the lines. Azad sensed the growth of Hindu right-wing forces and its sinister consequences. He took two steps. He gave up his presidentship of the Congress and ensured that Nehru, not Patel, succeeded him. In a partitioned India, he feared the fate of forty million Muslims. He made a last desperate attempt to save them by his plan, which the cabinet mission took over, with Pakistan hidden inside it to make it palatable to Jinnah. His attempt was doomed to failure. Congress wanted a strong centre; Jinnah, no centre worth the name. Maulana sorrowfully blamed his dear friend. But Nehru's outburst was a calculated indiscretion; he was determined to shape to his liking the India over which he could exercise effective control.[1]

Patel was a realist. He came from a peasant stock – the pattidars of Charottarin Gujarat – and he had the peasant's uncanny shrewdness, tenacity of purpose, and cunning. He had a sense of timing. He honestly believed that Jinnah had not the quality in him to lead a mass movement nor the nerve to send people to destruction. But when Jinnah did produce the joker from the pack, by calling out the Muslim mob and commencing civil war, Patel took due notice. And when the Leaguers joined the central government in October 1946 and split the government into two hostile factions, he made up his mind that partition was inevitable, if the British were to be got out. He accepted early in 1947 V. P. Menon's formula of two dominions for demission of power by Britain. Behind the scenes he arranged the steps towards partition – the details of which may never be known.

It is tempting to see one of the 'ifs' of Indian history in March 1946. Congress could have picked up the Rajagopalachari formula and told the three wise men from Britain: 'we agree to separate; let us consider if after

[1] [Editors' note: cf. this estimate with B. R. Nanda, above, pp. 178–82.]

separation we can find some common ground to maintain our common integrity.' Maybe some kind of confederation would have emerged. Maybe the Muslims would have responded to a frank gesture by Congress. Maybe Jinnah would have been accommodating. The crucial province of Punjab was not then in his bag. Here was a possible slender last chance for sanity. On the other hand, it must be remembered that the father-image of Gandhi had a strangulating hold on Nehru, Patel and the party. Nehru must have felt himself inhibited in making any moves of constructive leadership. It took another year for Nehru and Patel to push aside Gandhi; it was too late then.

Congress chose to sit pretty, throwing the onus on the cabinet mission to find a way out. Congress argued that since the British were in favour of democracy and shared the Congress ideal of unity for the sub-continent, it was Britain's business to bring round Jinnah to give effect to the commonly shared desires. Secondly, Congress leaders, in spite of their anti-British sentiments, had respect for British cleverness in state-craft. Leave it to the British to find a way out. In 1949, I put it to a Congressman of U.P. that it seemed impracticable for a monarchical Commonwealth to admit republican India as a member. He said: 'Don't worry. The British are clever – they will find a formula.' Thirdly, the two protagonists could always seem to disagree; each party was free to take up irreconcilable positions. At all costs they must be able to save their faces and be able to say to their followers that they had agreed to nothing on their own accord. Pethick-Lawrence put the position neatly to Attlee: 'No one seems to expect us to succeed in getting the parties to agree among themselves. Most Indians seem to assume that it will be the English who will settle the matter for them and then no doubt they will continue to make Aunt Sally of us – our latest effort in this Alice in Wonderland croquet party.'

Till the very end partition was made to appear a British performance, never an Indian responsibility. Mountbatten had to announce the decision to partition India. Congress was seen with reluctance and a heavy heart to accept partition. Jinnah merely nodded his assent with difficulty. Mountbatten had to perform the surgical operation. Radcliffe had to draw the boundary between the two states on a topo-sheet. The Hindus, Muslims and Sikhs reserved to themselves the right to contribute to the blood bath.

Fourthly, Congress never assessed the significance of the 1937 election, confirmed in 1946, which etched the maximum extent of Congress power in the sub-continent. Under more normal conditions Congress and League leaders would have calmly examined the situation. Congress was fantastically unreal in its estimate that it had the strength to envelop the Muslim majority areas. Pakistan had to come because Congress failed and Jinnah triumphed. In the tug-of-war between Congress and Jinnah, the Indian rope broke.

THE BRITISH

Unlike Congress, which had it in its power to retrieve the situation and stop the progress down the inclined plane towards partition at least on three occasions – certainly in 1939 and 1942, possibly in 1946 – the British had their chance, as an imperial power, only from 1935 to the fall of the Chamberlain government in 1940. By 1942, the British government seemed to have made up its mind to give up India after the war. This fact was gloomily disclosed to the King by Churchill at one of their Tuesday luncheons in July 1942.[1] Thereafter the British could not influence the course of events which rapidly passed out of their control.

For over a century the aristocratic ruling class of Britain had given consistency to imperial rule. Baldwin, Chamberlain, Hoare, and Zetland, did not realize in 1935 that the purpose of this class was soon to be exhausted. They were far from thinking that the Indian empire was a wasting asset; certainly the time had not come to dispose of it. The credo of the imperialist was simple, by no means wrong. In the East, either you govern or you go. Imperialism was a highly competitive business, a function of power. The imperialist had no faith in the Acts of 1919 and 1935. He honestly did not understand the sentiments of Indian or Asian nationalism; he was not even aware that it existed. Only Attlee was to declare in 1937 that a Labour government would always prefer to err in being too soon rather than too late in the granting of self-government to India. Attlee was to remember this in 1947.

Curzon had said, 'in Britain there are no two parties about India'. Perhaps so; but a fatal flaw in the Act of 1935 was that it embodied an 'odd melange of the many once-good ideas' due to factious fights within the Conservative party, with the result that concessions were made to the irrelevancies of Churchill's onslaught on the India Bill. As it happened, the British started the limited advance in reforms against time – the time being regulated not by Britain, but by Hitler in Europe. The Conservative government could have shown imagination in sending over a viceroy with imagination, human and competent in gaining a friendly understanding of the mind of the recalcitrant Indian political leaders. They sent as viceroy a land-owning aristocrat who believed the abiding purpose of his class in ruling India would endure for as long a time as he could foresee. We find him writing to Zetland, early in 1940, before Chamberlain's government fell; 'It is not part of our policy, I take it, to expedite in India constitutional changes for their own sake, or gratuitously hurrying the handing over of controls to Indian hands at any pace faster than we regard as best calculated on a long view to hold India to the Empire.'

Linlithgow loved the pomp and power of his office. Nehru met him on several occasions before 1940; and he has left a good description of the viceroy in the *Discovery of India*.[2] Linlithgow reminded some Indians of a viceroy, in one of Kipling's stories, who brought out with him a turbulent private secretary, a hard man with a soft manner and a morbid passion for work. 'No wise man has a policy', said the viceroy in the story, 'A policy is the blackmail levied on the fool by the unforeseen. I am not the former and and I do not believe in the latter.' The 'Linlithwaite' rule of seven and half years was a barren one, a period of political and moral bankruptcy, from the consequences of which rescue came to the British people, at the end of the

[1] J. Wheeler-Bennett, *King George VI*, pp. 702–3.
[2] See 1st ed., 1946, p. 528.

war, through their wise instinct, 'dimly, inarticulately, unconsciously', telling them that choice lay between retaining the empire by force and relinquishing it on grounds of moral conscience.

After installing the provincial ministries in office, the viceroy ploddingly worked hard to lure the princes into federation. The princes needed to be charmed by a charmer like Mountbatten, who could have won them over. Alternatively, they could have been coaxed, even mildly coerced. In true oriental fashion, viceregal emissaries were sent to the courts of Indian princes. Each ruler clung to his 'dynastic sovereignty' – a quasi-proprietary right – resting on the territory of his state. He was afraid of his territory being absorbed in the federal structure. Like every one else in India, he too felt that the British were not going from India. The princes hesitated, delayed, procrastinated, bargained for impossible terms, and finally denounced the terms offered to them.

Failure to set up a federation by 1939 and the outbreak of world war underlined the importance of having a viceroy who would maintain a friendly dialogue with the leaders of the Congress and the League, and keep open channels of communication with them in the midst of the clashes and conflicts of the turbulent political currents.

Linlithgow presided over a war-time government which no one believed was strong enough to do what it pleased. He committed India to 'war with Hitler with a fiat, as Wellesley had once committed Bengal against Napoleon'. It is said of Wellesley that he regarded the ending of the Company's quarrel with Tipu's Mysore, once and for all, as his contribution to Bonaparte's defeat. Likewise, Linlithgow thought that a resolute quarrel with Congress was his contribution to the defeat of Hitler. He and his anti-Congress I.C.S. advisers were determined that there should be no compromise with Congress, no return of Congress inside government for the duration of the war. From this position begins the rapid decline of Britain's ability to control and direct the course of events leading to partition. As long as the war lasted the British could sit tight on the Indian lid; after that, one should expect a blow-up. Linlithgow departed from India, leaving the political situation in a complete deadlock, but with the assured conviction that the British held the initiative and could break it at their will.

Wavell seems to have given thought to the deadlock situation on becoming viceroy. As an act of great clemency he proposed the release of Gandhi and Nehru and to invite them to join his executive council. This made the King angry; London would not look at it. The British cabinet was, however, more responsive at the end of war in Europe. Wavell was instructed to go ahead with the idea of having Congress and League leaders in his council. Wavell held throughout his tenure to a single idea. The starting point should be to bring the leaders of both parties into the central government; then he would proceed to work out with their co-operation the constitutional problem of independence. Under normal conditions, it was a sensible, common-sense approach. Wavell was unable to grasp the abnormalities of Jinnah. Jinnah would not enter into a central government if he was denied his claim to be the leader of the ninety million Muslims. That claim – however untenable or incongruous it may seem – was the very prop of his demand for Pakistan, and was yet to be conceded. He broke up the Simla conference; any concession by him at that time would have weakened his position.

The Labour government in London did the obvious thing. It decided to gauge the strength of the two protagonists in a general election. The election was fought, not on the issue of independence, but on that of a united or divided India. The result of the election polarized the situation. The Muslim majority areas stood behind Jinnah. The British government drew the right conclusion; there were only two parties to deal with.

From March 1946 Attlee's government assumed full charge of the negotiations in India. According to one commentator, Wavell was holding the dirty end of the stick in India. He was 'ordered' by Attlee to instal Nehru in office in September 1946, ignoring Jinnah's attitude of non-participation, which only lasted for a few weeks. Wavell is reported to have remarked that he felt like a 'poor relation' when he was present at the conference in London in December 1946. He complained in writing to the king that His Majesty's ministers failed to lay down any definite policy for guidance. Attlee soon replaced him by Mountbatten.

There was little the viceroy could have done. The once powerful viceregal government had neither the initiative nor the influence to jolt political thinking to any fresh line of thought. It had no fresh cards to deal. The soldier-viceroy was a fish out of water in presiding over a civilian central government. Wavell's failure lay in his inability to mobilize the resourceful talent in his government in support of the efforts of the cabinet mission. He failed, at least, in three obvious responsibilities. On one occasion, Nehru complained to Whitehall that Wavell was a weak man, though honest and sincere, and that he was principally advised by two 'English Mullahs'. This was unfair. Wavell was a man of independent judgment, of 'valiant truth', of high moral courage. It never occurred to him to draw upon the experience of his very knowledgeable reforms commissioner. At any time for the asking V. P. Menon would have told him that the crux of the problem of setting up two independent governments in the sub-continent was the establishment of two central authorities backed up by the power of their own armies. In Indian conditions, only the authority of a strong central government can hold in check the centrifugal forces and prevent the parts from falling apart.

When Menon drew up his plan for the demission of power to two central governments on dominion status basis, which became the Mountbatten plan of June 1947, he was not producing a rabbit out of his hat – performing a magician's trick! Nor did he have to take, as Leonard Mosley has it, a stiff peg of whisky and four aspirins, 'to draw up a plan which was to change the face of India and the world'. The outlines of the plan, sketchy perhaps, were there in the viceroy's reforms office, one of the many exercises of a versatile civil service. It had only to be brought out, and worked upon in the light of the thinking at any particular time. Menon stood in the long line of British administrators representing the departmental wisdom and philosophy of the home and reforms office. The proof of the soundness of that wisdom was demonstrated soon after partition. The two governments after a very bad shake, felt strong enough to commit their forces in the Kashmir war; the Indian army marched into Hyderabad. The viceroy should have maintained close consultation with V. P. Menon and kept in his sleeve *a* Menon plan. V. P. Menon and Sir B. N. Rau were resourceful, very knowledgeable in constitutional problems, versatile in finding solutions to intricate problems, precise in drafting – they both possessed many admirable talents which were fully utilized by independent India. Rau was one of the very few Hindus for whom Jinnah had high personal regard.

Next, Wavell should have kept in readiness a detailed plan for the division of the Indian army. He should have swallowed his own emotions as a great soldier and asked his commander-in-chief to do the same. There is a reference by Mosley to a paper by General Tuker on the division of the army. The text of the paper is not available but it is suggestive of forward thinking on the part of a high ranking military officer.[1] Wavell may easily have consulted Sir C. M. Trivedi, who was Wavell's secretary in the war department, and sought his assistance to draw up a plan for the division of the army. At one time, Wavell wished to take Trivedi as his private secretary but Whitehall prevailed upon him to take Sir Evan Jenkins. Wavell failed to make use of the talents of another Indian official in whom he had shown confidence.

In March 1946, the retiring governor of the Punjab, Sir Bertrand Glancy – an antediluvian I.C.S. of the old Punjab school who had spent a lifetime in 'humbugging' the princes – handed over the provincial ministry to a Muslim rump headed by Khizr Hyat Khan Tiwana, condemning the majority Muslims, the Leaguers, into opposition. This grave mistake resulted in the terrific explosion in the Punjab a year later. Wavell showed supineness in not pulling up the governor who should have been advised to take over the administration as a temporary measure under section 93 of the Government of India Act, and pass on the responsibility for bringing in a ministerial government of the majority party of the Muslims, to his more knowledgeable, able successor, Sir Evan Jenkins who at that time occupied the key post of private secretary to the viceroy.

Wavell's government had ceased to think and was suffering from a creeping paralysis of thought. It is strange that at the seat of viceregal authority there should have been the muddled thinking of handing over power to the provinces – the source of which is not fully known. In the circumstances of 1946–7, no plan for demission of power would have worked which left the centre weak and divided, in pursuit of fictional unity on sentimental grounds. India would have been handed over to prolonged civil war and anarchy. Azad's plan, about which he is rapturous in his memoirs, was deceptive. It would not have brought about a centre, as functional parts were missing. There would have been warring provinces with autonomy to the communities to kill one another. A sad commentary on the British thinking of those days is the eagerness shown for dissolving the Indian state. Wavell's own plan – operation Ebb-Tide – a scheme for the evacuation of India by stages as a military operation, was termed by Attlee as 'defeatist' and by a later commentator as 'dangerous rubbish'. Attlee's declaration of February 20, 1947, contained the ambiguous phraseology that the powers of the central government would be handed over, on the due date, 'whether as a whole to some form of central government for British India or in some areas to the existing

[1] [Editors' note: see Wainwright, above, pp. 142–7.]

Provincial governments . . .' Though the texts of Mountbatten's different plans which he sent to Attlee are not available, the impression gathered from V. P. Menon's narrative is, that Mountbatten originally envisaged handing over power initially to the provinces, thinking possibly that it was in conformity with the British government's intentions of handing over power to provinces themselves.

Wavell stood on the side-lines during the cabinet mission's futile attempts to reconcile the irreconcilable. There was no one to tell the mission that it was too late in the day to reconvert the Muslims to accept the semblance of a united India even in a minimal form. The Labour government had enormous goodwill but it lacked Indian expertise. The mission took a false step in producing its own plan; it was in no position to enforce it. The measure of its failure lies in the tragic irony of its declaration; 'We are unable to advise the British government that the power which at present resides in British hands should be handed over to two entirely separate sovereign states.' The plan was unworkable; highly ingenious; as one writer puts it, 'a sort of a lawyer's brief for a test case in a legal text book'.

Ultimately, it was left to Jinnah to break the deadlock by bringing the joker out of his pack. This jolted Wavell into some clear thinking. Though Wavell was unable to assist the cabinet mission in India, he imparted some dynamism to the thinking of the government in London. He showed a realistic appreciation of the rundown condition of the Indian administration whose authority on the ground lay very thin. In February 1947, Cripps told the house of commons that the main reason for the early transfer of power was the impracticability on the one hand of recruiting new British officers and on the other hand of retaining the undivided loyalty of the Indian officers. Wavell showed foresight in recommending March 31, 1948 as the date for the final transfer of power.

What could the Labour government have done, anxious as they were to dispose of India? They could have replaced Wavell earlier instead of sacking him in 1947. Labour might not have easily found a man from its own ranks. Attlee's intuition in selecting Mountbatten was to come later. They should have picked up Leo Amery's excellent idea that the British should set a time limit to their stay in India and proceeded on that idea from the beginning of their involvement with the Indian problem on assuming office in 1945. Thirdly, Socialists should not have been unduly obsessed with the unity of India, which the British had brought about as an imperial power. Like Mountbatten, they should not have been sentimental of Britain's past in India; they should have had no qualms about the division of the Indian army; much of the mystique about it rested on the 'sentimental recollections of its proud and paternalistic British officers'. Fourthly, they should have subtly encouraged Nehru to bring up the Rajagopalachari formula for discussion during the work of the cabinet mission and persuaded the Congress to agree first to division and then to unite for a few common interests. To the Congress slogan; 'Quit India' and the League slogan: 'Divide and Quit', the British should have quietly planted the idea in the mind of Nehru: 'Divide first and then unite on the common integrity of India.' They should have aimed at a loose confederal India and Pakistan. These hard decisions may still have enabled Attlee's government to guide the blind irrational forces of India and Islamic nationalism heading for a violent collision.

Looking back to the 1930s: if the British government had set up during the viceroyalty of Lord Irwin, some kind of a dominion status government, a united India might have been the successor authority. It is sometimes argued that the introduction of democratic government resulted in partition. The British had given Indians the concept of a modern state. Nehru and the westernized elites held on to it against Gandhian onslaughts; it may be they sinned in being too western in developing the concept and in belittling the sentiments of the Muslims who violently reacted against the idea of majority rule implicit in the English pattern of parliamentary democracy. It is doubtful if the British were ever serious in working democratic institutions in partnership with Indians. According to Laski, who for a time assisted Hoare over the India Bill, 'the predominantly conservative cabinet felt a genuine repugnance to making a contract on equal terms with men of colour'. The English put not their trust in princes nor in the proletariat; till the end of their rule they remained convinced that the alien English alone could ensure good government.

The British used the reform acts as a rope ladder to get down from the back of the Indian elephant. Their policy was to shed power by stages. In so doing, they failed to see the inter-relation between power and influence. Irwin had realized that 'the choice lay between power, which had served us well from the days of Clive, and influence, which if we could use it aright in the changed conditions of the 20th century would serve us better. Of the two, influence, was the more securely founded and the more enduring.' In 1947, the British found that though they possessed physical force, that alone could not solve the Indian problem; in any case the British would not use force to that end. In the alternative, they found themselves bereft of influence.

In the ultimate analysis, it had not dawned upon any group of men in England that just as privilege and power are shed in favour of classes in one's own country, so also the same can be abandoned on moral grounds in favour of the subject peoples of the Empire. Marxists asserted that the imperialists would never voluntarily renounce power; the Marxist strand in Nehru's thinking deepened his inveterate distrust of British intentions. The realization came late to the British people, a close shave as Strachey put it. The realization, however, could not prevent partition; it was not apparent to any one in 1947, as it is now that Pakistan 'was in truth the product of a revolution within a revolution'.

THE MUSLIMS

The Muslims as a community were fated in turn to be disliked, hated, and feared. They were a fallen people, fallen as a ruling class, and bereft of political and economic power. Their adjustment to the ruling British was slow, hesitant, and painful; to the Hindus proving well-nigh impossible, as the rising new Hindu middle-classes were ahead of the Muslims in tackling the problem of modernization and in coming to terms with the modern way of life. At a rough estimate, the Muslim was behind the Hindu by at least twenty-five years, in education, in politics, and the competitive ways of life open under British rule. In the days of Muslim power and glory, the Hindu, in Muslim eyes, had been a second-class citizen. As the Hindus recovered strength through the Hindu renaissance and developed nationalism on western lines, the Muslims, in their eyes, were a minority community, politically important and significant, but nevertheless a minority. In India, the dominant political position belonged to the Hindu, an inescapable fact of the twentieth century modern world. At the Calcutta session of the Hindu Mahasabha in 1939, Savarkar, opposing the division of India into a Hindu India and a Muslim India, underlined the dominant position for the Hindus who constituted the majority. Congress, enunciating western democratic principles, asserted the same dominating position over the Muslims.

From the eighties of the last century, the Muslims were caught on the horns of a dilemma. If they sought protection for their interests within India, it could only be as a political minority. If they sought it in the wider area of Islamic brotherhood, it would have to be on the basis of pan-Islamism. Some groups, largely of the upper class, sought British protection; a smaller group, anti-British in sentiment, cherished pan-Islamic ideas. But when Turkey emerged as a modern secular state under Mustafa Kemal, Muslims of every group had to turn inward into India and seek accommodation within.

The so-called communal problem was in the main an expression of this dilemma and of a fear complex in an India entering into a reformist era. Muslims were assailed by a doubt that the British might not be permanently in India to guarantee their position. Their tactics were, therefore, to get something out of the British, and to ask the Hindus to safeguard it, as well as to concede something more. They hesitated to make common cause with the Hindus to displace the British because they had no faith in the dominant Hindu majority. The Muslim attitude was one of dignified arrogance, and this exasperated the Hindus. On their part the British made what proved to be their last attempt at a communal settlement, a communal award and the incorporation of certain safeguards into the Act of 1935. The experiences of 1937–9 again intensified the old dilemma; how could Muslims live under a central government which was bound to be Hindu dominated. Was there a way out? No one imagined that a breakthrough would ultimately hinge upon Jinnah's leadership.

Jinnah moved away from Congress as Gandhi moved in to take possession of it. In the mid-twenties, Jinnah's position appeared somewhat dubious. Still rated as a nationalist, he was seen in the role of a lawyer putting the Muslim brief to Congress. At the same time, Birkenhead was expounding to the viceroy, Lord Irwin, the 'policy of securing a solid Muslim support and leaving Jinnah high and dry'. Congress was soon to administer a severe rebuff to Jinnah when the all-parties convention was held in Calcutta in 1928, to consider the Nehru report. Not only were the fourteen points of Jinnah rejected one by one but Jinnah was 'taunted with having no right to represent the Muslims. It broke his heart and hurt his pride and he gave up all hope of Hindu–Muslim unity which was his life's mission. A Parsee friend of his says that on this occasion he saw the proud Jinnah weeping for the first time in his life.'[1]

[1] S. Abid Husain, *The Destiny of Indian Muslims* (1965), p. 73.

Jinnah was again left 'high and dry' when he attended the Round Table conference in London in the thirties. The British pitchforked the Aga Khan into the leadership of the Muslims. The Aga later complained in his *Memoirs* that the Indian bureaucracy disliked his leadership. The bureaucracy was building Muslim leadership in the Punjab; the Punjab Muslims were the pet of the British in India as Chiang-Kai-Shek was of the Americans. History was to record disillusionment in both cases.

Jinnah was cold, arrogant, and witheringly rude towards the British in India; on one occasion he accused Linlithgow of double-crossing him. The British, on their part, never suspected that this elegant, inordinately vain Bombay lawyer, would confront them claiming to be the leader of 90 million Muslims. Nehru and Congress underrated him as an opponent; this was their biggest mistake. Nehru had an *idée fixe* about Jinnah. His estimate of Jinnah in the *Discovery of India* shows the measure of Nehru's honest failure to understand him. In 1937, Jinnah appeared to both the British and to Congress, as the disaffected leader of a factious Muslim group, rapidly acquiring a nuisance value in the new democratic set-up in the provinces. Both had their respective calculations which held out little prospects for Jinnah achieving a consolidation of Muslim opinion under his sole leadership.

Congress tenaciously clung to its pretensions that a large number of progressive and nationalist Muslims were its colleagues. It claimed that Muslim organizations like Jamiat-ul-ulema, the All-India Shia conference, the Majlis-e-Ahrar, and the All-India Momin conference were the allies of Congress in the liberation struggle. In reality, in the opinion of an Indian scholar, they remained in practical politics a drag on the Congress. For, on one hand, they failed to convert any appreciable section of the Muslim community to Congress secularism and on the other, they virtually influenced the Congress decisions relating to communal settlements.[1]

The British kept a watchful eye on the Punjab, to them the 'key' Muslim majority area. Here power rested safely with the pro-British Muslim leaders and their Hindu and Sikh allies, representatives of the conservative rural Punjab. Congress and League were nowhere in the picture. The Punjab was impressively safe from the communal wrangles between Jinnah and the Congress. A minor worry and chagrin of the British was the affiliation of the Red Shirt Pathans with Congress. The politics of Bengal was a rich stew of its own. The main problem was to hold in check Hindu anarchists and terrorists. Jinnah's League mattered little in the volatile politics of Bengal.

Just as Jinnah was to establish a new sovereign state on an idea, so he began to establish his leadership on no recognizable and assessable foundation. Towards the end, Nehru oversimplified Jinnah's successful leadership by telling Mountbatten: 'The secret of his success and it has been tremendous, if only for its emotional intensity, was in his capacity to take up a permanently negative attitude.' To an onlooker, too, it appeared to be deceptively negative. Jinnah was building his leadership and the power that goes with it, like making bricks without straw. His Muslim League was not organized, like the Congress, at the grass-roots. It had a top structure which for long intervals

[1] Ram Gopal, *Indian Muslims* (1959), p. 294.

remained moribund. It had no ideology or cause to enthuse the Muslim intellectuals and the middle-class intelligentsia. His followers were not visible in numbers; they were hovering somewhere in the background. As a leader, he was cold, aloof, a distance away from his colleagues. He held the cards closely to his chest; none shared his inner thoughts. In the Muslim majority provinces, the ministries there had barred his entry into the arena of provincial authority. In the Congress provinces his opponents were in temporary honeymoon with British power.

Jinnah astutely exploited the opening moves made by Congress on assuming office in the provinces. They were three. Congress spurned the idea of coalition with the League; aimed at disrupting the emergence of the League as an all-India body, for Congress alone was to confront the British; and attempted to absorb Muslim leadership by the mass-contact programme in the U.P. Congress may not have intended them to be so. Jinnah said they were so; it well suited his purpose.

He opened an attack on the nationalist Muslims and the Muslim organizations in alliance with Congress. Several times he lost his temper when he was asked to negotiate with Congress through Azad, whom he attacked in 1940, calling him viciously 'a Muslim show-boy Congress President'. He took up the position that the League was the sole representative body of the Indian Muslims, by which he meant that he desired to play a major and decisive role in determining the fate of India. Congress wanted the League to form a common front with it in order to fight the British. Why should he oblige Congress? He knew Congress would never give up its Muslim allies, much less concede the League equality of status. If he kept up the quarrel, there might be a chance of detaching Muslims from Congress. He asked the viceroy to take note of Muslim dissatisfaction, demanding a royal commission to enquire into the complaints made by the League.

At the same time, Jinnah adopted the tactic of driving a wedge between the British and the Congress to prevent any possible coalescence of their power in the centre which the British then were anxious to set up under the 1935 Act. Jinnah, in a talk with Lord Brabourne, then governor of Bengal, in August 1938, is said to have made a startling suggestion that the British 'should keep Centre as it is now; that they should make friends with the Muslims by protecting them in the Congress provinces and if the British did that, the Muslims would protect the British in the Centre'. So says Zetland, who differing from Linlithgow, began to have a doubt whether the Muslims might not provide the biggest obstacle in the way of the achievement of federation.

The outbreak of Hitler's war paved the way for the decisive break-through of Jinnah's leadership and the ultimate resolution of the age-long dilemma of the Indian Muslims in the manner he wished. His call for a 'Deliverance Day' towards the end of 1939 was not an empty demonstration. He saw the realities of the situation which had now altered in his favour. Congress had given up power in the Hindu majority provinces where British rule had returned. War-time conditions made it inevitable for the British to depend on Muslim support. He need not openly fight the British. He could safely leave that to Congress. He had only to interpose himself between Congress and the British, and deprive them both of the initiative to make any move for a political settlement, without his concurrence. In October 1939, the Muslim League laid down this condition; it was to be the opening salvo of the war of succession in 1946–7: 'No declaration regarding the constitutional advance for India should be made without the consent and approval of the All-India Muslim League, nor any constitution be framed and finally adopted by His Majesty's Government and the British Parliament without such approval and consent.'

Jinnah had set up an effective road block in the path of any political settlement, present or future. He seems to have realized, unlike Congress, whose inveterate distrust of British intentions clouded the clarity of its judgment, that the British would go after the war; at any rate they would be in no position to protect Muslim interests. The working of the provincial part of the Act had shown the hollowness of British safeguards. Muslims had to rely on their own strength. Jinnah had also realized that Congress would never agree to give him the right of veto in the progress of constitutional questions. As an old nationalist, he would not say that the British should for ever remain in India. The British would demand of him an answer as to what sort of a centre would satisfy him and the League. There was no point in being exasperatingly negative; a positive declaration was imperative. On March 23, 1940, the Muslim League passed the resolution familiarly known as the Pakistan resolution. None bothered to study its implications, much less cared to understand what it really meant; it sounded so bizarre. Every one said that Jinnah had put up a very stiff price for his co-operation but that he was open to bargaining.

The U.P. Muslims forming only fourteen per cent of the population of the province, were not the primary beneficiaries of the Pakistan resolution. Yet they gave lot of support to it. The support came from three distinct groups. There was a considerable output of propagandist literature by the intellectuals of the Aligarh University. Its general tenor was how to render the Hindu-dominated India weak at the centre by suggesting all sorts of divisions, cutting the country into various bits and pieces. The generality of Muslims began to entertain the comforting feeling that the Hindus would now be cut down to size, in no position to lord it over them, compelled to share power on a basis of parity. Round about 1944–5 Muslim officials were secretly sympathizing with the Pakistan concept as they saw opportunities for wider employment in the highest offices without having to compete with the Hindus. They saw new vistas and horizons in a Muslim state. Here was an opportunity for the Muslims to work for an ideal, without begging for favours either from the British or the Hindus.

It is not known when Jinnah moved into a point of no return in relation to his demand for Pakistan. It is believed that he was not unalterably committed till Cripps came to India in 1942. It is also not known when he irrevocably dismissed the idea of a single centre and along with it some kind of association between the Muslims and the Hindus.

Jinnah might have made up his mind but he was far from certain that either the British or Congress would concede his demand. He distrusted both as intensely as ever. The advent of the socialist government in 1945 intensified his distrust. Nehru had personal contacts with the socialist leaders who were friendly to Congress. Jinnah appeared to them a troublesome communalist leader, using a minority group to veto the progress of the majority. The three-party parliamentary delegation which visited India in the winter of 1945 reached at least one specific conclusion – that Jinnah was not bluffing; he was serious about Pakistan.

His acceptance of the cabinet mission plan has been the subject of much curiosity and comment. Cripps had hidden inside the plan the outline of Jinnah's Pakistan – not the 'truncated' one which was finally accepted in 1947. Jinnah was certain that Congress would fight for a strong centre. He would start from the compulsory grouping and fight for a centre almost unrecognizable as a common centre. He was not giving away anything which mattered.

Looking back, it appears strange that Jinnah should have broken the deadlock, rather forced into that step, by summoning the Muslim mob in the call for a 'Direct Action Day', a weapon which Congress had excluded from Jinnah's armoury. Jinnah's timing in starting the war of succession showed his political astuteness. In 1946, the British had become weak; everyone knew the days of British administration were numbered. They were in no position to deal with civil disorder decisively. Regardless of consequences, Jinnah set the country on a disastrous course. The British were worried. On whom could they depend – police, Indian army, even British troops? Congress for a time seemed not worried, still hoping to push Jinnah aside. However, realization soon came as civil war spread over the Indo-Gangetic plain.

Another strange fact is that Jinnah's leadership, till the very end, had no base in the Muslim majority areas. True, he had roused the apprehensions of Muslims regarding their political future. He had imparted to the League the characteristics of a mass organization. He had kindled dynamism among the Muslim intelligentsia – the most important class in the liberation struggle in colonial countries. But the provincial governments of Bengal and Punjab had successfully kept him from making an inroad into their strong-holds. In the Punjab, the crucial area for Pakistan-to-be, certain fortuitous circumstances like the early demise of Mian Fazl-i-Husain and Sikandar Hyat assisted Jinnah in brow-beating the less experienced men in authority. There was a body of Punjabi Muslims who had not accepted the full implications of Pakistan. The external forces generated by Jinnah cracked the counter forces of sanity and moderation within the Punjab.

It is hard for an Indian to explain the motives of Jinnah. One can only surmise that he felt that he was an instrument in a noble cause, to secure for the Indian Muslims a homeland of their own, a room or two in the vast mansion of India. He became possessed of an idea, determined to achieve, against all odds, what he had set out to achieve. In his own mind he must have come to the conclusion that Pakistan was no longer the chimerical idea of a few young students at Cambridge as it had appeared to the Muslim elders attending the London Round Table conference. Pakistan could be a reality. It could exist side by side with big India. Jinnah did not have the broad sweep of ideas about the world outside India which Nehru had, but within his limited but practical mind Jinnah must have argued that Pakistan had a chance of survival in spite of the threat posed by India, which threat might be mitigated by the centrifugal forces inherent in Indian society, by the weakness of the central government subjected to the pressure of the anti-federal forces of princely India, and by the alienation of Britain, for it was then axiomatic that India would not remain in the Commonwealth.

THE FINALE

Partition came willy-nilly. Right-wing Hindus were enraged that the Muslims had once again had their own way, managing to slip out of the net. Nehru considered it a monstrous folly that in the twentieth century a nation state should have come into existence through medieval ideas of religion. Jinnah, a westernized elite, must be presumed to have worked for the *territorial* nationality of the Muslims, but the only cementing force for this Muslim territorial nationality was the spirit of Islam, apart from the dynamic will of Jinnah. Yet too much emphasis should not be laid on religious bigotry and religion as the basis for partition. Relations between India and Pakistan have been very bad for other reasons.

Inevitably, the process of partition under the leadership of Mountbatten has been dramatized. The scene is laid in the viceroy's house with the viceroy as the chief actor. In the last days of this historic office, Mountbatten brought into play his colourful personality, a new technique of public relations in place of the rigidity of the viceregal court etiquette, necessary showmanship to win over the confidence of distrustful Indian leaders, and even some salesmanship of the authentic Madison Avenue variety. Behind all this was the grimness of a harsh purpose.

The accession of princely India was an *entr'acte* between the administrative consequences of partition and the ghastly tragedy building up in the Punjab. The princely interlude falls within a small compass among the events of the period. There is reason to believe that Mountbatten had no particular love for the princely order. He began to take some interest in it when he realized that the delicate balance between the two new dominions might be upset by some foolish princely misadventure. The instrument of accession was sponsored by a group of Dewans of Rajasthan states, in association with the Dewan of Baroda, who met at Mount Abu in May 1947. They advised Sardar Patel that it was necessary to establish a very tenuous relationship with the Indian states after independence; otherwise the situation would be anomalous with hundreds of 'foreign jurisdictions' surrounding the Indian dominion. The first draft was made by Gopalaswami Ayyangar; it was subsequently embellished to make it attractive to the princes by affirming the sovereignty of the princes over their territories and ensuring their financial autonomy. Patel invited Mountbatten, as viceroy and a royalty, to persuade the princes to sign the instrument of accession.

A myth of this period is the so-called princely 'Third Force' and the machinations of certain officials; the confederation scheme of Jam Digvijai Sinhji of Jamnagar; and a few other princely castles in the air. The princes were aimlessly busy. Mercifully they did not know what was happening to them. Sardar had realized by May 1947, that Kashmir and Hyderabad might prove troublesome. He authorized Mountbatten to bring round the ruler of Kashmir to decide one way or the other and to play for time with the Nizam. Patel wisely said nothing about paramountcy. He had been advised that paramountcy was power. He who controls the central government and the army exercises paramountcy over the princes in his own way. As an astute power politician Patel understood the significance of it: he talked little and bided his time.

The transfer of power in 1947 must now be seen as having actually begun with the introduction of provincial autonomy in 1937: no one then would have thought it to have been so. It began a race against time: no one could have foreseen it. That events were rapidly overtaking a timetable was only realized when Attlee made the declaration of February 20, 1947. Nehru talked of a certain dynamism in the political situation. Mountbatten as viceroy with a mission dramatized it with his hustle and bustle. After June 2nd, it was one mad rush. Many things happened in the few remaining months, culminating in appalling human tragedy.

In the inquests so far held on the events of 1947, a few scapegoats have been discovered, some myths have been publicized, random judgments passed on various 'ifs' and 'might-have-beens' of one's choice. Strangely, the events have had no traumatic effect on Indians. Indian historiography was and remains a 'paltry affair': hence there has been no study of the events which led to the partition. Occasionally one hears among intellectuals a note of regret questioning whether all the sacrifices made by Indian nationalism were necessary; whether we could not have achieved what we got by other means.

In course of time historians will set out their judgments. It is appropriate to end with a note of impressions, if not of conclusion. In the final reckoning it is well to remember that the British were not dealing with politicians playing a parliamentary game of politics (with all those British ideas thrown in, distrust of logic, distaste for doctrine, gift for compromise, sense of fairplay, so notoriously hard to translate into foreign languages) but with the charismatic leaders of Indian and Islamic versions of western nationalism, worshippers of the Moloch of the modern nation state. With all their modern culture, their noble characters, their intellectual integrity, their strikingly high degree of sophistication as westernized elites, Jawaharlal Nehru and Muhammad Ali Jinnah had not fully assimilated the alien knowledge; they wandered between the two worlds and belonged to neither. They were unable to free themselves, granted their admitted greatness, from the 'schizophrenia fostered in deep-seated malaise which is one of the persistent features of the Asian social scene'. It is not a profitable endeavour to distribute proportionate shares of blame between Nehru, Jinnah and the British. None of them were in a position to find a way out of a revolutionary situation. All revolutionary changes exact their price. As the last viceroy bowed out of British Indian history; as the countryside in the Punjab went up in smoke and flame; as millions of peasants began to trek across the new borders; as innocent men, women and children faced doom and destruction, wondering why the Indian fates had suddenly turned their fury on them, an onlooker in Delhi, may have said to himself:

> 'For the unexpected, gods always find a way
> This is what the gods did here, today.'

A THIRD FORCE IN INDIA 1920–47: A STUDY IN POLITICAL ANALYSIS

by PERCIVAL SPEAR*

The purpose of this paper is to consider the role of non-political public opinion in shaping the events which led up to the partition of India. It is contended that this body of opinion was always an important, and sometimes a decisive influence in public affairs.

The source for this paper is essentially my own memories and experiences when a resident of Delhi between the years 1924–45. These have of course been supplemented by such reading of memoirs, histories, etc., and personal contacts as have come my way. But residence in a country does not in itself confer a title to speak about it and it therefore seems desirable to be more explicit about the special circumstances of my stay. My centre was Delhi nearly all this time and my milieu the College of St Stephen's and the University of Delhi up to 1940, and government service in Delhi and Simla from 1940–5. During these years St Stephen's College possessed certain characteristics which made it an unusually valuable point of observation. From the time of C. F. Andrews's association with the college a tradition had been established, not common at that time, of close contact between the English and Indian staff, who were mainly non-Christian and included both Hindu and Muslim members. At the same time, because of the relatively small size of the college, there was close contact with the students which was brought about in various ways. From these contacts came not only friendships with the Indian staff and their circles but contacts with the students' parents and their circles. In addition, in those days the college was closely connected with the University of Delhi in which I shared. In the history department there was also a system of inter-collegiate lectures which provided contacts with the sister Hindu College. Later there was a good deal of liaison with the new All-India Radio and its staff. Taking these conditions together they gave one the opportunity – if one cared to take advantage of it – of observing the flow of middle class opinion over a fairly wide range which included, beside the academic, samples of professional, commercial, official and rural opinion.

The special circumstances of the college and Delhi at that time made the range more catholic than might be supposed. To begin with, the proportion of Muslims to Hindus almost reached the national ratio. As the successor to the old Delhi College, St Stephen's attracted the conservative Delhi Muslims, whether politically or theologically, including members of the Mughal family, as being the least Hindu of the colleges available. Others including ex-khilafat non-co-operators came for the prospects it held out. Others came from the Punjab, from official or landed families. Then the rural classes were represented by the Jats, for whose higher education the

* Fellow of Selwyn College, Cambridge.

college had been a pioneer. The first Jat minister in the Punjab, Lal Singh, and the famous Choudhri Chothu Ram, were Stephanians. The college also benefited from the presence in Delhi of the imperial secretariat with its large Bengali and much smaller south Indian element. From this source came a Bengali colony in the college which was both lively and attractive, and a sprinkling of south Indians, Marathas and Parsis. There were also a number of Sikhs and a Jain group. While this did not amount to a microcosm of all India, as we liked to believe, it did provide something of a cross-section of north Indian society.

The opportunities provided by this home base, as it were, were increased by two factors. There were journeys and visits in connection with one's professional work, academic or student. In this way western and southern India, Bengal and the Punjab were covered. I was able to consort at various times with the poets and artists of Shantiniketan, the Pathans of the frontier, the Brahmins and social workers of Poona and Bombay; to see the civil disobedience movement of 1930 at its height in Bombay as well as communal riots in Delhi at first hand and the Mahatma emerging from one of his fasts or addressing meetings in Queen's Gardens. During the war, while in government service, the perspective of course altered. By that time there were in the secretariat many Indians in responsible positions as well as subordinate ones who essentially came from the same middle class; only the circle was wider and the grouping more miscellaneous or cosmopolitan. The circle then included, besides rule-bureaucrats, some very able administrators and open-minded officers, journalists and writers, film producers from Bombay, a poet from the Punjab, and business men and politicians from all quarters. The secretariat personnel was then so largely Indian that it served as a sounding board to echo round its walls the sounds of opinion from outside.

There was one further advantage of residence in Delhi at that time. Everyone came to it sooner or later. As often as not, when calling on someone in some distant place, one found that he was not available – because he was in Delhi. Specially was this true of the Christmas season when Delhi was a favourite haunt for 'All-India' conferences. And then there was the assembly, where I served during the war as a government whip for three sessions, with its pomp and bustle, its coming and going, its leaders, the animated speeches in the chamber, the gossip and arguments in the lobbies. This is the background from which comes what I have to say.

Before considering the role of non-political public opinion in Indian affairs it is necessary to have some idea of the content of public opinion itself. Only a small portion was articulate on national or even provincial affairs. It would perhaps be best to start by trying to define the nature of Indian public opinion itself. We can make a first distinction between the articulate and inarticulate classes. The former, broadly speaking, were the literate classes, whether in English or local languages. Their organs of expression were the press, books and pamphlets, the public lecture and meetings, conferences and private discussions. For all these media of expression there was a sufficient degree of civil liberty except for open incitements to violence or the overthrow of the government. Between them and the inarticulate classes, the public meetings formed a bridge of communication. We may next note a distinction between a permanent articulate opinion and a temporary one. The permanent group was again, in general, the literate classes. Temporary groups came from the illiterate classes who might be very vocal for a time on a particular issue and would then relapse into silence again. One of the arts of political management was to stir the inarticulate man and to bring as large a proportion as possible to the aid of an organized articulate group. By and large this is what Mahatma Gandhi managed to do on several occasions with his *hartals*, no rent proposals, and salt-making. But he had his failures too, as in 1932 and in 1940–1, and they are, in their way, as significant as his successes. When he succeeded, as in 1920–1 and in 1930–1, the Congress became an all-India movement, and when he failed it relapsed into an organ of the middle class. His overall achievement was to diffuse throughout Hindu India a general sense that Congress was the champion of something new called nationalism, and that this was in accord with the general principles of *dharma*. For the inarticulate classes nationalism in the hands of Congress was seen as a sort of supercaste Hinduism with the Mahatma as its patron saint, or *guru*, if not its *avatar*.

But Congress was not the sole or complete representative of the middle class, and here we come to the main contention of this paper. Let us look for a moment at the composition and characteristics of the middle class whose development has recently so suggestively been studied by Professor B. B. Misra. We have first the official hierarchy from the Indian civilian sitting in the seats of power to the *tahsildar* or *Kirnam* or police inspector of a sub-district headquarters. Under the rules, of course, they could take no part in political life. But their influence was nevertheless considerable. There were two reasons for this. Everyone in India loves discussion, and officials were no exceptions to the rule. If you can't hold a durbar, you become a durbari. They made a firm distinction between their duty to the government and their own opinions, and these, when they did not implicate their own position in society, they were very ready to express. The second was the Indian tendency to look upwards for guidance and enlightenment. India was still patriarchally minded, and the official, as the servant of the *raj*, traditionally enjoyed some of the religious mystique which distinguished his position from that of officials elsewhere. The British had succeeded the rajas it is true, but the Crown in the person of Queen Victoria, had acquired some of the veneration attached to the imperial throne from the time of Akbar. After the officials came the professional classes, the journalists, the teachers, the doctors and specially the lawyers. These were all more or less imbued with western ideas and, except for some teachers and doctors, were independent of government. Next we may list the mercantile class, from the Bombay operator to the village *bania*. These people had widely differing interests, and greatly varying levels of westernization. Yet all were literate and even the village *bania* would send his son to the district middle or high school if he could. All shared a certain awareness of what was going on in India and the world, and all had a certain interest in events. If the modern business man had his college education, his national newspapers and his stock reports to sustain him, the village trader had his regional language bi-weekly newspapers and those reports of friends and relations which are in perpetual circulation throughout India.

After the traders came the agriculturists. Not, of course, all agriculturists, the peasants or cultivators. But it is a mistake to suppose that there were no country people in the articulate class. There was, in fact, a whole heirarchy. At the top came the greater landholders like the *zamindars* of Bengal, Bihar and parts of the United Provinces and the Madras Presidency, the *talaqdars* of Oudh and others elsewhere. They were few in number and in some cases remarkably supine. But they were distinctly articulate and could exercise considerable influence in the council of state (which had a total electorate of between 17,000 and 20,000 voters) and the upper houses of the United Provinces and Bengal. They had formed the first Indian political body in the British India Association of 1853. They were generally conservative and sensitive of their *zamindari* rights, it is true, but they had also supplied from their *milieu* in the early days of nationalism such men as Surendranath Bannerji and Romesh Chander Dutt. Below them came the various gradations of landholders down to the 'yeomen' *zamindars* of the Punjab and village headmen. Not all the landholders were literate in English, nor all the lesser men literate at all. But they were nevertheless aware of events and issues and capable of expressing their views and promoting their interests, and must therefore be numbered in the articulate group.

This articulate class, heterogeneous as it was, had certain common characteristics. It is worth while pausing to note some of them, for they help to explain its reactions, sometimes surprising, to events. In the first place, they all shared the hierarchial leader principle which runs through Indian society. The village *bania* was something of an authority in his village on account of his superior knowledge, but he in turn would look up to the merchants and bankers in the towns. The landholder, while something of an oracle to those below him, was usually in awe of those above. The professional classes of the towns were more free of traditional restraints but they treated the national leaders with a deference which was more than loyalty. The tendency to defer to superior rank, which in India means caste, clan, and spiritual as well as material status, was at times an important factor in the behaviour of this group. There is no doubt that the 'mahatma' status of Gandhi was of the greatest assistance to him, while Motilal Nehru derived advantage from his brahminical status, as did Tilak from his membership of the Chitpavan section of the Maratha brahmins.

The second and third characteristics were inhibiting ones, which help to explain the conflicts which often occurred in the minds of this class. One of these was the sense of commitment. All these people were in their different ways, busy with responsible avocations, having a stake in society and dependents to support. Many had land to lose and so to cherish, others had trade to preserve and the professionals their careers. Hence that dichotomy between thought, speech and action which observers have often noticed in Indian politics, a certain unwillingness to act when it meant putting one's worldly prospects to the hazard. A notable example of this was the halting response to Gandhi's call to resign office as part of the non-co-operation movement. The men who came out of the services were men of character, but most of them preferred to sympathize from within. And when the circumstances are considered, they could hardly be blamed. But the students without much responsibility or many obligations, flocked out of the colleges, as the peasants would do from their fields in an off-season to attend a great political rally. Terrorists were usually young; Aurobindo Ghose was not the only one who became a sage or devotee in mature life. The characteristic which links with commitment is that of conservatism. The Indian people are temperamentally conservative, a trait which is promoted by the whole socio-religious structure of society, by the weight of custom, and by such theological presuppositions of life as caste, *karma*, *dharma* and rebirth. The current order of society is traditionally sacred, and still exercises a mesmeric effect on most Indians. Tilak for all his militant nationalism, was in other ways a traditionalist. Gandhi was neither a socialist nor a social revolutionary; he was neither an egalitarian nor a secularist. He sought to remove disabilities rather than abolish status, to lop off from society harmful accretions rather than to reform or refashion it. This innate conservatism tended to cause alarm as soon as any course of action seemed to be proceeding to extremes and threatening violence or social security. There had to be some overriding factor or emotion of great strength to set these cautionary feelings aside. There ran, for example, a ripple of anxiety over the face of Indian society on the news of the Moplah outbreak in 1921, again at the time of the Chauri Chaura burning, and at the proposal for no-tax campaigns in 1931.

There then come two characteristics which tended to unite this class and push it into action. The first was the sentiment of nationalism. For the more sophisticated this was a secular territorial sentiment borrowed from the west. Those of this type, who retained feelings for traditional cults, as did many in Bengal and Maharashtra, gave the sentiment a religious background with a goddess in the person of Mother India or Bharat Mata. An example of the former which readily comes to mind, is G. K. Gokhale and of the latter, his Maratha counterpart, B. G. Tilak. Bepin Chandra Pal and Aurobindo Ghose, whose youthful enthusiasm ran to extremes, are Bengali examples. The outlook of the Arya Samajis, personified in Lala Lajpat Rai, is another case of nationalism tinged by religion, in this case unconnected with a divine cult, but informed by the supposed spirit of primitive Hinduism. This national feeling was essentially a vague one and it was not easy at first to distinguish between imitations of the west, more or less counterfeit, and genuine sentiment containing some residual seed of action. It was often a moot question as to how far secular nationalism was seeking roots in traditional soil, or how far local cults were using secular nationalism as a stimulus and an advertisement. The difficulty of this stage of nationalism was that the traditional roots being local or sectional, the result of growth tended to be divisive. Thus Tilak appealed, in his pre-1914 days, to orthodox Hindu and Maratha anti-Muslim sentiment, which, raised to an all-India level, would have turned nationalism into a Brahminical and anti-Muslim movement. In Bengal at the partition of 1905 a great following was achieved by linking the cause with the great mother in her various forms. But this would not do for the rest of India. The same argument applied to the Arya Samaj with their policy of back to the Vedas. The theosophists tried to meet this divisive difficulty with their doctrine that Hinduism equals everything and everything equals Hinduism. But this was too obscure for the masses and either superfluous or insufficiently satisfying for the others. Nationalism threatened to divide into a number of cults which could either be set against each other or crushed separately if they strayed towards violence.

It was Gandhi who resolved this dilemma, at once committing Congress to Hinduism and embracing all Hindus in nationalism. He did this, in his magic way, by standing apart from all sectarian expressions of faith, and by emphasizing, by means of symbolic ritual as well as by speech, the essential values of Hinduism and the essential unity of all within its fold. By symbolic ritual I mean such things as the spinning qualification for Congress membership (Hindu simplicity), fasts as expressions of repentance, purification and protest, the *hartal* as an expression of moral indignation, the Harijan movement, with its sharing of wells and temples, as an expression of Hindu brotherhood, the wearing of the loin cloth and the salt march as an expression of community with the Hindu cultivator. His prayer meetings and his *bhajjans* emphasized this in the religious field in spite of the inclusion of Christian hymns and Christian and Muslim prayers. These latter were an expression of toleration and brotherliness towards others, but did not affect the overwhelming Hindu trend of the rest of the ritual. It is true that Gandhi maintained that nationalism was for Muslims and Christians as well as Hindus, and the rituals just mentioned were perhaps gestures in this direction. At the back of his mind he perhaps conceived of two rings of nationalism, the one containing all Hindus, and the other the remaining Indians as well. But India was for him the land of the sacred mother, and the Hindu socio-religious system, as renovated to his design, its sacred heritage. The others were certainly brothers, but not quite to the same degree. All men are brothers, he might have said, but some are more brotherly than others. They were more than tolerated, they were even loved in his view, but they were in a category which a theologian would describe as 'separated brethren'.

It was this nationalism which swept the articulate classes from the 1920s and in a vaguer and more diffused way spread to the masses as well. To the Hindu members of the former class, it gave an assurance of a connection both with past history and past custom. They could be proud of the past and its achievements, and in that assurance make adjustments to meet the problems of the present and import from the west to build for the future. It was an outlook which encouraged action, self-reliance and unity; it gave a feeling of both solidarity and confidence. The social structure could be pruned, but would not be destroyed; innovations could be grafted on to it and would grow in time into typical Indian shapes. Gandhi's nationalism was a *tour de force* in supplying a sense of unity to a world of social diversity and historic tensions.

The last of these characteristics was a sense of self-respect. In the Indian articulate class this has taken a peculiar form arising from the circumstances of recent history. Indians, like the members of other nations with a long history, have a natural pride in their past and its unique contribution to the world. But in the case of India this was undermined by the long centuries of foreign domination by Turk, Mughal and Briton. Political domination need not affect national self-esteem if it is merely a recognition of *force majeure*. But in the nineteenth century this was reinforced by the cultural claims of an intrusive and aggressive westernism. It was as if the west was saying, like the Red Queen in *Alice*, 'Now we are five times as strong as you are *and* five times as clever!' And it was not only a matter of argument, but of demonstration also, as western institutions and techniques obtruded into the east and ideas from the west seeped into eastern minds. The Indian loyally attached to his own tradition was faced with the overbearing claims of the west and he badly needed reassurance. Was his own culture obsolete as he was told? Was his fate to become a poor relation of the west in a sort of regional cultural suburb? The Hindu revival movements of the nineteenth century were the first answer to this mood of depression. As their symbol we may take Swami Vivekananda's appearance at the Chicago parliament of religions in 1894. Next came national movements in the far and middle east and the defeat of Russia by Japan in 1904–5. The real break-through was the collapse of the west itself into internecine strife in the first world war which shattered the myth of western moral superiority and convinced India that her only disadvantages lay in the world of technology and physical force. Yet her past experience and self-doubts meant that she still needed re-assurance. It left on the Indian mind both a determination to be on terms with the west in every particular and a nervous sensitivity in matters of equality and self-respect. Things must not only be equal but be seen and felt to be equal. The unforgivable sin in a foreigner was an assumption of superiority or a hint of inequality. An example of this attitude in practice can be seen in the discussions about dominion status and independence. In the thirties and forties many logical and verbal hairs were split on this subject, the fact being that however independent the content of dominion status might be (after the statute of Westminster of 1931) it was not seen and felt to be independence. This attitude explains both the eventual adoption of the republican form and the subsequent damping down of demands for leaving the Commonwealth.

The Muslims of India require separate treatment. While the broad division between the articulate and inarticulate classes and the play of western influences on the former was the same as in the case of the Hindus, the circumstances of their community and history gave them special characteristics which caused them to react differently to identical stimuli. In the first place, the articulate class was much smaller than that of the Hindus, arising from the fact that in Mughal times Muslims tended to be either executives or peasants and soldiers, the middling ranks and jobs being filled by Hindus. This small articulate class had also been influenced by secular western nationalism, but only a minority had gone far enough to find an easy meeting point with the secular wing of Hindu nationalism. There was thus a relationship but an uneasy one, between this Muslim class and the corresponding Hindu one. These Muslims had also an uneasy relationship with the very large inarticulate class. This class was still under the influence of the medieval minded *ulema*, exponents of traditional Islam. While intellectual Muslim modernism emanated from Aligarh it was, if one may use the term, a layman's doctrine, and had little influence on the learned of Deoband. There was not the same bridging between the traditional and the modern as was happening within Hinduism with the various reform movements of the nineteenth century. The Muslim secularist therefore had the sense of insecurity of a man who feels that he has no solid community support. He was susceptible to the charge of infidelity and the reproach or smear of the cry *Kafir*. Within this class we must further distinguish. There were those who saw the relation of Indian nationalism to Islam along the lines of Ataturk in Turkey. Religion was a personal and group matter apart from politics; these men formed the core of the nationalist Muslims, men like Dr Ansari, Sir Mirza Ismail, the Raja of Mahmudabad and M. A. Jinnah himself until about 1930. There were those who saw Indian Islam as a community within India, Indian but separate from the Hindus and not to be swallowed up by them. Sir Syed Ahmad represented this view which prompted the formation of the Muslim League and led on to the Pakistan movement. And there were those, more traditionally minded, for whom Muslim India was a province of world Islam and for whom nationalism was subordinate to religion. The Ali brothers were connected with this view. They found a convenient bridge between nationalism and pan-Islam in the *Khilafat* movement and when this broke down tended actively to promote Muslim separatism.

All three sections faced the problem of communication with the great inarticulate mass. Clearly what would move a Muslim peasant would differ from what would move a Hindu peasant, but how to move him at all? There were only two answers, a threat to his land which provided his livelihood, and a threat to his religion which gave his life meaning and which was cherished the more firmly the harsher and more precarious his life. To arouse his feelings, he must be made to feel that Islam was in danger, for which his antipathy to certain aspects of Hinduism was a convenient instrument. The Muslim peasant remained largely impervious to the end of the period for his land was not in danger but it was easier to arouse the town-dwellers. In this respect the 'pan-Islamists' had an advantage for they had no scruples in fomenting riots by means of anti-Hindu propaganda, using fanatics and small traders as agents, the butcher and local *badmashes* as their spearhead.

It was for the allegiance of the articulate class in both communities that the various political parties contended. My case is that they never possessed the permanent allegiance of more than a fraction of the class, and that it was the uncommitted majority which influenced events by moving or not moving in ways unpredictable by the party managers. The most important of the parties was of course the Congress; indeed it may be called the only real party of significance at the national level. The Communist party, in spite of governmental alarums, was too small; the Mahasabha, with wide connections it is true, was more of a social than a political organization. The only other real parties, in the sense of having local organizations and a grass roots appeal, were the provincial Justicites of Madras and the Unionists of the Punjab. The Liberals or Moderates had no serious organization and were admittedly a group of officers without troops. Moreover they did not even obey the same general. They were divided into genuine liberals like Sir Tej Bahadur Sapru and C. Y. Chintamani, who sincerely desired political advance along constitutional lines, and virtual conservatives or whigs, who regarded the 'Montford' reforms as a stopping place rather than a starting point. Their nervousness about mass reactions inhibited their zeal for further reform. Their fear of the masses hamstrung their leadership of the classes. Sir Surendranath Bannerjea in his later years was one of these, and I think also the silver-tongued Srinivasa Sastri. And there were others who were frankly hangers on of government and hopers for office. Bodies like the responsivists were transitory splinter groups, the politicians delight but indifferent to the public.

The Congress then, was the only body which could make a claim to the permanent allegiance of the articulate public. It had a nation wide organization with local branches going down to the villages. It had a four-anna membership ticket. It had the *mystique* of being the nation building body of forty years standing and the prestige built up for it by men like Bannerjea, and Gokhale and Tilak. Above all it was bathed in the new radiance shed on it by Mahatma Gandhi, who now presented it as a sort of incarnation of Mother India, with himself as the chief *pujari*. It had a core of devoted workers for whom the Gandhi cap and *Khadi dhoti* were more than a mere uniform, and it had its inner ring of *satyagrahis*, the specially trained devotees of the Mahatma and the missionaries, as it were, of his doctrine. It had distinguished leadership in men like C. R. Das and Motilal Nehru and it now commanded considerable funds from industrialists as well as from the small subscriber.

On paper, therefore, the Congress should have swept the articulate public and have been sure of its unswerving support, while also making forays into the wider field of the masses. But in fact this did not happen. Instead we have the spectacle of rapid changes in the degree of the public support for Congress, with corresponding spectacular changes in its fortunes. At the time it was easy to say that this was due to the machinations of the alien government, the forces of darkness frustrating the children of light. But this was only a party talking point and known to be such. More relevant were the gaps which from time to time appeared in the Congress ranks. At one time Gandhi was disavowed (at the Gaya Congress); at another he used to insist that he was not even a four-anna member. At one time the parliamentary swarajists were jettisoned and later the activist left wing deflected if it did not dictate policy until the open break with Subhas Chandra Bose in 1939. But these clashes of personality and disagreements on policy between groups are not the whole of the story; they are common in all big parties and do not explain the mercurial rise and fall in the party's fortunes. In my view the explanation is rather to be found in the incomplete accord or *rapport* between the Congress and the middle class. Virtually the whole of this class were supporters or sympathizers with Congress (except communalists here and there, Jat farmers in the Punjab and Justicite non-Brahmins in Madras). So long as it kept to moderate courses it had their support and approval. But with more extreme policies it was a different matter. This class, if it was to be moved at all, had to be swept off its feet by some powerful wave of emotion, and even then it could not be relied on for long. The wave would break, ripple up the shore a little further than before and then recede to leave a litter of resentment and carry a backwash of depression. Congress had the support of all the class some of the time and of some of the class all the time, but never the whole class all the time.

The secret of this behaviour by the articulate class is to be found, not in the vagaries of leadership, nor in the opposition of the government, which was a pre-determining factor, a fixed point known to all. It is to be found in the make-up or psychology of this class, which caused it to react in particular ways to particular situations. The proof of this contention can only lie in a study of the classes actual political conduct in the period 1920–47.

We begin with the non-co-operation movement of 1920 which confirmed Gandhi's ascendancy over the Indian public and swept Congress from a class to a national stage. In each episode we may note the motives for the various reactions of this class to events. Prior to 1919 the middle class had been not only moderate but cautious, disliking the Bengal terrorists almost as much as the British, regarding them as a threat to their hard earned property and position. But by 1919 they were moved by many new and powerful emotions. There was war weariness with its irritation at shortages. More important, there was the new sense of self-respect and maturity born of wartime disillusionment with Europe, the Russian revolution and president Wilson's fourteen points. To this new sense the Amritsar massacre, and even more its open justification in England a year later, was a deadly provocation. At the same time Muslim emotions were stirred by the Turkish question and the *Khilafat* issue, so that for a brief moment there appeared to be unanimity in the articulate class and well beyond it too. This was what induced the middle class to support non-co-operation. But at once reservations appeared. The response to the call of resignation from office was poor, while students flocked from the schools and colleges. The first elections were not boycotted sufficiently to prevent the new councils from functioning. The reason is clear: the young with few responsibilities, were willing to go the whole way with Congress policy: their elders, with more at stake, were not prepared to throw in everything, including their careers. This mood of reluctance to extreme action deepened to disquiet and then alarm at the successive developments of the Moplah rising, the Prince of Wales riots, the proposal for a no-tax campaign and the Chauri-Chaura burning. There was much more talk among these people about the sins of the government than the means of chastising it. Just before Gandhi's arrest in February 1922 it seemed as though he might secure the support of the masses at the cost of the loss of the classes. In the event he had, for a time, the veneration of both and the support of neither.

The reaction which followed Gandhi's arrest was a manifestation in political form of these inner feelings. The class would make a dramatic protest against such a blatant assault on its new found self-esteem as Amritsar, but it would not go into permanent or revolutionary opposition to the government. It consistently preferred half a loaf to no bread and so it virtually accepted the reforms in spite of Gandhi and the no-changers.

In 1924–5 there was much talk in this class of the sins of the government and much veneration for Gandhi, but Lord Reading's policy was in fact accepted as liberal if over cautious. At the centre there had been a number of liberal gestures such as the repeal of the Rowlatt Act, the declaration of the fiscal autonomy convention and the setting up of the tariff board (which pleased Bombay), the announcement of the fifty-fifty Indo-British ratio as the target for higher appointments and the holding of I.C.S. examinations in Delhi as well as London (welcome to the whole middle class), the championing of Indian rights in South Africa by Srinivasa Sastri, and Indian membership of the new League of Nations (for Indian feelings of *amour propre*). In the provincial field the Justice and Unionist parties in Madras and the Punjab respectively had shown that the new constitution had possibilities when subject to determined leadership. The 'No-Changers' made no headway. The swarajists themselves suffered defections, not only from the individual office-seekers but from organized groups who in the Central Provinces and Bombay borrowed Tilak's slogan of 'responsive co-operation' as responsivists. Lord Reading threw some of this advantage away by doubling the salt tax in 1925 for this touched the self-respect 'complex' of the articulate though individually they suffered little by it. Nevertheless this situation broadly continued until late 1927.

It seemed in 1926 as though a bold initiative by the new viceroy (Irwin) might attract a body of opinion to the government. But all he did in this direction was to plead for communal unity, which was considered part of the stock-in-trade of incoming viceroys. Then descended, like a clap of thunder from a clear sky, the appointment of the all-white Simon commission. The reaction was spontaneous and profound; the articulate class was virtually unanimous in rejection and protest. The reason for this was that this action touched, and less lightly than in the case of the salt tax, on that same sensitive spot of the post-world-war-one sense of self-respect. In people's minds and feelings this was a throwback to the pre-war days of European superiority and Curzonian imperialism, and as such it was not to be borne. A part of this class was ready for stronger action and indeed with the young leaders Bose and Nehru, called for it. But the rest were still ready for compromise because they had too much to lose by extremism. The class thus divided again on Lord Irwin's dominion status and Round Table declaration of October 1929. There is no doubt that the uncommitted public hoped for a settlement at this time. Whether Gandhi really determined on civil disobedience in order to forestall a violent upheaval by the left wing of Congress has still to be revealed. But it is certain that in the first three months of 1930 the uncommitted public was very reluctant to embark on an anti-government campaign. Their sympathy was enlisted *after* the march to Dandi by Gandhi's handling of the campaign and the general distaste for police methods, another throwback to the old days of remembered humiliation. The class drew back again as soon as an opportunity was presented by Irwin's Simla speech of early July. This resilement made the first Round Table conference possible and in turn led on to the Gandhi–Irwin truce of March 1931. By the beginning of that year Gandhi knew that public support was flagging; he knew that a welcome awaited a successful outcome of the negotiations. And welcome indeed there was. The middle class as a whole had had enough; they were quite content with the next slice of the loaf and would brandish the bread knife no longer. The wounds to their self-respect had been healed or at least treated and bandaged; their normal preference for gradual reform and fear of violent upheaval had therefore resumed their sway. This mood accounts for the failure of the renewed civil disobedience movement of January 1932 in spite of the provocative government action. It was virtually over in six months, not because of police severity, but because the middle class as a whole had no heart in it. It was really the left-wing of Congress which went to prison on that occasion.

Then Willingdon's government made a fundamental miscalculation in trying to suppress Congress altogether between 1932 and 1934. The fact that the middle class as a whole would not go to prison or jeopardize their careers at the Congress bidding did not mean that they withheld their general approval. Government action achieved its purpose on the surface, but it made the Congress leaders into martyrs and consolidated long-term general support for them. It also deprived the Government of any respect it had once enjoyed from this class. That is why the Congress sprang to full strength the moment it emerged from its legal banning in 1934 and won notable successes in the 1937 elections. The class had now virtually no alternative between support for Congress and inaction. The Liberals were by now a scattered remnant and the communalists were distasteful to most of the class. This was the new pattern for which Lord Willingdon was responsible.

The Government of India Act of 1935 was the next issue, and raised again the old issue of direct action or constitutional criticism. I suggest that the decision to accept office in 1937 was a piece of realism by Congress marking a realization by its leaders of the limits of its control of this class. The outbreak of the second world war in September 1939 added a new issue, and perhaps dimension, to Indian politics, for everyone knew at once that there must be big changes after the war. In general, excepting perhaps Subhas Chandra Bose and his followers, there was sympathy with the British stand against Hitler and the dictators. There was, however, an immediate crisis over the viceroy's method of declaring India's participation in the war, which led to the resignation of the Congress ministries. Some British observers have found it difficult to understand the depth of feeling aroused by Lord Linlithgow's clumsiness. But the reaction in fact exactly fitted into the pattern already described. The brusque announcement without any form of consultation or 'by your leave' touched again the now well-established Indian pride. On the other hand the Congress withdrawal from provincial office was considered unrealistic by the average man and aroused no enthusiasm. Nor did Gandhi's selective civil disobedience in the following year; it was, in fact, a damp political squib. Some may think that the reason for this half-hearted action was precisely because Gandhi knew that the public would not back anything bigger.

The collapse of France in 1940 and the threatened invasion of Britain was a profound shock to this class for they felt the apparently stable though much criticized British *raj* to be threatened by an external force, and with it their own security. They were correspondingly heartened by Britain's stand and her success in the battle of Britain. Even Winston Churchill, the old avowed enemy of Indian freedom, became for the moment a hero. Henceforward there was a growing ambivalence in this class until the end of the war: a sympathy with the allied struggle with Germany and Japan which enabled the government to recruit large numbers for all kinds of war service despite the Congress and League bans, and a growing impatience amounting to exasperation at the government political inaction in India. This was coupled with a rising suspicion that the British did not mean what they said when they talked of self-government 'after the war' and would slip out of their obligations if they could. Yet this class still objected to extreme courses and would have welcomed a moderate settlement with the British. This statement is confirmed by the two dramatic incidents which stand out in the six war years of political frustration. The first was the Cripps mission of March–April 1942 with its Cripps offer. The enthusiasm which the mission excited and the pitch to which expectations were raised were convincing proof of the general public's desire for an amicable *modus vivendi* with the British. The depression at the failure of the mission was correspondingly great. The second was the Congress 'rebellion' of August 1942, which followed Gandhi's description of his resolution as 'after all, this is open rebellion', and his internment along with the Congress working committee, in the Aga Khan's palace at Poona. There was a rising, presumably engineered by the left wing of Congress, now freed for a moment from Gandhian shackles; there was widespread violence, specially in the United Provinces and Bihar. But what was more noteworthy was the failure of the middle class as a whole to lend support. No bombs were thrown, no offices resigned, no legal disobedience offered. The limit of their action was talk of a police *raj* and the use of government typewriters to produce 'Quit India' notices. The class was exasperated with its ambivalent position and inevitably blamed the government, but it still stopped short of violence or revolution.

After the war, the general desire for a settlement with the British was expressed by the Congress. But the public again resiled from any resort to a short-cut of violence as was shown by its reaction to the Bombay naval mutiny in early 1946. Suspicion of British intentions was largely removed by the conduct of the cabinet mission later in that year. But the demand for independence by consent then clashed with the League demand for Pakistan and the issues became too complicated for further analysis. But one thing was clear in the welter of negotiations, charges and counter-charges and riots, the articulate class as a whole was still moderate in outlook. It still preferred the half-loaf of achievement if a whole one involved violence and a risk to their security. As once the Round Table conference and the 1935 Act were preferred to direct action for independence now, so in 1946–7 partition was preferred to *purna swaraj* at the price of continuing massacres and incalculable civil war.

If this analysis is correct, there has always been, down to independence, a public opinion of the articulate classes in India over which the Congress as well as other political groups, had a very incomplete control. The gap between speech and action in this group varied in direct proportion to Congress approaches to illegality or violence. Verbal support of Congress objectives or assent to their polemics often misled Congress leaders, Gandhi included, into overestimating the degree of support they could command, *and retain*, in pursuing extra-constitutional courses. But for Gandhi's genius in finding the *via media* of non-violent non-co-operation, and of *civil* disobedience Congress might well have stumbled, in the hands of men like Bose or the younger Nehru into a head-on clash with government which would have destroyed the unity of the articulate class and put back freedom for many years. As it was, they often miscalculated because they did not understand the psychology of this class. With its periodical silent withdrawals of support this class performed a service to the country by restraining the Congress before its activist wing could stage the clash with government for which it was straining, a clash which would have alienated it from the body of the articulate class and broken up the Congress. The pity of it was that this class was wholly unorganized politically on an all-India scale, either in the form of a party external to Congress, or of a pressure group within. We therefore have to trace its views by the rise and fall of the individuals who from time to time reflected its views most accurately. A Srinivasa Sastri, a Sapru, a Rajagopalachari for a time successively played this role, and Gandhi himself voiced their feelings at times, notably at the time for the Gandhi–Irwin truce negotiations. As a whole this class therefore acted as the makeweight or stabilizer of Indian politics, its method being the negative one of 'thou shalt not'. But though amorphous in composition, indefinite in policy, undefinable in terms of numbers or of programmes and negative in action, it is to the actions, and still more the non-actions of this class that India owes a freedom from violent revolution during the twentieth century.

PROSPECTS FOR A UNITED INDIA AFTER THE CESSATION OF BRITISH RULE, AS THESE APPEARED IN SIND 1930–46[1]

by H. T. LAMBRICK*

(N.B. The term 'India', throughout this paper, means British India together with the Indian states – in the old sense of 'state' – within the frontiers as they stood in 1946. The matter within square brackets is subsequent comment on the original diary.)

The province of Sind was unique, in that it alone, among all the provinces of British India, had not been under Hindu rule since A.D. 712. For the next 1,130 years it had been ruled by Muslim sovereigns; and that long period was followed immediately by nearly a century of British rule. The North West Frontier Province might be regarded as even more of a Muslim country than Sind, but it should be remembered that a substantial portion of the territory composing it, Peshawar included, was conquered by the Sikhs and remained under their domination for fifteen years (1834–49). No such phase intervened between Muslim and British rule in Sind.

The population of Sind, including that of Khairpur state which is as Sindhi as the rest, amounted in 1931 to roughly 3 million Muslims and 1 million Hindus. Only in the North West Frontier Province was there a greater disparity in favour of the Muslims. Moreover, the distribution of the two communities was peculiar. The vast majority of the Hindus lived in the towns or in substantial villages, while the vast majority of the Muslims lived in small villages, hamlets and farmsteads scattered all over the countryside.

British rule in Sind, too, had certain peculiarities. After its annexation the country was first governed as a separate province for four years, and was thereafter united, purely on grounds of administrative convenience and in particular because it was a deficit province, with the Bombay presidency. The two areas had then virtually nothing in common. The individuality of the indigenous institutions of Sind was such that many of the most important Bombay laws and regulations were inapplicable there. And, of course, Sind already had developed its own rules and regulations in revenue, criminal and other matters, which had no connection with those in force in Bombay.

The immediate head of the Sind administration, as part of the presidency of Bombay, was the commissioner-in-Sind, who was really much more like a deputy governor without an executive council. For instance, he was ex-officio inspector-general of police in Sind, and though subordinate to the government of Bombay exercised directly a number of the powers of that government.

After the Montagu-Chelmsford reforms, the Bombay legislative council

[1] Read 7th December, 1966.

* Fellow of Oriel College, Oxford. Member of I.C.S. serving in Sind, 1927–47.

included a certain number of members elected in Sind, and there were similarly one or two in the central legislative assembly. Not unnaturally, the reported deliberations of these bodies sitting several hundred miles away from Sind, and not very often concerned with Sind affairs, aroused relatively little interest within that province. People of all classes continued to look up to the commissioner.

Another curious feature in the province was that although its Muslim population outnumbered the Hindus by about three to one, the ratio by community employed in all grades of the government services other than the police, was almost the reverse. This was partly because the Hindus had taken more readily to western education than the Muslims, but also because a section of the Hindu community had a tradition of government service going back long before British rule. The civil service of the Talpur Baluch rulers of Sind had been staffed almost entirely by these Amils of Hyderabad.

I have already mentioned that Hindus in Sind were almost all townsmen, with the Muslims living all over the countryside. So here were elements which were likely to have a rather peculiar influence in the event of a 'national' civil disobedience movement; or again on provincial autonomy, if Sind were separated from Bombay. Their effect for the time being was to confer on the district officers a degree of influence which was probably greater than in most provinces of British India.

Who were those district officers? So far as the European element goes, they were men who came out to India at the age of twenty-two or twenty-three direct from British universities. Their ideas about politics and administration were liable to be derived from Plato's *Republic*, Aristotle, the works of Hobbes and Rousseau, and Burke's speeches. For the most part they arrived in India completely innocent of politics and administration in a practical point of view. They knew that their duty was not to dabble in Indian politics, but to be impartial administrators, and threw themselves into the business of learning that job by doing it. In the districts they very soon learned the facts of life and the springs of men's actions. And they became aware that for the purposes of their daily work, Aesop's *Fables* were a far more valuable compendium of political philosophy than all the books over which they had argued at the university. Some forgotten genius had prescribed Aesop, translated into Sindhi, as the set book for the higher standard language examination which we had to pass before we could obtain a district charge. One might have thought that the fables had originated in Sind (they *are* known to have an ancient *Indian* origin) so apt were these parables in portraying the country and the people; and no language could convey their spirit as well as does colloquial Sindhi.

And here I wish to add a rider to my theorem of the curious innocence in which we began our work of administration. British officers were liable constantly to inveigh against the graft, nepotism, improper influence, use of a public position for private advantage and similar phenomena which they encountered among politicians, in local self government, and elsewhere in Sind – no doubt in other parts of India – and to talk rather as if such things were peculiar to those countries and unknown in England! This was simply because few of us really knew anything about local government in England or about its other institutions, except schools and universities; and learned very little more about them when we were on leave. It was a different matter when we had lived some time in England after retirement! Suffice it that a friend of mine who had for several years administered the town of 'Z' in Sind, in supersession of its notorious municipality, and thought he had become a perfect connoisseur of *daggābazi*, told me many years later, after experience in an appointment in an institution of considerable status in England, that what he found went on there made him feel as naïve as a child in these matters.

I trust that forbearance will be shown towards the aforementioned intolerant trait, characteristic of the outlook of the junior British officer, when it appears in the letters from which I am going to quote. For my coverage of the subject of this paper is to be entirely extracts from what I wrote home at the time – that is, periodically during the years from 1930 to 1946. These letters were all preserved, but I only re-read them within the last few months, more than twenty years after the last of them was written and more than thirty-six years after the date of the first. It is not that I think them particularly prescient or judicious, but because each of them reflects how affairs appeared to me at the time it was written. At least there is no wisdom after the event, no re-interpretation by hindsight, no unconscious perversion of my contemporary views by faulty memory.

I have not *altered* a word, though I have *omitted* occasional words and phrases which added nothing but emphasis to my ideas; and I propose to string together these extracts with brief factual remarks to place them in context. The reason why I have chosen so long a period for the purpose of my subject is that it was in 1930 that people in Sind seriously began to consider the question what would happen when the British left, and at that same time the beginnings of the answer could be discerned.

I therefore begin with Gandhi's breaking of the salt law and the civil disobedience movement of 1930. I was then assistant collector and sub-divisional magistrate in a district in Upper Sind.

* * *

Larkana
25 April, 1930

The Satyagraha movement goes on somewhat languidly up here. . . . People are making salt . . . from 'kalar' soil out of which they got salt in the Mirs' time. The Excise people confiscated the stuff but did not arrest the man – we don't want to make a hero of him. There is speechifying and they sing some rather good songs. One of them has this refrain every other line:

'Qaido lun johbhago bhago: Angrez Hind man bhago bhago'

– a pun on bhago, which is the past tense of two verbs, to run away and to break. It means 'The salt law has been broken, broken. The English have run, run from India.'

Camp, Kambar
13 May, 1930

. . . The political question as far as Larkana is concerned is fairly simple . . . those who have joined in the non-co-operation movement are insignificant, and have no influence except over school boys and obscure people. The

Mussalmans are taking practically no notice of it, and the zemindars in particular know where their advantages lies. But I fear they must be losing to some degree their confidence in Government.

Camp, Miro Khan
24 May, 1930

. . . We are in no danger of serious trouble in Larkana and I am inclined to doubt whether our tyrannies will achieve the notoriety of discussion in any but the local rags. I am inclined to predict an outcome similar to that of the 1921–22 troubles. Non-violence is impossible – the mob and bad characters everywhere seize the opportunity to prey on society – outrages like those in Chittagong and Sholapur frighten the leaders and alienate their supporters among the moderates – and so it ends, after causing another storm of bloodshed and ill-feeling, inflicted on the wretched country by its so-called liberators, who then turn round on the 'satanic' Government because they forced it into taking drastic measures to preserve order. No respectable Englishman can be out of sympathy with aspirations towards freedom . . . the disproportion between theory and practice is the difficulty in this country.

Larkana
8 June, 1930

. . . Today is the last and principal celebration of Mohurram, and with the Congress propaganda being solely confined to the more quarrelsome Hindus of the place, you may imagine that we are anxious. . . . I think our precautions should be adequate. Luckily the Congress people have enough sense to refrain from processions and speechifying today; and on the whole things should pass off well. But tomorrow they will be at it again, and are likely to provoke a clash with the Mussulmans of a village near, whose zemindar refused to have them making nuisances of themselves there, and kicked them out. They have said they will go back with about 300 volunteers – so you can imagine we are ready for a row there. . . .

[later]

Mohurram passed off very well – the people were good humoured and surpassed all our expectations. The Hindus weren't afraid after all but watched the tamāsha both from their houses and in the streets. . . . However, we are back to where we started again, as regards the machinations of the Congress. The attack on the village referred to earlier on is almost certain: as soon as it is, I am going to arrest the two worst men.

[A week or more passed without any developments, and I went for a few days to Karachi.]

Larkana
25 June, 1930

Actually a row of sorts took place here while I was in the train coming back, the Congress volunteers being foolish enough to go to the village of Lahori beyond my bungalow on the same side of the canal, with the result that they had a trouncing from Mussulman toughs waiting there. . . .

Though glad in a way that these Congress fools showed their cowardice (they ran on the shouts of 'Allah Akbar', not because they were hit – they *were* beaten a bit as they ran!) I don't like the look of it. Even if we Government people do not get the credit of staging the whole show – as we shall among the extremists – it will be thought by everyone that we are afraid to take action ourselves and the zemindars consequently take the law into their own hands, to deal with the movement. . . . The intimidation Ordinances have been extended to this place – we have arrests everywhere else in Sind and producing good effects – why not here?

Larkana
2 July, 1930

. . . Our little Larkana trouble . . . has produced a very quietening effect on the Congress people, and the panchāyat soon found that they could not go through with a week's 'hartāl' and see the Mussulmans drive a roaring trade while they lost money. So the position is much better.

Larkana
16 July, 1930

. . . I was at Ratodero getting the measure of the political question there. Things had improved, for the people we sent to jail from there have apologized and are willing to give any pledge, if they are let out – the first volunteers to 'rat' in Sind, though others have elsewhere.

[Now came news of the great Sukkur riots of August 1930. Muslims in Sukkur town attacked the Hindus and looted them. Disturbances went on for three days, in spite of the most drastic action by police and para-military forces. And significantly, this wave of robbery, dacoity and murder spread all over Sukkur district; that is to say, the Hindu population in many towns and villages were attacked.]

Karachi
21 August, 1930

. . . What an astounding business that is! Nothing on such a scale has happened in Sind since the Conquest. The worst feature is that the rumour has gone round, and is believed *bona fide* by the dacoits themselves, that Government has no objection to the Hindus being attacked and robbed! I think some zemindar who has been made to eat dirt by the Congress has tipped the wink to his *badmāshes* to spread the idea. The wretched Government is held to blame, at any rate, as for everything else.

[I was appointed special magistrate to try the riot and dacoity cases, and wrote, before taking up the work:]

Sukkur
10 September, 1930

. . . I believe the evidence will be pretty rotten – identification very shaky – and so forth: all the Hindus in Sind will be clamouring for convictions, and the Mussulmans working hard for acquittals.

[After the trials had gone on for six months, with varying results, there was a general demand that the residue should be settled by arbitration, to allay the bitterness. I was appointed assistant commissioner-in-Sind. The civil disobedience movement was continuing elsewhere.]

Camp of the Commissioner-in-Sind
27 January, 1932

... The political situation so far as Sind is concerned is perfectly quiet and well in hand. In fact I feel that we are using a sledge hammer to kill flies, with these savage ordinances. They are necessary, of course, elsewhere; but the 'movement' in Sind never really had much guts. The zemindars and merchants of standing are with the Government to a man ... many loyal but shrewd and time-serving people in Karachi wish that we had been firm with Congress before: but I don't agree. It was necessary to give them a chance to co-operate ... in order to secure moderate opinion here and at home.

[I have already mentioned that Sind was a deficit province: that is to say, its revenue did not equal the expenditure of administration – at the time when it was attached to the Bombay presidency. In spite of great improvements in irrigation during the eighty-five years that followed, it remained a deficit province, in 1932. But with the inauguration of the Lloyd barrage and canals in that year there were prospects that Sind would soon become self supporting, and the question whether it should be constituted a separate province was reopened.]

Government House
Karachi.
31 March, 1932

... We are all wondering what the new Sind Separation Conference will bring forth. The matter is developing in a new direction however; Bombay, having woken up to the fact that Sind is costing them a crore yearly will want to get rid of us; and not only for financial reasons – the presence of the (comparatively) pro-Government *bloc* of Sindhi members in the Legislative Council has long been felt a drag on the go-ahead-and-damn-the-risk element in the Presidency. So not only the Sind Mussalman, but the Presidency Mussulman and many Hindus will be glad to get rid of us.[1] The Hindus there of course will be somewhat restrained by the bogy of Mussulman tyranny over their co-religionists in Sind under the new régime.

Government House
Karachi.
19 May 1932

... We cannot quite pierce the veil which enshrouds the Secretary of State's and Viceroy's high policy, but one thing is certain – if for the furtherance of that policy it is necessary that Sind should be made one of a chain of Muslim provinces, it will be separated however large the subvention it may need to keep it going.... I get the impression that after having been accused of 'dividing and ruling' – most unjustly accused – ever since Indians became vocal, we have at last got to do it in sober fact – not in everyday administration but up at the top of things. The reason is the transference of so much power into the hands of those who are utterly and radically divided among

[1] *Sic*, in original. The sense requires, after 'Sind Mussulman' the words 'wants to be free from Bombay'.

themselves. We may well have an India split into Muslim provinces and Hindu provinces; the dividing line being softened and a certain unity maintained by the presence of enormous communities as hostages on each of the 'wrong' sides of the line . . . it seems cynical; but it is a solution thoroughly in keeping with the genius of the country, which may be summed up in one word – disintegration.

To make what seems very clear out here clearer to you at home: – you have a predominantly Muslim legislature and executive in, say, Sind. The only thing that will stop them from passing discriminatory laws, not exactly *against* the Hindus *per se*, but laws which work out in favour of Muslims, is the fact that in, say, Orissa, the Hindus can and will retaliate, if their minority rights are not respected in Sind. Of course the pan-Muslim belt from Kashmir, through half the Panjab, N.W.F.P., Baluchistan and Sind looks rather like a pistol aimed at the heart of India, with behind it the Khilāfat and the Jehād. It is Shaukat Ali's dream, and when we are slanged in the Hindu papers for pampering the Muslims, we can't help feeling a little uncomfortable. As I said at the beginning, it is in high places only that this divide-and-rule seems to be becoming more than a stock denunciatory slogan. For all ordinary purposes the dividing is kindly done for us. . . . We are committed to a policy of political advance for the benefit of the intelligentsia, and down below there is social stagnation, the only reactions of which are communal. Messrs. Lansbury and Maxton meet Indians who are clever committee men, shrewd business men, eloquent speakers – thorough politicians in a word. . . . It is not that these individuals are not capable each of doing his job well in any individual position, but where is the foundation? – on which they would be able to stand if they were Englishmen filling such posts in England: where is sane national feeling, where is the common sense of the man in the street, where is public opinion? Democratic Government cannot succeed without these things, and they do not exist in India. Can you imagine a minister in a British Cabinet mistrusted because he was a Lancastrian or a Devonian?

Government House
Karachi.
18 August, 1932

. . . We have just got down to arranging for the 'Communal Award' being given wide publicity. I think it is a very fair distribution of seats among the various communities and interests, and ought to work as the best *modus vivendi* that we can expect. Of course it will please nobody generally and only a very few locally: majorities will say their actual numerical majority has been whittled down till they have to fight to keep it, while minorities will say that they haven't a chance to make their voice heard. But it is a good thing that, e.g., the Muslims in Bengal will have to work to maintain their position as a majority community. . . .

Of course one can easily say that it is nothing but a 'scrap of paper' – an artificial, mathematical, arm-chair document; but the peoples of India must realize that it is their . . . lack of unity that has forced us to impose a settlement upon them based on statistics and little else, to try to make them work together without letting one or the other community run amuck. . . . My fears are for the Panjab. . . . The Sikhs are in a ferment – and do you know what they are saying among themselves, if not openly? That they do not mind living under British domination, but will never live under Muslim domination. That, I fancy, is the feeling of every minority in every corner of India, though Indians (the vocal and politically-minded) are chary of admitting it.

Government House
Karachi.
23 March, 1933

. . . The White Paper is much what we expected; really the large emergency powers given to Governors and the Viceroy are a pleasant surprise, and look like an indication that Churchill has done some good among the immense harm that his outbursts must do us, in what they call 'political circles' out here. But there is one snag in it. If, in a so-called constitutional Government you give the Head a dictator's powers, albeit they may not often be needed, we must have good men as Governors. The time has passed when we could get along with a third-rate politician from home . . . we can't have rubbish any longer, when the new régime begins. I wonder if those in High Places realize this. *Entre nous*, the Viceroy told R - - - - that when he first came out he didn't think Indian Civil Servants ought to become Governors: but that after a year he found that the I.C.S. Governors' provinces – Panjab, U.P. and C.P., at any rate – were much the best-run!

[In 1935 I was transferred from Upper Sind frontier, where I was deputy commissioner, to act as deputy secretary, political and reforms department, Bombay. At this time the debates on the Government of India Bill were on.]

Bombay
23 May, 1935

I must say that the last effort of the die-hards, in regard to excluding certain areas from the scope of the Constitution, was pretty unscrupulous, and unworthy: fancy suggesting that the whole of Surat district should be administered *à la* Political Agent! U.S.F. contains sufficiently wild and violent people, but I should never dream of trying to mollycoddle them at the expense of those who are more advanced.

Poona
1 (?) June, 1935

. . . Why do not Congress speakers see the irony, and indeed absurdity, in their invoking the example of Ireland – her long struggle for Home Rule, and England's eventual surrender? Nothing could be more damaging to their own case. The lesson of Ireland for India can be summed up in one word – Ulster. England, or at least Asquith, wanted to give Home Rule to Ireland – the whole of Ireland. But Protestant Ulster made it absolutely clear that she would fight rather than submit to Catholic Dublin. And now we see what came of it all. Do our politicians at home appreciate the analogy? And have they the courage to say so?

[After a further spell in Upper Sind frontier I was posted as collector and district magistrate of Sholapur, in the Deccan. The headquarters is a large industrial city, with many cotton mills. Meanwhile Sind had been constituted a separate province, under an interim government pending inauguration of provincial autonomy under the Government of India Act, 1935.]

Sholapur
18 December, 1936

. . . No one seems to appreciate the significance of the fact that Kabul and Delhi were under the same sovereignty for just as long as they have since been separated – two centuries, under the Moghals. And after that you had the Panjab and Sind united with Afghanistan under Nadir Shah and Ahmed Shah Abdali. That seems to me a perfectly natural combination, looking up there from this new viewpoint in the Maratha country.

Camp, Pandharpur
28 February, 1937

Well, it looks as if the Congress will accept office in the six provinces in which they have an absolute majority: and I fancy they will set about bringing a deadlock and forcing the Governor to use his special powers at once. They will then resign and go into opposition, and defeat any other Ministry, so the Governor will still have to keep using the aforesaid powers. They will then appeal to 'the Country' that the new Constitution is an engine of tyranny. But mark you, this programme has its dangers. In the Panjab and Sind, and I expect Bengal – possibly one or two other provinces – there will be Ministries that will work the Constitution, and the people of these provinces will enjoy the boon of Democracy (for what it is worth). And if I am not much mistaken, the result will be that Muslim India will be governing itself and Hindu India, thanks to the Congress, will have less say in its own governing than it has now! This may, after a few years, result in 'the country' rejecting the Congress and turning to something a little more reasonable.

But of course my calculations may be quite wrong. In any case, I am sure that we shall have a packet of trouble in the not too remote future. The Communist candidate got into the Mill constituency by a huge majority.

Sholapur
22 October, 1937

. . . You will have seen how the Muslims have rallied to the banner of the Crescent and Star. It was the inevitable result of Congress' inconsiderate and pig-headed tactics. I fancy we shall have commun*AL* trouble all over India, not only Commun*IST*, the two communities being more sharply divided than ever. The radical and axiomatic principle in Indian politics is that the Muslims will not stand Hindu Raj over all – I don't mean locally, in States, etc. So we are boiling up for a first class row. The Congress want to get the Muslims into their fold but their methods are not at all happy – they bribe religious leaders and the unprincipled rag-tag and bobtail but when the cry of 'Islam in danger' goes up, as it has now done at the big meeting of the

Muslim League in Lucknow, we shall soon see whether 'Congress-ki-jai' or 'Allah-u-Akbar' will rally the Muslims.

It is the fault of the Congress entirely for adopting the principle that it alone speaks for the whole of India, and ignoring the existence of the League as long as it could: it can do so no longer now.

Camp, Salsa
2 December, 1937

. . . we are passing from the Iron age (of the 'Steel Frame'!) to that of Lead – Saturn is in the ascendant. One thing that seems to me a most curious feature in the political evolution of this country is the utter and most salutary and essential isolation of the Army. It stands still in its loyalty; those Indians who enter it as Commissioned Officers become, so far as I know, more English than the English in their *political* views; and everything else is moving so fast. The traditional thing for the Indian Dictator, or Tyrant-raja to do – ? our friend Jawaharlal, when with his Jacobins he mops up the Girondists of the Congress right wing? – is to gain the army. But this would seem impossible; so where will revolution get a hold, when the worst comes to the worst?

[On the outbreak of war in 1939 I was re-posted to Sind, and in 1940 was travelling all over the province, as superintendent of the census.]

Camp, Thariri Mohbat
26 January, 1940

. . . Hindus everywhere tell me that they have no sense of security in the smaller villages since Provincial Autonomy was introduced, and one of their Members is actually tabling a motion that the constitution be suspended and the Governor take over the administration, as Law and Order is non-existent! This is pretty good from the Hindus, who have for the most part been the most vocal in demanding constitutional reform, Indianization, etc. All are asking for European officers now: and another indication of the way things are going is that there is a motion to extend the provisions of the Sind Frontier Regulation to the whole of Sind, whereas the previous clamour was for its abolition. It applies to the Frontier talukas of Upper Sind Frontier, Larkana and Dadu Districts, to control the Baluch tribes there, and permit their blood-feuds etc. to be settled by tribal custom, in Jirgas; in which, mark you, no Advocates are permitted to appear: hence the previous outcries against it!

Now most officials who have had to administer the Jirga system have found it liable to become, in spite of them, a great engine of oppression: and I for one am highly scandalized at the proposal to extend rather than abridge its limits.

Karachi
10 September, 1940

. . . The Muslim League is now co-operating in the war-effort – but its demands so far as the future constitution goes are really more extreme than those of the Congress and other parties; and if through pique they joined with the Congress in Civil Disobedience (very unlikely, I think) they would never agree about the constitution which was to replace 'British Imperialism'. I think even some of the Manchester Guardian staff may be getting a glimmering of the truth – viz. that India is not a Nation but a Continent; but that the *Muslims in India* are something *very like a nation.*

Camp, Ghaibidero
7 December, 1940

... You will have been wondering how the Satyagraha campaign is affecting things here. The Congress High Command have decided that in view of the delicate state of things in Sind they should not have their people here courting jail. I feel that all we need do in India is to remain firm and let it be known that we shall stand no nonsense. The Muslim League, though they do not like us, like the Congress still less, and the latter know it.

Camp, Shah Hassan
1 January, 1941

... I hold no brief for the Muslim League as portrayed by its local protagonists, but in sober fact the whole of *inarticulate* Muslim India is behind it. The majority of Congress Muslims are either cranks or the hirelings of the Congress . . . it was because the Congress Muslim Mass Contact movement was mainly bribery and because they had secured Muslim religious leaders by the same means that the Muslims are so bitter against the Congress. But they are *so ashamed* of the fact that some of their people stooped so low that they dare not give publicity to the fact – which destroys their most powerful argument, and they have fallen back on the most trivial reasons for complaint against the Congress Ministries. It is as well to remember this. The 'New Statesman and Nation' seems to have no idea that the Muslims have a very good case for 'Pakistan', and that it is utterly impossible for them to submit to Hindu 'Raj' in the Central Government.

Karachi
7 February, 1941

... My impression is that the Congress is steadily losing its influence: of course it never had any in this Province.

[Early in 1942 disturbances created by the fanatical Hur sect in Sind with the object of compelling the provincial government to release their *pir*, who had been sent into detention outside Sind, attained the proportions of a terrorist rebellion. I was placed on special duty to concert operations to suppress it. The Congress meanwhile promoted a new civil disobedience movement in other parts of India.]

Hyderabad, Sind.
3 September, 1942

... Conditions in India are interesting now, when one considers what repercussions they may produce on her political future. The Muslims have stood utterly aloof from the Non-Violent (*lucus a non lucendo*!) movement of Hindu hooliganism. As a result, I suppose we shall, after it is over, lean a still more attentive ear to the Congress . . . at the same time retaining sufficient say in matters to prevent the sword of the Muslim exacting a little natural justice.

Hyderabad, Sind
21 May 1944

. . . Gandhi's release took most of us here completely by surprise, and apart from officials many Muslims were disgusted by our weakness. The good people in Parliament, the Manchester Guardian and the New Statesman, who harp on this appeasement of the Congress, who still put implicit trust in what men *say* they are, and pay no attention to what they *do* – these people I should like to have with me in the Makhi area for a time . . . and let them see a little life in India in the rough.

Hyderabad, Sind.
30 July, 1944

. . . I wonder if the English papers reproduce such things as the furious resolutions passed by the Hindu Māhāsābhā in Bengal and all over the country, denouncing Gandhi as the betrayer of Hinduism, and saying they will fight to the last ditch before they allow Muslims self-determination, etc. What can one do? Why does not someone get up and say what the real Indian problem is – to make leopards change their spots?

[Operations against the bands of Hur outlaws in Sind and the adjoining states continued unremittingly. They for their part kept up the 'war', murdering and looting Hindu shopkeepers, Muslim landholders, and others, with apparent impartiality, and sabotaging irrigation canals. It was necessary to put under restraint a large number of non-active members of the sect who harboured the gangs and gave them intelligence. These measures occasioned a new development.]

Camp, via Hyderabad Sind
27 January, 1946

. . . The Congress have started to espouse the cause of the Hurs. (They are as suitable bed-fellows as the 'Indian National Army' men: though the Hurs have not yet learned the 'palāver' about the 'Nation'!)

I shall probably be issuing a statement to the Press about it.

Camp, Sanghar.
21 February, 1946

. . . What do you think of the (at this moment) latest development in affairs here – the mutinies in the Royal Indian Navy? This is the fruit of our 'appeasing' the forces of disorder and indiscipline, letting the I.N.A. be pampered while the men who remained staunch under every kind of torture and hardship are virtually cold-shouldered: the old, old policy of sacrificing our friends in this country – a rapidly decreasing number, and no wonder! – and sucking up to our enemies. The R.A.F. set a precious example with their strikes – men in comparatively comfortable transit centres preventing their comrades coming from unpleasant places in East Asia for some well-earned leave or demobilization, from getting home, because they, many of them out here only two or three years, were 'browned off'. . . . I'm afraid there is little hope of my getting away before June. They require me to put in order the complicated structure which I have contributed to make, during these last years, owing to the exigencies of the Hur problem.

The other day I silenced ignorant Press critics (including J. Nehru) by an exposition of some sides of the problem and the reasons for our measures. I should not feel happy if I left much for others to disentangle.

[Pandit Nehru had, in the course of a visit to Sind, been misinformed by his hosts as to the nature of the Hurs' activities and of our proceedings against them. His public references to the Hurs' showing 'their amazing strength' appeared to me particularly unfortunate, seeing that among the many hundred persons they had slaughtered was one former prime minister of the Sind government, and the son of another, both killed; not to mention loss constantly inflicted on the people and the revenues by sabotage of canals and railways. Their 'movement' was not anti-British in character, but the anarchy of primitive fanaticism.

Having obtained the approval of government I issued a press statement for the first and last occasion during my service in India.

I was on leave in England in 1947. It is perhaps superfluous to add, after all that I have set before you, that to me the principal and most painful events of that year in India appeared the natural and ineluctable consequences of the cessation of British rule over the sub-continent.]

FEDERAL NEGOTIATIONS IN INDIA 1935–9, AND AFTER

by SIR FRANCIS WYLIE*

An impression seems to be gaining ground that it was principally due to the dilatory methods pursued by Lord Linlithgow that an Indian federation, in terms of the 1935 Act, was not created in the years immediately preceeding the outbreak of the second world war. During the war too Linlithgow is apparently accused in certain quarters of obstructing essential political reform. K. M. Panikkar [1] for instance wrote in 1953:

'The determined opposition of the nationalists and the claims of the Muslims for a separate state with complete independence [*sc.* from India?] rendered the Act of 1935 abortive. Realizing the failure of their efforts the British Government through Sir Stafford Cripps offered complete Dominion Status with certain temporary limitations [*sic*] during the period of the war, but the scheme failed to materialize owing to the intransigence of the Civil Service and the then Governor General Lord Linlithgow.'

These are serious charges. Whether they are well founded or not it will not be possible to say definitely till the day comes when all the papers are available – which may not be long now. In the meantime, however, it may be worthwhile to draw attention to some aspects of the problem which have a bearing on the pace of political developments in India between the passing of the 1935 Act and September 1939 when the war broke out. The Act received the royal assent on August 4, 1935.

THE PROBLEM

In 1935 British India was organized in sixteen separate administrative units. The population of each of these units according to the 1941 census was as follows (Muslim percentage in brackets):

Madras	49,341,610	(7·9%)
Bombay	20,849,840	(9·2%)
* Bengal	60,306,523	(54·9%)
United Provinces	55,020,617	(15·3%)
* Punjab	28,418,819	(51·1%)
Bihar	36,340,151	(13%)
Central Provinces and Berar	16,813,584	(4·7%)
* Assam	10,204,733	(33·7%)

* I.C.S. 1914–47: Indian Political Service 1919–38; Governor of Central Provinces and Berar 1938–40; Political Adviser to the Crown Representative 1940–41 and 1943–5; Governor of the United Provinces 1945–47

1 *Asia and Western Dominance*, p, 274.

* N.W.F.P.	3,038,067 (91·8%)
Orissa	8,728,544 (31·9%)
* Sind	4,535,008 (72%)
Ajmer-Merwara	583,693 (15·3%)
* Baluchistan	501,631 (87·4%)
Coorg	168,706 (3·3%)
* Delhi	917,939 (33·1%)
Panthpipluda	5,367 (24%)

I have extracted these figures from the Census Report though everybody who has had anything to do with the Indian problem must by now know them practically by heart. Commentators however – particularly perhaps commentators in England – tend to discuss the Indian sub-continent as if it was one nice homogeneous entity over which a constitution – written thousands of miles away – could be fitted just like a hat or a cap. The problem was of course much more subtle than that.

The total population of British India at this census was 386,666,623 of which the Muslim community constituted twenty-four per cent. There were in addition some 660 Indian states with a total population of 90,857,901 and a Muslim percentage of 13·3. The latter was provided almost entirely by the states situated in the extreme north-west of the country. The units with a large and, as it proved later, an indigestible religious and cultural minority are marked with an asterisk. With the possible exception of the Sikhs the non-Muslim minorities were politically speaking unimportant. I do not myself regard the so-called untouchables as a minority in this context. They constituted a social and economic problem certainly, but essentially a problem which a free India would one day have to solve for herself. Nobody else could do it for her.

The problem which the 1935 Act purported to solve was therefore the governance, with due regard to the preservation of British power and the protection of British interests, of a country with upwards of 400 million inhabitants divided into a multiplicity of linguistic groups and including a religious and cultural minority of no less than 90 million souls. Posterity may wonder at the hardihood of the British parliament in thinking that such a feat was possible. To solve the problem they relied on the – in England – well tried expedient of parliamentary democracy plus federation. Apart however from the fact that constitutions do not necessarily export well there were in the India of 1935 historical and administrative circumstances which militated against the success of the federal principle and indeed against the very system of parliamentary democracy in the proposed autonomous units as well. The countries which have so far evolved a federal system of government – a very sophisticated governmental expedient – consisted previously of separate areas possessing some at any rate of the attributes of sovereignty, areas which had already attracted some degree of local loyalty from their inhabitants. These units felt spontaneously the need for a closer union than can be achieved by, for instance, alliances between sovereign states. This was not true in India. What the 1935 Act attempted to do in fact, so far as British India was concerned, was to impose a quasi-federal system of government on a previously existing unitary state. The provinces of this state not only had never possessed any of the distinctive attributes of sovereign states, but they had most of them been created haphazard as British conquest spread itself over the Indian peninsula. Or some of them, the North West Frontier Province for instance, had been created by ukase purely for administrative convenience and with no discernible political end in view. Inter-provincial boundaries were often anomalous. The eastern parts of the United Provinces, for example, would have been better accommodated in Bihar while east Punjab and west United Provinces had linguistic and cultural affinities which would, if they had been joined together, have qualified them for the role of a federal unit. The Punjab itself, where some degree of provincial loyalty and provincial pride was said to exist, contained no less than three separate and potentially antagonistic communities – Muslims, Hindus and Sikhs. When the strain came, as one day it had to, these disparate elements fell apart with results that are painfully obvious to us now. In the south of India the same anomalies were present, Gujaratis and Mahrattas in Bombay, parts of the Central Provinces which should have been in the United Provinces and so on. That these conditions will right themselves one day seems certain, we may hope without entailing the disruption of the Indian union in the process. For the moment it is only necessary to note that the state of affairs I have tried to describe inevitably made for unstable political conditions at the provincial level. So long as the Indian Nation Congress remains the only well organized political party in what we may call Hindu India – with the prestige of its leadership in the national struggle to sustain it – the damaging effect of the anomalous structure of the old British provinces may not be too much in evidence. What needs emphasis here is the fact that nowhere in these prospective federal units was it possible for real local loyalty to emerge – a loyalty cemented by common religious, linguistic or cultural affinities. Bengal may be cited as an exception. In Bengal there was certainly a common language and to some extent a common culture, but in Bengal fifty-five per cent of the population was Muslim and the rest Hindu. Such were some of the difficulties attending the creation of federal units out of the existing provinces of British India.

Which brings me to the question of the Indian states (old parlance). It was clear to us all that if India was to advance to dominion status the Indian states must somehow or other be brought in. Here was a real problem. There were some 660 so-called Indian states, surely the oddest political set-up that the world has ever seen. As everybody knows the vast majority of these miscellaneous territories were quite unfitted to be adequate administrative let alone federal units. The half dozen states which, by reason of their size, might have qualified for either role exhibited as often as not the same anomalous structure as has been noted already in the case of the British Indian provinces. Both Hyderabad and Kashmir, the two largest of these units, were notable examples of this anomaly. The 1935 Act, however, afforded no remedy for the existence of 660 separate administrative units, the vast majority of them minuscule. In fact by prescribing representation for all of them in the federal legislature the bland suggestion was offered that they had on their merits a claim to indefinite continued existence. This was false and constitutes a real blemish in the Act. Nor was any serious attempt made to expedite political (*sc.* democratic) reform in any of these curious territories. The vast majority of them were in any case far too small to support a parliamentary system of government. In the federal legislature, the representatives of the population of all these heterogeneous areas were to be nominated by the rulers, a derisive proposal from the point of view of the Indian National Congress. The latter it is true had always treated the states question delicately. Probably because they knew that the princely territories would one day in the natural order of things merge with British India and maybe also because some princes – probably quite a lot of them – helped with Congress funds.

When at the first Round Table conference in 1930 Tej Bahadur Sapru came out with the then novel suggestion for an Indian federation, the proposal was immediately accepted – there was certainly collusion here – on behalf of the princes by Bikaner followed by Alwar, Rewa and Sangli. It is ironical to note that two of these rulers – Alwar and Rewa – had later to be deprived of their powers for gross misrule. All the four princes mentioned were in fact petty people ruling over tiny principalities each with less than one million inhabitants. The great states, Hyderabad, Mysore and the rest were of course also represented at the Round Table conference, but their representatives seem to have kept discreetly in the background on this issue. That a little prince like Bikaner should have spoken first on such a momentous issue I trace to the influence of K. M. Panikkar who was at the time secretary of the chamber of princes and who later became prime minister first in Patiala and then in Bikaner. It is just possible too that these small but active princes, knowing nothing of the real nature of a federal government, welcomed the federal proposal because somebody had put it into their heads that, if they joined an Indian federation, they would thereby free themselves from the odious supervision of the viceroy's political department.

I visited Bikaner among many other states to explain to the Maharaja and his government the implications of the federal chapters of the 1935 Act. This was no less than six years after the first Round Table conference, where Bikaner had made his historic pronouncement, but only a few months after the arrival in India of Lord Linlithgow. Unfortunately by the time the viceroy's special representatives embarked on their mission the smaller states – Bikaner among them – had joined together to provide themselves with a whole battery of lawyers including some very loud-mouthed American experts. These people reaped a rich harvest all through the winter of 1936–7 and in the process confused the minds of the poor princes mightily. In the 1935 Act, the proposed division of powers between the federation and the states was as explicit as skilful drafting and careful consideration could make it. This did not, however, prevent, in all the small states I visited, long orations on the perils of 'eminent domain' and other esoteric excrescences which were described as inevitable by-products of the federal system of government. It should be said too that the Davidson committee's report on the financial aspects of the proposed federation, as these affected the Indian states, made ominous and sometimes very abstruse reading for the princes who were most of them more concerned to keep their 'privy purses' intact than to speculate on the intricacies of federal constitutions. It was only in the small states that this train of lawyers followed the viceroy's special representatives around. The half dozen big states had their own advisers. Hyderabad for instance had the late Walter Monckton specially retained during the whole period when the federal discussions were in progress and in fact right up till 1947. Monckton was there not only for his skill as a lawyer but because the Nizam thought he had influence in the Conservative party in England. The Nizam of course had never any intention of joining an Indian federation though he scrupulously avoided saying so. What he wanted was independence when the British went with, if possible, the present of an Indian port from them before they went to give him an outlet to the sea.

The most important states I personally visited were Baroda and Kashmir. The Baroda discussions were both difficult and highly technical, but the strong impression I got was that Krishnamachari the Diwan, an old deputy collector from Madras, a cautious man and very conceited, was highly dubious about the whole thing. The Gaekwar himself was away racing in Bombay and anyway cared for none of those things. In Kashmir where the discussions took place in the presence of a bored and sulky Hari Singh the whole matter took on, even for me, an air of complete unreality.

If there is truth in the allegation that in 1936–7 Lord Linlithgow dragged his feet then perhaps the charge may be held to stick over these visits by special representatives to all the important Indian states and incidentally to many that were of no importance at all. For the representatives had no instructions to try and persuade rulers to join the federation. They were to explain the provisions of the Act and that was all. If Lord Linlithgow was at fault there, however, the home government were in on it too. For anything like pressure on the princes to join was very delicate ground. They had many allies in England both in parliament and outside it and they had cried so often and so stridently that their relations were with the British Crown alone and that their treaties had been described by successive viceroys as 'inviolate and inviolable' that many people thought obscurely that they must have right on their side, to the point that 'the Princes' came to be thought of as great powerful rulers – all 660 of them. That only about six of them had any claim to serious consideration at all as potential federal units was a fact about which even viceroys of India had to be constantly reminded.

The special representatives completed their mission by the spring of 1937. They had, of course, kept the viceroy and the secretary of state informed of the result of their visit to each state, but their reports had to be collated and some impression formed of the likely intentions of the princes. In the early summer of 1937 I was posted to other duties and I do not know what measures, if any, Lord Linlithgow took after that to hurry the deliberations along. In retrospect, however, I would say that, if they were left to their own devices, there was never the slightest chance of getting rulers representing fifty per cent of the population of the princely states to sign instruments of accession before the second world war broke out in September 1939. The only way, so far as the British government were concerned, if they genuinely wanted to expedite the creation of the federation, would have been to take the princes by the neck and compel them to come in. This is what Patel and V. P. Menon did later on. What Patel and Menon did in 1948, the Indian National Congress could very possibly have arranged in 1937–8 if they had wanted to. I am not sure myself that they did.

THE INDIAN NATIONAL CONGRESS

Would the Congress have worked a federal government 1935 model at the centre if somehow or other the necessary princely adhesion had been secured? It is a moot question. Nehru [1] says 'The Act of 1935 was bitterly opposed by all sections of Indian opinion'. This is an exaggeration, but it is certainly true that the Congress high command was altogether opposed both to the federal sections of the Act and to the sections dealing with the so-called provincial autonomy. At the centre it was the reservations over defence, finance and foreign affairs, read with the whole corpus of the governor-general's special responsibilities – *inter alia* to protect the princes – which riled them. In the provinces the governors' special responsibilities were regarded as an anachronism and insulting anachronism at that. As Pandit Pant – the ablest and best of the Congress politicians I came across – said to me much later 'Under the 1935 Act we seem to need more supervision than we did under dyarchy'. At the centre again the notion of a democratic parliament which included in the council of state forty per cent and in the house of assembly thirty-three per cent of members nominated by obscurantist despotic rulers of sometimes extremely petty Indian states was just anathema. On the reverse of the medal it may be noted that what stuck in the gullets of many princes was this very provision. They would not hear of their representatives being elected – most of them had no representative institutions in their states anyway – but they knew their men and feared that anybody they sent to Delhi to represent them would come back a flaming 'red'. Nehru again hated in his very bones the whole principle of communal electorates. To him it did not matter that the principle of communal electorates dated from 1906 or even that the principle had been sanctified by the Lucknow pact of 1916. Himself a humanist, that a man's politics should depend on his religion struck him as an absurdity while the divisive dangers for the country he thought of as lethal.

In spite of all these difficulties I think personally that, after much haggling and possibly after securing some face-saving pronouncements by the British government, maybe even some amendments to the Act, the Congress would have agreed to work it, having arranged at the same time for the necessary quota of princes to sign instruments of accession. Ever since 1928 the declared goal of the Indian National Congress had, of course, been independence. But political advance in India had always been by stages. The Congress leaders were also not fools. They saw well enough the difficulties of the problem even if they derided the British government for making too much of them.

THE MUSLIM LEAGUE

And what of the Muslims? The timing of events is here crucial. Popular ministries were formed in seven provinces in July 1937 just about the time

[1] *The Discovery of India*, p. 319.

when the reports of the viceroy's special representatives about the attitude of the princes were being digested. In the 1937 elections the Muslim League did badly. Even in the North West Frontier Province (91·8 per cent Muslim) they could not gain a majority though the so-called Congress vote in that province was perhaps more in the nature of a protest against a flaccid and inexpert administration, too much and too long under the influence of the local Khans (landlords), than a mature political judgment on the part of an inexperienced and highly volatile electorate. Nehru's satisfaction at the Congress performance at this election, in an almost exclusively Muslim area, was deliberately played up to buttress his own political attitude and the Congress claim to represent all India. Then came provincial autonomy in seven Indian provinces which brought not only the League but the whole Muslim community face to face, almost for the first time, with political reality. The accusations of gross anti-Muslim bias on the part of the Congress ministries were of course moonshine, but Muslims everywhere were brought to realize what it meant to be in a perpetual minority under democratic conditions. Government after all does not consist only of impartial administration of the actual law. There is the prestige attaching to the holding of office, perks and small favours abound while the mere exclusion from the dispensing of patronage can do much to make people feel themselves second class citizens.

Nevertheless it was only in 1940 that a Muslim League resolution formally demanded the creation of a separate state though the idea had been talked of, particularly among Muslim intellectuals, for years before that. I doubt myself if say in 1938 – the necessary adhesion of the princes could never have been secured before that – the Muslims could have been brought to co-operate in the creation of the federation except after long and arduous haggling while the war, we must remember, broke out in September 1939. My conclusion therefore is that it was not only the delay in securing the adhesion of the princes that prevented the creation of an Indian federation in the years 1937–9. Time was painfully short, but other attendant difficulties were also formidable.

Les rois ne lâchent que quand
le peuple arrache(?)

Which brings me to the question of tempo. Before the outbreak of war there was little sign of a real revolutionary mentality in India. The Indian National Congress certainly had not got it or it was well muffled under Gandhi's leadership. The 1935 Act represented an important stage in the steady advance of India towards self-government. It was far, however, from being a revolutionary document. British interests and the reality of British power in India were firmly protected. No one on the British side in the years I am reviewing thought of independence for India as an early possibility. Lord Halifax apparently wrote to Lord Zetland sometime in 1937 'A stone-walling policy shows a lack of imagination and will get us nowhere'. Torn from its context it is difficult to know what exactly the noble Earl meant by this sentence. He certainly did not mean immediate surrender to the Congress demand for independence. He was not at all that sort of man even if on a day many years before he had allowed the 'naked faquir' to stride up the steps of the viceroy's house in New Delhi. A real revolutionary atmosphere – and in my present view there was at that stage no solution of the Indian problem without it – was created for the first time by Clement Attlee's announcement in the British house of commons on February 20, 1947, that by hook or by crook the British government intended to hand over power in India 'not later than June 1948'. Lord Mountbatten arrived in India on March 22, 1947, to put the transfer of power through, and the British were in fact out by August 15th of the same year. This dazzling performance has I think helped to focus criticism on the deliberate – some would say dilatory – processes followed by the British government – and by and large regarded as natural by the Indian people – between 1930 and 1939. The implied contrast here is fallacious. Mountbatten had not to provide the Indian subcontinent with a constitution. Nor had he – a principal difficulty in all the long discussions between London and Delhi in the pre-war years – to find constitutional means of protecting British interests in the country. The service he rendered to India – and it was a real service given that the job had to be done at all – was to cut her in two with maximum speed. And it was brilliantly done. George Merrill and I – he was the American envoy in Delhi at the time – decided one evening when we were watching Lord Louis and his consort in action that in all history no revolution had perhaps ever been put through with so much grace. On his return to England Mountbatten is said to have told the East Indian Association 'It took two years to separate Sind from Bombay. We separated 400 million people in two and a half months.' Before he made that statement somebody should have advised him to define his terms.

THE CRIPPS OFFER

It remains to consider the *obiter dictum* of K. M. Panikkar, quoted in the first paragraph of this note. He calls the Cripps offer of 1942 'complete Dominion Status with certain temporary limitations during the period of the war'. Actually the offer was a good deal less than that. I was in Afghanistan in 1942 and can write of the offer from memory only. It produced, of course, the Mahatma's famous quip about a post-dated cheque and in truth the Cripps offer dealt mostly in promises – extensive promises it is true – about post-war concessions to Indian demands. There was to be complete dominion status, with the right of secession from the Commonwealth, an exclusively Indian constituent assembly followed by a bilateral treaty with Britain, etc., etc. I have never heard myself that Lord Linlithgow and his advisers did anything to discourage or delay this plan. No immediate fundamental constitutional change was in any case envisaged. It was hoped to secure Indian co-operation in the war effort at the price of very real concessions at the war's end. But the Congress, maybe rightly from their point of view, wanted the substance of power at once. They demanded that the executive council should have immediately the full powers of a dominion cabinet. That way lay chaos and if, in the circumstances of the time, Lord Linlithgow resisted the demand I would find it very difficult to disagree with him. Lord

Mountbatten's experience at a much later stage with an interim government formed from warring Hindu and Muslim politicians points the moral. My recollection is, however, that Cripps said one important thing about the Indian states which should not be allowed to escape notice. The princes were to be free to join the proposed post-war dominion government and *in any case their treaties would be revised to meet the new situation.* If the viceroy's special representatives had been allowed to say that in 1936–7 the necessary quota of princes might have been frightened into signing instruments of accession. After all when it came to the bit in 1947 these famous treaties were unilaterally renounced without causing any particular tremor anywhere. Incidentally there is one minor point about the Congress demand for a dominion status type of cabinet in 1942 which deserves notice. If the demand had been accepted the governor-general's power to keep the ramshackle Indian states structure in being – power which rested on sub section 12(g) read with sections 285–287 of the 1935 Act – would almost certainly have been lost, with possibly disastrous consequences to the internal peace of India in the very middle of a war. I find it very difficult to believe that a dominion type cabinet at the centre would ever have allowed sections 285–287 to be used.

PAKISTAN?

Anyone who has persevered so far with the reading of this note is I think entitled to know what my own attitude was in these high matters. I should explain to begin with that I was never an active participant in the viceroy's deliberations. A custom had grown up by which the political problem was dealt with by the viceroy in a very personal way. In what follows, therefore, it should be understood that I do not write as one who was at the real centre of affairs. I had been of course always myself in favour of satisfying India's national – and natural – aspirations as expeditiously as possible though I hoped always that this could be done without damaging the fabric of the administration irretrievably. On the other hand I was altogether opposed to the partition of the country. My only direct attempt at intervention in the argument was in 1945 when I circulated a paper arguing that means simply must be found to avoid the carving up of the country. A complete rearrangement of the map of India was necessary I wrote to create federal units based on linguistic, cultural *and religious* affinities. The federal concept was still capable of all sorts of extensions. Why should not the Muslim units, once their limits had been established, be allowed to maintain their separate armed forces, fly the flag of the union with some added emblem that would satisfy their susceptibilities, etc., etc. Always provided that the federal government had effective control at least of defence, foreign affairs and, if possible, communications. The Indian states should, I suggested, be left alone for the time being, but should be told straight away that their future lay with the Indian union and that, when this was established, their special relationship with the British Crown would be terminated. The rearrangement of provincial boundaries should, I wrote, be entrusted to a Royal Commission consisting exclusively of Indian members. It will not be forgotten that the creation of linguistic provinces was an old demand of the Indian National Congress. Nevertheless in retrospect these proposals of mine seem now to be unpractical and almost naive. The intention behind them was however fair enough. It was of course to get religion away from the centre of the storm. The cabinet mission were attracted by them for twenty-four hours and then sent for me to say that they would not do at all. There was not enough time. Nehru, with whom I discussed the idea of a Royal Commission, was very cold about it. He detected in it I think a wheeze to delay the transfer of power and he boggled particularly at the notion of a separate flag for a federal unit. He probably realized even then that the creation of linguistic provinces, though at one time it had been a Congress demand, was in fact political dynamite. We all know this now after the Bombay upheaval and we may get further proof of it if the Indian government persists with its policy – enshrined in the constitution – of forcing the whole country to do its public business in Hindi. As a small sidelight on feeling in the United Provinces about Pakistan I should mention that with the prominent Muslims I met there – unfortunately they were not many in the twilight of the *raj* – I made no secret of my opposition to the partition of the country. Not one of them disagreed with me and many of them agreed emphatically. It was not I suppose that they enjoyed the prospect of living under a perpetual Hindu majority but that, if Jinnah had his way, their community, in what was left of the country, would be so weakened that in the end it might be completely submerged.

CONCLUSION

I now come back to the two charges levelled against Lord Linlithgow. Till all the papers are available it is not possible to be sure but for the moment I would say myself that the verdict must be the Scottish one 'Not Proven'.

SOME THOUGHTS ON BRITISH POLICY AND THE INDIAN STATES, 1935–47,

in reply to questions put to

SIR CONRAD CORFIELD*

THE APPROACH TO THE STATES FOLLOWING THE GOVERNMENT OF INDIA ACT, 1935

As federation could not come into being without the consent of the rulers, and this consent only be secured by the Crown representative, it was assumed by Sir Bertrand Glancy, who was then political adviser, that Lord Linlithgow would make use of the political department to approach the rulers. It was suggested that the residents and political agents should be carefully briefed on the problems involved, whilst the experts prepared the instruments of accession which would have to be signed by each ruler. Political officers were in close touch with the rulers and knew their individual reactions. Moreover, they were known to be in favour of personal rule in principle, and would not be open to the suspicion of trying to extract more concessions from the rulers than were essential to establish federation. They were also on the spot to deal with particular problems as they arose. Linlithgow, however, was so impressed with the complicated issues involved that he decided to appoint a special group of three officers to take charge of the negotiations. Only two of these, Sir Arthur Lothian and Sir Courtenay Latimer, knew the states intimately. The other, Sir Francis Wylie, though a political officer, was conversant mainly with frontier problems. Their colleague, Sir Eric Conran-Smith, was the expert from the reforms office, where much of the detailed work of the new Act had to be done.

As soon as this decision was announced the rulers took alarm. They were already under pressure from the Congress politicians through the praja mandals to surrender internal power. It now appeared that they were going to be under pressure from the paramount power to surrender more to the future federation than they had bargained for. So they decided to meet this frontal attack by employing top-level constitutional experts from England to negotiate on their behalf. As a result, long, detailed wrangles developed and it was two years before draft instruments of accession were prepared.

It would have helped, of course, if Whitehall had not treated the negotiations as a chance to tidy up the whole structure of accessions. The states were too varied in size, geographical position and internal development not to present an untidy picture. This had been accepted for generations and could not be altered in a few months. The attempt bred delay and suspicion.

It would also have helped if the approach had been made through the residents and political agents. I can vouch for this because I was officiating as

* I.C.S. 1920–47: political department, 1925–47: political adviser to the crown representative, 1945–7.

resident for Rajputana when the time came for the rulers to decide whether they would sign the instrument of accession or not. Most of the rulers in Rajputana (except for the Maharaja of Bikaner, who had been the protagonist for federation at the second Round Table conference but had since become so disillusioned that he was now leading the opposition to it) asked me for advice. They had no wish to discuss details. In any case the instruments were so legalistic as to be almost incomprehensible. What each wanted to know was whether he was being faithless to the long history, tradition and integrity of his state if he signed. I believed that in the long run more of the individuality of each state would be preserved by relinquishing the proposed powers to the federation than by refusing to sign. But each ruler had to be persuaded of this in the light of his particular circumstances, not in the light of legal constitutional formulae.

For instance, one ruler had recently succeeded, but without full powers because of misgovernment by his predecessor which had to be put right. I knew that his over-riding wish was to have these restrictions on his powers removed. When he asked whether he should sign or not I suggested that the Crown representative would be impressed by his wisdom and ability if he did. Another ruler, whose state had once been the accepted leader of Rajpatana, was impressed with the suggestion that if he became the first to sign he would be giving a valuable lead to his brother Rajput princes. A third ruler accepted the view that he could hardly do better than take the advice of his British chief minister, who had served him so wisely over the years.

Whether these individual suggestions were decisive or not I cannot tell, because the rulers' replies were never published, but Linlithgow did tell me that Rajputana was the only area from which the necessary fifty per cent acceptance had been received. I have little doubt myself that if the procedure proposed by Sir Bertrand Glancy had been adopted the negotiations would have been swifter and the results more favourable to federation. In that case the federation of all India could have been established before the war and India might have joined willingly in the war against nazism instead of having war declared on its behalf by the viceroy without the consent of its leaders. And under the influence of the joint war effort the federation might have learned how to overcome Hindu–Muslim antagonism without partition and how to integrate the states without eliminating their value. As it was, federation had to be put into the refrigerator for the duration and never revived.

My view then was, and still is, that if the problem had been treated on a personal and not a constitutional basis, adherence could have been obtained before the war from a sufficient number of rulers to start the ball rolling. There is always a tendency to climb on the bandwagon. But Linlithgow had no confidence in the personal touch. Once the negotiations had opened on a legalistic basis, the chances were negligible.

THE RÔLE OF POLITICAL ADVISER, 1945–7

I took over as political adviser in June 1945. My first aim was to re-establish relations with the standing committee of the chamber of princes. The ground had been prepared because, first, Lord Wavell had promised that 'the paramount power would not hand over its control to any other authority without their consent', and secondly, Sir Francis Wylie, who was unsympathetic to the rulers had left. There was still, however, suspicion. So I entered into personal discussions with the chancellor, the nawab of Bhopal. My attitude was that provided the interests of the country and its people as a whole were not jeopardized the rulers had every right to expect from the paramount power all the freedom to which they were entitled under their treaties. When the chancellor and his colleagues were persuaded that this would be the future attitude, peace was restored and negotiations could begin.

The aims of British policy pursued between 1945 and 1947 should I think have been the same as I put to a gathering of the Punjab states rulers in 1943 when I was their resident. Only the third aim contained anything novel. The aims were: (1) closer contacts with their subjects, leading to some form of constitutional monarchy, (2) grouping of states into larger units, not only for administrative but also for political purposes, and (3) a legal separation of the privy purse allotment from state funds *after* classifying the kind of expenditure rightly debitable to the privy purse and transferring all balances to a development fund. One ruler wished to know if this meant that the paramount power intended to break treaties in order to enforce these aims. My reply was that they were aims which I thought the rulers themselves should adopt if they wished to survive under post-war conditions. Years later, another of these rulers when on a visit to England admitted that if these aims had been adopted the states would not have been obliterated after independence.

I was able to persuade a number of the Punjab rulers to inaugurate development funds, but a budget classification of privy purse expenditure continued to be a problem. My predecessor as political adviser had discussed privy purse expenditure with the standing committee of the chamber on more than one occasion, but no agreement was reached. I revived the discussions. There had been for many years an accepted formula as to the percentage of state revenue which privy purse expenditure should not exceed. Budget classification of this expenditure had, however, not been discussed, which of course meant that the percentage formula was valueless. The standing committee needed much persuasion before a classification was accepted. The Indian states department subsequently made use of the formula and I hope also of the classification which I had with so much difficulty persuaded the standing committee to accept.

I had always been unhappy about the functions of the chamber of princes ever since I first attended a meeting of the chamber in 1921 when I was assistant private secretary to the viceroy, Lord Reading. The chamber was supposed to take counsel with the viceroy about matters of common interest to India as a whole, but it hardly ever did. Consequently this duty was left to the political department. It was not easy, however, for a viceroy who was the sole representative of the states in the governor-general's council to fulfil this duty when matters of common concern were on the council's agenda. So it was decided to create under the Federal Act a new appointment of political adviser to the Crown representative, who would have cabinet rank and be entitled to attend the governor-general's council in order to put forward the states' views on matters of common interest. My predecessors did not make use of this power and relied on interdepartmental consultation. I determined to use it. But after attending a number of council meetings I soon realized that, though the presence of the political adviser at cabinet discussions did help to remind the members of council that there were questions of policy on which they were not entitled to make decisions without taking into consideration the interests of the states, these interests could not be fully protected by the political adviser alone.

I therefore drafted a scheme for a joint consultative council on which selected chief ministers of the states could sit with members of the governor-general's council in order to discuss matters of common concern. Unfortunately there was some delay in pursuing this proposal, whilst I was on short leave, and the approval of the secretary of state was not received until Wavell had persuaded the Congress and Muslim League to share the portfolios of the central government.

This proposal for a joint consultative council was included as the first item on the agenda of the first meeting of the new cabinet. I was in attendance as usual to represent the states point of view. Except for the viceroy himself and his private secretary, George Abell, I was the only Britisher present, and it fell to me to explain the proposal and to stress its importance as a clearing house for future development. It was greeted with stony silence. Though the Congress members had agreed with reluctance to share portfolios with the Muslim League it was clear that neither side was prepared to share with states' representatives any of its power to influence future events. The silence was eventually broken by a Muslim Congress member who ignored the proposal and told the viceroy that he thought it was quite unsuitable for the states' points of view in the cabinet to be put forward by a British officer, and asked when an Indian could be appointed political adviser. It was hardly for me to comment, but subsequently, when Wavell asked me what I thought of the suggestion, I said there was much to be said for it, if someone could be found whom the rulers would trust and the Congress and Muslim League leaders would agree upon. He smiled, and we heard no more of the suggestion. But there was no doubt that my value to the states as their representative in the British Indian cabinet was now at an end.

RELATIONS BETWEEN THE POLITICAL DEPARTMENT AND LORD MOUNTBATTEN

Lord Mountbatten's policy towards the states was dictated by the necessity for a British India solution, and his aim was to secure the assent of the rulers to new agreements which would subordinate them to the successor governments. I took my stand on the 1946 cabinet mission memorandum regarding the lapse of paramountcy. It was based on a draft by Sir Stafford Cripps, who accepted some of my amendments. In my view it was clear that an exercise of paramountcy by the Crown representative (before paramountcy lapsed) which hampered the states in their negotiations for future political arrangements with the new dominions was contrary to the letter and spirit of that memorandum, which had been accepted as a basis for the final settlement. I considered any such action a breach of faith.

Mountbatten ceased to listen to the political department from the day he made his bargain with Vallabhbhai Patel about promoting a limited adherence, which I could not support. Mountbatten told me that he had succeeded in persuading Patel to limit adherence to defence, external affairs and communications. I pointed out that he had agreed to use his influence as the representative of the paramount power to recommend a bargain which could not be guaranteed after independence, and which would inevitably be extended. V. P. Menon was virtually his political adviser from that date, and had had considerable influence before that date. I remember the day but not the date when I gave Mountbatten the facts of a certain case and he said I must be wrong because Nehru had told him otherwise. I don't know if Menon had briefed Nehru.

My main difference with Mountbatten was when he agreed to use his influence as Crown representative and as a royal personage with the rulers to ensure adherence before the lapse of paramountcy. Incidentally, when I asked him what should be said to rulers who wished for some guarantee that their personal connection with the Crown should never be severed, he wished me to assure rulers that this connection was safe because they would be adhering to a dominion which accepted the monarch as king. On a further question whether, if the dominion declared a republic, the rulers could then technically withdraw their adherence, he replied that he felt sure that the cabinet would accept this and I could assure the rulers accordingly. But I felt unable to do so!

I had other differences with him over Kashmir and Hyderabad. I suggested that, if these two states were left to bargain after independence, it would be quite possible for India and Pakistan to come to an agreement. The two cases balanced each other, with a Hindu ruler over mainly Muslim subjects and a Muslim ruler over mainly Hindu subjects, neither of them having access to the sea and both providing valuable amenities over water and communications to both the new dominions. But Mountbatten did not listen to me and when he visited Kashmir he did not even invite his political adviser to accompany him, as was the custom. Anything that I said to Mountbatten about Kashmir carried no weight against the long-standing determination of Nehru to keep it in India.

It is sometimes forgotten that the Crown representative was under the direct control of the secretary of state. After my last residents' conference at the end of March 1947 (which Mountbatten opened but did not attend) the proceedings were recorded and forwarded to the India Office. I was anxious to obtain as soon as possible some instructions on the points raised in these proceedings. Mountbatten was too busy negotiating with the Congress and Muslim League leaders to give any attention to the states problem, so I gladly accepted the offer to accompany Ismay to London when he was taking to the cabinet Mountbatten's final plan, which Nehru turned down whilst Ismay was still in London. As regards this plan, all I wanted to do was to make sure that the cabinet memorandum of May 1946 was referred to and endorsed. This was done in paragraph 18 of the statement of June 3rd.

On the points arising from the residents' conference I had separate discussions with the secretary of state and his India Office advisers. Decisions were made and I returned to India to carry them out. I did not see Mountbatten on my return as he left at once for London with his revised plan. There was no time to lose and I went ahead to implement the secretary of state's instructions. So far as I was concerned, these represented H.M.G.'s policy. Whether H.M.G. had formulated any other policy for the so-called princely states I do not know. If they did, I had no inkling of it from Mountbatten.

THE STATES IN AN INDEPENDENT INDIA

Independence for individual states or for regional groupings was quite impractical. The exercise of paramountcy had welded the continent into too firm a structure, and the political department never supported the idea of a separate entity for the states. However, regional *merger* schemes which we did support, and which were essential to the survival of small states, may well have led outsiders to believe that a grouping of all states was also favoured.

It was the threat of the states' independence that the Congress leaders were really afraid of, because this strengthened the states' bargaining power over future political relations. If the states were committed beforehand these political relations could be quickly adapted to suit the central government. It was for this reason that I could not be enthusiastic when Mountbatten agreed to use his influence to ensure adherence before the lapse of paramountcy. I think the process of adherence to the new dominions would have been very similar if it had taken place after independence, though it would have required more understanding from the Congress leaders, and in the process of bargaining more of the values of personal indigenous rule might have been preserved. These values are not negligible and should not, I think, have been obliterated.

I have no doubt that a standstill agreement (such as that drawn up by my joint secretary, E. B. Wakefield) to ensure that the economic life of the country could continue intact until new agreements were made, leaving new political arrangements to be negotiated after the lapse of paramountcy, would have been more in accord with H.M.G.'s policy as expressed in the cabinet mission memorandum than the policy which Mountbatten was persuaded by Menon and Patel to adopt, namely to make use of the influence of paramountcy and his own personal prestige to press the rulers to accept an entirely new political relationship in advance of the lapse of paramountcy, especially so when his pressure was reinforced by a bargain which he could not guarantee, and which clearly Menon and Patel had no intention of keeping.

I know nothing of the nawab of Bhopal's attempt, shortly before the transfer of power, to form a union consisting of a number of states in central India. It was, I imagine a last minute attempt to fortify the bargaining power of these states. It had no substance to the best of my knowledge. I had already discouraged a similar scheme in the Deccan states which the resident had inadvisedly supported. These and similar schemes were not real mergers and offered no solution to the problem of viable units.

I had held for some years that mergers must be real. When I was officiating as resident for Rajputana in 1939 I came across a case in which I believed that a real merger was practicable. The small state of Nimrana was a tributary of Alwar and there were strong historical links. Personal persuasion and careful negotiations led to a merger agreement which was accepted by the two rulers. But when this reached the then political adviser it was turned down because the problem was so large and complicated that it ought to be dealt with on an all-India basis. My little pilot scheme, which might have provided valuable seed, fell on barren soil. The Maharaja of Alwar was disappointed and the Raja of Nimrana rather relieved. The story got around.

The most disappointing development during my two years as political adviser was the failure of the states negotiating committee, established under paragraph four of the cabinet mission memorandum, to hold together. After considerable discussion and negotiation the nawab of Bhopal, chancellor of the chamber of princes, managed to form a committee which for the first time was accepted as representative even by the major states who usually took no share in the chamber of princes. This was a great achievement and one on which I congratulated the rulers when I addressed their gathering in Bombay at their invitation.

When the Muslim League accepted the cabinet mission plan the states negotiating committee had already been formed. It was my hope that if the committee held together and retained the rulers' rights to nominate representatives to the constituent assembly, the Muslim League might be persuaded to be represented on that assembly. Perhaps this was a forlorn hope, but it was surely a British officer's duty to do everything he could to avoid the partition of a great country which the British had been the first to create. A 'conservative' representation of the states and the Muslims in the constituent assembly might well have been a valuable counterweight to Congress dictation. I know that the Muslim League did consider this aspect but, when the states negotiating committee disintegrated on communal lines, the hope was quite dead, perhaps feeble though it was.

When the committee met the Congress leaders it was able to impress them with its unanimity. The Congress leaders did not appreciate what they considered to be this *obstacle*. Individual approaches to members of the committee were then made and it was even suggested to some of them that it was unwise to unite under the leadership of a 'Muslim' chairman, who might be more in sympathy with Pakistan than with India. Some rulers were also persuaded (often by their ministers, whose ambitions lay with an independent central government) to join the constituent assembly whatever their negotiating committee recommended. The committee then began to disintegrate and when the nawab asked me what he should do I said he could but resign, since in his capacity as chancellor he was no longer able to influence the negotiations: he must now concentrate on the interests of his own state. The same applied to all the other rulers. Mountbatten then accepted the challenge and instructed me to invite the rulers to meet him. I fixed July 25th for this purpose and left India on July 23rd.

BRITISH POLICY TOWARDS THE STATES

The great failing of British policy, as I saw it, was to continue to provide protection to the rulers' dynasties without a reasonable *quid pro quo*. It had so often been stated that protection had to be deserved. It was not a difficult step from that position to specify how it should be deserved. The premier requirement was to introduce reasonable checks on undiluted autocracy. There were some who thought it more in accord with the treaty position for the paramount power itself to impose checks when necessary. But such external checks could only be temporary and they created more and more suspicion without providing a long-term cure.

I saw no reason why the paramount power should not have offered to withdraw the interference of paramountcy in return for internal checks. I tried this in Datia state in 1946 and it succeeded. The ruler accepted internal checks and I withdrew our restrictions. But the main snag was that the form which these constitutional checks should take was never clarified. I tried (when I was the resident in Jaipur) to frame a model Act which could be used by the ruler for this purpose. I even had it printed at my expense and sent to headquarters. It was treated as an improper suggestion. But we were continually advising the rulers to constitutionalize and when they asked how, we said it was for them to decide. They needed guidance; but democracy was suspect, and alternatives which entrenched personal rule too dangerous to attract any secretary of state, whose position and power was of course based on democracy. I think the risk would have been worth running, because the creation of viable state units would have provided stability for the future India.

The official view was that agreements and sanads which the paramount power had negotiated were sacrosanct, and mergers, which I advocated, as mentioned above, could not be political and real without breaking faith. But as already stated, the duty of protection carried with it in my view a reciprocal duty of viability, and viability could have been gradually implemented by the paramount power. It could have been impressed on the larger states that their safety depended on the viability of *all* the states and that these real mergers were in their own ultimate interests. Sudden pressure for mergers naturally created alarm, as it did over the attachment scheme in Kathiawar. But, when I took over, time was short, and shorter than anyone supposed.

THE PARLIAMENTARY DELEGATION TO INDIA, JANUARY 1946

by LORD SORENSEN*

INDIA AND THE NEW 1945 LABOUR GOVERNMENT

High among the formidable tasks confronting the British government and cabinet under prime minister Clement Attlee in 1945 was that of meeting the imperative demand of India for national independence. This was no less clamant than the ultimate settlement of European affairs after the collapse of the vanquished Axis powers, the necessity of defeating Japan, our economic rehabilitation, progressive demobilization and the fulfilment of the Labour government's domestic programme. Moreover, the situation in India could itself aggravate all other problems unless speedily resolved.

There was no lack of will on the part of that government to secure peace with India on the basis of her national freedom and complete self-government, for the prime minister had long demonstrated his entire sympathy with Indian political aspirations, many of his cabinet and government colleagues had in the past been prominent pro-Indian advocates and the Labour party conference had pledged the party to strive for the liberation of India from British imperial domination. There were a few party elements who were critical, particularly of the Indian National Congress, but overwhelmingly it was taken for granted that the Labour government would honour its obligation in respect of India. Frederick Pethick-Lawrence was appointed secretary of state for India and his many years of support for Indian aspirations strengthened the confidence that the government 'meant business'.

Pre-eminently, however, the crucial difficulty of composing acute difficulties between the Indian National Congress and the Muslim League remained a grim obstacle, and this was appreciated by those familiar with Indian politics, even if some dismissed it as a secondary matter that could be surmounted by negotiation and meanwhile was exploitable by those who sought to frustrate the inevitable. Nevertheless, Sir Stafford Cripps, whose past support for Indian freedom was well known, had been baffled in his own efforts on behalf of His Majesty's previous government to promote Indian communal agreement. Attlee, since his experience with the 1928 Simon commission was thoroughly aware of this problem.

Not as a device to play for time, but as a possible interim means of encouraging confidence in its resolute intentions both in India and among its supporters the government decided to send to India a goodwill mission comprising M.P.s of all parties.

THE PARLIAMENTARY DELEGATION

On December 12, 1945 Herbert Morrison, lord president of the council, announced this proposal in the house of commons. The delegation, he

* Labour M.P., 1929–31 and 1935–64. Chairman of the India League.

declared, would 'be able to convey in person the general wish and desire of the people of this country that India should speedily attain her full and rightful position as an independent partner State in the British Commonwealth'. He also intimated the delegation would go under Empire (now Commonwealth) Parliamentary Association auspices, but Anthony Eden and others expressed doubts on the suitability of that excellent organization. On reflection the government agreed that as the mission had more political significance than a normal E.P.A. friendly tour it would be a specific parliamentary delegation.

When asked about its terms of reference Morrison emphasized it was not to be an official enquiry or commission and would make no formal report, but that its function was 'First of all to convey the goodwill of the British Parliament and also to make contacts, to get information and to assess the situation'.

Names of those to be selected for the mission floated about the corridors of the house of commons, but conjecture and rumour dissolved with the official announcement that the ten members would consist of Professor Robert Richards M.P., a former under-secretary of state for India, Arthur Bottomley M.P., Mrs Muriel Wallhead Nichol M.P., Woodrow Wyatt M.P., myself and Lord Chorley, all of the Labour party; R. Low M.P. (now Lord Arlington), Godfrey Nicholson M.P., Lord Munster, also a former secretary of state for India, who were Conservatives, and R. Hopkin Morris M.P. a Liberal. Here may I be permitted a personal allusion? Although it was firmly assumed I would be one of the delegation actually this was not confirmed until almost the last minute after I had been approached by an intermediary M.P. on behalf of the cabinet.

Embarrassingly he enquired if I had personally received any financial inducement from Indian sources to serve Indian political interests, which I suppose in vulgar idiom means 'bribe'. To that, no doubt motivated by a laudable desire to keep the party clean, I replied with an indignant negative and speedily my name, now with detergent purity, was added to the list of those with probity unquestioned. I mention this trivial incident only because it is not unrelated to the India League about which I must appropriately make brief reference shortly. Meanwhile this supplies evidence of the care taken to ensure the delegation was worthily representative of diverse dispositions in a double sense.

At its preliminary briefing meeting the delegation appreciated fully that it had no plenipotentiary powers enwrapped within its terms of reference, but was vested solely with the responsibility of making human contact with Indian leaders and organizations great or small, seeing and judging personally the contemporary Indian scene and as far as possible nourishing goodwill. Professor 'Bob' Richards was nominated leader, an urbane, genial colleague who seasoned his abundant store of goodwill with delectable, if sometimes slightly disconcerting touches of naivité. He seemed unaware that much water had flowed in the Ganges since he had been at the India Office over twenty years before, but his heart was sufficiently in the right place to keep us in collective amity and I greatly mourned his demise a few years later. With little embellishment of our somewhat ambiguous brief we left Poole in

Dorset on January 2, 1946 in a Sunderland flying-boat, reached Karachi several hours later and arrived in Delhi on January 4th to be greeted by a vast excited crowd. On February 12th we arrived again in England after an exhausting, enlightening tour.

THE INDIA LEAGUE

I must explain my reference to the India League lest it be thought extraneous to the basic theme of my discourse. That organization, of which I was firstly honorary (and I stress the 'Honorary') parliamentary secretary and then chairman, had campaigned for many years for Indian self-government and independence, for the most part having as its secretary, also honorary in fact, V. K. Krishna Menon. It did an amazing job if for no other reason because Krishna Menon was and is an amazing person in his intellectual brilliance, his dynamic devotion and – his capacity for needlessly making enemies as well as friends. What was more amazing than this fascinating exasperating personality was the strenuous propaganda the League pursued with the support of a medley of dedicated enthusiasts in London and about the country who arranged meetings, conferences and the dissemination of literature that had widespread cumulative influence. Notwithstanding dark insinuations to me by Ernest Bevin when a government minister that he knew 'where you get your money to pay for your propaganda' the League's funds were secured entirely from collections, subscriptions and donations from individuals in this country. When I attempted to assure Mr Bevin of this and challenged him to prove the contrary he rose from the chair at the small gathering where he had met me and a few colleagues and mutely lumbered off. Later I had confirmation of my presumption that the totally unfounded suspicion hinted by the massive ex-trade union leader was shared by some other members of the government, and if my previously-mentioned confrontation with its intermediary had issued in an unfavourable report I would not have been in the position to write this paper.

After the conclusion of the war against the European axis powers and the establishment of Labour government the India League felt it would be appropriate that Krishna Menon, A. Dobbie M.P., who was a prominent member of the national union of railwaymen, and myself should visit India. At that time it was necessary to secure a permit for travel to Asia, but our application was refused together with the intimation that probably the government would be proposing a delegation to India of members of parliament. Ultimately, when I was included in that delegation my League associates were very gratified. My inclusion apparently created particular interest in India where, to my surprise, I discovered on my arrival there that my pro-Indian activities were extensively known.

I trust I am not being unwarrantably egotistical by stating that my apparent digression from my main theme is justified because of its bearing on the initial reception of the delegation. To my alarm I was smothered in garlands on reaching Indian soil and besieged by a host of journalists and others, my colleagues submitting to a less effusive floral welcome. It took me some time to surmount emotional confusion and realize that I was the victim of discrimination, which was both embarrassing to me and discouraging to our joint prospects of proffering our abundant stock of goodwill. Indeed, there were disconcerting omens of a low temperature awaiting the mission in that meteorologically hot Indian climate. Our Leader, 'Bob' Richards hoped for the best, but we wondered a little about our fortune in the days ahead.

Among the bubbling throng of the first days suddenly appeared Miss Agatha Harrison, whom I had known well in London as a shrewd, unconventional Quaker and member of the Friends (Quaker) India conciliation group whose chairman was their highly-esteemed Carol Heath. This small company of Quakers had privately and unobtrusively been very active in nourishing better Anglo-Indian understanding and had made numerous contacts with Indian leaders, including Gandhi whose religious emphasis on non-violence the group felt, had strong affinity with the spirit and discipline of Quakerism. Miss Harrison had been several times to India and was on terms of personal friendship with Mahatma Gandhi, and her group had decided she should fly to India in the belief that she could be of service and possibly assist in unofficial liaison between our delegation and the Mahatma and other leaders.

Unknown as she was to my colleagues the frequent sight of her, sometimes smoking a Woodbine cigarette, evoked their response of critical puzzlement, and I began to surmise they imagined she was a motherly maiden lady who had arrived to supervise my personal welfare. I appreciated their concern even if they misunderstood that her own concern was not merely with me, but with the purpose we hoped to serve, and at my tactful suggestion thenceforth cheerfully she fulfilled her altruistic task less visibly. I also strove to convey to my friends that she had no sinister ulterior motives, but while charitably they accepted my assurance nonetheless their relief at the nominal withdrawal of the lady they referred to as 'Aunt Agatha' was very clear. Perhaps if her parents had given her a different Christian name they would have been less apprehensive. Probably they never realized adequately that because of her remarkable personal contacts she did very much behind the scenes to remove prejudices from the path of the mission.

It was not solely due to her that soon the original human climate definitely improved, for I know that Pandit Nehru himself took measures to ensure this, though there were dusty patches of dubiety we had to traverse. On my part I persisted, if not always successfully, in my efforts to avoid becoming detached from the rest of the team.

SCOPE OF THE TOUR

We were over two hours late at Delhi airport after leaving the flying boat at Karachi and had to scramble through an assembled multitude then to be driven with imperious speed to the viceroy's house and hurriedly prepare for a much-delayed opulent, official dinner with Lord and Lady Wavell. Our first scheduled meeting with Indians was at a packed press conference. Professor Richards was benignly avuncular in the chair and after expressing felicitations and our sense of great responsibility he innocently brought us to the verge of havoc, if not disaster, by blandly asserting that in his opinion

India 'was certainly entitled to a measure of Home Rule'. The vocal reaction to this from the audience appeared to paralyse the chairman who could not comprehend why his employment of a hoary, obsolete political phrase should have produced an explosive outburst. Silently I squirmed, scrutinized my colleagues who registered imperturbability as a British example of behaviour under such circumstances and decided I should intervene. I explained that the journalists should not misinterpret the chairman's allusion which was only an old-fashioned description of what now signified independent self-government. Apparently, this placated them in some measure, but the avalanche of questions continued for a long time to need deft, diplomatic treatment charged with cordiality to allay suspicion and convince the questioners that we came simply as friendly enquirers anxious to learn all we could.

I feared my intervention might bring on my head the charge that I had no right to be so specific in my translation of the chairman's words, but there was no disciplinary sequel. I had no doubt, however, that my companions were rather fearful that I might commit an indiscretion and equally no doubt that my translation had been salutary. Intent as I was not to leave a false impression of the purport of our visit, in all honesty when asked if I had an open mind on the issue of Indian freedom and independence I had to reply that as one answer could imply that my mind was empty as far as I personally was concerned my mind had long since been filled with conviction on the justice of the Indian demand.

The itinerary sketched to us was certainly very exhaustive, and yet as we pursued our course there were many accretions and we were kept at the job from early morning to midnight. We had three or four meetings with the viceroy and governor-general, Lord Wavell, conversations with numerous British provincial governors, administrative officers, civil servants, judges and business men, we met the full Congress working committee twice and individual members of it several times, including Jawaharlal Nehru, we spent a long morning with the Muslim League leader, 'Qaid-i-Azam' Muhammad Ali Jinnah, and had several meetings with other Muslim League representatives or groups and with leaders or adherents of other religious communities, Hindhu, Christian, Parsee, Sikh, Jain and Buddhist. Of course we had discussions with many political organizations, including with Dr Ambedkar, an 'outcaste' himself and spokesman of a small movement severely critical of Gandhi's alleged patronizing attitude to the 'Harijans', and with others outside Congress, socialist and otherwise. We met trade unionists, co-operative society representatives, merchants and industrialists, men and women social workers, aboriginals, sadhus, prison officers, village elders, rajas and maharajas and a sprinkling of very dotty suppliants.

We visited most main cities from Peshawar to Madras and Bombay to Calcutta and a score of villages. Twice I set off in a car and haphazardly called at villages with an interpreter, sometimes at villages where both Hindus and Muslims dwelt together apparently amicably, and we inspected factories, industrial plants, as at Jamshedpur Tata steel works, slums, hospitals, schools and colleges, mosques, temples, churches and famous archaeological treasures. This may sound like a typical tourist whirlwind, nonetheless we encompassed the lot together with many, many hours of talk and conference. Beyond this I received, as did my colleagues to a less degree, shoals of petitions, memoranda, appeals and correspondence. At every stopping place I had to grant interviews to scores of people apart from those we saw collectively.

In New Delhi I was privileged to be the guest of *Manchester Guardian* correspondent B. Shiva Rao and his wife from whom I gained much information and with whom was also staying his brother Sir Benegal Rau, an eminent lawyer engaged on proposals for amending drastically Indian matrimonial and kindred laws. There I met in the pre-breakfast queue seeking interviews with me my Danish namesake who lives in a Himalayan cavern and two face-painted holy men who beseeched me with streaming tears to prevent interference with their ancient matrimonial code, unaware that my fellow-guest was the culprit. I confess I drank avidly everything I could of Indian life and culture because I was convinced that the political issue could not be divorced from its economic, cultural and religious contexts. Since my first association with the India League I had read widely not only on Indian politics, whether left or right biased, propagandist, objective or academic, but also on Indian history, philosophy, culture and economics. It was thus inevitable for me to revel in the world with which by reading I was familiar and was now surrounding me.

Our comprehensive experience had individual reactions and interpretations with each of us. It could be said that I was a biased participant in so far as I had been pro-Indian in my India League activities in the United Kingdom and so could not exercise dispassionate judgment, but this had some advantage for the mission. Because of my presence Indians could feel we were not simply a band of political sight-seers superficially inspecting the strange ways of the natives in their natural habitat. This was false in any case, for my companions also in varying degree had acquainted themselves with the sociological background on India. My value to them lay in the link I provided between them and Indians because of my known past activities. This did not mean I could not be objective or judiciously appreciate facts. On the contrary a subordinate reason to my paramount conviction that India must be independent was my belief that until India had full responsibility for her own life she would be unready to face facts fairly and squarely and continue to blame the British for all the ills she suffered, from floods and droughts and Muslim–Hindu tensions to excessive fecundity.

My colleagues also had their biases. Some had residual imperialist nostalgia, some were critical of Congress and some of Gandhi, but all were genuinely anxious alike for the sake of India and Britain to discover and commend what might be the best way out of the existing impasse toward Indian self-government. I did not identify myself with the Indian Congress, nor nominally did the India League, although it seemed to me beyond doubt that Congress did represent overwhelmingly the Indian nationalist movement. What I found gratifying was that if there had been any among the delegation who had been hesitant about Indian independence, expediency itself was compelling them to admit its necessity. As one important British administrator confessed to me, 'Gandhi's "Quit India" is inescapable. We must clear out.' Of that there appeared to be no question, the vitally important question being 'How?'

Twice we met Mohandas Karamchand Gandhi. I had met him previously during a Round Table conference when he lodged at Kingsley Hall settlement in Bow, and in addition to our corporate interviews with him I spent an early morning hour with him on the rooftop of his host's house, I think in Bombay. Most of that time he talked not on politics, but on his family and his religious outlook. I held and hold him in high esteem, yet not sycophantly, for while he was truly a saintly man I consider some of his judgments to have been wrong. Mystics can be subtle despots, and though Gandhi had real humility and magnanimity that perilous despotism could be assertive. His simple dhoti, celibate asceticism and his personal identification with the peasant masses was not a self-conscious pose and both his deep religious faith and love of humanity were utterly sincere. Yet I think he insufficiently realized that what was his own spiritual necessity was not therefore appropriate for others and that at the temple of truth wherein he worshipped there were many political as well as religious doors. However, the supreme fact remains that his teaching on *ahimsa* and *satyagraha* had for some time an immense influence in guiding most of the Indian nationalist movement away from violent hatred. With all his human shortcomings I contend he was a truly rare, noble personality.

I think some of my colleagues thought of him as a queer, exotic fish, very agile and even a bit slippery, but requiring cautious respect such as must be accorded any eminent leader who can wield great power. All were impressed by him, whatever their reservations, and appreciated his titanic influence. On the other hand we perceived that Pandit Nehru was the mass political focus, also exercising great power and influence, and I think my colleagues found it more fruitful to converse with him because he, like them, was a political animal. His patrician bearing and Harrovian education, his nationalist and socialist outlook, his clear English speech and cogent argumentation had more variegated appeal to ten British parliamentarians than the earnest mental convolutions of a Mahatma.

At Allahabad I stayed in Nehru's home and there met for the first time Madame Pandit who had recently returned from America. He talked much on the India League and Krishna Menon, on the futility of Pakistan and on his hopes for Indian political and economic emancipation leading to a happier relationship with my own country. I saw something of the adulation Indian masses poured on him when he took me to the junction of the sacred Ganges and Jumna where a million pilgrims had gathered. When he was recognized they swarmed like a cloud of locusts over him amid a dense cloud of dust until literally he had to fight his way back to his car and return home. Even there a vast throng waited patiently in and around his garden, to the angry mutterings of the gardener until intermittently he appeared at the porch to smile and murmur a few words. I knew that those two men, Gandhi and Nehru, represented an irresistible force, and steadily I felt that this was being endorsed by my colleagues.

Our meeting with the members of the Congress working committee was fascinating both because we met face to face others, all ex-prisoners, who directed the mass movement and because of the diverse reactions of their personalities. At our initial meeting I could feel the suspicious reserve behind the veil of courtesy and as we exchanged thoughts the veil was penetrated with blunt questions and harsh complaints, particularly from Patel, an Indian prototype of Ernest Bevin. Asaf Ali, a Muslim, was suavely critical, Kripalani I thought slightly derisive and the poetess, Mrs Naidu, eased the situation by her gay little jokes. The British press had reported that Nehru considered our mission 'a huge hoax' (or joke) and although he stated he had been misreported I conjectured that this was what the Congress working committee approximately thought it to be. That was the measure of the mood we had somehow to disperse if our task was not to report a fiasco.

Other political personalities whom we met outside the Congress orbit included C. Rajagopalachari, Sir Tej Bahadur Sapru, a Liberal leader, and Bhulabhai Desai, these diverging from the Congress in many respects, but equally devoted to Indian national freedom. They, too, like the others hardly referred to Indian partition, as if any thought of this was verging on intolerable treachery. I was myself strongly opposed to that proposal as economically calamitous, ethnically incongruous and politically provocative, but I was well aware of the Pakistan concept and its Muslim communal appeal.

THE MUSLIM LEAGUE

Some years before, a Cambridge student had forwarded to me his plan for a separate Muslim state to be carved out of India and designated 'Pakistan' derived from the initials of predominate Muslim areas. This had been adopted by M. A. Jinnah and the Muslim League and had now become the hypnotic slogan and goal of the League among many Muslims. I was acquainted with the many reasons advanced in its support – the alleged incompatability of Hinduism and Islam, their diverse cultures and interests, and the bitter resentment against the alleged intolerance, arrogance and nepotic, ruthless economic repression of Muslims by forceful Hindus.

Against this, I also knew the Muslim League did not embrace all Muslims, some of whom were desirous of fostering communal social integration and others feared the economic loss involved with the advent of Pakistan. There were devout Muslims among Congress leaders, the scholarly Maulana Abul Kalam Azad being Congress president at the time of our tour, and Asaf Ali a member of its working committee. The Muslim Momins, the Syed group in Sind, the Bengal followers of Fazlul Haq and the Khudai Khitmatgars or 'Servants of God' in the then North West Frontier Province kept aloof from the Muslim League. We spent a day in and near the Khyber Pass and I had some hours with Gaffar Khan, the 'Frontier Gandhi' and leader of the Khudai Khitmatgars, a tall, impressive figure by whose side I sat on the truck from which he addressed an admiring crowd accompanied by alarming saluting rifle shots. In the gathering dusk of his bungalow he emphasized his disagreement with the objective of the Muslim League.

Despite this evidence that the Muslim League had its Muslim critics, increasingly I came to realize that however theoretically sound was the case against the Pakistan thesis yet emotionally it was exceedingly powerful, much more so than I had appreciated. On reaching Lahore by train during our travels we found the railway station and its vicinity flooded with a human sea waving little green flags. For a delusory moment we had the assumption that this was to welcome our arrival until we swiftly discovered that unknown to us Jinnah had been on the train and as the vociferous welcome was directed to him we were merely an ignored eddy on the edge of the flood. This put us properly in our place and also demonstrated how deep the Pakistan appeal had gone into that local section of the Muslim community. Nor was this the only sign that awakened me to the intensity of an emotional reality that overwhelmed rational considerations. Again and again gregarious emotion has had to be accepted as a sociological determinative fact in human affairs, and in India I was impressed with this phenomenon now operating not only through the Indian Congress, but also the rival Muslim League.

At our interview with Jinnah in a Delhi garden I had a personal conversation with the Muslim League leader. His sincerity and integrity were no less than Gandhi's or Nehru's, nor was his sway over the community he inspired. Lean, tall, with long, stern, proud features and sartorially immaculate he provided a complete contrast with the Mahatma and indeed with his associates, for he was not a pious Muslim and probably privately treated Gandhi's metaphysical, moralistic flights into the realm of political agitation with ironical impatience if not disdain. He was aloofly polite as I talked with him, but absolutely implacable in his unswerving dedication to the attainment of Pakistan, and I felt I was arguing with a steel rod. As he wished me goodbye he said with an eloquent inflection 'Well, Mr Sorensen, it's up to you', by which I knew he meant it was up to me to recognize an inflexible fact and amend the policy I had pursued of advocating a united, independent Indian government, for he would never alter his own conviction. Without the magnetic, resolute leadership of Muhammad Ali Jinnah Muslim League aspirations might have been compromised, but with his leadership I came to believe there would be no deviation from unremitting determination to reach his goal.

I still hoped, however, that he would achieve this within a federation or confederation that gave him and the League autonomous power wherein to preserve Islamic values and to implement a Muslim social order without Hindu interference or domination. This I felt would have to be conceded, even though I shared strongly Congress antipathy to the formation of virtually a theocratic state. There ought to be a constitutional arrangement by which the emotional, cultural realities would be embodied and yet without the complete severance that would be economically dangerous and potent for deplorable accentuation of communal distinctions. Transcending the tragic schism, our mission appreciated the unqualified inter-communal conviction that geographical India must be released from our centuries-long imperial rule, for the profound differences could no longer be used as an excuse for delay and temporary alliance would be formed against its prolongation.

LESSONS WE LEARNED

I have mentioned dissident groups within the Muslim community, but notwithstanding my propagandist elaboration of this it grew clear that no dissidents possessed the strength of the Muslim League or were much more than incidental to the crucial internal political Indian conflict, much as I had presumed and desired otherwise. There were other internal conflicts brought to our consideration, such as the claim of the Indian princes that as Britain traditionally had always respected the constitutional difference between 'British India' and 'Princes India' so remained its obligation to preserve the historic rights and privileges of those Indian states over which ruled maharajas and rajas. There was also the claim of the millions of pariahs, outcastes or Gandhi's Harijans for liberation from ancient gross subjugation and there was the clamour of the Sikhs for special recognition.

All this came within our cognizance, and so did the appalling poverty of India, whether basically due to natural causes or, as frequently alleged, aggravated by past British policy and recent negligence. Both in town slums and in mud villages where live eighty-five per cent of the Indian people the squalor, malnutrition, infirmities and primitive conditions contrasted savagely with the concentrated luxury of a small wealthy minority. The decorated elephants upon which I and Brigadier Low rode through Hyderabad to a lavish lunch, the rich carpets and adornments in the palace at Mysore, the intricate carvings on temples and the sedate, spacious homes of city merchants could not screen that mass Indian poverty. In one village I asked a company of skinny, bearded inhabitants (no women) if they wanted Indian national freedom, and on receiving a stout affirmative I enquired what they thought this would mean to them? Whereat they replied through a grinning interpreter, 'More rice'. I took this as symptomatic of the assumption of vast numbers in the nationalist movement that with the departure of the British their age-long burdens would miraculously vanish.

Absorbed though we all were with the manifold facets of the Indian scene, toward the end of six weeks we were becoming physically and mentally weary and were more than eager to return home. We had learned a great deal during our good-will tour, or had amplified what we had thought we knew. We had been impressed by the emotional intensity of Indian nationalism and its demand for national freedom, and with the capacity of its leaders. We had become very conscious of the strength of Jinnah and the Muslim League within the Indian Muslim community, and while we would not venture on any proposals regarding this we hoped most earnestly that an accommodation would be reached between the Congress and the Muslim League by which India could avoid complete separation. We recognized the gravity of this problem and that many strenuous efforts to solve it had failed not through lack of intention, but we agreed that nothing less than assurance of immediate independent self-government was essential. Further, we realized that Indian poverty would demand from a national government the utmost exertions to ensure some rise in the standard of living of its people.

All this might seem an underlining of the obvious, but it had psychological value for the British government nonetheless, and we were satisfied that our mission had on the whole succeeded in fracturing the barriers of suspicion and hostility behind which India fretfully awaited a response to her sustained demand. If my own position in the delegation has obtruded unduly I am sorry, but I trust my explanation of this is appreciated as being relevant to the task of establishing on behalf of the government the goodwill that was a precondition for negotiations at the highest level. The human contacts made were invaluable and I hope without stupid conceit this was made a little more possible by my own previous activities in respect of the liberation of India, which I had undertaken as an expression of my ethical and political faith. But I do not over-rate this beyond a small contribution.

On reaching London again, with rich memories of warm personal kindness from our Indian hosts and of the fascinating Indian scene, Arthur Henderson, under secretary of state for India, met us and requested us forthwith proceed to Downing Street. It was evening and we strongly resisted the request, but agreed to attend in the morning, which we did.

The prime minister and other cabinet ministers were present as the delegation assembled around the long table. Professor Richards gave his outline of our experiences and his informal report, stressing foremostly our unanimous decision that India must be guaranteed immediately her national freedom and sovereign rights. After much interrogation and the voicing of individual opinions the meeting closed, and with it our collective endeavour to fulfil our task of encouraging Anglo-Indian goodwill in order to fortify the government's intention to transfer power to the Indian people.

Of my several overseas tours that one with my Labour, Conservative and Liberal friends will ever be the most momentous. If little has emerged of value in my broad description of its scope and nature, and if some human aspects have been disproportionate to the academic need to know more of its significance in the historic drama, I can only remind readers of the limits of our terms of reference and also that even those human episodes can give political illumination. The mission will have barely a footnote in the history of that drama, but even footnotes can reveal something that elucidates obscurity in the main text. I am happy to think I may be a word in a ten-letter footnote.

IMPRESSIONS, 1938–47

by MAURICE AND TAYA ZINKIN

I. MAURICE ZINKIN*

EARLY DAYS

When I arrived in India in 1938, there was a very interesting mixture of attitudes among the people I met.

The older British government officials felt that it would be years before India was ready for complete self-government. They were frequently profoundly hostile to what they regarded as the weakness of the government at home, which would make concessions just when some civil disobedience movement had been fully mastered. They were not, in Bombay at least, very race-conscious; they all had Indian friends. But a good deal of their lives outside work was spent in a limited circle of people like themselves, mostly British, and, while their understanding of the peasant and the countryside was often profound, they often neither liked nor understood the merchant, the clerk and the lawyer. Their opposition to early self-government was never based on any sense of British economic interests of which they understood nothing. It was sometimes based on a more general feeling that Britain's great place in the world depended on holding India. But essentially it was the result of a deep feeling for India. They were afraid that an independent India would split up, that there would be great communal troubles, that corruption and nepotism would spread, that government would be run in the interest of the banias and the English-educated, that there would be faction and domination by political bosses, and that the peasant would suffer. Enough of their fears have come true to show that their concern was genuine. What they did not realize was that India needed much more active policies in economic development and social reform, and that these were possible only to an Indian government.

The younger British officials found this attitude too static. Many of them would have liked to see some reasonably whole-hearted compromise with the Congress which would permit a combined attack on such problems as debt and poverty and untouchability. They mostly accepted the inevitability of self-government at some time during their career, though they thought of it as coming at the end rather than at the beginning and hoped that they would be able to serve on under an independent government.

To all the British, old and young, in Bombay at least, two facts seemed evident. First, there could be no settlement without the Congress. A future Indian government was bound to be largely Congress; the government of Bombay already was Congress. Secondly, the Congress did not, as they claimed, represent the whole nation. The Muslims, even in 1938 and even in

* Formerly member of the I.C.S.

low-temperature Bombay, were on the whole anti-Congress, though usually not yet Muslim League. They saw the Congress as a Hindu organization, which did not consider their special interests. They objected to the Mahatma's Hindu religious symbolism and to the use of 'Bande Mataram' as a national song. The untouchables were often clearly behind Dr Ambedkar. The Bhil tribesmen of West Khandesh followed their own leaders, the Mahratta peasants of Sholapur were as often anti-Brahmin as pro-Congress.

Above all, the British official could see that the British government still had a great deal of support. Certain of its virtues were widely appreciated, often in the most touching way by Congressmen themselves. In Bombay, at least, there was very little hatred, and a great deal of affection. The peasant was always disarmingly willing to give one credit for good intentions. The old-fashioned, the landowners, the princes, the pious (not the rich; the businessmen were Congress) preferred the British to a Congress they saw as iconoclastic. The lower-rank Indian official frequently despised and disliked Congressmen, partly out of loyalty, partly because the British provided an India more to his taste, more modern than the Congress India of hand-spinning, prohibition and self-sufficient village republics.

The British official's inoculation into Indian nationalism came mainly from his contemporaries in his own service and services of similar rank. They were nationalist almost to a man, though profoundly ambivalent about the Congress. They wanted an India which they would run, not a Gandhian India. Their choice amongst Congressmen was Nehru, because he seemed to them a modernizer, because he talked the same language that they had learned at the university. Only a minority fully appreciated the greatness of Gandhi.

In 1938 the services and the Congress ministry were still getting to know each other, and they were beginning to form some mutual respect. Men like Morarji Desai and K. M. Munshi were good administrators, and most people admired B. G. Kher's character. Despite considerable friction and suspicion, by the time the war came, a reasonable working relationship had been established, and most officials were sorry when the Congress government resigned. Certainly the advisers' regime which followed leant over backwards not to change Congress policy or give offence to Congress feeling, and the 1940 civil disobedience movement was handled with tact and care and good-feeling on both sides.

THE WAR

The war changed everything.

For the first time it created a very large body of Indians with all the modern skills, as officers, managers and officials. It also brought to India far more middle-class Englishmen than had ever come before. There was, therefore, an unprecedented mingling of British and Indians. The old complexes, on both sides, largely died away.

Because Indians thus became much more confident that they could do the job themselves, and because they were fighting a war for democracy and self-determination, the support for the British government dropped away.

The immense voluntary effort of the war was the last spurt. By the end of the war the great majority of Indians, at least above the level of sub-inspector of police or subedar-major, wanted to be left to run things their way.

As this desire grew stronger, politics polarized. This happened fairly gradually. None of one's Muslim friends regarded Pakistan as anything but a pipe-dream in 1940. By 1942–3 some of them were toying with the idea. By 1945 many were in favour of it, especially amongst those who had not been to a British university. The I.C.S. held out longest. I do not remember any Muslim I.C.S. who was in favour before 1946.

Amongst non-Muslims, there was an increasing drift to Congress sympathies. Nobody else by the mid forties counted. The average army officer or official was no more tempted by Gandhianism than he had been, but, as against the departing British and the increasingly assertive Muslims, he really had nowhere else to go. Nehru was here of crucial importance. He had the right modern image, and by the end of the war everybody was socialist – Nehru on many points of policy never went further left than Lord Wavell.

British reactions were more complicated. After the Cripps offer, to the I.C.S. at least, it was clear the days of the *raj* were numbered, though nobody would have given it quite as short a run as it turned out to have. Up to 1942, those whose service had been in the provinces of the peninsula in particular often sympathized with the Congress, and nobody was in favour of Pakistan. The troubles of August 1942, however, alienated many British officials fatally, and they were further alienated by Nehru's support of the I.N.A. officers who were put on trial after the war. Many continued, like Lord Wavell, to regard a united India as Britain's greatest achievement. Others were prepared to support anyone who had been pro- the war effort. Gandhi's alleged remark about a 'post-dated cheque on a crashing bank' in 1942, however apocryphal it may have been, also had a great effect in alienating many people. They did not therefore become pro-Jinnah – but they were prevented from being as anti-Jinnah as their desire to hand on an undiminished heritage would otherwise have made them.

I have said nothing about the viceroy and the government of India. That is because throughout Lord Linlithgow's time they were hopelessly negative. Linlithgow was an admirable administrator; but from the time the war broke out it seemed to us younger civil servants that he made no political move worthy of the name. Since this was matched by an almost equal Congress ineffectiveness – they did not co-operate with the war, but, on the whole, they did not sabotage it either – a vacuum was created which gave Jinnah more of an opportunity than he would otherwise have had.

AFTER THE WAR

1945–7 was only the working-out of trends already well in action when the war ended. By 1946 the polarization of politics was virtually complete. People were either Congress, more or less, or League, more or less. Those British who were in any way at the centre of power knew that they could not last much longer, and were concerned only to get a final settlement which would make a glorious, rather than a shameful, climax to Britain's long rule.

Pakistan might not have come out without a long series of favourable accidents – the murder of Allah Bakhsh, the erosion of Congress support in the N.W.F.P., the failure of the Muslims in what was to remain India to ask themselves what would happen to them, the impetuosity of Nehru. But, by sometime in 1946, it seemed to me, I remember, the probable solution. The government was not powerful enough to coerce the Muslim majority areas, Jinnah had inflamed the always strong Muslim sense of separateness. The Congress had shown itself totally helpless to handle the situation, I think for two reasons. They did not believe the British were going until the last minute; they were therefore more concerned with running a movement than with negotiating. They did not understand the power of religion in creating *political* entities; when one talked of Ireland (which is a reasonably exact parallel) to a Congressman or even to a non-Muslim member of the I.C.S., one was met with blank incomprehension. To bring religion into politics was mediaeval. It must be some British or land-owners' trick to postpone handing over power. The Hindus, themselves all-inclusive, simply did not understand the exclusiveness of Islam. They could not believe that men whom they saw as fellow-Indians, fellow-Punjabis or Bengalis, who spoke the same language and ate the same food, could feel themselves separate and different. A true dialogue between the Muslim League and the Congress was not possible, because the League believed the Congress to be Hindu, which it was not, and the Congress believed the League to be a stooge of the British and the zamindars, which it equally was not.

By the beginning of 1947, in the central secretariat where I was, it was clear that there were only two questions. How quickly could the British go? and, could any unity, at least the unity of the army, be preserved? As it became daily more obvious to everybody (except perhaps Nehru) that the British really were going, and going soon, their power to influence events steadily diminished. Every secretariat decision was taken with its effect on a future Pakistan or India in everybody's minds. The Muslim Leaguers and the Congressmen in the government behaved as two totally separate groups, and under the strain even the I.C.S. began to split into its component parts – the Muslims of the audit and accounts service had been strong partisans from 1945 at the latest, but they were exceptional.

After June, when partition was agreed, the secretariat was virtually paralysed. Nobody thought of anything except how to bring partition about. The wonder is not that a certain amount of loose ends were left, but that there were not many more Some of the credit for this must go to the efficiency of men like H. M. Patel and Osman Ali. More goes to Mountbatten's speed. People were not given the time to find points over which to quarrel.

The massacres were unexpected. The assumption was that, once partition had been achieved, everything would quieten down. The minorities on both sides of the line were so large that oppression of them would obviously be foolish; and nobody doubted the goodwill on this issue of either Jinnah or the Congress. The politicians had never handled violence (except perhaps for Suhrawardy in Calcutta) and they neither expected it nor (except for Gandhi) knew what to do about it. The British were equally taken unawares.

I do not remember any of our favourite prophets of doom anticipating the scale of the Punjab killings.

At the end everything got swept away in a torrent. Nothing had really been worked out. When I did a calculation of the Indian and Pakistani balance of payments in my spare time, I found that everybody accepted my figures because nobody else, least of all the Muslim League, had bothered to do it. But probably that is the only way the great revolutions can be achieved. If one counts all the costs, one will never be revolutionary.

One last personal view. I believe that if Vallabhbhai Patel had been in charge of the Congress from 1945, a deal might conceivably have been done with the League. But Gandhi was too big a man, in everybody's eyes, for it to be possible for him to do a deal; and to Nehru, with his socialism and his secularism, the League was like the scarlet woman of Rome to an Orangeman.

II. TAYA ZINKIN

Until I arrived in India in 1945 I knew practically nothing about India, being French and not interested in politics. In any case, as with most people what focused my attention was not India but the progress of the war.

In the fall of 1944 I became engaged to a British member of the Indian Civil Service. I left the USA where I was in early 1945 to join him in England to get married and I did not get to India before October 1945. Because I knew so little about the problems of Indo-British relations, I was struck with great force by my own impressions and still remember quite a lot of what it felt like. Some of my recollections may act as a useful corrective to the analysis of scholars and historians who were not there at the time and are trying to reconstruct events with hindsight and research.

In my American university I had been friendly with an Indian Ph.D. from Madras who was, like myself, doing research in biochemistry. We had been sharing a lab for a year when I told him I was getting engaged to a Briton in the I.C.S. His reaction was very puzzling for I did not even know what I.C.S. really meant, and my knowledge of India was entirely confined to Kipling; I only read Forster after getting engaged. 'You will become a memsaheb and if I call on you in Delhi, you will keep me waiting in the verandah and treat me like a servant', and from then on my colleague became obsequious. It was quite clear from his behaviour that he thought, as indeed I did, that India would remain British for ever. The same lack of foresight over the coming of independence was exhibited by a cousin of my husband's, then first secretary in the British embassy in Washington, and by the staff of the British consulate in New York who arranged for me to go to England on a troopship. To them, and to most of the people I met in England, and I met many people including my husband's very large family, the *raj* seemed doomed to a long life. Everyone greeted me as one who was going out to India for life and would end as the wife of a very senior member of the Indian Civil Service indeed, a member with a good chance to end up as finance minister or governor of the reserve bank. Even Sir Ardeshir Dalal who had come to England as the head of a purchasing mission, spoke as if the British would stay in India for a very long time, certainly as long as my husband's career.

On the other hand my husband, coming as he did from India, took a quite different view. He felt sure the British would be going, the question was only when. To ensure his redeployability, in case the *raj* did not last his time he had got into the finance and commerce pool in 1942; and during his leave in 1945 made contacts with various organizations in England so that he would be in a better position to change career if necessary. Against the background of what he felt I found the ignorance, lack of interest and blimpishness of Britons most intriguing. Most people behaved towards India like the proverbial ostrich. This was true of my husband's relations, of his Cambridge friends and it was particularly true of the officials in the India Office. My husband was preaching the need for Indianization to all the people he met, and I remember his being invited to address the overseas committee of Unilever, in April 1945, and urging them to Indianize their Indian subsidiary, this at a time when an official of the India Office was seriously arguing to him that India would never be allowed to become independent since it would cut off the supply of Gurkhas to the army. And when I had to arrange for my passage to India in the fall, the quite senior official of the India Office who dealt with my case kindly warned me: 'Things are changing out there in India. I am afraid, from what I have been told, that when you get there you will have to mix with Indians, sometimes; you may even have to invite them to tea!' (He was not all that ridiculous for only a very short time before that, when Lord Linlithgow had given a large party for his officials in Simla, Indians were served in the garden and on the verandah, only white faces were allowed inside; this I was told, as a matter of fact, by the wife of a senior member of the Indian Civil Service (Indian) who told her husband she would never accept a viceregal invitation again.)

On the troopship going out to India to join my husband I met many army officers who were rejoining their regiments in the Punjab; they certainly talked as if the Indian army was there to stay, and stay with British officers. If they were blind, what about the British government who recruited to the I.C.S. as late as the spring of 1946. My husband's youngest brother had the rare distinction of joining the I.C.S. and retiring from it with compensation for loss of career all within a few weeks; his retirement took place in the late spring of 1946.

Yet, by October, when I arrived in India, it had become quite obvious to all but the confirmed blimps that the end of British rule was but a matter of time. Pakistan, a word I had never heard before, because my interests were medical and not political, had by then become an accepted concept.

The only questions which were being asked everywhere I went were 'Where' and 'How'. The Indians seemed to me to be as naïve as the Britons in Britain were indifferent. Hindus would go on for hours arguing that nobody had ever heard of a country being divided on religious grounds since the dark ages of the crusades. I kept saying that they were wrong, that religion is precisely what divides people most easily and used the Irish parallel as an example; but Ireland was always indignantly rejected by Indians as irrelevant. The way Indians, Hindu and Muslim alike, talked about their future, even about their grievances against the British, the perfidious Albion (being French, I too believed Albion to be perfidious and never hesitated to say so), the language they used made me realize how innocent India was of the facts of terror, civil war, repression and totalitarianism. I had experiences of the Spanish civil war, Hitler's regime, the bombings and torpedoing of the second world war, and the entire Indian dialogue seemed almost unreal in its gentility. The Calcutta killings of 1946 did introduce them to the horrors of civil war.

Firmly entrenched in a fool's paradise were the Sikhs and the princes, both confident that the British would not abandon their favoured sons, both confident to the point of intransigence, both unable to strike a profitable bargain. I remember Master Tara Singh trying to make a deal with Jinnah while Sardar Panikkar kept preventing Jinnah's intrigues with the princes from going too far. But whereas the Sikhs were, by and large, united, the princes were too busy quarrelling over gun salutes and such foolish things, to have any hope of survival. But they did not understand this; the world was still the one where they had been descended from the sun and the moon. I remember Panikkar inviting us to stay in Bikaner in the winter of 1945 with specific instructions to talk sense into the maharaja over dinner. But his highness was so bored with politics that my husband had to give up and the prince, a great *shikar*, only revived when I began to talk to him about the film 'Trader Horn'. This was 1945. In 1946 his highness invited us to the imperial sand grouse shoot. It was quite eerie the way his world had not caught up with events; that week was like a Rip Van Winkle expedition in reverse. But the rulers were not to blame. After all the resident in Indore, whom we saw a great deal of during *Easter 1947* was still talking as if Britain would remain paramount for ever.

To go back to 1945–6 in Delhi, what struck one was that the Hindus were so distrustful of British intentions that they could not see that time *was* running out. They still behaved as if they were playing a political game, and this went on till Mountbatten announced a date for the transfer of power.

This feeling that the British would manage to hang on somehow was shared by all except those Muslims who were in Jinnah's orbit (as distinct from the Muslims who supported him but did not really believe he would succeed; this was true of most Muslims). Jinnah's orbit as I would call it, consisted of a core of people ranging from Liaqat Ali Khan and Chaudhuri Muhammad Ali, both of whom we knew, to my munshi who was the cousin of somebody who was a clerk at Jinnah house. This inner core had no doubt that the British would go, and go soon and from the way my munshi talked before and after direct action day I got the feeling that direct action day was the Muslim League's 'Quit India' equivalent. This may be hindsight, but I think I felt, on the two occasions when I met Jinnah, that he was very ruthless, practical, and that he no longer treated the British as overlord, but more like tenants whose lease had run out. The Jinnah core always spoke of what would happen 'when' the British go; the Hindus always spoke of what would happen 'if' the British went. The Hindus saw the British as victorious imperialists; the Jinnah core saw them as exhausted allies of the Americans. There were, it must be remembered, plenty of Americans in Delhi at the time and they used to behave with an ebulliance which looked full of vitality compared to the way the British behaved.

As far as partition was concerned, once it become accepted as a possibility, I do not think that anyone anticipated what it would be like; not even after the Calcutta killings of 1946 and the ensuing pendulum of communal war. Partition was not a new concept to Indians, Bengal had been partitioned before, and Sind had been partitioned from Bombay. It all felt like one of those operations on paper (despite Gandhi's talk of vivisection) by which an administrative or electoral boundary had been shifted or created. The officials certainly did not anticipate what happened. Thus a friend of ours who was in the I.C.S. opted for Pakistan although his family were in Bombay, because he happened to be posted in Sind at the time. He was a Parsi. Muslims by and large did opt for Pakistan and Hindus for India, but this was not in anticipation of events, but simply because this seemed the rational thing to do for Hindus and the patriotic one for Muslims. Hindus and Sikhs from Pakistan did not move their belongings or their families until they were driven out and lost their belongings. Khushwant Singh took a job in London at our suggestion, just before partition, but made no arrangements to protect his properties, and his family was, like so many others, stranded in Simla. If officials and politicians made no arrangements why should businessmen make arrangements. We used to know Hindu and Muslim businessmen and industrialists; they never gave economic consideration a thought and let themselves be guided by their emotions. Yet I have time and again found a tendency amongst scholars to endeavour to substantiate their belief in the crucial influence of vested interests on the historical process.

Beside the power of vested interests, which are usually credited with a foresight they lack, scholars like to find in published documents and by their research support for their belief in the inevitability of history. There may be an inevitability of history but the actors on the stage at the time did not behave like actors who have learnt their part and were preparing the audience for what would come next, they behaved rather like blindfolded people in search, not only of an author but of an audience and a part. To those who have been trying to bring some sense into the resulting chaos I would only say that I fully subscribe to the remark of Sir Archibald Nye [1] 'Maybe, but I was there at the time and it did not *feel* like that'. Indeed, it did not feel, taste or smell, like tidy historians would have one believe.

Most people involved at the time were very much in the position of Ian Stephens [2] whose main preoccupation was not to record history in the making but to see that his paper came out, that there were not too many misprints, that he got the newsprint and that distribution went on come what may, even if his staff was being stoned or killed. Historians may succeed in providing history with inevitability but that this is only a *tour de force* is perhaps best illustrated by the fact that Stephen Garvin who was a contemporary of my husband's put the point of no return from partition firmly at the failure of the Simla conference [3] while my husband puts it fully one year earlier. And if one remembers that Jinnah already had cancer can one be sure that history would have taken the same turn if he had died one or two years earlier?

[1] At a partition seminar meeting.
[2] Editor of *The Statesman* (Calcutta) at this time.
[3] During partition seminar meetings.

CHRONOLOGY, 1935–47

1935

2 August	Government of India Act received royal assent.
6 August	Marquess of Linlithgow appointed to succeed Lord Willingdon as viceroy from April 1936.
5 September	Nehru released from prison: flew to Europe to his wife.
17–18 October	All-India Congress Committee meeting at Madras resolved not to come to any decision on question of acceptance of office.

1936

16 February	All-India Muslim conference met in New Delhi, Aga Khan in the chair. Question of amalgamating with Muslim League left over for decision by Muslims elected to new provincial legislatures.
12 March	Nehru returned to India.
21–24 March	Congress working committee met in Delhi.
1 April	Inauguration of new province of Sind.
6 April	Inauguration of Orissa province.
6–7 April	Congress working committee met in Allahabad.
9–15 April	All-India Congress Committee met at Lucknow: Nehru took over presidentship: new working committee appointed.
11–12 April	24th session of the All-India Muslim League meeting in Bombay attacked federal scheme in new Act but decided to work provincial scheme. Central parliamentary board formed to contest coming elections, Jinnah president: authorized to organize provincial parliamentary boards.
12–14 April	49th session of Indian National Congress at Lucknow rejected new constitution and demanded constituent assembly, but decided to take part in elections to provincial legislatures. Committee appointed to consider mass contact.
18 April	Marquess of Linlithgow installed as viceroy.
27–29 April	New Congress working committee met at Wardha. Parliamentary committee constituted to organize elections.
28 May	Nehru began tour in Delhi and Punjab.
11 June	Election manifesto of Muslim League issued from Lahore.
12 June	Muslim League declared that they would use new constitution to further their objective of full and complete home rule for India.

29 June–1 July	Congress working committee met at Wardha.
1–2 July	Congress parliamentary committee met at Wardha.
9 July	Death of Fazl-i-Husain.
13 July	Executive council of Bengal United Moslem party invited Jinnah to visit Calcutta in connection with elections.
18–26 July	Nehru toured Sind.
27 July–5 August	Nehru visited Punjab.
August	Jinnah addressed meetings in U.P. and Bengal.
18–23 August	Congress parliamentary committee, working committee, and A.I.C.C. met at Bombay. Election manifesto adopted.
19 September	Meeting of Muslim League central parliamentary board at Simla. Jinnah announced that strong provincial boards had been established in U.P., Madras, Bombay and Assam; situation in Punjab not satisfactory; no progress in Frontier, Sind, Bihar and Orissa.
3 October	First session of Bihar United Muslim conference held at Patna.
24 October	Conference of C.P. Muslims considered formation of Muslim League parliamentary board in province.
24–25 October	C.P. Muslim political conference at Nagpur called on Muslims to unite under banner of Muslim League and Jinnah. Provincial branch of League formed.
30–31 October	Joint conference of Indian princes and their ministers held in Bombay to consider federation: committee appointed to examine provisions of the Act.
2 November	Fazlul Haq leader of the Praja Socialist party in Bengal removed from membership of Muslim League central parliamentary board.
9–11 December	Congress working committee met in Bombay: Nehru re-elected president of Congress: working committee passed resolution reiterating determination of Congress to reject new constitution.
23–29 December	Congress working committee, A.I.C.C., and Congress met at Faizpur.
27–28 December	50th session of Congress at Faizpur reiterated its rejection of Act, but decided to contest elections to provincial legislatures.
December	Electioneering in full swing.

1937

January–February	Elections held for provincial assemblies (electorate, 37,000,000).
2 January	Viceroy's representative discussed with large number of princes in Calcutta, question of their accession to the Indian federation.

3 January	Jinnah spoke at Calcutta: warned Congress not to interfere in Muslim affairs. He then toured Bengal on behalf of League candidates.
17 January	Polling began in Calcutta for Bengal legislative assembly.
18 January	Polling in Calcutta for general seats in Bengal assembly.
21 January	Elections in Punjab, accompanied by rowdy incidents.
25 January	Constitution committee of chamber of princes met in Delhi to consider all-India federation.
27 January	Khwaja Sir Nazimuddin, member of Bengal executive council, defeated by Fazlul Haq, Praja party leader.
3 February	Fazlul Haq outlined his party's programme at Munshiganj.
15 February	Executive committee of Praja party ratified agreement reached between leaders of the party and Muslim League for purpose of working new constitution.
17 February	Sir Sikandar Hayat Khan invited to form ministry in Punjab.
17 February	Constitution committee of chamber of princes submitted its first recommendations.
24–25 February	14th session of the chamber of princes in Delhi.
27 February–1 March	Meeting of Congress working committee at Wardha. 'The Congress has entered the legislatures not to co-operate . . . but to combat the Act. . . .' 'The objective of the Congress is . . . complete independence. . .' 'The immediate objective of the Congress in the Legislatures is to fight the new constitution. . . .'
6 March	Fazlul Haq agreed to form ministry in Bengal.
16 March	Congress working committee passed resolution recommending conditional acceptance of office.
18 March	All-India Congress Committee meeting at Delhi passed resolution authorizing conditional acceptance of office in provinces.
1 April	Provincial responsible government came into force.
8 April	Lord Zetland in house of lords, and R. A. Butler in house of commons defined H.M.G.'s attitude to political impasse.
10 April	Gandhi made statement in reply to Lord Zetland.
19 April	Jinnah criticized Congress attempt to divide Muslim ranks.
26 April	R. A. Butler made statement on political impasse.
22 April	Nehru announced Muslim mass-contact programme.
26 April	Nehru and Jinnah issued counter-statements on Congress bid to capture Muslim support.
28 April	Resolution of Congress working committee on political deadlock.
May	Nehru visited Burma and Malaya.
May	Neville Chamberlain succeeded Stanley Baldwin as prime minister. Zetland remained India secretary.

8 May	Statement by Lord Zetland on constitutional impasse.
21 June	Viceroy, Lord Linlithgow, issued statement interpreting constitution – on special powers of governors.
5–8 July	Congress working committee met at Wardha and resolved to accept office.
July	Congress ministries formed in Bihar, Orissa, C.P., U.P., Bombay and Madras.
25 July	Jinnah issued statement urging Hindu–Muslim unity. Called on Muslims to consolidate their strength for coming struggle.
14–17 August	Congress working committee met at Wardha and discussed general policy to be followed by Congress ministers.
15–18 October	25th session of All-India Muslim League at Lucknow. Premiers of Punjab and Bengal joined League; resolution passed opposing introduction of federation. League decided to frame comprehensive social, economic and educational programme to win support of Muslim masses.
22–23 October	Wardha educational conference.
29–31 October	All-India Congress Committee met at Calcutta.
22 November	Congress membership 3,134,249.
27–28 December	First session of All-India Muslim students federation held in Calcutta: Jinnah president.
1938	
1 January	National Liberal federation of India meeting in Calcutta resolved to support federation scheme in new constitution.
1 January	Hindu Mahasabha at its concluding session urged government to expedite introduction of federation.
2–4 January	Congress working committee met in Bombay.
5 January	Jinnah speaking at Allahabad urged settlement of minorities problem.
18 January	Subhas Chandra Bose elected president of the Congress.
3 February	Congress working committee met at Wardha. Premiers of seven Congress provinces had been invited to attend: C. Rajagopalachari from Madras and N. B. Khare from C.P. did so.
4 February	Congress working committee passed resolution reiterating opposition to federation.
5 February	Gandhi and Nehru wrote to Jinnah asking for definite statement of League's demands.
6 February	Congress working committee decided not to set up Congress organizations in Indian states.
15 February	Bihar and U.P. ministries resigned over question of release of political prisoners.
19–21 February	51st session of Indian National Congress at Haripura in Gujarat.
25 February	Constitutional crisis in U.P. ended.
26 February	Bihar cabinet withdrew resignation.

March	Congress ministry formed in Assam.
21 March	Sind ministry resigned. Leader of United party formed new ministry in coalition with Hindu Independent party.
10 April	Subhas Chandra Bose urged mass contact with Muslims and scheduled castes.
14 April	Subhas Chandra Bose appealed to Muslims to join Congress.
17–18 April	Special session of Muslim League at Calcutta. Jinnah reported on success of League in organizing Muslims since last session in October 1937. Appealed to both communities to realize their moral obligations to each other.
21 April	Death of Sir Muhammad Iqbal.
24 April	Bengal Hindu Mahasabha in Calcutta appealed to Gandhi not to conclude his negotiations with Jinnah without consulting non-Congress political organizations.
28 April	Gandhi had interview with Jinnah in Bombay on communal question: sequel to correspondence between Jinnah, Nehru and Gandhi which had gone on for some months past. Joint statement issued.
1–8 May	Gandhi carried out an extensive tour in Frontier province.
11–12 May	Subhas Chandra Bose, Congress president, had discussions with Jinnah in Bombay on communal question.
12–14 May	Conference of premiers of seven Congress provinces and members of Congress parliamentary sub-committee in Bombay. Conference called by president of Congress to consider general questions of co-ordination and co-operation among Congress provinces. Among other matters it was decided to introduce Wardha education scheme in the seven provinces.
14 May	Congress leaders drafted memorandum in reply to Jinnah's point in connection with communal talks – taken to Jinnah by Subhas Bose when talks resumed.
20 May	Gandhi had talk with Jinnah in Bombay.
26 May	Talks between Jinnah and Subhas Bose continued.
2 June	Under-secretary of state for India stated in house of commons that no date had yet been fixed for inauguration of federation.
2 June	Nehru left Bombay for Europe. Returned in November.
4 June	Council of the Muslim League discussed Congress memorandum on communal peace terms and authorized Jinnah to send reply to Congress president.
11 June	Reorganization committee of chamber of princes decided to constitute a committee to deal with matters of common interest to Indian states as regarded federation.
15 June	Full text of Gandhi–Jinnah and Jinnah–Nehru correspondence released.
20 June	Vallabhbhai Patel and Subhas Chandra Bose called at Wardha to decide on reply to Jinnah's letter.

20 June	Sheriff of Bombay disputed Jinnah's claim to be sole representative of Muslims.
22 June	Fazlul Haq resigned and then formed new ministry.
24 June	Subhas Bose and other leaders discussed Congress–League negotiations with Gandhi at Wardha.
25 June	Viceroy left Bombay for England. Lord Brabourne acting viceroy.
1 July	Nehru had long interview with Lord Halifax in London.
7 July	Two Muslim organizations opposed to League established in Bihar, viz. Jamiat-ul-ulema and Momin Jamiat.
23–27 July	Congress working committee met at Wardha.
25 July	Gandhi dictated letter to be sent to Jinnah on communal problem. Congress unable to accept Jinnah's claim that League should be recognized as sole representative of Muslim population.
31 July	League working committee replied to Congress president's letter on communal settlement and criticized attitude adopted by Congress.
16 August	Subhas Chandra Bose, with Jinnah's permission, released correspondence between himself and Jinnah about Hindu–Muslim settlement.
24–26 September	A.I.C.C. met at Delhi. Resolution condemning negotiations with Jinnah defeated.
2 October	All-India Muslim educational conference rejected Wardha scheme.
5 October	Gandhi began Frontier Province tour which continued throughout October.
8–15 October	Sind Muslim League conference at Karachi. Jinnah strongly criticized Congress attitude to Muslim interests and accused Congress executive of wanting to divide Muslims.
9 October	Bengal and Punjab premiers speaking at Sind Muslim League conference challenged claim of Congress to represent Indian nation.
10 October	Sind Muslim League conference discussed resolution urging that India be divided into two federations, one for Muslims and the other for non-Muslim groups.
12 October	Negotiations for League ministry in Sind broke down.
24 October	Viceroy returned to India.
17 November	Nehru returned to India.
28 November–1 December	Informal conference of rulers and their ministers held in Bombay.
11–16 December	Congress working committee met at Wardha and passed resolution declaring Hindu Mahasabha and Muslim League communal organization (15 December). Hindu–Muslim question discussed. Correspondence of president of Congress with Jinnah closed.

18 December	Liaqat Ali Khan, secretary of Muslim League, said at Nagpur that no agreement with Congress was possible so long as Congress was not prepared to recognize League as only representative organization of Indian Muslims.
19 December	Viceroy made statement on prospects of federation at opening of annual meeting of associated chambers of commerce in Calcutta.
20 December	Jinnah issued statement on viceroy's appeal to give federal scheme a trial. Criticized working of provincial autonomy in provinces.
26–29 December	26th session of Muslim League held at Patna. Jinnah attacked Gandhi for giving to Congress Hindu outlook and Hindu ideals. Resolution passed favouring launching of civil disobedience in Bihar, U.P. and C.P. League established committee of enquiry into alleged Congress persecution of Muslims.
30 December	Hindu Mahasabha at Nagpur passed resolution accepting federation.
31 December	Speakers at National Liberal federation criticized Congress executive for interfering in administration of ministries in the provinces.
1939	
end January	Princes received from viceroy draft instrument of accession.
30 January	Subhas Chandra Bose re-elected Congress president. Members of working committee resigned.
9 March	At annual session of Congress at Tripuri, C.P., Subhas Chandra Bose resigned and Rajendra Prasad elected president in his stead.
13 March	Viceroy inaugurated session of chamber of princes in Delhi.
April	Council of Muslim League meeting in Delhi passed resolution objecting to intensive propaganda of Congress in efforts to establish Hindu hegemony all over India.
June	Princes and their ministers meeting in Bombay pronounced terms in instrument of accession unacceptable. Time limit for replies extended to 1 September.
3 September	Viceroy announced that India was at war with Germany.
4 September	Viceroy saw Gandhi, Jinnah and chancellor of the chamber of princes.
8–14 September	Congress working committee met at Wardha in emergency session.
10 September	Nehru returned to India from China.
11 September	Negotiations with princes over 1935 Act suspended and federation postponed.
14 September	Resolution of Congress working committee on war crisis and India required declaration of war aims from British government.

18 September	Resolution of League working committee on war crisis.
26 September	Viceroy had meeting of over three hours with Gandhi.
2 October	Viceroy interviewed Rajendra Prasad and Nehru.
October	Viceroy had series of interviews with leaders of other political parties, including Jinnah.
10 October	A.I.C.C. passed resolution dealing with situation arising out of the war, endorsing working committee's statement of 14 September and requesting declaration from British government of its war aims.
18 October	Viceroy made statement on war aims and war effort.
22–23 October	Congress working committee met at Wardha and issued manifesto calling on Congress ministries to resign.
22 October	Manifesto by Muslim League asking for further discussion and clarification.
by end October	Ministries in all Congress provinces had resigned. Governors assumed control under Section 93 of Government of India Act, except in Assam where coalition ministry formed under Sir Mahomed Saadullah. Bengal, Punjab and Sind continued as before.
1 November	Gandhi, Rajendra Prasad and Jinnah had interviews with viceroy to discuss proposal for expanding executive council.
5 November	Viceroy made statement on correspondence with Prasad, Gandhi and Jinnah, and published correspondence.
19–23 November	Meeting of Congress working committee passed resolution demanding constituent assembly.
22 December	Observed as 'Deliverance Day' by followers of Muslim League throughout India.
1939	During this year partition schemes were put forward by Dr Syed Abdul Latif, Sir Sikandar Hyat Khan and Professor Syed Zafarul Hasan, and Dr Muhammad Afzal Husain Qadri.
1940	
6 January	Viceroy in speech at Nagpur regretted interruption, because of resignation of Congress ministries, in orderly progress of India towards goal of dominion status.
7 January	Jinnah released correspondence between himself and Nehru on Congress–League differences.
7 January	Jinnah reiterated League demand for recognition as authoritative and representative organization of Muslims in India. Nehru stated that Congress did not recognize League as sole representative of Muslims. Negotiations discontinued.
10 January	Nehru at Gaziabad said that there could be no question of settlement with government or of return of Congress ministries to office until question of India's freedom finally settled.
13 January	Viceroy saw Jinnah and Bhulabhai Desai in Bombay.

17 January	Viceroy at Baroda stated that federation had been suspended not abandoned.
19–21 January	Congress working committee met at Wardha. Gandhi authorized to seek from viceroy clarification of certain points in his speech of 10 January.
25 January	Viceroy saw Sir Sikandar Hyat Khan.
3 February	Viceroy saw premiers of Punjab and Bengal – Sir Sikandar Hyat Khan and Fazlul Haq – together.
3–6 February	League working committee met in New Delhi. Jinnah stated that western democracy was unsuited for India.
4 February	Fazlul Haq, in New Delhi, suggested setting up of coalition governments in provinces for duration of war.
5 February	Viceroy saw Gandhi in attempt to break political deadlock. Gandhi issued statement to press next day.
6 February	Viceroy saw Jinnah.
11 February	Lord Zetland in interview in *Sunday Times* made appeal to leaders of Congress to 'escape from the tyranny of phrases'.
16 February	Abul Kalam Azad elected president of Congress.
25 February	Council of Muslim League met at New Delhi.
28 February	Congress working committee met in Patna to decide on resolution to be put forward at forthcoming Congress session at Ramgarh.
1 March	Congress working committee at Patna passed resolution declaring determination of party to resort to civil disobedience as soon as organization fit enough.
13 March	Viceroy saw Jinnah.
13 March	Sir Michael O'Dwyer shot dead, and Lord Zetland wounded, at meeting of East India Association at Caxton Hall in London.
15 March	Congress working committee met at Ramgarh.
19–20 March	53rd session of Congress held at Ramgarh. Patna resolution of working committee carried by large majority. Complete independence and constituent assembly demanded.
22–24 March	27th session of Muslim League held at Lahore.
22 March	Jinnah suggested division of India into two autonomous national states.
23 March	'Lahore resolution' of Muslim League.
31 March	Jinnah issued statement from New Delhi appealing to Hindus and Sikhs to give serious consideration to League scheme of partition.
3 April	Lord Zetland broadcast on Britain's policy towards India.
8 April	Vallabhbhai Patel in Ahmedabad stated a fight inevitable: question was when to start the fight.
10 April	White Paper on 'India and the War' issued: sought approval of parliament for continuance of section 93 proclamations in the seven provinces (approved 18 April).

15 April	Congress working committee met at Wardha.
15 April	Master Tara Singh, presiding at first U.P. Sikh conference at Lucknow, said 'If the Moslem League want to establish "pakistan" they will have to pass through an ocean of Sikh blood'.
18 April	Lord Zetland reviewed in house of lords position of India.
27 April–1 May	Azad Muslim conference, Allah Baksh, premier of Sind, president, met in Delhi. Disputed claim of Muslim League to be only representative of Muslims and condemned demand for partition.
6 May	Nehru in Poona said that neither Mahasabha nor League had positive programme. Characterized Pakistan scheme as foolish and said that it would not last 24 hours.
10 May	Winston Churchill replaced Neville Chamberlain as prime minister. L. S. Amery succeeded Lord Zetland as secretary of state (19 May).
10 May	German armies invaded Holland and Belgium.
19 May	Hindu Mahasabha condemned Pakistan scheme as 'anti-Hindu and therefore anti-national'.
23 May	Amery in commons stated that attainment by India of full and equal partnership in Commonwealth was goal of British policy.
27 May–3 June	British army evacuated from Dunkirk.
10 June	Italy declared war on allies.
16 June	League working committee endorsed Jinnah's policy and authorized him to continue his negotiations with viceroy.
17 June	Fall of France.
17–21 June	Congress working committee met at Wardha and announced (21 June) that it could not accept Gandhi's extreme stand on non-violence.
27 June	Parliament passed India and Burma (Emergency Provisions) Act providing 'in the event of a complete breakdown of communications with the United Kingdom' for transfer to governor-general of powers normally exercised by secretary of state.
27 June	Viceroy interviewed Jinnah.
29 June	Viceroy saw Gandhi at Simla.
1 July	Subhas Chandra Bose arrested.
3 July	Gandhi issued appeal 'To Every Briton' to accept method of non-violence and lay down his arms.
3–7 July	Emergency meeting of Congress working committee in Delhi renewed demand for immediate declaration of full independence for India, with provisional national government constituted at centre.
July	A.I.C.C. meeting at Poona ratified resolution of working committee.

7 August	Viceroy made statement on India's constitutional development – the 'August Offer' – and announced that executive council would be expanded and war advisory council established.
8 August	Viceroy's statement read in commons by secretary of state.
11 & 13 August	Viceroy saw Jinnah.
13 August	V. D. Savarkar saw viceroy and later accepted August offer on behalf of Hindu Mahasabha, as did Sikhs, scheduled castes and other organizations.
13 August–15 September	Battle of Britain.
18–22 August	Congress working committee met at Wardha and sent reply to viceroy (20 August) rejecting August offer.
23 August	Rajagopalachari made his 'sporting offer' to promote agreement with League.
29 August	Correspondence between viceroy and Azad released for publication.
31 August–2 September	League working committee met in Bombay to consider viceroy's offer and passed resolution stating that League's full co-operation in war effort would be conditional on viceroy clearing certain points with Jinnah.
7 September-16 May 1941	'Blitz' on London, industrial centres and western ports.
15 September	A.I.C.C met in Bombay and rejected August offer. Gandhi assumed active leadership of Congress.
24 September	Viceroy had long discussion with Jinnah
27 September	Viceroy saw Gandhi
28 September	Working committee of League met in New Delhi and rejected August offer.
29 September	Council of League passed resolution rejecting August offer.
13 October	Congress working committee at Wardha approved Gandhi's plan of individual civil disobedience. Vinoba Bhave selected to inaugurate movement.
17 October	Individual civil disobedience movement started by Vinoba Bhave.
21 October	Vinoba Bhave arrested. Nehru chosen to follow him.
31 October	Nehru arrested and sentenced to four years' imprisonment.
mid-November	Second stage of civil disobedience movement began.
17 November	Sardar Patel arrested.
20 November	Viceroy announced that he would not proceed with enlargement of executive council or establishment of war advisory council as major political parties had rejected August offer.
21 November	Secretary of state in London appealed to Indians to study afresh constitutional problem of India.
5 December	Subhas Chandra Bose released.

8 December	Fazlul Haq appealed to Jinnah to reopen negotiations with Congress.
31 December	Abul Kalam Azad arrested.

1941

5 January	Third stage of civil disobedience campaign began.
27 January	Subhas Chandra Bose escaped to Germany.
22 February	League working committee re-affirmed basic principles laid down in Lahore resolution of 1940.
11 March	Sir Sikandar Hyat Khan, premier of Punjab, explained his attitude to Pakistan in debate in Punjab legislative assembly.
13–14 March	Non-party conference in Bombay, Tej Bahadur Sapru president, proposed reconstruction of viceroy's executive council.
April	Fourth stage of civil disobedience campaign began.
22 April	Amery commented in commons on non-party scheme and civil disobedience campaign.
May	Statement by Jinnah on Sapru proposals.
1 July	Wavell appointed c. in c. India.
21 July	Governor-general's council reconstituted to consist of 8 Indians, 3 Britons, governor-general and commander-in-chief. National defence council of 30 members set up.
22 July	Both Gandhi and Jinnah reacted unfavourably to Simla announcement on expansion of viceroy's executive council.
26–27 July	Non-party political leaders conference, Sapru president, met at Poona.
30 July	Jinnah threatened disciplinary action against members of Muslim League who joined viceroy's executive council and national defence council.
19 August	Provincial prime ministers invited by viceroy to join national defence council. They accepted.
24 August	League working committee ordered three League premiers of Punjab, Bengal and Assam to resign from national defence council. Fazlul Haq resigned from working committee and council of League in protest. Sir Sultan Ahmed refused to resign from executive council and Begum Shah Nawaz from national defence council; both expelled from League.
August	'Atlantic Charter': joint declaration by Roosevelt and Churchill.
9 September	Churchill in house of commons said Atlantic charter did not qualify in any way various statements of policy relating to India.
10 September	Fazlul Haq resigned from national defence council.
6 October	First session of national defence council held at Simla.
26 October	*Dawn* began publication from Delhi (weekly).

by mid-October	Expansion of viceroy's executive council completed.
by mid-October	Many Congressmen who had taken part in individual civil disobedience had been released. Section of Congress suggested that Congress should take back power in provinces: Gandhi refused to yield.
26 October	Council of Muslim League endorsed decisions made by working committee in August.
23 November	Ministry sworn in in Orissa and proclamation under Section 93 revoked.
1 December	Fazlul Haq's ministry resigned, but he returned as head of coalition cabinet of 9 members (5 Muslims, 4 Hindus) on 11 December.
3 December	Civil disobedience prisoners, including Nehru and Azad, set free.
6 December	Japanese destroyed American fleet at Pearl Harbour.
11 December	Fazlul Haq expelled from League.
13 December	Saadullah's ministry fell in Assam and was followed by governor's rule (until August 1942).
23 December	Congress working committee met at Bardoli. Gandhi retired from leadership of Congress.

1942

January	A.I.C.C. met at Wardha.
1 February	Gandhi inaugurated All-India Goseva Sangh conference at Wardha.
15 February	Fall of Singapore.
8 March	Fall of Rangoon.
11 March	Statement by prime minister in house of commons announcing decision to send Cripps mission to India.
22 March	Cripps arrived in Delhi and began series of conversations with leaders of all political parties.
29 March	Cripps held press conference on his draft declaration.
30 March	Draft declaration for discussion with Indian leaders published.
2 April	Congress working committee passed resolution rejecting proposals put forward by Cripps mission.
2 April	League working committee passed resolution rejecting proposals put forward by Cripps mission.
3 April	Colonel Louis Johnson, President Roosevelt's personal envoy, arrived in Delhi.
4 April	Gandhi left Delhi after advising Cripps to take first plane home.
4 April	Indian leaders saw commander-in-chief.
7 April	Cripps wrote to Azad and Jinnah on question of Indian defence member.
8 April	Cripps finalized his formula.
9 April	Azad and Nehru approached Cripps on question of cabinet government.

10 April	Azad wrote to Cripps demanding cabinet government. Cripps replied on same day taking Azad's letter as rejection by Congress working committee of draft declaration. Negotiations terminated.
11 April	Resolutions of Congress working committee and of League rejecting the proposals were published.
11 April	Cripps held press conference and later broadcast on breakdown of discussions.
12 April	Cripps left India for England.
23 April	Rajagopalachari got resolution passed by Congress members in Madras legislature recommending to A.I.C.C. that Congress should acknowledge Muslim League's claim for separation and start negotiations with League.
26 April	In the *Harijan* Gandhi pleaded for British withdrawal from India, and in following issues explained and elaborated his 'Quit India' programme.
28 April	Amery made statement in house of commons on failure of Cripps mission.
29 April–2 May	A.I.C.C. met at Allahabad. Rajagopalachari's Madras resolution rejected by large majority, and counter-resolution on 'unity of India' passed. Resolution calling for non-co-operation and non-violent resistance to invader passed.
10 May	Gandhi in Bombay called on Britain to 'Leave India to God. If that is too much, then leave her to anarchy.'
11 May	Gandhi wrote an appeal 'To Every Briton' to retire from every Asian and African possession, at least from India.
18 May	Gandhi answered questions at press conference on his demand for British withdrawal from India and on Congress–League stalemate.
May–June	Rajagopalachari campaigned in Madras for forging of national front, establishment of national government and mobilization of country for defence.
20 June	Fall of Tobruk to the German army. British army retreated to El Alamein.
2 July	Viceroy's executive council expanded from 12 to 15 members: 11 non-official Indian, 1 non-official European, and 3 European officials (including the c. in c.).
6–14 July	Congress working committee met at Wardha and passed resolution demanding withdrawal of British rule from India and determining on mass civil disobedience campaign under Gandhi's leadership if demand not complied with.
July	Jinnah, Hindu Mahasabha, Liberals, Communists, and other leaders dissented from Congress appeal for civil disobedience.
15 July	Rajagopalachari resigned from Congress.

25 July	Rommel stopped at El Alamein.
27 July	Amery in house of commons and Cripps in broadcast to America denounced Congress demand.
7 August	A.I.C.C. met in Bombay.
8 August	A.I.C.C. endorsed working committee's resolution demanding withdrawal of British power from India and sanctioned beginning of mass struggle under Gandhi's leadership.
9 August	Gandhi and members of Congress working committee arrested, followed by arrest of all important Congress leaders. Congress committees declared unlawful associations.
August–September	Disturbances throughout India continued until end of September.
16–20 August	League working committee met at Bombay and deplored decision of A.I.C.C. to launch open rebellion. Muslims called upon to abstain from participation.
August	Sir Mahomed Saadullah took office in Assam.
10 October	Allah Bakhsh, premier of Sind, dismissed by the governor, Sir Hugh Dow. Sir Ghulam Hussain Hidayatullah took office with support of Muslim League.
23 October–4 November	Battle of El-Alamein.
early November	Rajagopalachari had talks with Jinnah.
7 November	Anglo-American forces landed in French North Africa.
12 November	Rajagopalachari saw viceroy and asked for permission to see Gandhi. Permission refused.
December	Council of Muslim League passed resolution stating that Muslims were entitled to homelands in NW and NE of India where they were in majority.
late December	Death of Sir Sikandar Hyat Khan.
31 December–8 February	Correspondence between Gandhi and viceroy.

1943

29 January	Gandhi informed viceroy of his intention to fast.
8 February	Government of India offered to release Gandhi for duration of fast: offer refused.
9 February–3 March	Gandhi's fast.
10 February	Government issued statement on fast and events leading up to it.
17 February	Three members of viceroy's executive council resigned over Gandhi's fast.
19 February	Non-party conference, Sapru chairman, met in Delhi, and urged Gandhi's immediate release. Jinnah refused to attend.
22 February	Government issued paper on Congress responsibility for disturbances in 1942.

March	Rajagopalachari's formula approved by Gandhi during fast.
28 March	Fazlul Haq forced to resign as premier of Bengal. Governor's rule continued until April 24th.
24 April	Sir Nazimuddin formed mainly Muslim League ministry in Bengal.
end April	At annual session of Muslim League announced that all Muslim majority provinces were now under control of League ministries.
May	Allah Bakhsh, ex-premier of Sind, murdered.
May	Muslim League ministry took office in N.W.F.P. under Aurangzeb Khan.
9 July	Allied forces landed in Sicily.
August–November	Bengal famine.
20 October	Lord Wavell succeeded Lord Linlithgow as viceroy of India.
December	Muslim League meeting at Karachi resolved to establish committee of action to organize Muslims all over India to resist imposition of unitary constitution and to prepare for coming struggle for achievement of Pakistan.

1944

17 February	Wavell addressing joint session of central legislature stated Cripps offer still open. Said India a natural unit.
February	Wavell visited famine-afflicted areas.
March	Japanese advanced into Assam assisted by I.N.A.
8 April	Rajagopalachari's formula communicated to Jinnah, followed by discussions and correspondence. Jinnah agreed to place formula before League.
April	Jinnah went to Lahore to talk with Khizr Hyat Khan, chief minister of Punjab.
April/May	Non-party conference at Lucknow authorized its president, Sapru, to prepare memorandum to be submitted to viceroy.
6 May	Gandhi released unconditionally on medical grounds.
6 May	Allied armies landed in France – D Day.
June	Japanese defeated at Imphal.
17 June	Gandhi wrote to viceroy requesting permission to interview members of Congress working committee and asking for meeting with viceroy. Permission refused.
20 June	Government published correpondence which had passed between Linlithgow, Wavell, Government of India, and Gandhi during his detention.
10 July	Rajagopalachari's formula made public for first time.
12 July	Gandhi at press conference gave authentic version of his interview with Stewart Gelder published in *Times of India*, previous day. He would be satisfied with national

	government in full control of civil administration; viceroy and c. in c. to have complete control of military operations.
15 July	Gandhi wrote to Wavell asking to see members of working committee and for an interview with viceroy.
17 July	Gandhi wrote to Jinnah suggesting meeting: Jinnah replied that he would be glad to receive Gandhi at his house in Bombay on his return from Kashmir.
27 July	Gandhi in letter to Wavell made proposals to bring about a Congress–Government understanding. Prepared to renounce civil disobedience and give full co-operation to war effort if declaration of immediate Indian independence was made and national government formed.
28 July	In house of commons secretary of state state said Gandhi's proposals did not even form starting-point for profitable discussion.
30 July	League working committee meeting at Lahore gave Jinnah full authority to negotiate with Gandhi. Jinnah dismissed Rajagopalachari formula.
15 August	Wavell replied to Gandhi that it was impossible to alter constitution during war.
August	Wavell at conference of governors stated that after the war promises made to India would have to be redeemed. Governors advised that positive move essential.
9–27 September	Gandhi–Jinnah talks. Correspondence released on 27 September.
October	Wavell sent proposals to Churchill and secretary of state.
19 November	Standing committee of non-party conference decided to appoint committee to examine communal and minorities question: members not to be actively associated with any recognized party.
3 December	Sapru announced names of members of committee. Jinnah refused to recognize committee or to meet Sapru.
1945	
20 January	Bhulabhai Desai saw viceroy and told him of Desai–Liaqat Ali pact, approved by Gandhi. (Jinnah disclaimed all knowledge of pact.)
February	Governor of Bombay saw Jinnah about Desai proposals. Jinnah said they had been made without any authority from League.
February	League ministry in Sind, led by Sir Ghulam Hussain Hidayatullah, defeated. Proposal to form coalition ministry upset by Jinnah.
12 March	Muslim League ministry in N.W.F.P. defeated. Dr Khan Sahib, leader of Congress party, invited to form new government.
14 March	Sir Ghulam Hussain Hidayatullah formed new ministry in Sind.

23 March	Wavell went to London, accompanied by V. P. Menon and Sir Evan Jenkins, for discussions with secretary of state and India committee.
28 March	Nazimuddin's ministry defeated in Bengal: governor took over administration of province under section 93.
March	In Assam Sir Mahomed Saadullah formed coalition cabinet with Gopinath Bardolai, Congress leader.
3 May	British forces entered Rangoon.
7 May	Germany surrendered.
23 May	Caretaker government formed in London.
4 June	Wavell returned to Delhi.
14 June	Wavell broadcast his proposals to advance India towards full self-government, and announced conference to be held at Simla. Amery announced in commons that viceroy had been empowered to make proposals on composition of interim government in India.
June	Viceroy sent invitations to all political leaders, and carried on correspondence with Gandhi, who issued various press statements.
15 June	Nehru and other Congress leaders released from prison.
24 June	Viceroy had separate interviews with Azad, Gandhi and Jinnah.
25 June–14 July	Simla conference.
3–6 July	Congress working committee selected panel of names to submit to viceroy.
5 July	General election in Britain.
6 July	League working committee met.
7 July	Jinnah wrote to viceroy.
8 July	Viceroy had prolonged discussions with Jinnah.
9 July	Viceroy sent Jinnah written reply.
11 July	Viceroy saw Jinnah. Conference failed.
11 July	Viceroy saw Gandhi and told him that conference had failed.
14 July	Fifth and last session of conference: Wavell announced failure of conference, because League claimed right to nominate all Muslim members of executive council.
26 July	Labour government came into power in Britain, C. R. Attlee prime minister, Lord Pethick-Lawrence secretary of state for India.
6 August	Jinnah demanded fresh elections.
August	Wavell convened meeting of governors at which it was agreed that elections would be held as soon as possible.
14 August	Japanese surrendered.
21 August	Wavell summoned to London for discussions. Announced that general elections would he held in winter.
24 August	Wavell left for London, accompanied by V. P. Menon and Sir Evan Jenkins, for discussions with secretary of state and India committee.

late August	Azad approached Gandhi with plan for communal settlement.
16 September	Wavell returned to India.
19 September	Wavell made statement on elections and his plans for summoning constitution-making body.
21 September	A.I.C.C. meeting at Bombay passed resolution characterizing Wavell's proposal as 'vague and inadequate and unsatisfactory'.
November	I.N.A. trials began in Red Fort, Delhi.
4 December	Secretary of state in house of lords announced that parliamentary delegation would be visiting India.
7 December	Congress working committee meeting in Calcutta reaffirmed its faith in non-violence.
late December	Results of elections to central legislative assembly announced.

1946

5 January	Parliamentary delegation, led by Professor Robert Richards, arrived in India.
11 January	Day celebrated by Muslim League as day of victory.
28 January	Viceroy addressed newly-elected central legislature.
January	R.A.F. strike.
11–15 February	Riots in Calcutta.
18–23 February	R.I.N. mutiny.
19 February	Secretary of state announced that cabinet mission was to visit India.
16 March	Debate in house of commons on cabinet mission's visit to India.
25 March	Cabinet mission arrived in Delhi.
3–17 April	Cabinet mission saw Indian leaders.
	Congress case put to mission by Azad.
	Gandhi interviewed immediately afterwards (3 April).
	Mission interviewed Jinnah (4 April).
	Mission interviewed representative of Sikhs, Scheduled Castes, Depressed Classes, Hindu Mahasabha, and Liberals.
10 April	Jinnah called together in Delhi convention of over 400 members of various legislatures recently elected on Muslim League ticket. Resolution passed calling for independent Pakistan.
16 April	Mission saw Jinnah again.
17 April	Mission saw Azad again.
17–23 April	Mission went to Kashmir to rest.
24 April	Cabinet mission scheme put before Jinnah and rejected. Rejected also by Congress leaders.
26 April	Cripps saw Azad who raised question of three-tier constitution. Cripps also saw Jinnah.

27 April	Letters sent by secretary of state to presidents of Congress and League inviting them each to send four negotiators to meet mission.
5–12 May	Second Simla conference between cabinet mission and Azad, Nehru, Patel, Abdul Ghaffar Khan, and Jinnah, Muhammad Ismail Khan, Liaqat Ali Khan, Abdur Rab Nishtar. Conference failed.
16 May	Cabinet mission put out statement in which it presented its own scheme.
16 May	Broadcast by secretary of state and statement by Cripps at press conference.
17 May	Broadcasts by Cripps and viceroy.
17 May	Cabinet mission held press conference on its plan.
22 May	Jinnah made statement on cabinet mission statement of 16 May.
24 May	Congress working committee adopted resolution raising various points in regard to cabinet mission plan and putting its own interpretation on paragraph 15.
25 May	Cabinet mission and viceroy issued statement saying that Congress interpretation of paragraph 15 was not in accordance with mission's intentions.
25 May	Azad wrote to viceroy asking for written confirmation that interim government would have same powers as a dominion cabinet. Viceroy denied ever having said that it would.
6 June	Council of Muslim League passed resolution accepting cabinet mission's scheme of 16 May.
10 June	Representative conference of Sikhs at Amritsar rejected cabinet mission's proposals and appointed committee of action under ex-I.N.A. officer to fight plan.
12 June	Viceroy saw Nehru. Meeting followed by meetings and correspondence over composition of interim government with Jinnah, etc. Deadlock.
16 June	Cabinet mission presented its own scheme for formation of interim government at centre.
June	Sikhs rejected interim proposals and refused to agree to any Sikh representative joining executive council.
19 June	Jinnah wrote to viceroy asking for clarification of points in statement of 16 June. Viceroy replied. Gist of correspondence communicated to Azad.
22 June	Viceroy wrote to Jinnah saying that he and cabinet mission could not accept Congress request for Muslim of their choice to be included in interim government.
25 June	Congress working committee meeting in Delhi passed resolution rejecting proposals for interim government but decided that Congress should join proposed constituent assembly.
25 June	League working committee passed resolution agreeing to join interim government on basis of statement of 16 June.

25 June	Azad in communicating Congress resolution to viceroy stated that Congress accepted proposals in 16 May statement but adhered to own interpretation.
25 June	Cabinet mission saw Jinnah and informed him that scheme of 16 June had fallen through, but since Congress and League had both accepted 16 May statement it was proposed to set up coalition government.
26 June	Last meeting between cabinet mission and party leaders. Negotiations for interim government had failed.
29 June	Cabinet mission left India.
6 July	A.I.C.C. meeting in Bombay ratified resolution of working committee accepting cabinet mission plan. Nehru took over Congress presidentship from Azad.
6 July	Nehru made statement in which he said 'We are not bound by a single thing except that we have decided for the moment to go to the Constituent Assembly'. Jinnah characterized Nehru's statement as 'a complete repudiation of the basic form upon which the long term scheme rests . . .'.
18 July	Pethick-Lawrence in lords and Cripps in commons reaffirmed cabinet mission plan, denying Congress interpretation.
22 July	Viceroy wrote to presidents of Congress and League putting forth proposals for interim coalition government.
23 July	Nehru replied that he was unable to co-operate in formation of government on lines suggested by viceroy.
27 July	At meeting of council of Muslim League in Bombay Jinnah accused cabinet mission of bad faith and condemned Congress. League had no alternative but to adhere once more to national goal of Pakistan.
29 July	Council of League passed resolution retracting its acceptance of cabinet mission plan, and another calling for 'direct action'. Working committee called upon Muslims throughout India to observe 16 August as 'Direct Action Day'.
	Viceroy saw Nehru after League resolution and asked him to give assurances to League: Nehru replied that he did not see what assurances he could give.
by end July	Elections completed for the 296 seats assigned in the constituent assembly to British–Indian provinces. Congress won all general seats except 9, and League won all Muslim seats except 5.
31 July	Jinnah replied to viceroy's letter of 22 July that his working committee could not accept viceroy's proposals.
6 August	Viceroy wrote to Nehru inviting him to make proposals for formation of interim government.
8 August	Viceroy replied to Jinnah's letter of 31 July saying that he had decided to invite Congress to form interim government.

8 August	Congress working committee met at Wardha and decided to accept invitation to form interim government. Passed resolution making it clear that Congress accepted the 16 May statement in its entirety, but interpreted it so as to resolve inconsistencies contained in it. Congress hoped that League would join constituent assembly.
12 August	Viceroy issued communiqué announcing his invitation to president of Congress to form provisional government.
13 August	Nehru wrote to Jinnah suggesting personal discussion.
14 August	Sikh panthic board accepted statement of 16 May.
15 August	Jinnah replied to Nehru, followed by more correspondence and meeting. Nehru offered Jinnah 5 seats in interim government of 14. No result.
16 August	'Direct Action Day': public holiday in Bengal and Sind.
16–18 August	Great Calcutta killing.
17 August	Nehru explained to viceroy that he would include in government six Congress nominees and three minority representatives and fill five Muslim seats with non-League Muslims – viceroy averse to this.
18 August	Nehru met viceroy on question of further approach to Jinnah.
19 August	Nehru wrote to viceroy confirming his view on composition of government.
19 August	Jinnah issued statement to press.
19–22 August	Discussions between viceroy, Azad and Nehru.
22 August	Nehru wrote to viceroy on question of coalition with League. Against 'appeasement' of League.
24 August	Press communiqué issued stating that King had accepted resignations of governor-general's executive council and that Nehru, Patel, Prasad, Asaf Ali, Rajagopalachari, Sarat Chandra Bose, Matthai, Baldev Singh, Shafaat Ahmed Khan, Jagjivan Ram, Syed Ali Zaheer, and C. H. Bhabha, had been nominated in their place.
24 August	Viceroy broadcast on formation of interim government.
24 August	Jinnah after viceroy's broadcast reiterated demand for division of India.
24/25 August	Wavell flew to Calcutta. Met Khwaja Nazimuddin.
27 August	Wavell met Gandhi and Nehru on his return from Calcutta. Advocated setting up of coalition governments both in Bengal and at the centre. Asked Congress to accept formula on grouping accepting mission's meaning. Could not summon constituent assembly until this was settled.
27 August	Gandhi wrote to viceroy. Viceroy wrote to Nehru asking him to place his formula before Congress working committee.
28 August	Nehru replied to viceroy that working committee was surprised at sudden change in his approach. Congress

	position with regard to grouping clear. Unable to accept viceroy's proposal.
2 September	Interim government took office without League.
early September	Communal clashes in Bombay and Ahmedabad.
7 September	Nehru broadcast on constituent assembly.
8 September	Jinnah gave interview to *Daily Mail* stating that Nehru had made no definite proposals to him.
September	Viceroy had discussions with Nehru and Rajagopalachari.
16 September	Viceroy saw Jinnah but no agreement reached.
25 September	Viceroy saw Jinnah: interim government discussed.
26 September	Viceroy saw Nehru and Gandhi.
2 October	Viceroy informed Jinnah that he had failed to secure any concession from Congress over nationalist Muslim issue. Asked League to come into government. Jinnah agreed to summon working committee. Jinnah then sent viceroy note setting out nine points for elucidation.
4 October	Viceroy consulted Nehru on Jinnah's points and then replied to Jinnah.
4 October	Nehru wrote to viceroy stating that cabinet must be able to function together.
10–20 October	Communal disturbances in Noakhali.
12 October	Viceroy wrote to Jinnah.
13 October	Jinnah wrote to Wavell that League had decided to join interim government. He and Liaqat had interview with viceroy.
14 October	Viceroy informed Nehru of his meeting with League leaders.
14 October	Jinnah submitted five names for interim government.
15 October	Press communiqué issued on decision of League to join interim government.
23 October	Gandhi in statement on grouping clause said that no law-giver could give an authoritative interpretation of his own law. A duly constituted court of law must decide it.
25 October	Interim government reconstituted.
26 October	Muslim League members of interim government took office.
29 October	Gandhi arrived in Calcutta from Delhi.
30 October–7 November	Bihar outbreak. Viceroy, Nehru and Rajendra Prasad all visited the province.
6 November	Gandhi left Calcutta for Noakhali. Remained there until 2 March.
6–15 November	Communal outbreak at Garhmukteswar.
17 November	Jinnah wrote to viceroy arguing that Congress had not accepted statement of 16 May and therefore it would be futile for him to summon his council. Urged viceroy to postpone meeting of constituent assembly.
18/19 November	Viceroy saw Jinnah and Nehru about constituent assembly.

20 November	Viceroy issued invitations for meeting of constituent assembly. Jinnah called on League representatives not to participate.
November	Annual session of Congress at Meerut demanded that League should either accept cabinet mission plan and come into constituent assembly or quit interim government.
26 November	Viceroy saw Nehru, Liaqat and Baldev Singh and invited them to London for discussions. Nehru refused invitation. Attlee sent personal invitation to Nehru, who then accepted. Attlee also sent personal invitation to Jinnah.
2 December	Wavell, Nehru, Baldev Singh, Jinnah and Liaqat arrived in London.
3–6 December	London conference. No agreement reached.
6 December	Government put out statement clarifying cabinet mission plan.
7 December	Nehru and Baldev Singh returned to India. Jinnah and Liaqat stayed in England.
9 December	Constituent assembly met without League members, and adjourned until 20 January.
18 December	Attlee made his first approach to Mountbatten to succeed Wavell.
22 December	Congress working committee issued statement clarifying its attitude towards H.M.G.'s statement of 6 December.
late December (or early January)	V. P. Menon had lengthy discussion with Vallabhbhai Patel suggesting that power should be transferred to two central governments on basis of dominion status. Patel agreed and Menon sent outline of his plan to secretary of state, but no action was taken.

1947

January	Jinnah returned to India: ill, took no part in affairs until early March.
5 January	A.I.C.C. met in Delhi and endorsed statement of working committee of 22 December: resolution passed 7 January.
20 January	Constituent assembly met.
25 January	Liaqat Ali Khan issued statement putting various questions to Congress.
29 January	League working committee met in Karachi: called upon government to declare that plan of 16 May had failed, and demanded that constituent assembly should be dissolved.
February	Communal rioting in Punjab.
1 February	Nehru had interview with viceroy.
5 February	Viceroy received demand from Congress and minority members for resignation of League representatives from interim government.
6 February	Viceroy saw Liaqat.

7 February	Liaqat wrote to viceroy about Congress demand for resignation of League members: stated that Congress had not accepted 16 May statement.
13 February	Nehru wrote to viceroy and again demanded resignation of League members from interim government.
15 February	Vallabhbhai Patel stated that Congress would withdraw from interim government if League members remained.
20 February	Prime Minister made statement to parliament announcing British intention of leaving India by June 1948. Mountbatten to succeed Wavell as viceroy.
21 February	Wavell urged Nehru to get League into constituent assembly. He also saw Liaqat.
March	Food shortage; industrial unrest; strikes; communal rioting in Punjab.
March	League organized demonstrations against Congress ministry in N.W.F.P. Large scale arrest of Leaguers.
2 March	Khizr Hyat Khan resigned as premier of Punjab. Khan of Mamdot (League) failed to form ministry.
2 March	Gandhi left Noakhali for Bihar.
5 March	Sir Evan Jenkins, governor of Punjab, took over administration of province under Section 93.
5 March	Congress working committee met to consider statement of 20 February: invited League to discuss transfer of power: called for partition of Punjab and Bengal.
9 March	Nehru wrote to Wavell enclosing copies of resolutions of working committee.
March	Liaqat's budget proposals called for a twenty-five per cent tax on business profits of more than Rs. 100,000.
22 March	Lord Mountbatten arrived in Delhi. Wrote to Gandhi and Jinnah inviting them to Delhi for discussions.
23 March	Wavell left Delhi.
24 March	Mountbatten sworn in as viceroy.
March–April	Mountbatten had talks with all party leaders.
24 March	Mountbatten had interviews with members of interim government, especially Nehru and Liaqat over budget proposals – percentage of tax reduced.
25 March	Mountbatten saw Patel.
30 March	Gandhi left Bihar for Delhi.
31 March	Mountbatten saw Gandhi.
1 April	Gandhi in second interview with Mountbatten suggested that viceroy should dismiss existing cabinet and invite Jinnah to form new one.
2 April	Mountbatten saw Gandhi again.
2 April	Lord Pethick-Lawrence resigned as Secretary of State for India and was succeeded by Lord Listowel.
5 April	Mountbatten met Jinnah for first time.
8 April	Viceroy received letter from Liaqat asking for armed forces to be reorganized so that they could be more readily

split between Pakistan and Hindustan. Mountbatten said there could be no splitting of Indian army before withdrawal of British.

April — Communal disturbances in Punjab and adjoining provinces, including Delhi. Agitation against Congress ministry in N.W.F.P. Congress government in N.W.F.P. decided to release political prisoners, but they refused to accept their freedom unless ministry resigned.

8 April — Mountbatten raised with Jinnah question of appeal by both major parties for truce in communal disturbances.

9 April — British Residents in Indian states conferred in Delhi.

12 April — Gandhi wrote to Viceroy that his plan to hand over to Jinnah was not acceptable to Congress and that he was handing over all future negotiation to working committee.

14 April — Gandhi returned to Bihar.

15 April — Joint statement signed by Gandhi and Jinnah issued deploring violence and denouncing use of force for achievement of political ends.

15–16 April — Viceroy's plan put before governors' conference in New Delhi.

18 April — Mountbatten interviewed Sikh leaders who insisted that Punjab must be partitioned.

20 April — Nehru said Muslim League could have Pakistan on condition that they did not take away other parts of India which did not wish to join Pakistan.

24 April — Jinnah put out an appeal to reason in N.W.F.P.

28 April — Rajendra Prasad, president of constituent assembly, accepted principle of partition.

28 April — Gandhi returned to Delhi.

28–30 April — Mountbatten visited the N.W.F.P.

2 May — Ismay and Abell flew to London with first draft of the Mountbatten plan (revised version of plan discussed with governors in April).

4 May — Gandhi and Jinnah met while visiting viceroy, their first meeting for three years.

6 May — Gandhi had three-hour meeting with Jinnah at Jinnah's house.

7 May — Mountbatten with V. P. Menon and Mièville, arrived in Simla.

7 May — V. P. Menon asked to prepare paper on demission of power under present constitution.

8 May — Gandhi left Delhi for Calcutta.

8 May — Nehru, with Krishna Menon, arrived in Simla: guests of viceroy at Viceregal Lodge.

9 May — Vallabhbhai Patel made statement suggesting that power be transferred to Indian government on basis of dominion status.

10 May	Viceroy called conference attended by Nehru, Mièville and V. P. Menon to discuss Menon's plan.
10 May	Mountbatten received from London plan taken by Ismay, as approved by British cabinet.
10 May	It was announced that viceroy would meet Jinnah, Liaqat, Nehru, Patel and Baldev Singh in Delhi on 17 May to present to them plan for transfer of power.
10 May	Mountbatten showed plan to Nehru who rejected it.
11 May	Meeting with leaders postponed until 2 June.
11 May	V. P. Menon prepared draft of his own plan.
14 May	Mountbatten returned to Delhi.
14 May	Gandhi left Calcutta for Patna.
15 May	Mountbatten summoned to London for consultations.
15 May	Mountbatten saw Patel and Liaqat.
16 May	V. P. Menon drew up draft of eight 'Heads of Agreement' which was approved by Viceroy and shown to all leaders.
16 May	Viceroy had consultations with leaders. New plan finalized. Nehru accepted it in writing; Jinnah verbally.
18 May	Mountbatten left Delhi for London, taking V. P. Menon and Erskine-Crum with him.
19 May	Mountbatten arrived in London.
19–30 May	Discussions between Mountbatten, Attlee, India and Burma committee, and opposition leaders. Nehru and Jinnah kept informed of progress of discussions.
22 May	Jinnah demanded an 800-mile corridor to link East and West Pakistan.
24 May	Gandhi left Bihar for Delhi.
25 May onwards	Gandhi at prayer meetings spoke in favour of a united India.
31 May	Mountbatten returned to India with final plan approved by British cabinet.
2 June	Meeting between Viceroy and Indian leaders. Viceroy saw Gandhi after main meeting.
2 June	Congress working committee met and decided to accept plan: Kripalani wrote to Viceroy.
2 June	Baldev Singh accepted plan on behalf of Sikhs.
2 June (midnight)	Viceroy saw Jinnah who gave verbal assurances about his acceptance of plan.
3 June	Second meeting between Mountbatten and Indian leaders, who agreed to plan. They were presented with paper on administrative consequences of partition.
3 June	Members of states negotiating committee were told of plan.
3 June	Plan announced over all-India radio by Viceroy: followed by Nehru, Jinnah and Baldev Singh. Plan also announced in House of Commons.
4 June	Mountbatten held press conference, at which he gave first formal indication that transfer of power would take place on 15 August 1947 and not June 1948.

4 June	Viceroy saw Gandhi just before his prayer meeting.
4 June	Bhopal resigned as Chancellor of Chamber of Princes.
5 June	Mountbatten held third meeting with Indian leaders to discuss administrative consequences of partition.
after 3 June	Muslim League mass movements in Assam and N.W.F.P. abandoned.
8 June	At a meeting of interim government formula found for submitting policy decisions and high grade appointments direct to Viceroy to avoid dissension.
10 June	Plan ratified by council of Muslim League.
June	Joint conference of Sikh organizations in Lahore welcomed division of Punjab.
13 June	Partition committee of interim government formed, with steering committee of two senior civil servants to coordinate work of expert committees charged with specific facets of partition.
14 June	A.I.C.C. meeting in Delhi ratified plan.
19–23 June	Mountbatten visited Kashmir.
20 June	Bengal Legislative Assembly opted for partition.
23 June	Mountbatten asked Jinnah for his decision on governor-general question.
23 June	Punjab legislative assembly opted for partition.
26 June	Sind legislative assembly opted for Pakistan.
27 June	Partition committee gave way to partition council of wider authority. Council decided that Sir Cyril Radcliffe should be invited to serve as Chairman of Punjab and Bengal Boundary Commissions.
30 June	Partition council agreed to procedure for division of armed forces. Auchinleck to remain as supreme commander after 15 August under joint defence council. Arbitral tribunal set up, Sir Patrick Spens President.
June	Baluchistan opted for Pakistan.
June	Violence in Punjab.
2 July	Mountbatten showed draft Indian Independence Bill to Indian leaders, and to Gandhi, for comment.
2 July	Jinnah told Mountbatten that he himself wished to be Governor-General of Pakistan.
4 July	Indian Independence Bill introduced into House of Commons.
5 July	Liaqat asked Mountbatten to recommend Jinnah's name as Governor-General of Pakistan. He hoped that Mountbatten would remain as Governor-General of India.
5 July	New states department inaugurated by Vallabhbhai Patel.
5 July	Ismay and Campbell-Johnson left Delhi for London.
6–7 July	Referendum held in Sylhet, which decided to join East Bengal.
6–17 July	Referendum held in N.W.F.P. which decided to join Pakistan.

7 July	Ismay arrived in London and saw Attlee.
8 July	Attlee consulted opposition leaders over question of Mountbatten remaining as Governor-General of India. All agreed.
10 July	Debate on second reading of Indian Independence Bill in Commons – small attendence.
by mid-July	All disputed areas had chosen and fresh elections were then held there for election of representatives to respective constituent assemblies.
14 July	Constituent Assembly began its fourth session attended by League members from non-Pakistan provinces.
16 July	Indian Independence Bill passed its third reading.
16–24 July	Bengal Boundary Commission in session.
18 July	Indian Independence Act received royal assent.
19 July	Mountbatten announced establishment of two separate provisional governments, one for India and one for Pakistan.
21 July	Union constitution committee presented to Constituent Assembly draft constitution.
21–31 July	Punjab Boundary Commission in session.
22 July	Ismay and Campbell-Johnson arrived in Delhi from London.
22 July	Members of partition council announced a Punjab boundary force to be set up. Both governments pledged themselves to accept awards of Boundary Commission, and guaranteed protection of minorities.
25 July	Mountbatten addressed Chamber of Princes.
30 July	Mountbatten visited Calcutta.
end July	Gandhi paid brief visit to Kashmir and N.W.F.P.
1 August	Punjab boundary force set up.
4–6 August	Bengal Boundary Commission in session to consider Sylhet.
5 August	Viceroy told Patel, Jinnah and Liaqat of information implicating Sikh leaders in sabotage plans.
6 August	Partition Council met for last time.
7 August	Jinnah flew to Karachi.
9 August	Gandhi arrived in Calcutta.
11 August	Constituent Assembly of Pakistan met and elected Jinnah President.
12 August	Bengal and Punjab awards complete. Sylhet award not yet ready.
13 August	Radcliffe award ready.
13 August	Mountbatten flew to Karachi.
14 August	Mountbatten addressed Pakistan Constituent Assembly and then flew back to Delhi.
15 August	India and Pakistan became independent. Jinnah sworn in as Governor-General of Pakistan and Mountbatten as

	Governor-General of India. Pakistan cabinet headed by Liaqat; Indian cabinet by Nehru.
16 August	Mountbatten handed the Radcliffe award to the leaders of both dominions in Delhi.
17 August	Radcliffe award published.

SELECT BIBLIOGRAPHY OF WORKS IN ENGLISH

BIBLIOGRAPHIES

Case, Margaret H. *South Asian History 1750–1950. A Guide to Periodicals, Dissertations and Newspapers* (Princeton, 1968).

Deshpande, P. G. *Gandhiana* (Ahmedabad, 1948).

Ghani, A. R. *Pakistan: A Select Bibliography* (Lahore, 1951).

Moreland G. and Sidiqui, A. N. *Star and Crescent: An Annotated Bibliography of Pakistan* (Karachi, 1956).

Morris, M. D. and Stein, B. 'The economic history of India, a bibliographical essay', *Journal of Economic History*, xxi (June 1961), 179–207.

Sharma, J. S. *Mahatma Gandhi, A Descriptive Bibliography* (Delhi, 1955).

Jawaharlal Nehru, A Descriptive Bibliography (Delhi, 1959).

Indian National Congress, A Descriptive Bibliography (Delhi, 1959).

Wilson, P. *Government and Politics of India and Pakistan, 1885–1955: A Bibliography of Works in Western Languages* (Berkeley, Cal., 1956).

UNPUBLISHED SOURCES

There is a vast amount of unpublished official source material in Great Britain, India and Pakistan for the years covered by this study. Where the thirty-year rule applies this material is gradually becoming available for consultation. In addition there are many collections of private papers, many still in private ownership, to which access depends on permission being obtained from the owners. This note is intended only to draw attention to the major collections, and indicate where further information might be obtained.

The official records of the department of the Secretary of State for India are in the custody of the India Office Library in London and are subject to the thirty-year rule, that is, they are open to inspection thirty years after the date of origin. Documents relating to the transfer of power in India are being prepared for publication under the general editorship of Professor P. N. S. Mansergh. The India Office Library also has the custody of many collections of private papers, including those of secretaries of state, viceroys, governors, and others. For information, and details of access, enquiries should be made to the Librarian. The Library also collects information about relevant private papers deposited in other institutions or remaining in private hands.[1]

The thirty-year rule applies also to the records of other departments of state, deposited at the Public Record Office, and to the cabinet papers.[2]

The official records of the government of India are deposited at the National Archives of India in New Delhi.[3] Some of the records for the period 1935–47 are open: for details and information on access application should be made

[1] See *Guide to the India Office Library*, new edn (1967), and the *Annual Reports* of the Library.

[2] See *Guide to the Contents of the Public Record Office*, 2 vols (1963).

[3] See Low, Iltis and Wainwright, *Government Archives in South Asia* (1969).

to the Director of Archives. The National Archives also has some collections of private papers, of which that of M. R. Jayakar might be mentioned here, and collects information as to the location of papers in other repositories, as well as of those still in private hands, though there has so far been no systematic attempt to collect information about private papers in India.

The records of the Congress working committee have been deposited at the Nehru Memorial Museum and Library in New Delhi, and this library also has custody of a large collection of Nehru letters, as well as papers of other nationalist leaders. Enquiries as to holdings and access should be made to the Director. Correspondence and papers of Mahatma Gandhi will be found in the Gandhi Samarak Nidhi in Delhi, and the National Library in Calcutta also has a few collections of private papers, the most important being that of Tej Bahadur Sapru.

The records of the All-India Muslim League have been deposited at Karachi University, where they are in process of being sorted and arranged for the use of scholars. Other collections of private papers have also been rescued and deposited at Karachi University and will become available in due course.[1] The private papers of M. A. Jinnah are in the custody of the Government of Pakistan, but will eventually be housed at Karachi University with the Muslim League papers.

PUBLISHED SOURCES

A. *British Official*

1. Acts of Parliament

   The Government of India Act, 23 December 1919. 9 & 10 Geo. V, c. 101.

   The Government of India Act, 2 August 1935. 26 Geo. V, c. 2.

   The Indian Independence Act, 18 July 1947. 10 & 11 Geo. VI, c. 30.
2. Parliamentary Debates, 1935–47.
3. Minutes and Debates of the Legislative Council of India and its successors, 1854–1947.
4. Parliamentary Papers (including some non-Parliamentary Papers).

   Cd. 9109 (1918). Report on Indian Constitutional Reforms (Montagu-Chelmsford Report).

   Cd. 9190 (1918). Report of the Indian Sedition Committee (Rowlatt Committee Report).

   H.C. 203 (1919). Report of the Joint Select Committee on the Government of India Bill, 1919.

   Cmd. 681 (1920). Report of the Committee Appointed to Investigate Disturbances in the Punjab (Hunter Committee Report).

   Cmd. 1552 (1921). East India (Moplah Rebellion).

   Cmd. 2360 (1925). Majority Report, Reforms Enquiry Committee (Muddiman Committee Report).

   Cmd. 2986 (1927). Indian Statutory Commission. Statement published on 8 November 1927 by the Governor-General of India.

[1] Z. H. Zaidi, working under the auspices of the School of Oriental and African Studies, London, has been responsible for collecting many of the papers now deposited at Karachi University.

Cmd. 3302 (1928–9). Report of the Indian States Committee.
Cmd. 3451 (1929). Report of the Indian Central Committee.
Cmd. 3525 (1930). Supplementary Note by Dr A. Suhrawardy to the Report of the Indian Central Committee.
Cmd. 3568 (1930). Report of the Indian Statutory Commission (Simon Commission). Vol. I, Survey.
Cmd. 3569 (1930). Report of the Indian Statutory Commission. Vol. II, Recommendations.
Report of the Indian Statutory Commission. Vols IV–XIV. Memoranda Submitted by the Government of India and the India Office, and by Provincial Governments (HMSO, 1930).
Cmd. 3778 (1931). Proceedings of the Indian Round Table Conference, First Session, 12 November 1930–19 January 1931.
Cmd. 3997 (1932). Proceedings of the Indian Round Table Conference, Second Session, 7 September 1931–1 December 1931.
Indian Round Table Conference, Second Session: Proceedings of the Federal Structure Committee and Minorities Committee, 1932. (HMSO, 1932), 3 vols.
Cmd. 4086 (1932). Report of the Indian Franchise Committee.
Cmd. 4147 (1932). East India (Constitutional Reforms): Communal Decision.
Cmd. 4238 (1933). Reports and Proceedings of the Indian Round Table Conference, Third Session, 17 November 1932–24 December 1932.
Joint Committee on Indian Constitutional Reform (Session 1932–33): Report with Minutes of Evidence and Records. 6 vols. (HMSO, 1933–4).
Joint Committee on Indian Constitutional Reform (Session 1933–34): Report. 2 vols. (HMSO, 1934).
Return showing the Results of the Election in India, 1937 (1937).
Cmd. 6121 (1939). India and the War: Statement Issued by the Governor-General of India on 17 October 1939: with Appendices.
Cmd. 6129 (1939). India and the War: Announcement Published by the Governor-General of India on 6 November 1939, and Correspondence Connected Therewith.
Cmd. 6196 (1939–40). India and the War: Communiqué Issued by the Governor-General and Resolutions by the Indian National Congress, the All-India Moslem League and the Chamber of Princes.
Cmd. 6219 (1939–40). India and the War: Statement by the Governor-General, 8 August 1940.
Cmd. 6235 (1940). India and the War: Statement by the Governor-General, 20 November 1940.
Cmd. 6293 (1941). India and the War: Announcement Issued by the Governor-General, 22 July 1941.
Cmd. 6350 (1942). India (Lord Privy Seal's Mission) 1942. Statement and Draft Declaration by His Majesty's Government with Correspondence Connected Therewith.

Cmd. 6430 (1943). India: Statement on the Congress Party's Responsibility for Disturbances in 1942–3. March 1943.

Cmd. 6652 (1945). India: Statement of Policy of His Majesty's Government.

Cmd. 6821 (1946). India: Statement by the Cabinet Mission and His Excellency, the Viceroy.

Cmd. 6829 (1946). Correspondence and Documents connected with the Conference between the Cabinet Mission and His Excellency the Viceroy and Representatives of the Congress and the Muslim League, May 1946.

Cmd. 6835 (1946). India: Statement by the Cabinet Mission, 25 May 1946.

Cmd. 6861 (1946). India: Statement by the Cabinet Mission.

Cmd. 6862 (1946). India (Cabinet Mission): Papers Relating to (*a*) the Sikhs, (*b*) the Indian States, and (*c*) the European Community. May–June 1946.

Cmd. 7047 (1947). Indian Policy Statement. 20 February 1947.

Cmd. 7136 (1947). Indian Policy Statement. 3 June 1947.

India in [1917/18–1934/35]: Statements Prepared for Presentation to Parliament in Accordance with the Requirements of the 26th Section of the Government of India Act (5 & 6 Geo. V, c. 61). 1919–37. 17 vols.

B. *Indian Conference Proceedings, Reports, etc.*

1. Indian National Congress publications

Reports (Annual). 1885–1947.

Resolutions of the Indian National Congress. 1928–46.

Twenty-seven Months of Service; being a Brief Account of what the Congress Ministries did from July 1937–October 1939. (Bombay, 1939.)

The War Crisis; Statement issued by the Congress Working Committee at Wardha on September 14, 1939, in regard to the War Crisis and India. (Allahabad, 1939.)

Congress and the War Crisis. (Allahabad, 1940.)

March of Events, being the Case of the Indian National Congress vis-à-vis the Present World Crisis. 3 vols. (Bombay, 1940, 1945, 1946.)

Poverty and Partition; being a Brief Account of the Economic Implications of Pakistan. (Bombay, 1946.)

Congress Ministries at Work, April 1946–April 1947 (Allahabad, 1947).

2. All-India Muslim League publications

The Constitution and Rules of the All-India Muslim League (Delhi).

List of the Members of the Council of the All-India Muslim League (Delhi).

Resolutions of the All-India Muslim League, May 1924–December 1946. Compiled by Liaqat Ali Khan. 6 vols. (Delhi, n.d., 1944, n.d., n.d., n.d., n.d.)

Presidential Address of Dr Sir Muhammad Iqbal Delivered at the Allahabad Session of the All-India Muslim League, December 1930.

Presidential Addresses of Qaid-e-Azam, M. A. Jinnah, Delivered at the Sessions of the All-India Muslim League [1937–43] (Delhi, 1946).

Re Hindu–Muslim Settlement: Correspondence between Mr Gandhi and Mr Jinnah, Pandit Nehru and Mr Jinnah and between Mr S. Bose and Mr Jinnah (Delhi, 1938).

Report of the Enquiry Committee appointed by the Council of the All-India Muslim League to enquire into Muslim Grievances in Congress Provinces, 15 November 1938 (Pirpur Report) (Delhi, 1938).

All-India Muslim League (Bihar Province) Publicity Committee: Report . . . on some Grievances of the Muslims, 1938–9. President S. M. Shareef. (Shareef Report). 2 vols. (Patna, 1940).

Report of the Committee appointed by the Council of the All-India Muslim League to examine the Wardha Scheme (Lucknow, n.d.).

The War! Problem of India's Future Constitution! What Muslim India and its Leader Mr M. A. Jinnah Think (Delhi, 1940).

Jinnah–Gandhi Talks (September 1944). Text of Correspondence. . . . (Delhi, 1944).

It Shall Never Happen Again. [32 articles originally published in *Dawn*] (Delhi, 1946).

How Much Is The Difference? by Humayun Akhtar (Delhi, 194?).

3. All-Parties Conference publications

Report of the Committee appointed by the Conference to Determine the Principles of the Constitution for India (Nehru Report). (Allahabad, 1928).

Proceedings of the All-Parties Convention, 22 December 1928-1 January 1929 (Allahabad, 1929).

4. Non-Party Political Conference publications

Proceedings of the Non-Party Political Conference held at Bombay on 13 & 14 March 1941 (Delhi, 1941).

Proceedings of the Second Session of the Non-Party Political Conference held at Poona on 26 & 27 July 1941 (Allahabad, 1941).

A National Government: Answer to Criticism: Statements issued by the President and Standing Committee of the Non-Party Political Conference, and other papers (Allahabad, 1941).

Proceedings of the Third Session. . . . (Allahabad, 1942).

Constitutional Proposals of the Sapru Committee. 1945 (Moradabad, 1946).

5. All-India Hindu Mahasabha

Savarkar, Vinayak Damodar. *Hindu Rashtra Darshan: a Collection of the Presidential Speeches delivered from the Hindu Mahasabha platform* (Bombay, 1949).

6. Indian Princes

Proceedings of the Meetings of the Chamber of Princes (Narendra Mandal). February 1930, March 1940, January 1946 (Simla).

Report of the Speeches delivered at the Conference of Indian Princes held at Bombay, February 25th, 1935 (London, 1935).

A Handbook of the Chamber of Princes (Simla, 1942).

7. Constituent Assembly of India
Debates. 1947.
Documents Relating to Statements by His Majesty's Government on 6 December 1946, 20 February 1947 and 3 June 1947 (New Delhi, 1947).

C. *Newspapers and Journals*

1. In Britain
The Times (London).
The Daily Telegraph & Morning Post (London).
The Manchester Guardian (Manchester).
The Daily Mail (London).
The New Statesman & Nation (London).
2. In India (English language only).
Amrita Bazar Patrika (Calcutta).
Civil and Military Gazette (Lahore).
Dawn (Delhi).
Harijan (Ahmedabad).
The Hindu (Madras).
The Hindustan Times (Delhi).
The Leader (Allahabad).
The Modern Review (Calcutta).
The Morning News (Calcutta).
Muslim Outlook (Lahore).
The People's Age (Bombay).
The Pioneer (Allahabad).
The Star of India (Calcutta).
The Statesman (Calcutta).
The Times of India (Bombay).
The Tribune (Lahore).
Young India (Ahmedabad).

D. *Other contemporary materials*

1. *The Indian Annual Register:* an annual digest of public affairs in India, ed. by N. N. Mitra. 1919–47 (Calcutta).
2. Selections of documents
Banerjee, A. C., ed. *Indian Constitutional Documents*, Vol. III, 1917–39 (Calcutta, 1949).
Banerjee, A. C. and Bose, D. R., eds *The Cabinet Mission in India* (Calcutta, 1946).
Gwyer, M. and Appadorai, A., eds. *Speeches and Documents on the Indian Constitution 1921–47*, 2 vols. (London, 1957).
Philips, C. H., ed. *The Evolution of India and Pakistan 1858–1947* (London, 1962).
3. Collected writings, correspondence and speeches
Afzal, M. R., ed. *Selected Speeches and Statements of the Qaid-i-Azam Mohammad Ali Jinnah* (*1911–34 and 1947–48*) (Lahore, 1966).

Ahmad, Jamil-ud-din, edn. *Some Recent Speeches and Writings of Mr Jinnah*, Vol. I (Lahore, 1943; 6th edn, 1960); Vol. II (Lahore, 1947; 6th edn, 1964).

Amery, L. S. *India and Freedom* [speeches, 1940–42] (London, 1942).

Bose, N. K. *Selections from Gandhi*, 2nd edn (Ahmedabad, 1957).

Bose, S. C. *Crossroads:* being *Works, 1938–40*, compiled by the Netaji Research Bureau (Calcutta).

Bright, J. S., ed. *Important Speeches of Jawaharlal Nehru . . ., 1922–46*, 2nd edn (Lahore, n.d.).

Chatterjee, N. C. *Hindu Politics, the Message of the Mahasabha: a Collection of Speeches and Addresses* (Calcutta, ?1945).

Gandhi, M. K. *Collected Works of Mahatma Gandhi*, Vol. I – , in progress (Govt. of India, New Delhi).

Gandhi–Linlithgow Correspondence (Jubbulpore, 1943).

Correspondence with Mr. Gandhi, August 1942–April 1944 (Delhi, 1944).

Gandhi–Jinnah Talks, July–October 1944 (New Delhi, 1944).

Letters to Sardar Patel (Ahmedabad, 1957).

Ghosha, M. L. *Speeches and Writings* (Calcutta, 1935).

Hoare, Sir S. *Speeches 1931–5*.

Iqbal, A., ed. *Selected Writings and Speeches of Maulana Mohamed Ali* (Lahore, 1936).

Iqbal, M. *Letters of Iqbal to Jinnah . . . conveying his views on the political future of Muslim India* (Lahore, 1943).

Irwin, Lord. *Speeches*, Vols I and II (Simla, 1930–31).

Jinnah, M. A. *Writings*, 2 vols (Ahmedabad, 1947).

Mohamed Ali Jinnah: An Ambassador of Unity: His Speeches and Writings 1912–17: With a Biographical Appreciation by Sarojini Naidu (Madras, n.d.).

Pakistan, the Muslim Charter [speech to the University Union] (Aligarh, 194?).

Speeches by Qaid-i-Azam Mohamed Ali Jinnah, Governor General of Pakistan: 3rd June 1947 to 14 August 1948 (Karachi, n.d.).

Jung, N. Y., ed. *The Pakistan Issue, being the correspondence between Sayyid Abdul Latif and M. A. Jinnah on the one hand, and between him and Maulana Abul Kalam Azad, Rajendra Prasad and Jawaharlal Nehru on the other, and connected papers on . . . Pakistan* (Lahore, 1943).

Khan, A. M., ed. *Leader by Merit, a study of the career and character of Sardar Patel . . . including all his important speeches from 1921 to 1946* (Lahore, 1946).

Life and Speeches of Sardar Patel . . . including his important speeches until his death (New Delhi, 1951).

Linlithgow, Marquess of. *Speeches and Statements, 1936–43* (New Delhi, 1945).

Maudoodi, A. A. *The Political Theory of Islam, being an address delivered at Shah Chiragh Mosque, Lahore, in October, 1939* (Lahore, 1939).

Mookerji, S. P. *Awake Hindusthan:* 'a collection of my speeches delivered in connection with Hindu Mahasabha movement' (Calcutta, ?1945).

Mountbatten, Earl. *Time Only to Look Forward:* speeches as Viceroy of India and Governor-General of the Dominion of India, 1947–8 (London, 1949).

Nehru, J. *Recent Essays and Writings on the Future of Indian Communalism, Labour and Other Subjects* (Allahabad, 1937).

Nehru–Jinnah Correspondence, including Gandhi–Jinnah and Nehru–Nawab Ismail Correspondence (Allahabad, 1938).

The Unity of India, Collected Writings 1937–40 (London, 1941).

A Bunch of Old Letters (Bombay, 1958).

Norman, Dorothy. *Nehru: the First Sixty Years* [a selection of Nehru's political writings], 2 vols (London, 1965).

Panikkar, K. M. and Pershad, A., eds *The Voice of Freedom: Selected Speeches of Pandit Motilal Nehru* (Bombay, 1961).

Pirzada, S. S., ed. *Leaders' Correspondence with Mr Jinnah* (Bombay, 1944).

Qaid-e-Azam Jinnah's Correspondence (Karachi, 1966).

Pyrelal, U. N., ed. *Gandhiji's Correspondence with the Government, 1942–44, 1944–47* (Ahmedabad, 1957–59).

'Shamloo', ed. *Speeches and Statements of Iqbal*, 2nd edn (Lahore, 1948).

Singh, Durlab. *A Complete Record of Unity Talks* (Lahore, 1945).

Sinha, S. *A Selection from the Speeches and Writings of Sachchidanand Sinha* (Calcutta, 1942).

Wavell, Lord. *Speeches, 1943–47* (New Delhi, 1948).

Willingdon, Lord. *Speeches* (Simla, 1935–7).

4. Contemporary books and pamphlets

Adhikari, G. M. *Pakistan and Indian National Unity* (London, 1943).

Pakistan and National Unity; the Communist Solution, 2nd edn (1944).

The Imperialist Alternative: Churchill: Cripps Conspiracy for a New Communal Award, 4th edn (Bombay, 1945).

Agarwala, R. M. *The Hindu–Muslim Riots, Their Causes and Cures* (Lucknow, 1943).

Ahmad, Jamil-ud-din. *Muslim India and its Goal* (Aligarh, 1940).

Through Pakistan to Freedom (Lahore, 1944).

Ahmad, K. A. *The Founder of Pakistan, through Trial to Triumph* (Cambridge, 1942).

Ahmad, N. *The Basis of Pakistan* (Calcutta, 1947).

Ahmad, T. *Responsible Government and the Solution of the Hindu–Muslim Problem* (London, 1928).

Ahmed, Sir A. *The Indian Minorities Problem* (1932).

Ahmed, Sir S. S. *A Treaty between India and the United Kingdom*, 2nd edn (New Delhi, 1945).

Aiyangar, N. R. *The Government of India Act, 1935* (Madras, 1937).

Aiyar, V. *After the Reforms. Communal versus Democratic Psychology* (Karur, 1939).

Aiyer, H. R. *Why Pakistan?* (Trivandrum, 1945).
Aiyer, P. S. S. *Indian Constitutional Problems* (Bombay, 1928).
Akbar Pasha, M. *Pakistan Achieved* (Madras, 1947).
Alexander, H. G. *Congress Rule in India: a Study in Social Reform* (Fabian Research Bureau publication, 1938).
India Since Cripps (London, 1944).
Ambedkar, B. R. *Thoughts on Pakistan* [Report submitted to the Executive Council of the Independent Labour Party] (Bombay, 1941).
Ranade, Gandhi and Jinnah (Bombay, 1943).
What Congress and Gandhi have done to the Untouchables, 2nd edn (Bombay, 1946).
Pakistan or the Partition of India, 3rd edn (Bombay, 1946).
Angadi, S. N. *I Differ from Congress* (Belgaum, 1936).
Ansari, S. *Pakistan; the Problem of India* (Lahore, 1944), 2nd edn, 1945.
Arslan, A. *Pakistan Explained* (Lahore, 1945).
Ashraf, K. M. *Pakistan: Foreward* [*sic*] (Delhi, 1940).
Ashraf, M. ed. *Cabinet Mission and After* (Lahore, 1946).
Azad, A. K. *India's Choice* (London, 1940).
Banerjea, N. *Psychotherapy of Indian Riots, a Study of the Causes, the Consequences and the Remedies of the Communal Riots in India* (Calcutta, 1941).
Banerjea, S. N. *A Nation in Making* (London, 1931).
Bannerjee, D. N. 'India's Case for Independence', *Current History*, xxxviii (May, 1933).
Partition or Federation? (Calcutta, 1945).
Bapat, N. S. *Nationalism versus Communalism* (*An Essay on Hindu–Muslim Unity*), 3rd edn (Poona, 1943).
Birdwood, Lord. *A Continent Experiments* (London, 1945).
Bose, S. C. *The Indian Struggle* (London, 1935).
Bose, S. M. *The Working Constitution of India* (Calcutta, 1939).
Brailsford, H. N. *Democracy for India* (London, 1939).
Subject India (London, 1943).
Brown, W. N. 'India's Pakistan Issue', *Proc. of Amer. Phil. Soc.* xci (April 1947), 162–80.
Chakrabarti, A. *Hindus and Musalmans of India* (Calcutta, 1940).
Not By Politics Alone (Calcutta, 1944).
Chaudhuri, B. M. *Muslim Politics in India* (Calcutta, 1946).
Chintamani, C. Y. *Indian Politics since the Mutiny* (London, 1937).
Chintamani, C. Y. and Masani, M. R. *India's Constitution at Work* (Bombay, 1940).
Confederacy of India, by 'A Punjabi' (Lahore, 1939).
Coupland, R. *The Cripps Mission* (London, 1942).
Report on the Constitutional Problem in India, 3 pts (London, 1942–3).
The Future of India (London, 1943).
Indian Politics, 1936–1942 (London, 1943).
India: A Re-Statement (London, 1945).
Dalal, Sir A. R. *An Alternative to Pakistan* (New Delhi, 1945).

Dalal, M. N. *Whither Minorities?* (Bombay, 1940).
Dar, B. A. *Why Pakistan?* (Lahore, 1946).
Desai, B. *I.N.A. Defence.*
Desai, M. *Maulana Abul Kalam Azad* (Agra, 1946).
Devi, S. *A Warning to the Hindus.*
Durrani, F. K. K. *The Meaning of Pakistan* (Lahore, 1944).
The Future of Islam in India (Lahore, ?1946).
Communalism (Lahore, n.d.).
Dutt, R. P. *A Guide to the Problem of India* (London, 1942).
Freedom for India: the Truth about the Cabinet Mission's Visit (London, C.P. 1946).
A New Chapter in Divide and Rule (Bombay, 1946).
Eddy, J. P. and Lawton, F. H. *India's New Constitution* (London, 1935).
Fazl-ul Huq, A. K. *Muslim Sufferings under Congress rule* (? Calcutta, 1939).
Gandhi, M. K. *To the Protagonists of Pakistan* (Karachi, 1947).
Communal Unity (Ahmedabad, 1949).
Gandhi–Muslim Conspiracy, by a Hindu Nationalist. Foreword by J. M. Mehta (Poona, 1941).
Gauba, K. L. *The Consequences of Pakistan* (Lahore, 1946).
Graham, G. F. I. *The Life and Work of Syed Ahmed Khan* (Edinburgh, 1885).
Griffiths, P. J. *The British in India* (London, 1946).
el Hamza. *Pakistan, A Nation* (Lahore, 1st edn 1941, 2nd edn 1942, 3rd edn 1944).
Haq, Ch. A. *Pakistan and Untouchability* (Lahore, 1941).
Hasan, S. Z. and Qadri, M. A. *The Problem of the Indian Muslims and its Solution.*
Hyder, S. *Progress of Pakistan* (Lahore, 1947).
Iftikhar-ul-Haq. *Pakistan and Constituent Assembly . . .* (Lahore, 1946).
India's Problem of her Future Constitution. All-India Muslim League's Lahore resolution, popularly known as 'Pakistan'; an unbiased scientific and analytical study, being a collection of essays by various authors. Preface by M. A. Jinnah (Bombay, 1940).
Iqbal, Sir M. *Islam and Ahmadism, with a Reply to Questions raised by Pandit Jawaharlal Nehru . . .* (Lahore, 1936).
Ismail, Sir M. *Suggestions for a Constitution for India* (1938).
Jinnah, M. A. 'Two Nations in India', *Time and Tide*, xxi (1940), 10.
Johnston, J. *Hindu Domination in India: an Examination of the Origin, Objects, and Results of the Government Proposals* (Southend, 1935).
Can the Hindus Rule India? (London, 1935).
Joshi, P. C. *They Must Meet Again* (Bombay, 1944).
Kabir, H. *Muslim Politics, 1906–1942* (Calcutta, 1943).
Karim, R. *For India and Islam* (Calcutta, 1937).
Pakistan Examined, with the Partition Schemes of Dr Latif, Sir Sikandar Hyat Khan and Others (Calcutta, 1941).
Muslims and the Congress (Calcutta, 1941).
Kaushik, B. G. *The House that Jinnah Built* (Bombay, 1944).

Khan, A. M. *The Communalism in India, its Origin and Growth* (Lahore, 1944).
Vital Islam (Lahore, 1946).
Khan, M. H. *The Case for Pakistan* (? 1941).
Khan, Sir S. A. *What are the Rights of the Muslim Minority in India?* (Allahabad, 1928).
Khan, Sir S. H. *Outlines of a Scheme of Indian Federation* (Lahore).
Khanna, M. *Muslim Demand for Pakistan* (1942).
Pakistan: A Hindu View (1942).
Kidwai, M. H. *Pan-Islamism and Bolshevism* (London, 1937).
Kotewal, J. F. *The Indian Charter, being a Description of the Vicious Circles, Small and Great, Constituting the Indian Political Deadlock; including an Exposition of the Hindu–Muslim Communal Problem, and its Corollary – Pakistan* (Karachi, 1944).
Kripalani, J. B. *Indian National Congress* (1946).
Krishna, J. B. *The Problem of Minorities* (London, 1939).
Kulakarni, V. B. *Is Pakistan Necessary?* (Bombay, 1944).
Kumarappa, J. M. *Can India Be United?* (1945).
Latif, S. A. *The Muslim Problem of India* (Bombay, 1939).
The Great Leader (Lahore, 1947).
Madhok, B. *Hindusthan on the Crossroads, being a Historical Study of the Communal and Constitutional Problem of India* (Lahore, 1946).
Manshardt, C. *The Hindu–Muslim Problem of India* (London, 1936).
Maudoodi, A. A. *Nationalism and India*, 2nd edn (Pathankot, Punjab, 1947).
Meherally, Y. *A Trip to Pakistan* (1st edn 1943, 2nd edn 1944).
Mehta, A. and Patwardhan, A. *The Communal Triangle in India* (Allahabad, 1942).
Mehtar, M. A. *Whys of the Great Indian Conflict* (Lahore, 1947).
Mookerji, R. K. *A New Approach to Communal Problem* (Bombay, 1943).
Moon, P. *Strangers in India* (New York, 1945).
The Future of India (London, 1945).
Mukerjee, R. *The Economist Looks at Pakistan* (Bombay, 1944).
Mukerji, N. C. *The Revolutionary Mind in India Today* (Allahabad, 1937).
Mukherji, S. *Communalism in Muslim Politics* (Calcutta, 1947).
Munshi, K. M. *I Follow the Mahatma* (Bombay, 1940).
Akhand Hindustan (Bombay, 1942).
The Indian Deadlock (Allahabad, 1945).
The Changing Shape of Indian Politics (Poona, 1945).
Narayan, J. P. *Towards Struggle* (Bombay, 1946).
Nehru, J. 'The Solidarity of Islam', *Modern Review*, November 1935.
'His Highness the Aga Khan', *Modern Review*, November 1935.
'The Orthodox of All Regions, Unite', *Modern Review*, December 1935.
Indian and the World (London, 1936).
The Question of Language (Allahabad, 1937).

Eighteen Months in India, 1936–37 (Allahabad, 1938).
Where Are We? (Allahabad, 1938).
The Discovery of India (London, 1946).
Nichols, B. *Verdict on India* (Bombay, 1944).
Noman, M. *Muslim India: Rise and Growth of the All-India Muslim League* (Allahabad, 1942).
Noman, M., ed. *Our Struggle, 1857–1947. A Pictorial Record of the Pakistan Movement* (Karachi, 1947).
'Pakistan' in *Encyclopaedia of Islam* (Leiden, 1937).
Pakistan Literature Series
1. *National States and National Minorities.* By M. A. S. Kheiri (Lahore, 1947).
2. *The Communal Pattern of India.* By K. S. Ahmad (Lahore, 1947).
3. *Some Aspects of Pakistan.* By Jamil-ud-din Ahmad (Lahore, 1947).
4. *Politico-regional Division of India.* By K. S. Ahmad (Lahore, 1945).
6. *Is India Geographically One?* By K. S. Ahmad (Lahore, 1945).
7. *Muslim Educational Problems.* By Liaqat Ali Khan (Lahore, 1945).
9. *The Development of Islamic Culture in India.* By I. H. Qureshi (Lahore, 1946).
12. *Economic Basis of Pakistan.* By A. I. Qureshi (Lahore, 1947).
13. *Are the Indian Muslims a Nation?* By 'a Student of International History' (Lahore, 1947).
Prakash, I. *Where Do We Differ? The Congress and the Hindu Mahasabha* (New Delhi, 1942).
Prasad, B. *The Hindu–Muslim Question* (Allahabad, 1941).
India's Hindu–Muslim Question (Allahabad, 1946).
Prasad, R. *India Divided* (Bombay, 1947).
Puckle, Sir F. 'The Pakistan Doctrine: Its Origins and Power', *Foreign Affairs*, xxiv (April, 1946).
Qadri, S. N. A. . . . *A Moslem's Inner Voice* . . . (Lahore, 1944).
Qureshi, A. I. *Economic Basis of Pakistan* (Lahore, 1947).
Rahmat Ali, C. *What does the Pakistan National Movement stand for?* 1st ed. (1933).
Pakistan, the Fatherland of the Pak Nation, 3rd edn (Cambridge, 1947).
Rai, G. *Pakistan X-rayed* (Lahore, 1946).
Rajput, A. B. *Muslim League, Yesterday and Today* (Lahore, 1946).
Raman, T. A. *What Does Gandhi Want?* (N.Y., 1945).
Rizvi, Begum F. *Pakistan Defined* (Lahore, ? 1945).
Roy, Sir B. P. S. *Parliamentary Government in India* (Calcutta, 1943).
Saiyid, M. H. *Mohammad Ali Jinnah* (Lahore, 1945).
Schuster, G. and Wint, G. *India and Democracy* (London, 1941).
Sen, D. *The Problem of Minorities* (Calcutta, 1940).
Seth, H. L. *The Khaksar Movement under Searchlight and the Story of its Leader Allama Mushraqi* (Lahore, 1943).

Shafi, Sir M. M. *Some Important Indian Problems* (Lahore, 1930).
Shah, I. A. *Pakistan: a Plan for India* (London, 1944).
Shah, K. T. *Why Pakistan? and Why Not?* (Bombay, 1944).
Singh, Darbara. *Indian Struggle, 1942* (Lahore, 1944).
Singh, Tara. *Why We Must Avoid a Civil War in India* (Lahore, 1946).
Sinha, K. K. *Communal Problem: a Fresh Approach* (Lucknow, 1946).
Sitaramayya, P. *The History of the Indian National Congress*, 2 vols (Bombay, 1946–7).
Smith, R. A. *Divided India* (New York, 1947).
Smith, W. C. *Modern Islam in India* (London, 1946).
Smith, W. R. *Nationalism and Reform in India* (New Haven, 1938).
Sufi, G. M. *Commonsense on Pakistan* Rev. & enl. edn (Bombay, 1946).
Suleri, Z. A. *The Road to Peace and Pakistan* (Lahore, 1944).
My Leader, 3rd edn (Lahore, 1946).
Sundaram, L. *A Secular State for India . . .* (Delhi, 1944).
Tyabji, H. B. *Why Mussulmans Should Oppose Pakistan* (Bombay, 1946).
Tyson, G. *India Arms for Victory* (Allahabad, 1943).
M.R.T. *Nationalism in Conflict in India* (Bombay, 1943).
Pakistan and Muslim India; with a Foreword by Qaid-i-Azam, Mr M. A. Jinnah (Bombay, 1943).
Union of Democratic Control. *India and the War* (1941).
Vairanapillai, M. S. *Are We Two Nations?* (Lahore, 1946).
Whyte, F. *India, a Federation?* (Calcutta, 1925).
Yunus, M. *Frontier Speaks* (Bombay, 1947).
Zaheer, S. *A Case for Congress–League Unity* (Bombay, 1944).
Zetland, 2nd Marquess of. *Steps Toward Indian Home Rule* (London, 1935).

E. Memoirs and Autobiographies

Aga Khan, The. *Memoirs* (London, 1954).
Ali, Chaudhri Muhammad. *The Emergence of Pakistan* (New York, 1967).
Ali, Mohamed. *My Life: A Fragment* (Lahore, 1942).
Amery, L. S. *My Political Life*, 4 vols (London, 1953–55).
Attlee, C. R. *As It Happened* (London, 1954).
Azad, A. K. *India Wins Freedom* (Bombay, 1959).
Birla, G. D. *In The Shadow of the Mahatma: A Personal Memoir* (Bombay, 1953).
Bose, N. K. *My Days with Gandhi* (Calcutta, 1953).
Campbell-Johnson, A. *Mission With Mountbatten* (London, 1951).
Casey, R. G. *An Australian in India* (London, 1947).
Chaudhuri, N. C. *An Autobiography of an Unknown Indian* (London, 1951).
Dwarkadas, K. *India's Fight for Freedom* (Bombay, 1966).
Gandhi, M. K. *An Autobiography or the Story of My Experiments with Truth* (Ahmedabad, 1940).
Delhi Diary (Ahmedabad, 1948).
Ghosh, S. *Gandhi's Emissary* (London, 1967).

Halifax, Lord. *Fulness of Days* (London, 1957).
Iqbal, M. *Stray Reflections* (Lahore, 1961).
Ismail, Sir M. *My Public Life* (London, 1954).
Ismay, Lord. *Memoirs* (London, 1960).
Ispahani, M. A. H. *Qaid-e-Azam Jinnah As I Knew Him* (Karachi, 1966).
Jayakar, M. R. *The Story of My Life*, 2 vols (Bombay, 1958–9).
Khaliquzzaman, C. *Pathway to Pakistan* (Lahore, 1961).
Montagu, E. S. *An Indian Diary* (London, 1930).
Munshi, K. M. *Pilgrimage to Freedom* (Bombay, 1967).
Nehru, J. *An Autobiography* (London, 1936).
Prasad, R. *Autobiography* (Bombay, 1957).
Reed, S. *The India I Knew, 1897–1947* (London, 1952).
Russell, W. W. *Indian Summer* (Bombay, 1951).
Setalvad, C. *Recollections and Reflections* (Bombay, 1946).
Stephens, I. *Monsoon Morning* (London, 1966).
Templewood, Visc. (Sir S. Hoare). *Nine Troubled Years* (London, 1954).
Tuker, Sir F. *While Memory Serves* (London, 1950).
Winterton, Earl. *Orders of the Day* (London, 1953).
Fifty Tumultuous Years (London, 1955).
Young, D. *Try Anything Twice* (London, 1965).
Zetland, 2nd Marquess of. '*Essayez*' (London, 1956).

SECONDARY WORKS

Adam, C. F. *Life of Lord Lloyd* (London, 1948).
Agarwalla, N. *The Hindu–Muslim Question* (Calcutta, 1951).
Ahmad, A. *Islamic Modernism in India and Pakistan, 1857–1964* (London, 1967).
Ahmad, Jamil-ud-din. *Final Phase of Struggle for Pakistan* (Karachi, 1964).
Albiruni, A. H. [pseud. of S. M. Ikram]. *Makers of Pakistan and Modern Muslim India* (Lahore, 1950).
Ashe, G. *Gandhi: A Study in Revolution* (London, 1968).
Aziz, K. K. *Britain and Muslim India, 1857–1947* (London, 1963).
The Making of Pakistan: A Study in Nationalism (London, 1967).
Background to Mass Murder. An account of what led up to the disorders that attended the partition of India (New Delhi Foreign Relations Soc. of India, 1950).
Bahadur, L. *The Muslim League, its History, Activities and Achievements* (Agra, 1954).
Bhagat, K. P. *A Decade of Indo-British Relations, 1937–1947* (Bombay, 1959).
Binder, L. *Religion and Politics in Pakistan* (Berkeley, Cal., 1961).
Birdwood, Lord. *Two Nations and Kashmir* (London, 1956).
Birkenhead, Lord. *Halifax* (London, 1965).
Blunt, Sir E. *The I.C.S.: The Indian Civil Service* (London, 1937).
Bolitho, H. *Jinnah: Creator of Pakistan* (London, 1954).
Bose, N. K. *Studies in Gandhism*, 3rd edn (Calcutta, 1962).
Brecher, M. *Nehru: a Political Biography* (London, 1959).
Brittain, Vera. *Pethick-Lawrence: A Portrait* (London, 1963).
Callard, K. *Pakistan, A Political Study* (London, 1957).

Chatterji, A. *The Constitutional Development in India: 1937–1947* (Calcutta, 1958).
Cooke, C. *Life of Richard Stafford Cripps* (London, 1957).
Connell, J. *Auchinleck* (London, 1959).
Das, M. N. *The Political Philosophy of Jawaharlal Nehru* (London, 1961).
Davis, K. 'India and Pakistan – The Demography of Partition', *Pacific Affairs*, xxii, September 1949.
Edwardes, M. *The Last Years of British India* (London, 1963).
Estorick, E. *Stafford Cripps: A Biography* (London, 1949).
Faruqui, Z. *The Deoband School and the Demand for Pakistan* (London, 1963).
Fischer, L. *The Life of Mahatma Gandhi* (New York, 1950).
Furnivall, J. S. *Colonial Policy and Practice* (Cambridge, 1948).
Gopal, R. *Indian Muslims: A Political History* (Bombay, 1959).
Gopal, S. *The Viceroyalty of Lord Irwin, 1926–1931* (Oxford, 1957).
Griffiths, P. J. *The British Impact on India*, 2nd edn (London, 1965).
Modern India (London, 1957).
Hamid, A. *A Brief Survey of Muslim Separatism in India* (Asia Publishing House, 1968).
Hancock, W. K. *Survey of British Commonwealth Affairs* (1936–42), 2 vols (London).
Haq, M. *Muslims in India* (Delhi, 1964).
Husain, A. *Sir Fazl-i-Husain: A Political Biography* (Bombay, 1946).
Husain, S. A. *The Destiny of Indian Muslims* (1965).
Husain, M., *et al.*, eds *A History of the Freedom Movement, 1707–1947*, 4 vols (Karachi, 1957–61).
Jain, A. P. *Rafi Ahmad Kidwai* (Asia Publishing House, 1965).
Jeffries, C. *The Transfer of Power* (London, 1960).
Jennings, W. I. *The Approach to Self-Government* (Cambridge, 1956).
Kabir, H., ed. *Maulana Abul Kalam Azad: A Memorial Volume* (Bombay, 1959).
Khosla, G. D. *Stern Reckoning; A Survey of the Events Leading Up To and Following the Partition of India* (New Delhi, ?1949).
Lumby, E. W. R. *The Transfer of Power in India, 1945–47* (London, 1954).
Mackenzie, W. J. M. 'Representation in Plural Societies', *Political Studies*, February 1954, pp. 54–69.
Majumdar, A. K. *Advent of Independence* (Bombay, 1963).
Majumdar, R. C. *History of the Freedom Movement* (Calcutta, 1962 *et seq.*).
Majumdar, S. K. *Jinnah and Gandhi: Their Rôle in India's Quest for Freedom* (Calcutta, 1966).
Malik, H. *Moslem Nationalism in India and Pakistan* (Washington, D.C., 1963).
Mansergh, P. N. S. *Survey of British Commonwealth Affairs, 1939–1952* (London, 1958).
The Commonwealth and the Nations (London, 1958).
Masani, R. P. *Britain in India* (London, 1960).
Mellor, A. *India Since Partition* (New York, 1951).
Menon, V. P. *The Transfer of Power in India* (London, 1957).
The Story of the Integration of the Indian States (New York, 1956).

Michel, A. A. *The Indus Rivers. A Study of the Effects of Partition* (Newhaven, Conn., 1967).
Moon, P. *Divide and Quit* (London, 1961).
Mosley, L. *The Last Days of the British Raj* (London, 1961).
Mujeeb, M. *The Indian Muslims* (London, 1967).
Murphy, G. *In the Minds of Men* (New York, 1953).
Nanda, B. R. *Mahatma Gandhi* (London, 1958).
The Nehrus, Motilal and Jawaharlal (London, 1962).
Nicholson, M. *Self Government and the Communal Problem* (London, 1948).
Nicholson, H. *King George the Fifth: His Life and Reign* (London, 1952).
O'Malley, L. S. S. *The Indian Civil Service, 1601–1930* (London, 1931).
Panjabi, K. L. *The Indomitable Sardar* (Bombay, 1962).
Parikh, N. D. *Sardar Vallabhbhai Patel* (Ahmedabad, 1953).
Philips, C. H. *The Partition of India, 1947* (Leeds, 1967).
Pirzada, S. S. *Evolution of Pakistan* (Lahore, 1963).
Prakash, I. *A Review of the History and Work of the Hindu Mahasabha* (New Delhi, 1952).
Prakasa, Sri. *Pakistan's Birth and Early Days* (Meerut, 1965).
Pyrelal, U. N. *Mahatma Gandhi: The Last Phase* (Ahmedabad, 1956–58).
Qureshi, I. H. *The Muslim Community of the Indo-Pakistan Sub-Continent* ('s-Gravenhage, 1962).
Rajput, A. B. *Muslim League Yesterday and Today* (London, 1948).
Rahman, F. 'Muslim Modernism in Indo-Pakistan Sub-Continent', *BSOAS*, xxi (1958), No. 1, pp. 82–99.
Rao, P. Kodanda. *Rt Hon. V. S. Srinivasa Sastri: A Political Biography* (Bombay, 1963).
Saiyid, M. H. *Mohammad Ali Jinnah* (*A Political Biography*) (Lahore, 1953).
Saksena, R. N. *Refugees: A Study in Changing Attitudes* (Asia Publishing House, 1961).
Sayed, G. M. *Struggle for New Sind* (Karachi, 1949).
Sayeed, K. B. *Pakistan: The Formative Phase*, 2nd edn (London, 1968).
The Political System of Pakistan (Boston, 1967).
Sen, S. *The Birth of Pakistan* (Calcutta, 1955).
Sengupta, P. *Sarojini Naidu: A Biography* (Asia Publishing House, 1966).
Shafi, A. M. A. *Haji Sir Abdoola Haroon. A Biography* (Karachi, n.d.).
Sharma, J. S. *India's Struggle for Freedom* (Delhi, 1962).
Sinha, S. *Indian Independence in Perspective* (London, 1964).
Smith, W. C. 'Hyderabad: Muslim Tragedy', *Middle East Journal*, iv (January 1950).
Modern Islam in India (Lahore, 1954).
Islam in Modern History (London, 1957).
Spear, T. G. P. *India, Pakistan and the West*, 3rd edn (London, 1958).
Stephens, I. *Pakistan* (London, 1963).
Symonds, R. *The Making of Pakistan* (London, 1950).
Tendulkar, D. G. *Mahatma: Life of Mohandas Karamchand Gandhi*, 8 vols (Bombay, 1951–4).
Tinker, H. *Experiment With Freedom: India and Pakistan 1947* (London, 1967).

Toye, H. *Springing Tiger, A Study of Subhas Chandra Bose* (London, 1959).
Trumbull, R. *India Since Partition* (New York, 1954).
Tyabji, H. B. *Badruddin Tyabji: A Biography* (Bombay, 1952).
Waheed Khan, A. *India Wins Freedom, The Other Side* (Karachi, 1961).
Waheed-uz-Zaman. *Towards Pakistan* (Lahore, 1964).
Wheeler-Bennett, J. *King George VI: His Life and Reign* (London, 1958).
Sir John Anderson (London, 1962).
Williams, F. *A Prime Minister Remembers* (London, 1961).
Williams, L. F. Rushbrook. *The State of Pakistan*, rev. edn (London, 1966).
Woodruff, P. [pseud. of Philip Mason]. *The Men Who Ruled India*, Vol. II *The Guardians* (London, 1954).

INDEX